WESTERN CANON SERIES

The Western Canon's value is self-evident. Its status, however, has been under threat since the middle of the 20th century. Feminists, Marxists, intersectionalists, and others deny the Canon's existence by refusing to observe its traditional boundaries, throwing the borders open to invite all manner of second- and third-rate material. They intentionally misread the Canon, deconstructing it and looking for incoherence where men have only ever found genius.

Imperium Press' Western Canon series reclaims the Canon from the forces hostile to it. The series offers not only definitive versions of these works, but also supplementary material placing them at the centre of our aesthetic, intellectual, and spiritual life—where they belong.

HOMER is both a shadowy figure and the generally acknowledged supreme genius of Western literature. No record of his life survives. Tradition places him some time in the 9th or 8th centuries BCE, and attributes to him *Iliad*, *Odyssey*, thirty-three *Hymns*, and a number of lesser works. The question of who he was—or who they were—fills out innumerable volumes and an entire branch of classical scholarship. All agree, however, that his influence on the Western literary tradition has been incalculable.

WILLIAM CULLEN BRYANT was an American poet, journalist, and editor of the New York *Evening Post*, called "the Founding Father of American poetry," and "the first American writer of verse to win international acclaim" for his *Thanatopsis*. He resides squarely within the Romantic poetic tradition, anticipating other American poets in this by over a decade. A fierce proponent of American literary nationalism, he earned the admiration of Edgar Allen Poe and served as literary mentor to Walt Whitman. Of his translations of *Iliad* and *Odyssey*, completed at the height of his poetic maturity, it has been said that "nothing can be more clear and fascinating than Mr. Bryant's narrative, conveyed in the true epic manner with regard to directness and nobility of style."

ILIAD

HOMER

Translated into English blank verse by
WILLIAM CULLEN BRYANT

Foreword by
RICARDO DUCHESNE

PERTH
IMPERIUM PRESS
2019

Published by Imperium Press

www.imperiumpress.org

First published by Fields, Osgood & Co. 1871

Foreword © Ricardo Duchesne, 2018
The moral rights of the author have been asserted
Used under license to Imperium Press

Map of the Ægean and Asia Minor © Alamy Ltd.
All rights reserved
Used under license to Imperium Press

All rights are reserved. No part of this publication may be reproduced, stored in a retrieval system, or transmitted in any form or by any means, electronic, mechanical, photocopying, recording, or otherwise, without prior permission of Imperium Press. Enquiries concerning reproduction outside the scope of the above should be directed to Imperium Press.

FIRST EDITION

A catalogue record for this
book is available from the
National Library of Australia

ISBN 978-0-6486905-0-4 Paperback

Imperium Press has no responsibility for the persistence or accuracy of URLs for external or third-party Internet websites referred to in this publication and does not guarantee that any content on such websites is, or will remain, accurate or appropriate.

CONTENTS

Foreword: The Iliad and the Invention of
Consciousness   vii
Translator's Preface   xxxvii
Map of the Ægean and Asia Minor   xlvi

ILIAD
  Book I   3
  Book II   24
  Book III   53
  Book IV   68
  Book V   87
  Book VI   117
  Book VII   135
  Book VIII   151
  Book IX   170
  Book X   193
  Book XI   211
  Book XII   239
  Book XIII   254
  Book XIV   282
  Book XV   299
  Book XVI   324
  Book XVII   353
  Book XVIII   377
  Book XIX   397

Book XX	411
Book XXI	428
Book XXII	448
Book XXIII	465
Book XXIV	494
Genealogies	521
Bibliography	525
Glossary of Names	529

THE ILIAD AND THE INVENTION OF CONSCIOUSNESS

HOMER THE INVENTOR OF LITERARY PERSONALITIES

THE *Iliad*, a poem composed sometime between 725 and 675 BC by a man named "Homer," is the first extant work of Western literature. It is acknowledged by many, in the words of William Cullen Bryant, "to be the greatest production of poetic genius that the world had seen." The names most often listed in the hierarchies of poetic genius I have seen are Homer, Virgil, Shakespeare, Dante, and Milton. The American poet and critic Ezra Pound once said that if there is a man where you can nearly get "all of poetry" it is Homer.[1] For Tolstoy, when one compares Shakespeare with Homer, "the infinite distance separating true poetry from its imitation emerges with special vividness".[2] The 18th century English poet, Alexander Pope, whose translation of the *Iliad* Bryant read with "avidity," believed it was Homer's "invention" that made him "the greatest of poets". It is "invention," he

---

1 Ezra Pound, "Homer or Virgil," in *Homer: A Collection of Critical Essays*. Edited by George Steiner and Robert Fagles (Englewood Cliffs, New Jersey: Prentice-Hall, 1962).
2 Leo Tolstoy, "Homer and Shakespeare," in *Homer: A Collection of Critical Essays*.

said, "that distinguishes all great geniuses: the utmost stretch of human study, learning, and industry."

> Whatever praises may be given to works of judgment, there is not even a single beauty in them to which the invention must not contribute [...] It is to the strength of this amazing invention we are to attribute that unequalled fire and rapture which is so forcible in Homer, that no man of a true poetical spirit is master of himself while he reads him. What he writes is of the most animated nature imaginable; everything moves, everything lives, and is put in action. If a council be called, or a battle fought, you are not coldly informed of what was said or done as from a third person; the reader is hurried out of himself by the force of the poet's imagination, and turns in one place to a hearer, in another to a spectator [...] This fire is discerned in Virgil, but discerned as through a glass, reflected from Homer, more shining than fierce, but everywhere equal and constant: in Lucan and Statius it bursts out in sudden, short, and interrupted flashes: In Milton it glows like a furnace kept up to an uncommon ardour by the force of art: in Shakespeare it strikes before we are aware, like an accidental fire from heaven: but in Homer, and in him only, it burns everywhere clearly and everywhere irresistibly.[3]

For me, as a historian and a sociologist, rather than a translator or a poet, what surprised me most about Homer's *Iliad*, in comparison to the major writings which preceded him, songs or recitations of various kinds, including the celebrated "epic" of Gilgamesh, from civilizations in Mesopotamia, from the "eternal" Egyptian world of the Pharaohs, and from Asia generally, is the presence of vivid characters with identifiable personalities, capable of introspection and deliberation. The variety of personalities, of men who can be distinguished from each other because they exhibit a certain capacity for free individuality, is also what Alexander Pope means by Homer's inventiveness as a poet:

> We come now to the characters of his persons; and here we shall find no author has ever drawn so many, with so visible and surprising a variety, or given us such lively and affecting

---

3 *The Iliad of Homer in the English Verse Translation by Alexander Pope* (New York: The Heritage Press, [1720] 1943), v-vi.

impressions of them. Everyone has something so singularly his own, that no painter could have distinguished them more by their features, than the poet has by their manners. Nothing can be more exact than the distinctions he has observed in the different degrees of virtues and vices. The single quality of courage is wonderfully diversified in the several characters of the *Iliad*. That of Achilles is furious and intractable; that of Diomede forward, yet listening to advice, and subject to command; that of Ajax is heavy and self-confiding; of Hector, active and vigilant: the courage of Agamemnon is inspirited by love of empire and ambition; that of Menelaus mixed with softness and tenderness for his people: we find in Idomeneus a plain direct soldier; in Sarpedon a gallant and generous one.[4]

We should not assume, however, that Homer was an artist who invented personalities out of his peculiar genius. When we refer to "Homer" we are not talking about an isolated creator but about a man who captured in the highest poetic form the aristocratic spirit of the ancient Greeks and of Indo-Europeans generally. The *Iliad* is the first literary expression of the European soul, the point when this soul, precisely and only because it is European, attains consciousness of the human self in contradistinction to the surrounding world, including the body, within which all living beings, and non-Europeans, are enveloped, cocooned, and forever trapped. This nascent European self is not the universal abstract individual of modern liberalism who wilfully rejects his collective ancestry, common traditions, and ethnic kinship, but is rather the unique production of a collectivity of people starting to deliberate on their cultural values, religious beliefs, and on the "external forces" impinging on their thoughts. What we witness in the *Iliad* is the beginning of the European self's autonomy from all blind determinations and suppositions. Just the beginning in what would be an incredible journey in the developing of this self and the arrival of the "I" of German Idealism when an "I" unconditionally posits his own existence. The *Iliad* is the beginning, and beginnings are always the hardest and most important to understand.

---

4 *The Iliad of Homer in the English Verse Translation by Alexander Pope*, viii.

SNELL AND JAYNES

They say that Homer's *Iliad* and *Odyssey* "exist to be translated". The *Iliad* has been translated into English countless times since the first translation in 1581, more than 40 in the 19th century, another 30 in the 20th, and 16 so far in the 21st century.[5] Homer has been studied, annotated, and interpreted since antiquity. Not even experts can show command of the vast number of studies written over the centuries. They prefer to study limited periods, such as "eighteenth-century notions of the early Greek epic (1688-1798)".[6] But while Sir John L. Myres was complaining in the 1930s that "it is not easy to say anything new about Homer",[7] the number of "new" interpretations actually accelerated after WWII. In my estimation the most fruitful interpretations are contained in Bruno Snell's *The Discovery of the Mind*, and in Julian Jaynes' *The Origins of Consciousness in the Breakdown of the Bicameral Mind*.[8]

The odd thing is that these authors contradict my view that Homer is the first writer in whom we find emerging signs of human deliberation and recognizable personalities. Snell writes:

> ...Homer does not know genuine personal decisions; even where a hero is shown pondering two alternatives the intervention of the gods plays the key role [...] Mental and spiritual acts are due to the impact of external factors, and man is the open target of a great many forces which impinge on him, and penetrate his very core.[9]

---

5 For these numbers I am relying on Adam Nicolson, "A new translation of the Iliad," review of The Iliad, Homer: A New Translation, by Peter Green, *The Spectator*, August 2015; and Ian Johnston, "Published English Translations of Homer's Iliad and Odyssey," http://johnstoniatexts.x10host.com/homer/homertranslations.htm
6 Kristi Simonsuuri, *Homer's Original Genius. Eighteenth-century notions of the early Greek epic 1688-1798* (London: Cambridge University Press, 1979).
7 Sir John L. Myres, *Homer and His Critics*. Edited by Dorothea Gray. (London: Routledge & Kegan Paul, 1958), 1. This book was constructed from research and writings Myres completed in the 1930s.
8 Bruno Snell *The Discovery of the Mind* (New York: Harper & Row Publishers, 1960). Julian Jaynes, *The Origins of Consciousness in the Breakdown of the Bicameral Mind*. (Toronto: University of Toronto Press, 1976).
9 Snell, *Discovery of the Mind*, 20.

Jaynes writes:

> The characters of the *Iliad* do not sit down and think out what to do. They have no conscious minds such as we say we have, and certainly no introspection. It is impossible for us with our subjectivity to appreciate what it was like. When Agamemnon, king of men, robs Achilles of his mistress, it is a god that grasps Achilles by his yellow hair and warns him not to strike Agamemnon [...] Iliadic men have no will of their own and certainly no notion of free will [...] Iliadic man [...] had no awareness of his awareness of the world, no internal mind-space to introspect upon.[10]

What makes Snell and Jaynes invaluable, notwithstanding their underestimation of subjective consciousness in Homeric heroes, is their appreciation of the fact that consciousness is not a naturally given attribute acquired by humans through natural selection. The creation of a self "that is responsible and can debate within itself [...] is the product of culture".[11] I will explain below why Homer's characters did show some degree of subjectivity. We don't have space here to get into the rich intricacies of Snell's and Jaynes' arguments. I will only say, first, in the case of Snell, that once his book moves past Homer, it is a most penetrating illumination of the development of free consciousness among ancient Greeks. *The Discovery of the Mind* tells us that it was in the archaic period of Greek history, between 650 and 500 BC, that we see characters becoming more conscious of their personality, with the rise of lyric poets expressing "a more precise appreciation of the self," the "inwardly felt emotions" of the poet.[12] This is the beginning of what would become an ever more definite crystallization of the difference between the inner self and the outer world, between mind and matter, through the tragic characters of Aeschylus, Sophocles and Euripides in fifth century BC, who are faced with the dire predicament of a choice between equally compelling moral outcomes, all the way to the writings of the Ionian natural philosophers, who gradually succeeded in depriving the gods of their control over natural phenomena, leading to the eventual replacement of myth

---

10 Jaynes, *The Origins of Consciousness*, 70-75.
11 ibid., 79.
12 Snell, *The Discovery of the Mind*, 44-48.

by logical and scientific reasoning in the writings of Aristotle.

The flaw in Snell is that there is no explanation for the appearance of poets "conscious of their individuality". He seems to imply that poets, literary writers, and philosophers somehow managed through their artistic and philosophical creativity to bring about the liberation of the subject from its prior imprisonment to external forces and gods.

Jaynes offers an explanation of "how consciousness began" but not a persuasive one. He says that it began sometime around 1400-600 B.C. when men were compelled by the chaos of wars, catastrophes, and national migrations induced by overpopulation, and by the widespread use of writing, to question their "bicameral" mentality and to voice their own internally generated thoughts.[13] We don't need to get into the neurology underlying the term "bicameral" to understand that this is a mentality in which humans are ruled by the voices of gods, fear of repression and rigid theocratic norms and controls. Jaynes emphasizes in particular how the development of writing in the second millennium, combined with the weakening and collapse of theocratic empires, as well as the intermingling of peoples from different nations with different beliefs, weakened the "auditory" power of the gods and the rigid norms occupying the brains of peoples during this epoch.

Jaynes does not mean any type of writing, not the writing that was first invented in Mesopotamia around 3500-3000 BC as an inventory device, a way of recording the collection of taxes and god-commanded events. He seems to mean the writing found in the "narratization of epics" in which an "I" of ourselves "doing this or that," and thus making "decisions on the basis of imagined outcomes" makes an appearance.[14] He further explains that human introspection and self-visualization first emerged through the making of metaphors and analogies, metaphors of "me" and of "analog I". Humans came to experience consciousness of themselves as generators of their own thoughts only when they had developed a language sophisticated enough to produce metaphors and analogical models, that is, figures of speech containing an implied comparison, in which a phrase commonly used of one thing

---

13 Jaynes, *The Origins of Consciousness*, 204-222.
14 ibid., 63.

is applied to express another phrase in which some further similarity exists.

But as Jaynes admits, what he presents by way of historical examples of this metaphorical thinking are a "few suggestions".[15] He focuses on historical examples of the bicameral mind, as well as bicameral aspects of contemporary hypnosis, hallucinations, and schizophrenia. What I find perplexing is his choice of the *Iliad* as a key example of the bicameral mind when the *Iliad* was in fact the most advanced and sophisticated example in the "narratization of epic", a poem written towards the end of the very period Jaynes said the bicameral mind broke down.[16] However, commentators have tended to ignore some important qualifications Jaynes makes about his claim that the *Iliad* lacked free individuality. He actually says that we should not be surprised to find in the *Iliad* signs of the breakdown of the bicameral mind given the date of its origins. He cites the famous statement by Achilles against Agamemnon: "Hateful to me as the gates of Hades is the man who hides one thing in his heart and speaks another"—as an "indication of subjective consciousness".[17] He cites the words in which both Agenor and Hector exclaim "the same astonished words"—"But wherefore does my life say this to me?"—as clear intimations of introspection. But in the end Jaynes concludes that these were exceptional expressions possibly added later after Homer.[18]

One has to ask: if Greek literature after the *Iliad*, as Jaynes says, "very quickly became a literature of consciousness," as Snell distinctly shows, and if "we may regard the *Iliad* as standing at the great turning of the times",[19] the breakdown of the bicameral mind, why would it not be reasonable to suppose that the *Iliad* was a transitional work in which certain bicameral aspects co-existed along a newly emerging subjective consciousness? Why does Jaynes insist that the *Iliad* must be seen "as a window back into those unsubjective times when every kingdom was in essence a theocracy"?[20] Why not as a window into an emerging metaphor-

---

15 ibid., 216.
16 ibid., 217-18.
17 ibid., 82.
18 ibid., 82.
19 Jaynes, *The Origins of Consciousness*, 83.
20 ibid., 83.

ical mentality?

More questions are begged by Jaynes' sudden statement that in Homer's *Odyssey* there is a sharp distancing from the bicameral mentality of the *Iliad* "toward subjective consciousness [...] increasing use of spatial interiority and personification [...] a new mentality" (276). The only way he can account for this break is to argue that the *Odyssey* was not the work of one man named Homer but of a succession of poets writing "at least a century later". The *Odyssey*, I would say, does exhibit a clearer tendency toward introspection by way of its central character, Odysseus, who is able to exercise greater control over his passions away from the self-destructive and blind tendencies of Achilles. Odysseus was not a warrior at the level of Achilles, but he was more strategic and calculating in the conduct of war, the one who came up with the idea of a Trojan Horse. These are the works of the same author Homer. In the *Iliad* he is already pointing to the weaknesses and excessive nature of warriors like Achilles, admired though he was for being the greatest fighter, and for showing some clemency towards Priam, the father of Hector. But what ultimately distinguishes Achilles was the thymotic part of his soul, a part that Plato would later identify with the "spirited" or passionate side of males with overweening pride. This part of the soul was intensified by the aristocratic lifestyle of Europeans, and insomuch as the rational side of the soul was undeveloped, and one was lacking in reflection or introspection, the pursuit of "immortal glory" would manifest itself in too rash, impulsive, and cruel a fashion.

The society depicted in the *Iliad* was not, as Jaynes says, "quite similar to the contemporary divinely ruled kingdoms of Mesopotamia".[21] The *Iliad* grew out of a prototypical Indo-European aristocratic society, Mycenae, in which the king was first among equals. Mycenaeans are the first people in human history to have created a true aristocratic civilization in which "some men," not just the king, were free to deliberate over major issues affecting the group and free to aspire for heroic greatness. As I argued in *The Uniqueness of Western Civilization* (2012), and in *Faustian Man in a Multicultural Age* (2017), the material origins of this aristocratic individualist ethos are to be found in the pastoral lifestyle of the IEs,

---

21 ibid., 80.

their original domestication and riding of horses, their invention of wheeled vehicles in the fourth millennium BC, together with the efficient exploitation of the "secondary products" of domestic animals (dairy products, textiles, harnessing), all of which gave IEs a more robust physical anthropology and the most dynamic way of life in their time. To be worthy of an aristocratic status one had to demonstrate one's capacity for heroic action, one's ability to differentiate oneself from the others as a fighter and a man of the highest honor. This relentless obsession with their status, with their pride, to be honored by their peers, intensified the natural inclination that men have to become men.[22] It also engendered an introspective and metaphorical style of speaking and writing. The *Iliad* is packed with metaphors and analogies, and with identifiable personalities with differentiated psychological dispositions.

EUROPEAN MALE NATURE, NOT "HUMAN NATURE"

As serious a scholar as Snell was, and incredibly important as Jaynes' book is, they were not able in the era that they were living, in the aftermath of the defeat of the "worst evil in history," the Nazi movement, to contemplate the notion that Europeans were a whole new breed of human beings. Belonging to a generation prohibited from speaking about Europe's superior culture, and compelled by external (bicameral) factors to speak of the "human race" as a homogeneous species, Snell and Jaynes examined the origins of consciousness as if they were examining a phenomenon occurring among humans as such, rather than among a most singular people. Snell knows that the Greeks invented the literary genres of

---

22 The biology of men is such that throughout history, cross-culturally, they have had to prove to other men that they are men, reliable, courageous, manly, and tough. (I need hardly say that this requirement "to become a man" has declined dramatically in the West in recent decades). I examine the way in which the aristocratic culture of Indo-Europeans intensified and individualized this need by men to demonstrate the veracity of their sexual biological state of being in "The Masculine Preconditions of Individualism, the Indo-Europeans, and the Modern Hegelian Concept of Collective Freedom" *Council of European Canadians* (May 1, 2018), https://www.eurocanadian.ca/2018/05/masculine-preconditions-of-individualism-indo-europeans-hegelian-concept-collective-freedom.html

the epic, lyric poetry, and dramatic tragedy. He knows that they invented prose writing, discovered the mind, how to write proper history based on evidence rather than hearsay, invented logic and deductive reasoning, as well as inductive reasoning. But then Snell takes the Greek invention of "*humanitas*" to mean that the Greeks were starting to think that "each and every human being has his own share of dignity and of freedom",[23] confounding the Greek idea that humans are beings with potentialities that can be developed through a proper education with the post-WWII human rights idea that all humans are equally born with inherent rights.

In speaking of "*humanitas*" the Greeks actually took themselves to be the embodiment of what is potentially highest among humans in contrast to the barbarians. It is true that with Euripides (and others) they were projecting onto humans generally their own pursuit of excellence, their own admiration for humans as beings capable of excellence, and their own respect for individuality and for the humanity of non-aristocrats in a more democratic Greece; however, it is a far cry to attribute to the ancient Greeks any modern notion of human rights and equality. It is more accurate to say the Greeks were seeing themselves as a frame of reference, the standard for humanity, without realizing it. They were ethnocentrically projecting their universalism onto others.

This ethnocentrism has reached high levels of convoluted proportions in our times. Current classicists, in the same vein as they endorse the enriching differences of non-Western cultures, unconsciously portray the particular values of the West as "human values". When charged that they are "cultural imperialists," they resort to the historically fabricated claim that Western works are not really "Western" but part of a world of "intermingling races" and trade networks. This confabulated mentality, combined with the ever growing influence of the Darwinian claim that all humans developed a *uniform and ready-made* conscious equipment (albeit with variations in IQ among races) in the pursuit of survival strategies, has made it very difficult for scholars to give a proper account of the incredibly different mentality Europeans have exhibited since ancient times away from the bicameral cultures of the non-European world. Only Europeans became conscious and the

---

23 Snell, *The Discovery of the Mind*, 263.

causes of this consciousness need an explanation. The *Iliad* is the first work in Western literature and it is the first exhibiting consciousness.

The academic situation as it now stands is that the *Iliad* is a work that bespeaks of "human truths". Take Bernard Knox's "Introduction" to Robert Fagles' 1990 translation of the *Iliad*. This otherwise learned Introduction abounds in statements that seek to portray the *Iliad* as a poem written by and for humanity. Everyone after WWII was expected to write with a view to improving the "human condition," and the *Iliad*, or so we are told, contains moral messages by and for humanity. Here are some passages from this Introduction:

> The Iliad accepts violence as a permanent factor in *human life* and accepts it without sentimentality, for it is just as sentimental to pretend that war does not have its monstrous ugliness as it is to deny that is has its own strange and fatal beauty.
>
> The tragic course of Achilles' rage, his final recognition of *human values*—this is the guiding theme of the poem, and it is developed against a background of violence and death. But the grim progress of the war is interrupted by scenes which remind us that the brutality of war, though an integral part of *human life*, is not the whole of it...
>
> These two poles of the *human condition*, war and peace, with their corresponding aspects of *human nature*, the destructive and creative, are implicit in every situation and statement of the poem.[24]

This is confounding because the violence of the *Iliad* can only be fully comprehended in the context of a culture dominated by free aristocrats, because the values of the *Iliad* are not "human values" but European aristocratic values, because there is no tragic literature outside the West, because the *Iliad* testifies to the singular discovery of the mind in the West, and because in the West the destructive and creative are not two corresponding aspects of human nature but are instead inextricably dependent upon each other. Destructive warfare is the activity where ancient Greeks, before the full discovery of the mind, realized their potential for the highest

---

24 Bernard Knox, "Introduction" in *Homer: The Iliad*, trans. Robert Fagles.

in man. It was through their pursuit of heroic deeds that Europeans first achieved their individuality and started a process in which Europeans began to overcome the dark world of mysterious forces and unquestioned norms enveloping the subjective consciousness of humans. It is not just that war "releases essential creative instincts [...] heightens man's sense of life, his joy in his humanness, his sense of beauty in the world, and his love and respect for his fellow man".[25] It is that warfare carried by aristocratic men was the primordial foundation for the emergence of consciousness and the incredible cultural efflorescence of ancient Greece. It is very misleading to talk about "human values" and "fellow man" when the *Iliad* was singularly a product of a particular culture.

What makes this all the more intractable is that, in the same vein as the *Iliad* has been portrayed as a work that speaks about "the human condition," the literature of the non-Western world has been increasingly interpreted as if it were part of the same set of cultural values that made the West. Perhaps the best way to start bringing home how different the first book of Western civilization is, the *Iliad*, from all prior works produced by the surrounding bicameral civilizations, is to compare it to the Epic of Gilgamesh, seen as the greatest literary work produced in the East, and the "first heroic epic".

THE EPIC OF GILGAMESH IS NOT A HEROIC TRAGEDY

The story of Gilgamesh is not a heroic tragedy because the world this story grew from was not aristocratic. The upper classes of the Near Eastern world were not free; sovereignty in these states belonged to either god-kings or kings considered the viceroys of the gods. Yet, in our multicultural universities where "diversity" programs are the order of the day, and superficial variations are celebrated, the current trend among classicists has been to argue that *Gilgamesh* is an epic with "striking similarities" to the *Iliad* and to other Western poems such as *Beowulf*. A known expert on Homer,

---

(New York: Viking, 1990), 3-64.
25 Ian C. Johnston, *The Ironies of War: An Introduction to Homer's Iliad*. (Boston: University Press of America, 1988).

Jasper Griffin, in a long review of Stephen Mitchell's *Gilgamesh: A New English Version*, states that the heroic themes of the *Iliad* were predated by over a thousand years in "an extraordinary epic poem" known as *Gilgamesh*.[26] Similarly, N. K. Sanders, in an earlier English translation of this epic, informs us that the king Gilgamesh is "the first tragic hero."[27] I cannot agree with these classicists. We can agree with Walter Burkert's sensible enough point that in both the Homeric poems and *Gilgamesh* we have "epic" narratives which employ long verses repeated indefinitely, dealing with gods, sons of gods, and great men from the past.[28] We can agree as well both epics employ similar traits of style, standard epithets, formulaic verses, repetition of verses, and typical scenes. Up to a point, Burkert may be right also, at least on the surface, that the central characters in *Gilgamesh* and in Homer's epics are warriors who perform great deeds. But the differences, I would suggest, are far more striking than the resemblances.

To start with, the "hero" Gilgamesh appears, from the very beginning, as a typical Eastern ruler who claims to have achieved all the great things for his society, and that no one else has any achievements to their names. The only other fighting man in this epic is Enkidu, a wild man who lacks nobility. Unlike the *Iliad*, which consists of battle scenes constructed largely out of individual encounters designed to enhance the specific deeds of singular heroes, there are no individuals with identifiable biographies in *Gilgamesh*. The ruler, a king of Uruk or Erech, a city of Mesopotamia, first appears as a despot, in contradistinction to the ideal ruler who should be a Shepherd of the city; and, although it is the case that this was an ideal that motivated Eastern rulers to show concern for righteousness, consider the following acts attributed to Gilgamesh in the opening scenes, which clearly give him a tyrannical touch: "...his lust leaves no virgin to her lover, neither the warrior's daughter nor the wife of the noble."[29] As this passage

26 Jasper Griffin, "The True Epic Vision" review of Gilgamesh: A New English Version, *New York Review of Books*, March 9, 2006.
27 In the following assessment of Gilgamesh I will be relying on this translation, *The Epic of Gilgamesh*, translated with an Introduction by N. K. Sanders (Penguin Edition, 1981).
28 Walter Burkert, *The Orientalizing Revolution* (Cambridge, UK: Cambridge University Press, 1992).
29 Sanders, "Introduction", *The Epic of Gilgamesh*, 62.

suggests, even the daughters of warriors and the wives of nobles were not safe from the whims and appetites of kings. In stark contrast, Agamemnon, King of Mycenae, appears in the opening pages of the *Iliad* facing the fury and insubordination of his most important vassal, Achilles, with all his followers, for having offended his honor in taking a girl Achilles had earned as a prize from his army. Although Achilles is "the best of the Achaeans," the performer of "the greatest deeds of martial valor," the *Iliad* devotes long sketches to the personal ancestries of other aristocrats including, for example, Diomedes in Book 5, Patroclus in Book 16, and Menelaus in Book 17. Even warriors who are not major figures are identified by name, their parents, wife, and children, and their homelands.

In Homer's vision of the Mycenaean past, Agamemnon is surrounded by free, prideful men who are always deliberating and debating their actions rather than subserviently following the commands of an autocratic king. The king Agamemnon, writes Martin Nilsson, "was no Pharaoh nor was he a king by divine right like the Hellenistic kings and the late Roman Emperors".[30] The right to attend the popular assembly was restricted to those who risked their lives in battle. The chiefs were the representatives of their contingents and spoke in their name. Freedom of speech was inherent at the assembly. Much of the *Iliad* consists of speeches by aristocratic warriors arguing over strategies, and debating the king's proposals over the conduct of the war. The *Iliad* is abundant in the creation of "some two dozen finely individualized major characters" in addition to numerous minor figures. No single autocrat made all the decisions and boasted about his deeds without challengers.[31]

---

30 Martin Nilsson, *Homer and Mycenae* (London: Metheun and Co., [1933] 1968), 233

31 Actually, as M.L. West observes: "A king may himself be a hero, but in most cases the roles are distinct. The outstanding hero—one may think of Achilles, Hector, Jason, Heracles, Arjuna, Beowulf, Cu Chulainn, Lancelot—is usually not identified with the king. The king is remembered for kingly virtues such as justice, prosperity, liberality or his lack of them." A hero in Indo-European poetry was "generally a man of supreme physical strength and endurance allied to moral qualities such as fearlessness, determination, and a propensity for plunging into dangerous and daunting enterprises" See *Indo-European Poetry and Myth* (Oxford: Oxford University Press, 2007), 411.

Now, to be sure, the relation of the *Iliad* to historical reality has long been a matter of scholarly interest. A few scholars have claimed that what Homer really mirrors is his own contemporary world of the 8th century, while others have argued that his epics call back the world of "Dark Age" Greece around 1050-900 BC. The stronger consensus is that Homer's poems reflect the central cultural values of the Mycenaean Age of about 1400-1100 BC. There are a variety of elements in his epics representing different periods regarding the types of weapons, shields, and metals mentioned in the poems. But the social structures and values are still drawn primarily from the world of late aristocratic Mycenae.[32]

Oswyn Murray thinks that Mycenaean states were rather similar to the "oriental despotisms" of Mesopotamia and Egypt.[33] He may be correct that the warrior people who founded Mycenae came to be influenced by the centralized palace economies of the Near East. I tend to favor the view that the political structure of the Greek mainland during the 2nd millennium was one of autonomous "feudal" warlords surrounded by aristocratic retainers under the nominal overlordship of Mycenae. The king was the overlord or the *wanax* of other lords. Mycenaean records do refer to a class called *hepetai* or "followers" who formed the court circle but these were also identified as the "companions" of the king. There are references as well to warriors called *telestai*, or men of telos, who were similarly wealthy aristocrats, masters of parcels of land which they had obtained in return for military undertakings with the king.[34]

With the collapse of Mycenaean culture around 1100 BC, and the destruction of Mycenae and the administrators who managed the centralizing palaces of the overlord, the distinction between the overlord and the vassal noble chieftains disappeared, and instead of a political order centered around an overlord-monarch,

---

32 J. V. Luce, *Homer and the Heroic Age* (New York: Harper & Row, 1975), 69-72. John Chadwick, *The Mycenaean World* (Cambridge: Cambridge University Press, 2005), 180-6.
33 Murray Oswyn, *Early Greece* (London: Fontana Paperbacks, 1980), 18
34 Luce, *Homer and the Heroic Age*, 79-80; Cyril Robinson, *A History of Greece* (New York, Methuen, 1983), 12-18; Chadwick, *The Mycenaean World*, 72; M.T.W. Arnheim, *Aristocracy in Greek Society* (London: Thames and Hudson, 1977), 15-17.

one finds in Greece many decentralized petty chiefdoms.[35] This may explain why in Homer's poems—to the degree that they partly reflect the preceding Dark Age—the king Agamemnon is portrayed as having very limited powers. Be that as it may, in Homer's time, which is known as the Archaic Age (roughly between 800 and 500 BC) aristocrats expected kings to consult a council consisting of the heads of the noble families. "Debate within the council or before the people was the basis of decision-making".[36]

I would insist that the crucial difference comes down to the absence of personal tragedy in *Gilgamesh*. I do not believe we can talk of heroism and tragedy when there is only one ruler with the chance to claim fame without peers to challenge him, question his deeds, and put him to the test. Burkert equates Gilgamesh's longing for immortality with the Homeric heroes' longing for "imperishable glory".[37] It is true that Gilgamesh longs for eternity, and on his journey, at the last moment, he finds a secret herb that promises the gift of eternal youth; but then a snake, a reptile, takes the herb as he is asleep, and so he fails to achieve eternity. The suggestion seems to be that even the king's destiny is ultimately decided by arbitrary (bicameral) forces or accidental events. Where is the heroism in a situation in which a snake decides the outcome? The message that death is the lot of mankind is decided by a snake. Moreover, while Gilgamesh is a hero who "wishes to make for himself a name" and in his journey defeats the giant monster Humbaba, it is noteworthy that what he yearns for is everlasting life, weeping bitterly when the snake steals the herb; which is, again, in direct contrast to the pursuit of personal immortality by Homer's Mycenaean warriors, who sought above all else, above comfort and life, to be renowned for glorious deeds. Indeed, whereas Gilgamesh yearned for everlasting life, the Greek heroes consciously rejected a long life without memorable deeds for a short life with immortal deeds. The contrast could not be greater.[38]

---

35 Victor Ehrenberg, *The Greek State* (New York: Norton Library, 1964), 17-20; Arnheim, *Aristocracy in Greek Society*, 38-39.
36 Oswyn, *Early Greece*, 58.
37 Walter Burkert, *Babylon, Memphis, Persepolis, Eastern Contexts of Greek Culture* (Cambridge, Mass.: Harvard University Press, 2004), 27.
38 Although Samuel Kramer tries as best as possible to mirror Gilgamesh as the "first heroic epic", he acknowledges that in comparison to the "written epics of the three Indo-European Heroic Ages" (the Greek, Indian, and Teutonic) "there

Sandars defines the tragic in *Gilgamesh* as "the conflict between the desires of the god and the destiny of man".[39] Griffin concludes with these words of "wisdom": "the highest nobility and the deepest truth are inseparable, in the end, from failure—however heroic—from defeat, and from death".[40] Griffin would have us believe that *Gilgamesh* and the *Iliad* are in the end inseparable. There is a tragic element in both: no matter what their heroes accomplish, the same end awaits them, namely defeat and death. Burkert thinks that the main message of both epics is the ethos of the mortality of humans in contrast to the enduring life of gods.[41] Again, I disagree. The gods of Mesopotamia were mysterious forces in the sight of which men felt fear and trepidation; they were gods lacking human traits yet in control of human destiny, responsible for the precariousness of life, military defeats, epidemics, floods and droughts.[42]

This was not so with the Greeks and their gods. Their gods were human-like in their desires and looks, lacking in terror and mystery; and, for all the tragic fate that awaited Achilles and the many other heroes, it was not a fate brought on by snakes stealing herbs, but a self-chosen fate by proud men who knew that men who yearn for greatness will be invaded by passions which appear as impersonal forces, sometimes as gods, which take over the individual in directions beyond their control. Yes, there is a common theme or atmosphere of fatalism and gloom in the *Iliad*, a keen awareness that those who strive for achievement in war pursue a course whose characteristic end is a "short-lived" life. But there is also a spirit of overweening confidence in man's capacity to strive, in the midst of moments of fear and doubt, against the most difficult obstacles.

Griffin writes that "there is no happy ending" in *Gilgamesh* just

---

is little characterization and psychological penetration in the Sumerian material. The heroes tend to be broad types, more or less undifferentiated, rather than highly personalized individuals". See *History Begins at Sumer* (New York: Anchor Books, 1959), 203.
39 Sandars, "Introduction" *The Epic of Gilgamesh*, 21.
40 Griffin, "The True Epic Vision".
41 Burkert, *Babylon, Memphis, Persepolis, Eastern Contexts of Greek Culture*, 26.
42 Herbert Muller, *Freedom in the Ancient World* (New York: Harper & Brothers, 1961).

as in the *Iliad* (and the *Song of Roland* and other heroic sagas of the West). I would say that the ending of *Gilgamesh* seems to be that the ways of men are unchangeable, and that it is not for men to ever comprehend the ultimate meaning of life, the unfathomable ways of the gods; all humans, "the master and the servant," are the same before the destinies decided by mysterious gods. This same Sumerian outlook remains in all the other versions of *Gilgamesh* from Babylonian to Assyrian times. In contrast, in the Iliad, as Katherine King writes, "it is only because death in its myriad forms is inescapable that it behooves a man to attempt to win honor, that is, to win the right to have the tangible good things of life—ranking place, rich meat, choice wine, and a good farmland—and to be looked up to as the gods one cannot be".[43] Humans are mortal; they are not gods, but they can win honor, a good farmland for their families and a good name, which lives on after their death.

Greek heroes sometimes asked for visible signs of divine support; signs which cannot be willed by human effort to show up at the desired time, but which might nevertheless happen by a happy coincidence. In the *Iliad* there are gods behind every event, what happens between humans down on earth appears to be planned and brought forth by gods located on a higher, exalted level. But when the gods present themselves to the aristocrats to deliver their wishes, they do so in a way that does not reduce them to a state of fright and feebleness. The gods speak as if they were speaking to peers, "with chivalrous courtesy," offering their advice, telling them it is better to follow the gods, if they wish, while the heroes communicate and react to the gods without losing their freedom and honor.

PLATO'S SELF-MASTERY

The exalted state of berserker inspiration associated with the fight for pure prestige, together with the entire IE aristocratic way of life, had a profound effect on the constitution of the human personality, awakening within it a sense of human "inwardness" and

---

43 Katherine King, *Achilles: Paradigms of the War Hero from Homer to the Middle Ages* (Berkeley: University of California, 1987), 5-7.

thereby the "discovery of the mind" and the restless rationality of the West. The evolution of a rational self has been debated under various headings, including "the evolution of the concept of the Greek psyche," "the early Greek concept of the soul," the Socratic ideal "know thyself," and "Plato's Self-Mastery". I will examine this complex discussion as they relate to the unique evolution of a Western self increasingly aware of the distinction between personal agency (or acting under one's initiative) and extraneous forces (or acting under the influence of gods and bodily organs or processes). I will begin with Charles Taylor's major philosophical work, *Sources of the Self*. This book, as the subtitle indicates, is mostly on *The Making of the Modern Identity*. I am only concerned here with the origins of consciousness and individual identity in a literary work, the *Iliad*, and will focus on that part of Taylor's book. According to Taylor, it was Plato who developed the idea of a "self-collected" character capable of ordering and controlling his extraneous appetites and emotions. He did so by articulating a concept of a "unified self" consisting of three parts—bodily appetites, emotions, and reason—of which reason was master of appetites and emotions.[44] As Plato explained it in his *Republic*, this tripartite self was said to be unified to the extent that reason was performing its proper virtue, namely wisdom. The emotional part (or "spirited" element) was guided by reason in the performance of its virtues of courage and fortitude.[45] The appetitive part was performing its functions in a manner consistent with the virtue of temperance.

Taylor informs us that Plato's concept of the self was not "modern" in that its ultimate criterion as to what constituted a self was defined as an order that was seen as outside us—in the Good or the Forms—rather than within us. It was Augustine who later introduced the inside/outside dichotomy and bequeathed to the West "the inwardness of radical reflexivity".[46] This insight eventually led to the development of the Kantian idea that humans are truly free only when they come to legislate for themselves the normative

---

44 Charles Taylor, *Sources of the Modern Self: The Making of the Modern Identity* (Cambridge, MA: Harvard University Press, 1991), 115-126.
45 *The Republic of Plato*. Translated with Introduction by Francis Conford (Oxford University Press, 1977), 129-143.
46 Taylor, *Sources of the Self*, 131.

ordering they wish to follow. Nevertheless, without Plato's concept of the "unified self" as a necessary means by which to come to terms with the proper cultivation of one's self-mastery, "the modern notion of interiority could never have developed".[47]

Taylor draws a sharp contrast between Plato's moral doctrine of self-mastery and Homer's concept of the self. He explains that in the modern West we take it for granted that "our thoughts, ideas, or feelings are 'within' us, while the objects in the world these mental states reflect on are 'without'".[48] This way of localizing ourselves inside ourselves is so bound up with our modern ways of growing up as singular personalities (with our own projects and inner life experiences) that we now think of this as natural. He clarifies that, on one basic level, humans at all times and places have had a sense that there is person "A" and person "B" to whom different physical attributes, actions, and momentary expressions can be attributed. Alongside this basic perception, there is, however, a newer and uniquely Western sense of agency that had its origins in ancient Greece. Plato represents the paradigmatic expression of the distinction between what is "inside" and what is "outside" a person. But this was not the way the self was viewed in Homeric times. Drawing on the commentaries of Snell and Richard Onians[49] on the *Iliad* and the *Odyssey*, Taylor notes the absence in these epics of words that could be translated in a way that clearly designated the "thoughts," "psyche," "feelings," and bodily sensations of each character. The meanings of these words portray characters with a fragmented and quasi-independent self. They lack a clear sense of the mental, emotional, and bodily components of their selves. The word "psyche," for instance, rather than designating the site of thinking and feeling, appears to designate a life force that enters the body and flees from it at death through the mouth.

Taylor makes reference to Snell's observation that Homeric heroes were driven to perform impressive deeds by a surge of energy and manic enthusiasm. This energy and enthusiasm was thought to be infused into them by gods. He compares these heroes to

---

47 ibid., 120.
48 ibid., 111.
49 Richard Onians, *The Origins of European Thought* (New York: Arno Press, [1951] 1973).

berserkers in "primitive" Scandinavian and early Celtic cultures; they too were filled by a kind of raging madness on the battle field—a psychic state ostensibly incompatible with the reflective and self-collected stance Plato envisioned as the ideal person in the *Republic*.

In other words, according to Taylor, in the Homeric epics, and in the berserker cultures of Europe, there were no fully integrated, autonomous agents or heroic characters capable of clearly distinguishing for themselves what was "inside" and what was "outside". He reads Plato's philosophy as an effort to subordinate the warrior-citizen morality of strength, courage, and glory—which grew out of the berserker barbarian past—to a philosophical morality of dispassionate deliberation. The part of the soul dealing with desire (*thymos*), which Plato associated with the warrior function, was thus relegated to a subordinate function in his Republic, secondary to the part of the soul dealing with reason, which he associated with the ruler function.

Taylor distinguishes, albeit broadly, between a Platonic (or Western-to-become-Modern) view of the self and a traditional view which prevailed everywhere else, including berserker/Homeric warrior cultures. He refers, in this context, to Geertz's anthropological reports from Java (Bali). In these reports, Geertz pointed to the absence in the language of Balinese people of words drawing a clear distinction between individual and group actions, between what was "inside" and "outside" the individual. He pointed to the way Balinese culture did not think of individuals as isolated, detachable beings, but as persons whose individualities were inextricably connected to the community and its way of life.

Insofar as Taylor's argument explains that a notion of the self is not given naturally to us, and that introspection is a Western achievement alone, I agree with Taylor. But his reading of the *Iliad* is flawed. Homeric man was already becoming "self-conscious" of his individuality. Self-consciousness was not the achievement of some philosopher sitting quietly; it was initiated by Indo-European berserkers obsessed with their individual deeds; they laid the groundwork for the dialectical evolution of the Western spirit towards ever higher levels of heightened self-awareness. Let us go directly to Geertz's argument, which Taylor barely touches upon, in order to highlight the contrast I see between Geertz's Balinese subjects and Indo-European or Homeric warriors. Geertz's familiar essay is entitled "'From the Native's Point of View': On the Nature of Anthropological Understanding".[50] The central passage of this article, on the "Javanese sense of what a person is," is the following:

> The "inside"/"outside" words, batin and lair [...] refer on the one hand to the felt realm of human experience and on the other to the observed realm of human behavior... Batin, the "inside" word, does not refer to a separate seat of encapsulated spirituality detached or detachable from the body, or indeed to a bounded unit at all, but to the emotional life of human beings taken generally. It consists of the fuzzy, shifting flow of subjective feeling perceived directly in all its phenomenological immediacy but considered to be, at its roots at least, identical across all individuals, whose individuality it thus effaces. And similarly, lair, the "outside" word, has nothing to do with the body as an object, even an experienced object. Rather, it refers to that part of human life which, in our culture, strict behaviorists limit themselves to studying—external actions, movements, postures, speech—again conceived as in its essence invariant from one individual to the next.

In contrast to modern Western individuals, Balinese men (and Geertz makes similar observations about other Near Eastern places) "do not float as bounded psychic entities, detached from their backgrounds and singularly named...[T]heir identity is an attribute they borrow from their setting."

Similarly, it has been a common perception that Homeric men, as well as European barbarians, understood themselves to be members of a close-knit group. As Aaron Gurevich has observed about the characters portrayed in Scandinavian Sagas, the "mental categories used are those of the unit, the individuals' own group: they look at themselves from outside as it were, through the eyes of society".[51] M.I. Finley has also written, regarding Homer's society, that its "basic values [...] were given, predetermined and so

---

50 Clifford Geertz, "From the Native's Point of View: On the Nature of Anthropological Understanding. *American Academy of Arts and Sciences*, 28, No.1 (1974).
51 Aaron Gurevich, *The Origins of European Individualism* (Oxford: Blackwell, 1995), 53.

were a man's place in the society and the privileges and duties that followed from his status".[52] Every individual had a given role and status within a well-defined cultural order. A warrior was thus expected to perform the role of a warrior, to show excellence in the performance of the martial virtues. Alasdair Macintyre, in his highly celebrated book *After Virtue* (originally published in 1981), follows Finley's idea that in Homeric society, as in other heroic societies like Iceland or Ireland, every individual acted "within a well-defined and highly determinate system of roles and statuses." He says that "it is only within their framework of rules and precepts that they [the characters of the *Iliad*] are able to frame purposes at all." He contrasts this "traditional" world of prescribed roles to the modern "capacity to detach oneself from any particular standpoint or point of view, to step backwards, as it were, and view and judge that standpoint or point of view from the outside".[53]

It is also the case that Snell and Onians, as Taylor points out, have argued that Homeric man constantly felt himself decisively influenced by gods and passions beyond his control. The Homeric self was likewise seen as fragmented, determined by the flux and fusion of "inside" and "outside" forces. Snell writes: "Mental and spiritual acts are due to the impact of external factors, and man is the open target of a great many forces which impinge on him and penetrate his very core".[54] Their bodily parts are not just physical but act as agents charged with an overflowing energy. Man was undifferentiated. The *noos* is mentioned in contexts that relate to "intellectual functions," "thinking," but at the same time one can hardly speak of Homeric individuals as having a separate faculty of thought, since *noos* is also mentioned in contexts whereby men are emotionally roused to action. *Noos* is not mere intellect; it is dynamic [...] and emotional.[55] Yet *thymos* is also a term used mainly in reference to emotional issues; in numerous passages in the *Iliad* it is the seat of joy, pleasure, love, etc., but in others it is

---

52 M.I. Finley, *The World of Odysseus* (New York: Viking, 1954), 134.
53 Alasdair MacIntyre, *After Virtue* (University of Notre Dame Press, 2003), 121-130.
54 Snell, *The Discovery of the Mind*, 20.
55 Onians, *The Origins of European Thought*, 83.

the organ of "knowledge".⁵⁶ Mental acts like "thinking," "desiring," and "feeling" are ascribed to physical organs. Onians writes that the organ of mind in Homer is in the lungs; the mind or the "stuff of consciousness" is identical with breath.⁵⁷ The "psyche" is a word used to characterize the soul, and something that is the prize of battle, which is risked and saved in battle, but it is also a word used to denote the breath of life which departs through the mouth.⁵⁸

THE BEGINNINGS OF SELFHOOD IN THE ILIAD

Thus, according to Snell and Onians, Homeric vocabulary showed an absence of awareness of a unitary self. Therefore, it would seem to follow (against what I have been arguing) that the notion of the "I" as seat of self-consciousness cannot be attributed to Indo-European/Homeric heroes. There are several reasons why these observations are only half the story. First, the interpretation that is now commonly associated with the name of Snell has not gone unchallenged. For example, Jan Bremmer, in his book *The Early Greek Concept of the Soul*, believes that Homeric heroes are frequently portrayed using the personal pronoun, saying "I wish" or "I thought", which consequently suggests that they "must have had a general sense of psychic coherence and, at least, an imperfect notion of the unity of the personality".⁵⁹ He also thinks that Snell ignored Homer's focus on individually named heroes, as well as the numerous heroes who defy the norms of gods and men, such as Ajax and Achilles. One should not be surprised by Bremmer's qualification that "in Homer's time the individual did not yet know of the will as an ethical factor, nor did he distinguish between what was inside and outside himself as we do".⁶⁰ Nevertheless, Bremmer believes that in Homer there was already a tendency to dematerialize mental attributes or words. He notes that psyche

---

56 Snell, *The Discovery of the Mind*, 13.
57 Onians, *The Origins of European Thought*, 32-33, 51-52.
58 Snell, *The Discovery of the Mind*, 9.
59 Jan Bremmer, *The Early Greek Concept of the Soul* (Princeton University Press, 1983, 66-7.
60 Bremmer, *The Early Greek Concept of the Soul*, 67.

has mostly a non-physical mode of existence,[61] that *noos* is "never conceived as something material," and that *thymos* is, "above all, the source of emotions".[62]

Secondly, as Malcolm Schofield has pointed out, the *Iliad* was structured around deliberation and clashes of views about what course of action should be taken in any given circumstance and about what values should be followed. While there is no question that in Homer's time one's class or status carried strong normative requirements, and that, in this respect, decisions cannot be seen as autonomous acts of self-legislation, but must be interpreted in reference to status-based considerations, the existence of debate and disagreement is a notorious feature of Homer's epics. Finley exaggerates when he writes that the obligation to abide by the norms associated by one's status "were not subject to analysis or debate... [but] left only the narrowest margin for the exercise of what we should call judgment".[63] It is best to think there was an aristocratic code that celebrated competition for great deeds by free men with characters that would not submit to despotic rulers, to impersonal collective norms.

Expanding on Schofield, Christopher Gill examines four deliberative monologues in Homer's epics in which chieftains are clearly seen to face dilemmas over the proper course of action they should take, reasoning through alternative possibilities rather than acting as if their choices were settled definitely by the requirements of their status. He questions the assumption that status-based values such as *aristeuein* ("to be best" or "to win honor") were rigid codes which settled dilemmas unquestionably. He shows how four chieftains in the *Iliad* and *Odyssey*, including three major ones, Hector, Odysseus, and Menelaus, faced comparable dilemmas yet reached "different conclusions by different reasoning".[64] Although none of these characters disowns the "thick values" associated with their status, Gill's conclusion, after carefully examining each monologue, is that there was a kind of self-conscious

---

61 ibid., 16-18
62 ibid., 57, 54.
63 As cited in M. Schofield, "Euboulia in the Iliad" *Classical Quarterly* 36 (1986): 6-31.
64 Christopher Gill, *Personality in Greek Epic, Tragedy and Philosophy. The Self in Dialogue* (Oxford University Press, 1996), 71

agent involved in determining what "being best" meant in different situations.⁶⁵ Gill also detects, particularly in the case of Hector's monologue regarding what course of action to take in his role as Troy's defender, and in response to alternative choices offered to him by members of his household, a "psychological agent who acts on the basis of reasons and reasoning." It is worth quoting this passage for the support it gives to the argument I am making on the birth of selfhood:

> The self involved is also an ethical agent whose reasons and reasoning are informed by the action-guiding beliefs of his community and by his engagement with his social role. It is this kind of 'self' of which Hector's monologue shows 'consciousness', and whose 'responsibility' is acknowledged. This kind of self-consciousness is displayed partly by the significant use of internalized dialogue. It is also displayed by other distinctive features [...] One is the use of the deliberative formula, 'that would be much better'..."⁶⁶

Finally, it is strange that the same Jaynes who says that in trying to understand the origins of consciousness we should pay attention to the use of metaphors in ancient writings, does not have a word to say about the continuous use of metaphors in the *Iliad*. I will only bring up a simple point in what is a very complicated topic in need of much analysis. According to Jaynes, "understanding a thing is to arrive at a metaphor for that thing by substituting something more familiar to us".⁶⁷ Drawing a connection or a comparison with something that is familiar to us is what allows us, and what shows to others, understanding of what we are speaking about. We use metaphors to try to convey to others what we are thinking, what's in our minds, which is an act of introspection, of inventing a subjective mind space inside our own heads, metaphorically seeing something by describing it in words familiar to us. When we imagine ourselves "doing" this or that heroic action, and "making" decisions on the basis of imagined "outcomes," we are imagining our "selves" behaving in an imagined world. We are seeing the reality we are describing, or ourselves "moving about

---

65 ibid., 70-93.
66 ibid., 85-6.
67 Jaynes, *The Origins of Consciousness*, 52.

in our imagination "by way of analogy, by way of constructing an analog space with an analog 'I' that can observe that space, and move metaphorically in it".⁶⁸

Now, if Jaynes does not bring up a single metaphor from the *Iliad*, Snell dedicates many pages to the use of metaphors, but rather than framing this discussion in relation to the origins of consciousness, he gets into an intricate discussion of how Greek thought moved from Homeric analogies and metaphorical phrases "to the analogies of science and philosophy".⁶⁹ He says that in Homer "the mind is understood by analogy with the physical organs and their function".⁷⁰ The motions of the soul are metaphorically described or made familiar by analogy with animal life. The hero rushes upon the enemy as a lion rushes upon the herd. A man who walks like a lion has a very healthy thymotic impulse, strength and courage. Yet, from what we have said above, there is some degree of introspection in the *Iliad* in which heroes do seem to deliberate about what is the proper course of action to take, whether he ought to do this or that. While it is true that the scenes of reflection and resolution are stereotypical, and gods intervene to help bring about the choice, we do sense an "I" that imagines different outcomes as a result of different choices. Achilles imagines himself dying as a young man in a *blaze* of glory or living a long and *obscure* life. All the heroes come to the same fatal decision and the decision in this sense seems predetermined. Nevertheless this is a culture in which men have decided to strive for heroism and immortality rather than give way to the appetitive instinct for comfort, or to the fear of death. It is not that they have fatalistically chosen a short life but that they understand that violence and a shorter life are an inescapable reality of a heroic life in their world.

CONCLUDING THOUGHTS

The increasing detachment of the self from the ensemble of the surrounding world manifested itself in different degrees by different sides of the human personality in multiple cultural ways during

---

68 ibid., 65.
69 ibid., 191.
70 ibid., 198.

the course of Western history. There is a biological starting point, a necessary biological precondition, which consists in the fact that a man is not born a man but must become a man. Throughout history, across all cultures, men became men only by proving their masculinity in risky contests with the surrounding environment and with other adversarial men. It is this struggle to become a man in the eyes of other men that sets the preconditions for the conscious differentiation of the male ego from the enveloping womb-like environment. But this precondition and embryonic differentiation cannot be seen as the first cultural sign of an emerging human personality; it is only a necessary precondition, a very important one, in making us realize that we must avoid looking at some religious experience, some intellectual or artistic movement, for the first ushering of individualism. We must look instead for what is today seen as the least civilized aspect of human nature: the contesting and violent struggle of men to become men.

The first signs of individualism are to be witnessed among the horse riding Indo-European aristocratic warriors who originally came storming out of the Pontic Steppes in the fourth millennium BC. This obsession with proving oneself a man was intensified within the aristocratic polities of Indo-Europeans, which afforded "some men", not just a despotic ruler, the opportunity to pursue individual glory and immortal fame. The struggle for honor and recognition by one's aristocratic peers, which is a struggle for an immaterial form of validation by other men, and against the biological fear of death, nurtured an awareness among aristocrats that each hero is not just a body with appetites and limbs but also a character, an individual with an *immaterial psyche* that is risked in battle, and with a *thymos* that is "spirited" and causes intense emotions, and with a *noos* that represents a separate faculty of thinking. While the distinction between the soul, the intellect, and the bodily organs is not well crystallized in Homer's *Iliad*, individuals with outstanding feats associated with their particular names are beginning to be recognized, and not just in the *Iliad*, but in all the earliest sagas, myths, and heroic accounts of Indo-Europeans. We find in these heroic tales individuals with private grudges, private frustrations, and private internal spaces, even if we have to wait for Plato to witness a clear distinction between bodily appetites, thymotic emotions, and mental faculties.

We can see early on in history how the individualism of aristocrats was democratized in the Greek hoplite citizen soldiers who defeated the Persian invaders, the independent farmer who owns his land and "suffers no master, speaks his due, fights his own battles, and leaves an imprint of self-reliance and non-conformity, a legacy of independence that is the backbone of Western society". This legacy continued through the small holding farmers who made up the Roman legions and fought as citizens, the free peasants of Medieval Europe with their self-governing communes, to the citizens of modern states demanding representation. In Homeric man there is a latent awareness, but still nebulous articulation, of the human personality as an "I" that is not the plaything of irrational or mysterious forces but is capable of some deliberation among alternative choices. Decisions are indeed shaped by the gods but the Olympian gods "carry the graceful stamp of an aristocratic society [...] when a god associates with a man, he elevates him, and makes him free, strong, courageous, certain of himself [...] far removed from the mysteries of chthonic darkness and ecstasy".[71]

In the next archaic period of Greek history, between 650 and 500 BC, we see characters becoming more conscious of their personality, with the rise of the lyric poets, Sappho and Archilochus, in their regular use of phrases expressing "a more precise appreciation of the self," the "inwardly felt" emotions of the poet.[72] With the tragedians of the next generation, Aeschylus and Sophocles, we witnessed for the first time in history the interpretation of human action in the light of individual choice: "what am I to do?" This process of detachment from the ensemble of external forces and determinations is taken one step further by the characters in Euripides, who ask whether their actions were just in a more real-

---

71 Snell, *The Discovery of the Greek Mind*, 23-42. I should add here that Snell, like Jaynes, does not say outright that the Iliad is devoid of "human intellection". "The heroes of the Iliad, however, no longer feel that they are the playthings of irrational forces; they acknowledge their Olympian gods who constitute a well-ordered and meaningful world" (22). "It would be absurd to suppose that Apollo or Athena could have regarded the intellect as their enemy" (39). "Homer's myths reveal two features which anticipate the subsequent enlightenment [...] They encourage self-knowledge in the spirit of the Delphic motto: 'Know thyself,' and thus they extol measure, order, and moderation" (207).
72 Snell, 47-48.

istic setting than the solemn ostentation found in Aeschylus.

A history of individualism in all its expressions in literature, both in depth and complexity of characters, as well as in the persistent emergence of new styles of writing, has yet to be written. The same is true for painting, philosophy, law, political theory, historical writing, and scientific knowledge. No one in our universities wants to talk about the immense originality of Europeans because it is an embarrassment to the incredible poverty of multiculturalism. A history of sculpture alone would have to acknowledge the amazing breakthrough of the Greeks in detaching themselves from the unchanging styles of the Orient and making the discovery of foreshortening, in building "in marble and with a splendour and nobility never known before," and in learning to seize, towards the end of the fourth century, "the individual character of a physiognomy", a style that would be advanced by the Roman realistic portraiture of private individuals "in which every line, crease, wrinkle, and even blemish was ruthlessly recorded".

There is an immense complexity in the development of many forms of European individualism through the Roman discovery of the legal persona, the Christian emphasis on the inner conscience of the believer, through the Renaissance all the way into the Cartesian method, in which only the veracity of the thinking self is demonstrated, and only exact mathematical truths are accepted. Multiple explanations have been offered for this individualism, always in a truncated way, each specialist emphasizing one period and one dimension of this individualism. The only way we can comprehend this history is by going back to the beginnings, to the *Iliad* where we witness the first literary instance of individualism and consciousness in history by a unique collectivity of people known as "Europeans".

RICARDO DUCHESNE.

MAY, 2018.

TRANSLATOR'S PREFACE

HAVING now nearly completed my translation of the Iliad of Homer, I sit down to write the Preface, that it may be prefixed to the first volume. To this task of translation, which I began in 1865, I afterwards gave myself the more willingly because it helped in some measure to divert my mind from a great domestic sorrow. I am not sure that, when it shall be concluded, it may not cost me some regret to part with so interesting a companion as the old Greek poet, whose thoughts I have, for four years past, been occupied, though with interruptions, in the endeavor to transfer from his own grand and musical Greek to our less sonorous but still manly and flexible tongue.

In what I shall say of my own translation I do not mean to speak in disparagement of any of the previous English versions of the Iliad, nor to extenuate my obligations to some of them. I acknowledge that although Homer is, as Cowper has well observed, the most perspicuous of poets, I have been sometimes, perhaps often, guided by the labors of my predecessors to a better mode of dealing with certain refractory passages of my author than I should otherwise have found. Let me, without detracting from their merits, state what I have endeavored to do. I have endeavored to be strictly faithful in my rendering; to add nothing of my own, and to give the reader, so far as our language would allow, all that I found in the original. There are, however, in Homer, frequently recurring, certain expressions which are merely a kind of poetical finery, introduced when they are convenient to fill out a line or to give it a sonorous termination, and omitted when they are not needed for this purpose. The Greeks, for example, almost whenever they are spoken of are magnanimous, or valiant, or warlike, or skilled in taming steeds: the Trojans are magnanimous also, and valiant, and warlike, and equally eminent in horsemanship. The warriors of the Iliad are all sons of some magnanimous or warlike parent. Achilles is the son of Peleus, and Peleus is magnanimous; and these epithets are repeated upon page after page throughout the poem. Achilles is spoken of as swift-footed or godlike almost whenever he appears, and sometimes is honored by both epithets. Hector is illustrious, and knightly, and distinguished by his beamy crest. Even the coxcomb Paris, for whom Homer seems to entertain a proper contempt, is godlike. These complimentary additions to the name of the warrior are, however, dispensed with whenever the hexameter is rounded to a well-sounding conclusion without them. Where they appear in the Greek, I have in nearly all instances retained them, making Achilles swift-footed and Ulysses fertile in resources, to the end of the poem; but in a very few cases, where they embarrassed the versification, I have used the liberty taken by Homer himself, and left them out. Everywhere else it has been my rule not to exclude from the translation anything which I found in the text of my author.

There is another point in regard to which I have taken equal pains, and which seems to me equally important. I have endeavored to preserve the simplicity of style which distinguishes the old Greek poet, who wrote for the popular ear and according to the genius of his language, and I have chosen such English as offers no violence to the ordinary usages and structure of our own. I have sought to attain what belongs to the original,—a fluent narrative style, which shall carry the reader forward without the impediment of unexpected inversions and capricious phrases, and in which, if he find nothing to stop at and admire, there will at least be nothing to divert his attention from the story and the characters of the poem, from the events related and the objects described. I think that not many readers of the present day would agree with Pope, who, as Spence relates, after remarking that he had nothing to say for rhyme, went on to observe that he doubted whether a poem could be supported without it in our language, unless it were stiffened with such strange words as would destroy our language itself. It is remarkable that this should have been said by one who had given the reading world an edition of Shakespeare, in whose dramas are to be found passages of blank-verse which might be instanced as the perfection of that form of versification,—not to be excelled in sweetness of modulation, and grace and freedom of language,—without a single harsh inversion, or any of that clumsy stiffening which Pope so disapproved, yet seemed to think so necessary. The other dramatists of the Elizabethan period also supply examples of the same noble simplicity of language and construction, suited to the highest poetry. In this translation the natural order of the words has been carefully preserved, as far as the exigencies of versification would allow, and I have ventured only upon those easy deviations from it which form no interruptions to the sense, and at most only remind the reader that he is reading verse.

I have chosen blank-verse for this reason among others, that it enabled me to keep more closely to the original in my rendering, without any sacrifice either of ease or of spirit in the expression. The use of rhyme in a translation is a constant temptation to petty infidelities, and to the employment of expressions which have an air of constraint, and do not the most adequately convey the thought. I had my reasons also for not adopting the ballad measure, which some have thought to allow the nearest approach to the manner of Homer. There are, it is true, certain affinities between the style of Homer and that of the old ballad poems of Great Britain. Both were the productions of a rude age; both were composed to be sung to public audiences; and this gave occasion to certain characteristics in which they resemble each other. But the Homeric poems, as it seems to me, are beyond the popular ballads of any modern nation in reach of thought and in richness of phraseology; and if I had adopted that form of poetry there would have been, besides the disadvantage of rhyme, a temptation to make the version conform in style and spirit to the old ballads of our own literature, in a degree which the original does not warrant, and which, as I think, would lead to some sacrifice of its dignity. I did not adopt the hexameter verse, principally for the reason that in our language it is confessedly an imperfect form of versification, the true rhythm of which it is difficult for those whose ear is accustomed only to our ordinary metres to perceive. I found that I could not possibly render the Greek hexameters line for line, like Voss in his marvellous German version, in which he has not only done this, but generally preserved the pauses in the very part of the line in which Homer placed them. We have so many short words in English, and so few of the connective particles which are lavishly used by Homer, that often when I reached the end of the Greek line I found myself only in the middle of my line in English. This difficulty of subduing the thought—by compression or expansion of phrase—to the limits it must fill would alone have been sufficient to deter me from attempting a translation in hexameters. I therefore fell back upon blank-verse, which has been the vehicle of some of the noblest poetry in our language; both because it seemed to me by the flexibility of its construction best suited to a narrative poem, and because, while it enabled me to give the sense of my author more perfectly than any other form of verse, it allowed me also to avoid in a greater degree the appearance of constraint which is too apt to belong to a translation.

I make no apology for employing in my version the names Jupiter, Juno, Venus, and others of Latin origin, for Zeus, Here, Aphrodite, and other Greek names of the deities of whom Homer speaks. The names which I have adopted have been naturalized in our language for centuries, and some of them, as Mercury, Vulcan, and Dian, have even been provided with English terminations. I was translating from Greek into English, and I therefore translated the names of the gods, as well as the other parts of the poem.

In explanation of what may appear to some readers an unauthorized abridgment of the famous simile of the moon and stars at the end of the Eighth Book, I will mention here, by way of note,—the only one which I shall have occasion to make,—that in translating I have omitted two lines of the text, which the best critics regard as not properly belonging to it, but as transferred by some interpolator from another simile in the Sixteenth Book, where they are found in their proper place.

In the intimate acquaintance with the Iliad which the work of translation has given me, an impression has been revived which was made upon my mind when in my boyhood I first read that poem in an English version. I recollect very well the eager curiosity with which I seized upon the translation of Pope when it came within my reach, and with what avidity I ran through the pages which rendered into our language what was acknowledged to be the greatest production of poetic genius that the world had seen. I read with a deep interest for the fate of Troy, and with a kindly feeling toward Hector, whose part I took warmly against the bloodthirsty Achilles; and great as might have been the guilt of Paris, I read with an earnest wish that Troy might be delivered from its besiegers. When I came to the end of the poem, I laid it down with a feeling of disappointment. I was not told, save in certain dim predictions, what became of Troy, which the Greeks had mustered from so many regions to besiege, nor what was the fate of the mild and venerable Priam, and the aged Hecuba, and Andromache, the gentle and affectionate wife, and her infant son,—personages for whose fortunes the poet had so powerfully awakened my concern and my curiosity. Helen, to recover whom the war was waged, was still in Troy, and Paris, her effeminate husband, was still alive and unharmed. Why the Trojans, who hated Paris—why Hector and the other sons of Priam, who disapproved of their brother's conduct—why Priam himself, who is never said to have approved of it, did not insist that the seducer should restore Helen to her first and proper husband, for whom she seems to have still entertained a lingering regard, I could never imagine. Particularly strange it seemed that Paris was not forced by his countrymen to give up Helen after the combat between him and Menelaus, in which he was clearly overcome, and by the terms of the solemn treaty which preceded the duel was bound to restore his stolen bride and her wealth to the Greeks. The poet has chosen to leave that circumstance without adequate explanation. The breaking of the truce by Pandarus, and the sudden renewal of the war in consequence, does not explain it, for afterwards, in the Seventh Book, we have Antenor proposing, in council, to restore Helen and her wealth, as a certain way of ending the war,—a proposal which is not adopted simply because Paris objects to it. Paris would not consent to restore Helen, and the Trojan princes and leaders, as if Paris were their absolute monarch, allowed him to have his way, and to prolong a war which Hector foresaw—as he says in the famous interview with Andromache—was to end in the destruction of Troy. The impression to which I refer has been confirmed by the minute study which I have recently made of the poem. I can make nothing of it but a detached chapter of the poetic history of the Trojan war,—an episode in the narrative of that long siege which was to be concluded by a greater event than any recorded in the Iliad, the taking of the city of Troy;—a work of an inexhaustible imagination, with characters vigorously drawn and finely discriminated, and incidents rapidly succeeding each other and infinitely diversified,—everywhere a noble simplicity, mellifluous numbers, and images of beauty and grandeur; yet everywhere indications that the poem had a continuation. It is full of references to events which are yet to be related, and provokes a desire for further disclosures, which it fails to gratify. There are frequent allusions to the brief term of life allotted to Achilles, and several, one of which I have already mentioned, to the final capture of Troy. Thetis predicts that her son, perishing almost immediately after taking the life of Hector, will not live to see the fall of the besieged city. The audiences before whom the books of the Iliad were recited by the minstrels would naturally say: "You speak of the capture of Troy; tell us how it was taken at last. Achilles, the mightiest of warriors, you say, was to be slain soon after the death of Hector. Relate the manner of his death, and how it was received by the Greeks and the Trojans. Describe his funeral, as you described those of his friend Patroclus and his adversary Hector. Tell us what became of Andromache, and Astyanax, her son, and all the royal family of Priam." Thus may we suppose that, until Aristotle arose to demonstrate the contrary, the fable of the Iliad must have appeared to the general mind to be incomplete.

Let me say a word or two of the personage whom the critics call the hero of the Iliad. Achilles is ill-used by Agamemnon, the general-in-chief of the Greeks,—and so far he has the sympathy of the reader; but he is a ferocious barbarian at best, and as the narrative proceeds, he loses all title to our interest. His horrid prayer that the Greeks may be slaughtered by thousands until they learn to despise a monarch who has done him a personal injury, and his inhuman delight in the havoc made of them by the Trojans under Hector, cause us to turn from him with the horror and aversion due to a selfish and cruel nature which imposes no reserve or restraint upon its own impulses. His warm affection for his gentle friend and companion, Patroclus, partly restores him to our favor; but his pitiless treatment of the Trojans who supplicate him for quarter, and his capture of twelve Trojan youths in order to cut their throats at the funeral pile of Patroclus, as he afterwards does in cold blood, bring back our disgust; and when Hector with his dying voice warns him of his approaching death, the reader has no objection to offer. If Achilles be the hero of the poem, the poet has not succeeded in obtaining for him either our good opinion or our good wishes. In the fortunes of Hector, however, whose temper is noble and generous, who while grieving at the crime of Paris defends his country with all his valor, whose character is as gentle and affectionate as it is spirited and manly, it is impossible for the reader not to feel a strong interest. The last book of the Iliad relates the recovery of his dead body from the Greeks, and the celebration of his funeral in Troy. In this book, also, the character of Achilles appears less unamiable, since he grants the rites of hospitality to Priam, and is persuaded by his entreaties to restore, for a princely ransom, the dead body of Hector, contrary to his first resolution. It is to be observed, however, that he is moved to this, not by his own native magnanimity, but by considerations which indirectly relate to himself,—that is to say, by being artfully led to think of his own father, Peleus, an aged man like Priam, anxiously waiting in his distant palace for the return of his son from the war, and fearing that he may never behold him again. Once in the interview with Priam the fierce and brutal nature of Achilles breaks out in threats, which terrify the old king into silence. Priam is himself warned by the gods that he is not safe in remaining overnight in the tent of Achilles, and, lest he should not be protected from the ferocity of Agamemnon, withdraws by stealth in the darkness and returns to Troy.

    I have no answer to make to those who regard it as a blemish in the great work of Homer that he represents the gods in their dealings with men as governed, for the most part, by motives either mean and base, or frivolous and childish. In the Trojan war everything happens by their direction or their prompting. In the system of Homer it is they who stir up men to strife, who bring on the battles, promote the slaughter, and bring it to an end, urge the personages of the fable to ruinous follies and imprudences, and give or withhold victory at their pleasure; and in all this their rule is not one of justice and beneficence, but of caprice. Their favor is purchased by hecatombs, and their hatred incurred by acts which have no moral quality that should give offence to an upright judge. They are debauched, mercenary, rapacious, and cruel; they dwell in a world in which the rules of right and the maxims necessary to the well-being of human society find no recognition. It was for this reason that Plato, the earliest author of an *Index expurgatorius* forbade the circulation of the writings of the Greek poets in his imaginary commonwealth.

Yet let me say this in favor of my author, that in one part of the poem the absolute rectitude of the Divine government is solemnly recognized. In the Third Book of the Iliad, a truce is agreed upon between the Trojans and the Greeks, while Menelaus and Paris are to decide by single combat the quarrel which has occasioned the siege of Troy. A compact is made, according to which the victor is to possess Helen and her wealth, and the Trojans and Greeks are ever afterward to remain friends and allies. The gods are invoked to be witnesses of the treaty, and to pursue with their vengeance those by whom it shall be violated, whether they be Greeks or Trojans. Few passages in the Iliad are more striking or of graver import than this appeal to the justice of the gods,—this testimony, given by two warring nations, of their confidence in the equity with which the immortals govern the world. Paris is overcome by Menelaus in the combat; the truce is broken by a Trojan, who wounds Menelaus severely; the treaty is not fulfilled by delivering up Helen; and, as the action of the poem proceeds in the next book, Agamemnon exhorts the Greeks to fight valiantly, in the full assurance that Jupiter and the other gods will never permit treachery to remain unpunished; and accordingly he predicts a terrible retribution already hanging over Troy. And whatever may be our admiration for the amiable and noble qualities of Hector, and our sympathy for the thousands of innocent persons dwelling in his populous city, it cannot be denied that the interference of the gods in the affairs of Troy leads in the end to a great result consistent with substantial justice. Paris, the violator of the laws of hospitality, the adulterer and robber, is sheltered, protected, and countenanced in Troy,—the Trojan people make themselves partakers in his guilt; and in the end they share in its punishment. Hector, the prop of their state, the champion in whom they put their trust, is slain; and we are allowed, by means of predictions, a glimpse of the coming destruction of Troy, and learn that the sceptre of the kingdom will pass from the house of Priam, whose son committed the crime which led to the war, and will be swayed by the posterity of the blameless Æneas.

Here I leave my translation in the hands of the reading public, who, if they do not wholly neglect it, will judge whether I have made any approach toward the fulfilment of the design set forth in the beginning of this Preface.

W. C. BRYANT.

DECEMBER, 1869.

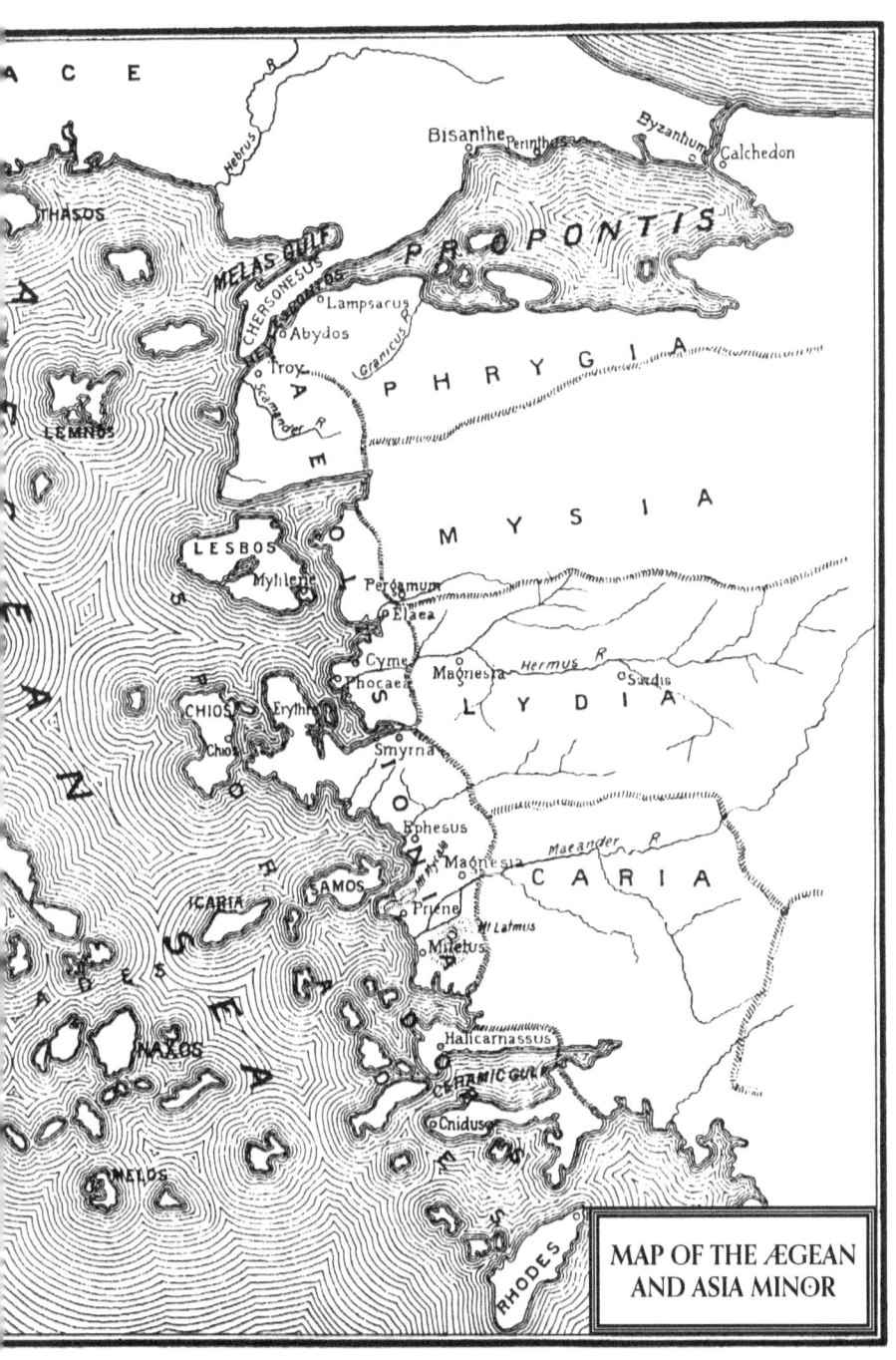

ILIAD

BOOK I

O Goddess! sing the wrath of Peleus' son,
Achilles; sing the deadly wrath that brought
Woes numberless upon the Greeks, and swept
To Hades many a valiant soul, and gave
Their limbs a prey to dogs and birds of air,—   5
For so had Jove appointed,—from the time
When the two chiefs, Atrides, king of men,
And great Achilles, parted first as foes.
   Which of the gods put strife between the chiefs,
That they should thus contend? Latona's son   10
And Jove's. Incensed against the king, he bade
A deadly pestilence appear among
The army, and the men were perishing.
For Atreus' son with insult had received
Chryses the priest, who to the Grecian fleet   15
Came to redeem his daughter, offering
Uncounted ransom. In his hand he bore
The fillets of Apollo, archer-god,
Upon the golden sceptre, and he sued
To all the Greeks, but chiefly to the sons   20
Of Atreus, the two leaders of the host:—
   "Ye sons of Atreus, and ye other chiefs,
Well-greaved Achaians, may the gods who dwell
Upon Olympus give you to o'erthrow
The city of Priam, and in safety reach   25
Your homes; but give me my beloved child.

And take her ransom, honoring him who sends
His arrows far, Apollo, son of Jove."
   Then all the other Greeks, applauding, bade
Revere the priest and take the liberal gifts 30
He offered, but the counsel did not please
Atrides Agamemnon; he dismissed
The priest with scorn, and added threatening words:—
   "Old man, let me not find thee loitering here,
Beside the roomy ships, or coming back 35
Hereafter, lest the fillet thou dost bear
And sceptre of thy god protect thee not.
This maiden I release not till old age
Shall overtake her in my Argive home,
Far from her native country, where her hand 40
Shall throw the shuttle and shall dress my couch.
Go, chafe me not, if thou wouldst safely go."
   He spake; the aged man in fear obeyed
The mandate, and in silence walked apart,
Along the many-sounding ocean-side, 45
And fervently he prayed the monarch-god,
Apollo, golden-haired Latona's son:—
   "Hear me, thou bearer of the silver bow,
Who guardest Chrysa, and the holy isle
Of Cilla, and art lord in Tenedos, 50
O Smintheus! if I ever helped to deck
Thy glorious temple, if I ever burned
Upon thy altar the fat thighs of goats
And bullocks, grant my prayer, and let thy shafts
Avenge upon the Greeks the tears I shed." 55
   So spake he supplicating, and to him
Phœbus Apollo hearkened. Down he came,
Down from the summit of the Olympian mount,
Wrathful in heart; his shoulders bore the bow
And hollow quiver; there the arrows rang 60
Upon the shoulders of the angry god,
As on he moved. He came as comes the night,
And, seated from the ships aloof, sent forth
An arrow; terrible was heard the clang
Of that resplendent bow. At first he smote 65

The mules and the swift dogs, and then on man
He turned the deadly arrow. All around
Glared evermore the frequent funeral piles.
Nine days already had his shafts been showered
Among the host, and now, upon the tenth, 70
Achilles called the people of the camp
To council. Juno, of the snow-white arms,
Had moved his mind to this, for she beheld
With sorrow that the men were perishing.
And when the assembly met and now was full, 75
Stood swift Achilles in the midst and said:—
   "To me it seems, Atrides, that 'twere well,
Since now our aim is baffled, to return
Homeward, if death o'ertake us not; for war
And pestilence at once destroy the Greeks. 80
But let us first consult some seer or priest,
Or dream-interpreter,—for even dreams
Are sent by Jove,—and ask him by what cause
Phœbus Apollo has been angered thus;
If by neglected vows or hecatombs, 85
And whether savor of fat bulls and goats
May move the god to stay the pestilence."
   He spake, and took again his seat; and next
Rose Calchas, son of Thestor, and the chief
Of augurs, one to whom were known things past 90
And present and to come. He, through the art
Of divination, which Apollo gave,
Had guided Iliumward the ships of Greece.
With words well ordered courteously he spake:—
   "Achilles, loved of Jove, thou biddest me 95
Explain the wrath of Phœbus, monarch-god,
Who sends afar his arrows. Willingly
Will I make known the cause; but covenant thou,
And swear to stand prepared, by word and hand,
To bring me succor. For my mind misgives 100
That he who rules the Argives, and to whom
The Achaian race are subject, will be wroth.
A sovereign is too strong for humbler men,
And though he keep his choler down awhile,

It rankles, till he sate it, in his heart. 105
And now consider: wilt thou hold me safe?"
   Achilles, the swift-footed, answered thus:—
"Fear nothing, but speak boldly out whate'er
Thou knowest, and declare the will of Heaven.
For by Apollo, dear to Jove, whom thou, 110
Calchas, dost pray to, when thou givest forth
The sacred oracles to men of Greece,
No man, while yet I live, and see the light
Of day, shall lay a violent hand on thee
Among our roomy ships; no man of all 115
The Grecian armies, though thou name the name
Of Agamemnon, whose high boast it is
To stand in power and rank above them all."
   Encouraged thus, the blameless seer went on:—
"'Tis not neglected vows or hecatombs 120
That move him, but the insult shown his priest,
Whom Agamemnon spurned, when he refused
To set his daughter free, and to receive
Her ransom. Therefore sends the archer-god
These woes, and still will send them on the Greeks, 125
Nor ever will withdraw his heavy hand
From our destruction, till the dark-eyed maid
Freely, and without ransom, be restored
To her beloved father, and with her
A sacred hecatomb to Chrysa sent. 130
So may we haply pacify the god."
   Thus having said, the augur took his seat.
And then the hero-son of Atreus rose,
Wide-ruling Agamemnon, greatly chafed.
His gloomy heart was full of wrath, his eyes 135
Sparkled like fire; he fixed a menacing look
Full on the augur Calchas, and began:—
   "Prophet of evil! never hadst thou yet
A cheerful word for me. To mark the signs
Of coming mischief is thy great delight. 140
Good dost thou ne'er foretell nor bring to pass.
And now thou pratest, in thine auguries,
Before the Greeks, how that the archer-god

Afflicts us thus, because I would not take
The costly ransom offered to redeem 145
The virgin child of Chryses. 'Twas my choice
To keep her with me, for I prize her more
Than Clytemnestra, bride of my young years,
And deem her not less nobly graced than she,
In form and feature, mind and pleasing arts. 150
Yet will I give her back, if that be best;
For gladly would I see my people saved
From this destruction. Let meet recompense,
Meantime, be ready, that I be not left,
Alone of all the Greeks, without my prize. 155
That were not seemly. All of you perceive
That now my share of spoil has passed from me."
   To him the great Achilles, swift of foot,
Replied: "Renowned Atrides, greediest
Of men, where wilt thou that our noble Greeks 160
Find other spoil for thee, since none is set
Apart, a common store? The trophies brought
From towns which we have sacked have all been shared
Among us, and we could not without shame
Bid every warrior bring his portion back. 165
Yield, then, the maiden to the god, and we,
The Achaians, freely will appoint for thee
Threefold and fourfold recompense, should Jove
Give up to sack this well-defended Troy."
   Then the king Agamemnon answered thus:— 170
"Nay, use no craft, all valiant as thou art,
Godlike Achilles; thou hast not the power
To circumvent nor to persuade me thus.
Think'st thou that, while thou keepest safe thy prize,
I shall sit idly down, deprived of mine? 175
Thou bid'st me give the maiden back. 'Tis well,
If to my hands the noble Greeks shall bring
The worth of what I lose, and in a shape
That pleases me. Else will I come myself,
And seize and bear away thy prize, or that 180
Of Ajax or Ulysses, leaving him
From whom I take his share with cause for rage.

Another time we will confer of this.
Now come, and forth into the great salt sea
Launch a black ship, and muster on the deck 185
Men skilled to row, and put a hecatomb
On board, and let the fair-cheeked maid embark,
Chryseis. Send a prince to bear command,—
Ajax, Idomeneus, or the divine
Ulysses;—or thyself, Pelides, thou 190
Most terrible of men, that with due rites
Thou soothe the anger of the archer-god."
  Achilles the swift-footed, with stern look,
Thus answered: "Ha, thou mailed in impudence
And bent on lucre! Who of all the Greeks 195
Can willingly obey thee, on the march,
Or bravely battling with the enemy?
I came not to this war because of wrong
Done to me by the valiant sons of Troy.
No feud had I with them: they never took 200
My beeves or horses, nor, in Phthia's realm,
Deep-soiled and populous, spoiled my harvest fields.
For many a shadowy mount between us lies,
And waters of the wide-resounding sea.
Man unabashed! we follow thee that thou 205
Mayst glory in avenging upon Troy
The grudge of Menelaus and thy own,
Thou shameless one! and yet thou hast for this
Nor thanks nor care. Thou threatenest now to take
From me the prize for which I bore long toils 210
In battle; and the Greeks decreed it mine.
I never take an equal share with thee
Of booty when the Grecian host has sacked
Some populous Trojan town. My hands perform
The harder labors of the field in all 215
The tumult of the fight; but when the spoil
Is shared, the largest share of all is thine,
While I, content with little, seek my ships,
Weary with combat. I shall now go home
To Phthia; better were it to return 220
With my beaked ships; but here, where I am held

In little honor, thou wilt fail, I think,
To gather, in large measure, spoil and wealth."
  Him answered Agamemnon, king of men:—
"Desert, then, if thou wilt; I ask thee not 225
To stay for me; there will be others left
To do me honor yet, and, best of all,
The all-providing Jove is with me still.
Thee I detest the most of all the men
Ordained by him to govern; thy delight 230
Is in contention, war, and bloody frays.
If thou art brave, some deity, no doubt,
Hath thus endowed thee. Hence, then, to thy home,
With all thy ships and men! there domineer
Over thy Myrmidons; I heed thee not, 235
Nor care I for thy fury. Thus, in turn,
I threaten thee; since Phœbus takes away
Chryseis, I will send her in my ship
And with my friends, and, coming to thy tent,
Will bear away the fair-cheeked maid, thy prize, 240
Briseis, that thou learn how far I stand
Above thee, and that other chiefs may fear
To measure strength with me and brave my power."
  The rage of Peleus' son, as thus he spake,
Grew fiercer; in that shaggy breast his heart 245
Took counsel, whether from his thigh to draw
The trenchant sword, and, thrusting back the rest,
Smite down Atrides, or subdue his wrath
And master his own spirit. While he thus
Debated with himself, and half unsheathed 250
The ponderous blade, Pallas Athene came,
Sent from on high by Juno, the white-armed,
Who loved both warriors and made both her care.
She came behind him, seen by him alone,
And plucked his yellow hair. The hero turned 255
In wonder, and at once he knew the look
Of Pallas and the awful-gleaming eye,
And thus accosted her with wingèd words:—
"Why com'st thou hither, daughter of the god
Who bears the ægis? Art thou here to see 260

The insolence of Agamemnon, son
Of Atreus? Let me tell thee what I deem
Will be the event. That man may lose his life,
And quickly too, for arrogance like this."
    Then thus the goddess, blue-eyed Pallas, spake:— 265
"I came from heaven to pacify thy wrath,
If thou wilt heed my counsel. I am sent
By Juno the white-armed, to whom ye both
Are dear, who ever watches o'er you both.
Refrain from violence; let not thy hand 270
Unsheathe the sword, but utter with thy tongue
Reproaches, as occasion may arise,
For I declare what time shall bring to pass;
Threefold amends shall yet be offered thee,
In gifts of princely cost, for this day's wrong. 275
Now calm thy angry spirit, and obey."
    Achilles, the swift-footed, answered thus:—
"O goddess, be the word thou bring'st obeyed,
However fierce my anger; for to him
Who hearkens to the gods, the gods give ear." 280
    So speaking, on the silver hilt he stayed
His strong right hand, and back into its sheath
Thrust his good sword, obeying. She, meantime,
Returned to heaven, where ægis-bearing Jove
Dwells with the other gods. And now again 285
Pelides, with opprobrious words, bespake
The son of Atreus, venting thus his wrath:—
    "Wine-bibber, with the forehead of a dog
And a deer's heart! Thou never yet hast dared
To arm thyself for battle with the rest, 290
Nor join the other chiefs prepared to lie
In ambush,—such thy craven fear of death.
Better it suits thee, midst the mighty host
Of Greeks, to rob some warrior of his prize
Who dares withstand thee. King thou art, and yet 295
Devourer of thy people. Thou dost rule
A spiritless race, else this day's insolence,
Atrides, were thy last. And now I say,
And bind my saying with a mighty oath:

By this my sceptre, which can never bear   300
A leaf or twig, since first it left its stem
Among the mountains,—for the steel has pared
Its boughs and bark away, to sprout no more,—
And now the Achaian judges bear it,—they
Who guard the laws received from Jupiter,—   305
Such is my oath,—the time shall come when all
The Greeks shall long to see Achilles back,
While multitudes are perishing by the hand
Of Hector, the man-queller; thou, meanwhile,
Though thou lament, shalt have no power to help, 310
And thou shalt rage against thyself to think
That thou hast scorned the bravest of the Greeks."
  As thus he spake, Pelides to the ground
Flung the gold-studded wand, and took his seat.
Fiercely Atrides raged; but now uprose   315
Nestor, the master of persuasive speech,
The clear-toned Pylian orator, whose tongue
Dropped words more sweet than honey. He had seen
Two generations that grew up and lived
With him on sacred Pylos pass away,   320
And now he ruled the third. With prudent words
He thus addressed the assembly of the chiefs:—
  "Ye gods! what new misfortunes threaten Greece!
How Priam would exult and Priam's sons,
And how would all the Trojan race rejoice,   325
Were they to know how furiously ye strive,—
Ye who in council and in fight surpass
The other Greeks. Now hearken to my words,—
Ye who are younger than myself,—for I
Have lived with braver men than you, and yet   330
They held me not in light esteem. Such men
I never saw, nor shall I see again,—
Men like Pirithoüs and like Druas, lord
Of nations, Cæneus and Exadius,
And the great Polypheme, and Theseus, son   335
Of Ægeus, likest to the immortal gods,
Strongest of all the earth-born race they fought—
The strongest with the strongest of their time—

With Centaurs, the wild dwellers of the hills,
And fearfully destroyed them. With these men 340
Did I hold converse, coming to their camp
From Pylos in a distant land. They sent
To bid me join the war, and by their side
I fought my best, but no man living now
On the wide earth would dare to fight with them. 345
Great as they were, they listened to my words
And took my counsel. Hearken also ye,
And let my words persuade you for the best.
Thou, powerful as thou art, take not from him
The maiden; suffer him to keep the prize 350
Decreed him by the sons of Greece; and thou,
Pelides, strive no longer with the king,
Since never Jove on sceptred prince bestowed
Like eminence to his. Though braver thou,
And goddess-born, yet hath he greater power 355
And wider sway. Atrides, calm thy wrath—
'Tis I who ask—against the chief who stands
The bulwark of the Greeks in this fierce war."
   To him the sovereign Agamemnon said:—
"The things which thou hast uttered, aged chief, 360
Are fitly spoken; but this man would stand
Above all others; he aspires to be
The master, over all to domineer,
And to direct in all things; yet, I think,
There may be one who will not suffer this. 365
For if by favor of the immortal gods
He was made brave, have they for such a cause
Given him the liberty of insolent speech?"
   Hereat the great Achilles, breaking in,
Answered: "Yea, well might I deserve the name 370
Of coward and of wretch, should I submit
In all things to thy bidding. Such commands
Lay thou on others, not on me; nor think
I shall obey thee longer. This I say,—
And bear it well in mind,—I shall not lift 375
My hand to keep the maiden whom ye gave
And now take from me; but whatever else

May be on board that swift black ship of mine,
Beware thou carry not away the least
Without my leave. Come, make trial now,   380
That these may see thy black blood bathe my spear."
  Then, rising from that strife of words, the twain
Dissolved the assembly at the Grecian fleet.
Pelides to his tents and well-mannered ships
Went with Patroclus and his warrior friends,   385
While Agamemnon bade upon the sea
Launch a swift bark with twenty chosen men
To ply the oar, and put a hecatomb
Upon it for the god. He thither led
The fair-cheeked maid Chryseis; the command   390
He gave to wise Ulysses; forth they went,
Leader and crew, upon their watery path.
Meanwhile, he bade the camp be purified;
And straight the warriors purified the camp,
And, casting the pollutions to the waves,   395
They burned to Phœbus chosen hecatombs
Of bulls and goats beside the barren main,
From which the savor rose in smoke to heaven.
  So was the host employed. But not the less
Did Agamemnon persevere to urge   400
His quarrel with Pelides; and he thus
Addressed Talthybius and Eurybates,
His heralds and his faithful ministers:—
  "Go ye to where Achilles holds his tent,
And take the fair Briseis by the hand,   405
And bring her hither. If he yield her not,
I shall come forth to claim her with a band
Of warriors, and it shall be worse for him."
  He spake, and sent them forth with added words
Of menace. With unwilling steps they went   410
Beside the barren deep, until they reached
The tents and vessels of the Myrmidons,
And found Achilles seated by his tent
And his black ship; their coming pleased him not.
They, moved by fear and reverence of the king,   415
Stopped, and bespake him not, nor signified

Their errand; he perceived their thought and said:—
  "Hail, heralds, messengers of Jove and men!
Draw near; I blame you not. I only blame
Atrides, who hath sent you for the maid.   420
Noble Patroclus! bring the damsel forth,
And let them lead her hence. My witnesses
Are ye, before the blessed deities,
And mortal men, and this remorseless king,
If ever he shall need me to avert   425
The doom of utter ruin from his host.
Most sure it is, he madly yields himself
To fatal counsels, thoughtless of the past
And of the future, nor forecasting how
The Greeks may fight, unvanquished, by their fleet." 430
  He spake. Meantime Patroclus had obeyed
The word of his beloved friend. He brought
The fair-cheeked maid Briseis from the tent,
And she was led away. The messengers
Returned to where their barks were moored, and she 435
Unwillingly went with them. Then in tears
Achilles, from his friends withdrawing, sat
Beside the hoary ocean-marge, and gazed
On the black deep beyond, and stretched his hands,
And prayed to his dear mother, earnestly:—   440
  "Mother! since thou didst bring me forth to dwell
Brief space on earth, Olympian Jupiter,
Who thunders in the highest, should have filled
That space with honors, but he grants them not.
Wide-ruling Agamemnon takes and holds   445
The prize I won, and thus dishonors me."
  Thus, shedding tears, he spake. His mother heard,
Sitting within the ocean deeps, beside
Her aged father. Swiftly from the waves
Of the gray deep emerging like a cloud,   450
She sat before him as he wept, and smoothed
His brow with her soft hand, and kindly said:—
  "My child, why weepest thou? What grief is this?
Speak, and hide nothing, so that both may know."
  Achilles, swift of foot, sighed heavily,   455

And said: "Thou know'st already. Why relate
These things to thee, who art apprised of all?
 "To Thebè, to Eëtion's sacred town,
We marched, and plundered it, and hither brought
The booty, which was fairly shared among 460
The sons of Greece, and Agamemnon took
The fair-cheeked maid Chryseis as his prize.
But Chryses, priest of Phœbus, to the fleet
Of the Achaian warriors, brazen-mailed,
Came, to redeem his daughter, offering 465
Ransom uncounted. In his hand he bore
The fillets of Apollo, archer-god,
Upon the golden sceptre, and he sued
To all the Greeks, but chiefly to the sons
Of Atreus, the two leaders of the host. 470
Then all the other chiefs, applauding, bade
Revere the priest and take the liberal gifts
He offered; but the counsel did not please
Atrides Agamemnon: he dismissed
The priest with scorn, and added threatening words. 475
The aged man indignantly withdrew
And Phœbus—for the priest was dear to him—
Granted his prayer and sent among the Greeks
A deadly shaft. The people of the camp
Were perishing in heaps. His arrows flew 480
Among the Grecian army, far and wide.
A seer expert in oracles revealed
The will of Phœbus, and I was the first
To counsel that the god should be appeased.
But Agamemnon rose in sudden wrath, 485
Uttering a threat, which he has since fulfilled.
And now the dark-eyed Greeks are taking back
His child to Chryses, and with her they bear
Gifts to the monarch-god; while to my tent
Heralds have come, and borne away the maid 490
Briseis, given me by the sons of Greece.
But succor thou thy son, if thou hast power;
Ascend to heaven and bring thy prayer to Jove,
If e'er by word or act thou gav'st him aid.

For I remember, in my father's halls 495
I often heard thee, glorying, tell how thou,
Alone of all the gods, didst interpose
To save the cloud-compeller, Saturn's son,
From shameful overthrow, when all the rest
Who dwell upon Olympus had conspired 500
To bind him,—Juno, Neptune, and with them
Pallas Athene. Thou didst come and loose
His bonds, and call up to the Olympian heights
The hundred-handed, whom the immortal gods
Have named Briareus, but the sons of men 505
Ægeon, mightier than his sire in strength;
And he, rejoicing in the honor, took
His seat by Jove, and all the immortals shrank
Aghast before him, and let fall the chains.
Remind him of all this, and, sitting down, 510
Embrace his knees, and pray him to befriend
The Trojans, that the Greeks, hemmed in and slain
Beside their ships and by the shore, may learn
To glory in their king, and even he,
Wide-ruling Agamemnon, may perceive 515
How grievous was his folly when he dared
To treat with scorn the bravest of the Greeks."
   And Thetis answered, weeping as she spake:—
"Alas, my son, why did I rear thee, born
To sorrow as thou wert? O would that thou 520
Unwronged, and with no cause for tears, couldst dwell
Beside thy ships, since thou must die so soon.
I brought thee forth in an unhappy hour,
Short-lived and wronged beyond all other men.
Yet will I climb the Olympian height among 525
Its snows and make my suit to Jupiter
The Thunderer, if haply he may yield
To my entreaties. Thou, meanwhile, abide
By thy swift ships, incensed against the Greeks,
And take no part in all their battles more. 530
But yesterday did Jove depart to hold
A banquet far in Ocean's realm, among
The blameless Ethiopians, and with him

Went all the train of gods. Twelve days must pass
Ere he return to heaven, and I will then 535
Enter his brazen palace, clasp his knees,
And hope to move his purpose by my prayers."
    So saying, she departed, leaving him
In anger for the shapely damsel's sake,
Whom forcibly they took away. Meantime 540
Ulysses, with the sacred hecatomb,
Arrived at Chrysa. Entering the deep port,
They folded up the sails and laid them down
In the black ship, and lowering the mast,
With all its shrouds, they brought it to its place. 545
Then to the shore they urged the bark with oars,
And cast the anchors and secured the prow
With fastenings. Next, they disembarked and stood
Upon the beach and placed the hecatomb
In sight of Phœbus, the great archer. Last, 550
Chryseis left the deck, and, leading her
Up to the altar, wise Ulysses gave
The maid to her dear father, speaking thus:—
    "O Chryses! Agamemnon, king of men,
Sends me in haste to bring this maid to thee 555
And offer up this hallowed hecatomb
To Phœbus, for the Greeks; that so the god,
Whose wrath afflicts us sore, may be appeased."
    So speaking, to her father's hands he gave
The maiden; joyfully the priest received 560
The child he loved. Then did the Greeks array
The noble hecatomb in order round
The sculptured altar, and with washen hands
They took the salted meal, while Chryses stood
And spread abroad his hands and prayed aloud:— 565
    "Hear me, thou bearer of the glittering bow,
Who guardest Chrysa and the pleasant isle
Of Cilia and art lord in Tenedos!
Already hast thou listened to my prayer
And honored me, and terribly hast scourged 570
The Achaian people. Hear me yet again,
And cause the plague that wastes the Greeks to cease."

So spake he, supplicating, and to him
Phœbus Apollo hearkened. When the prayers
Were ended, and the salted meal was flung, 575
Backward they turned the necks of the fat beeves,
And cut their throats, and flayed the carcasses,
And hewed away the thighs, and covered them
With caul in double folds; and over this
They laid raw fragments of the other parts. 580
O'er all the aged priest poured dark red wine,
And burned them on dry wood. A band of youths
With five-pronged spits, beside him, thrust these through
The entrails, which they laid among the flames.
And when the thighs were all consumed, and next 585
the entrails tasted, all the rest was carved
Into small portions and transfixed with spits
And roasted with nice care and then withdrawn
From the hot coals. This task performed, they made
The banquet ready. All became its guests 590
And all were welcome to the equal feast.
And when their thirst and hunger were allayed,
Boys crowned the ample urns with wreaths, and served
The wine to all, and poured libations forth.
Meantime the Argive youths, that whole day long, 595
Sang to appease the god; they chanted forth
High anthems to the archer of the skies.
He listened to the strain, and his stern mood
Was softened. When, at length, the sun went down
And darkness fell, they gave themselves to sleep 600
Beside the fastenings of their ships, and when
Appeared the rosy-fingered Dawn, the child
Of Morning, they returned to the great host
Of the Achaians. Phœbus deigned to send
A favoring breeze; at once they reared the mast 605
And opened the white sails; the canvas swelled
Before the wind, and hoarsely round the keel
The dark waves murmured as the ship flew on.
So ran she, cutting through the sea her way.
But when they reached the great Achaian host, 610
They drew their vessel high upon the shore

Among the sands, and underneath its sides
They laid long beams to prop the keel, and straight
Dispersed themselves among the tents and ships.
   The goddess-born Achilles, swift of foot,   615
Beside his ships still brooded o'er his wrath,
Nor came to council with the illustrious chiefs,
Nor to the war, but suffered idleness
To eat his heart away: for well he loved
Clamor and combat. But when now, at length,   620
The twelfth day came, the ever-living gods
Returned together to the Olympian mount
With Jove, their leader. Thetis kept in mind
Her son's desire, and, with the early morn,
Climbed the great heaven and the high mount, and found   625
All-seeing Jove, who, from the rest apart,
Was seated on the loftiest pinnacle
Of many-peaked Olympus. She sat down
Before the son of Saturn, clasped his knees
With her left arm, and lifted up her right   630
In supplication to the Sovereign One:—
   "O Jupiter, my father, if among
The immortals I have ever given thee aid
By word or act, deny not my request.
Honor my son, whose life is doomed to end   635
So soon; for Agamemnon, king of men,
Hath done him shameful wrong: he takes from him
And keeps the prize he won in war. But thou,
Olympian Jupiter, supremely wise,
Honor him thou, and give the Trojan host   640
The victory, until the humbled Greeks
Heap large increase of honors on my son."
   She spake, but cloud-compelling Jupiter
Answered her not; in silence long he sat.
But Thetis, who had clasped his knees at first,   645
Clung to them still, and prayed him yet again:—
   "O promise me, and grant my suit; or else
Deny it,—for thou need'st not fear,—and I
Shall know how far below the other gods
Thou holdest me in honor." As she spake,   650

The Cloud-compeller, sighing heavily,
Answered her thus: "Hard things dost thou require,
And thou wilt force me into new disputes
With Juno, who will anger me again
With contumelious words; for ever thus, 655
In presence of the immortals, doth she seek
Cause of contention, charging that I aid
The Trojans in their battles. Now depart,
And let her not perceive thee. Leave the rest
To be by me accomplished; and that thou 660
Mayst be assured, behold, I give the nod;
For this, with me, the immortals know, portends
The highest certainty: no word of mine
Which once my nod confirms can be revoked,
Or prove untrue, or fail to be fulfilled." 665
   As thus he spake, the son of Saturn gave
The nod with his dark brows. The ambrosial curls
Upon the Sovereign One's immortal head
Were shaken, and with them the mighty mount
Olympus trembled. Then they parted, she 670
Plunging from bright Olympus to the deep,
And Jove returning to his palace home;
Where all the gods, uprising from their thrones,
At sight of the Great Father, waited not
For his approach, but met him as he came. 675
   And now upon his throne the Godhead took
His seat, but Juno knew—for she had seen—
That Thetis of the silver feet, and child
Of the gray Ancient of the Deep, had held
Close council with her consort. Therefore she 680
Bespake the son of Saturn harshly, thus:—
   "O crafty one, with whom, among the gods,
Plottest thou now? Thus hath it ever been
Thy pleasure to devise, apart from me,
Thy plans in secret; never willingly 685
Dost thou reveal to me thy purposes."
   Then thus replied the Father of the gods
And mortals: "Juno, do not think to know
All my designs, for thou wilt find the task

Too hard for thee, although thou be my spouse, 690
What fitting is to be revealed, no one
Of all the immortals or of men shall know
Sooner than thou; but when I form designs
Apart from all the gods, presume thou not
To question me or pry into my plans." 695
  Juno, the large-eyed and august, rejoined:—
"What words, stern son of Saturn, hast thou said!
It never was my wont to question thee
Or pry into thy plans, and thou art left
To form them as thou wilt; yet now I fear 700
The silver-footed Thetis has contrived—
That daughter of the Ancient of the Deep—
To o'erpersuade thee, for, at early prime,
She sat before thee and embraced thy knees;
And thou hast promised her, I cannot doubt, 705
To give Achilles honor and to cause
Myriads of Greeks to perish by their fleet."
  Then Jove, the cloud-compeller, spake again:—
"Harsh-tongued! thou ever dost suspect me thus,
Nor can I act unwatched; and yet all this 710
Profits thee nothing, for it only serves
To breed dislike, and is the worse for thee.
But were it as thou deemest, 'tis enough
That such has been my pleasure. Sit thou down
In silence, and obey, lest all the gods 715
Upon Olympus, when I come and lay
These potent hands on thee, protect thee not."
  He spake, and Juno, large-eyed and august,
O'erawed, and curbing her high spirit, sat
In silence; meanwhile all the gods of heaven 720
Within the halls of Jove were inly grieved.
But Vulcan, the renowned artificer,
Sought to console his mother in her grief,—
The white-armed Juno,—and thus interposed:—
  "Great will the evil be and hard to bear, 725
If, for the sake of mortals, ye are moved
To such contention and the assembled gods
Disturbed with discord. Even the pleasant feast

Will lose its flavor when embittered thus.
And let me warn my mother while I speak, 730
Wise as she is, that she defer to Jove,
Lest the All-Father angrily again
Reply, and spoil the banquet of the day.
The Thunderer of Olympus, if he choose
To make a wreck of all things, wields a power 735
Far greater than we all. Accost him thou
With gentle speeches, and the Lord of heaven
Will then regard us in a kindly mood."
 As thus he spake, he gave into the hands
Of his beloved mother the round cup 740
Of double form, and thus he spake again:—
 "Mother, be patient and submit, although
In sadness, lest these eyes behold thee yet
Beaten with stripes, and though I hold thee dear
And grieve for thee, I cannot bring thee help; 745
For hard it is to strive with Jupiter.
Already once, when I took part with thee,
He seized me by the foot and flung me o'er
The battlements of heaven. All day I fell,
And with the setting sun I struck the earth 750
In Lemnos. Little life was left in me,
What time the Sintians took me from the ground."
 He spake, and Juno, the white-shouldered, smiled,
And smiling took the cup her son had brought;
And next he poured to all the other gods 755
Sweet nectar from the jar, beginning first
With those at the right hand. As they beheld
Lame Vulcan laboring o'er the palace-floor,
An inextinguishable laughter broke
From all the blessed gods. So feasted they 760
All day till sunset. From that equal feast
None stood aloof, nor from the pleasant sound
Of harp, which Phœbus touched, nor from the voice
Of Muses singing sweetly in their turn.
 But when the sun's all-glorious light was down, 765
Each to his sleeping-place betook himself;
For Vulcan, the lame god, with marvellous art,

Had framed for each the chamber of his rest.
   And Jupiter, the Olympian Thunderer,
Went also to his couch, where 'twas his wont,   770
When slumber overtook him, to recline.
And there, beside him, slept the white-armed queen
Juno, the mistress of the golden throne.

BOOK II

ALL other deities, all mortal men,
Tamers of war-steeds, slept the whole night
through;
But no sweet slumber came to Jove; his thoughts
Were ever busy with the anxious care
To crown with honor Peleus' son, and cause
Myriads to perish at the Grecian fleet.
At last, this counsel seemed the best,—to send
A treacherous dream to Agamemnon, son
Of Atreus. Then he called a Dream, and thus
Addressing it with wingèd words, he said:—
   "Go, fatal Vision, to the Grecian fleet,
And, entering Agamemnon's tent, declare
Faithfully what I bid thee. Give command
That now he arm, with all the array of war,
The long-haired Greeks, for lo, the hour is come
That gives into his hands the city of Troy
With all its spacious streets. The powers who dwell
In the celestial mansions are no more
At variance; Juno's prayers have moved them all,
And o'er the Trojans hangs a fearful doom."
   So spake the God; the Vision heard, and went
At once to where the Grecian barks were moored,
And entered Agamemnon's tent and found
The king reposing, with the balm of sleep
Poured all around him. At his head the Dream

Took station in the form of Neleus' son,
Nestor, whom Agamemnon honored most
Of all the aged men. In such a shape
The heaven-sent Dream to Agamemnon spake:—
    "O warrior-son of Atreus, sleepest thou?
Tamer of steeds! It ill becomes a chief,
Who has the charge of nations and sustains
Such mighty cares, to sleep the livelong night.
Give earnest heed to me, for I am come
A messenger from Jove, who, though far off,
Takes part in thy concerns and pities thee.
He bids thee arm, with all the array of war,
The long-haired Greeks, for now the hour is come
Which gives into thy hands the city of Troy
With all its spacious streets. The powers that dwell
In the celestial mansions are no more
At variance; Juno's prayers have moved them all,
And o'er the Trojans hangs a fearful doom,
Decreed by Jove. Bear what I say in mind,
And when thy sleep departs forget it not."
    He spake, and, disappearing, left the king
Musing on things that never were to be;
For on that very day he thought to take
The city of Priam. Fool! who little knew
What Jupiter designed should come to pass,
And little thought by his own act to bring
Great woe and grief on Greeks and Trojans both
In hard-fought battles. From his sleep he woke,
The heavenly voice still sounding in his ears,
And sat upright, and put his tunic on,
Soft, fair, and new, and over that he cast
His ample cloak, and round his shapely feet
Laced the becoming sandals. Next, he hung
Upon his shoulders and his side the sword
With silver studs, and took into his hand
The ancestral sceptre, old, but undecayed,
And with it turned his footsteps toward the fleet
Of the Achaian warriors brazen-mailed.
    Now Dawn, the goddess, climbed the Olympian height,

Foretelling Day to Jupiter and all 65
The immortal gods, when Agamemnon bade
The shrill-voiced heralds call the long-haired Greeks
Together; they proclaimed his will, and straight
The warriors came in throngs. But first he bade
A council of large-minded elders meet 70
On Pylian Nestor's royal bark, and there
Laid his well-pondered thought before them thus:—
  "My friends, give ear: a Vision from above
Came to me sleeping in the balmy night;
Most like to noble Nestor was its look,— 75
Its face, its stature, and its garb. It stood
Beside me at my head, and thus it spake:—
  "'O warrior-son of Atreus, sleepest thou?
Tamer of steeds! It ill becomes a chief,
Who has the charge of nations and sustains 80
Such mighty cares, to sleep the livelong night.
Give earnest heed to me, for I am come
A messenger from Jove, who, though far off,
Takes part in thy concerns and pities thee.
He bids thee arm, with all the array of war, 85
The long-haired Greeks, for now the hour is come
Which gives into thy hands the city of Troy
With all its spacious streets. The powers who dwell
In the celestial mansions are no more
At variance; Juno's prayers have moved them all, 90
And o'er the Trojans hangs a fearful doom,
Decreed by Jove. Bear what I say in mind.'
  "It spake and passed away, and with it fled
My slumbers. Now must we devise a way
To bring into the field the sons of Greece. 95
I first will try, as best I may, with words,
And counsel flight from Troy with all our ships.
Ye each, with different counsels, do your part."
  He spake, and took his seat, and after him
Nestor, the king of sandy Pylos, rose, 100
With well-considered words. "O friends," he said,
"Leaders and princes of the Grecian race,
Had any other of the Argive host

Related such a dream, we should have said
The tale is false, and spurned the counsel given. 105
But he has seen it who in rank and power
Transcends us all, and ours it is to see
How we may arm for war the sons of Greece.'
   He spake, and left the council, and the rest,
All sceptred kings, arose, prepared to obey 110
The shepherd of the people. All the Greeks
Meanwhile came thronging to the appointed place.
As, swarming forth from cells within the rock,
Coming and coming still, the tribe of bees
Fly in a cluster o'er the flowers of spring, 115
And some are darting out to right and left,
So from the ships and tents a multitude
Along the spacious beach, in mighty throngs,
Moved toward the assembly. Rumor went with them,
The messenger of Jove, and urged them on. 120
And now, when they were met, the place was stunned
With clamor; earth, as the great crowd sat down,
Groaned under them; a din of mingled cries
Arose; nine shouting heralds strove to hush
The noisy crowd to silence, that at length 125
The heaven-descended monarchs might be heard.
   And when the crowd was seated and had paused
From clamor, Agamemnon rose. He held
The sceptre; Vulcan's skill had fashioned it,
And Jove bestowed it on his messenger, 130
The Argos-queller Hermes. He in turn
Gave it to Pelops, great in horsemanship;
And Pelops passed the gift to Atreus,
The people's shepherd. Atreus, when he died,
Bequeathed it to Thyestes, rich in flocks; 135
And last, Thyestes left it to be borne
By Agamemnon, symbol of his rule
O'er many isles and all the Argive realm.
Leaning on this, he spake these wingèd words:—
   "Friends, Grecian heroes, ministers of Mars, 140
Saturnian Jove hath in an evil net
Entangled me most cruelly. He gave

His promise and his nod, that, having razed
Troy with her strong defences, I should see
My home again; but now he meditates 145
To wrong me, and commands me to return,
With lessened glory and much people lost,
To Argos. Thus hath it seemed good to Jove
The mighty, who hath overthrown the towers
Of many a city, and will yet o'erthrow. 150
The ages yet to come will hear with shame
That such a mighty army of the Greeks
Have waged a fruitless war, and fought in vain
A foe less numerous; yet no end appears
To this long strife. Should Greeks and Trojans make 155
A treaty, faithfully to number each,
And should the Trojans count their citizens,
And we the Greeks, disposed in rows of tens,
Should call the Trojans singly to pour out
The wine for us, full many a company 160
Often would lack its cup-bearer; so far,
I judge, the sons of Greece outnumber those
Who dwell in Troy. But they have yet allies
From many a city, men who wield the spear,
Withstanding my attempt to overthrow 165
That populous town. Nine years of mighty Jove
Have passed already, and the planks that form
Our barks are mouldering, and the cables drop
In pieces, and our wives within their homes,
With their young children, sit expecting us; 170
Yet is the enterprise for which we came
Still unperformed. Now let us all obey
The mandate I reveal, and hasten hence,
With all our fleet, to our beloved homes;
For Troy with her broad streets we cannot take." 175
　　He spake, and in the bosoms of the crowd
Stirred every heart; even those who heard him not
Were moved: the assembly wavered to and fro
Like the long billows of the Icarian Sea,
Roused by the East wind and the South, that rush 180
Forth from the cloudy seat of Father Jove;

Or like the harvest-field, when west winds stoop
Suddenly from above, and toss the wheat.
So was the whole assembly swayed; they ran
With tumult to the ships; beneath their feet   185
Rose clouds of dust, and each exhorted each
To seize the ships and drag them to the deep.
They cleared the channels mid the clamorous cries
Of multitudes, who hastened to return,
And drew the props from underneath their barks.   190
  Then had the Greeks returned before their time
If Juno had not to Minerva said:—
  "Unconquerable child of Jove! What change
Is this? Shall then the Argive army thus
Flee to their homes across the deep and leave   195
Glory to Priam, and to Ilium's sons
The Argive Helen, for whose sake have died
So many Greeks upon the Trojan strand,
Far from the land they loved? But hasten thou
To the host of Argive warriors mailed in brass,   200
And with persuasive words restrain their men.
Nor let them launch their barks upon the sea."
  She spake; nor did the blue-eyed Pallas fail
To heed the mandate, but with quick descent
She left the Olympian height and suddenly   205
Stood by the swift ships of the Grecian host.
She found Ulysses there, the man endowed
With wisdom like to Jove's; he had not touched
His well-appointed bark, for grief had seized
The hero's heart. The blue-eyed goddess took   210
Her place beside him, and addressed him thus:—
  "Son of Laertes, nobly born and sage
Ulysses, will ye, entering your good ships,
Return in flight to your own land and leave
Glory to Priam, and to Ilium's sons   215
The Argive Helen, for whose sake have died
So many Greeks upon the Trojan strand,
Far from the land they loved? Go thou at once
And seek the Argive warriors and restrain
With thy persuasive words the impatient men,   220

Nor let them launch their well-appointed ships."
   She spake; Ulysses knew the heavenly voice,
And hastened back, and as he ran cast by
His cloak. Eurybates of Ithaca,
The herald, caught it up, and followed him.   225
And now before Atrides, king of men,
The warrior stood, and from his hand received
The ancestral sceptre, old, but undecayed;
And bearing this, he went among the ships
Which brought the Achaian army, mailed in brass;   230
And whomsoe'er he met upon his way,
Monarch or eminent among the host,
He stopped him, and addressed him blandly, thus:—
   "Good friend, this eager haste as if from fear
Befits thee not. Sit down, and cause the rest   235
To sit. What Agamemnon's will may be
Thou canst not yet be certain; he intends
To try the Greeks, and soon will punish those
Who act amiss. We cannot all have heard
What he has said; beware, then, lest his wrath   240
Fall heavily upon the sons of Greece.
The monarch, foster-child of Jupiter,
Is terrible enraged. Authority
Is given by Jove, all-wise, who loves the king."
   But when he found one of the lower sort   245
Shouting and brawling, with the royal wand
He smote him, and reproved him sharply, thus:—
   "Friend, take thy seat in quiet, and attend
To what thy betters say; thou art not strong
Nor valiant, and thou art of mean repute   250
In combat and in council. We, the Greeks,
Cannot be all supreme in power. The rule
Of the many is not well. One must be chief
In war, and one the king, to whom the son
Of Saturn gives the sceptre, making him   255
The lawgiver, that he may rule the rest."
   Thus did he act the chief, and make the host
Obey his word; they to the council ground
Came rushing back from all the ships and tents

With tumult, as, on the long-stretching shore   260
Of ocean many-voiced, his billows fling
Themselves in fury, and the deep resounds.
   All others took their seats and kept their place;
Thersites only, clamorous of tongue,
Kept brawling. He, with many insolent words,   265
Was wont to seek unseemly strife with kings,
Uttering whate'er it seemed to him might move
The Greeks to laughter. Of the multitude
Who came to Ilium, none so base as he,—
Squint-eyed, with one lame foot, and on his back   270
A lump, and shoulders curving towards the chest;
His head was sharp, and over it the hairs
Were thinly strewn. He hated most of all
Achilles and Ulysses, and would oft
Revile them. He to Agamemnon now   275
Called with shrill voice and taunting words. The Greeks
Heard him impatiently, with strong disgust
And vehement anger, yet he shouted still
To Agamemnon, and kept railing on:—
   "Of what dost thou complain; what wouldst thou more,   280
Atrides? In thy tents are heaps of gold;
Thy tents are full of chosen damsels, given
To thee before all others, by the Greeks,
Whene'er we take a city. Dost thou yet
Hanker for gold, brought by some Trojan knight,   285
A ransom for his son, whom I shall lead—
I, or some other Greek—a captive bound?
Or dost thou wish, for thy more idle hours,
Some maiden, whom thou mayst detain apart?
Ill it beseems a prince like thee to lead   290
The sons of Greece, for such a cause as this,
Into new perils. O ye coward race!
Ye abject Greeklings, Greeks no longer, haste
Homeward with all the fleet, and let us leave
This man at Troy to win his trophies here,   295
That he may learn whether the aid we give
Avails him aught or not, since he insults
Achilles, a far braver man than he;

And yet, Achilles is not moved by this
To anger: he is spiritless, or else,   300
Atrides, this injustice were thy last."
   Taunting the shepherd of the people thus,
Thersites shouted to the king of men.
But great Ulysses, coming quickly up,
Rebuked him with a frown: "Thou garrulous wretch!   305
Glib as thou art of tongue, Thersites, cease,
Nor singly dare to seek dispute with kings.
There came, I deem, no viler wretch than thou
To Troy with Agamemnon. Prate no more
Of kings, reviling them, and keeping watch   310
For pretexts to return. We know not yet
Whether to go or to remain were best.
Thou railest at the shepherd of the host,
Atrides Agamemnon, for thou seest
The Grecian heroes load him with rewards,   315
While thou insultest him with scurrilous words,
I tell thee now,—and I shall keep my word,—
If e'er again I find thee railing on,
As now thou dost, then let Ulysses wear
His head no longer, let me not be called   320
The father of Telemachus, if I
Shall fail to seize thee, and to strip thee bare
Of cloak and tunic, and whatever else
Covers thy carcass, and to send thee forth,
Howling, to our swift barks upon the shore,   325
Scourged from the council with a storm of blows."
   He spake, and with his sceptre smote the back
And shoulders of the scoffer, who crouched low
And shed a shower of tears. A bloody whelk
Rose where the golden sceptre fell. He took   330
His seat, dismayed, and still in pain wiped off
The tears from his smutched face. The multitude
Around him, though in anxious mood, were moved
To smiles, and one addressed his neighbor thus:—
   "Strange that Ulysses does a thousand things   335
So well,—so wise in council, and in war
So brave; and for the Grecian army now

He does the best of all, in silencing
The chatter of this saucy slanderer,
Whose acrid temper will not soon again   340
Move him to rail with insolent speech at kings."
  So talked the multitude. Ulysses then,
Holding the sceptre, rose, and by his side
The blue-eyed Pallas, in a herald's form,
Commanded silence, that the Argive host—   345
The mightiest and the meanest—might attend
To what should now be said, and calmly weigh
The counsel given them. With a prudent art
Ulysses framed his speech, and thus he spake:—
  "The Greeks, O Atreus' son, would bring on thee   350
Dishonor in the eyes and speech of men,
Breaking the promise made when first they came
From Argos, famed for steeds, that, having spoiled
This well-defended Troy, thou shouldst return
A conqueror. And now, like tender boys   355
Or widowed women, all give way to grief
And languish to return. 'Twere hard to bear
If, after all our sufferings and our toils,
We go back now. And yet, whoe'er remains
A single month away from wife and home   360
Chafes if the winter storms and angry sea
Detain him still on board his well-oared bark;
And we have seen the ninth full year roll round
Since we came hither. Therefore blame I not
The Greeks if they in their beaked ships repine   365
At this delay. But then it were disgrace
To linger here so long and journey home
With empty hands. Bear with us yet, and wait
Till it be certain whether Calchas speaks
Truly or not. For we remember well,   370
And all of you whom cruel death has spared
Are witnesses with me, that when the ships
Of Greece—it seems as if but yesterday—
Mustered in Aulis on their way to bring
Woe upon Priam and the town of Troy,   375
And we, beside a fountain, offered up

On sacred altars chosen hecatombs,
Under a shapely plane-tree, from whose root
Flowed the clear water, there appeared to us
A wondrous sign. A frightful serpent, marked 380
With crimson spots, which Jupiter sent forth
To daylight from beneath the altar-stone,
Came swiftly gliding toward the tree, whereon
A sparrow had her young—eight unfledged birds—
Upon the topmost bough and screened by leaves; 385
The mother was the ninth. The serpent seized
The helpless brood and midst their piteous cries
Devoured them, while the mother fluttered round,
Lamenting, till he caught her by the wing;
And when he had destroyed the parent bird 390
And all her brood, the god who sent him forth
Made him a greater marvel still. The son
Of crafty Saturn changed the snake to stone;
And we who stood around were sore amazed.
Such was the awful portent which the gods 395
Showed at that sacrifice. But Calchas thus
Instantly spake, interpreting the sign:—
   "'O long-haired Greeks,' he said, 'why stand ye thus
In silence? All-foreseeing Jupiter
Hath sent this mighty omen; late it comes 400
And late will be fulfilled, yet gloriously,
And with a fame that never shall decay.
For as the snake devoured the sparrow's brood,
Eight nestlings, and the mother-bird the ninth,—
So many years the war shall last; the tenth 405
Shall give into our hands the stately Troy.'
   "So spake the seer; thus far his words are true.
Bide ye then here, ye well-greaved sons of Greece,
Until the city of Priam shall be ours."
   He spake, and loud applause thereon ensued 410
From all the Greeks, and fearfully the ships
Rang with the clamorous voices uttering
The praises of Ulysses and his words.
   Then Nestor, the Gerenian knight, arose
And thus addressed them: "Strangely ye behave, 415

Like boys unwonted to the tasks of war.
Where now are all your promises and oaths?
Shall all our councillings and all our cares,
Leagues made with wine, religiously outpoured,
And plightings of the strong right hand, be cast   420
Into the flames? Idly we keep alive
A strife of words, which serves no end though long
We loiter here! But thou, Atrides, firm
Of purpose, give command that now the Greeks
Move to the war, and leave to meet their fate   425
Those—one or more—who, parting from our host,
Meditate—but I deem in vain—to flee
Homeward to Argos ere they are assured
Whether the word of Jove omnipotent
Be false or true. For when the Greeks embarked   430
In their swift ships, to carry death and fate
To Ilium's sons, almighty Jupiter
Flung down his lightnings on the right and gave
Propitious omens. Therefore let no Greek
Go home till he possess a Trojan wife   435
And ye have signally avenged the wrongs
And griefs of Helen. Yet, if one be here
Who longs to go, let him but lay his hand
On his black ship, prepared to cross the deep,
And he shall die before the rest. But thou,   440
O king, be wisely counselled, lend an ear
To others, nor neglect what I propose.
Marshal the Greeks by tribes and brotherhoods,
That tribe may stand by tribe, and brotherhoods
Succor each other; if thou thus command   445
And they obey, thou shalt discern which chief
Or soldier is faint-hearted, which is brave,
For each will fight his best, and thou shalt know
Whether through favor of the gods to Troy,
Or our own cowardice and shameful lack   450
Of skill in war, the town is not o'erthrown."
   In turn the monarch Agamemnon spake:—
"O aged warrior, thou excellest all
The Greeks in council. Would to Jupiter,

To Pallas and Apollo, that with me 455
There were but ten such comrades. Priam's town
Would quickly fall before us and be made
A desolation. But the god who bears
The ægis, Saturn's son, hath cast on me
Much grief, entangling me in idle strifes 460
And angry broils. Achilles and myself
Have quarrelled for a maid with bitter words,
And I was first incensed. But if again
We meet and act as friends, the overthrow
That threatens Ilium will not be delayed,— 465
Not for an hour. Now all to your repast!
And then prepare for battle. First let each
See that his spear be sharp, and put his shield
In order, give to his swift-footed steeds
Their ample forage, and o'erlook his car 470
That it be strong for war; for all the day
Shall we maintain the stubborn fight, nor cease
Even for a moment, till the night come down
To part the wrathful combatants. The band
Of each broad buckler shall be moist with sweat 475
On every breast, and weary every arm
That wields the spear, and every horse that drags
The polished chariot o'er the field shall smoke
With sweat. But whosoever shall be found
By the beaked ships and skulking from the fray 480
Shall be the feast of birds of prey and dogs!"

   He spake; the Argives raised a mighty shout,
Loud as when billows lash the beetling shore,
Rolled by the south wind toward some jutting rock
On which the waves, whatever wind may blow, 485
Beat ceaselessly. In haste the people rose
And went among the ships, and kindled fires
Within their tents and took their meal. And one
Made offerings to one god; another paid
Vows to another of the immortal race; 490
And all implored deliverance from death
And danger. Agamemnon, king of men,
Offered a fatted ox of five years old

To Jupiter Almighty, summoning
The elder princes of the Grecian host,—   495
Nestor the first, the king Idomeneus,
And then the warriors Ajax and the son
Of Tydeus, with Ulysses, like to Jove
In council, sixth and last. Unbidden came
The valiant Menelaus, for he knew   500
The cares that weighed upon his brother's heart.
Then, as they stood around the fatted ox
And took in hand the salted barley-meal,
King Agamemnon in the circle prayed:—
    "O Jove, most great and glorious! who dost rule   505
The tempest,—dweller of the ethereal space!
Let not the sun go down and night come on
Ere I shall lay the halls of Priam waste
With fire, and give their portals to the flames,
And hew away the coat of mail that shields   510
The breast of Hector, splitting it with steel.
And may his fellow-warriors, many a one,
Fall round him to the earth and bite the dust.

    He spake; the son of Saturn hearkened not,
But took the sacrifice and made more hard   515
The toils of war. And now when they had prayed,
And strown the salted meal, they drew the neck
Of the victim back and cut the throat and flayed
The carcass, hewed away the thighs and laid
The fat upon them in a double fold,   520
On which they placed raw strips of flesh, and these
They burned with leafless billets. Then they fixed
The entrails on the spits and held them forth
Above the flames, and when the thighs were burned
And entrails tasted, all the rest was carved   525
Into small portions and transfixed with spits
And roasted carefully and drawn away.
And when these tasks were finished and the board
Was spread, they feasted; from that equal feast
None went unsated. When they had appeased   530
Their thirst and hunger, the Gerenian knight
Nestor stood forth and spake: "Most glorious son

Of Atreus, Agamemnon, king of men!
Waste we no time in prattle, nor delay
The work appointed by the gods, but send 535
The heralds of the Achaians, brazen-mailed,
To call the people to the fleet, while we
Pass in a body through their vast array
And wake the martial spirit in their breasts."
    He spake, and Agamemnon, king of men, 540
Followed the counsel. Instantly he bade
The loud-voiced herald summon to the war
The long-haired Argives. At the call they came,
Quickly they came together, and the kings,
Nurslings of Jupiter, who stood beside 545
Atrides, hastened through the crowd to form
The army into ranks. Among them walked
The blue-eyed Pallas, bearing on her arm
The priceless ægis, ever fair and new,
And undecaying; from its edge there hung 550
A hundred golden fringes, fairly wrought,
And every fringe might buy a hecatomb.
With this and fierce, defiant looks she passed
Through all the Achaian host, and made their hearts
Impatient for the march and strong to endure 555
The combat without pause,—for now the war
Seemed to them dearer than the wished return,
In their good galleys, to the land they loved.
    As when a forest on the mountain-top
Is in a blaze with the devouring flame 560
And shines afar, so, while the warriors marched,
The brightness of their burnished weapons flashed
On every side and upward to the sky.
    And as when water-fowl of many tribes—
Geese, cranes, and long-necked swans—disport themselves 565
In Asia's fields beside Caÿster's streams,
And to and fro they fly with screams, and light,
Flock after flock, and all the fields resound;
So poured, from ships and tents, the swarming tribes
Into Scamander's plain, where fearfully 570
Earth echoed to the tramp of steeds and men;

And there they mustered on the river's side,
Numberless as the flowers and leaves of spring.
And as when flies in swarming myriads haunt
The herdsman's stalls in spring-time, when new milk   575
Has filled the pails,—in such vast multitudes
Mustered the long-haired Greeks upon the plain,
Impatient to destroy the Trojan race.
  Then, as the goatherds, when their mingled flocks
Are in the pastures, know and set apart   580
Each his own scattered charge, so did the chiefs,
Moving among them, marshal each his men.
There walked King Agamemnon, like to Jove
In eye and forehead, with the loins of Mars,
And ample chest like him who rules the sea.   585
And as a bull amid the hornèd herd
Stands eminent and nobler than the rest,
So Jove to Agamemnon on that day
Gave to surpass the chiefs in port and mien.
  O Muses, goddesses who dwell on high,   590
Tell me,—for all things ye behold and know,
While we know nothing and may only hear
The random tales of rumor,—tell me who
Were chiefs and princes of the Greeks; for I
Should fail to number and to name them all,—   595
Had I ten tongues, ten throats, a voice unapt
To weary, uttered from a heart of brass,—
Unless the Muses aided me. I now
Will sing of the commanders and the ships.
  Peneleus, Prothoënor, Leïtus,   600
And Clonius, and Arcesilaus led
The warriors of Bœotia, all who dwelt
In Hyria and in rocky Aulis, all
From Schœnus and from Scolus and the hill
Of Eteonus and Thespeia's fields,   605
And Graia and the Mycalesian plain,
All who from Herma and Ilesius came,
And Erythræ, and those who had their homes
In Eleon, Hyla, and Ocalea,
And Peteona, and the stately streets   610

Of Medeon, Copæ, Thisbè full of doves,
And those whose dwelling-place was Eutresis,
And Coronæa, and the grassy lawns
Of Haliartus, all the men who held
Platæa, or in Glissa tilled the soil,   615
Or dwelt in Hypothebæ nobly built,
Or in Onchestus with its temple-walls
Sacred to Neptune, or inhabited
Arnè with fruitful vineyards, Midea
And Nyssa the divine, and Anthedon   620
The distant,—fifty were their barks, and each
Held sixscore youths of the Bœotian race.
 Next, over those who came from Aspledon
And from Orchomenus in Minyas
Ascalaphus ruled with his brother chief   625
Ialmenus,—two sons of mighty Mars.
These, in the halls of Actor, Azis' son,
Astyoche bore to the god of war,
Who met by stealth the bashful maid, as once
She sought the upper palace-rooms. Their ships   630
Were thirty, ranged in order on the shore.
 Then Schedius and Epistrophus, two chiefs
Born to Iphitus, son of Naubolus
The large of soul, led the Phocean host,
Those who in Cyparissus had their homes,   635
In Panope and Crissa the divine
And Daulis, or about Hyampolis
Anemoreia, and upon the banks
Of broad Cephissus, and with them the race
Who held Lilæa by Cephissus' springs.   640
With these came forty ships. Their leaders went
Among them, ranging them in due array
And close to the Bœotians on the left.
 Ajax the swift of foot, Oïleus' son,
Was leader of the Locrians,—less in limb   645
And stature than the other Ajax,—nay,
Much smaller than that son of Telamon,
Wearing a linen corselet; but to wield
The spear he far excelled all other men

Of Hellas and Achaia. Those who dwelt 650
In Cynus, Opus, Bessa, and the fields
Of Calliarus, Scarpha, and the green
Augeia, Tarpha, and the meadows where
Boagrius waters Thronium, followed him
With forty dark-hulled Locrian barks, that came 655
From coasts beyond Eubœa's sacred isle.
   The Eubœans breathing valor, they who held
Chalcis, Eretria, and the vineyard slopes
Of Histiæa, and the lofty walls
Of Dium and Cerinthus by the sea, 660
And Styra, and Earystus; these obeyed
Elphenor of the line of Mars, and son
Of Chalcodon large-souled, a prince who ruled
The Abantes. Him with loosely-flowing locks
The Abantes followed, swift of foot and fierce 665
In combat, and expert to break the mail
Upon the enemies' breasts with ashen spears;
With forty dark-hulled barks they followed him.
   Next they who came from Athens nobly built,
The city of Erechtheus, great of soul, 670
Son of the teeming Earth, whom Pallas reared,
That daughter of the Highest, and within
Her sumptuous temple placed him, where the sons
Of Athens, with the circling year's return,
Paid worship at her altars, bringing bulls 675
And lambs to lay upon them; these obeyed
Menestheus, son of Peteus, whom no chief
On earth could equal in the art to place
Squadrons of men and horse in due array
For battle. Nestor only sought to share 680
This praise, but Nestor was the elder chief.
Fifty dark galleys with Menestheus came.
   Ajax had brought twelve ships from Salamis,
And these he stationed near the Athenian host.
   But they who dwelt in Argos, or within 685
The strong-walled Tiryns, or Hermione
And Asine with their deep, sheltering bays,
Trœzene and Eïonæ, and hills

Of Epidaurus planted o'er with vines,
And they who tilled Ægina and the coast 690
Of Mases,—Grecian warriors,—over these
Brave Diomed bore sway, with Sthenelus,
Beloved son of far-famed Capaneus,
And, third in rule, Euryalus, who seemed
Like to a god, Mecisteus' royal son 695
Who sprung from Talaus; yet the chief command
Was given to Diomed, the great in war.
A fleet of eighty galleys came with them.
   The dwellers of Mycenæ nobly built,
Of Corinth famed for riches, and the town 700
Of beautiful Cleonæ, they who tilled
Orneia, Aræthyrea's pleasant land,
And Sicyon, where of yore Adrastus reigned,
And Hyperesia and the airy heights
Of Gonoessa, and Pellenè's fields, 705
And they who came from Ægium and the shores
Around it, and broad lands of Helicè,—
These had a hundred barks, and over them
Atrides Agamemnon bore command;
And with him came the largest train of troops 710
And bravest. He was cased in gleaming mail,
And his heart gloried when he thought how high
He stood among the heroes,—mightier far
In power, and leader of a mightier host.
   Then they who dwelt within the hollow vale 715
Of queenly Lacedæmon, they who held
Phare and Sparta, Messa full of doves,
Bryseiæ, and Augeia's rich domain,
Amyclæ and the town of Helos, built
Close to the sea, and those who had their homes 720
In Läas and the fields of Œtylus;
All these obeyed the brother of the king,
The valiant Menelaus. Sixty ships
They brought, but these he ranged apart from those
Of Agamemnon. Through the ranks he went, 725
And, trusting in his valor, quickened theirs
For battle; for his heart within him burned

To avenge the wrongs of Helen and her tears.
   Then came the men who tilled the Pylean coast
And sweet Arenè, Thrya at the fords 730
Of Alpheus, and the stately palace homes
Of Æpy, or in Cyparissus dwelt,
Or in Amphigeneia, Pteleum,
Helos and Dorium, where the Muses once
Met, journeying from Œcalian Eurytus, 735
The Thracian Thamyris, and took from him
His power of voice. For he had made his boast
To overcome in song the daughters nine
Of Jove the Ægis-bearer. They in wrath
Smote him with blindness, took the heavenly gift 740
Of song away, and made his hand forget
Its cunning with the harp. All those were led
By Nestor, the Gerenian knight, who came
To war on Troy with fourscore ships and ten.
   The Arcadians, dwelling by the lofty mount 745
Cyllene, near the tomb of Epytus,
Warriors who combat hand to hand, and they
Who tilled the fields of Pheneus and possessed
Orchomenus with all its flocks, or dwelt
In Ripa and in Stratia, and the bleak 750
Enispe, beaten with perpetual winds,
And in Tegea, and the lovely land
Of Mantinea, and in Stymphalus
And in Parrhasia, came in sixty ships
To Troy, with Agapenor for their chief, 755
Son of Ancæus. Every ship was thronged
With warriors of Arcadia, for the king
Of men, Atrides, gave them well-cared barks
To cross the dark blue deep, since not to them
Pertained the cares and labors of the sea. 760
   Then from Buprasium and the sacred coast
Of Elis, from Hyrmine and remote
Myrsinus and the Olenian precipice,
And from Alisium came, with chieftains four,
The warriors, ten swift galleys following 765
Each chieftain, crowded with Epean troops.

And part obeyed Amphimacus, the son
Of Cteatus, and part with Thalpius came,
The son of Eurytus Actorides,
And part with brave Diores, of the line 770
Of Amarynceus. Last, Polyxenus,
The godlike offspring of Agasthenes,
Whose father was Augeias, led the rest.
   They from Dulichium and the Echinades,
Those holy isles descried from Elis o'er 775
The waters, had for leader Megas, brave
As Mars,—the son of Phyleus, dearly loved
By Jove. He left his father's house in wrath
And dwelt within Dulichium. With the troops
Of Megas came a fleet of forty ships. 780
   Ulysses led the Cephallenian men,
Who dwelt in Ithaca, or whose abode
Was leafy Neritus, and those who came
From Crocyleia, and from Ægilips
The craggy, and Zacynthus, and the isle 785
Of Samos, and Epirus, and from all
The bordering lands. O'er these Ulysses ruled,
A chief like Jove in council, and with him
There came twelve galleys with their scarlet prows.
   Then with the Ætolians came Andræmon's son 790
Thoas, their leader. With him were the men
Of Pleuron and Pylene, Olenus,
And Chalcis on the sea-coast and the rocks
Of Calydon; for now no more the sons
Of large-souled Œneus were alive on earth, 795
Nor lived the chief himself, and in his tomb
Was Meleager of the golden hair;
And thus the Ætolian rule to Thoas came,
A fleet of fourscore galleys followed him.
   Idomeneus, expert to wield the spear, 800
Commanded those of Crete, the men who dwelt
In Cnosus or Gortyna, strongly walled
Lyctus, Miletus, and the glimmering
Lycastus, Phæstus, Rhytium's populous town,
And all the warrior train inhabiting 805

The hundred towns of Crete. Idomeneus
The mighty spearman, and Meriones,
Fierce as the god of war, commanded these,
And came to Troy with eighty dark-ribbed barks.
   Tlepolemus, a warrior of the stock 810
Of Hercules, was leader of the troops
Of Rhodes, and brought nine vessels to the war,
Manned with the haughty Rhodians. These were ranged
In threefold order: those of Lindus, those
Who dwell in white Camirus, lastly those 815
Of Ialassa. These Tlepolemus,
The valiant spearman, ruled. Astyoche
Bore him to mighty Hercules, who led
The maid from Ephyra, upon the banks
Of Selleïs, to be his wife, what time 820
His valor had overthrown and made a spoil
Of many a city full of noble youths.
Tlepolemus, when in the palace-halls
He grew to manhood, slew an aged man,
An uncle of his father, whom he loved, 825
Lycimnius, of the line of Mars, and straight
He rigged a fleet of ships and led on board
A numerous host and fled across the sea.
For fearful were the threats of other sons
And grandsons of the mighty Hercules. 830
In Rhodes they landed after wanderings long
And many hardships. There they dwelt in tribes,—
Three tribes,—and were beloved of Jupiter,
The ruler over gods and men, who poured
Abundant riches on their new abode. 835
   Nireus with three good ships from Syma came,—
Nireus, Aglaia's son by Charopus
The monarch,—Nireus who in comeliness
Surpassed all Greeks that came to Ilium, save
The faultless son of Peleus. Yet was he 840
Unwarlike and few people followed him.
   The dwellers of Nisyrus, Crapathus,
And Cos, the city of Eurypylus,
Casus, and the Calydnian isles, obeyed

Phidippus and his brother Antiphus, 845
Sons of the monarch Thessalus, who sprang
From Hercules. With thirty ships they came.
   But those who held Pelasgian Argos, those
Who dwelt in Alos, Trachys, Alope,
Phthia, and Hellas full of lovely dames,— 850
Named Myrmidons, Achaians, Hellenes,—
Achilles led their fifty ships; but they
Now heeded not the summons to the war,
For there was none to form their ranks for fight.
The great Achilles, swift of foot, remained 855
Within his ships, indignant for the sake
Of the fair-haired Briseis, whom he brought
A captive from Lyrnessus after toils
And dangers many. He had sacked and spoiled
Lyrnessus, and o'erthrown the walls of Thebes 860
And smitten Mynes and Epistrophus,
The warlike sons of King Evenus, sprung
From old Selapius. For this cause he kept
Within his ships, full soon to issue forth.
   The men of Phylacè, of Pyrasus,— 865
Sacred to Ceres and o'erspread with flowers,
And of Itona, mother of white flocks,
Antrona on the sea, and Pteleum green
With herbage,—over these while yet he lived
The brave Protesilaüs ruled; but now 870
The dark earth covered him, and for his sake
His consort, desolate in Phylacè,
Tore her fair cheeks, and all unfinished stood
His palace, for a Dardan warrior slew
Her husband as he leaped upon the land, 875
The foremost of the Achaians. Yet his troops
Were not without a leader, though they mourned
Their brave old chief. Podarces, loved by Mars,—
Son of Iphiclus, rich in flocks, who sprang
From Phylacus,—led them and formed their ranks. 880
A younger brother of the slain was he.
The slain was braver. Though the warriors grieved
To lose their glorious chief, they did not lack

A general. Forty dark ships followed him.
    Then they who dwelt in Pheræ, by the lake   885
Bœbeis, and in Bœbe, Glaphyræ,
And nobly built Iolchos, came to Troy,
Filling eleven galleys, and obeyed
Eumelus, whom Alcestis the divine
Bore to Admetus,—fairest, she, of all   890
The house of Pelias and of womankind.
    Those from Methonè, craggy Olizon,
And Melibœa and Thaumacia, filled
Seven ships, with Philoctetes for their chief;
A warrior skilled to bend the bow. Each bark   895
Held fifty rowers, bowmen all, and armed
For stubborn battle. But their leader lay
Far in an island, suffering grievous pangs,—
The hallowed isle of Lemnos. There the Greeks
Left him, in torture from a venomed wound   900
Made by a serpent's fangs. He lay and pined.
Yet was the moment near when they who thus
Forsook their king should think of him again.
Meantime his troops were not without a chief;
Though greatly they desired their ancient lord,   905
For now the base-born Medon marshalled them,
Son of Oïleus. Rhene brought him forth
To that destroyer of strong fortresses.
    The men of Tricca and Ithome's hills,
And they who held Œchalia and the town   910
Of Eurytus the Œchalian, had for chiefs
Two sons of Æsculapius, healers both,
And skilful,—Podalirius one, and one
Machaon. Thirty hollow barks were theirs.
    The dwellers of Ormenium, they whose homes   915
Were by the Hyperian fount, and they
Who held Asterium and the snowy peaks
Of Titanus, obeyed Eurypylus,
Evæmon's son, and far renowned. A fleet
Of forty dark-ribbed vessels followed him.   920
    Those who possessed Argissa, those who held
Gyrtonè, Orthè, and Helonè, those

Who dwelt in Oloösson with white walls,
The sturdy warrior Polypœtes led,
Son of Pirithoüs, who derived his birth 925
From deathless Jove. Hippodameia bore
The warrior to Pirithoüs on the day
When he took vengeance on the shaggy brood
Of Centaurs, and from Pelion drove them forth
To Æthicæ. Yet not alone in rule 930
Was Polypœtes, for Leonteus, sprung
From the large-souled Coronus, Cæneus' son,
Shared with him the command. With them a fleet
Of forty dark-hulled vessels came to Troy.

Then Guneus came, with two and twenty ships 935
From Cythus. Under his command he held
The Enienes, and that sturdy race,
The Peribœan warriors, and the men
Who built on cold Dodona, or who tilled
The fields where pleasant Titaresius flows 940
And into Peneus pours his gentle stream,
Yet with its silver eddies mingles not,
But floats upon the current's face like oil,—
A Stygian stream by which the immortals swear.

With Prothoüs, Tenthredon's son, there came 945
The warriors of Magnesia, who abode
By Peneus, and by Pelion hung with woods;
Swift-footed Prothoüs led these. They came
With forty dark-hulled galleys to the war.

These were the chiefs and princes of the Greeks. 950
Say, Muse, who most excelled among the kings,
And which the noblest steeds, of all that came
With the two sons of Atreus to the war?
The noblest steeds were those in Pheræ bred,
That, guided by Eumelus, flew like birds,— 955
Alike in hue and age; the plummet showed
Their height the same, and both were mares, and, reared
By Phœbus of the silver bow among
The meadows of Pieria, they became
The terror of the bloody battle-field. 960
The mightiest of the chiefs, while yet in wrath

Achilles kept aloof, was Ajax, son
Of Telamon; yet was Pelides far
The greater warrior, and the steeds which bore
That perfect hero were of noblest breed. 965
In his beaked galleys, swift to cut the sea,
Achilles lay, meanwhile, and nursed the wrath
He bore to Agamemnon, Atreus' son,
The shepherd of the people. On the beach
His warriors took their sport with javelins 970
And quoits and bows, while near the chariots tied
The horses, standing, browsed on lotus-leaves
And parsley from the marshes. But beneath
The tents the closely covered chariots stood,
While idly through the camp the charioteers, 975
Hither and thither sauntering, missed the sight
Of their brave lord and went not to the field.

   The army swept the earth as when a fire
Devours the herbage of the plains. The ground
Groaned under them as when the Thunderer Jove 980
In anger with his lightnings smites the earth
About Typhœus—where they say he lies—
In Arimi. So fearfully the ground
Groaned under that swift army as it moved.

   Now to the Trojans the swift Iris came 985
A messenger from ægis-bearing Jove,
Tidings of bale she brought. They all had met—
Old men and youths—in council at the gates
Of Priam's mansion. There did Iris take
Her station near the multitude, and spake, 990
In voice and gesture like Polites, son
Of Priam, who, confiding in his speed,
Had stood a watcher for the sons of Troy
On aged Æsyeta's lofty tomb,
To give them warning when the Achaian host 995
Should issue from their galleys. Thus disguised,
Swift Iris spake her message from the skies:—

   "Father! thou art delighted with much speech,
As once in time of peace, but now 'tis war,
Inevitable war, and close at hand. 1000

I have seen many battles, yet have ne'er
Beheld such armies, and so vast as these,—
In number like the sands and summer leaves.
They march across the plain, prepared to give
Battle beneath the city walls. To thee,   1005
O Hector, it belongs to heed my voice
And counsel. Many are the allies within
The walls of this great town of Priam, men
Of diverse race and speech. Let every chief
Of these array his countrymen for war,   1010
And give them orders for the coming fight."
  She spake, and Hector heeded and obeyed
The counsel of the goddess; he dismissed
The assembly; all the Trojans rushed to arms,
And all the gates were opened. Horse and foot   1015
Poured forth together in tumultuous haste.
  In the great plain before the city stands
A mound of steep ascent on every side;
Men named it Batiea, but the gods
Called it the swift Myrinna's tomb; and here   1020
Mustered the sons of Troy and their allies.
  Great Hector of the beamy helm, the son
Of Priam, led the Trojan race. The host
Of greatest multitude was marshalled there,
And there the bravest, mighty with the spear.   1025
  Æneas marshalled the Dardanian troops,—
The brave son of Anchises. Venus bore
The warrior to Anchises on the heights
Of Ida, where the mortal lover met
The goddess. Yet he ruled them not alone;   1030
Two chiefs, Antenor's sons Archelochus
And Acamas, were with him in command,
Expert in all the many arts of war.
  The Trojans from Zeleia, opulent men,
Who drank the dark Æsepus,—over these   1035
Ruled Pandarus, Lycaon's valiant son,
To whom the god Apollo gave his bow.
  The troops from Adrasteia, they who dwelt
Within Apæsus' walls, or tilled the soil

Of Pityeia and Tereia's heights,   1040
Were led by Amphius and Adrastus, clad
In linen corslets for the war, the sons
Of Merops the Percosian, skilled beyond
All other men in the diviner's art.
Nor would he that his sons should seek the field   1045
Of slaughter. They obeyed him not; the fates
Decreed their early death and urged them on.
   The dwellers of Percote, Practium,
And Sestus, and Abydus, and divine
Arisba, followed Asius, great among   1050
The heroes and the son of Hyrtacus,—
Asius, who came with strong and fiery steeds,
Borne from Arisba and from Selleïs' banks.
   Hippothoüs over the Pelasgian tribes—
Skilled spearman, who abode among the fields   1055
Of the deep-soiled Larissa—bore command,—
Hippothoüs with Pylæus, who derived
Their race from Mars, and for their father claimed
Pelasgian Lethus, son of Teutamus.
   And Acamas, and Peiroüs, valiant chief,   1060
Were captains of the Thracian men, whose fields
Were bounded by the rushing Hellespont.
Euphemus came with his Cicones, skilled
To wield the spear in fight. The nobly-born
Trœzenus was his father. Ceas' son   1065
Pyræchmes with Pæonia's archers came
From the broad Axius in far Amydon,—
Axius, the fairest river of the earth.
   Pylæmenes, a chief of fearless heart,
Led from the region of the Eneti,   1070
Where first the stubborn race of mules was bred,
The Paphlagonian warriors, they who held
Cytorus, Sesamus, and fair abodes
Built where Parthenius wanders on, and those
Who dwelt in Cromna and Ægialus,   1075
And on the lofty Erythinian heights.
   And Hodius and Epistrophus led on
The Halezonians from the distant land

Of Alyba, where ores of silver lie.
And Chromis and the augur Ennomus 1080
Were leaders of the Mysians; but his skill
Saved not the augur from the doom of death,
Slain by the swift of foot, Æacides,
With other men of Troy where Xanthus flows.
And Phorcys, and Ascanius, who was like 1085
A god in beauty, led the Phrygian troops
From far Ascania, eager for the fray.
And Antiphus and Mesthles were the chiefs
Of the Mæonian warriors, reared beside
The ships of Tmolus. There Gygæa's lake 1090
Brought forth both chieftains to Pylæmenes.
   Nastes was leader of the Carian troops,
Who spake in barbarous accents and possessed
Miletus and the leafy mountain heights
Where dwell the Phthirians, and Mæander's stream, 1095
And airy peaks of Mycalè. O'er these
Amphimachus and Nastes held command,—
Amphimachus and Nastes, far renowned
Sons of Nomion, him who, madly vain,
Went to the battle pranked like a young girl 1100
In golden ornaments. They spared him not
The bitter doom of death; he fell beneath
The hand of swift Æacides within
The river's channel. There the great in war,
Achilles, spoiled Nomion of his gold. 1105
Sarpedon and the noble Glaucus bore
Rule o'er the Lycians coming from afar,
Where eddying Xanthus runs through Lycia's meads.

BOOK III

NOW when both armies were arrayed for war,
Each with its chiefs, the Trojan host moved on
With shouts and clang of arms, as when the cry
Of cranes is in the air, that, flying south
From winter and its mighty breadth of rain,   5
Wing their way over ocean, and at dawn
Bring fearful battle to the pigmy race,
Bloodshed and death. But silently the Greeks
Went forward, breathing valor, mindful still
To aid each other in the coming fray.   10
   As when the south wind shrouds a mountain-top
In vapors that awake the shepherd's fear,—
A surer covert for the thief than night,—
And round him one can only see as far
As one can hurl a stone,—such was the cloud   15
Of dust that from the warriors' trampling feet
Rose round their rapid march and filled the air.
   Now drew they near each other, face to face,
And Paris in the Trojan van pressed on,
In presence like a god. A leopard's hide   20
Was thrown across his shoulders, and he bore
A crooked bow and falchion. Brandishing
Two brazen-pointed javelins, he defied
To mortal fight the bravest of the Greeks.
   Him Menelaus, loved of Mars, beheld   25
Advancing with large strides before the rest;

And as a hungry lion who has made
A prey of some large beast—a hornèd stag
Or mountain goat—rejoices, and with speed
Devours it, though swift hounds and sturdy youths 30
Press on his flank, so Menelaus felt
Great joy when Paris, of the godlike form,
Appeared in sight, for now he thought to wreak
His vengeance on the guilty one, and straight
Sprang from his car to earth with all his arms. 35
  But when the graceful Paris saw the chief
Come toward him from the foremost ranks, his heart
Was troubled, and he turned and passed among
His fellow-warriors and avoided death.
As one who meets within a mountain glade 40
A serpent starts aside with sudden fright,
And takes the backward way with trembling limbs
And cheeks all white,—the graceful Paris thus
Before the son of Atreus shrank in fear,
And mingled with the high-souled sons of Troy. 45
Hector beheld and thus upbraided him
Harshly: "O luckless Paris, nobly formed,
Yet woman-follower and seducer! Thou
Shouldst never have been born, or else at best
Have died unwedded; better were it far, 50
Than thus to be a scandal and a scorn
To all who look on thee. The long-haired Greeks,
How they will laugh, who for thy gallant looks
Deemed thee a hero, when there dwells in thee
No spirit and no courage? Wast thou such 55
When, crossing the great deep in thy stanch ships
With chosen comrades, thou didst make thy way
Among a stranger-people and bear off
A beautiful woman from that distant land,
Allied by marriage-ties to warrior-men,— 60
A mischief to thy father and to us
And all the people, to our foes a joy,
And a disgrace to thee? Why couldst thou not
Await Atrides? Then hadst thou been taught
From what a valiant warrior thou didst take 65

His blooming spouse. Thy harp will not avail,
Nor all the gifts of Venus, nor thy locks,
Nor thy fair form, when thou art laid in dust.
Surely the sons of Troy are faint of heart,
Else hadst thou, for the evil thou hast wrought, 70
Been laid beneath a coverlet of stone."
    Then Paris, of the godlike presence, spake
In answer: "Hector, thy rebuke is just;
Thou dost not wrong me. Dauntless is thy heart;
'Tis like an axe when, wielded by the hand 75
That hews the shipwright's plank, it cuts right through,
Doubling the wielder's force. Such tameless heart
Dwells in thy bosom. Yet reproach me not
With the fair gifts which golden Venus gave.
Whatever in their grace the gods bestow 80
Is not to be rejected: 'tis not ours
To choose what they shall give us. But if thou
Desirest to behold my prowess shown
In combat, cause the Trojans and the Greeks
To pause from battle, while, between the hosts, 85
I and the warlike Menelaus strive
In single fight for Helen and her wealth.
Whoever shall prevail and prove himself
The better warrior, let him take with him
The treasure and the woman, and depart; 90
While all the other Trojans, having made
A faithful league of amity, shall dwell
On Ilium's fertile plain, and all the Greeks
Return to Argos, famed for noble steeds,
And to Achaia, famed for lovely dames." 95
    He spake, and Hector, hearing him, rejoiced,
And went between the hosts, and with his spear,
Held by the middle, pressed the phalanxes
Of Trojans back, and made them all sit down.
The long-haired Greeks meanwhile, with bended bows, 100
Took aim against him, just about to send
Arrows and stones; but Agamemnon, king
Of men, beheld, and thus he cried aloud:—
    "Restrain yourselves, ye Argives; let not fly

Your arrows, ye Achaians; Hector asks— 105
He of the beamy helmet asks to speak."
  He spake, and they refrained, and all, at once,
Were silent. Hector then stood forth and said:—
  "Hearken, ye Trojans and ye nobly-armed
Achaians, to what Paris says by me. 110
He bids the Trojans and the Greeks lay down
Their shining arms upon the teeming earth,
And he and Menelaus, loved of Mars,
Will strive in single combat, on the ground
Between the hosts, for Helen and her wealth; 115
And he who shall o'ercome, and prove himself
The better warrior, to his home shall bear
The treasure and the woman, while the rest
Shall frame a solemn covenant of peace."
  He spake, and both the hosts in silence heard. 120
Then Menelaus, great in battle, said:—
  "Now hear me also,—me whose spirit feels
The wrong most keenly. I propose that now
The Greeks and Trojans separate reconciled,
For greatly have ye suffered for the sake 125
Of this my quarrel, and the original fault
Of Paris. Whomsoever fate ordains
To perish, let him die; but let the rest
Be from this moment reconciled, and part.
And bring an offering of two lambs—one white, 130
The other black—to Earth and to the Sun,
And we ourselves will offer one to Jove.
And be the mighty Priam here, that he
May sanction this our compact,—for his sons
Are arrogant and faithless,—lest some hand 135
Wickedly break the covenant of Jove.
The younger men are of a fickle mood;
But when an elder shares the act he looks
Both to the past and future, and provides
What is most fitting and the best for all." 140
  He spake, and both the Greeks and Trojans heard
His words with joy, and hoped the hour was come
To end the hard-fought war. They reined their steeds

Back to the ranks, alighted, and put off
Their armor, which they laid upon the ground   145
Near them in piles, with little space between.
   Then Hector sent two heralds forth with speed
Into the town, to bring the lambs and call
King Priam. Meanwhile Agamemnon bade
Talthybius seek the hollow ships and find   150
A lamb for the altar. He obeyed the words
Of noble Agamemnon, king of men.
   Meanwhile to white-armed Helen Iris came
A messenger. She took a form that seemed
Laodice, the sister of Paris, whom   155
Antenor's son, King Helicaon, wed,—
Fairest of Priam's daughters. She drew near
To Helen, in the palace, weaving there
An ample web, a shining double-robe,
Whereon were many conflicts fairly wrought,   160
Endured by the horse-taming sons of Troy
And brazen-mailed Achaians for her sake
Upon the field of Mars. Beside her stood
Swift-footed Iris, and addressed her thus:—
   "Dear lady, come and see the Trojan knights   165
And brazen-mailed Achaians doing things
To wonder at. They who, in this sad war,
Eager to slay each other, lately met
In murderous combat on the field, are now
Seated in silence, and the war hath ceased.   170
They lean upon their shields; their massive spears
Are near them, planted in the ground upright.
Paris, and Menelaus, loved of Mars,
With their long lances will contend for thee,
And thou wilt be declared the victor's spouse."   175
   She said, and in the heart of Helen woke
Dear recollections of her former spouse
And of her home and kindred. Instantly
She left her chamber, robed and veiled in white,
And shedding tender tears; yet not alone,   180
For with her went two maidens,—Æthra, child
Of Pitheus, and the large-eyed Clymene.

Straight to the Scæan gates they walked, by which
Panthoüs, Priam, and Thymœtes sat,
Lampus and Clytius, Hicetaon sprung 185
From Mars, Antenor and Ucalegon,
Two sages,—elders of the people all.
Beside the gates they sat, unapt, through age,
For tasks of war, but men of fluent speech,
Like the cicadas that within the wood 190
Sit on the trees and utter delicate sounds.
Such were the nobles of the Trojan race
Who sat upon the tower. But when they marked
The approach of Helen, to each other thus
With wingèd words, but in low tones, they said:— 195
   "Small blame is theirs, if both the Trojan knights
And brazen-mailed Achaians have endured
So long so many evils for the sake
Of that one woman. She is wholly like
In feature to the deathless goddesses. 200
So be it: let her, peerless as she is,
Return on board the fleet, nor stay to bring
Disaster upon us and all our race."
   So spake the elders. Priam meantime called
To Helen: "Come, dear daughter, sit by me. 205
Thou canst behold thy former husband hence,
Thy kindred and thy friends. I blame thee not;
The blame is with the immortals who have sent
These pestilent Greeks against me. Sit and name
For me this mighty man, the Grecian chief, 210
Gallant and tall. True, there are taller men;
But of such noble form and dignity
I never saw: in truth, a kingly man."
   And Helen, fairest among women, thus
Answered: "Dear second father, whom at once 215
I fear and honor, would that cruel death
Had overtaken me before I left,
To wander with thy son, my marriage-bed,
And my dear daughter, and the company
Of friends I loved. But that was not to be; 220
And now I pine and weep. Yet will I tell

What thou dost ask. The hero whom thou seest
Is the wide-ruling Agamemnon, son
Of Atreus, and is both a gracious king
And a most dreaded warrior. He was once   225
Brother-in-law to me, if I may speak—
Lost as I am to shame—of such a tie."
   She said, the aged man admired, and then
He spake again: "O son of Atreus, born
Under a happy fate, and fortunate   230
Among the sons of men! A mighty host
Of Grecian youths obey thy rule. I went
To Phrygia once,—that land of vines,—and there
Saw many Phrygians, heroes on fleet steeds,
The troops of Otreus, and of Mygdon, shaped   235
Like one of the immortals. They encamped
By the Sangarius. I was an ally;
My troops were ranked with theirs upon the day
When came the unsexed Amazons to war.
Yet even there I saw not such a host   240
As this of black-eyed Greeks who muster here."
   Then Priam saw Ulysses, and inquired:—
"Dear daughter, tell me also who is that,
Less tall than Agamemnon, yet more broad
In chest and shoulders. On the teeming earth   245
His armor lies, but he, from place to place,
Walks round among the ranks of soldiery,
As when the thick-fleeced father of the flocks
Moves through the multitude of his white sheep."
   And Jove-descended Helen answered thus:—   250
"That is Ulysses, man of many arts,
Son of Laertes, reared in Ithaca,
That rugged isle, and skilled in every form
Of shrewd device and action wisely planned."
   Then spake the sage Antenor: "Thou hast said   255
The truth, O lady. This Ulysses once
Came on an embassy, concerning thee,
To Troy with Menelaus, great in war;
And I received them as my guests, and they
Were lodged within my palace, and I learned   260

The temper and the qualities of both.
When both were standing 'mid the men of Troy,
I marked that Menelaus's broad chest
Made him the more conspicuous, but when both
Were seated, greater was the dignity   265
Seen in Ulysses. When they both addressed
The council, Menelaus briefly spake
In pleasing tones, though with few words,—as one
Not given to loose and wandering speech,—although
The younger. When the wise Ulysses rose,   270
He stood with eyes cast down, and fixed on earth,
And neither swayed his sceptre to the right
Nor to the left, but held it motionless,
Like one unused to public speech. He seemed
An idiot out of humor. But when forth   275
He sent from his full lungs his mighty voice,
And words came like a fall of winter snow,
No mortal then would dare to strive with him
For mastery in speech. We less admired
The aspect of Ulysses than his words."   280
 Beholding Ajax then, the aged king
Asked yet again: "Who is that other chief
Of the Achaians, tall, and large of limb,—
Taller and broader-chested than the rest?"
 Helen, the beautiful and richly-robed,   285
Answered: "Thou seest the mighty Ajax there,
The bulwark of the Greeks. On the other side,
Among his Cretans, stands Idomeneus,
Of godlike aspect, near to whom are grouped
The leaders of the Cretans. Oftentimes   290
The warlike Menelaus welcomed him
Within our palace, when he came from Crete.
I could point out and name the other chiefs
Of the dark-eyed Achaians. Two alone,
Princes among their people, are not seen,—   295
Castor the fearless horseman, and the skilled
In boxing, Pollux,—twins; one mother bore
Both them and me. Came they not with the rest
From pleasant Lacedæmon to the war?

Or, having crossed the deep in their good ships, 300
Shun they to fight among the valiant ones
Of Greece, because of my reproach and shame?"
   She spake; but they already lay in earth
In Lacedæmon, their dear native land.
   And now the heralds through the city bore 305
The sacred pledges of the gods,—two lambs,
And joyous wine, the fruit of Earth, within
A goat-skin. One of them—Idæus—brought
A glistening vase and golden drinking-cups,
And summoned, in these words, the aged king:— 310
   "Son of Laomedon, arise! The chiefs
Who lead the Trojan knights and brazen-mailed
Achaians pray thee to descend at once
Into the plain, that thou may'st ratify
A faithful compact. Alexander now 315
And warlike Menelaus will contend
With their long spears for Helen. She and all
Her treasures are to be the conqueror's prize;
While all the other Trojans, having made
A faithful league of amity, shall dwell 320
On Ilium's fertile plain, and all the Greeks
Return to Argos, famed for noble steeds,
And to Achaia, famed for lovely dames."
   He spake, and Priam, shuddering, heard and bade
The attendants yoke the horses to his car. 325
Soon were they yoked; he mounted first and drew
The reins; Antenor took a place within
The sumptuous car, and through the Scæan gates
They guided the fleet coursers toward the field.
   Now when the twain had come where lay the hosts 330
Of Trojans and Achaians, down they stepped
Upon the teeming earth, and went among
The assembled armies. Quickly, as they came,
Rose Agamemnon, king of men, and next
Uprose the wise Ulysses. To the spot 335
The illustrious heralds brought the sacred things
That bind a treaty, and with mingled wine
They filled a chalice, and upon the hands

Of all the kings poured water. Then the son
Of Atreus drew a dagger which he wore 340
Slung by his sword's huge sheath, and clipped away
The forelocks of the lambs, and parted them
Among the Trojan and Achaian chiefs,
And stood with lifted hands and prayed aloud:—
   "O Father Jupiter, who rulest all 345
From Ida, mightiest, most august! and thou,
O all-beholding and all-hearing Sun!
Ye Rivers, and thou Earth, and ye who dwell
Beneath the earth and punish after death
Those who have sworn false oaths, bear witness ye, 350
And keep unbroken this day's promises.
If Alexander in the combat slay
My brother Menelaus, he shall keep
Helen and all her wealth, while we return
Homeward in our good ships. If, otherwise, 355
The bright-haired Menelaus take the life
Of Alexander, Helen and her wealth
Shall be restored, and they of Troy shall pay
Such fine as may be meet, and may be long
Remembered in the ages yet to come. 360
And then if, after Alexander's fall,
Priam and Priam's sons refuse the fine,
I shall make war for it, and keep my place
By Troy until I gain the end I seek."
   So spake the king, and with the cruel steel 365
Cut the lambs' throats, and laid them on the ground,
Panting and powerless, for the dagger took
Their lives away. Then over them they poured
Wine from the chalice, drawn in golden cups,
And prayed to the ever-living gods; and thus 370
Were Trojans and Achaians heard to say:—
   "O Jupiter most mighty and august!
Whoever first shall break these solemn oaths,
So may their brains flow down upon the earth,—
Theirs and their children,—like the wine we pour, 375
And be their wives the wives of other men."
   Such was the people's vow. Saturnian Jove

Confirmed it not. Then Priam, of the line
Of Dardanus, addressed the armies thus:—
"Hear me, ye Trojans, and ye well-greaved Greeks! 380
For me I must return to wind-swept Troy.
I cannot bear, with these old eyes, to look
On my dear son engaged in desperate fight
With Menelaus, the beloved of Mars.
Jove and the ever-living gods alone 385
Know which of them shall meet the doom of death."
  So spake the godlike man, and placed the lambs
Within his chariot, mounted, and drew up
The reins. Antenor by him took his place
Within the sumptuous chariot. Then they turned 390
The horses and retraced their way to Troy.
  But Hector, son of Priam, and the great
Ulysses measured off a fitting space,
And in a brazen helmet, to decide
Which warrior first should hurl the brazen spear, 395
They shook the lots, while all the people round
Lifted their hands to heaven and prayed the gods;
And thus the Trojans and Achaians said:—
  "O Father Jove, who rulest from the top
Of Ida, mightiest one and most august! 400
Whichever of these twain has done the wrong,
Grant that he pass to Pluto's dwelling, slain,
While friendship and a faithful league are ours."
  So spake they. Hector of the beamy helm
Looked back and shook the lots. Forth leaped at once 405
The lot of Paris. Then they took their seats
In ranks beside their rapid steeds, and where
Lay their rich armor. Paris the divine,
Husband of bright-haired Helen, there put on
His shining panoply,—upon his legs 410
Fair greaves, with silver clasps, and on his breast
His brother's mail, Lycaon's, fitting well
His form. Around his shoulders then he hung
His silver-studded sword, and stout, broad shield,
And gave his glorious brows the dreadful helm, 415
Dark with its horse-hair plume. A massive spear

Filled his right hand. Meantime the warlike son
Of Atreus clad himself in like array.
   And now when both were armed for fight, and each
Had left his host, and, coming forward, walked   420
Between the Trojans and the Greeks, and frowned
Upon the other, a mute wonder held
The Trojan cavaliers and well-greaved Greeks.
There near each other in the measured space
They stood in wrathful mood with lifted spears.   425
   First Paris hurled his massive spear; it smote
The round shield of Atrides, but the brass
Broke not beneath the blow; the weapon's point
Was bent on that strong shield. The next assault
Atrides Menelaus made, but first   430
Offered this prayer to Father Jupiter:—
   "O sovereign Jove! vouchsafe that I avenge
On guilty Paris wrongs which he was first
To offer; let him fall beneath my hand,
That men may dread hereafter to requite   435
The friendship of a host with injury."
   He spake, and flung his brandished spear; it smote
The round shield of Priamides; right through
The shining buckler went the rapid steel,
And, cutting the soft tunic near the flank,   440
Stood fixed in the fair corslet. Paris bent
Sideways before it and escaped his death.
Atrides drew his silver-studded sword,
Lifted it high and smote his enemy's crest.
The weapon, shattered to four fragments, fell.   445
He looked to the broad heaven, and thus exclaimed:—
   "O Father Jove! thou art of all the gods
The most unfriendly. I had hoped to avenge
The wrong by Paris done me, but my sword
Is broken in my grasp, and from my hand   450
The spear was vainly flung and gave no wound."
   He spake, and, rushing forward, seized the helm
Of Paris by its horse-hair crest, and turned
And dragged him toward the well-armed Greeks. Beneath
His tender throat the embroidered band that held   455

The helmet to the chin was choking him.
And now had Menelaus dragged him thence,
And earned great glory, if the child of Jove,
Venus, had not perceived his plight in time.
She broke the ox-hide band; an empty helm 460
Followed the powerful hand; the hero saw,
Swung it aloft and hurled it toward the Greeks,
And there his comrades seized it. He again
Rushed with his brazen spear to slay his foe.
But Venus—for a goddess easily 465
Can work such marvels—rescued him, and, wrapped
In a thick shadow, bore him from the field
And placed him in his chamber, where the air
Was sweet with perfumes. Then she took her way
To summon Helen. On the lofty tower 470
She found her, midst a throng of Trojan dames,
And plucked her perfumed robe. She took the form
And features of a spinner of the fleece,
An aged dame, who used to comb for her
The fair white wool in Lacedæmon's halls, 475
And loved her much. In such an humble guise
The goddess Venus thus to Helen spake:—
  "Come hither, Alexander sends for thee;
He now is in his chamber and at rest
On his carved couch; in beauty and attire 480
Resplendent, not like one who just returns
From combat with a hero, but like one
Who goes to mingle in the choral dance,
Or, when the dance is ended, takes his seat."
  She spake, and Helen heard her, deeply moved; 485
Yet when she marked the goddess's fair neck,
Beautiful bosom, and soft, lustrous eyes,
Her heart was touched with awe, and thus she said:—
  "Strange being! why wilt thou delude me still?
Wouldst thou decoy me further on among 490
The populous Phrygian towns, or those that stud
Pleasant Mæonia, where there haply dwells
Some one of mortal race whom thou dost deign
To make thy favorite. Hast thou seen, perhaps,

That Menelaus, having overpowered 495
The noble Alexander, seeks to bear
Me, hated as I must be, to his home?
And hast thou therefore fallen on this device?
Go to him, sit by him, renounce for him
The company of gods, and never more 500
Return to heaven, but suffer with him; watch
Beside him till he take thee for his wife
Or handmaid. Thither I shall never go,
To adorn his couch and to disgrace myself.
The Trojan dames would taunt me. O, the griefs 505
That press upon my soul are infinite!"
    Displeased, the goddess Venus answered: "Wretch,
Incense me not, lest I abandon thee
In anger, and detest thee with a zeal
As great as is my love, and lest I cause 510
Trojans and Greeks to hate thee, so that thou
Shalt miserably perish." Thus she spake;
And Helen, Jove-begotten, struck with awe,
Wrapped in a robe of shining white, went forth
In silence from amidst the Trojan dames, 515
Unheeded, for the goddess led the way.
    When now they stood beneath the sumptuous roof
Of Alexander, straightway did the maids
Turn to their wonted tasks, while she went up,
Fairest of women, to her chamber. There 520
The laughing Venus brought and placed a seat
Right opposite to Paris. Helen sat,
Daughter of ægis-bearing Jove, with eyes
Averted, and reproached her husband thus:—
    "Com'st thou from battle? Rather would that thou 525
Hadst perished by the mighty hand of him
Who was my husband. It was once, I know,
Thy boast that thou wert more than peer in strength
And power of hand, and practice with the spear,
To warlike Menelaus. Go then now, 530
Defy him to the combat once again.
And yet I counsel thee to stand aloof,
Nor rashly seek a combat, hand to hand,

With fair-haired Menelaus, lest perchance
He smite thee with his spear and thou be slain." 535
    Then Paris answered: "Woman, chide me not
Thus harshly. True it is, that, with the aid
Of Pallas, Menelaus hath obtained
The victory; but I may vanquish him
In turn, for we have also gods with us. 540
Give we the hour to dalliance; never yet
Have I so strongly proved the power of love,—
Not even when I bore thee from thy home
In pleasant Lacedæmon, traversing
The deep in my good ships, and in the isle 545
Of Cranaë made thee mine,—such glow of love
Possesses me, and sweetness of desire."
    He spake, and to the couch went up; his wife
Followed, and that fair couch received them both.
    Meantime Atrides, like a beast of prey, 550
Went fiercely ranging through the crowd in search
Of godlike Alexander, None of all
The Trojans, or of their renowned allies,
Could point him out to Menelaus, loved
Of Mars; and had they known his lurking-place 555
They would not for his sake have kept him hid,
For like black death they hated him. Then stood
Among them Agamemnon, king of men,
And spake: "Ye Trojans and Achaians, hear,
And ye allies. The victory belongs 560
To warlike Menelaus. Ye will then
Restore the Argive Helen and her wealth,
And pay the fitting fine, which shall remain
A memory to men in future times."
    Thus spake the son of Atreus, and the rest 565
Of the Achaian host approved his words.

BOOK IV

MEANTIME the immortal gods with Jupiter
Upon his golden pavement sat and held
A council. Hebe, honored of them all,
Ministered nectar, and from cups of gold
They pledged each other, looking down on Troy.   5
When, purposely to kindle Juno's mood
To anger, Saturn's son, with biting words
That well betrayed his covert meaning, spake:—
   "Two goddesses—the Argive Juno one,
The other Pallas, her invincible friend—   10
Take part with Menelaus, yet they sit
Aloof, content with looking on, while still
Venus, the laughter-loving one, protects
Her Paris, ever near him, warding off
The stroke of fate. Just now she rescued him   15
When he was near his death. The victory
Belongs to Menelaus, loved of Mars.
Now let us all consider what shall be
The issue,—whether we allow the war,
With all its waste of life, to be renewed,   20
Or cause the warring nations to sit down
In amity. If haply it shall be
The pleasure and the will of all the gods,
Let Priam's city keep its dwellers still,
And Menelaus lead his Helen home."   25
   He spake, but Juno and Minerva sat,

And with closed lips repined, for secretly
They plotted evil for the Trojan race.
Minerva held her peace in bitterness
Of heart and sore displeased with Father Jove. 30
But Juno could not curb her wrath, and spake:—
   "What words, austere Saturnius, hast thou said!
Wilt thou then render vain the toils I bear,
And all my sweat? My very steeds even now
Are weary with the mustering of the host 35
That threaten woe to Priam and his sons.
Yet do thy will; but be at least assured
That all the other gods approve it not."
   The cloud-compelling Jupiter replied
In anger: "Pestilent one! what grievous wrong 40
Hath Priam done to thee, or Priam's sons,
That thou shouldst persevere to overthrow
His noble city? Shouldst thou through the gates
Of Ilium make thy way, and there devour,
Within the ramparts, Priam and his sons 45
And all the men of Troy alive, thy rage
Haply might be appeased. Do as thou wilt,
So that this difference breed no lasting strife
Between us. Yet I tell thee this,—and thou
Bear what I say in mind: In time to come, 50
Should I design to level in the dust
Some city where men dear to thee are born,
Seek not to thwart my vengeance, but submit.
For now I fully yield me to thy wish,
Though with unwilling mind. Wherever dwell 55
The race of humankind beneath the sun
And starry heaven, of all their cities Troy
Has been by me most honored,—sacred Troy,—
And Priam, and the people who obey
Priam, the wielder of the ashen spear; 60
For there my altars never lacked their rites,—
Feasts, incense, and libations duly paid."
   Then Juno, the majestic, with large eyes,
Rejoined: "The cities most beloved by me
Are three,—Mycenæ, with her spacious streets, 65

Argos, and Sparta. Raze them to the ground,
If they be hateful to thee. I shall ne'er
Contend to save them, nor repine to see
Their fall; for, earnestly as I might seek
To rescue them from ruin, all my aid
Would not avail, so much the mightier thou.
Yet doth it ill become thee thus to make
My efforts vain. I am a goddess, sprung
From the same stock with thee; I am the child
Of crafty Saturn, and am twice revered,—
Both for my birth and that I am the spouse
Of thee who rulest over all the gods.
Now let us each yield somewhat,—I to thee
And thou to me; the other deathless gods
Will follow us. Let Pallas be despatched
To that dread battle-field on which are ranged
The Trojans and Achaians, and stir up
The Trojan warriors first to lift their hands
Against the elated Greeks and break the league."

   She ended, and the Father of the gods
And mortals instantly complied, and called
Minerva, and in wingèd accents said:—
"Haste to the battle-field, and there, among
The Trojan and Achaian armies, cause
The Trojan warriors first to lift their hands
Against the elated Greeks and break the league."

   So saying, Jupiter to Pallas gave
The charge she wished already. She in haste
Shot from the Olympian summits, like a star
Sent by the crafty Saturn's son to warn
The seamen or some mighty host in arms,—
A radiant meteor scattering sparkles round.
So came and lighted Pallas on the earth
Amidst the armies. All who saw were seized
With wonder,—Trojan knights and well-armed Greeks;
And many a one addressed his comrade thus:—

   "Sure we shall have the wasting war again,
And stubborn combats; or, it may be, Jove,
The arbiter of wars among mankind,

Decrees that the two nations dwell in peace." 105
  So Greeks and Trojans said. The goddess went
Among the Trojan multitude disguised;
She seemed Laodocus, Antenor's son,
A valiant warrior, seeking through the ranks
For godlike Pandarus. At length she found 110
Lycaon's gallant and illustrious son,
Standing with bucklered warriors ranged around,
Who followed him from where Æsepus flows;
And, standing near, she spake these wingèd words:—
  "Son of Lycaon! wilt thou hear my words, 115
Brave as thou art? Then wilt thou aim a shaft
At Menelaus; thus wilt thou have earned
Great thanks and praise from all the men of Troy,
And chiefly from Prince Paris, who will fill,
Foremost of all, thy hands with lavish gifts, 120
When he shall look on Menelaus slain—
The warlike son of Atreus—by thy hand,
And laid upon his lofty funeral pile.
Aim now at Menelaus the renowned
An arrow, while thou offerest a vow 125
To Lycian Phœbus, mighty with the bow,
That thou wilt bring to him a hecatomb
Of firstling lambs, when thou again shalt come
Within thine own Zeleia's sacred walls."
  So spake Minerva, and her words o'ercame 130
The weak one's purpose. He uncovered straight
His polished bow, made of the elastic horns
Of a wild goat, which, from his lurking-place,
As once it left its cavern lair, he smote,
And pierced its breast, and stretched it on the rock. 135
Full sixteen palms in length the horns had grown
From the goat's forehead. These an artisan
Had smoothed, and, aptly fitting each to each,
Polished the whole and tipped the work with gold.
To bend that bow, the warrior lowered it 140
And pressed an end against the earth. His friends
Held up, meanwhile, their shields before his face,
Lest the brave sons of Greece should lift their spears

Against him ere the champion of their host,
The warlike Menelaus, should have felt 145
The arrow. Then the Lycian drew aside
The cover from his quiver, taking out
A well-fledged arrow that had never flown,—
A cause of future sorrows. On the string
He laid that fatal arrow, while he made 150
To Lycian Phœbus, mighty with the bow,
A vow to sacrifice before his shrine
A noble hecatomb of firstling lambs
When he should come again to his abode
Within his own Zeleia's sacred walls. 155
Grasping the bowstring and the arrow's notch,
He drew them back, and forced the string to meet
His breast, the arrow-head to meet the bow,
Till the bow formed a circle. Then it twanged.
The cord gave out a shrilly sound; the shaft 160
Leaped forth in eager haste to reach the host.
   Yet, Menelaus, then the blessed gods,
The deathless ones, forgot thee not; and first,
Jove's daughter, gatherer of spoil, who stood
Before thee, turned aside the deadly shaft. 165
As when a mother, while her child is wrapped
In a sweet slumber, scares away the fly,
So Pallas turned the weapon from thy breast,
And guided it to where the golden clasps
Made fast the belt, and where the corslet's mail 170
Was doubled. There the bitter arrow struck
The belt, and through its close contexture passed,
And fixed within the well-wrought corslet stood,
Yet reached the plated quilt which next his skin
The hero wore,—his surest guard against 175
The weapon's force,—and broke through that alike;
And there the arrow gashed the part below,
And the dark blood came gushing from the wound.
As when some Carian or Mæonian dame
Tinges with purple the white ivory, 180
To form a trapping for the cheeks of steeds,—
And many a horseman covets it, yet still

It lies within her chamber, to become
The ornament of some great monarch's steed
And make its rider proud,—thy shapely thighs,   185
Thy legs, and thy fair ankles thus were stained,
O Menelaus! with thy purple blood.
    When Agamemnon, king of men, beheld
The dark blood flowing from his brother's wound,
He shuddered. Menelaus, great in war,   190
Felt the like horror; yet, when he perceived
That still the arrow, neck and barb, remained
Without the mail, the courage rose again
That filled his bosom. Agamemnon, then,
The monarch, sighing deeply, took the hand   195
Of Menelaus,—while his comrades round
Like him lamented,—sighing as he spake:—
    "Dear brother, when I sent thee forth alone
To combat with the Trojans for the Greeks,
I ratified a treaty for thy death,—   200
Since now the Trojans smite and under foot
Trample the league. Yet not in vain shall be
The treaty, nor the blood of lambs, nor wine
Poured to the gods, nor right hands firmly pledged;
For though it please not now Olympian Jove   205
To make the treaty good, he will in time
Cause it to be fulfilled, and they shall pay
Dearly with their own heads and with their wives
And children for this wrong. And this I know
In my undoubting mind,—a day will come   210
When sacred Troy and Priam and the race
Governed by Priam, mighty with the spear,
Shall perish all. Saturnian Jove, who sits
On high, a dweller of the upper air,
Shall shake his dreadful ægis in the sight   215
Of all, indignant at this treachery.
Such the event will be; but I shall grieve
Bitterly, Menelaus, if thou die,
Thy term of life cut short. I shall go back
To my dear Argos with a brand of shame   220
Upon me. For the Greeks will soon again

Bethink them of their country; we shall then
Leave Argive Helen to remain the boast
Of Priam and the Trojans,—while thy bones
Shall moulder, mingling with the earth of Troy,— 225
Our great design abandoned. Then shall say
Some haughty Trojan, leaping on the tomb
Of Menelaus: 'So in time to come
May Agamemnon wreak his wrath, as here
He wreaked it, whither he had vainly led 230
An army, and now hastens to his home
And his own land, with ships that bear no spoil,
And the brave Menelaus left behind.'
So shall some Trojan say; but, ere that time,
May the earth open to receive my bones!" 235
   The fair-haired Menelaus cheerfully
Replied: "Grieve not, nor be the Greeks alarmed
For me, since this sharp arrow has not found
A vital part, but, ere it reached so far,
The embroidered belt, the quilt beneath, and plate 240
Wrought by the armorer's cunning, broke its force."
   King Agamemnon took the word and said:—
"Dear Menelaus! would that it were so,
Yet the physician must explore thy wound,
And with his balsams soothe the bitter pain." 245
Then turning to Talthybius, he addressed
The sacred herald: "Hasten with all speed,
Talthybius; call Machaon, warrior-son
Of Æsculapius, that much-honored leech,
And bring him to the Achaian general, 250
The warlike Menelaus, whom some hand
Of Trojan or of Lycian, skilled to bend
The bow, hath wounded with his shaft,—a deed
For him to exult in, but a grief to us."
   He spake; nor failed the herald to obey, 255
But hastened at the word and passed among
The squadrons of Achaia, mailed in brass,
In search of great Machaon. Him he found
As midst the valiant ranks of bucklered men
He stood,—the troops who followed him to war 260

From Triccæ, nurse of steeds. Then, drawing near,
The herald spake to him in wingèd words:—
    "O son of Æsculapius, come in haste.
King Agamemnon calls thee to the aid
Of warlike Menelaus, whom some hand   265
Of Trojan or of Lycian, skilled to bend
The bow, hath wounded with his shaft,—a deed
For him to exult in, but a grief to us."
    Machaon's heart was touched, and forth they went
Through the great throng, the army of the Greeks.   270
And when they came where Atreus' warlike son
Was wounded, they perceived the godlike man
Standing amid a circle of the chiefs,
The bravest of the Achaians, who at once
Had gathered round. Without delay he drew   275
The arrow from the fairly-fitted belt.
The barbs were bent in drawing. Then he loosed
The embroidered belt, the quilted vest beneath,
And plate,—the armorer's work,—and carefully
O'erlooked the wound where fell the bitter shaft,   280
Cleansed it from blood, and sprinkled over it
With skill the soothing balsams which of yore
The friendly Chiron to his father gave.
    While round the warlike Menelaus thus
The chiefs were busy, all the Trojans moved   285
Into array of battle; they put on
Their armor, and were eager for the fight.
Then wouldst thou not have seen, hadst thou been there,
King Agamemnon slumbering, or in fear,
And skulking from the combat, but alert,   290
Preparing for the glorious tasks of war.
His horses, and his chariot bright with brass,
He left, and bade Eurymedon, his groom,
The son of Ptolemy Piraides,
Hold them apart still panting, yet with charge   295
To keep them near their master, till the hour
When he should need them, weary with the toil
Of such a vast command. Meantime he went
On foot among his files of soldiery,

And whomsoe'er he found with fiery steeds 300
Hasting to battle, thus he cheered them on:—
  "O Argives! let not your hot courage cool,
For Father Jove will never take the part
Of treachery. Whosoe'er have been the first
To break the league, upon their lifeless limbs 305
Shall vultures feast; and doubt not we shall bear
Away in our good ships the wives they love
And their young children, when we take their town."
  But whomsoe'er he saw that kept afar
From the dread field, he angrily rebuked:— 310
  "O Argives! who with arrows only fight,
Base as ye are, have ye no sense of shame?
Why stand ye stupefied, like fawns, that, tired
With coursing the wide pastures, stop at last,
Their strength exhausted! Thus ye stand amazed, 315
Nor think of combat. Wait ye for the hour
When to your ships, with their fair-sculptured prows,
Moored on the borders of the hoary deep,
The Trojans come, that haply ye may see
If the great hand of Jove will shield you then?" 320
  Thus Agamemnon, as supreme in power,
Threaded the warrior-files, until he came
Where stood the Cretans. All in arms they stood
Around Idomeneus, the great in war.
Like a wild boar in strength, he led the van, 325
And, in the rear, Meriones urged on
His phalanxes. The king of men rejoiced,
And blandly thus bespake Idomeneus:—
  "Idomeneus! I honor thee above
The other knights of Greece, as well in war 330
As in all other labors, and no less
In banquets, when the Achaian nobles charge
Their goblets with the dark-red mingled wine
In sign of honor. All the other Greeks
Drink by a certain measure, but thy cup 335
Stands ever full, like mine, that thou may'st drink
When thou desirest. Hasten to the war
With all the valor thou dost glory in."

The Cretan chief, Idomeneus, replied:—
"Atrides, I remain thy true ally, 340
As I have pledged my faith. But thou exhort
The other long-haired-Greeks, and bid them rush
To combat, since the Trojans break their oath.
For woe and death must be the lot of those
Who broke the peace they vowed so solemnly." 345
  He spake. The son of Atreus, glad at heart,
Passed on among the squadrons, till he came
To where the warriors Ajax formed their ranks
For battle, with a cloud of infantry.
As when some goatherd from the hill-top sees 350
A cloud that traverses the deep before
A strong west wind,—beholding it afar,
Pitch-black it seems, and bringing o'er the waves
A whirlwind with it; he is seized with fear,
And drives his flock to shelter in a cave,— 355
So with the warriors Ajax to the war
Moved, dense and dark, the phalanxes of youths
Trained for the combat, and their serried files
Bristling with spears and shields. The king of men
Saw with delight, and spake these wingèd words:— 360
  "O warriors Ajax, leaders of the Greeks
In brazen armor, I enjoin you not
To rouse the courage of your soldiery.
Such word would ill become me, for yourselves
Have made your followers eager to engage 365
In manful combat. Would to Jupiter,
To Pallas, and Apollo, that there dwelt
In every bosom such a soul as yours!
Then would the city of King Priam fall
At once, o'erthrown and levelled by our hands." 370
  Thus having said, he left them and went on
To others. There he found the smooth of speech,
Nestor, the Pylian orator, employed
In marshalling his squadrons. Near to him
Alastor and the large-limbed Pelagon, 375
Chromius, and Hæmon, prince among his tribe,
And Bias, shepherd of the people, stood.

The cavalry with steeds and cars he placed
In front. A vast and valiant multitude
Of infantry he stationed in the rear, 380
To be the bulwark of the war. Between
He made the faint of spirit take their place,
That, though unwillingly, they might be forced
To combat with the rest. And first he gave
His orders to the horsemen, bidding them 385
To keep their coursers reined, nor let them range
At random through the tumult of the crowd:—
   "And let no man, too vain of horsemanship,
And trusting in his valor, dare advance
Beyond the rest to attack the men of Troy, 390
Nor let him fall behind the rest, to make
Our ranks the weaker. Whoso from his car
Can reach an enemy's, let him stand and strike
With his long spear, for 'tis the shrewder way.
By rules like these, which their brave hearts obeyed, 395
The men of yore laid level towns and towers."
   The aged man, long versed in tasks of war,
Counselled them thus. King Agamemnon heard,
Delighted, and in wingèd words he said:—
   "O aged man, would that thy knees were firm 400
As is thy purpose, and thy strength as great!
But age, the common fate of all, has worn
Thy frame: would that some others had thy age,
And thou wert of the number of our youths!"
   Then answered Nestor, the Gerenian knight:— 405
"O son of Atreus, I myself could wish
That I were now as when of yore I struck
The high-born Ereuthalion down. The gods
Bestow not all their gifts on man at once.
If I were then a youth, old age in turn 410
Is creeping o'er me. Still I keep among
The knights, and counsel and admonish them,—
The office of the aged. Younger men,
They who can trust their strength, must wield the spear."
   He spake. The son of Atreus passed him by, 415
Pleased with his words, and, moving onward, came

Where—with the Athenians, ever prompt to raise
The war-cry, grouped around him—stood the knight
Menestheus, son of Peteus. Near to these
Was wise Ulysses, with his sturdy band   420
Of Cephalonians. None of these had heard
The clamor of the battle, for the hosts
Of Trojan knights and Greeks had just begun
To move, and there they waited for the advance
Of other squadrons marching on to charge   425
The Trojans and begin the war anew.
The king of men, Atrides, was displeased,
And spake, and chid them thus with wingèd words:—
 "O son of Peteus, foster-child of Jove,
And thou, the man of craft and evil wiles!   430
Why stand ye here aloof, irresolute,
And wait for others? Ye should be the first
To meet the foe and stem the battle's rage.
I bid you first to banquets which the Greeks
Give to their leaders, where ye feast at will   435
On roasted meats and bowls of pleasant wine.
Now, ere ye move, ye willingly would see
Ten Grecian squadrons join the deadly strife."
 The man of many arts, Ulysses, spake,
And frowned: "O Atreus' son! what words are these   440
Which pass thy lips? How canst thou say that we
Avoid the battle? Ever when the Greeks
Seek bloody conflict with the Trojan knights,
Thou, if thou wilt, and if thou givest heed
To things like these, shalt with thine eyes behold   445
The father of Telemachus engaged
In combat with the foremost knights that form
The Trojan van. Thou utterest empty words."
 King Agamemnon, when he saw the chief
Offended, changed his tone, and, smiling, said:—   450
 "Son of Laertes, nobly born and wise
Ulysses! It is not for me to chide
Nor to exhort thee, for thy heart, I know,
Counsels thee kindly toward me, and thy thought
Agrees with mine. We will discuss all this   455

Hereafter. If just now too harsh a word
Was uttered, may the immortals make it vain!"
   So saying, he departed, and went on
To others. By his steeds and by his car,
That shone with fastenings of brass, he found   460
The son of Tydeus, large-souled Diomed,
And Sthenelus, the son of Capaneus,
Standing beside him. Looking at them both,
King Agamemnon to Tydides spake
In wingèd words, and thus reproved the chief:—   465
   "O son of Tydeus, that undaunted knight!
What is there to appall thee? Why look through
The spaces that divide the warlike ranks?
Not thus did Tydeus feel the touch of fear,
But ever foremost of his warriors fought.   470
So they declare who saw his deeds, for I
Was never with him, nor have ever seen
The hero. Yet they say that he excelled
All others. Certain is it that he once
Entered Mycenæ as a friendly guest,   475
With no array of soldiery, but came
With godlike Polynices. 'Twas the time
When warrior-bands were gathered to besiege
The sacred walls of Thebes, and earnestly
They prayed that from Mycenæ they might lead   480
Renowned auxiliars to the war, and we
Would willingly have given the aid they asked,—
For we approved the prayer,—but Jove, with signs
Of angry omen, changed our purposes.
The chiefs departed, journeying on to where   485
Asopus flows through reeds and grass, and thence
The Achaians sent an embassy to Thebes
By Tydeus. There he met the many sons
Of Cadmus at the banquets in the hall
Of valiant Eteocles. Though alone   490
Among so many, and a stranger-guest,
The hero feared them not, but challenged them
To vie with him in games; and easily
He won the victory, such aid was given

By Pallas. Then the sons of Cadmus, skilled 495
In horsemanship, were wroth, and privily
Sent fifty armèd youths to lie in wait
For his return. Two leaders had the band,—
Maion, the son of Hæmon, like a god
In form, and Lycophontes, brave in war, 500
Son of Autophonos. A bloody death
Did Tydeus give the youths. He slew them all
Save Maion, whom he suffered to return,
Obedient to an omen from the gods.
Such was Ætolian Tydeus; but his son, 505
A better speaker, is less brave in war."
  He spake; and valiant Diomed, who heard
The king's reproof with reverence, answered not.
Then spake the son of honored Capaneus:—
  "Atrides, speak not falsely, when thou know'st 510
The truth so well. Assuredly we claim
To be far braver than our fathers were.
We took seven-gated Thebes with fewer troops
Than theirs, when, trusting in the omens sent
From heaven, and in the aid of Jupiter, 515
We led our men beneath the city walls
Sacred to Mars. Our fathers perished there
Through their own folly. Therefore never seek
To place them in the same degree with us."
  The brave Tydides with a frown replied: 520
"Nay, hold thy peace, my friend, and heed my words.
Of Agamemnon I will not complain,—
The shepherd of the people; it is his
To exhort the well-armed Greeks to gallant deeds.
Great glory will attend him if the Greeks 525
Shall overcome the Trojans, and shall take
The sacred Ilium; but his grief will be
Bitter if we shall fail and be destroyed.
Hence think we only of the furious charge!"
  He spake, and from his chariot leaped to earth 530
All armed; the mail upon the monarch's breast
Rang terribly as he marched swiftly on.
The boldest might have heard that sound with fear.

As when the ocean-billows, surge on surge,
Are pushed along to the resounding shore   535
Before the western wind, and first a wave
Uplifts itself, and then against the land
Dashes and roars, and round the headland peaks
Tosses on high and spouts its spray afar,
So moved the serried phalanxes of Greece   540
To battle, rank succeeding rank, each chief
Giving command to his own troops; the rest
Marched noiselessly: you might have thought no voice
Was in the breasts of all that mighty throng,
So silently they all obeyed their chiefs,   545
Their showy armor glittering as they moved
In firm array. But, as the numerous flock
Of some rich man, while the white milk is drawn
Within his sheepfold, hear the plaintive call
Of their own lambs, and bleat incessantly,—   550
Such clamors from the mighty Trojan host
Arose; nor was the war-cry one, nor one
The voice, but words of mingled languages,
For they were called from many different climes.
These Mars encouraged to the fight; but those   555
The blue-eyed Pallas. Terror too was there,
And Fright, and Strife that rages unappeased,—
Sister and comrade of man-slaying Mars,—
Who rises small at first, but grows, and lifts
Her head to heaven and walks upon the earth.   560
She, striding through the crowd and heightening
The mutual rancor, flung into the midst
Contention, source of bale to all alike.
  And now, when met the armies in the field,
The ox-hide shields encountered, and the spears,   565
And might of warriors mailed in brass; then clashed
The bossy bucklers, and the battle-din
Was loud; then rose the mingled shouts and groans
Of those who slew and those who fell; the earth
Ran with their blood. As when the winter streams   570
Rush down the mountain-sides, and fill, below,
With their swift waters, poured from gushing springs,

Some hollow vale, the shepherd on the heights
Hears the far roar,—such was the mingled din
That rose from the great armies when they met. 575
  Then first Antilochus, advancing, struck
The Trojan champion Echepolus down,
Son of Thalysius, fighting in the van.
He smote him on the helmet's cone, where streamed
The horse-hair plume; the brazen javelin stood 580
Fixed in his forehead, piercing through the bone,
And darkness gathered o'er his eyes. He fell
As falls a tower before some stubborn siege.
Then Elephenor, son of Chalcodon,
Prince of the brave Abrantes, by the foot 585
Seized the slain chieftain, dragging him beyond
The reach of darts, to strip him of his arms;
Yet dropped him soon, for brave Agenor saw,
And, as he stooped to drag the body, hurled
His brazen spear and pierced the uncovered side 590
Seen underneath the shield. At once his limbs
Relaxed their hold, and straight the spirit fled.
Then furious was the struggle of the Greeks
And Trojans o'er the slain; they sprang like wolves
Upon each other, and man slaughtered man. 595
  Then by the hand of Ajax Telamon
Fell Simoïsius, in the bloom of youth,
Anthemion's son. His mother once came down
From Ida, with her parents, to their flocks
Beside the Simoïs; there she brought him forth 600
Upon its banks, and gave her boy the name
Of Simoïsius. Unrequited now
Was all the care with which his parents nursed
His early years, and short his term of life,—
Slain by the hand of Ajax, large of soul. 605
For, when he saw him coming, Ajax smote
Near the right pap the Trojan's breast; the blade
Passed through, and out upon the further side.
He fell among the dust of earth, as falls
A poplar growing in the watery soil 610
Of some wide marsh,—a fair, smooth bole, with boughs

Only on high, which with his gleaming axe
Some artisan has felled to bend its trunk
Into the circle of some chariot-wheel;
Withering it lies upon the river's bank. 615
So did the high-born Ajax spoil the corpse
Of Simoïsius, Anthemion's son.
But Antiphus, the son of Priam, clad
In shining armor, saw, and, taking aim,
Cast his sharp spear at Ajax through the crowd. 620
The weapon struck him not, but pierced the groin
Of one who was Ulysses' faithful friend,—
Leucus,—as from the spot he dragged the dead;
He fell, the body dropping from his hold.
Ulysses, stung with fury at his fall, 625
Rushed to the van, arrayed in shining brass,
Drew near the foe, and, casting a quick glance
Around him, hurled his glittering spear. The host
Of Trojans, as it left his hand, shrank back
Upon each other. Not in vain it flew, 630
But struck Democoön, the spurious son
Of Priam, who, to join the war, had left
Abydos, where he tended the swift mares.
Ulysses, to revenge his comrade's death,
Smote him upon the temple with his spear. 635
Through both the temples passed the brazen point,
And darkness gathered o'er his eyes; he fell,
His armor clashing round him with his fall.
Then did the foremost bands, and Hector's self,
Fall back. The Argives shouted, dragging off 640
The slain, and rushing to the ground they won.
Then was Apollo angered, looking down
From Pergamus, and thus he called aloud:—
    "Rally, ye Trojans! tamers of fleet steeds!
Yield not the battle to the Greeks. Their limbs 645
Are not of stone iron, to withstand
The trenchant steel ye wield. Nor does the son
Of fair-haired Thetis now, Achilles, take
Part in the battle, but sits, brooding o'er
The choler that devours him, in his ships." 650

Thus from the city spake the terrible god.
Meantime Tritonian Pallas, glorious child
Of Jupiter, went through the Grecian ranks
Where'er they wavered, and revived their zeal.
    Diores, son of Amarynceus, then 655
Met his hard fate. The fragment of a rock
Was thrown by hand at his right leg, and struck
The ankle. Piroüs, son of Imbrasus,
Who came from Ænus, leading to the war
His Thracian soldiers, flung it; and it crushed 660
Tendons and bones, and down the warrior fell
In dust, and toward his comrades stretched his hands,
And gasped for breath. But he who gave the wound,
Piroüs, came up and pierced him with his spear.
Forth gushed the entrails, and the eyes grew dark. 665
    But Piroüs by Ætolian Thoas fell,
Who met him with his spear and pierced his breast
Above the pap. The brazen weapon stood
Fixed in the lungs. Then Thoas came and plucked
The massive spear away, and drew his sword, 670
And thrusting through him the sharp blade, he took
His life away. Yet could he not despoil
The slain man of his armor, for around
His comrades thronged, the Thracians, with their tufts
Of streaming hair, and, wielding their long spears, 675
Drove him away. And he, though huge of limb,
And valiant and renowned, was forced to yield
To numbers pressing on him, and withdrew.
Thus near each other stretched upon the ground
Piroüs, the leader of the Thracian band, 680
And he who led the Epeans, brazen-mailed
Diores, lay with many others slain.
    Then could no man, who near at hand beheld
The battle of that day, see cause of blame
In aught, although, unwounded and unbruised 685
By weapons, Pallas led him by the hand
In safety through the midst, and turned aside
The violence of javelins; for that day
Saw many a Trojan slain, and many a Greek,

Stretched side by side upon the bloody field. 690

BOOK V

THEN Pallas to Tydides Diomed
Gave strength and courage, that he might appear
Among the Achaians greatly eminent,
And win a glorious name. Upon his head
And shield she caused a constant flame to play, 5
Like to the autumnal star that shines in heaven
Most brightly when new-bathed in ocean tides.
Such light she caused to beam upon his crest
And shoulders, as she sent the warrior forth
into the thick and tumult of the fight. 10
 Among the Trojans, Dares was the priest
Of Vulcan, rich and blameless. His two sons
Were Phegeus and Idæus, trained in all
The arts of war. They left the host and came
To meet Tydides,—on the chariot they, 15
And he on foot; and now, as they drew near,
First Phegeus hurled his massive lance. It flew
O'er Diomed's left shoulder and struck not.
Tydides cast his spear, and not in vain;
It smote the breast of Phegeus in the midst, 20
And dashed him from his seat. Idæus leaped
To earth, and left the sumptuous car, nor dared
To guard the slain, yet would have met his death
If Vulcan had not borne him swiftly thence
Concealed in darkness, that he might not leave 25
The aged man, his father, desolate.

The son of Tydeus took the steeds, and bade
His comrades lead them to the fleet. Aghast
The valiant sons of Troy beheld the sons
Of Dares, one in flight, the other slain. 30
   Meantime the blue-eyed Pallas took the hand
Of Mars, and thus addressed the fiery god:—
   "Mars, Mars, thou slayer of men, thou steeped in blood,
Destroyer of walled cities! should we not
Leave both the Greeks and Trojans to contend, 35
And Jove to crown with glory whom he will,
While we retire, lest we provoke his wrath?"
   Thus having said, she led the violent Mars
From where the battle raged, and made him sit
Beside Scamander, on its grassy bank. 40
And then the Achaians put the sons of Troy
To flight: each leader slew a foe; and first
The king of men, Atrides, from his car
Struck down the huge-limbed Hodius, who was chief
Among the Halizonians. As he turned 45
To flee, the Achaian, smiting him between
The shoulders, drove the javelin through his breast.
Heavily clashed his armor as he fell.
   Then by Idomeneus was Phæstus slain,
Son of Meonian Borus, who had come 50
From Tarna, rich in harvests. As he sprang
Into his car, Idomeneus, expert
To wield the ponderous javelin, thrust its blade
Through his right shoulder. From the car he fell,
And the dark night of death came over him. 55
The Achaian warriors following spoiled the slain.
   The son of Atreus, Menelaus, slew
With his sharp spear Scamandrius, the son
Of Strophius, practised in the forest chase,
A mighty hunter. Him had Dian taught 60
To strike whatever beast the woody wild
Breeds on the hills; but now availed him not
The favor of Diana, archer-queen,
Nor skill to throw the javelin afar;
For Menelaus, mighty with the spear, 65

Followed him as he fled, and in the back
Smote him, between the shoulder-blades, and drave
The weapon through. He fell upon the ground
Headlong, his armor clashing as he fell.
And then Meriones slew Phereclus, 70
Son of Harmonius, the artificer,
Who knew to shape all works of rare device,
For Pallas loved him. It was he who built
The fleet for Paris,—cause of many woes
To all the Trojans and to him,—for ill 75
He understood the oracles of heaven.
Him did Meriones, pursuing long,
O'ertake, and, smiting him on the right hip,
Pierced through the part beneath the bone and near
The bladder. On his knees with sad lament 80
He fell, and death involved him in its shade.
   And then by Meges was Pedæus slain,
Antenor's base-born son, whom Threno reared—
The noble Threno—with as fond a care
As her own children, for her husband's sake. 85
And now the mighty spearman, Phyleus' son,
Drew near and smote him with his trenchant lance
Where meet the head and spine, and pierced the neck
Beneath the tongue; and forth the weapon came
Between the teeth. He fell, and in the fall 90
Gnashed with his teeth upon the cold bright blade.
   Then did Evæmon's son Eurypylus
Strike down Hypsenor, nobly born, the son
Of great Dolopion, Scamander's priest,
Whom all the people honored as a god. 95
Evæmon's gallant son, o'ertaking him
In flight, with one stroke of his falchion hewed
His brawny arm away. The bloody limb
Dropped to the ground, and the dark night of death
Came o'er his eyes: so cruel fate decreed. 100
   Thus toiled the heroes in that stubborn fight.
Nor would you now have known to which array—
Trojan or Greek—Tydides might belong;
For through the field he rushed with furious speed,

Like a swollen river when its current takes 105
The torrent's swiftness, scattering with a sweep
The bridges; nor can massive dikes withstand
Its fury, nor embankments raised to screen
The grassy meadows, while the rains of Jove
Fall heavily, and harvests, late the joy 110
Of toiling youth, are beaten to the ground.
Thus by Tydides the close phalanxes
Of Troy were scattered, nor could they endure,
All numerous as they were, his strong assault.
As Pandarus, Lycaon's eminent son, 115
Beheld Tydides rush athwart the field,
Breaking the ranks, he drew his crooked bow
And smote the chief's left shoulder as he came,
Striking the hollow corslet. The sharp point
Broke through, and blood came gushing o'er the mail. 120
Then called aloud Lycaon's eminent son:—
  "Brave Trojans, great in mastery of steeds,
Press on; the bravest of the Grecian host
Is smitten, nor, I think, can long survive
The grievous wound, if it be true that I, 125
At the command of Phœbus, son of Jove,
Have left my home upon the Lycian shore."
  Thus boastfully he spake; but his swift shaft
Slew not Tydides, who had now withdrawn.
And, standing by his steeds and chariot, spake 130
To Sthenelus, the son of Capaneus:—
"Haste down, kind Sthenelus, and with thy hand
Draw the sharp arrow from my shoulder here."
  He spake, and Sthenelus at once leaped down,
Stood by his side, and from his shoulder drew 135
The wingèd arrow deeply fixed within.
The blood flowed forth upon the twisted rings
Of mail, while Diomed, the valiant, prayed:—
  "Hear me, O child of ægis-bearing Jove,
Goddess invincible! if ever thou 140
Didst aid me or my father in the heat
Of battle, aid me, Pallas, yet again.
Give me to slay this Trojan; bring him near,

Within my javelin's reach, who wounded me,
And now proclaims—the boaster—that not long   145
Shall I behold the brightness of the sun."
   So prayed he, and Minerva heard his prayer
And lightened all his limbs,—his feet, his hands,—
And, standing near him, spake these wingèd words:—
   "War boldly with the Trojans, Diomed;   150
For even now I breathe into thy frame
The ancestral might and fearless soul that dwelt
In Tydeus, peerless with the steed and shield.
Lo! I remove the darkness from thine eyes,
That thou may'st well discern the gods from men; 155
And if a god should tempt thee to the fight,
Beware to combat with the immortal race;
Only, should Venus, child of Jupiter,
Take part in battle, wound her with thy spear."
   The blue-eyed Pallas spake, and disappeared;   160
And Diomed went back into the field
And mingled with the warriors. If before
His spirit moved him fiercely to engage
The men of Troy, a threefold courage now
Inspired him. As a lion who has leaped   165
Into a fold—and he who guards the flock
Has wounded but not slain him—feels his rage
Waked by the blow;—the affrighted shepherd then
Ventures not near, but hides within the stalls,
And the forsaken sheep are put to flight,   170
And, huddling, slain in heaps, till o'er the fence
The savage bounds into the fields again;—
Such was Tydides midst the sons of Troy.
Astynous first he slew, Hypenor next,
The shepherd of the people. One he pierced   175
High on the bosom with his brazen spear,
And smote the other on the collar-bone
With his good sword, and hewed from neck and spine
The shoulder. There he left the dead, and rushed
To Abas and to Polyeidus, sons   180
Of old Eurydamas, interpreter
Of visions. Ill the aged man had read

His visions when they joined the war. They died,
And Diomed, the valiant, spoiled the slain.
Xanthus and Thoön he encountered next, 185
The sons of Phænops, born in his old age.
No other child had he, to be his heir,
And he was worn with length of years. These two
Tydides smote and took their lives, and left
Grief to their father and regretful cares, 190
Since he no more should welcome their return
From war, and strangers should divide his wealth.
Then smote he Chromius and Echemon, sons
Of Dardan Priam, in one chariot both.
As on a herd of beeves a lion springs 195
While midst the shrubs they browse, and breaks their necks,—
Heifer or ox,—so sprang he on the twain
And struck them, vainly struggling, from their car,
And spoiled them of their arms, and took their steeds,
And bade his comrades lead them to the fleet. 200
 Æneas, who beheld him scattering thus
The embattled ranks before him, straightway went
Through the thick fight, amid encountering spears,
In search of godlike Pandarus. He found
Lycaon's blameless and illustrious son, 205
And stood before him, and addressed him thus:—
 "Where is thy bow, O Pandarus, and where
Thy wingèd arrows? Where the old renown
In which no warrior here can vie with thee,
And none upon the Lycian shore can boast 210
That he excels thee? Hasten, and lift up
Thy hands in prayer to Jupiter, and send
An arrow at this man, whoe'er he be,
Who thus prevails, and thus afflicts our host,
And makes the knees of many a strong man weak. 215
Strike him,—unless he be some god incensed
At Troy for sacrifice withheld, since hard
It is to bear the anger of a god."
 Lycaon's son, the far-renowned, replied:—
"Æneas, leader of the Trojans mailed 220
In brass, to me this man in all things seems

Like warlike Diomed. I know his shield,
High helm, and steeds, and yet I may not say
That this is not a god. But if he be
The chief of whom I speak, the warlike son   225
Of Tydeus, not thus madly would he fight,
Without some god to aid him. By his side
Is one of the immortals, with a cloud
About his shoulders, turning from its aim
The swiftly flying arrow. 'Twas but late   230
I aimed a shaft that pierced the hollow mail
On his left shoulder, and I thought him sent
To Pluto, but I slew him not. Some god
Must be offended with me. I have here
No steeds or car to mount. Far off at home   235
There stand within Lycaon's palace-walls
Eleven chariots, fair and fresh and new:
Each has an ample cover, and by each
Are horses yoked in pairs, that champ their oats
And their white barley. When I left my home,   240
Lycaon, aged warrior, counselled me,
Within his sumptuous halls, that with my steeds
And chariot I should lead the sons of Troy
In the fierce battle. I obeyed him not:
Far better if I had. I wished to spare   245
My horses, lest, so largely fed at home,
They might want food in the beleaguered town.
So, leaving them, I came on foot to Troy,
Confiding in my bow, which yet was doomed
To avail me little, for already I   250
Have smitten with my arrows the two chiefs,
Tydides and Atrides, and from both
Drew the red blood, but only made their rage
To flame the fiercer. In an evil hour
I took my bow and quiver from the wall   255
And came to lead the Trojans for the sake
Of Hector. But if ever I return
To see my native country and my wife
And my tall spacious mansion, may some foe
Strike off my head if with these hands I fail   260

To break my bow in pieces, casting it
Into the flames, a useless weapon now."
   The Trojan chief Æneas, answering, said:—
"Nay, talk not so; it cannot but be thus,
Until upon a chariot, and with steeds,   265
We try our prowess with this man in war.
Haste, mount my chariot here, and thou shalt see
How well are Trojan horses trained to range
The field of battle, in the swift pursuit
Hither and thither, or in rapid flight;   270
And they shall bring us safely to the town
Should Jove a second time bestow the meed
Of glory on Tydides. Haste, and take
The lash and well-wrought reins, while I descend
To fight on foot; or haply thou wilt wait   275
The foe's advance while I direct the steeds."
   Then spake again Lycaon's eminent son:—
"Keep thou the reins, Æneas, and still guide
The horses. With their wonted charioteer,
The better shall they bear away the car   280
Should we be forced to fly before the arm
Of Diomed; lest, taking flight, they range
Unmastered when they hear thy voice no more,
Nor bear us from the combat, and the son
Of Tydeus, having slain us, shall lead thence   285
Thy firm-hoofed coursers. Therefore guide them still,
Them and the chariot, while, with this keen spear,
I wait the Greek, as he is rushing on."
   They spake, and, climbing the magnificent car,
Turned toward Tydides the swift-footed steeds.   290
The noble son of Capaneus beheld,
And said in wingèd words to Diomed:—
   "Tydides Diomed, most dear of men!
I see two warriors, strong, immensely strong,
Coming to combat with thee. Pandarus   295
Is one, the skilled in archery, who boasts
To be Lycaon's son; and by his side
There comes Æneas, glorying that he sprang
From the large-souled Anchises,—borne to him

By Venus. Mount we now our car and leave 300
The ground, nor in thy fury rush along
The van of battle, lest thou lose thy life."
   The brave Tydides, with a frown, replied:—
"Speak not of flight; thou canst not yet persuade
My mind to that. To skulk or shrink with fear 305
In battle ill becomes me, and my strength
Is unexhausted yet. It suits me not
To mount the chariot; I will meet the foe
Just as I am. Minerva will not let
My spirit falter. Ne'er shall those swift steeds 310
Bear the two warriors hence,—if even one
Escapes me. One thing more have I to say;
And keep it well in mind. Should Pallas deign—
The wise, forecasting Pallas—to bestow
On me the glory of overcoming both, 315
Stop thy swift horses, and tie fast the reins
To our own chariot, and make haste to seize
The horses of Æneas, guiding them
Hence from the Trojan to the Grecian host;
For they are of the stock which Jupiter 320
The Thunderer gave to Tros. It was the price
He paid for Ganymede, and they, of all
Beneath the eye of morning and the sun,
Are of the choicest breed. The king of men,
Anchises, stealthily and unobserved, 325
Brought to the coursers of Laomedon
His brood-mare, and obtained the race. Six colts
Their offspring, in his courts were foaled. Of these,
Four for himself he kept, and in his stalls
Reared them, and two of them, both apt for war, 330
He gave Æneas. If we make them ours,
The exploit will bring us honor and renown."
   Thus they conferred. Meantime their foes drew near,
Urging their fiery coursers on, and first
Lycaon's eminent son addressed the Greek:— 335
   "My weapon, swift and sharp, the arrow, failed
To slay thee; let me try the javelin now,
And haply that, at least, may reach its mark."

He spake, and, brandishing his massive spear,
Hurled it against the shield of Diomed. 340
The brazen point broke through, and reached the mail.
Then shouted with loud voice Lycaon's son:—
    "Ha! thou art wounded in thy flank; my spear
Bites deep; nor long, I think, canst thou survive,
And great will be my glory gained from thee." 345
    But thus the valiant Diomed replied,
Incapable of fear: "Thy thought is wrong.
I am not wounded, and I well perceive
That ye will never give the conflict o'er
Till one of you, laid low amid the dust, 350
Pour out his blood to glut the god of war."
    He spake, and cast his spear. Minerva kept
The weapon faithful to its aim. It struck
The nose, and near the eye; then passing on
Betwixt the teeth, the unrelenting edge 355
Cleft at its root the tongue; the point came out
Beneath the chin. The warrior from his car
Fell headlong; his bright armor, fairly wrought,
Clashed round him as he fell; his fiery steeds
Started aside with fright; his breath and strength 360
Were gone at once. Æneas, with his shield
And his long spear, leaped down to guard the slain,
That the Achaians might not drag him thence.
There, lion-like, confiding in his strength,
He stalked around the corpse, and over it 365
Held his round shield and lance, prepared to slay
Whoever came, and shouting terribly.
    Tydides raised a stone,—a mighty weight,
Such as no two men living now could lift;
But he, alone, could swing it round with ease. 370
With this he smote Æneas on the hip,
Where the thigh joins its socket. By the blow
He brake the socket and the tendons twain,
And tore the skin with the rough, jagged stone.
The hero fell upon his knees, but stayed 375
His fall with his strong palm upon the ground;
And o'er his eyes a shadow came like night.

Then had the king of men, Æneas, died,
But for Jove's daughter, Venus, who perceived
His danger instantly,—his mother, she   380
Who bore him to Anchises when he kept
His beeves, a herdsman. Round her son she cast
Her white arms, spreading over him in folds
Her shining robe, to be a fence against
The weapons of the foe, lest some Greek knight   385
Should at his bosom aim the steel to take
His life. And thus the goddess bore away
From that fierce conflict her beloved son.
   Nor did the son of Capaneus forget
The bidding of the warlike Diomed,   390
But halted his firm-footed steeds apart
From the great tumult, with the long reins stretched
And fastened to the chariot. Next, he sprang
To seize the horses with fair-flowing manes,
That drew the chariot of Æneas. These   395
He drave away, far from the Trojan host,
To the well-greaved Achaians, giving them
In charge, to lead them to the hollow ships,
To his beloved friend Deipylus,
Whom he of all his comrades honored most,   400
As likest to himself in years and mind.
And then he climbed his car and took the reins,
And, swiftly drawn by his firm-footed steeds,
Followed Tydides, who with cruel steel
Sought Venus, knowing her unapt for war,   405
And all unlike the goddesses who guide
The battles of mankind, as Pallas does,
Or as Bellona, ravager of towns.
O'ertaking her at last, with long pursuit,
Amid the throng of warring men, the son   410
Of warlike Tydeus aimed at her his spear,
And wounded in her hand the delicate one
With its sharp point. It pierced the ambrosial robe,
Wrought for her by the Graces, at the spot
Where the palm joins the wrist, and broke the skin,   415
And drew immortal blood,—the ichor,—such

As from the blessed gods may flow; for they
Eat not the wheaten loaf, nor drink dark wine;
And therefore they are bloodless, and are called
Immortal. At the stroke the goddess shrieked, 420
And dropped her son. Apollo in his arms
Received and in a dark cloud rescued him,
Lest any of the Grecian knights should aim
A weapon at his breast to take his life.
Meantime the brave Tydides cried aloud:— 425
  "Leave wars and battle, goddess. Is it not
Enough that thou delude weak womankind?
Yet, if thou ever shouldst return, to bear
A part in battle, thou shalt have good cause
To start with fear, when war is only named." 430
  He spake; and she departed, wild with pain,
For grievously she suffered. Instantly
Fleet-footed Iris took her by the hand
And led her from the place, her heart oppressed
With anguish and her fair cheek deathly pale. 435
She found the fiery Mars, who had withdrawn
From that day's combat to the left, and sat,
His spear and his swift coursers hid from sight,
In darkness. At his feet she fell, and prayed
Her brother fervently, that he would lend 440
His steeds that stood in trappings wrought of gold:—
  "Dear brother, aid me; let me have thy steeds
To bear me to the Olympian mount, the home
Of gods, for grievously the wound I bear
Afflicts me. 'Twas a mortal gave the wound,— 445
Tydides, who would even fight with Jove."
  She spake; and Mars resigned to her his steeds
With trappings of bright gold. She climbed the car,
Still grieving, and, beside her, Iris took
Her seat, and caught the reins and plied the lash. 450
On flew the coursers, on, with willing speed,
And soon were at the mansion of the gods
On high Olympus. There the active-limbed,
Fleet Iris stayed them, loosed them from the car,
And fed them with ambrosial food. Meanwhile, 455

The goddess Venus at Dione's feet
Had cast herself. The mother round her child
Threw tenderly her arms, and with her hand
Caressed her brow, and spake, and thus inquired:—
   "Which of the dwellers of the skies, dear child,   460
Has dealt thus cruelly with thee, as one
Caught in the doing of some flagrant wrong?"
   And thus did Venus, queen of smiles, reply:—
"The son of Tydeus, arrogant Diomed,
Wounded me as I sought to bear away   465
From battle's dangers my beloved son
Æneas, dear beyond all other men:
For now no longer does the battle rage
Between the Greeks and Trojans, but the Greeks
Venture to combat even with the gods."   470
   Dione, great among the goddesses,
Rejoined: "Submit, my daughter, and endure,
Though inly grieved; for many of us who dwell
Upon the Olympian mount have suffered much
From mortals, and have brought great miseries   475
Upon each other. First, it was the fate
Of Mars to suffer, when Aloëus' sons,
Otus and mighty Ephialtes, made
Their fetters fast upon his limbs. He lay
Chained thirteen months within a brazen cell;   480
And haply there the god, whose thirst of blood
Is never cloyed, had perished, but for aid
Which Eribœa gave, the beautiful,
His step-mother. She made his miseries known
To Mercury, who set him free by stealth,   485
Withered and weak with long imprisonment.
And Juno suffered when Amphitryon's son,
The valiant, dared to plant in her right breast
A three-pronged arrow, and she writhed with pain.
And Pluto suffered, when the hero-son   490
Of Ægis-bearing Jove, with a swift shaft,
Smote him beside the portals of the dead,
And left him filled with pain. He took his way
To high Olympus and the home of Jove,

Grieving and racked with pain, for deep the dart 495
Had pierced his brawny shoulder, torturing him.
There Pæan with his pain-dispelling balms
Healed him, for he was not of mortal race.
O daring man and reckless, to make light
Of such impieties, and violate 500
The sacred persons of the Olympian gods!
It was the blue-eyed Pallas who stirred up
Tydides to assail thee thus. The fool!
He knew not that the man who dares to meet
The gods in combat lives not long. No child 505
Shall prattling call him father when he comes
Returning from the dreadful tasks of war.
Let then Tydides, valiant though he be,
Beware lest a more potent foe than thou
Encounter him, and lest the nobly-born 510
Ægialeia, in some night to come—
Wise daughter of Adrastus, and the spouse
Of the horse-tamer Diomed—call up
The servants of her household from their sleep,
Bewailing him to whom in youth she gave 515
Her maiden troth,—the bravest of the Greeks."
   She spake, and wiped the ichor from the hand
Of Venus; at her touch the hand was healed
And the pain left it. Meantime Pallas stood,
With Juno, looking on, both teasing Jove 520
With words of sarcasm. Blue-eyed Pallas thus
Addressed the god: "O Father Jupiter,
Wilt thou be angry at the word I speak?—
As Venus, wheedling some Achaian dame
To join the host she loves, the sons of Troy, 525
Caressed the fair, arrayed in gay attire,
A golden buckle scratched her tender hand."
   As thus she spake, the Father of the gods
And mortals, calling golden Venus near,
Said, with a smile: "Nay, daughter, not for thee 530
Are tasks of war; be gentle marriage-rites
Thy care; the labors of the battle-field
Pertain to Pallas and the fiery Mars."

Thus with each other talked the gods, while still
The great in battle, Diomed, pursued 535
Æneas, though he knew that Phœbus stretched
His arm to guard the warrior. Small regard
Had he for the great god, and much he longed
To strike Æneas down and bear away
The glorious arms he wore; and thrice he rushed 540
To slay the Trojan, thrice Apollo smote
Upon his glittering shield. But when he made
The fourth assault, as if he were a god,
The archer of the skies, Apollo, thus
With menacing words rebuked him: "Diomed, 545
Beware; desist, nor think to make thyself
The equal of a god. The deathless race
Of gods is not as those who walk the earth."
   He spake; the son of Tydeus, shrinking back,
Gave way before the anger of the god 550
Who sends his shafts afar. Then Phœbus bore
Æneas from the tumult to the height
Of sacred Pergamus, where stands his fane;
And there Latona and the archer-queen,
Diana, in the temple's deep recess, 555
Tended him and brought back his glorious strength.
Meantime the bowyer-god, Apollo, formed
An image of Æneas, armed like him,
Round which the Trojans and Achaians thronged
With many a heavy weapon-stroke that fell 560
Upon the huge orbs of their ox-hide shields
And lighter bucklers. Now to fiery Mars
Apollo spake: "Mars, Mars, thou plague of men,
Thou steeped in blood, destroyer of walled towns!
Wilt thou not force this man to leave the field? 565
Wilt thou not meet in arms this daring son
Of Tydeus, who would even fight with Jove?
Already has he wounded, in close fight,
The goddess Venus at the wrist, and since
Assaulted me as if he were a god." 570
   He said, and on the heights of Pergamus
Sat down, while the destroyer Mars went forth

Among the embattled Trojan ranks, to rouse
Their valor. In the form of Acamus,
The gallant Thracian leader, he bespake   575
The sons of Jove-descended Priam thus:—
   "O sons of Priam, him who claims descent
From Jupiter! how long will ye submit
To see your people slaughtered by the Greeks?
Is it until the battle-storm shall reach   580
Your city's stately portals? Even now
A hero whom we honor equally
With the great Hector, our Æneas, son
Of the large-souled Anchises, is struck down.
Haste, let us rescue our beloved friend."   585
   He spake, and into every heart his words
Carried new strength and courage. In that hour
Sarpedon chid the noble Hector thus:—
   "Where is the prowess, Hector, which was thine
So lately? Thou hast said that thou alone,   590
Thy kindred and thy brothers, could defend
The city, without armies or allies.
Now I see none of these; they all, like hounds
Before a lion, crouch and slink away,
While the confederates bear the brunt of war.   595
I am but an auxiliar come from far,
From Lycia, where the eddying Xanthus runs.
There left I a beloved wife, and there
An infant child, and large possessions, such
As poor men covet. Yet do I exhort   600
My Lycians to the combat, and myself
Would willingly engage this foe of Troy,
Although I here have nothing which the Greeks
Might bear or drive away. Thou standest still,
Meanwhile, nor dost thou bid the rest to keep   605
Their ground and bear the battle for their wives.
Yet have a care, lest, as if caught at length
In the strong meshes of a mighty net,
Ye find yourselves the captives and the prey
Of enemies, who quickly will destroy   610
Your nobly-peopled city. These are thoughts

That should engage thy mind by night and day,
And thou shouldst beg the chiefs of thine allies,
Called to thy aid from far, that manfully
They meet the foe, and foil his fierce attack, 615
And take the cause of this reproach away."

   Sarpedon spake; and Hector, all in arms,
Stung by his words, and leaping from his car,
Brandished his spears, and went among the hosts
And rallied them to battle. Terrible 620
The conflict that ensued. The men of Troy
Made head against the Greeks: the Greeks stood firm,
Nor ever thought of flight. As when the wind
Strews chaff about the sacred threshing-floors
While wheat is winnowed, and before the breeze 625
The yellow Ceres separates the grain
From its light husk, which gathers in white heaps,—
Even so the Greeks were whitened o'er with dust
Raised in that tumult by the horses' hoofs
And rising to the brazen firmament, 630
As toward the fight the charioteers again
Urged on their coursers. Yet the Greeks withstood
The onset, and struck forward with strong arms.
Meantime the furious Mars involved the field
In darkness, to befriend the sons of Troy, 635
And went through all the ranks, and well fulfilled
The mandate which Apollo gave the god
Who wields the golden falchion, bidding him
Kindle the courage of the Trojan host
Whene'er he saw the auxiliar of the Greeks, 640
Minerva, leave the combat. Then the god
Brought from the sanctuary's inner shrine
Æneas,—filling with recovered strength
That shepherd of the people. He beside
His comrades placed himself, and they rejoiced 645
To see him living and unharmed and strong
As ever; yet they questioned not; their task
Was different, set them by the god who bears
The silver bow, and Mars the slayer of men,
And raging Strife that never is appeased. 650

        The Ajaces and Ulysses and the son
Of Tydeus roused the Achaians to the fight.
For of the strength and clamor of the foe
They felt no fear, but calmly stood, to bide
The assault; as stand in air the quiet clouds   655
Which Saturn's son upon the mountain-tops
Piles in still volumes when the north wind sleeps,
And every ruder breath of blustering air
That drives the gathered vapors through the sky.
Thus calmly waited they the Trojan host,   660
Nor thought of flight. And now Atrides passed
In haste along their ranks, and gave command:—
    "O friends, be men, and let your hearts be strong,
And let no warrior in the heat of fight
Do what may bring him shame in others' eyes;   665
For more of those who shrink from shame are safe
Than fall in battle, while with those who flee
Is neither glory nor reprieve from death."
    So spake the king, and hurled his spear and smote
Deïcoön, the son of Pergasis,   670
A chief, and a companion in the war
Of the great-souled Æneas. He in Troy
Was honored as men honored Priam's sons,
For he was ever foremost in the fight.
The weapon struck his shield, yet stopped not there,   675
But, breaking through its folds and through the belt,
Transfixed the part beneath. The Trojan fell
To earth, his armor clashing with his fall.
    Æneas slew the sons of Diocles,—
Orsilochus and Crethon, eminent Greeks.   680
Their father dwelt in Pheræ nobly built,
Amid his riches. From Alpheius he
Derived his race,—a river whose long stream
Flows through the meadows of the Pylian land.
Orsilochus was to Alpheius born,   685
Lord over many men, and he became
The father of great Diocles, to whom
Twin sons were born, well trained in all the arts
Of warfare,—Crethon and Orsilochus.

These, in the prime of youth, with their black ships   690
Followed the Argives to the coast of Troy
Famed for its generous steeds. They left their home
To vindicate the honor of the sons
Of Atreus,—Agamemnon, king of men,
And Menelaus,—but they found their death.   695
   As two young lions, nourished by their dam
Amid the thickets of some mighty wood,
Seizing the beeves and fattened sheep, lay waste
The stables, till at length themselves are slain
By trenchant weapons in the shepherd's hand,   700
So by the weapons of Æneas died
These twain; they fell as lofty fir-trees fall.
But now, when Menelaus saw their fate,
The mighty warrior, deeply sorrowing, rushed
Among the foremost, armed in glittering brass,   705
And brandishing his spear; for Mars had roused
His soul to fury, trusting he would meet
Æneas, and would perish by his hand.
Antilochus, the generous Nestor's son,
Came also to the van, for anxiously   710
He feared mischance might overtake the king,
To make the toils of their long warfare vain;
And there he found the combatants prepared
For battle, with their trusty spears in hand,
And standing face to face. At once he took   715
His stand beside the monarch of the Greeks.
At sight of the two warriors side by side,
All valiant as he was, Æneas shunned
The encounter. They, when they had drawn the dead
Among the Grecian ranks, and to their friends   720
Given up the hapless brothers, turned to take
Their place among the foremost in the fight.
Then, too, Pylæmenes, a chief like Mars,
And leader of the Paphlagonian host,—
A valiant squadron armed with shields,—was slain.   725
Atrides Menelaus, skilled to wield
The javelin, gave his death-wound. He transfixed
The shoulder at the collar-bone. Meanwhile

Antilochus against his charioteer,
Mydon, the brave son of Atymnias, hurled   730
A stone that smote his elbow as he wheeled
His firm-paced steeds in flight. He dropped the reins,
Gleaming with ivory as they trailed in dust.
Antilochus leaped forward, smiting him
Upon the temples with his sword. He fell   735
Gasping amidst the sand, his head immersed
Up to his shoulders,—for the sand was deep,—
And there remained till he was beaten down
Before the horses' hoofs. Antilochus,
Lashing the horses, drave them to the Greeks.   740
    Hector beheld, and, springing with loud shouts,
Stood mid the wavering ranks. The phalanxes
Of the brave Trojans followed him, for Mars
And terrible Bellona led them on,—
Bellona bringing Tumult in her train,   745
And Mars with brandished lance—a mighty weight—
Now stalking after Hector, now before.
    Him when the valiant Diomed beheld,
He trembled; and, as one who, journeying
Along a way he knows not, having crossed   750
A place of drear extent, before him sees
A river rushing swiftly toward the deep,
And all its tossing current white with foam,
And stops and turns, and measures back his way,
So then did Diomed withdraw, and spake:—   755
    "O friends, how greatly must we all admire
This noble Hector, mighty with the spear
And terrible in war. There is some god
Forever near him, warding off the stroke
Of death; beside him yonder even now   760
Stands Mars in semblance of a mortal man.
Yield, then, and with your faces toward the foe
Fall back, and strive not with the gods of heaven."
    Even as he spake, the Trojan host drew near,
And Hector slew two warriors trained to arms,—   765
Menesthes and Anchialus,—who came
Both in one chariot to the war. Their fall

Ajax, the son of Telamon, beheld,
And pitied, and drew near, and stood, and hurled
His glittering spear. It smote Ampheius, son 770
Of Selagus, who, rich in lands and goods,
Abode in Pæsus. In an evil hour
He joined the cause of Priam and his sons.
Him at the belt the spear of Ajax smote,
And pierced the bowels. With a crash he fell. 775
Then hastened mighty Ajax to strip off
The armor, but the Trojans at him cast
Their pointed spears that glittered as they flew,
And many struck his shield. He pressed his heel
Against the slain, and from the body drew 780
His brazen spear, but could not from the breast
Loose the bright mail, so thick the weapons came,
And such the wary dread with which he saw
The bravest of the Trojans closing round,
Many and fierce, and all with spears outstretched; 785
And he, though strong and valiant and renowned,
Driven from the ground, gave way to mightier force.
   So toiled the warriors through that stubborn fight,
When cruel fate urged on Tlepolemus,
The great and valiant son of Hercules, 790
To meet Sarpedon, mighty as a god.
And now, as each to each advanced,—the son
And grandson of the cloud-compeller Jove,—
Thus first Tlepolemus addressed his foe:—
   "Sarpedon, Lycian monarch, what has brought 795
Thee hither, trembling thus, and inexpert
In battle? Lying flatterers are they
That call thee son of Jupiter who bears
The ægis; for unlike the heroes thou,
Born to the Thunderer in times of old, 800
Nor like my daring father, Hercules
The lion-hearted, who once came to Troy
To claim the coursers of Laomedon.
With but six ships, and warriors but a few,
He laid the city waste and made its streets 805
A desolation. Thou art weak of heart,

And round thee are thy people perishing;
Yet, even wert thou brave, thy presence here
From Lycia's coast would prove of small avail
To Troy; for, slain in combat here by me, 810
Thou to the gates of Hades shalt go down."
   Sarpedon, leader of the Lycians, thus
Made answer: "True it is, Tlepolemus,
That he laid waste the sacred city of Troy
For the base dealings of Laomedon, 815
The monarch who with railing words repaid
His great deservings, and kept back the steeds
For which he came so far. But thou—thy fate
Is slaughter and black death from this my spear;
And fame will come to me, and one more soul 820
Go down to Hades." As Sarpedon spake,
Tlepolemus upraised his ashen spear,
And from the hands of both the chiefs at once
Their massive weapons flew. Sarpedon smote
Full in the throat his foe; the cruel point 825
Passed through the neck, and night came o'er his eyes.
Tlepolemus, in turn, on the left thigh
Had struck Sarpedon with his ponderous lance.
The weapon, cast with vigorous hand and arm,
Pierced deep, and touched the bone; but Jupiter 830
Averted from his son the doom of death.
   His noble comrades raised and bore away
The great Sarpedon from the battle-field,
Trailing the long spear with them. Bitter pain
It gave him; in their haste they marked it not, 835
Nor thought to draw the ashen weapon forth,
That he might mount the car; so eagerly
His anxious bearers hurried from the war.
   On the other side the well-armed Greeks took up
The slain Tlepolemus, to bear him thence. 840
The great Ulysses, large of soul, beheld,
And felt his spirit moved, as anxiously
He pondered whether to pursue the son
Of Jove the Thunderer, or turn and take
The life of many a Lycian. Yet to slay 845

Jove's mighty son was not his destiny,
And therefore Pallas moved him to engage
The crowd of Lycian warriors. Then he slew
Cœranus and Alastor, Chromius,
Alcander, Halius, and Prytanis 850
Noëmon; and yet more the noble Greek
Had slain, if crested Hector, mighty chief,
Had not perceived the havoc and, arrayed
In shining armor, hurried to the van
Of battle, carrying terror to the hearts 855
Of the Achaians. As he saw him near,
Sarpedon was rejoiced, yet sadly said:—
   "O son of Priam, leave me not a prey
To these Achaians. Aid me, let me breathe
My latest breath in Troy, since I no more 860
Can hope, returning to my native land,
To gladden my dear wife and little son."
   He spake, and crested Hector answered not,
Still pressing forward, eager to drive back
The Greeks in quick retreat, and take the life 865
Of many a foe. Then did the noble band
Who bore the great Sarpedon lay him down
Beneath a shapely beech, a tree of Jove
The Ægis-bearer. There stout Pelagon,
His well-beloved comrade, from his thigh 870
Drew forth the sharp blade of the ashen spear.
Then the breath left him, and his eyes were closed
In darkness; but the light came back again
As, breathing over him, the fresh north wind
Revived the spirit in his laboring breast. 875
   But not for Mars nor Hector mailed in brass
Fled the Achaians to their fleet; nor yet
Advanced they on the foe, but step by step
Gave way before him, for they had perceived
The god of war was with the sons of Troy. 880
   Whom first, whom last did Hector, Priam's son,
And iron Mars lay low? The godlike chief
Teuthras, and—great among the Grecian knights—
Orestes, and the Ætolian Trechus, famed

As spearman, and Œnomaus, and the son 885
Of Œnops, Helemes, and after these
Belted Oresbius, who in Hyla made
His home, intent on gathering wealth beside
The Lake Cephissus, on whose borders dwelt
Bœotians many, lords of fertile lands. 890
  The white-armed goddess Juno, when she saw
The Argives falling in that cruel fray,
Addressed Minerva with these wingèd words:—
  "O thou unconquerable goddess, born
To Jove the Ægis-bearer! what is this? 895
It was an idle promise that we made
To Menelaus, that he should behold
Troy, with its strong defences, overthrown,
And reach his home again, if thus we leave
Mars the destroyer to his ravages. 900
Come, let us bring our friends effectual aid."
  So spake she, and her bidding was obeyed
By blue-eyed Pallas. Juno the august,
Daughter of mighty Saturn, laid in haste
The harness, with its ornaments of gold, 905
Upon the horses. Hebe rolled the wheels,
Each with eight spokes, and joined them to the ends
Of the steel axle,—fellies wrought of gold,
Bound with a brazen rim to last for aye,—
A wonder to behold. The hollow naves 910
Were silver, and on gold and silver cords
Was slung the chariot's seat; in silver hooks
Rested the reins, and silver was the pole
Where the fair yoke and poitrels, all of gold,
Were fastened. Juno, eager for the strife, 915
Led the swift-footed steeds beneath the yoke.
  Then Pallas, daughter of the god who bears
The ægis, on her father's palace-floor
Let fall in dainty folds her flowing robe
Of many colors, wrought by her own hand, 920
And, putting on the mail of Jupiter
The Cloud-compeller, stood arrayed in arms
For the stern tasks of war. Her shoulder bore

The dreadful ægis with its shaggy brim
Bordered with Terror. There was Strife, and there 925
Was Fortitude, and there was fierce Pursuit,
And there the Gorgon's head, a ghastly sight,
Deformed and dreadful, and a sign of woe
When borne by Jupiter. Upon her head
She placed a golden helmet with four crests 930
And fair embossed, of strength that might withstand
The armed battalions of a hundred towns;
Then stepped into her shining car, and took
Her massive spear in hand, heavy and huge,
With which whole ranks of heroes are o'erthrown 935
Before the daughter of the Mighty One
Incensed against them. Juno swung the lash
And swiftly urged the steeds. Before their way,
On sounding hinges, of their own accord,
Flew wide the gates of heaven, which evermore 940
The Hours are watching,—they who keep the mount
Olympus and the mighty heaven, with power
To open or to close their cloudy veil.
Thus through the gates they drave the obedient steeds,
And found Saturnius, where he sat apart 945
From other gods, upon the loftiest height
Of many-peaked Olympus. Juno there,
The white-armed goddess, stayed her chariot-wheels,
And, thus accosting Jove, she questioned him:—
 "O Father Jupiter, does not thy wrath 950
Rise at those violent deeds of Mars? Thou seest
How many of the Achaians he has slain,
And what brave men. Nay, thus it should not be.
Great grief is mine; but Venus and the god
Phœbus, who bears the silver bow, rejoice 955
To see this lawless maniac range the field,
And urge him on. O Father Jupiter,
Wilt thou be angry with me if I drive
Mars, sorely wounded, from the battle-field?"
 The cloud-compelling Jupiter replied:— 960
"Thou hast my leave; but send to encounter him
Pallas the spoiler, who has many a time

Brought grievous troubles on the god of war."
   He spake, and white-armed Juno instantly
Obeyed him. With the scourge she lashed the steeds,   965
And not unwillingly they flew between
Earth and the starry heaven. As much of space
As one who gazes on the dark-blue deep
Sees from the headland summit where he sits—
Such space the coursers of immortal breed   970
Cleared at each bound they made with sounding hoofs;
And when they came to Ilium and its streams,
Where Simoïs and Scamander's channels meet,
The white-armed goddess Juno stayed their speed,
And loosed them from the yoke, and covered them   975
With darkness. Simoïs ministered, meanwhile,
The ambrosial pasturage on which they fed.
   On went the goddesses, with step as light
As timid doves, and hastened toward the field
To aid the Achaian army. When they came   980
Where fought the bravest warriors in a throng
Around the great horse-tamer Diomed,
Like ravenous lions or wild boars whose rage
Is terrible, the white-armed goddess stood,
And called aloud,—for now she wore the form   985
Of gallant Stentor, in whose brazen voice
Was heard a shout like that of fifty men:—
   "Shame on you, Argives,—wretches, who in form,
And form alone, are heroes. While we yet
Had great Achilles in the war, the men   990
Of Ilium dared not pass beyond their gates,
So much they feared his mighty spear; but now
They push the battle to our hollow ships,
Far from the town." As thus the goddess spake,
New strength and courage woke in every breast.   995
   Then blue-eyed Pallas hastened to the son
Of Tydeus. By his steeds she found the king,
And by his chariot, as he cooled the wound
Made by the shaft of Pandarus. The sweat
Beneath the ample band of his round shield   1000
Had weakened him, and weary was his arm.

He raised the band, and from the wounded limb
Wiped off the clotted blood. The goddess laid
Her hand upon the chariot-yoke, and said:—
  "Tydeus hath left a son unlike himself;
For he, though low in stature, was most brave;
And when he went, an envoy and alone,
To Thebes, the populous Cadmean town,
And I, enjoining him to keep aloof
From wars and rash encounters, bade him sit
Quietly at the feasts in palace-halls,
Still, to his valiant temper true, he gave
Challenges to the Theban youths, and won
The prize with ease in all their games, such aid
I gave him. Now I stand by thee in turn,
Protect thee, and exhort thee manfully
To fight against the Trojans; but to-day
Either the weariness of toil unnerves
Thy frame, or withering fear besets thy heart.
Henceforth we cannot deem thee, as of late,
The offspring of Œnides skilled in war."
  And then the valiant Diomed replied:—
"I know thee, goddess, daughter of great Jove
The Ægis-bearer; therefore will I speak
Freely and keep back nothing. No base fear
Unmans me, nor desire of ease; but well
I bear in mind the mandate thou hast given.
Thou didst forbid me to contend with gods,
Except that if Jove's daughter, Venus, joined
The battle, I might wound her with my spear.
But now I have withdrawn, and given command
That all the Greeks come hither; for I see
That Mars is in the field and leads the war."
  Again the blue-eyed Pallas, answering, said:—
"Tydides Diomed, most dear of men,
Nay, fear thou nothing from this Mars, nor yet
From any other of the gods; for I
Will be thy sure defence. First urge thy course
Full against Mars, with thy firm-footed steeds.
Engage him hand to hand; respect him not,—

The fiery, frantic Mars, the unnatural plague
Of man, the fickle god, who promised me
And Juno, lately, to take part with us
Against the Trojans and befriend the Greeks.
Now he forgets, and joins the sons of Troy." 1045
  She spake, and laid her hand on Sthenelus,
To draw him from the horses; instantly
He leaped to earth; the indignant deity
Took by the side of Diomed her place;
The beechen axle groaned beneath the weight 1050
Of that great goddess and that man of might.
Then Pallas seized the lash and caught the reins,
And, urging the firm-footed coursers, drave
Full against Mars, who at that moment slew
Huge Periphas, the mightiest one of all 1055
The Ætolian band,—Ochesius' famous son.
While bloody-handed Mars was busy yet
About the slain, Minerva hid her face
In Pluto's helmet, that the god might fail
To see her. As that curse of humankind 1060
Beheld the approach of noble Diomed,
He left the corpse of Periphas unspoiled
Where he had fallen, and where he breathed his last,
And came in haste to meet the Grecian knight.
And now, when they were near, and face to face, 1065
Mars o'er the chariot-yoke and horses' reins
First hurled his brazen spear, in hope to take
His enemy's life; but Pallas with her hand
Caught it and turned it, so that it flew by
And gave no wound. The valiant Diomed 1070
Made with his brazen spear the next assault,
And Pallas guided it to strike the waist
Where girded by the baldric. In that part
She wounded Mars, and tore the shining skin,
And drew the weapon back. The furious god 1075
Uttered a cry as of nine thousand men,
Or of ten thousand, rushing to the fight.
The Greeks and Trojans stood aghast with fear,
To hear that terrible cry of him whose thirst

Of bloodshed never is appeased by blood. 1080
   As when, in time of heat, the air is filled
With a black shadow from the gathering clouds
And the strong-blowing wind, so furious Mars
Appeared to Diomed, as in a cloud
He rose to the broad heaven and to the home 1085
Of gods on high Olympus. Near to Jove
He took his seat in bitter grief, and showed
The immortal blood still dropping from his wound,
And thus, with wingèd words, complaining said:—
   "O Father Jupiter! does not thy wrath 1090
Rise at these violent deeds? 'Tis ever thus
That we, the gods, must suffer grievously
From our own rivalry in favoring man;
And yet the blame of all this strife is thine,
For thou hast a mad daughter, ever wrong, 1095
And ever bent on mischief. All the rest
Of the immortals dwelling on this mount
Obey thee and are subject to thy will.
Her only thou hast never yet restrained
By word or act, but dost indulge her freaks 1100
Because the pestilent creature is thy child.
And now she moves the insolent Diomed
To raise his hand against the immortal gods.
And first he wounded Venus in the wrist,
Contending hand to hand; and then he sought 1105
To encounter me in arms, as if he were
The equal of a god. My own swift feet
Carried me thence, else might I long have lain,
In anguish, under heaps of carcasses,
Or helplessly been mangled by his sword." 1110
   The Cloud-compeller, Jove, replied, and frowned:—
"Come not to me, thou changeling, to complain.
Of all the gods upon the Olympian mount
I like thee least, who ever dost delight
In broils and wars and battles. Thou art like 1115
Thy mother Juno, headstrong and perverse.
Her I can scarcely rule by strict commands,
And what thou sufferest now, I deem, is due

To her bad counsels. Yet 'tis not my will
That thou shouldst suffer longer, who dost share   1120
My lineage, whom thy mother bore to me.
But wert thou born, destroyer as thou art,
To any other god, thou hadst long since
Lain lower than the sons of Uranus."

  So spake he, and to Pæon gave command   1125
To heal the wound; and Pæon bathed the part
With pain-dispelling balsams, and it healed;
For Mars was not to die. As, when the juice
Of figs is mingled with white milk and stirred,
The liquid gathers into clots while yet   1130
It whirls with the swift motion, so was healed
The wound of violent Mars. Then Hebe bathed
The god, and robed him richly, and he took
His seat, delighted, by Saturnian Jove.

  Now, having forced the curse of nations, Mars,   1135
To pause from slaughter, Argive Juno came,
With Pallas, her invincible ally,
Back to the mansion of imperial Jove.

BOOK VI

NOW from that stubborn conflict of the Greeks
And Trojans had the gods withdrawn. The fight
Of men encountering men with brazen spears
Still raged from place to place upon the plain
Between the Xanthus and the Simoïs.   5
   And first of all did Ajax Telamon,
The bulwark of the Achaians, break the ranks
Of Troy and raise the hopes of those who fought
Beside him; for he smote the bravest man
Of all the Thracian warriors,—Acamas,   10
Son of Eussorus, strong and large of limb.
His spear-head, through the plumed helmet's cone
Entering the forehead of the Thracian, pierced
The bone, and darkness gathered o'er his eyes.
The valiant Diomed slew Axylus,   15
The son of Teuthras. To the war he came
From nobly-built Arisba; great his wealth,
And greatly was he loved, for courteously
He welcomed to his house beside the way
All comers. None of these could interpose   20
Between him and his death, for Diomed
Slew him and his attendant charioteer,
Calysius; both went down below the earth.
   And then Euryalus struck Dresus down,
And smote Opheltius and went on to slay   25
Æsepus and his brother Pedasus;—

A river-nymph, Abarbareïa, bore
Both children to Bucolion the renowned.
Bucolion was the eldest of the sons
Of great Laomedon. His mother reared   30
The boy in secret. While he fed his sheep,
He with the river-nymph was joined in love
And marriage, and she bore him twins; and these,
Brave and of shapely limb, Mecisteus' son
Struck down, and from their shoulders tore the mail.   35
The warlike Polypœtes overthrew
Astyalus; Ulysses smote to earth
Pidytes the Percosian with the spear,
And Teucer Aretaon, nobly born.
The glittering javelin of Antilochus,   40
The son of Nestor, laid Ablerus low;
And Agamemnon, king of men, struck down
Elatus, who on lofty Pedasus
Dwelt, by the smoothly flowing Satnio's stream.
Brave Leïtus slew Phylacus in flight,   45
And by Eurypylus Melanthius fell.
Then valiant Menelaus took alive
Adrastus, whose two coursers, as they scoured
The plain in terror, struck against a branch
Of tamarisk, and, there entangled, snapped   50
The chariot pole, and, breaking from it, fled
Whither were others fleeing. From the car
Adrastus to the dust beside the wheel
Fell, on his face. There, lifting his huge spear,
Atrides Menelaus o'er him stood.   55
Adrastus clasped the warrior's knees and said:—
    "O son of Atreus, take me prisoner,
And thou shalt have large ransom. In the house
Of my rich father ample treasures lie,—
Brass, gold, and tempered steel,—and he shall send   60
Gifts without end when he shall hear that I
Am spared alive and in the Grecian fleet."
    He spake, and moved the conqueror, who now
Was minded to give charge that one among
His comrades to the Grecian fleet should lead   65

The captive. Agamemnon came in haste,
And, lifting up his voice, rebuked him thus:—
   "O Menelaus, soft of heart, why thus
Art thou concerned for men like these? In sooth,
Great are the benefits thy household owes   70
The Trojans. Nay, let none of them escape
The doom of swift destruction by our hands.
The very babe within his mother's womb,
Even that must die, and all of Ilium born
Perish unburied, utterly cut off."   75
   He spake; the timely admonition changed
The purpose of his brother, who thrust back
The suppliant hero with his hand; and then
King Agamemnon smote him through the loins,
And prone on earth he fell. Upon the breast   80
Of the slain man Atrides placed his heel,
And from the body drew the ashen spear.
   Then Nestor to the Argives called aloud:—
"Friends, Grecian heroes, ministers of Mars!
Let no man here through eagerness for spoil   85
Linger behind the rest, that he may bear
Much plunder to the ships; but let us first
Strike down our enemies, and afterward
At leisure strip the bodies of the dead."
   Thus speaking, he revived in every breast   90
Courage and zeal. Then had the men of Troy
Sought refuge from the Greeks within their walls,
O'ercome by abject fear, if Helenus,
The son of Priam, and of highest note
Among the augurs, had not made his way   95
To Hector and Æneas, speaking thus:—
   "O Hector and Æneas, since on you
Is laid the mighty labor to command
The Trojans and the Lycians,—for the first
Are ye in battle, and in council first,—   100
Here make your stand, and haste from side to side,
Rallying your scattered ranks, lest they betake
Themselves to flight, and, rushing to their wives,
Become the scorn and laughter of the foe.

And then, so soon as ye shall have revived   105
The courage of your men, we here will bide
The conflict with the Greeks, though closely pressed;
For so we must. But, Hector, thou depart
To Troy and seek the mother of us both,
And bid her call the honored Trojan dames   110
To where the blue-eyed Pallas has her fane,
In the high citadel, and with a key
Open the hallowed doors, and let her bring
What she shall deem the fairest of the robes,
And amplest, in her palace, and the one   115
She prizes most, and lay it on the knees
Of the bright-haired Minerva. Let her make
A vow to offer to the goddess there
Twelve yearling heifers that have never borne
The yoke, if she in mercy will regard   120
The city, and the wives and little ones
Of its defenders; if she will protect
Our sacred Ilium from the ruthless son
Of Tydeus, from whose valor armies flee,
And whom I deem the bravest of the Greeks.   125
For not so greatly have we held in dread
Achilles, the great leader, whom they call
The goddess-born; but terrible in wrath
Is Diomed, nor hath his peer in might."
   He spake, and Hector of his brother's words   130
Was not unmindful. Instantly he leaped,
Armed, from his chariot, shaking his sharp spears;
And everywhere among the host he went,
Exhorting them to combat manfully;
And thus he kindled the fierce fight anew.   135
They, turning from the flight, withstood the Greeks.
The Greeks fell back and ceased to slay; they thought
That one of the immortals had come down
From out the starry heaven to help the men
Of Troy, so suddenly they turned and fought.   140
Then Hector to the Trojans called aloud:—
   "O valiant sons of Troy, and ye allies
Summoned from far! Be men, my friends; call back

Your wonted valor, while I go to Troy
To ask the aged men, our counsellors, 145
And all our wives, to come before the gods
And pray and offer vows of sacrifice."
  So the plumed Hector spake, and then withdrew,
While the black fell that edged his bossy shield
Struck on his neck and ankles as he went. 150
  Now came into the midst between the hosts
Glaucus, the offspring of Hippolochus,
And met the son of Tydeus,—both intent
On combat. But when now the twain were near,
And ready to engage, brave Diomed 155
Spake first, and thus addressed his enemy:—
  "Who may'st thou be, of mortal men? Most brave
Art thou, yet never in the glorious fight
Have I beheld thee. Thou surpassest now
All others in thy daring, since thou com'st 160
Within the reach of my long spear. The sons
Of most unhappy men are they who meet
My arm; but—if thou comest from above,
A god—I war not with the gods of heaven;
For even brave Lycurgus lived not long, 165
The son of Dryas, who engaged in strife
With the celestial gods. He once pursued
The nurses of the frantic Bacchus through
The hallowed ground of Nyssa. All at once
They flung to earth their sacred implements, 170
Lycurgus the man-slayer beating them
With an ox-driver's goad. Then Bacchus fled
And plunged into the sea, where Thetis hid
The trembler in her bosom, for he shook
With panic at the hero's angry threats. 175
Thenceforward were the blessed deities
Wroth with Lycurgus. Him did Saturn's son
Strike blind, and after that he lived not long,
For he was held in hate by all the gods.
So will I never with the gods contend. 180
But if thou be indeed of mortal race,
And nourished by the fruits of earth, draw near;

And quickly shalt thou pass the gates of death."
    Hippolochus's son, the far-renowned,
Made answer thus: "O large-souled Diomed, 185
Why ask my lineage? Like the race of leaves
Is that of humankind. Upon the ground
The winds strew one year's leaves; the sprouting grove
Puts forth another brood, that shoot and grow
In the spring season. So it is with man: 190
One generation grows while one decays.
Yet since thou takest heed of things like these,
And askest whence I sprang,—although to most
My birth is not unknown,—there is a town
Lapped in the pasture-grounds where graze the steeds 195
Of Argos, Ephyra by name, and there
Dwelt Sisyphus Æolides, most shrewd
Of men; his son was Glaucus, and the son
Of Glaucus was the good Bellerophon,
To whom the gods gave beauty and the grace 200
Of winning manners. Prœtus sought his death
And banished him, for Prœtus was the chief
Among the Argives; Jupiter had made
That people subject to his rule. The wife
Of Prœtus, nobly-born Anteia, sought 205
With passionate desire his secret love,
But failed to entice, with all her blandishments,
The virtuous and discreet Bellerophon.
Therefore went she to Prœtus with a lie,—
    "'Die, Prœtus, thou, or put Bellerophon 210
To death, for he has offered force to me.'
    "The monarch hearkened, and was moved to wrath;
And then he would not slay him, for his soul
Revolted at the deed; he sent him thence
To Lycia, with a fatal tablet, sealed, 215
With things of deadly import writ therein,
Meant for Anteia's father, in whose hand
Bellerophon must place it, and be made
To perish. So at Lycia he arrived
Under the favoring guidance of the gods; 220
And when he came where Lycian Xanthus flows,

The king of that broad realm received his guest
With hospitable welcome, feasting him
Nine days, and offering up in sacrifice
Nine oxen. But when rosy-fingered morn 225
Appeared for the tenth time, he questioned him
And bade him show the token he had brought
From Prœtus. When the monarch had beheld
The fatal tablet from his son-in-law,
The first command he gave him was, to slay 230
Heaven-born Chimæra, the invincible.
No human form was hers: a lion she
In front, a dragon in the hinder parts,
And in the midst a goat, and terribly
Her nostrils breathed a fierce, consuming flame; 235
Yet, trusting in the portents of the gods,
He slew her. Then it was his second task
To combat with the illustrious Solymi,—
The hardest battle he had ever fought—
So he declared—with men; and then he slew— 240
His third exploit—the man-like Amazons.
Then he returned to Lycia; on his way
The monarch laid a treacherous snare. He chose
From his wide Lycian realm the bravest men
To lie in ambush for him. Never one 245
Of these came home again,—Bellerophon
The matchless slew them all. And when the king
Saw that he was the offspring of a god,
He kept him near him, giving him to wife
His daughter, and dividing with him all 250
His kingly honors, while the Lycians set
Their richest fields apart—a goodly spot,
Ploughlands and vineyards—for the prince to till.
And she who now became his wife brought forth
Three children to the sage Bellerophon,— 255
Isandrus and Hippolochus; and, last,
Laodameia, who in secret bore
To all-providing Jupiter a son,—
Godlike Sarpedon, eminent in arms.
But when Bellerophon upon himself 260

Had drawn the anger of the gods, he roamed
The Aleian fields alone, a prey to thoughts
That wasted him, and shunning every haunt
Of humankind. The god whose lust of strife
Is never sated, Mars, cut off his son 265
Isandrus, warring with the illustrious race
Of Solymi; and Dian, she who guides
Her car with golden reins, in anger slew
His daughter. I am of Hippolochus;
From him I claim my birth. He sent me forth 270
To Troy with many counsels and commands,
Ever to bear myself like a brave man,
And labor to excel, and never bring
Dishonor on the stock from which I sprang,—
The bravest stock by far in Ephyra 275
And the wide realm of Lycia. 'Tis my boast
To be of such a race and such a blood."

   He spake. The warlike Diomed was glad,
And, planting in the foodful earth his spear,
Addressed the people's shepherd blandly thus:— 280
"Most surely thou art my ancestral guest;
For noble Œneus once within his halls
Received the blameless chief Bellerophon,
And kept him twenty days, and they bestowed
Gifts on each other, such as host and guest 285
Exchange; a purple baldric Œneus gave
Of dazzling color, and Bellerophon
A double golden goblet; this I left
Within my palace when I came to Troy.
Of Tydeus I remember nothing, since 290
He left me, yet a little child, and went
To Thebes, where perished such a host of Greeks.
Henceforward I will be thy host and friend
In Argos; thou shalt be the same to me
In Lycia when I visit Lycia's towns; 295
And let us in the tumult of the fray
Avoid each other's spears, for there will be
Of Trojans and of their renowned allies
Enough for me to slay whene'er a god

Shall bring them in my way. In turn for thee 300
Are many Greeks to smite whomever thou
Canst overcome. Let us exchange our arms,
That even these may see that thou and I
Regard each other as ancestral guests."
   Thus having said, and leaping from their cars, 305
They clasped each other's hands and pledged their faith.
Then did the son of Saturn take away
The judging mind of Glaucus, when he gave
His arms of gold away for arms of brass
Worn by Tydides Diomed,—the worth 310
Of fivescore oxen for the worth of nine.
   And now had Hector reached the Scæan gates
And beechen tree. Around him flocked the wives
And daughters of the Trojans eagerly;
Tidings of sons and brothers they required, 315
And friends and husbands. He admonished all
Duly to importune the gods in prayer,
For woe, he said, was near to many a one.
   And then he came to Priam's noble hall,—
A palace built with graceful porticos, 320
And fifty chambers near each other, walled
With polished stone, the rooms of Priam's sons
And of their wives; and opposite to these
Twelve chambers for his daughters, also near
Each other; and, with polished marble walls, 325
The sleeping-rooms of Priam's sons-in-law
And their unblemished consorts. There he met
His gentle mother on her way to seek
Her fairest child, Laodice. She took
His hand and held it fast, while thus she spake:— 330
   "Why art thou come, my child, and why hast left
The raging fight? Full hard these hateful Greeks
Press us, in fighting round the city-walls.
Thy heart, I know, hath moved thee to repair
To our high citadel, and lift thy hands 335
In prayer to Jupiter. But stay thou here
Till I bring pleasant wine, that thou may'st pour
A part to Jove and to the other gods,

And drink and be refreshed; for wine restores
Strength to the weary, and I know that thou   340
Art weary, fighting for thy countrymen."
  Great Hector of the crested helm replied:—
"My honored mother, bring not pleasant wine,
Lest that unman me, and my wonted might
And valor leave me. I should fear to pour   345
Dark wine to Jupiter with hands unwashed.
Nor is it fitting that a man like me,
Defiled with blood and battle-dust, should make
Vows to the cloud-compeller, Saturn's son.
But thou, with incense, seek the temple reared   350
To Pallas the despoiler,—calling first
Our honored dames together. Take with thee
What thou shalt deem the fairest of the robes,
And amplest, in thy palace, and the one
Thou prizest most, and lay it on the knees   355
Of the bright-haired Minerva. Make a vow
To offer to the goddess in her fane
Twelve yearling heifers that have never borne
The yoke, if she in mercy will regard
The city, and the wives and little ones   360
Of its defenders; if she will protect
Our sacred Ilium from the ruthless son
Of Tydeus, from whose valor armies flee.
So to the shrine of Pallas, warrior-queen,
Do thou repair, while I depart to seek   365
Paris, if he will listen to my voice.
Would that the earth might open where he stands,
And swallow him! Olympian Jupiter
Reared him to be the bane of all who dwell
In Troy, to large-souled Priam and his sons.   370
Could I behold him sinking to the shades,
My heart would lose its sense of bitter woe."
  He spake. His mother, turning homeward, gave
Charge to her handmaids, who through all the town
Passed, summoning the matrons, while the queen   375
Descended to her chamber, where the air
Was sweet with perfumes, and in which were laid

Her rich embroidered robes, the handiwork
Of Sidon's damsels, whom her son had brought—
The godlike Alexander—from the coast 380
Of Sidon, when across the mighty deep
He sailed and brought the high-born Helen thence.
One robe, most beautiful of all, she chose,
To bring to Pallas, ampler than the rest,
And many-hued; it glistened like a star, 385
And lay beneath them all. Then hastily
She left the chamber with the matron train.
   They reached Minerva's temple, and its gates
Were opened by Theano, rosy-cheeked,
The knight Antenor's wife and Cisseus' child, 390
Made priestess to the goddess by the sons
Of Troy. Then all the matrons lifted up
Their voices and stretched forth their suppliant hands
To Pallas, while the fair Theano took
The robe and spread its folds upon the lap 395
Of fair-haired Pallas, and with solemn vows
Prayed to the daughter of imperial Jove:—
   "O venerated Pallas, Guardian-Power
Of Troy, great goddess! shatter thou the lance
Of Diomed, and let him fall in death 400
Before the Scæan gates, that we forthwith
May offer to thee in thy temple here
Twelve yearling heifers that have never worn
The yoke, if thou wilt pity us and spare
The wives of Trojans and their little ones." 405
   So spake she, supplicating; but her prayer
Minerva answered not; and while they made
Vows to the daughter of Almighty Jove,
Hector was hastening to the sumptuous home
Of Alexander, which that prince had built 410
With aid of the most cunning architects
In Troy the fruitful, by whose hands were made
The bed-chamber and hall and ante-room.
There entered Hector, dear to Jove; he bore
In hand a spear eleven cubits long: 415
The brazen spear-head glittered brightly, bound

With a gold circle. In his room he there
Found Paris, busied with his shining arms,—
Corslet and shield; he tried his curvèd bow;
While Argive Helen with the attendant maids   420
Was sitting, and appointed each a task.
Hector beheld, and chid him sharply thus:—
  "Strange man! a fitting time indeed is this,
To indulge thy sullen humor, while in fight
Around our lofty walls the men of Troy   425
Are perishing, and for thy sake the war
Is fiercely blazing all around our town.
Thou wouldst thyself reprove him, shouldst thou see
Another warrior as remiss as thou
In time of battle. Rouse thee, then, and act,   430
Lest we behold our city all in flames."
  Then answered Paris of the godlike form:—
"Hector! although thou justly chidest me,
And not beyond my due, yet let me speak.
Attend and hearken. Not in sullenness,   435
Nor angry with the Trojans, sat I here
Within my chamber, but that I might give
A loose to sorrow. Even now my wife
With gentle speeches has besought of me
That I return to battle; and to me   440
That seems the best, for oft doth victory
Change sides in war. Remain thou yet awhile,
Till I put on my armor; or go thou,
And I shall follow and rejoin thee soon."
  He ended. Hector of the beamy helm   445
Heard him, and answered not; but Helen spake,
And thus with soothing words addressed the chief:—
  "Brother-in-law,—for such thou art, though I
Am lost to shame, and cause of many ills,—
Would that some violent blast when I was born   450
Had whirled me to the mountain wilds, or waves
Of the hoarse sea, that they might swallow me,
Ere deeds like these were done! But since the gods
Have thus decreed, why was I not the wife
Of one who bears a braver heart and feels   455

Keenly the anger and reproach of men?
For Paris hath not, and will never have,
A resolute mind, and must abide the effect
Of his own folly. Enter thou meanwhile,
My brother; seat thee here, for heavily   460
Must press on thee the labors thou dost bear
For one so vile as I, and for the sake
Of guilty Paris. An unhappy lot,
By Jupiter's appointment, waits us both,—
A theme of song for men in time to come."   465
  Great Hector of the beamy helm replied:—
"Nay, Helen, ask me not to sit; thy speech
Is courteous, but persuades me not. My mind
Is troubled for the Trojans, to whose aid
I hasten, for they miss me even now.   470
But thou exhort this man, and bid him haste
To overtake me ere I leave the town.
I go to my own mansion first, to meet
My household,—my dear wife and little child;
Nor know I whether I may come once more   475
To them, or whether the great gods ordain
That I must perish by the hands of Greeks."
  So spake the plumèd Hector, and withdrew,
And reached his pleasant palace, but found not
White-armed Andromache within, for she   480
Was in the tower, beside her little son
And well-robed nurse, and sorrowed, shedding tears.
And Hector, seeing that his blameless wife
Was not within, came forth again, and stood
Upon the threshold questioning the maids.   485
  "I pray you, damsels, tell me whither went
White-armed Andromache? Has she gone forth
To seek my sisters, or those stately dames,
My brothers' wives? Or haply has she sought
The temple of Minerva, where are met   490
The other bright-haired matrons of the town
To supplicate the dreaded deity?"
  Then said the diligent housewife in reply:—
"Since thou wilt have the truth,—thy wife is gone

Not to thy sisters, nor those stately dames, 495
Thy brothers' wives; nor went she forth to join
The other bright-haired matrons of the town,
Where in Minerva's temple they are met
To supplicate the dreaded deity.
But to the lofty tower of Troy she went 500
When it was told her that the Trojan troops
Lost heart, and that the valor of the Greeks
Prevailed. She now is hurrying toward the walls,
Like one distracted, with her son and nurse."
  So spake the matron. Hector left in haste 505
The mansion, and retraced his way between
The rows of stately dwellings, traversing
The mighty city. When at length he reached
The Scæan gates, that issue on the field,
His spouse, the nobly-dowered Andromache, 510
Came forth to meet him,—daughter of the prince
Eëtion, who, among the woody slopes
Of Placos, in the Hypoplacian town
Of Thebè, ruled Cilicia and her sons,
And gave his child to Hector great in arms. 515
She came attended by a maid, who bore
A tender child—a babe too young to speak—
Upon her bosom,—Hector's only son,
Beautiful as a star, whom Hector called
Scamandrius, but all else Astyanax,— 520
The city's lord,—since Hector stood the sole
Defence of Troy. The father on his child
Looked with a silent smile. Andromache
Pressed to his side meanwhile, and, all in tears,
Clung to his hand, and, thus beginning, said:— 525
  "Too brave! thy valor yet will cause thy death.
Thou hast no pity on thy tender child,
Nor me, unhappy one, who soon must be
Thy widow. All the Greeks will rush on thee
To take thy life. A happier lot were mine, 530
If I must lose thee, to go down to earth,
For I shall have no hope when thou art gone,—
Nothing but sorrow. Father have I none,

And no dear mother. Great Achilles slew
My father when he sacked the populous town   535
Of the Cilicians,—Thebè with high gates.
'Twas there he smote Eëtion, yet forbore
To make his arms a spoil; he dared not that,
But burned the dead with his bright armor on,
And raised a mound above him. Mountain-nymphs,   540
Daughters of ægis-bearing Jupiter,
Came to the spot and planted it with elms.
Seven brothers had I in my father's house,
And all went down to Hades in one day.
Achilles the swift-footed slew them all   545
Among their slow-paced bullocks and white sheep.
My mother, princess on the woody slopes
Of Placos, with his spoils he bore away,
And only for large ransom gave her back.
But her Diana, archer-queen, struck down   550
Within her father's palace. Hector, thou
Art father and dear mother now to me,
And brother and my youthful spouse besides.
In pity keep within the fortress here,
Nor make thy child an orphan nor thy wife   555
A widow. Post thine army near the place
Of the wild fig-tree, where the city-walls
Are low and may be scaled. Thrice in the war
The boldest of the foe have tried the spot,—
The Ajaces and the famed Idomeneus,   560
The two chiefs born to Atreus, and the brave
Tydides, whether counselled by some seer
Or prompted to the attempt by their own minds."
   Then answered Hector, great in war: "All this
I bear in mind, dear wife; but I should stand   565
Ashamed before the men and long-robed dames
Of Troy, were I to keep aloof and shun
The conflict, coward-like. Not thus my heart
Prompts me, for greatly have I learned to dare
And strike among the foremost sons of Troy,   570
Upholding my great father's fame and mine;
Yet well in my undoubting mind I know

The day shall come in which our sacred Troy,
And Priam, and the people over whom
Spear-bearing Priam rules, shall perish all. 575
But not the sorrows of the Trojan race,
Nor those of Hecuba herself, nor those
Of royal Priam, nor the woes that wait
My brothers many and brave,—who all at last,
Slain by the pitiless foe, shall lie in dust,— 580
Grieve me so much as thine, when some mailed Greek
Shall lead thee weeping hence, and take from thee
Thy day of freedom. Thou in Argos then
Shalt, at another's bidding, ply the loom,
And from the fountain of Messeis draw 585
Water, or from the Hypereian spring,
Constrained unwilling by thy cruel lot.
And then shall some one say who sees thee weep,
'This was the wife of Hector, most renowned
Of the horse-taming Trojans, when they fought 590
Around their city.' So shall some one say,
And thou shalt grieve the more, lamenting him
Who haply might have kept afar the day
Of thy captivity. O, let the earth
Be heaped above my head in death before 595
I hear thy cries as thou art borne away!"
   So speaking, mighty Hector stretched his arms
To take the boy; the boy shrank crying back
To his fair nurse's bosom, scared to see
His father helmeted in glittering brass, 600
And eying with affright the horse-hair plume
That grimly nodded from the lofty crest.
At this both parents in their fondness laughed;
And hastily the mighty Hector took
The helmet from his brow and laid it down 605
Gleaming upon the ground, and, having kissed
His darling son and tossed him up in play,
Prayed thus to Jove and all the gods of heaven:—
    "O Jupiter and all ye deities,
Vouchsafe that this my son may yet become 610
Among the Trojans eminent like me,

And nobly rule in Ilium. May they say,
'This man is greater than his father was!'
When they behold him from the battle-field
Bring back the bloody spoil of the slain foe,— 615
That so his mother may be glad at heart."
   So speaking, to the arms of his dear spouse
He gave the boy; she on her fragrant breast
Received him, weeping as she smiled. The chief
Beheld, and, moved with tender pity, smoothed 620
Her forehead gently with his hand and said:—
   "Sorrow not thus, beloved one, for me.
No living man can send me to the shades
Before my time; no man of woman born,
Coward or brave, can shun his destiny. 625
But go thou home, and tend thy labors there,—
The web, the distaff,—and command thy maids
To speed the work. The cares of war pertain
To all men born in Troy, and most to me."
   Thus speaking, mighty Hector took again 630
His helmet, shadowed with the horse-hair plume,
While homeward his beloved consort went,
Oft looking back, and shedding many tears.
Soon was she in the spacious palace-halls
Of the man-queller Hector. There she found 635
A troop of maidens,—with them all she shared
Her grief; and all in his own house bewailed
The living Hector, whom they thought no more
To see returning from the battle-field,
Safe from the rage and weapons of the Greeks. 640
   Nor waited Paris in his lofty halls,
But when he had put on his glorious arms,
Glittering with brass, he traversed with quick steps
The city; and as when some courser, fed
With barley in the stall, and wont to bathe 645
In some smooth-flowing river, having snapped
His halter, gayly scampers o'er the plain,
And in the pride of beauty bears aloft
His head, and gives his tossing mane to stream
Upon his shoulders, while his flying feet 650

Bear him to where the mares are wont to graze,—
So came the son of Priam—Paris—down
From lofty Pergamus in glittering arms,
And, glorious as the sun, held on his way
Exulting and with rapid feet. He found   655
His noble brother Hector as he turned
To leave the place in which his wife and he
Had talked together. Alexander then—
Of godlike form—addressed his brother thus:—
 "My elder brother! I have kept thee here   660
Waiting, I fear, for me, though much in haste,
And came less quickly than thou didst desire."
 And Hector of the plumèd helm replied:—
"Strange being, no man justly can dispraise
Thy martial deeds, for thou art truly brave.   665
But oft art thou remiss and wilt not join
The combat. I am sad at heart to hear
The Trojans—they who suffer for thy sake
A thousand hardships—speak so ill of thee.
Yet let us go: we will confer of this   670
Another time, if Jove should e'er vouchsafe
That to the immortal gods of heaven we pour
In our own halls the cup of liberty
When we have chased the well-armed Greeks from Troy."

BOOK VII

THE illustrious Hector spake, and rapidly
  Passed through the gate, and with him issued forth
His brother Alexander,—eager, both,
For war and combat. As when God bestows,
To glad the long-expecting mariners,
A favorable wind while wearily
They beat the ocean with their polished oars,
Their arms all nerveless with their length of toil,—
Such to the expecting Trojans was the sight
Of the two chiefs. First Alexander slew
Menesthius, who in Arnè had his home,
A son of Areïthoüs the king.
Large-eyed Philomedusa brought him forth
To the mace-bearer Areïthoüs.
And Hector smote Eïoneus, the spear
Piercing his neck beneath the brazen casque,
And straightway he dropped lifeless. Glaucus then—
Son of Hippolochus, and chief among
The Lycians—in that fiery onset slew
Iphinous, son of Dexius, with his spear.
It pierced the warrior's shoulder as he sprang
To mount his rapid car, and from the place
He fell to earth, his limbs relaxed in death.
Now when Minerva of the azure eyes
Beheld them in the furious combat thus
Wasting the Grecian host, she left the peaks

Of high Olympus, and came down in haste
To sacred Ilium. Straight Apollo flew
To meet her, for he marked from Pergamus
Her coming, and he greatly longed to give   30
The victory to the Trojans. As they met
Beside the beechen tree, the son of Jove,
The king Apollo, spake to Pallas thus:—
    "Why hast thou, daughter of imperial Jove,
Thus left Olympus in thine eager haste?   35
Seek'st thou to turn in favor of the Greeks
War's wavering chances?—for I know too well
Thou hast no pity when the men of Troy
Are perishing. But, if thou wilt give ear
To me, I shall propose a better way.   40
Cause we the conflict for this day to cease,
And be it afterward renewed until
An end be made of Troy, since it hath pleased
You, goddesses, to lay the city waste."
    And blue-eyed Pallas answered: "Be it so,   45
Mighty Archer. With a like intent
I left Olympus for this battle-field
Of Greeks and Trojans. But by what device
Think'st thou to bring the combat to a pause?"
    Then spake the king Apollo, son of Jove,   50
In turn to Pallas: "Let us seek to rouse
The fiery spirit of the Trojan knight
Hector, that he may challenge in the field
Some Greek to meet him, singly and alone,
In mortal combat. Then the well-armed Greeks,   55
Stung by the bold defiance, will send forth
A champion against Priam's noble son."
    He spake. The blue-eyed goddess gave assent;
And straightway Helenus, beloved son
Of Priam, in his secret mind perceived   60
The purpose of the gods consulting thus,
And came and stood by Hector's side and said:—
    "O Hector, son of Priam, and like Jove
In council, wilt thou hearken to my words
Who am thy brother? Cause the Trojans all   65

And all the Greeks to sit, while thou shalt stand
Proclaiming challenge to the bravest man
Among the Achaians to contend with thee
In mortal combat. It is not thy fate
To fall and perish yet, for thus have said   70
The ever-living gods, whose voice I heard."
   He spake; and Hector, hearing him, rejoiced,
And went between the hosts. He bore his spear,
Holding it in the middle, and pressed back
The ranks of Trojans, and they all sat down.   75
And Agamemnon caused the well-armed Greeks
To sit down also. Meantime Pallas sat,
With Phœbus of the silver bow, in shape
Like vultures, on the boughs of the tall beech,—
The tree of Father Jupiter who bears   80
The ægis,—and they looked with great delight
Upon the array of warriors in thick rows,
Horrid with shields and helms and bristling spears.
As when the west wind, rising fresh, breathes o'er
The deep, and darkens all its face with waves,   85
So seemed the Greeks and Trojans as they sat
In ranks upon the field, while Hector stood
Between the armies and bespake them thus:—
   "Ye Trojans, and ye well-armed Greeks, give ear
To what my spirit bids me speak. The son   90
Of Saturn, throned on high, hath not vouchsafed
To ratify the treaty we have made,
But meditates new miseries for us both,
Till ye possess the towery city of Troy,
Or, vanquished, yield yourselves beside the barks 95
That brought you o'er the sea. With you are found
The bravest sons of Greece. If one of these
Is moved to encounter me, let him stand forth
And fight with noble Hector. I propose,
And call on Jove to witness, that if he   100
Shall slay me with the long blade of his spear,
My arms are his to spoil and to bestow
Among the hollow ships; but he must send
My body home, that there the sons of Troy

And Trojan dames may burn it on the pyre.　　　　　105
But if I take his life, and Phœbus crown
My combat with that glory, I will strip
His armor off and carry it away
To hallowed Ilium, there to hang it high
Within the temple of the archer-god　　　　　　　110
Apollo; but his body I will send
Back to the well-oared ships, that on the beach
The long-haired Greeks may hold his funeral rites,
And rear his tomb by the wide Hellespont.
And then, in time to come, shall some one say,　　115
Sailing in his good ship the dark-blue deep,
'This is the sepulchre of one who died
Long since, and whom, though fighting gallantly,
Illustrious Hector slew.' So shall he say
Hereafter, and my fame shall never die."　　　　　120
　　He spake; but utter silence held them all,—
Ashamed to shun the encounter, yet afraid
To meet it,—till at length, with heavy heart,
Rose Menelaus from his seat, and thus
Bespake the army with reproachful words:—　　　125
　　"O boastful ones, no longer to be called
Greek warriors, but Greek women! a disgrace
Grievous beyond all others will be ours,
If none be found in all the Achaian host
To meet this Hector. May you, every one,　　　　130
There where ye now are sitting, turn to earth
And water, craven as ye are, and lost
To sense of glory! I will arm myself
For this encounter. With the immortal gods
Alone it rests to give the victory."　　　　　　135
　　He spake, and put his glorious armor on.
Then, Menelaus, had the Trojan's hand
Ended thy life, for he was mightier far
Than thou, had not the Achaian kings at once
Uprisen to hold thee back, while Atreus' son,　　140
Wide-ruling Agamemnon, took thy hand
In his, and made thee listen while he spake:—
　　"Sure, noble Menelaus, thou art mad.

Such frenzied daring suits not with the time.
Restrain thyself, though thou hast cause for wrath; 145
Nor in thy pride of courage meet in arms
One so much mightier,—Hector, Priam's son,
Whom every other chief regards with fear,
Whom even Achilles, braver far than thou,
Dreads to encounter in the glorious fight. 150
Withdraw, then, to thy comrades, and sit down.
The Greeks will send some other champion forth
Against him; and though fearless, and athirst
For combat, he, I deem, will gladly bend
His weary knees to rest should he escape 155
From that fierce conflict in the lists alive."
    With words like these the Grecian hero changed
The purpose of his brother, who obeyed
The prudent counsel; and with great delight
The attendants stripped the armor from his breast. 160
Then Nestor rose amid the Greeks and said:—
    "Ye gods! a great calamity hath fallen
Upon Achaia. How the aged chief
Peleus, the illustrious counsellor and sage,
Who rules the Myrmidons, will now lament!— 165
He who once gladly in his palace-home
Inquired of me the race and pedigree
Of the Greek warriors. Were he but to know
That all of them are basely cowering now
In Hector's presence, how would he uplift 170
His hands and pray the gods that from his limbs
The parted soul might pass to the abode
Of Pluto! Would to Father Jupiter
And Pallas and Apollo that again
I were as young as when the Pylian host 175
And the Arcadians, mighty with the spear,
Fought on the banks of rapid Celadon
And near to Phæa and Iardan's streams.
There godlike Ereuthalion stood among
Our foremost foes, and on his shoulders bore 180
The armor of King Areïthoüs,—
The noble Areïthoüs, whom men

And graceful women called the Mace-bearer;
For not with bow he fought, nor ponderous lance,
But broke the phalanxes with iron mace. 185
Lycurgus slew him, but by stratagem,
And not by strength; he from a narrow way,
Where was no room to wield the iron mace,
Through Areïthoüs thrust the spear: he fell
Backward; the victor took his arms, which Mars 190
The war-god gave, and which in after-time
Lycurgus wore on many a battle-field.
And when within his palace he grew old,
He gave them to be worn by one he loved,—
To Ereuthalion, who attended him 195
In battle, and who, wearing them, defied
The bravest of our host. All trembled; all
Held back in fear, nor dared encounter him.
But me a daring trust in my own strength
Impelled to meet him. I was youngest then 200
Of all the chiefs; I fought, and Pallas gave
The victory over him, and thus I slew
The hugest and most strong of men; he lay
Extended in vast bulk upon the ground.
Would I were young as then, my frame unworn 205
By years! and Hector of the beamy helm
Should meet an adversary soon; but now
No one of all the chieftains here, renowned
To be the bravest of the Achaian race,
Hastens to meet in arms the Trojan chief." 210
 Thus with upbraiding words the old man spake;
And straight arose nine warriors from their seats.
The first was Agamemnon, king of men;
The second, brave Tydides Diomed;
And then the chieftains Ajax, bold and strong; 215
And then Idomeneus, with whom arose
Meriones, his armor-bearer, great
As Mars himself in battle. After them,
Eurypylus Evæmon's valiant son,
And Thoas, offspring of Andræmon, rose, 220
And the divine Ulysses,—claiming all

To encounter noble Hector in the lists.
But then spake Nestor the Gerenian knight:—
  "Now let us cast the lot for all, and see
To whom it falls; for greatly will he aid   225
The nobly-armed Achaians, and as great
Will be his share of honor should he come
Alive from the hard trial of the fight."
  Then each one marked his lot, and all were cast
Into the helm of Agamemnon, son   230
Of Atreus. All the people lifted up
Their hands in prayer to the ever-living gods,
And turned their eyes to the broad heaven, and said:—
  "Grant, Father Jove, that Ajax, or the son
Of Tydeus, or the monarch who bears rule   235
In rich Mycenæ may obtain the lot."
  Such was their prayer, while the Gerenian knight,
Old Nestor, shook the lots; and from the helm
Leaped forth the lot of Ajax, as they wished.
A herald took it, and from right to left   240
Bore it through all the assembly, showing it
To all the leaders of the Greeks. No one
Knew it, and all disclaimed it. When at last,
Carried through all the multitude, it came
To Ajax the renowned, who had inscribed   245
And laid it in the helmet, he stretched forth
His hand, while at his side the herald stood,
And took and looked upon it, knew his sign,
And gloried as he looked, and cast it down
Upon the ground before his feet, and said:—   250
  "O friends! the lot is mine, and I rejoice
Heartily, for I think to overcome
The noble Hector. Now, while I put on
My armor for the fight, pray ye to Jove,
The mighty son of Saturn, silently,   255
Unheard by them of Troy, or else aloud,
Since we fear no one. None by strength of arm
Shall vanquish me, or find me inexpert
In battle, nor was I to that degree
Ill-trained in Salamis, where I was born.   260

He spake; and they to Saturn's monarch-son
Prayed, looking up to the broad heaven, and said:—
  "O Father Jove! most mighty, most august!
Who rulest from the Idæan mount, vouchsafe
That Ajax bear away the victory 265
And everlasting honor; but if thou
Dost cherish Hector and protect his life,
Give equal strength to both, and equal fame."
Such were their words, while Ajax armed himself
In glittering brass; and, when about his limbs 270
The mail was buckled, forward rushed the chief.
As moves the mighty Mars to war among
The heroes whom the son of Saturn sends
To struggle on the field in murderous strife,
So the great Ajax, bulwark of the Greeks, 275
With a grim smile came forward, and with strides
Firm-set and long, and shook his ponderous spear.
The Greeks exulted at the sight; dismay
Seized every Trojan: even Hector's heart
Quailed in his bosom; yet he might not now 280
Withdraw through fear, nor seek to hide among
The throng of people, since himself had given
The challenge. Ajax, drawing near, upheld
A buckler like a rampart, bright with brass,
And strong with ox-hides seven. The cunning hand 285
Of Tychius, skilled beyond all other men
In leather-work, had wrought it at his home
In Hyla. He for Ajax framed the shield
With hides of pampered bullocks in seven folds,
And an eighth fold of brass,—the outside fold. 290
This Telamonian Ajax held before
His breast, as he approached, and threatening said:—
  "Now shalt thou, Hector, singly matched with me,
Learn by what chiefs the Achaian host is led
Besides Achilles, mighty though he be 295
To break through squadrons, and of lion-heart.
Still in the beakèd ships in which he crossed
The sea he cherishes his wrath against
The shepherd of the people,—Atreus' son.

But we have those that dare defy thee yet,	300
And they are many. Let the fight begin."
   Then answered Hector of the plumèd helm:—
"O high-born Ajax, son of Telamon,
And prince among thy people, think thou not
To treat me like a stripling weak of arm,	305
Or woman all untrained to tasks of war.
I know what battles are and bloody frays,
And how to shift to right and left the shield
Of seasoned hide, and, unfatigued, maintain
The combat; how on foot to charge the foe	310
With steps that move to martial airs, and how
To leap into the chariot and pursue
The war with rushing steeds. Yet not by stealth
Seek I to smite thee, valiant as thou art,
But in fair open battle, if I may."	315
   He spake, and, brandishing his ponderous lance,
Hurled it; and on the outer plate of brass,
Which covered the seven bullock-hides, it struck
The shield of Ajax. Through the brass and through
Six folds of hides the irresistible spear	320
Cut its swift way, and at the seventh was stopped.
Then high-born Ajax cast his massive spear
In turn, and drove it through the fair, round shield
Of Priam's son. Through that bright buckler went
The rapid weapon, pierced the well-wrought mail,	325
And tore the linen tunic at the flank.
But Hector stooped and thus avoided death.
They took their spears again, and, coming close,
Like lions in their hunger, or wild boars
Of fearful strength, joined battle. Priam's son	330
Sent his spear forward, striking in the midst
The shield of Ajax, but it broke not through
The brass; the metal turned the weapon's point.
While Ajax, springing onward, smote the shield
Of Hector, drave his weapon through, and checked	335
His enemy's swift advance, and wounded him
Upon the shoulder, and the black blood flowed.
Yet not for this did plumèd Hector cease

From combat, but went back, and, lifting up
A huge, black, craggy stone that near him lay,   340
Flung it with force against the middle boss
Of the broad sevenfold shield that Ajax bore.
The brass rang with the blow. Then Ajax raised
A heavier stone, and whirled it, putting forth
His arm's immeasurable strength; it brake   345
Through Hector's shield as if a millstone's weight
Had fallen. His knees gave way; he fell to earth
Headlong; yet still he kept his shield. At once
Apollo raised him up; and now with swords,
Encountering hand to hand, they both had flown   350
To wound each other, if the heralds sent
As messengers from Jupiter and men
Had not approached,—Idæus from the side
Of Troy, Talthybius from the Grecian host,—
Wise ancients both. Betwixt the twain they held   355
Their sceptres, and the sage Idæus spake:—
   "Cease to contend, dear sons, in deadly fray;
Ye both are loved by cloud-compelling Jove,
And both are great in war, as all men know.
The night is come; be then the night obeyed."   360
   And Telamonian Ajax answered thus:—
"Idæus, first let Hector speak of this,
For he it was who challenged to the field
The bravest of the Grecian host, and I
Shall willingly obey if he obeys."   365
   To him in turn the plumèd Hector said:—
"Ajax, although God gave thee bulk and strength
And prudence, and in mastery of the spear
Thou dost excel the other Greeks, yet now
Pause we from battle and the rivalry   370
Of prowess for this day. Another time
We haply may renew the fight till fate
Shall part us and bestow the victory
On one of us. But now the night is here,
And it is good to obey the night, that thou   375
May'st gladden at the fleet the Greeks and all
Thy friends and comrades, and that I in turn

May give the Trojan men and long-robed dames,
In the great city where King Priam reigns,
Cause to rejoice,—the dames who pray for me,   380
Thronging the hallowed temple. Let us now
Each with the other leave some noble gift,
That all men, Greek or Trojan, thus may say:
'They fought indeed in bitterness of heart,
But they were reconciled, and parted friends.'"   385
   He spake, and gave a silver-studded sword
And scabbard with its fair embroidered belt;
And Ajax gave a girdle brightly dyed
With purple. Then they both departed,—one
To join the Grecian host, and one to meet   390
The Trojan people, who rejoiced to see
Hector alive, unwounded, and now safe
From the great might and irresistible arm
Of Ajax. Straightway to the town they led
Him for whose life they scarce had dared to hope.   395
And Ajax also by the well-armed Greeks,
Exulting in his feats of arms, was brought
To noble Agamemnon. When the chiefs
Were in his tents, the monarch sacrificed
A bullock of five summers to the son   400
Of Saturn, sovereign Jupiter. They flayed
The carcass, dressed it, carved away the limbs,
Divided into smaller parts the flesh,
Fixed them on spits, and roasted them with care,
And drew them from the fire. And when the task   405
Was finished, and the banquet all prepared,
They feasted, and there was no guest who lacked
His equal part in that repast. The son
Of Atreus, Agamemnon, brave, and lord
Of wide dominions, gave the chine entire   410
To Ajax as his due. Now when the calls
Of thirst and hunger ceased, the aged chief
Nestor, whose words had ever seemed most wise,
Opened the council with this prudent speech:—
   "Atrides, and ye other chiefs of Greece!   415
Full many a long-haired warrior of our host

Hath perished. Cruel Mars hath spilt their blood
Beside Scamander's gentle stream; their souls
Have gone to Hades. Give thou, then, command
That all the Greeks to-morrow pause from war, 420
And come together at the early dawn,
And bring the dead in chariots drawn by mules
And oxen, and consume them near our fleet
With fire, that we, when we return from war,
May carry to our native land the bones, 425
And give them to the children of the slain.
And then will we go forth and heap from earth,
Upon the plain, a common tomb for all
Around the funeral pile, and build high towers
With speed beside it, which shall be alike 430
A bulwark for our navy and our host.
And let the entrance be a massive gate,
Through which shall pass an ample chariot-way.
And in a circle on its outer edge
Sink we a trench so deep that neither steeds 435
Nor men may pass, if these proud Trojans yet
Should, in the coming battles, press us sore."

   He spake; the princes all approved his words.
Meanwhile, beside the lofty citadel
Of Ilium and at Priam's palace-gates 440
In turbulence and fear the Trojans held
A council, and the wise Antenor spake:—

   "Hearken, ye Trojans, Dardans, and allies,
To what my sober judgment bids me speak.
Send we the Argive Helen back with all 445
Her treasures; let the sons of Atreus lead
The dame away; for now we wage the war
After our faith is broken, and I deem
We cannot prosper till we make amends."

   He spake, and sat him down. The noble chief 450
Paris, the fair-haired Helen's husband, rose
To answer him, and spake this wingèd speech:—

   "Thy words, Antenor, please me not. Thy skill
Could offer better counsels. If those words
Were gravely meant, the gods have made thee mad. 455

But let me here, amid these knights of Troy,
Speak openly my mind. Give up my wife
I never will; but all the wealth I brought
With her from Argos I most willingly
Restore, with added treasures of my own." 460
 He said, and took his seat, and in the midst
Dardanian Priam rose, a counsellor
Of godlike wisdom, and thus sagely spake:—
 "Hear me, ye Trojans, Dardans, and allies!
I speak the thought that rises in my breast. 465
Take now, as ye are wont, your evening meal,
And set a watch and keep upon your guard;
But let Idæus to the hollow ships
Repair at morning, and to Atreus' sons—
To Agamemnon and his brother king— 470
Make known what Paris, author of this strife,
Proposes, and with fairly ordered speech
Ask further if they will consent to pause
From cruel battle till we burn the dead:
Then be the war renewed till fate shall part 475
The hosts and give to one the victory."
 He spake. The assembly listened and obeyed;
All through the camp in groups they took their meal.
But with the morn Idæus visited
The hollow ships, and found the Achaian chiefs, 480
Followers of Mars, in council near the prow
Of Agamemnon's bark; and, standing there,
The loud-voiced herald spake his message thus:—
 "Ye sons of Atreus, and ye other chiefs
Of all the tribes of Greece, I come to you 485
From Priam and the eminent men of Troy,
To say, if it be pleasing to your ears,
What Alexander, author of the war,
Proposes. All the wealth which in his ships
He brought to Troy—would he had perished first!— 490
He will, with added treasures of his own,
Freely restore; but her who was the wife
Of gallant Menelaus he denies
To render back, though all who dwell in Troy

Join to demand it. I am furthermore 495
Bidden to ask if you consent to pause
From cruel battle till we burn our dead:
Then be the war renewed till fate shall part
The hosts and give to one the victory."
   He spake; and all were silent for a space. 500
Then spake at length the valiant Diomed:—
   "Let none consent to take the Trojan's goods,
Nor even Helen; for a child may see
The utter ruin hanging over Troy."
   He spake. The admiring Greeks confirmed with shouts 505
The words of Diomed the knight, and thus
King Agamemnon to Idæus said:—
   "Idæus, thou thyself hast heard the Greeks
Pronounce their answer. What to them seems good
Pleases me also. For the slain, I give 510
Consent to burn them; to the dead we bear
No hatred; when they fall the rite of fire
Should soon be paid. Let Juno's husband, Jove
The Thunderer, bear witness to our truce."
   The monarch spake, and raised to all the gods 515
His sceptre, while Idæus took his way
To hallowed Ilium. There in council sat
Trojans and Dardans, waiting his return.
He came, and standing in the midst declared
His message. Then they all went forth in haste, 520
Some to collect the slain and some to fell
Trees in the forest. From their well-benched ships
The Achaians also issued, some to bring
The dead together, some to gather wood.
   Now from the smooth deep ocean-stream the sun 525
Began to climb the heavens, and with new rays
Smote the surrounding fields. The Trojans met,
But found it hard to know their dead again.
They washed away the clotted blood, and laid—
Shedding hot tears—the bodies on the cars. 530
And since the mighty Priam's word forbade
All wailing, silently they bore away
Their slaughtered friends, and heaped them on the pyre

With aching hearts, and, when they had consumed
The dead with fire, returned to hallowed Troy. 535
The nobly-armed Achaians also heaped
Their slaughtered warriors on the funeral pile
With aching hearts; and when they had consumed
Their dead with fire they sought their hollow ships.
   And ere the morning came, while earth was gray 540
With twilight, by the funeral pile arose
A chosen band of Greeks, who, going forth,
Heaped round it from the earth a common tomb
For all, and built a wall and lofty towers
Near it,—a bulwark for the fleet and host. 545
And in the wall they fitted massive gates,
Through which there passed an ample chariot-way;
And on its outer edge they sank a trench,—
Broad, deep,—and planted it with pointed stakes.
So labored through the night the long-haired Greeks. 550
   The gods who sat beside the Thunderer Jove
Admired the mighty labor of the Greeks;
But Neptune, he who shakes the earth, began:—
   "O Father Jove, henceforth will any one
Of mortal men consult the immortal gods? 555
Seest thou not how the long-haired Greeks have reared
A wall before their navy, and have drawn
A trench around it, yet have brought the gods
No liberal hecatombs? Now will the fame
Of this their work go forth wherever shines 560
The light of day, and men will quite forget
The wall which once we built with toiling hands—
Phœbus Apollo and myself—around
The city of renowned Laomedon."
   And cloud-compelling Jove in wrath replied:— 565
"Earth-shaking power! what words are these? Some god
Of meaner rank and feebler arm than thou
Might haply dread the work the Greeks have planned.
But as for thee, thy glory shall be known
Wherever shines the day; and when at last 570
The crested Greeks, departing in their ships,
Shall seek their native coasts, do thou o'erthrow

The wall they built, and sink it in the deep,
And cover the great shore again with sand.
Thus shall their bulwark vanish from the plain." 575
   So talked they with each other while the sun
Was setting. But the Achaians now had brought
Their labors to an end; they slew their steers
Beside the tents and shared the evening meal,
While many ships had come to land with store 580
Of wine from Lemnos, which Euneus sent,—
Euneus whom Hypsipyle brought forth
To Jason, shepherd of the people. These
Brought wine, a thousand measures, as a gift
To Agamemnon and his brother king, 585
The sons of Atreus. But the long-haired Greeks
Bought for themselves their wines; some gave their brass,
And others shining steel; some bought with hides,
And some with steers, and some with slaves, and thus
Prepared an ample banquet. Through the night 590
Feasted the long-haired Greeks. The Trojan host
And their auxiliar warriors banqueted
Within the city-walls. Through all that night
The Great Disposer, Jove, portended woe
To both with fearful thunderings. All were pale 595
With terror; from their beakers all poured wine
Upon the ground, and no man dared to drink
Who had not paid to Saturn's mighty son
The due libation. Then they laid them down
To rest, and so received the balm of sleep. 600

BOOK VIII

NOW morn in saffron robes had shed her light
O'er all the earth, when Jove the Thunderer
Summoned the gods to council on the heights
Of many-peaked Olympus. He addressed
The assembly, and all listened as he spake:— 5
  "Hear, all ye gods and all ye goddesses!
While I declare the thought within my breast.
Let none of either sex presume to break
The law I give, but cheerfully obey,
That my design may sooner be fulfilled. 10
Whoever, stealing from the rest, shall seek
To aid the Grecian cause, or that of Troy,
Back to Olympus, scourged and in disgrace,
Shall he be brought, or I will seize and hurl
The offender down to rayless Tartarus, 15
Deep, deep in the great gulf below the earth,
With iron gates and threshold forged of brass,
As far beneath the shades as earth from heaven.
Then shall he learn how greatly I surpass
All other gods in power. Try if ye will, 20
Ye gods, that all may know: suspend from heaven
A golden chain; let all the immortal host
Cling to it from below: ye could not draw,
Strive as ye might, the all-disposing Jove
From heaven to earth. And yet, if I should choose 25
To draw it upward to me, I should lift,

With it and you, the earth itself and sea
Together, and I then would bind the chain
Around the summit of the Olympian mount,
And they should hang aloft. So far my power   30
Surpasses all the power of gods and men."
　　He spake; and all the great assembly, hushed
In silence, wondered at his threatening words,
Until at length the blue-eyed Pallas said:—
　　"Our Father, son of Saturn, mightiest   35
Among the potentates, we know thy power
Is not to be withstood, yet are we moved
With pity for the warlike Greeks, who bear
An evil fate and waste away in war.
If such be thy command, we shall refrain   40
From mingling in the combat, yet will aid
The Greeks with counsel which may be their guide,
Lest by thy wrath they perish utterly."
　　The Cloud-compeller Jove replied, and smiled:—
"Tritonia, daughter dear, be comforted.   45
I spake not in the anger of my heart,
And I have naught but kind intents for thee."
　　He spake, and to his chariot yoked the steeds,
Fleet, brazen-footed, and with flowing manes
Of gold, and put his golden armor on,   50
And took the golden scourge, divinely wrought,
And, mounting, touched the coursers with the lash
To urge them onward. Not unwillingly
Flew they between the earth and starry heaven,
Until he came to Ida, moist with springs   55
And nurse of savage beasts, and to the height
Of Gargarus, where lay his sacred field,
And where his fragrant altar fumed. He checked
Their course, and there the Father of the gods
And men released them from the yoke and caused   60
A cloud to gather round them. Then he sat,
Exulting in the fulness of his might,
Upon the summit, whence his eye beheld
The towers of Ilium and the ships of Greece.
　　Now in their tents the long-haired Greeks had shared 65

A hasty meal, and girded on their arms.
The Trojans, also, in their city armed
Themselves for war, as eager for the fight,
Though fewer; for a hard necessity
Forced them to combat for their little ones   70
And wives. They set the city-portals wide,
And forth the people issued, foot and horse
Together, and a mighty din arose.
And now, when host met host, their shields and spears
Were mingled in disorder; men of might   75
Encountered, cased in mail, and bucklers clashed
Their bosses; loud the clamor: cries of pain
And boastful shouts arose from those who fell
And those who slew, and earth was drenched with blood.
   While yet 'twas morning, and the holy light   80
Of day grew bright, the men of both the hosts
Were smitten and were slain; but when the sun
Stood high in middle heaven, the All-Father took
His golden scales, and in them laid the fates
Which bring the sleep of death,—the fate of those   85
Who tamed the Trojan steeds, and those who warred
For Greece in brazen armor. By the midst
He held the balance, and, behold, the fate
Of Greece in that day's fight sank down until
It touched the nourishing earth, while that of Troy   90
Rose and flew upward toward the spacious heaven.
With that the Godhead thundered terribly
From Ida's height, and sent his lightnings down
Among the Achaian army. They beheld
In mute amazement and grew pale with fear.   95
   Then neither dared Idomeneus remain,
Nor Agamemnon, on the ground, nor stayed
The chieftains Ajax, ministers of Mars.
Gerenian Nestor, guardian of the Greeks,
Alone was left behind, and he remained   100
Unwillingly. A steed of those that drew
His car was sorely wounded by a shaft
Which Alexander, fair-haired Helen's spouse,
Sent from his bow. It pierced the forehead where

The mane begins, and where a wound is death. 105
The arrow pierced him to the brain; he reared
And whirled in torture with the wound, and scared
His fellow-coursers. While the aged man
Hastened to sever with his sword the thongs
That bound him to the car, the rapid steeds 110
Of Hector bore their valiant master on
With the pursuing crowd. The aged chief
Had perished then, if gallant Diomed
Had not perceived his plight. He lifted up
His voice, and, shouting to Ulysses, said:— 115
  "High-born Ulysses, man of subtle shifts,
Son of Laertes, whither dost thou flee?
Why like a coward turn thy back? Beware,
Lest there some weapon smite thee. Stay and guard
This aged warrior from his furious foe." 120
  So spake he; but the much-enduring man,
Ulysses, heard not the reproof, and passed
Rapidly toward the hollow ships of Greece.
Tydides, single-handed, made his way
Among the foremost warriors, till he stood 125
Before the horses of the aged son
Of Neleus, and in wingèd accents said:—
  "The younger warriors press thee sore, old chief!
Thy strength gives way; the weariness of age
Is on thee; thy attendant is not strong; 130
Thy steeds are slow. Mount, then, my car, and see
What Trojan horses are; how rapidly
They turn to right and left, and chase and flee.
I took them from the terror of the field,
Æneas. To our servants leave thine own, 135
While we with these assault the Trojan knights,
And teach even Hector that the spear I wield
Can make as furious havoc as his own."
  He spake; and Nestor, the Gerenian knight,
Complied. The two attendants, valiant men,— 140
Sthenelus and the good Eurymedon,—
Took charge of Nestor's steeds. The chieftains climbed
The car of Diomed, and Nestor took

Into his hand the embroidered reins and lashed
The horses with the scourge. They quickly came 145
To Hector. As the Trojan hastened on,
The son of Tydeus hurled a spear; it missed,
But spared not Eniopeus, him who held
The reins, the hero's charioteer, and son
Of brave Thebæus. In the breast between 150
The paps it smote him; from the car he fell,
And the swift horses started back; his soul
And strength passed from him. Hector bitterly
Grieved for his death, yet left him where he fell,
And sought another fitting charioteer. 155
Nor had the fiery coursers long to wait
A guide, for valiant Archeptolemus,
The son of Iphitus, was near at hand.
And him he caused to mount the chariot drawn
By his fleet steeds, and gave his hand the reins. 160
  Then great had been the slaughter; fearful deeds
Had then been done; the Trojans had been scared
Into their town like lambs into the fold,—
Had not the Father of the immortal gods
And mortal men beheld, and from on high 165
Terribly thundered, sending to the earth
A bolt of fire. He flung it down before
The car of Diomed; and fiercely glared
The blazing sulphur; both the frightened steeds
Cowered trembling by the chariot. Nestor's hand 170
Let fall the embroidered reins; his spirit sank
With fear, and thus he said to Diomed:—
  "Tydides, turn thy firm-paced steeds, and flee.
Dost thou not see that victory from Jove
Attends thee not? To-day doth Saturn's son 175
Award the glory to the Trojan chief.
Hereafter he will make it ours, if such
Be his good pleasure. No man, though he be
The mightiest among men, can thwart the will
Of Jupiter, with whom abides all power." 180
  The great in battle, Diomed, replied;—
"Truly, O ancient man, thou speakest well;

But this it is that grieves me to the heart,—
That Hector to the Trojan host will say,
'I put to flight Tydides, and he sought 185
Shelter among his ships.' Thus will he boast
Hereafter; may earth open then for me!"
    And Nestor, the Gerenian knight, rejoined:—
"What, son of warlike Tydeus, hast thou said?
Though Hector call thee faint of heart, and weak 190
The Trojans and Dardanians, and the wives
Of the stout-hearted Trojans armed with shields,
Whose husbands in their youthful prime thy hand
Hath laid in dust, will not believe his words."
    Thus having said, he turned the firm-paced steeds 195
Rearward, and mingled with the flying crowd.
And now the Trojans and their leader gave
A mighty cry, and poured on them a storm
Of deadly darts, and crested Hector raised
His thundering voice and shouted after them:— 200
    "O son of Tydeus! the swift-riding Greeks
Have honored thee beyond all other men,
At banquets, with high place and delicate meats
And flowing cups. They will despise thee now,
For thou art like a woman. Timorous girl! 205
Take thyself hence, and never think that I
Shall yield to thee, that thou may'st climb our towers
And bear away our women in thy ships;
For I shall give thee first the doom of death."
    He spake; and Diomed, in doubtful mood, 210
Questioned his spirit whether he should turn
His steeds and fight with Hector. Thrice the thought
Arose within his mind, and thrice on high
Uttered the all-forecasting Jupiter
His thunder from the Idæan mount, a sign 215
Of victory changing to the Trojan side.
Then Hector to the Trojans called aloud:—
    "Trojans and Lycians all, and ye who close
In deadly fight, the sons of Dardanus!
Acquit yourselves like men, my friends; recall 220
Your fiery valor now, for I perceive

The son of Saturn doth award to me
Victory and vast renown, and to the Greeks
Destruction. Fools! who built this slender wall   225
Which we contemn, which cannot stand before
The strength I bring; our steeds can overleap
The trench they digged. When I shall reach their fleet,
Remember the consuming power of fire,
That I may give their vessels to the flames,
And hew the Achaians down beside their prows,   230
While they are wrapped in the bewildering smoke."
   He spake; and then he cheered his coursers thus:—
"Xanthus, Podargus, Lampus nobly-bred,
And Æthon, now repay the generous care,
The pleasant grain which my Andromache,   235
Daughter of great Eëtion, largely gives.
She mingles wine that ye may drink at will
Ere yet she ministers to me, who boast
To be her youthful husband. Let us now
Pursue with fiery haste, that we may seize   240
The shield of Nestor, the great fame of which
Has reached to heaven,—an orb of massive gold
Even to the handles. Let us from the limbs
Of Diomed, the tamer of fleet steeds,
Strip off the glorious mail that Vulcan forged: 245
This done, our hope may be that all the Greeks
Will climb their galleys and depart to-night."
   So boasted he; but queenly Juno's ire
Was kindled, and she shuddered on her throne
Till great Olympus trembled. Thus she spake   250
To Neptune, mighty ruler of the deep:—
   "Earth-shaker! thou who rulest far and wide!
Is there no pity for the perishing Greeks
Within that breast of thine? They bring to thee
At Helicè and Ægæ costly gifts   255
And many, wherefore thy desire should be
That they may win the victory. If the gods
Who favor the Achaians should combine
To drive the Trojans back, and hold in check
High-thundering Jupiter, the God would sit   260

In sullen grief on Ida's top alone."
    Earth-shaking Neptune answered in disdain:—
"O Juno, rash in speech! what words are these?
Think not that I can wish to join the gods
In conflict with the monarch Jupiter,   265
The son of Saturn, mightier than we all."
    So held they colloquy. Meanwhile the space
Betwixt the galleys and the trench and wall
Was crowded close with steeds and shielded men;
For Hector, son of Priam, terrible   270
As Mars the lightning-footed, drave them on
Before him. Jove decreed him such renown.
And now would he have given that noble fleet
To the consuming flame, if Juno, queen
Of heaven, had not beheld, and moved the heart   275
Of Agamemnon to exhort the Greeks
That they should turn and combat. With quick steps
He passed beside the fleet, among the tents,
Bearing in his strong hand his purple robe,
And climbed the huge black galley which had brought   280
Ulysses to the war,—for in the midst
It lay, and thence the king might send his voice
To either side, as far as to the tents
Of Ajax and Achilles, who had moored
Their galleys at the different extremes   285
Of the long camp, confiding in their might
Of arm and their own valor. Thence he called,
With loud, clear utterance, to the Achaian host:—
    "O Greeks! shame on ye! cravens who excel
In form alone! Where now are all the boasts   290
Of your invincible valor,—the vain words
Ye uttered pompously when at the feast
In Lemnos sitting ye devoured the flesh
Of hornèd beeves, and drank from bowls of wine,
Flower-crowned, and bragged that each of you would be   295
A match for fivescore Trojans, or for twice
Fivescore? And now we all are not a match
For Hector singly, who will give our fleet
Soon to consuming flames. O Father Jove,

Was ever mighty monarch visited
By thee with such affliction, or so robbed
Of high renown! And yet in my good ship,
Bound to this luckless coast, I never passed
By thy fair altars that I did not burn
The fat and thighs of oxen, with a prayer
That I might sack the well-defended Troy.
Now be at least one wish of mine fulfilled,—
That we may yet escape and get us hence;
Nor let the Trojans thus destroy the Greeks."
   He spake, and wept. The All-Father, pitying him,
Consented that his people should escape
The threatened ruin. Instantly he sent
His eagle, bird of surest augury,
Which, bearing in his talons a young fawn,
The offspring of a nimble-footed roe,
Dropped it at the fair altar where the Greeks
Paid sacrifice to Panomphæan Jove.
   And they, when they beheld, and knew that Jove
Had sent the bird, took courage, rallying,
And rushed against the Trojans. Then no chief
Of all the Greeks—though many they—could boast
That he before Tydides urged his steeds
To sudden speed and drave them o'er the trench,
And mingled in the combat. First of all
He struck down Agelaus, Phradmon's son,
Armed as he was, who turned his car to fly,
And as he turned, Tydides with his spear
Transfixed his back between the shoulder-blades,
And drave the weapon through his breast. He fell
To earth, his armor clashing with his fall.
Then Agamemnon followed, and with him
His brother Menelaus; after these
The chieftains Ajax, fearful in their strength;
Idomeneus, and he who bore his arms,—
Meriones, like Mars in battle-field;
Eurypylus, Evæmon's glorious son;
And ninthly Teucer came, who bent his bow
Beneath the shield of Ajax Telamon,—

For Ajax moved his shield from side to side,
And thence the archer looked abroad, and aimed 340
His arrows thence. Whoever in the throng
Was struck fell lifeless. Teucer all the while,
As hides a child behind his mother's robe,
Sheltered himself by Ajax, whose great shield
Concealed the chief from sight. What Trojan first 345
Did faithful Teucer slay? Orsilochus,
Dætor, and Ophelestes, Ormenus,
Chromius, and Lycophontes nobly born,
And Hamopaon, Polyæmon's son,
And Melanippus,—one by one the shafts 350
Of Teucer stretched them on their mother earth.
Then Agamemnon, king of men, rejoiced
As he beheld him, with his sturdy bow,
Breaking the serried phalanxes of Troy;
And came, and, standing near, bespake him thus:— 355
  "Beloved Teucer! son of Telamon,
Prince of the people! ever be thy shafts
Aimed thus, and thou shalt be the light and pride
Of Greece, and of thy father Telamon,
Who reared thee from a little child with care 360
In his own halls, though spurious was thy birth.
Go on to do him honor, though he now
Be far away. And here I say to thee,—
And I will keep my word,—if Jupiter
The ægis-bearer and Minerva deign 365
To let me level the strong walls of Troy,
To thee will I assign the noblest prize
After my own,—a tripod, or two steeds
And chariot, or a wife to share thy bed."
  And thus the blameless Teucer made reply:— 370
"Why, glorious son of Atreus, wouldst thou thus
Admonish me, while yet I do my best,
And pause not in the combat? From the time
When we began to drive the enemy back
To Ilium, I have smitten and have slain 375
Their warriors with my bow. Eight barbed shafts
I sent, and each has pierced some warlike youth;

But this fierce wolf-dog have I failed to strike."
    He spake, and sent another arrow forth
At Hector with an eager aim. It missed 380
Its mark, but struck Gorgythion down, the brave
And blameless son of Priam; through his breast
The arrow went. Fair Castianira brought
The warrior forth,—a dame from Æsyma,
Beautiful as a goddess. As within 385
A garden droops a poppy to the ground,
Bowed by its weight and by the rains of spring,
So drooped his head within the heavy casque.
    Again did Teucer send another shaft
At Hector, eager still to smite. It missed 390
Its aim again, for Phœbus turned aside
The arrow, but it struck the charioteer
Of Hector, Archeptolemus the brave,
When rushing to the fight, and pierced his breast
Close to the nipple; from the car he fell, 395
The swift steeds started back, and from his limbs
The life and strength departed. A deep grief
For his slain charioteer came darkly o'er
The mind of Hector, yet, though sorrowing,
He left him where he fell, and straightway called 400
Cebriones, his brother, who was near,
To mount and take the reins. Cebriones
Heard and obeyed. Then from the shining car
Leaped Hector with a mighty cry, and seized
A ponderous stone, and, bent to crush him, ran 405
At Teucer, who had from his quiver drawn
One of his sharpest arrows, placing it
Upon the bowstring. As he drew the bow,
The strong-armed Hector hurled the jagged stone,
And smote him near the shoulder, where the neck 410
And breast are sundered by the collar-bone,—
A fatal spot. The bowstring brake; the arm
Fell nerveless; on his knees the archer sank,
And dropped the bow. Then did not Ajax leave
His fallen brother to the foe, but walked 415
Around him, sheltering him beneath his shield,

Till two dear friends of his—Menestheus, son
Of Echius, and Alastor nobly born—
Approached, and took him up and carried him,
Heavily groaning, to the hollow ships. 420
   Then did Olympian Jove again inspire
The Trojan host with valor, and they drave
The Achaians backward to the yawning trench.
Then Hector came, with fury in his eyes,
Among the foremost warriors. As a hound, 425
Sure of his own swift feet, attacks behind
The lion or wild boar, and tears his flank,
Yet warily observes him as he turns,
So Hector followed close the long-haired Greeks,
And ever slew the hindmost as they fled. 430
Yet now, when they in flight had crossed again
The trench and palisades, and many a one
Had died by Trojan hands, they made a halt
Before their ships, and bade each other stand,
And lifted up their hands and prayed aloud 435
To all the gods; while Hector, urging on
His long-maned steeds, and with stern eyes that seemed
The eyes of Gorgon or of murderous Mars,
Hither and thither swept across the field.
   The white-armed Juno saw, and, sorrowing, 440
Addressed Minerva with these wingèd words:—
   "Ah me! thou daughter of the God who bears
The ægis, shall we not descend to aid
The perishing Greeks in their extremity?
A cruel doom is theirs, to fall, destroyed 445
By one man's rage,—the terrible assault
Of Hector, son of Priam, who has made
Insufferable havoc in the field."
   And thus in turn the blue-eyed Pallas spake:—
"That warrior long ere this had lost his life, 450
Slain by the Greeks on his paternal soil,
But that my father's mind is warped by wrath.
Unjust to me and harsh, he thwarts my aims,
Forgetting all I did for Hercules,
His son,—how often, when Eurystheus set 455

A task too hard for him, I saved his life.
To heaven he raised his eyes and wept, and Jove
Despatched me instantly to succor him.
And yet if I, in my forecasting mind,
Had known all this when he was bid to bring 460
From strong-walled Erebus the dog of hell,
He had not safely crossed the gulf of Styx.
But now Jove hates me; now he grants the wish
Of Thetis, who hath kissed his knees and touched
His beard caressingly, and prayed that he 465
Would crown the overthrower of walled towns,
Achilles, with great honor. Well, the time
Will come when he shall call me yet again
His dear Minerva. Hasten now to yoke
For us thy firm-paced steeds, while in the halls 470
Of ægis-bearing Jupiter I brace
My armor on for war,—and I shall see
If Hector of the beamy helm, the son
Of Priam, will rejoice when we appear
Upon the field again. Assuredly 475
The men of Troy shall die, to feast the birds
Of prey and dogs beside the Grecian fleet."

   She ended, and the white-armed deity
Juno obeyed her. Juno the august,
The mighty Saturn's daughter, hastily 480
Caparisoned the golden-bitted steeds.
Meanwhile, Minerva on the palace-floor
Of Jupiter let drop the gorgeous robe
Of many hues, which her own hands had wrought,
And, putting on the Cloud-compeller's mail, 485
Stood armed for cruel war. And then she climbed
The glorious car, and took in hand the spear—
Huge, heavy, strong—with which she overthrows
The serried phalanxes of valiant men
Whene'er this daughter of the Almighty One 490
Is angered. Juno bore the lash, and urged
The coursers to their speed. The gates of heaven
Opened before them of their own accord,—
Gates guarded by the Hours, on whom the care

Of the great heaven and of Olympus rests, 495
To open or to close the wall of cloud.
Through these they guided their impatient steeds.
   From Ida Jupiter beheld, in wrath,
And summoned Iris of the golden wings,
And bade her do this errand: "Speed thee hence, 500
Fleet Iris! turn them back; allow them not
Thus to defy me: it is not for them
To engage with me in war. I give my word,—
Nor shall it lack fulfilment,—I will make
The swift steeds lame that draw their car, and hurl 505
The riders down, and dash the car itself
To fragments. Ten long years shall wear away
Before they cease to suffer from the wounds
Made by the thunderbolt. Minerva thus
May learn the fate of those who strive with Jove. 510
With Juno I am less displeased, for she
Is ever bent to thwart my purposes."
   He spake; and Iris, with the tempest's speed
Departing, bore the message from the heights
Of Ida to the great Olympus, where, 515
Among the foremost passes of the mount,
All seamed with hollow vales, she met and stayed
The pair, delivering thus the word of Jove:—
   "Now whither haste ye? What strange madness fires
Your breasts? The son of Saturn suffers not 520
That ye befriend the Greeks. He threatens thus,—
And will fulfil his threat,—that he will make
The coursers lame that draw your car, and hurl
The riders down, and dash the car itself
To fragments, and that ten long years must pass 525
Ere ye shall cease to suffer from the wounds
Made by the thunderbolt. So shalt thou learn,
O Pallas! what it is to strive with Jove.
With Juno is he less displeased, for she
Is ever bent to thwart his purposes; 530
But thou, he says, art guilty above all,
And shameless as a hound, if thou dare lift
Thy massive spear against thy father Jove."

So spake fleet-footed Iris, and withdrew;
And thus again to Pallas Juno said:—   535
"Child of the Ægis-bearer! let us strive
With Jove no longer for the sake of men,
But let one perish and another live,
As chance may rule the hour, and let the God,
Communing with his secret mind, mete out   540
To Greeks and Trojans their just destiny."
 She spake, and turned the firm-paced coursers back,
The coursers with fair-flowing manes. The Hours
Unyoked them, bound them to the ambrosial stalls,
And leaned against the shining walls the car;   545
While Juno and Minerva went among
The other deities and took their place
Upon their golden seats, though sad at heart.
Then with his steeds, and in his bright-wheeled car,
Came Jove from Ida to the dwelling-place   550
Of gods upon Olympus. There did he
Who shakes the islands loose the steeds and bring
The chariot to its place, and o'er it spread
Its covering of lawn. The Thunderer
Seated himself upon his golden throne,   555
The great Olympus trembling as he stepped;
While Juno and Minerva sat apart
Together, nor saluted him, nor asked
Of aught; but he perceived their thoughts and said:—
 "Juno and Pallas! why so sad? Not long   560
Ye toiled in glorious battle to destroy
The Trojans, whom ye hold in bitter hate:
This strength of mine, and this invincible arm
Not all the gods upon the Olympian mount
Can turn to flight, while your fair limbs were seized   565
With trembling ere ye entered on the shock
And havoc of the war. Now let me say—
And well the event would have fulfilled my words—
That, smitten with the thunder from my hand,
Your chariots never would have brought you back   570
To this Olympus and the abode of gods."
 He spake; while Pallas and the queen of heaven

Repined with close-pressed lips, and in their hearts
Devised new mischiefs for the Trojan race.
Silent Minerva sat, nor dared express 575
The anger that she bore her father Jove;
But Juno could not curb her wrath, and spake:—
    "What words, austere Saturnius, hast thou said?
Thou art, we know, invincible in might;
Yet must we sorrow for the heroic Greeks, 580
Who, by a cruel fate, are perishing.
We stand aloof from war, if thou require;
Yet would we counsel the Achaian host,
Lest by thy wrath they perish utterly."
    And then the Cloud-compeller, answering, said:— 585
"O Juno, large-eyed and august, if thou
Look forth to-morrow, thou shalt then behold
The all-powerful son of Saturn laying waste
With greater havoc still the mighty host
Of warlike Greeks. For Hector, great in war, 590
Shall pause not from the conflict, till he rouse
The swift-paced son of Peleus at the ships,
When, pent in narrow space, the armies fight
For slain Patroclus: such the will of fate.
As for thyself, I little heed thy rage: 595
Not even shouldst thou wander to the realm
Where earth and ocean end, where Saturn sits
Beside Iapetus, and neither light
Of overgoing suns nor breath of wind
Refreshes them, but gulfs of Tartarus 600
Surround them,—shouldst thou even thither bend
Thy way, I shall not heed thy rage, who art
Beyond all others shamelessly perverse."
    He ceased; but white-armed Juno answered not.
And now into the sea the sun's bright light 605
Went down, and o'er the foodful earth was drawn
Night's shadow. Most unwillingly the sons
Of Troy beheld the sunset. To the Greeks
Eagerly wished the welcome darkness came.
    Then from the fleet illustrious Hector led 610
The Trojans, and beside the eddying stream,

In a clear space uncumbered by the slain,
Held council. There, alighting from their cars,
They listened to the words that Hector spake,—
Hector, beloved of Jove. He held a spear, 615
In length eleven cubits, with a blade
Of glittering brass, bound with a ring of gold.
On this he leaned, and spake these wingèd words:—
    "Hear me, ye Trojans, Dardans, and allies.
But now I thought that, having first destroyed 620
The Achaian host and fleet, we should return
This night to wind-swept Ilium. To their aid
The darkness comes, and saves the Greeks, and saves
Their galleys ranged along the ocean-side.
Obey we, then, the dark-browed night; prepare 625
Our meal; unyoke the steeds with flowing manes,
And set their food before them. Bring at once
Oxen and fatlings of the flock from town,
And from your dwellings bread and pleasant wine.
And let us gather store of wood, to feed 630
A multitude of blazing fires all night,
Till Morning, daughter of the Dawn, appear,—
Fires that shall light the sky, lest in the hours
Of darkness with their ships the long-haired Greeks
Attempt escape across the mighty deep. 635
And, that they may not climb their decks unharmed,
Let every foeman bear a wound to cure
At home,—an arrow-wound or gash of spear,
Given as he leaps on board. So other foes
Shall dread a conflict with the knights of Troy. 640
And let the heralds, dear to Jove, command
That all grown youths and hoary-headed men
Keep watch about the city in the towers
Built by the gods; and let the feebler sex
Kindle large fires upon their hearths at home; 645
And let the guard be strengthened, lest the foe
Should steal into the city while its sons
Are all abroad. Thus let it be till morn,
Brave Trojans! I but speak of what the time
Requires, and on the morrow I shall speak 650

Of what the Trojan knights have then to do.
My prayer to Jove and to the other gods,
And my hope is, that I may drive away
These curs, brought hither by an evil fate
In their black ships. All night will we keep watch,   655
And, arming, with the early morn renew
The desperate conflict at the hollow ships.
Then shall I see if valiant Diomed
Tydides has the power to make me leave
The Grecian galleys for the city-walls,   660
Or whether I shall slay him with my spear
And take his bloody spoils. To-morrow's sun
Will make his valor known, if he withstand
The assault of this my weapon. Yet I think
The sunrise will behold him slain among   665
The first, with many comrades lying round.
Would that I knew myself as certainly
Secure from death and the decays of age,
And to be held in honor like the gods
Apollo and Minerva, as I know   670
This day will bring misfortune to the Greeks!"

  So Hector spake, and all the Trojan host
Applauded; from the yoke forthwith they loosed
The sweaty steeds, and bound them to the cars
With halters; to the town they sent in haste   675
For oxen and the fatlings of the flock,
And to their homes for bread and pleasant wine,
And gathered fuel in large store. The winds
Bore up the fragrant fumes from earth to heaven.

  So, high in hope, they sat the whole night through   680
In warlike lines, and many watch-fires blazed.
As when in heaven the stars look brightly forth
Round the clear-shining moon, while not a breeze
Stirs in the depths of air, and all the stars
Are seen, and gladness fills the shepherd's heart,   685
So many fires in sight of Ilium blazed,
Lit by the sons of Troy, between the ships
And eddying Xanthus: on the plain there shone
A thousand; fifty warriors by each fire

Sat in its light. Their steeds beside the cars— 690
Champing their oats and their white barley—stood,
And waited for the golden morn to rise.

BOOK IX

THE Trojans thus kept watch; while through the night
The power of Flight, companion of cold Fear,
Wrought on the Greeks, and all their bravest men
Were bowed beneath a sorrow hard to bear.
As when two winds upturn the fishy deep,— 5
The north wind and the west, that suddenly
Blow from the Thracian coast; the black waves rise
At once, and fling the sea-weed to the shore,—
Thus were the Achaians troubled in their hearts.
   Atrides, deeply grieving, walked the camp, 10
And bade the clear-voiced heralds call by name
To council all the chiefs, but not aloud.
The king himself among the foremost gave
The summons. Sadly that assembly took
Their seats; and Agamemnon in the midst 15
Rose, shedding tears,—as down a lofty rock,
Darkening its face, a fountain's waters flow,—
And, deeply sighing, thus addressed the Greeks:—
   "O friends! the chiefs and princes of the Greeks!
Saturnian Jove hath in an evil snare 20
Most cruelly entangled me. He gave
His promise once that I should overthrow
This strong-walled Ilium, and return; but now
He meditates a fraud, and sends me back
To Argos without glory, and with loss 25
Of many warriors. Thus doth it seem good

Doubtless to Jove Almighty, who hath cast
The towers of many a city down to earth,
And will cast others down,—his might excels
All other might. But let us now obey, 30
As I shall counsel you, and in our ships
Haste to our own dear country; for I see
That Troy with its broad streets can ne'er be ours."
   He spake; and all were silent. Silent long
Remained the sorrow-stricken sons of Greece, 35
Till Diomed, the brave in battle, spake:—
   "First of the chiefs I speak, to disapprove,
Atrides, thy rash purpose: 'tis my right
In council; nor, O king, be thou displeased.
Thou first among the Greeks hast taunted me 40
With lack of valor, calling me unapt
For war and weak of arm. The young and old
Have heard the taunt. One of two gifts the son
Of wily Saturn hath bestowed on thee:
High rank and rule o'er all the rest he gave, 45
But gave thee not the nobler quality
Of fortitude. Dost thou then truly deem
The Greeks unapt for war and weak of arm,
As thou hast said? Thou longest to return:
Go, then; the way is open; by the sea 50
The barks that brought thee from Mycenæ lie,
A numerous fleet. Yet others will remain—
Long-haired Achaians—till we overthrow
The city. Should they also pine for home,
Then let them flee, with all their ships; while I 55
With Sthenelus fight on until we make
An end of Troy,—for with the gods we came."
   He spake. The Greeks applauded; all admired
The words of the horse-tamer Diomed.
Nestor the knight then rose, and thus he spake:— 60
   "O son of Tydeus, eminently brave
Art thou among thy comrades in the field,
And great in council. No one here condemns
The sentence thou hast given; among the Greeks
Is no one who denies what thou hast said; 65

Yet hast thou not said all. Thy years are few,—
So few, thou mightest be my youngest son;
And yet thou speakest wisely to the kings
Of Greece, and thy discourse is just and right.
Now I, who boast of far more years than thou, 70
Will speak of this that yet remains, and none—
Not even Agamemnon—will gainsay
What I advise. A wretch without a tie
Of kin, a lawless man without a home,
Is he who takes delight in civil strifes. 75
But let us now give way to the dark night,
And make our banquets ready. Let the guards
Lie down within the trenches which we digged
Without the wall: be this the young men's charge.
And thou, Atrides, do thou now begin, 80
Who art supreme, and make a feast for all
The elder chiefs; it shall become thee well:
Thy tents are full of wine, which ships from Thrace
Bring every day across the mighty deep,
And thou hast all things ready, and a host 85
Of menials. Then, when many throng the board,
Thou shalt defer to him who counsels thee
Most wisely; for the Greeks have urgent need
Of prudent counsels, when the foe so close
Beside our galleys lights his multitude 90
Of watch-fires. Who that sees them can rejoice?
This night will rescue or destroy our host."
   He spake. They listened all, and willingly
Obeyed him. Forth in armor went the guards,
Led by the chieftain Thrasymedes, son 95
Of Nestor, by Ascalaphus, who claimed
His birth from Mars, and by Ialmenus
His brother, and Deïpyrus, with whom
There followed Aphareus, Meriones,
And Lycomedes, Creon's noble son. 100
Seven were the leaders of the guards; with each
A hundred youths in warlike order marched,
Bearing long spears; and when they reached the space
Between the trench and wall they sat them down,

And kindled fires and made their evening meal.   105
   Atrides brought the assembled elder chiefs
To his pavilion, and before them set
A generous banquet. They put forth their hands
And shared the feast; and when the calls of thirst
And hunger ceased, the aged Nestor first   110
Began to counsel them; the chief, whose words
Had lately seemed of wisest import, now
Addressed the assembly with well-ordered speech:—
   "Atrides Agamemnon, glorious king!
What I shall say begins and ends with thee,   115
For thou dost rule o'er many nations. Jove
Hath given to thee the sceptre, and the power
To make their laws, that thou may'st seek their good.
Thou, therefore, of all men, shouldst speak and hear
In council, and shouldst follow willingly   120
Another's judgment when it best promotes
The general weal; for all depends on thee.
Now let me say what seems to me most wise;
For better counsel none can give than this
Which now I meditate, and which to give   125
I purposed from the hour when thou, great king,
Didst bear the maid Briseis from the tent
Of the enraged Achilles, unapproved
By me, who strove to change thy rash design.
Then didst thou yield thee to thy haughty will,   130
And didst dishonor a most valiant man,
Whom the immortals honor. Thou didst take
And still dost keep the prize he fairly won.
Let it be now our study to appease
The hero with large gifts and soothing words."   135
   Then Agamemnon, king of men, replied:—
"O ancient man, most truly hast thou named
My faults. I erred, and I deny it not.
That man indeed is equal to a host
Whom Jupiter doth love and honor thus,   140
Humbling the Achaian people for his sake.
And now, since, yielding to my wayward mood,
I erred, let me appease him, if I may,

With gifts of priceless worth. Before you all
I number them,—seven tripods which the fire 145
Hath never touched, six talents of pure gold,
And twenty shining caldrons, and twelve steeds
Of hardy frame, victorious in the race,
Whose feet have won me prizes in the games.
No beggar would he be, nor yet with store 150
Of gold unfurnished, in whose coffers lay
The prizes those swift steeds have brought to me.
Seven faultless women, skilled in household arts,
I give moreover,—Lesbians, whom I chose
When he o'erran the populous Lesbian isle,— 155
Damsels in beauty who excel their sex.
These I bestow, and with them I will send
Her whom I took away,—Briseis, pure—
I swear it with a mighty oath—as pure
As when she left his tent. All these I give 160
At once; and if by favor of the gods
We lay the mighty city of Priam waste,
He shall load down his galley with large store
Of gold and silver, entering first when we,
The Greeks, divide the spoil. Then may he choose 165
Twice ten young Trojan women, beautiful
Beyond their sex save Helen. If we come
Safe to Achaian Argos, richly stocked
With milky kine, he may become to me
A son-in-law, and cherished equally 170
With my sole son Orestes, who is reared
Most royally. Three daughters there within
My stately palace-walls,—Chrysothemis,
Laodice, and Iphianassa,—dwell,
And he may choose among them, and may lead 175
Home to the house of Peleus her who best
Deserves his love. Nor need he to endow
The bride, for I will give an ampler dower
Than ever father to his daughter gave,—
Seven cities with thronged streets,—Cardamyle, 180
Enope, grassy Hira, Pheræ famed
Afar, Antheia with rich pasture-fields,

Æpeia beautiful, and Pedasus
With all its vineyards; all are near the sea,
And stand the last before you reach the coast 185
Of sandy Pylos. Rich in flocks and herds
Their dwellers are, and they will honor him
As if he were a god, and, ruled by him,
Will pay large tribute. These will I bestow,
Let but his anger cool and his resolve 190
Give way. 'Tis Pluto who is deaf to prayer
And ne'er relents, and he, of all the gods,
Most hateful is to men. Now let the son
Of Peleus yield at length to me, who stand
Above him in authority and years." 195
   Then answered Nestor the Gerenian knight:—
"Atrides Agamemnon! glorious king!
Gifts not to be contemned thou offerest
To Prince Achilles. Let us now despatch
A chosen embassy, who shall proceed 200
At once to where Pelides holds his tent.
I name the men; and cheerfully will they
Perform the duty: Phœnix, dear to Jove,
Shall be their leader, mighty Ajax next,
And then high-born Ulysses; heralds twain 205
Shall follow,—Hodius and Eurybates.
And now be water brought to cleanse our hands,
And charge be given that no ill-omened word
Be uttered, while we pray that Jupiter,
The son of Saturn, will assist our need." 210
   He spake; and all approved the words he said.
Then poured the heralds water on the hands
Of those who sat. The young men crowned with wine
The goblets, and in seemly order passed
The brimming cups, distributing to each. 215
Part to the gods they poured, and next they drank
As each might choose, and then the embassy
Hastened from Agamemnon's tent. To each
Gerenian Nestor spake in turn, and fixed
His eyes on each intently,—most of all 220
Upon Ulysses,—and with many a charge

To turn Pelides from his angry mood.
Along the edge of the resounding deep
They went, and as they walked they offered prayer
To earth-embracing Neptune, that their words   225
Might move the great soul of Æacides.
And now they came where lay the Myrmidons
Among their tents and ships. Achilles there
Drew solace from the music of a harp
Sweet-toned and shapely, in a silver frame,   230
Part of the spoil he took when he o'erthrew
Eëtion's town. To soothe his mood he sang
The deeds of heroes. By him sat alone
Patroclus, silent till the song should cease.
On moved the messengers,—before them walked   235
High-born Ulysses,—till they stood beside
Achilles. He beheld, and with the harp
Sprang from his seat, surprised. Patroclus saw
The heroes also, and arose. Their hands
The swift Achilles took in his, and said:—   240
  "Welcome! Ye come as friends. Some pressing cause
Must surely bring you hither, whom I prize,
Wronged as I am, beyond all other Greeks."
  Thus speaking, the great son of Peleus led
His guests still farther on, and seated them   245
On couches spread with purple coverings,
And thus addressed Patroclus, who was near:—
  "Son of Menœtius, bring a larger vase,
And mingle purer wine, and place a cup
For each, since these are most beloved friends,—   250
These warriors who now sit beneath my roof."
  He spake. Patroclus hearkened, and obeyed
His well-beloved friend, who meantime placed
A block beside the fire, and on it laid
Chines of a sheep and of a fatling goat,   255
And of a sow, the fattest of her kind.
Automedon stood by and held them fast;
Achilles took the knife and skilfully
Carved them in portions, and transfixed the parts
With spits. Patroclus, the divine in form,   260

Woke to a blaze the fire; and when the flame
Had ceased to rise he raked the glowing coals
Apart, and o'er them stretched the spits, and strewed,
Raising the flesh, the sacred salt o'er all.
And when he had made ready and had spread 265
The banquet on the board, Patroclus took
The bread and offered it to all the guests
In shapely canisters. Achilles served
The meats, and took his seat against the wall,
In front of great Ulysses. There he bade 270
His friend Patroclus offer sacrifice,
Casting the first rich morsels to the flames.
The guests put forth their hands and shared the feast;
And when the calls of hunger and of thirst
Were felt no longer, Ajax gave a nod 275
To Phœnix, which divine Ulysses saw,
And filled his cup and drank to Peleus' son:—
  "Thy health, Achilles! Princely feasts like this
Attend us both in Agamemnon's tent
And here,—for here is all that makes a feast 280
Complete; yet now is not the time to think
Of pleasant banquets, for our thoughts are turned—
O Jove-born warrior!—to a fearful time
Of slaughter, and the fate of our good ships,—
Whether we save them harmless, or the foe 285
Destroy them, if thou put not on thy might.
For now the haughty Trojans, and the troops
Who come from far to aid them, pitch their camp
Close to our fleet and wall, and all around
Kindle their many fires, and boast that we 290
No longer have the power to drive them back
From our black galleys. Jupiter, the son
Of Saturn, shows them favorable signs
With lightnings from above; and, terrible
In aspect and in valor, Hector makes 295
Sad havoc, trusting in the aid of Jove,
And neither reverences gods nor men,—
Such rage possesses him. He prays that soon
The morn may rise, that he may hew the prows

From all our ships and give them to the flames, 300
And slay the Greeks, bewildered with the smoke.
For me, I greatly fear the gods will grant
That he fulfil his threat, and that our doom
Will be to perish on the Trojan coast,
And far away from Argos famed for steeds. 305
Rise, then, though late,—rise with a resolute mind,
And from the hard-pressed sons of Greece drive back
The assailing Trojans. Thou wilt else lament
Hereafter, when the evil shall be done
And shall admit no cure. Bethink thee well 310
How from the Greeks thou may'st avert the day
Of their destruction. O my friend, when first
He sent thee forth to Agamemnon's help
From Phthia's coast, thy father Peleus said:—
"'My child, from Juno and Minerva comes 315
The gift of valor, if they choose to give.
But curb thou the high spirit in thy breast,
For gentle ways are best, and keep aloof
From sharp contentions, that the old and young
Among the Greeks may honor thee the more.' 320
"Such was the old man's charge, forgotten now.
Yield, then, and lay thy wrath aside. Large gifts
Doth Agamemnon offer, to appease
Thy wounded spirit. Hear me, if thou wilt,
Recount what gifts the monarch in his tent 325
Hath promised thee:—Seven tripods which the fire
Hath never touched; six talents of pure gold;
And twenty shining caldrons; and twelve steeds
Of hardy frame, victorious in the race,
Whose feet have won him prizes in the games. 330
No beggar would he be, nor yet with store
Of gold unfurnished, in whose coffers lay
The prizes those swift-footed steeds have won.
Seven faultless women, skilled in household arts,
He offers,—Lesbians, whom he chose when thou 335
Didst overrun the populous Lesbian isle,—
In beauty eminent among their sex.
These he bestows, and with them he will send

Her whom he took away,—Briseis, pure—
He swears it with a mighty oath—as pure   340
As when she left thy tent. All these he gives
At once; and if, by favor of the gods,
We lay the mighty city of Priam waste,
Thou shalt load down thy galley with large store
Of gold and silver, entering first when we,   345
The Greeks, divide the spoil. Then may'st thou choose
Twice ten young Trojan women, beautiful
Beyond their sex save Helen. If we come
Safe to Achaian Argos, richly stocked
With milky kine, thou may'st become to him   350
A son-in-law, and cherished equally
With his sole son Orestes, who is reared
Right royally. Three daughters there, within
The monarch's stately halls,—Chrysothemis,
Laodice, and Iphianassa,—dwell,   355
And thou may'st choose among them, and may'st lead
Home to the house of Peleus her who best
Deserves thy love. Nor needest thou endow
The bride, for he will give an ampler dower
Than ever father to his daughter gave,—   360
Seven cities with thronged streets,—Cardamyle,
Enope, grassy Hira, Pheræ famed
Afar, Antheia with rich pasture-grounds,
Æpeia beautiful, and Pedasus
With all its vineyards; all are near the sea,   365
And stand the last before you reach the coast
Of sandy Pylos. Rich in flocks and herds
Their dwellers are, and they will honor thee
As if thou wert a god, and, ruled by thee,
Will pay large tribute. These will he bestow,   370
Let but thine anger cease. But if the son
Of Atreus and his gifts still move thy hate,
At least have pity on the afflicted Greeks,
Pent in their camp, who now would honor thee
As if thou wert a god; and thou shalt gain   375
Great glory as their champion, and shalt slay
This Hector, who even now is close at hand,

And in a murderous frenzy makes his boast
That none of all the chieftains whom the fleet
Of Greece brought hither equals him in might." 380
   The swift Achilles answered him and said:—
"Son of Laertes, nobly-born, and versed
In wise devices, let me frankly speak
Just as I think, and just as I shall act.
Hateful to me, as are the gates of hell, 385
Is he who, hiding one thing in his heart,
Utters another. I shall speak as seems
To me the best; nor deem I that the son
Of Atreus or the other Greeks can move
My settled purpose, since no thanks are paid 390
To him who with the enemy maintains
A constant battle: equal is the meed
Of him who stands aloof and him who fights
Manfully; both the coward and the brave
Are held in equal honor, and they die 395
An equal death,—the idler and the man
Of mighty deeds. For me there is no store
Of wealth laid up from all that I have borne,
Exposing life in battle. As a bird
Brings to her unfledged young the food she finds, 400
Though she herself be fasting, so have I
Had many a night unvisited by sleep,
And passed in combat many a bloody day,
Fighting beside these warriors for their wives.
Twelve cities have I with my fleet laid waste, 405
And with my Myrmidons have I o'erthrown
Eleven upon this fertile Trojan coast.
Full many a precious spoil from these I bore,
And to Atrides Agamemnon gave.
He, loitering in his fleet, received them all; 410
Few he distributed, and many kept.
To chiefs and princes he indeed assigned
Prizes, which now they hold. From me alone
Of all the Greeks he takes my prize; he takes
My bride, whom well I loved;—and let him keep 415
The damsel. But what need is there that Greeks

Wage war against the Trojans? For what cause
Did Agamemnon, gathering from our realms
An army, lead it hither? Was it not
Because of fair-haired Helen? Are the sons   420
Of Atreus, then, the only men on earth
Who love their wives? Nay, every good man loves
And cherishes his spouse; and mine I loved
Tenderly, though the captive of my spear:
And now, since he hath taken my reward   425
Away and treacherously dealt with me,
Let him not try again, for I am warned,
And he will not persuade me. Let him take
Counsel with thee, Ulysses, and the rest,
How to drive back the enemy and save   430
The fleet from flames. Already has he done
Much without me; a rampart he has raised,
And round it dug a deep, broad trench, and filled
The trench with palisades. Yet can he not
Resist the man-destroyer Hector thus.   435
This Hector, when I fought among the Greeks,
Never would fight at distance from the walls,
And ventured not beyond the Scæan gates
And beechen tree. There waited he for me
Upon a time, and scarce escaped with life   440
From my assault. Now, since I do not choose
To fight with noble Hector, I shall pay,
To-morrow, sacrifice to Jupiter
And all the gods, and load my galleys well,
And draw them to the water. Then shalt thou   445
See—if thou care for such a sight—my ships
Sailing upon the fishy Hellespont
At early morning, with their crews on board
Eager to pull the oar; and if the god
Of ocean grant a prosperous voyage, then   450
On the third day we reach the fertile coast
Of Phthia. Large possessions left I there
When I came hither in an evil hour;
And thither I shall carry with me gold
And ruddy brass, and women of fair forms,   455

And burnished steel,—the spoils I won in war.
The prize he gave me, Agamemnon, son
Of Atreus, takes, with many insults, back.
Bear him this message,—give it openly,
That others of the Greeks may be like me   460
Indignant should he impudently dare
To wrong them also:—Let him ne'er again,
Though shameless, dare to look me in the face.
I will not join in council or in act
With him: he has deceived and wronged me once,   465
And now he cannot wheedle me with words.
Let once suffice. I leave him to himself,
To perish. All-providing Jupiter
Hath made him mad. I hate his gifts; I hold
In utter scorn the giver. Were his gifts   470
Tenfold,—nay, twenty-fold,—the worth of all
That he possesses, and with added wealth
From others,—all the riches that flow in
Upon Orchomenus, or Thebes, the pride
Of Egypt, where large treasures are laid up,   475
And through whose hundred gates rush men and steeds,
Two hundred through each gate;—nay, should he give
As many gifts as there are sands and dust
Of earth,—not even then shall Atreus' son
Persuade me, till I reap a just revenge   480
For his foul contumelies. I will wed
No child of Agamemnon. Even though
She vied with golden Venus in her charms,
And with the blue-eyed Pallas in her skill,
I would not wed her. Let him choose among   485
The Greeks a fitter husband,—one whose rule
Is wider than my own. For if the gods
Preserve me, and I reach my home again,
My father, Peleus, will bestow on me
A consort. Many are the Achaian maids,   490
Daughters of chiefs who hold our citadels
In Hellas and in Phthia, and of these,
Her who shall most delight me I will make
My well-beloved wife. My soul has longed

BOOK IX 183

Earnestly, with a fitting spouse betrothed 495
Duly, to make my dwelling there, and there
Enjoy the wealth which aged Peleus won;
For not to be compared with life is all
The wealth which, as men say, was treasured up
In Ilium's populous town in time of peace, 500
Ere the Greeks came, nor all the stores contained
Within the stony threshold of the god
Who bears the bow, Apollo, on the coast
Of rocky Pytho. We may gather spoil
Of oxen and of fatling sheep, and bring 505
Tripods from war, and yellow-manèd steeds:
The breath of man no force can seize or hold,
And when it leaves the enclosure of the teeth
It comes not back. My mother said to me—
The goddess, silver-footed Thetis, said— 510
A twofold fate conducts me to my death;—
If I remain to fight beneath the walls
Of Ilium, my return will be cut off,
But deathless my renown; if I return
To the dear land in which my fathers dwell, 515
My glory will be nought, but long my life,
And late will come to me the stroke of death.
And now I counsel all to sail for home,
For never will ye see the overthrow
Of lofty Ilium. Jove the Thunderer 520
Stretches his great hand o'er her, and her sons
Take courage. Go ye now, and take with you
This message to the princes of the Greeks,—
As is the office of an embassy,—
And bid them meditate some wiser plan 525
To save their galleys and the host of Greeks
Within the hollow barks. The plan which brought
You hither cannot serve you while I keep
My anger unappeased. Let Phœnix stay
To pass the night with us, that he may sail 530
To-morrow, if it please him, to the land
We love; I take him not against his will."
  He ceased; and silent were the ambassadors,

Astonished at his passionate words. At last
Phœnix, the aged knight, with many tears 535
And sighs, took up the word, in grief and fear
Lest Hector should destroy the Grecian fleet:—
　"Illustrious son of Peleus, if indeed
Thou wilt return, nor carest to repel
From our swift galleys the consuming fire, 540
Because thou art offended, how shall I,
Dear child, remain without thee? When at first
Peleus, the aged knight, from Phthia sent
Thee, yet a boy, to Agamemnon's aid,
Unskilled as then thou wert in cruel war, 545
And martial councils,—where men also gain
A great renown,—he sent me with thee, charged
To teach thee both, that so thou might'st become
In words an orator, in warlike deeds
An actor. Therefore, my beloved child, 550
Not willingly shall I remain behind;
Not even though a god should promise me
That, overcoming the decays of age,
I might become a beardless youth again,
As when from Hellas and its companies 555
Of lovely maids I came a fugitive,
And left Amyntor, son of Ormenus,—
My father,—angry with me for the sake
Of a fair-tressèd wanton, whom he loved,
Treating my mother basely. To my knees 560
My mother came and prayed me ceaselessly,
First, to possess the woman, that she then
Might loathe the elder one; and I obeyed.
My father knew it, and with many a curse
Invoked the hateful furies to forbid 565
That any child who owed his birth to me
Should ever sit upon his knees. The gods—
The Jove of Hades and dread Proserpine—
Confirmed his curse. I could not brook to dwell
Within my father's palace while he thus 570
Was wroth with me. My kindred and my friends
Came round me, and besought me to remain,

And stayed beside me. Many a fatling ewe
And many a slow-paced ox with curving horns
They slew, and many a fattened swine they stretched   575
Over the flame of Vulcan. From the casks
Of the old chief his wine was freely drawn.
Nine nights they slept surrounding me, while each
Kept watch in turn: nor ever were the fires
Put out; one blazed beneath the portico   580
Of the fair hall, and near the chamber-door
Another glimmered in the vestibule.
But when upon me rose the tenth dark night,
I broke my aptly-jointed chamber-doors,
And issued forth, and easily o'erleaped   585
The wall around the palace, quite unseen
Of watching men and of the serving maids.
I fled through spacious Hellas to the fields
Of Phthia, nurse of flocks, and to her king,
Peleus, who kindly welcomed me, and loved   590
Me as a father loves his only son,
Born to large wealth in his declining years.
He made me rich, and gave me sovereign rule
Over much people. My abode was fixed
In farthest Phthia, where I was the prince   595
Of the Dolopians. As for thee, my care,
Godlike Achilles, made thee what thou art.
I loved thee from my soul: thou wouldst not go
With any other to the feast, nor take
Thy food at home until upon my knees   600
I placed thee, carved thy meats, and gave them thee,
And poured thy wine. The tunic on my breast
Was often wetted by thee when the wine
Gushed in thy petulant childhood from thy lips.
Thus many things did I endure for thee,   605
And many toils perform; and since the gods
Vouchsafed no son to me, it was my thought
To train thee as a son, that thou might'st be,
O godlike man! the bulwark of my age.
And now subdue that mighty spirit of thine: 610
Ill it becomes thee to be merciless:

The gods themselves are placable, though far
Above us all in honor and in power
And virtue. We propitiate them with vows,
Incense, libations, and burnt-offerings, 615
And prayers for those who have offended. Prayers
Are daughters of almighty Jupiter,—
Lame, wrinkled, and squint-eyed,—that painfully
Follow Misfortune's steps; but strong of limb
And swift of foot Misfortune is, and, far 620
Outstripping all, comes first to every land,
And there wreaks evil on mankind, which prayers
Do afterwards redress. Whoe'er receives
Jove's daughters reverently when they approach,
Him willingly they aid, and to his suit 625
They listen. Whosoever puts them by
With obstinate denial, they appeal
To Jove, the son of Saturn, and entreat
That he will cause Misfortune to attend
The offender's way in life, that he in turn 630
May suffer evil and be punished thus.
Wherefore, Achilles! do thou also yield
The honor due Jove's daughters, freely given
By other valiant men. If Atreus' son
Brought thee no gifts, nor promised others still, 635
But kept his anger, I would never ask
That thou shouldst lay aside thy wrath and come
To help the Argives in their bitter need.
But he bestows large gifts, and adds a pledge
Of others yet in store, and he hath sent 640
The best men of the army, who to thee
Are dearest, to entreat thee. Spurn thou not
These, nor their embassy, although at first
Thine anger was not causeless. We have heard
The praise of heroes of the elder time, 645
Inflamed to vehement anger, yet appeased
By gifts, and yielding to persuasive words.
One instance I remember: long ago
It happened, and I will relate it here
Among my friends. Around the city-walls 650

Of Calydon did the Curetes strive
In battle with the Ætolians; they destroyed
Each other fearfully. The Ætolians fought
To save the pleasant town of Calydon,
And the Curetes warred to lay it waste.   655
Diana of the golden throne had caused
The war, displeased with Œneus, who withheld
From her the first-fruits of his fertile field:
While hecatombs were burnt in sacrifice
To feast the other gods, to her—   660
Daughter of Jove—no offering was brought;
For either he forgot, or thought the rite
Of little moment; but he greatly erred.
And now the child of Jove, the archer-queen,
Incensed, sent forth against him from the wood   665
A white-tusked wild boar, which upon his lands
Entered, and ravaged them, and brought to earth
Many tall trees: tree after tree they fell,
With roots uptorn, and all the blossoms on,
That promised fruit. Him Meleager, son   670
Of Œneus, slew, with many hunters called
From neighboring cities, bringing many hounds.
A few could not subdue him: he had made
Many already mount the funeral pile.
Diana kindled round the boar a strife   675
For the beast's head and bristly hide,—a war
'Twixt the Curetes and the Ætolian band
Of braves. The war, while Meleager fought,
Went not with the Curetes, nor could they,
Though many, keep the field. But wrath at last   680
Seized Meleager,—wrath, which rages oft
Even in prudent minds. Incensed against
Althæa, his own mother, he remained
At home with Cleopatra, his young wife,
The beauteous, whom a delicate-footed dame,   685
Marpessa, daughter of Evenus, bore
To Idas, bravest in his time among
The sons of men,—so brave that once he drew
A bow against Apollo for the sake

Of his neat-footed bride. The honored pair 690
Within the palace used to call their child
Alcyone; for when the archer-god,
Apollo, from her husband bore away
The mother, Cleopatra sadly wailed,
As wails the halcyon. So beside his spouse 695
Dwelt Meleager, brooding ever o'er
The violent anger which his mother's curse
Had kindled. Grieving for a brother's death,
She supplicated heaven, and often struck
Her hands against the teeming earth, and called— 700
Kneeling, her bosom all bedewed with tears—
On Pluto and the cruel Proserpine,
To put her son to death. From Erebus
The pitiless Erinnys, wandering
In darkness, heard the prayer. Then straightway rose 705
A sound of fearful tumult at the gates:
The towers were battered, and the elder chiefs
Of the Ætolians hastened to entreat
The aid of Meleager, and they sent
Priests of the gods, a chosen band, to pray 710
That he would come to their defence. Large gifts
They promised. Where the soil of Calydon
Was best, they bade him choose a fruitful field
Of fifty acres, half for vines, and half,
Cleared of the trees, for tillage. Earnestly 715
Did aged Œneus, famed for horsemanship,
Beseech him; to the chamber of his son,
High-roofed, he climbed, and at the threshold shook
The massive doors with knocking as he sued.
His sisters and his reverend mother joined 720
Their supplications: he resisted still.
And much his friends, the dearest and most prized,
Besought him, but they vainly strove to swerve
His steadfast mind, till his own chamber felt
The assault, and the Curetes climbed the walls 725
To fire the populous city. Then the nymph,
His graceful wife, entreated him with tears,
And spake of all the horrors which o'ertake

A captured city,—all the men cut off
By massacre, the houses given to flames, 730
The children and deep-bosomed women dragged
Into captivity. Her sorrowful words
He heard; his spirit was disturbed; he went
To gird his glittering armor on, and thus
He saved the Ætolians from a fearful doom, 735
Obeying his own impulse. The reward
Of rare and costly gifts they gave him not,
Though thus he rescued them. Be not thy thought
Like his, my friend; let no invisible power
Persuade thee thus to act. Far worse it were, 740
To wait, and when our fleet is all on fire
Offer thy aid. Accept the gifts at once:
Then will the Greeks, as if thou wert a god,
Hold thee in honor. If without the gifts
Thou enter later on the field of fight, 745
Thou wilt not have like honor with the host,
Although thou turn the assault of battle back."
   Then did Achilles, swift of foot, reply:—
"O ancient Phœnix, father, loved of Jove,
Such honor need I not; for the decree 750
Of Jove, I deem, already honors me,
And will detain me by my beakèd ships
While breath is in my lungs, and I have power
To move these knees. Yet one thing I would say,—
And bear it thou in mind,—vex not my soul 755
With weeping and lamenting for the sake
Of Agamemnon; it becomes thee not—
Thou who art loved by me—to yield thy love
To him, unless thou wouldst incur my hate.
And thou shouldst be the enemy of him 760
Who wrongs me. Reign thou equally with me,
And share my honors. These will carry back
My answer. Thou remain, and, softly couched,
Sleep here: with early morn will we consult
Whether to leave this region or remain." 765
   He spake, and, nodding to Patroclus, gave
A signal to prepare an ample couch

For Phœnix, while the other chiefs prepared
To leave the tent. Then Ajax Telamon,
The godlike chief, addressed his comrades thus:— 770
   "Son of Laertes, nobly born, and skilled
In sage devices, let us now depart,
Since, as it seems, the end for which we came
Cannot be compassed thus, and we must bear
With speed the unwelcome answer to the Greeks, 775
Who sit expecting us; while in his breast
The implacable Achilles bears a fierce
And haughty heart, nor doth he heed the claim
Of that close friendship of his fellow-chiefs,
Which at the Grecian fleet exalted him 780
Above all others. Unrelenting one!
Even for a brother's death a price is paid,
Or when a son is slain: the slayer dwells
At home among his people, having made
The appointed expiation. He to whom 785
The fine is offered takes it, and his thirst
Of vengeance is appeased. But in thy heart
The gods have kindled an unquenchable rage,
All for a single damsel,—and behold,
Seven more we offer, passing beautiful, 790
With many gifts beside. Let, then, thy mood
Be softened: have respect to thine own roof;
For we are guests beneath it, sent from all
The assembled host, and strong is our desire
To be thy dearest and most cherished friends 795
Of all the Achaians, many as they are."
   Achilles the swift-footed answered thus:—
"Illustrious Ajax, son of Telamon,
Prince of the people! all that thou hast said,
I well perceive, is prompted by thy heart. 800
Mine swells with indignation when I think
How King Atrides mid the assembled Greeks
Heaped insults on me, as if I had been
A wretched vagabond. But go ye now
And bear my message. I shall never think 805
Of bloody war till noble Hector, son

Of Priam, slaughtering in his way the Greeks,
Shall reach the galleys of the Myrmidons,
To lay the fleet in flames. But when he comes
To my own tent and galley, he, I think, 810
Though eager for the combat, will desist."
    He spake. Each raised a double cup and poured
Libations to the gods; they then returned
Beside the fleet. Ulysses led the way.
    Patroclus bade the attendant men and maids 815
Strew with all speed a soft and ample bed
For Phœnix. They obeyed, and spread the couch
With skins of sheep, dyed coverlets, and sheets
Of lawn; and there the old man lay to wait
The glorious morn. Meantime Achilles slept 820
Within the tent's recess, and by him lay
Phorbas's daughter, whom he carried off
From Lesbos,—Diomedè, rosy-cheeked.
Upon the other side Patroclus lay,
With slender-waisted Iphis by his side, 825
Given by the great Achilles when he took
Scyros the tall, where Enyëus ruled.
    Now when the ambassadors were come within
The tent of Agamemnon, all the chiefs
Rose, one by one, and, lifting up to them 830
Their golden goblets, asked the news they brought;
And first Atrides, king of men, inquired:—
    "Renowned Ulysses, glory of the Greeks!
Tell me, will he protect our fleet from flames,
Or does he, in his wrath and pride, refuse?" 835
    Then spake the hardy chief Ulysses thus:—
"Atrides Agamemnon, glorious king
Of men! he will not let his wrath abate,
But rages yet more fiercely, and contemns
Thee and thy gifts. He leaves thee to consult 840
With thine Achaians by what means to save
The fleet and army; for himself he means
To-morrow, with the early dawn, to launch
His well-appointed galleys on the sea,
And will advise the other Greeks to spread 845

The sails for home, since they will never see
The overthrow of lofty Troy, for Jove
The Thunderer stretches his protecting hand
Above her, and her sons have taken heart.
Such are his words; and those who went with me 850
Are present,—Ajax and the heralds both,
Sage men,—the witnesses to what I say.
The aged Phœnix stays behind to sleep,
And on the morrow to attend his chief
To their beloved country,—if he will, 855
For else by no means will he take him hence."
　He spake; and all were silent, all amazed
At what they heard, for these were bitter words.
Long sat the sons of Greece in silent thought,
Till Diomed, the great in battle, spake:— 860
　"Atrides Agamemnon, glorious king
Of men! I would thou hadst not deigned to ask
The illustrious son of Peleus for his aid,
With offer of large gifts; for arrogant
He is at all times: thou hast made him now 865
More insolent. Now leave him to himself,
To go or to remain: he yet will fight
When his mood changes, or some god within
Shall move him. Let us do what I advise:—
Betake we all ourselves to rest, but first 870
Refresh ourselves with food and wine; in them
Is strength and spirit. When the rosy morn
Shall shine, command thou that the foot and horse
Be speedily drawn up before the fleet,
And thou encourage them with cheerful words, 875
And fight among them in the foremost rank."
　He spake. The kings assented, and admired
The words of the horse-tamer Diomed;
And, pouring out libations, to their tents
They all departed, and lay down to rest, 880
And took into their souls the balm of sleep.

BOOK X

ALL the night long the captains of the Greeks
Slept at the ships, and pleasant was their sleep,—
Save only Agamemnon, Atreus' son,
The shepherd of the people. Not to him—
Vexed with a thousand cares—came gentle sleep. 5
As when the husband of the light-haired queen
Of heaven sends forth his thunders, ushering in
Some wide-involving shower,—rain, hail, or snow
Whitening the fields,—or opening o'er some land
The ravenous jaws of unrelenting war,— 10
So frequent were the groans which from his heart
Atrides uttered; for within his breast
His heart was troubled. Looking toward the plain
Of Troy, he wondered at the many fires
Blazing before the city, and the sound 15
Of flutes and fifes, and tumult of the crowd.
But when he turned him toward the fleet and host
Of Greece, he tore his hair, and flung it up
To Jove, and vented his great heart in groans.
And now at length it seemed to him most wise 20
To seek Neleian Nestor, and with him
Devise some plan by which to turn aside
The threatened evil from the Greeks. He rose,
And drew his tunic o'er his breast, and laced
The graceful sandals to his well-shaped feet; 25
And o'er his shoulders threw the blood-stained hide

Of a huge tawny lion, that reached down
Even to the ground; and took in hand his spear.
Meantime with like uneasy thoughts oppressed
Was Menelaus, to whose eyes there came   30
No slumber,—dreading lest calamity
Should light upon the Greeks, who for his sake
Had crossed the sea to carry war to Troy.
And first he threw a leopard's spotted hide
O'er his broad back, and placed the brazen helm   35
Upon his head, and took in his strong grasp
A spear, and went to bid his brother wake,—
His brother, the chief ruler over all
The men of Greece, and honored like a god.
He found him at his galley's prow in act   40
To sheath his shoulders in the shining mail,
And pleased to greet his coming. To the king
Thus Menelaus, great in battle, spake:—
    "Why arm thyself, my brother? Wouldst thou send
A warrior to explore the Trojan camp?   45
None will accept the task, I fear, to creep
Alone at dead of night, a spy, within
The hostile lines;—a bold man must he be."
    Then answered Agamemnon, king of men:—
"Most noble Menelaus, much we need   50
Wise counsel—thou and I—to save our men
And galleys from destruction, since the will
Of Jove is changed. Now hath the God respect
To Hector's sacrifices; for in truth
I never saw—I never heard of one   55
Who in one day performed such mighty deeds
As Hector, dear to Jove, just now hath wrought,
Though not the son of goddess or of god.
Those deeds will be, I deem, for many a day
A cause of bitter sorrow to the Greeks,—   60
Such evil hath he wrought. Now go at once,
And from their galleys call Idomeneus
And Ajax; while to noble Nestor's tent
I go, and pray that he will rise and give
Their orders to the sacred band of guards;—   65

For they will hearken to him, since his son
Commands them jointly with Meriones,
The armor-bearer of Idomeneus,—
Both named by us to that important trust."
   Then Menelaus, great in battle, said:—   70
"What wilt thou, then, and what dost thou command,—
That I remain with them until thou come,
Or, having given the message, seek thee here?"
   Again the monarch Agamemnon spake:—
"Wait there, lest as we go I meet thee not,   75
For many ways are through the camp. But thou,
In going, shout aloud and bid them all
Be vigilant, accosting every one
By his paternal name, and giving each
Due honor: bear thyself not haughtily: 80
We too must labor; for when we were born
Jove laid this hard condition on us all."
   So spake he, and, dismissing with that charge
His brother, hastened to where Nestor lay,
The shepherd of his people. Him he found   85
On his soft couch within his tent beside
His dark-brown ship. Around him scattered shone
His arms,—a shield, two spears, a gleaming helm,
And pliant belt, with which the ancient man
Girded himself when arming to lead on   90
His men to murderous fight;—for not to age
The warrior yielded yet. He raised his head,
And, leaning on his elbow, questioned thus
Atrides: "Who art thou that traversest
The camp beside the fleet at dead of night,   95
Alone, while others sleep? Com'st thou to find
One of the guardsmen, or a comrade? Speak;
Come not in silence thus: what wouldst thou have?"
   Then answered Agamemnon, king of men:—
"O Nestor, son of Neleus, whom the Greeks   100
All glory in! thou certainly wilt know
Atrides Agamemnon, whom the will
Of Jove hath visited with hardships great
Beyond what others bear, to last while breath

Is in my lungs, and while my knees can move.   105
I wander thus abroad because sweet sleep
Comes not to close my eyelids, and the war
And slaughter of the Greeks distress me sore.
For them I greatly fear, my heart is faint,
My mind confounded. In my breast the heart   110
Pants, and my limbs all tremble. If thou wilt,—
For, as I see, thou also dost not sleep,—
Come with me to the guards, that we may know
Whether, o'ercome by toil and weariness,
They give themselves to slumber and forget   115
Their watch. The foe is near us in his camp,
And how know we that even now by night
He plans not, to attack us in our tents?"
 Then Nestor, the Gerenian knight, replied:—
"Atrides Agamemnon, glorious king   120
Of men, almighty Jove will not perform
For Hector all that Hector plans and hopes;
And heavier cares, I think, will yet be his
When once Achilles' wrath is turned away.
Yet willingly I join thee. Let us call   125
The other chiefs,—Ulysses, Diomed,
Both mighty spearmen; Ajax, swift of foot;
And the brave son of Phyleus. It were well
To send and bid the mightier Ajax come,
And King Idomeneus, for farthest off   130
The ships of both are stationed. I shall chide
Thy brother Menelaus—though he be
Honored and dear, and though it please thee not—
For sleeping, while he leaves such toils as these
To thee alone. He should be here among   135
The chiefs, exhorting them to valiant deeds;
For now the hour of bitter need is come."
 Again spake Agamemnon, king of men:—
"At other times, old chief, I would have begged
That thou shouldst blame him: he is oft remiss,   140
And late to act; but not because of sloth,
Or want of spirit,—but he looks to me
And waits for my example. Yet to-night

He rose before me, sought me, and is sent
To call the chiefs whom thou hast named; and now   145
Let us go on, and meet them where they wait,
Among the guards and just before the gates,—
For I appointed that the trysting-place."
   And Nestor, the Gerenian knight, replied:—
"Then let no Greek condemn him, or refuse   150
To heed and to obey when he shall speak."
   He spake, and drew his tunic o'er his breast,
Laced the fair sandals to his shapely feet,
And round him fastened, with a clasp, his cloak,—
A double web of purple, with full folds   155
And flowing pile. He grasped a massive spear,
Its blade of trenchant brass. And first he sought
The galleys of the Achaians brazen-mailed.
There shouted Nestor the Gerenian knight,
To raise Ulysses, best of counsellors,   160
Jove-like in wisdom; who perceived the voice,
And issued from his tent in haste, and said:—
   "What brings you forth to walk the camp at night,
Beside the ships alone; what urgent cause?"
   Then answered Nestor the Gerenian knight:—   165
"Son of Laertes, nobly born, and skilled
In wise devices, be thou not displeased:
A fearful woe impends above the Greeks:
Come, then, and call the other chiefs, to give
Their counsel whether we shall flee or fight."   170
   He spake; and wise Ulysses, entering
His tent again, upon his shoulders laid
His well-wrought shield, and joined them as they went,
Till, coming to Tydides Diomed,
They found him by his tent among his arms,   175
His comrades sleeping round him with their shields
Beneath their heads. Their spears were set upright,
The nether points in earth. The polished brass
Gleamed like the lightnings of All-Father Jove.
In sleep the hero lay; a wild bull's hide   180
Was spread beneath him, and a carpet dyed
With glowing colors propped his head. The knight,

Gerenian Nestor, touched him with his foot
And roused him, and addressed him chidingly:—
   "O son of Tydeus! wilt thou calmly sleep   185
All the night long? And hast thou, then, not heard
That on a height amidst the plain the sons
Of Troy are stationed, near the ships, and small
The space that parts the enemy's camp from ours?"
   He spake. The son of Tydeus sprang from sleep   190
At once, and answered him with wingèd words:—
   "Thy labors are too constant, aged man;
Thou shrinkest from no hardship. Are there not
Young men among the Greeks to walk the camp
And call the kings? Thou never takest rest."   195
   And Nestor, the Gerenian knight, replied:—
"Well hast thou said, my friend, for I have sons
Without reproach, and I have many troops;
And any one of these might walk the camp
And give the summons. But to-night there lies   200
A hard necessity upon the Greeks,
And their destruction and their rescue hang
Balanced on a knife's edge. Come then, since thou
Art younger, call swift Ajax and the son
Of Phyleus, if thou wouldst relieve my age."   205
   He spake; and Diomed around him flung
A tawny lion's ample hide, that reached
Down to his feet, and took his spear and went
And summoned the two kings, and brought them forth.
   Now when they came among the assembled guard,   210
Its leaders were not slumbering; every man
Sat watchful and in arms. As dogs that guard
Flocks in a sheepfold hear some savage beast
That comes through thickets down the mountain-side;
Loud is the clamor of the dogs and men,   215
And sleep is frightened thence,—so gentle sleep
Fled from the eyes of those who watched, that night,
Sadly, with eyes turned ever toward the plain,
Intently listening for the foe's approach.
The aged Nestor saw them, and rejoiced,   220
And thus encouraged them with wingèd words:—

"Watch thus, dear youths, let no one yield to sleep,
Lest we become the mockery of the foe."
　　He spake, and crossed the trench; and with him went
The Grecian leaders, they who had been called
To council. With them went Meriones
And Nestor's eminent son, for they had both
Been summoned. Crossing to the other side
Of that deep trench, they found an open space
Clear of the dead, in which they sat them down,—
Just where the fiery Hector, having slain
Many Achaians, turned him back when night
Came o'er him. There they sat to hold debate;
And thus spake Nestor the Gerenian knight:—
　　"Friends! is there none among you who so far
Trusts his own valor that he will to-night
Venture among the Trojans? He perchance
Might capture on the borders of the camp
Some foeman wandering, or might bring report
Of what they meditate, and whether still
They mean to keep their station far from Troy
And near our ships, or, since their late success,
Return to Ilium. Could he safely bring
This knowledge back to us, his meed were great,—
Glory among all men beneath the sky,
And liberal recompense. As many chiefs
As now command our galleys, each would give
A black ewe with a suckling lamb,—such gifts
No one hath yet received,—and he should sit
A guest at all our banquets and our feasts."
　　He spake; and all were silent for a space.
Then Diomed, the great in battle, said:—
　　"Nestor, my resolute spirit urges me
To explore the Trojan camp, that lies so near;
Yet, were another warrior by my side,
I should go forth with a far surer hope,
And greater were my daring. For when two
Join in the same adventure, one perceives
Before the other how they ought to act;
While one alone, however prompt, resolves

More tardily and with a weaker will."
  He spake; and many a chief made suit to share
The risk with Diomed. The ministers
Of Mars, the chieftains Ajax, asked to go;
Meriones desired it; Nestor's son   265
Greatly desired to join the enterprise;
Atrides Menelaus, skilled to wield
The spear, desired it; and that hardy chief,
Ulysses, longed to explore the Trojan camp,
For full of daring aims was the great soul   270
Within his bosom. Agamemnon then,
The king of men, took up the word and said:—
  "Tydides Diomed, most dear of men,
Choose from the many chiefs, who ask to bear
A part with thee, the bravest. Be not moved   275
By deference to take the worse and leave
The abler warrior. Pay no heed to rank,
Or race, or wide extent of kingly rule."
  Thus spake the king; for in his heart he feared
For fair-haired Menelaus. Diomed,   280
The great in battle, then addressed them all:—
  "Ye bid me choose: how, then, can I o'erlook
Godlike Ulysses, prudent in resolve,
And firm in every danger, well-beloved
By Pallas. Give me him, and our return   285
Is sure, though from consuming flames; for he
Is wise to plan beyond all other men."
  Ulysses, nobly born and hardy, spake
In turn: "Tydides, praise me not too much,
Nor blame me, for thou speakest to the Greeks,   290
Who know me. Meantime let us haste to go,
For the night wears away, and morn is near.
The stars are high, two thirds of night are past,—
The greater part,—and scarce a third remains."
  He spake; and both arrayed themselves for fight.   295
The mighty warrior Thrasymedes gave
The two-edged sword he wore to Diomed,—
Whose own was at the galleys,—and a shield.
The hero then put on his helmet, made

Of tough bull-hide, with neither cone nor crest,— 300
Such as is worn by beardless youths. A bow,
Quiver, and sword Meriones bestowed
Upon Ulysses, placing on his brows
A leathern helmet, firmly laced within
By many a thong, and on the outer side 305
Set thickly with a tusky boar's white teeth,
Which fenced it well and skilfully. A web
Of woollen for the temples lined the work.
This helm Autolycus once bore away
From Eleon, the city where he sacked 310
The stately palace of Amyntor, son
Of Ormenus. The captor gave the prize
To the Cytheran chief, Amphidamas,
Who bore it to Scandeia, and in turn
Bestowed it upon Molus as his guest, 315
And Molus gave it to Meriones,
His son, to wear in battle. Now at last
It crowned Ulysses' temples. When the twain
Were all accoutred in their dreadful arms,
Forward they went, and left the assembled chiefs, 320
While, sent by Pallas forth, upon their right
A heron flew beside their path. The bird
They saw not, for the night was dark, but heard
Its rustling wings. Ulysses at the sound
Rejoiced, and supplicated Pallas thus:— 325
  "Hear! daughter of the Ægis-bearer Jove!
Thou who art near me in all dangers, thou
Whose eye is on me wheresoe'er I go,
Befriend me, Pallas, yet again, and grant
That, laden with great glory, we return 330
Safe to the galleys, mighty deeds performed,
And woe inflicted on the Trojan race."
  Next Diomed, the great in battle, prayed:—
"Daughter invincible of Jove, give ear
Also to me. Be with me now, as once 335
Thou didst attend on Tydeus nobly born,
My father, when he bore an embassy
To Thebe from the Achaians. He beside

The Asopus left the Achaians mailed in brass,
And bore a friendly message to the sons   340
Of Cadmus, and on his return performed
Full many a mighty deed with aid from thee,
Great goddess! for thou stoodest by his side.
Stand now by me; be thou my shield and guard;
And I, in turn, will offer up to thee   345
A yearling heifer, broad between the horns,
Which never ploughman yet hath tamed to bear
The yoke. Her to thine altar will I bring,
With gilded horns, to be a sacrifice."
  So prayed they. Pallas listened to their prayers;   350
And, having supplicated thus the child
Of Jove Almighty, the two chiefs went on
Like lions through the darkness of the night,
Through slaughter, heaps of corses, and black blood.
  Nor now had Hector suffered the brave sons   355
Of Troy to sleep, but summoned all the chiefs,
Leaders, and princes of the host, and thus
Addressed the assembly with well-ordered words:—
  "Who of you all will promise to perform
The task I set him, for a large reward?   360
For ample shall his meed be. I will give
A chariot and two steeds with lofty necks,
Swifter than the swift galleys of the Greeks.
Great glory will be his whoever dares
Approach those ships and bring the knowledge thence 365
Whether the fleet is guarded as before,
Or whether, yielding to our arms, the foe
Is meditating flight, and, through the night
O'ercome with weariness, keeps watch no more."
  He spake; and all were silent for a space.   370
Now there was one, among the Trojan chiefs,
Whose father was Eumedes, of the train
Of reverend heralds. Dolon was his name,
And he was rich in gold and brass, deformed
In face but swift of foot, an only son   375
Among five sisters. He stood forth among
The Trojans, and replied to Hector thus:—

"My daring spirit, Hector, urges me
To visit the swift ships and learn the state
Of the Greek host. But hold thy sceptre forth,   380
And solemnly attest the gods that thou
Wilt give to me the horses, and the car
Engrailed with brass, which bear the illustrious son
Of Peleus. I shall not explore in vain,
Nor balk thy hope of me; for I will pass   385
Into the camp until I reach the ship
Of Agamemnon, where the chiefs are now
Debating whether they shall fly or fight."

   He spake; and Hector held the sceptre forth,
And swore: "Be Jupiter the Thunderer,   390
Husband of Juno, witness, that those steeds
Shall bear no other Trojan than thyself.
That honor I confirm to thee alone."

   He spake. It was an idle oath, yet gave
New courage to the spy, who instantly   395
Upon his shoulders hung his crooked bow,
And round him flung a gray wolf's hide, and placed
A casque of otter-skin upon his head,
And took his pointed javelin, and made haste
To reach the Grecian fleet. Yet was he doomed   400
Never to leave that fleet again, nor bring
Tidings to Hector. Soon was he beyond
The crowd of men and steeds, and eagerly
Held on his way. Ulysses first perceived
His coming, and thus spake to Diomed:—   405

   "Some one, Tydides, from the enemy's camp
Is coming, either as a spy, or else
To spoil the dead. First let us suffer him
To pass us by a little on the plain,
Then let us rush and seize him. Should his speed   410
Be greater than our own, let us attack
The fugitive with spears, and drive him on
To where our ships are lying, from his camp,
Lest, flying townward, he escape our hands."

   He spake; and both lay down without the path,   415
Among the dead, while he unwarily

Passed by them. When he now had gone as far
As two yoked mules might at the furrow's end
Precede a pair of oxen,—for by mules
The plough is drawn more quickly through the soil   420
Of the deep fallow,—then they rose, and rushed
To seize him. As he heard their steps he stopped,
In hope that his companions had been sent
From Troy by Hector to conduct him back.
But when they came within a javelin's cast,   425
Or haply less, he saw that they were foes,
And moved his nimble knees, and turned to flee,
While rapidly they followed. As two hounds,
Sharp-toothed, and trained to track their prey, pursue
Through forest-grounds some fawn or hare that runs   430
Before them panting, so did Diomed
And terrible Ulysses without stop
Follow the fugitive, to cut him off
From his own people. In his flight he came
Where soon he would have mingled with the guards,   435
Close to the fleet. Then Pallas breathed new strength
Into Tydides, that no other Greek
Might boast that he had wounded Dolon first,
And steal the honor. Therefore, with his spear
Uplifted, Diomed rushed on and spake:—   440
    "Stop, or my spear o'ertakes thee, nor wilt thou
Escape a certain death from this right hand."
    He spake, and hurled his spear—but not to smite—
At Dolon, over whose right shoulder passed
The polished weapon, and, descending, pierced   445
The ground. Then Dolon, pale and fear-struck, stopped,
And quaked, with chattering teeth and stammering speech.
They, breathless with the chase, came up and seized
His hands, while, bursting into tears, he spake:—
    "Take me alive, and ye shall have from me   450
A ransom: there is store of brass and gold
And well-wrought steel, of which a princely share
My father will bestow when he shall hear
Of me alive and at the Grecian fleet."
    The crafty chief Ulysses answered thus:—   455

"Take heart, and cease to think of death, but tell,
And truly, why thou earnest to our fleet:
Was it to strip the bodies of the dead?
Camest thou, sent by Hector, as a spy
Among our ships, or of thine own accord?"   460
    And Dolon answered, trembling still with fear:—
"Hector, against my will and to my hurt,
Persuaded me. He promised to bestow
On me the firm-paced coursers, and the car
Engrailed with brass, which bear the illustrious son   465
Of Peleus, and enjoined me, by the aid
Of darkness to approach the foe and learn
Whether ye guard your galleys as before,
Or, overcome by us, consult on flight,
And, wearied with the hardships of the day,   470
Have failed to set the accustomed nightly watch."
    The man of craft, Ulysses, smiled, and said:—
"Truly, thy hope was set on princely gifts,—
The steeds of war-renowned Æacides,
Hard to be reined by mortal hands, or driven   475
By any, save by Peleus' son himself,
Whom an immortal mother bore. But come,
Tell me,—and tell the truth,—where hast thou left
Hector, the leader of the host, and where
Are laid his warlike arms; where stand his steeds;   480
Where are the sentinels, and where the tents
Of other chiefs? On what do they consult?
Will they remain beside our galleys here,
Or do they meditate, since, as they say,
The Greeks are beaten, a return to Troy?"   485
    Dolon, Eumedes' son, made answer thus:—
"What thou requirest I will truly tell.
Hector is with his counsellors, and now,
Apart from all the bustle, at the tomb
Of Ilus the divine, he plans the war.   490
Sentries, of whom thou speakest, there are none;
No chosen band, O hero! has in charge
To guard the camp. By all their blazing fires,
Constrained by need, the Trojans keep awake,

And each exhorts his fellow to maintain 495
The watch: not so the auxiliar troops who came
From far: they sleep, and since they have no wives
Nor children near, they let the Trojans watch."
　Then thus the man of wiles, Ulysses, spake:—
"How sleep they,—mingled with the knights of Troy, 500
Or by themselves? Tell me, that I may know."
　Dolon, Eumedes' son, made answer thus:—
"What thou requirest I will truly tell.
On one hand, toward the sea, the bowmen lie
Of Caria and Pæonia, and with them 505
Lelegans, Caucons, and the gallant tribe
Of the Pelasgians. On the other hand,
Toward Thymbra, are the Lycians, the proud race
Of Mysia, Phrygia's knights, and cavalry
Of the Mæonians. Why should ye inquire 510
The place of each? If ye design to-night
To penetrate into the Trojan camp,
There are the Thracians, newly come, apart
From all the others; with them is their king,
Rhesus, the son of Eioneus; his steeds 515
Are far the largest and most beautiful
I ever saw,—the snow is not so white,
The wind is not so swift. His chariot shines
With gold and silver, and the coat of mail
In which he came to Troy is all of gold, 520
And gloriously and marvellously bright,
Such as becomes not mortal men to wear,
But the gods only. Now to your swift ships
Lead me; or bind me fast with thongs, and here
Leave me till your return; and ye shall know 525
Whether the words I speak be true or false."
　Then sternly spake the gallant Diomed:—
"Once in our hands a prisoner, do not think,
O Dolon! to escape, though thou hast told
Things that shall profit us. For if we now 530
Release thee thou wilt surely come again
To the Greek fleet, a spy, or openly
To fight against us. If I take thy life,

'Tis certain thou wilt harm the Greeks no more."
 He spake. And as the suppliant took his chin 535
In his large hand, and had begun a prayer,
He smote him with his sword at the mid-neck,
And cut the tendons both; the severed head,
While yet he spake, fell, rolling in the dust.
And then they took his helm of otter-skin, 540
The wolf's-hide, sounding bow, and massive spear.
The nobly born Ulysses in his hand
Lifted the trophies high, devoting them
To Pallas, deity of spoil, and prayed:—
 "Delight thyself, O goddess, in these arms, 545
For thee we first invoke, of all the gods
Upon Olympus. Guide us now to find
The camp and coursers of the sons of Thrace."
 He spake; and, raising them aloft, he hung
The spoils upon a tamarisk, and brake 550
Reeds and the spreading branches of the tree,
To form a mark, that so on their return
They might not, in the darkness, miss the spot.
Then onward, mid strewn arms and pools of blood,
They went, and soon were where the Thracians lay. 555
There slept the warriors, overpowered with toil;
Their glittering arms were near them, fairly ranged
In triple rows, and by each suit of arms
Two coursers. Rhesus slumbered in the midst.
Near him were his fleet horses, which were made 560
Fast to the chariot's border by the reins.
Ulysses saw them first, and, pointing, said:—
 "This is the man, O Diomed, and these
The steeds, described by Dolon whom we slew.
Come, then; put forth thy strength of arm, for ill 565
Doth it become thee to stand idle here,
Armed as thou art. Loose thou the steeds; or else
Slay thou the men, and leave the steeds to me."
 He spake. The blue-eyed Pallas straightway gave
Strength to Tydides, who on every side 570
Dealt slaughter. From the smitten by the sword
Rose fearful groans; the ground was red with blood.

As when a ravening lion suddenly
Springs on a helpless flock of goats or sheep,
So fell Tydides on the Thracian band, 575
Till twelve were slain. Whomever Diomed
Approached and smote, the sage Ulysses seized,
And drew him backward by the feet, that thus
The flowing-manèd coursers might pass forth
Unhindered, nor, by treading on the dead, 580
Be startled; for they yet were new to war.
Now when the son of Tydeus reached the king,—
The thirteenth of his victims,—him he slew
As he breathed heavily; for on that night
A fearful dream, in shape Œnides' son, 585
Stood o'er him, sent by Pallas. Carefully
Ulysses meantime loosed the firm-paced steeds,
And, fastening them together, drave them forth,
Urging them with his bow: he had not thought
To take the showy lash that lay in sight 590
On the fair chariot-seat. In going thence
He whistled, as a sign to Diomed,
Who lingered, pondering on his next exploit,—
Whether to seize the chariot where was laid
The embroidered armor, dragging it away; 595
Or, lifting it aloft, to bear it thence;
Or take more Thracian lives. As thus his thoughts
Were busy, Pallas, standing near him, spake:—
  "O son of large-souled Tydeus, think betimes
Of thy return to where the galleys lie; 600
Else may some god arouse the sons of Troy,
And thou be forced to reach the ships by flight."
  She spake. He knew the goddess by her voice,
And leaped upon a steed. Ulysses lashed
The horses with his bow, and on they flew 605
Toward the swift galleys of the Grecian host.
  Apollo, bearer of the silver bow,
Kept no vain watch, and, angry when he saw
Minerva at the side of Diomed,
Down to the mighty host of Troy he came, 610
And roused from sleep a Thracian counsellor,—

Hippocoön, a kinsman of the house
Of Rhesus. Leaping from his couch, he saw
The vacant spot where the swift steeds had stood,
And, weltering in their blood, the dying chiefs. 615
He saw, and wept aloud, and called by name
His dear companion. Then a clamor rose,
And boundless tumult, as the Trojans came
All rushing to the spot, and marvelling
At what the daring warriors, who were now 620
Returning to the hollow ships, had done.
   And when these warriors now had reached the spot
Where Hector's spy was slain, Ulysses, dear
To Jupiter, reined in the fiery steeds,
And Diomed leaped down and took the spoil 625
Blood-stained, and gave it to Ulysses' hands,
And mounted. Then again they urged the steeds,
Which, not unwilling, flew along the way.
First Nestor heard the approaching sound, and said:—
   "Friends, chiefs and princes of the Greeks, my heart— 630
Truly or falsely—urges me to speak.
The trampling of swift steeds is in my ears.
O that Ulysses and the gallant son
Of Tydeus might be bringing at this hour
Firm-footed coursers from the enemy's camp! 635
Yet must I fear that these, our bravest chiefs,
Have met disaster from the Trojan crew."
   While he was speaking yet, the warriors came.
They sprang to earth; their friends, rejoicing, flocked
Around them, greeting them with grasp of hands 640
And with glad words, while the Gerenian knight,
Nestor, inquired: "Declare, illustrious chief,
Glory of Greece, Ulysses, how ye took
These horses: from the foe;—or did some god
Bestow them? They are glorious as the sun. 645
Oft am I midst the Trojans, for, though old,
I lag not idly at the ships; yet ne'er
Have my eyes looked on coursers like to these.
Some god, no doubt, has given them, for to Jove,
The God of storms, and Pallas, blue-eyed child 650

Of ægis-bearing Jove, ye both are dear."
   Then sage Ulysses answered: "Pride of Greece!
Neleian Nestor, truly might a god
Have given us nobler steeds than even these.
All power is with the gods. But these of which 655
Thou askest, aged man, are brought from Thrace,
And newly come. Brave Diomed hath slain
Their lord, and twelve companions by his side,—
All princes. Yet another victim fell,—
A spy whom, near our ships, we put to death,— 660
A man whom Hector and his brother chiefs
sent forth by midnight to explore our camp."
   He spake, and gayly caused the firm-paced steeds
To pass the trench; the other Greeks, well pleased,
Went with him. When they reached the stately tent 665
Of Diomed, they led the coursers on
To stalls where Diomed's fleet horses stood
Champing the wholesome corn, and bound them there
With halters neatly shaped. Ulysses placed
Upon his galley's stern the bloody spoil 670
Of Dolon, to be made an offering
To Pallas. Then, descending to the sea,
They washed from knees and neck and thighs the grime
Of sweat; and when in the salt wave their limbs
Were cleansed, and all the frame refreshed, they stepped 675
Into the polished basins of the bath,
And, having bathed and rubbed with fragrant oil
Their limbs, they sat them down to a repast,
And from a brimming jar beside them drew,
And poured to Pallas first, the pleasant wine. 680

BOOK XI

NOW did the Morning from her couch beside
Renowned Tithonus rise, that she might bring
The light to gods and men, when Jupiter
To the swift galleys of the Grecian host
Sent baleful Strife, who bore in hand aloft   5
War's ensigns. On the huge black ship that brought
Ulysses, in the centre of the fleet,
She stood, where she might shout to either side,—
To Telamonian Ajax in his tents
And to Achilles, who had ranged their ships   10
At each extreme of the Achaian camp,
Relying on their valor and strong arms.
Loud was the voice, and terrible, in which
She shouted from her station to the Greeks,
And into every heart it carried strength   15
And the resolve to combat manfully
And never yield. The battle now to them
Seemed more to be desired than the return
To their dear country in their roomy ships.
Atrides called aloud, exhorting them   20
To gird themselves for battle. Then he clad
Himself in glittering brass. First to his thighs
He bound the beautiful greaves with silver clasps,
Then fitted to his chest the breastplate given
By Cinyras, a pledge of kind intent;—   25
For, when he heard in Cyprus that the Greeks

Were bound for Ilium in their ships, he sent
This gift, a homage to the king of men;—
Ten were its bars of tawny bronze, and twelve
Were gold, and twenty tin; and on each side 30
Were three bronze serpents stretching toward the neck,
Curved like the colored bow which Saturn's son
Sets in the clouds, a sign to men. He hung
His sword, all glittering with its golden studs,
About his shoulders. In a silver sheath 35
It nestled, which was slung on golden rings.
And then he took his shield, a mighty orb,
And nobly wrought and strong and beautiful,
Bound with ten brazen circles. On its disk
Were twenty bosses of white tin, and one 40
Of tawny bronze just in the midst, where glared
A Gorgon's-head with angry eyes, round which
Were sculptured Fear and Flight. Along its band
Of silver twined a serpent wrought in bronze,
With three heads springing from one neck and formed 45
Into an orb. Upon his head he placed
A helmet rough with studs on every side,
And with four bosses, and a horse-hair plume
That nodded fearfully on high. He took
In hand two massive spears, brass-tipped and sharp, 50
That shone afar and sent their light to heaven,
Where Juno and Minerva made a sound
Like thunder in mid-sky, as honoring
The sovereign of Mycenæ rich in gold.
   Each chief gave orders to his charioteer 55
To stay his horses firmly by the trench,
While they rushed forth in arms. At once arose,
Ere yet the sun was up, a mighty din.
They marshalled by the trench the men on foot;
The horse came after, with short space between. 60
The son of Saturn sent among their ranks
Confusion, and dropped down upon the host
Dews tinged with blood, in sign that he that day
Would send to Hades many a valiant chief.
   The Trojans, on their side, in the mid-plain 65

Drew up their squadrons on a hill, around
The mighty Hector, and Polydamas
The blameless, and Æneas, who among
The sons of Troy was honored like a god,
And three sons of Antenor, who were named 70
Agenor and the noble Polybus
And the young Acamas of godlike bloom.
There Hector in the van uplifted bore
His broad round shield. As some portentous star
Breaks from the clouds and shines, and then again 75
Enters their shadow, Hector thus appeared
Among the foremost, issuing his commands,
Then sought the hindmost. All in brass, he shone
Like lightnings of the Ægis-bearer, Jove.
   As when two lines of reapers, face to face, 80
In some rich landlord's field of barley or wheat
Move on, and fast the severed handfuls fall,
So, springing on each other, they of Troy
And they of Argos smote each other down,
And neither thought of ignominious flight. 85
They met each other man to man; they rushed
Like wolves to combat. Cruel Strife looked on
Rejoicing; she alone of all the gods
Was present in the battle; all the rest,
Far off, sat quiet in their palaces, 90
The glorious mansions built for them along
The summits of Olympus. Yet they all
Blamed Saturn's son that he should honor thus
The Trojans. The All-Father heeded not
Their murmurings, but, seated by himself 95
Apart, exulting in his sovereignty,
Looked on the city of Troy, the ships of Greece,
The gleam of arms, the slayers, and the slain.
   While yet 'twas morn, and still the holy light
Of day was brightening, fast the weapons smote 100
On either side, and fast the people fell;
But at the hour when on the mountain-slope
The wood-cutter makes ready his repast,
Weary with felling lofty trees, and glad

To rest, and eager for the grateful meal, 105
The Greeks, encouraging each other, charged
And broke the serried phalanxes of Troy.
First Agamemnon, springing forward, slew
The shepherd of his people and their chief,
Bienor, and his trusty comrade next,— 110
The charioteer Oïleus, who had leaped
Down from his chariot to confront the king.
Him Agamemnon with his trenchant spear
Smote in the forehead as he came. The helm
Of massive brass was vain to stay the blow: 115
The weapon pierced it and the bone, and stained
The brain with blood; it felled him rushing on.
The monarch stripped the slain, and, leaving them
With their white bosoms bare, went on to slay
Isus and Antiphus, King Priam's sons,— 120
One born in wedlock, one of baser birth,—
Both in one chariot. Isus held the reins
While Antiphus, the high-born brother, fought.
These had Achilles once on Ida's height
Made prisoners, as they fed their flocks; he bound 125
Their limbs with osier bands, but gave them up
For ransom to the Trojans. Now the king
Of men, Atrides Agamemnon, pierced
Isus above the nipple with his spear,
And with his falchion smiting Antiphus 130
Beside the ear, he hurled him from his car.
Then hastening up, and stripping from the dead
Their shining mail, he knew them; he had seen
Both at the ships to which the fleet of foot,
Achilles, brought them bound from Ida's side. 135
As when a lion comes upon the haunt
Of a swift hind, to make an easy prey
Of her young fawns, and, with his powerful teeth
Seizing them, takes their tender lives; while she,
Though nigh, can bring no aid, but yields herself 140
To mortal fear, and, to escape his rage,
Flies swiftly through the wood of close-grown oaks,
With sweaty sides,—thus none of all the host

Of Trojans could avert from Priam's sons
Their fate, but fled in terror from the Greeks. 145
Next on Pisander and Hippolochus
Atrides rushed,—brave warriors both, and sons
Of brave Antimachus, the chief who took
Gold and rich gifts from Paris, and refused
To let the Trojans render Helen back 150
To fair-haired Menelaus. His two sons,
Both in one car, and reining their fleet steeds,
Atrides intercepted; they let fall
The embroidered reins, dismayed, as, lion-like,
Forward he came; and, cowering, thus they prayed:— 155
  "Take us alive, Atrides, and accept
A worthy ransom, for Antimachus
Keeps in his halls large treasures,—brass and gold,
And well-wrought steel; and he will send, from these,
Large ransom, hearing we are at the fleet 160
Alive. So prayed they with bland words, and met
Harsh answer: "Since ye call Antimachus
Your father, who in a Trojan council once
Proposed that Menelaus, whom we sent
A legate with Ulysses the divine, 165
Should not return to Greece, but suffer death,
Your blood must answer for your father's guilt."
  So spake the king, and, striking with his spear
Pisander's breast, he dashed him from the car.
Prone on the ground he lay. Hippolochus 170
Leaped down and met the sword. Atrides lopped
His hands and drave the weapon through his neck,
And sent the head to roll among the crowd.
And then he left the dead, and rushed to where
The ranks were in disorder; with him went 175
His well-armed Greeks: there they who fought on foot
Slaughtered the flying foot; the horsemen there
Clove horsemen down; the coursers' trampling feet
Raised the thick dust to shadow all the plain;
While Agamemnon cheered the Achaians on, 180
And chased and slew the foe. As when a fire
Seizes a thick-grown forest, and the wind

Drives it along in eddies, while the trunks
Fall with the boughs amid devouring flames,
So fell the flying Trojans by the hand 185
Of Agamemnon. Many high-maned steeds
Dragged noisily their empty cars among
The ranks of battle, never more to bear
Their charioteers, who lay upon the earth
The vulture's feast, a sorrow to their wives. 190
   But Jove beyond the encountering arms, the dust,
The carnage, and the bloodshed and the din
Bore Hector, while Atrides in pursuit
Was loudly cheering the Achaians on.
Meantime the Trojans fled across the plain 195
Toward the wild fig-tree growing near the tomb
Of ancient Ilus, son of Dardanus,—
Eager to reach the town; and still the son
Of Atreus followed, shouting, and with hands
Blood-stained and dust-begrimed. And when they reached 200
The Scæan portals and the beechen tree,
They halted, waiting for the rear, like beeves
Chased panting by a lion who has come
At midnight on them, and has put the herd
To flight, and one of them to certain death,— 205
Whose neck he breaks with his strong teeth and then
Devours the entrails, lapping up the blood.
Thus did Atrides Agamemnon chase
The Trojans; still he slew the hindmost; still
They fled before him. Many by his hand 210
Fell from their chariots prone, for terrible
Beyond all others with the spear was he.
But when he now was near the city-wall,
The Father of immortals and of men
Came down from the high heaven, and took his seat 215
On many-fountained Ida. In his grasp
He held a thunderbolt, and this command
He gave to Iris of the golden wings:—
   "Haste, Iris fleet of wing, and hear my words
To Hector:—While he sees the king of men, 220
Atrides, in the van and dealing death

Among the ranks of warriors, let him still
Give way, encouraging his men to hold
Unflinching battle with the enemy.
But when Atrides, wounded by a spear   225
Or arrow, shall ascend his chariot, then
Will I nerve Hector's arm with strength to slay
Until he come to the good ships of Greece,
And the sun set, and hallowed night come down."
   He spake; and she, whose feet are like the wind   230
In swiftness, heeded the command, and flew
From Ida's summit to the sacred town
Of Troy, and found the noble Hector, son
Of warlike Priam, standing mid the steeds
And the strong chariots, and, approaching, said:—   235
   "O Hector, son of Priam, and like Jove
In council! Jove the All-Father bids me say,
As long as thou shalt see the king of men,
Atrides, in the van, and dealing death
Among the ranks of warriors, thou shalt still   240
Give way, encouraging thy men to hold
Unflinching battle with the enemy;
But when Atrides, wounded by a spear
Or arrow, shall ascend his chariot, then
Will Jove endue thy arm with strength to slay   245
Until thou come to the good ships of Greece,
And the sun set, and hallowed night come down."
   So the fleet Iris spake, and went her way;
While Hector, leaping from his car in arms,
And wielding his sharp spears, went everywhere   250
Among the Trojan ranks, exhorting them
To combat, and renewed the stubborn fight.
They rallied and stood firm against the Greeks.
The Greeks, in turn, made strong their phalanxes.
The battle raged again, as front to front   255
They stood, while Agamemnon eagerly
Pressed forward, proud to lead the van in fight.
   Say, Muses, dwellers of Olympus! who
First of the Trojans or their brave allies
Encountered Atreus' son? Iphidamas,   260

Son of Antenor, strong and daring, bred
On the rich soil of Thrace, the nurse of flocks.
His grandsire Cisseus, from whose loins the fair
Theano sprang, had reared him from a child
Within his palace; and, when he attained   265
Youth's glorious prime, still kept him, giving him
His child to wife. He wedded her, but left
At once the bridal chamber when he heard
Of the Greek war on Ilium, and set sail
With twelve beaked galleys. These he afterward   270
Left at Percopè,—marching on to Troy.
And he it was who came to meet the son
Of Atreus. As the heroes now drew near
Each other, Agamemnon missed his aim;
His thrust was parried. Then Iphidamas   275
Dealt him beneath the breastplate on the belt
A vigorous blow, and urged the spear with all
His strength of arm; yet through the plated belt
It could not pierce, for there it met a plate
Of silver, and its point was turned like lead.   280
With lion strength, Atrides seized and drew
The weapon toward him, plucked it from the hand
That held it, and let fall his falchion's edge
Upon the Trojan's neck and laid him dead.
Unhappy youth! he slept an iron sleep,—   285
Slain fighting for his country, far away
From the young virgin bride yet scarcely his,
For whom large marriage-gifts he made,—of beeves
A hundred,—and had promised from the flocks
That thronged his fields a thousand sheep and goats.   290
Atrides Agamemnon spoiled the slain,
And bore his glorious armor off among
The Argive host. Antenor's elder son,
Illustrious Coön, saw, and bitter grief
For his slain brother dimmed his eyes. He stood   295
Aside, with his spear couched, while unaware
The noble Agamemnon passed, and pierced
The middle of the monarch's arm below
The elbow; through the flesh the shining point

Passed to the other side. The king of men,   300
Atrides, shuddered, yet refrained not then
From combat; but with his wind-seasoned spear
He rushed on Coön, who, to drag away
His father's son Iphidamas, had seized
The body by the feet, and called his friends,   305
The bravest, to his aid. Atrides thrust
His brazen spear below the bossy shield,
And slew him as he drew the corpse, and o'er
The dead Iphidamas struck off his head.
Thus were Antenor's sons—their doom fulfilled—   310
Sent by Atrides to the realm of death.
And then he ranged among the enemy's ranks
With wielded lance and sword and ponderous stones,
While yet the warm blood issued from his wound.
But when the wound grew dry, and ceased to flow   315
With blood, keen anguish seized his vigorous frame.
As when a woman feels the piercing pangs
Of travail brought her by the Ilythian maids,
Daughters of Juno, who preside at births,
And walk the ministers of bitter pains,—   320
Such anguish seized on Agamemnon's frame;
And, leaping to his chariot-seat, he bade
The guider of the steeds make haste to reach
The roomy ships, for he was overcome
With pain; but first he shouted to the Greeks:—   325
    "O friends, the chiefs and princes of the Greeks!
Yours is the duty to drive back the war
From our good ships, since all-disposing Jove
Forbids me, for this day, to lead the fight."
    He spake. The charioteer applied the lash,   330
And not unwillingly the long-maned steeds
Flew toward the hollow ships; upon their breasts
Gathered the foam; beneath their rapid feet
Arose the dust, as from the battle's din
They bore the wounded warrior. Hector saw   335
The flight of Agamemnon, and aloud
Called to the Trojans and the Lycians thus:—
    "Trojan and Lycian warriors, and ye sons

Of Dardanus, who combat hand to hand,
Be men; be mindful of your fame in war. 340
Our mightiest foe withdraws; Saturnian Jove
Crowns me with glory. Urge your firm-paced steeds
On the brave Greeks, and win yet nobler fame."
    He spake. His words gave courage and new strength
To every heart. As when a hunter cheers 345
His white-toothed dogs against some lioness
Or wild boar from the forest, Hector thus,
The son of Priam, terrible as Mars
The slayer of men, cheered on the gallant sons
Of Troy against the Greeks. Himself, inspired 350
With fiery valor, rushed among the foes
In the mid-battle foremost, like a storm
That swoops from heaven, and on the dark blue sea
Falls suddenly, and stirs it to its depths.
    Who then was slain the first, and who the last, 355
By Hector, Priam's son, whom Jove designed
To honor? First, Asæus; Dolops, son
Of Clytis; and Autonoüs; and then
Opites and Opheltius; next to whom
Æsymnus, Agelaus, Orus fell, 360
And resolute Hipponoüs the last.
All these, the princes of the Greeks, he slew,
Then smote the common crowd. As when a gale
Blows from the west upon the mass of cloud
Piled up before the south wind's powerful breath, 365
And tears it with a mighty hurricane,
While the swoln billows tumble, and their foam
Is flung on high before the furious blast,
So by the sword of Hector fell the heads
Of the Greek soldiery; and there had been 370
Ruin and ravage not to be repaired,
And the defeated Greeks had flung themselves
Into their ships, had not Ulysses then
Exhorted thus Tydides Diomed:—
    "Tydides! what has quenched within our hearts 375
Their fiery valor? Come, my friend, and take
Thy stand beside me: foul disgrace were ours

Should crested Hector make our fleet his prize."
  And thus the valiant Diomed replied:—
"Most willingly I stand, and bear my part 380
In battle; but with little hope, for Jove,
The God of storms, awards the day to Troy."
  He spake, and pierced Thymbræus with his spear
Through the left breast, and dashed him from his car.
Meanwhile Ulysses struck Molion down, 385
The prince's stately comrade. These they left
Never to fight again, and made their way
Through the thick squadrons, carrying, as they went,
Confusion with them. As two fearless boars
Rush on the hounds, so, mingling in the war, 390
They bore the foe before them, and the Greeks
Welcomed a respite from the havoc made
By noble Hector. Next they seized a car
Which bore two chiefs, the bravest of their host,—
Sons of Percosian Merops, who was skilled 395
Beyond all men in portents. He enjoined
His sons to keep aloof from murderous war.
Yet did they not obey him, for the fate
That doomed the twain to death impelled them on;
And Diomed, the mighty with the spear, 400
Spoiled them of life, and bore their armor off,
A glittering prize. Meantime Ulysses slew
Hippodamus, and next Hypirochus.
The son of Saturn looked from Ida's height,
And bade the battle rage on either side 405
With equal fury: both the encountering hosts
Slew and were slain. Tydides with his spear
Smote on the hip the chief Agastrophus,
The son of Pæon, thoughtless wretch, whose steeds
Were not at hand for flight; his charioteer 410
Held them at distance, while their master rushed
Among the foremost warriors till he fell.
Hector perceived his fall, as through the files
He looked, and straightway hastened to the spot
With shouts; and after him came rapidly 415
The phalanxes of Trojans. Diomed,

The great in battle, shuddered as he saw,
And thus addressed Ulysses, who was near:—
    "Lo! the destroyer, furious Hector, comes!
Let us stand firm, and face and drive him back."   420
    He said, and cast his brandished lance, nor missed
The mark: it smote the helm on Hector's head.
The brass glanced from the brass; it could not pierce
To the fair skin; the high and threefold helm—
A gift from Phœbus—turned the point aside.   425
The chief fell back, and, mingling with the throng,
Dropped on one knee, and yet upheld himself
With one broad palm upon the ground, while night
Darkened his eyes. The son of Tydeus sprang
To seize his spear, which now stood fixed in earth   430
Among the foremost warriors. In that time
Did Hector breathe again, and, having leaped
Into his chariot, he avoided death,
By mingling with the crowd; while, spear in hand,
Brave Diomed pursued him, shouting thus:—   435
    "This time, thou cur, hast thou escaped thy doom,
Though it was nigh thee. Phœbus rescues thee—
The god to whom thou dost address thy prayers—
Whene'er thou venturest mid the clash of spears.
Yet will I surely slay thee when we meet,   440
If any god be on my side; and now
I go to strike where'er I find a foe."
    He spake, and struck the son of Pæon down,
Skilful to wield the spear. But now the spouse
Of fair-haired Helen—Alexander—stood   445
Leaning against a pillar by the tomb
Of the Dardanian Ilus, who had been
An elder of the people; and he bent
His bow against the monarch Diomed,
Who at that moment knelt to strip the slain   450
Of the rich breastplate, and the shield that hung
Upon his shoulders, and the massive casque.
The Trojan drew the bow's elastic horn,
And sent an arrow that not vainly flew,
But, striking the right foot, pierced through, and reached   455

The ground beneath. Then Paris, with a laugh,
Sprang from his ambush, shouting boastfully:—
  "Lo, thou art smitten! Not in vain my shaft
Has flown; and would that it had pierced thy groin
And slain thee! Then the Trojans had obtained   460
Reprieve from slaughter,—they who dread thee now
As bleating goats a lion." Undismayed,
The valiant Diomed made answer thus:—
  "Archer and railer! proud of thy smart bow,
And ogler of the women! wouldst thou make   465
Trial of valor hand to hand with me,
Thy bow should not avail thee, nor thy sheaf
Of many arrows. Thou dost idly boast
That thou hast hit my foot. I heed it not.
It is as if a woman or a child   470
Had struck me. Lightly falls the weapon-stroke
Of an unwarlike weakling. 'Tis not so
With me, for when one feels my weapon's touch,
It passes through him, and he dies; his wife
Tears with her hands her cheeks; his little ones   475
Are orphans; earth is crimsoned with his blood;
And flocking round his carcass in decay,
More numerous than women, are the birds."
  He spake. Ulysses, mighty with the spear,
Came near and stood before him while he sat   480
Concealed, and drew the arrow from his foot.
Keen was the agony that suddenly
Shot through his frame: he leaped into his car,
And bade his charioteer make haste to reach
The roomy ships: the pain had reached his heart.   485
Ulysses, the great spearman, now was left
Alone, no Greek remaining by his side;
For fear had seized them all. With inward grief
The hero thus addressed his mighty soul:—
  "What will become of me? A great disgrace   490
Will overtake me if I flee in fear
Before this multitude; and worse will be
My fate if I am taken here alone,
While Jove has driven away the other Greeks

In terror. Why these questions, since I know 495
That cowards skulk from combat, while the brave,
Wounded or wounding others, keeps his ground?"
  While thus he reasoned with himself, the ranks
Of Trojans armed with bucklers came and closed
Around their dreaded enemy. As when 500
A troop of vigorous dogs and youths assail
From every side a wild boar issuing forth
From a deep thicket, whetting the white tusks
Within his crooked jaws; they press around,
And hear his gnashings, yet beware to come 505
Too nigh the terrible animal,—so rushed
The Trojans round Ulysses, the beloved
Of Jupiter. Then first the hero smote
Deïopites on the shoulder-blade,
And next struck Thoön down, and Ennomus, 510
And in the navel pierced Chersidamas
With his sharp spear, below the bossy shield,
When leaping from his chariot. In the dust
He fell, and grasped the earth with dying hands.
Ulysses left them there, and with his spear 515
He wounded Charops, son of Hippasus,
And brother of brave Socus. Socus saw,
And hastened to his aid, and, standing near,
The godlike chief bespake Ulysses thus:—
  "Renowned Ulysses! of whose arts and toils 520
There is no end, thou either shalt to-day
Boast to have slain two sons of Hippasus,
Brave as they are, and stripped them of their arms,
Or, smitten by my javelin, lose thy life."
  He spake, and smote the Grecian's orbèd shield. 525
The swift spear, passing through the shining disk,
And fixed in the rich breastplate, tore the skin
From all his side; yet Pallas suffered not
The blade to reach the inner parts. At once
The chief perceived that Socus had not given 530
A mortal wound, and, falling back a step,
Thus spake: "Unhappy youth, thy doom will soon
O'ertake thee. Though thou forcest me to pause

From combat with the Trojans, I declare,
This day thou sufferest the black doom of death.   535
Thou, smitten by my spear, shalt bring to me
Increase of glory, and shalt yield thy soul
To the grim horseman Pluto." Thus he spake,
While Socus turned to flee; and as he turned,
Ulysses with the spear transfixed his back,   540
And drave the weapon through his breast: he fell,
With armor clashing, to the earth, while thus
The great Ulysses gloried over him:—
　"O Socus! son of warlike Hippasus
The horseman! death has overtaken thee,   545
And thou couldst not escape. Unhappy one!
Now thou art dead thy father will not come
To close thy eyes, nor she, the honored one
Who gave thee birth; but birds of prey shall flap
Their heavy wings above thee, and shall tear   550
Thy flesh, while I in dying shall receive
Due funeral honors from the noble Greeks."
　He spake, and from his wounded side drew forth,
And from his bossy shield, the ponderous spear
Which warlike Socus threw, A gush of blood   555
Followed, and torturing pain. Now, when they saw
Ulysses bleed, the gallant sons of Troy
Called to each other, rushing in a crowd
To where he stood. Retreating as they came,
He shouted to his comrades. Thrice he raised   560
His voice as loud as human lungs could shout;
Thrice warlike Menelaus heard the cry,
And spake at once to Ajax at his side:—
　"Most noble Ajax, son of Telamon,
Prince of thy people! to my ear is brought   565
The cry of that unconquerable man,
Ulysses, seemingly as if the foe
Had hemmed him round alone, and pressed him sore
In combat. Break we through the crowd, and bring
Succor, lest harm befall him, though so brave,—   570
Fighting among the Trojans thus alone,—
And lest the Greeks should lose their mighty chief."

He spake, and led the way; his godlike friend
Followed. They found Ulysses, dear to Jove,—
The Trojans thronging round him like a troop   575
Of ravening jackals round an antlered stag
Which one who hunts upon the mountain-side
Hath stricken with an arrow from his bow:
By flight the stag escapes, while yet the blood
Is warm and easily the limbs are moved;   580
But when at last the shaft hath quelled his strength,
The hungry jackals in the forest-shade
Among the hills attack him, till by chance
The dreaded lion comes, alarmed, they flee,
And he devours the prey. So in that hour,   585
Many and brave, the sons of Troy pursued
Ulysses, skilled in war and wiles; while he
Wielded the spear and warded off the day
Of death. Then Ajax, coming near him, stood,
With his tall buckler, like a tower of strength   590
Beside him, and the Trojans fled in fear
On all sides. Warlike Menelaus took
Ulysses by the hand, and led him forth
From the thronged spot, while his attendant brought
The chariot near him. Ajax sprang upon   595
The Trojans, slaying Doryclus, a son
Of Priam, basely-born. Then Pandocus
He wounded; next he struck Lysander down,
Pyrasus and Pylartes. As a stream,
Swoln to a torrent by the showers of Jove,   600
Sweeps down, from hill to plain, dry oaks and pines,
And pours into the sea a muddy flood,
So mighty Ajax routed and pursued
The Trojans o'er the plain, and cut his way
Through steeds and warriors. Hector knew not this.   605
He fought where, on the battle's left, beside
The Xanthus, fastest fell the slain, and round
Great Nestor and the brave Idomeneus
Arose a mighty tumult. In that throng
Did Hector mingle with his spear and steeds,   610
Performing feats of valor, and laid waste

The ranks of youthful warriors. Yet the Greeks
Would not have yielded ground, if Paris, spouse
Of fair-haired Helen, had not forced the chief
Machaon, fighting gallantly, to pause; 615
For with an arrow triple-barbed he pierced
The chief's right shoulder, and the valiant Greeks
Feared lest the battle turn and he be slain.
And thus Idomeneus to Nestor said:—
"Neleian Nestor, glory of the Greeks, 620
Haste, mount thy chariot; let Machaon take
A place beside thee; urge thy firm-paced steeds
Rapidly toward the fleet; a leech like him,
Who cuts the arrow from the wound and soothes
The pain with balms, is worth a host to us." 625
    He spake; and the Gerenian knight obeyed,
And climbed the car in haste. Machaon, son
Of Æsculapius the peerless leech,
Mounted beside him; Nestor lashed the steeds,
And toward the roomy ships, which well they knew, 630
And longed to reach, they flew with eager speed.
    Meantime Cebriones, who had his seat
By Hector in the chariot, saw the ranks
Of Troy disordered, and addressed the chief:—
    "While we, O Hector, here are mid the Greeks 635
Just in the skirts of the tumultuous fray,
The other Trojans, men and steeds, are thrown
Into confusion where the warriors throng,
For Telamonian Ajax puts their ranks
To rout; I know him well by that broad shield 640
Borne on his shoulders. Thither let us drive
Our steeds and chariot, where in desperate strife
Meet horse and foot and hew each other down,
And a perpetual clamor fills the air."
    He spake; and with the whistling lash he struck 645
The long-maned steeds, and, as they felt the stroke,
Forward they flew with the swift car among
The Greeks and Trojans, trampling in their way
Corpses and shields. The axle underneath
Was steeped in blood; the rim of the chariot-seat 650

Was foul with the red drops which from their hoofs
The coursers sprinkled and the wheels threw up.
Then Hector strove, by rushing on the crowd,
To pierce it and break through it. To the Greeks
His coming brought destruction and dismay; 655
And well his spear was wielded. Through the ranks
Of other warriors with the spear he ranged,
With sword and ponderous stones; yet warily
He shunned the fight with Ajax Telamon.
　　Then Father Jove Almighty touched with fear 660
The heart of Ajax. All amazed he stood,
And cast his sevenfold buckler of bull's-hide
Upon his back, and, terrified, withdrew.
Now casting glances like a beast of prey
From side to side, he turned to right and left, 665
And, slowly yielding, moved knee after knee.
As when the rustics with their hounds drive off
A hungry lion from their stalls of kine,
Whom, watching all the night, they suffer not
To make their herd a prey; but he, intent 670
On ravin, rushes forward, yet in vain;
For many a javelin flies from daring hands
Against him, many a blazing torch is swung,
At which, though fierce, he trembles, and at morn
Stalks off in sullen mood;—so Ajax, sad 675
At heart, and fearing for the Grecian fleet,
Unwillingly fell back before the foe.
And as, when entering in a field, an ass
Slow-paced, whose flanks have broken many a shaft
To splinters, crops the harvest as it grows, 680
And boys attack him with their rods,—though small
Their strength,—but scarce, till he has browsed his fill,
Can drive him forth,—so did the gallant sons
Of Troy, and their allies from distant lands,
Continually pursue the mighty son 685
Of Telamon, and hurl their spears against
The centre of his shield. And now he wheeled,
As conscious of great valor, and repulsed
The crowding phalanxes; and now again

He turned to flee. And thus he kept the foe 690
From reaching the swift galleys, while he stood
Between the Greeks and Trojans, terrible
In wrath. The javelins hurled by daring hands
Against him—some hung fixed in his broad shield;
And many, ere they came to his fair skin, 695
Fell midway,—eager though they were to pierce
The warrior's side,—and plunged into the earth.
   Eurypylus, Evæmon's noble son,
Saw Ajax sorely pressed with many darts,
And came and stood beside him, taking aim 700
With his bright spear, and in the liver smote,
Beneath the midriff, Apisaon, son
Of Phausias, and a prince among his tribe.
His knees gave way, and down he sank in death.
But godlike Alexander, who beheld 705
The slayer stripping Apisaon's corpse
Of armor, at that moment bent his bow,
And pierced Eurypylus in the right thigh.
The reed brake in the wound. He writhed with pain,
And mingled with his fellows in the ranks, 710
Avoiding death, yet shouting to the Greeks:—
   "O friends, the chiefs and leaders of the Greeks,
Rally and keep your ground; ward off the fate
Of death from Ajax, who is sorely pressed
With darts, and, much I fear, may not escape 715
Safe from this stormy conflict. Stand ye firm
Around the mighty son of Telamon."
   So spake the wounded warrior; while his friends
Rallied around him, with their shields inclined
Against their shoulders, and with lifted spears. 720
And Ajax came and joined them; then he turned,
And firmly faced the foe. The Greeks renewed
The combat with a rage like that of fire.
   Now meantime the Neleian coursers, steeped
In sweat, were bearing Nestor and the prince 725
Machaon from the battle. On the prow
Of his great ship, Achilles, swift of foot,
Looked forth, and, gazing on the hard-fought fray

And the sad rout, beheld them. Then he called
His friend Patroclus, shouting from the ship.   730
Patroclus heard, within the tent, and came,
Glorious as Mars;—yet with that day began
His woes. The gallant Menœtiades
Made answer thus: "Why callest thou my name,
Achilles, and what needest thou of me?"   735
    And thus rejoined Achilles, swift of foot:—
"Son of Menœtius, nobly born, and well
Beloved by me, the Greeks, I deem, will soon
Be at my knees, imploring aid; for now
A hard necessity besets their host.   740
But go, Patroclus, dear to Jove, and ask
Of Nestor who it is that he hath brought
Thus wounded from the field. Seen from behind,
His form was like Machaon,—wholly like
That son of Æsculapius; but the face   745
I saw not, as the rapid steeds flew by."
    He spake. Patroclus hearkened to his friend,
And hastened to the Grecian tents and ships.
    Now when they reached the tent of Neleus' son,
The warriors in the chariot set their feet   750
Upon the nourishing earth. Eurymedon,
The old man's charioteer, took from the mares
Their harness; while the chieftains cooled themselves,
And dried their sweaty garments in the breeze,
Facing the border of the sea, and then,   755
Entering the tent of Nestor, sat them down
On couches. Hecamedè, bright of hair,
Prepared for them a mingled draught; the maid,
A daughter of the great Arsinoüs, came
From Tenedos with Nestor, when the town   760
Was ravaged by Achilles, and the Greeks
Gave her to Nestor, chosen from the rest
For him, as wisest of their counsellors.
First she drew forth a table fairly wrought,
Of polished surface, and with steel-blue feet,   765
And on it placed a brazen tray which bore
A thirst-provoking onion, honeycomb,

And sacred meal of wheat. Near these she set
A noble beaker which the ancient chief
Had brought from home, embossed with studs of gold. 770
Four were its handles, and each handle showed
Two golden turtles feeding, while below
Two others formed the base. Another hand
Could scarce have raised that beaker from its place,
But Nestor lifted it with ease. The maid, 775
Fair as a goddess, mingled Pramnian wine,
And grated o'er it, with a rasp of brass,
A goat's-milk cheese, and, sprinkling the white flour
Upon it, bade them drink. With this they quenched
Their parching thirst, and then amused the time 780
With pleasant talk. Patroclus to the door
Meantime, a godlike presence, came, and stood.
The old man, as he saw him, instantly
Rose from his princely seat and seized his hand,
And led him in and bade him sit; but he 785
Refused the proffered courtesy, and said:—
    "Nay, 'tis no time to sit: persuade me not,
Nursling of Jove; for he is to be feared,
And prone to wrath, who sent me to inquire
What wounded man is with thee; but I know,— 790
Now that I see Machaon sitting here,
The shepherd of the people. I must haste
Back to Achilles, bearing my report.
Thou knowest, ancient chief, how quick he is
To take offence and blame the innocent." 795
    Then Nestor, the Gerenian knight, rejoined:—
"Why does Achilles pity thus the sons
Of Greece when wounded? Little can he know
What sorrow reigns throughout the Grecian host
While, smitten in the close or distant fight, 800
Our bravest lie disabled in their ships.
The valiant son of Tydeus—Diomed—
Is wounded; wounded Agamemnon lies,
And the great wielder of the javelin,
Ulysses. By an arrow in the thigh 805
Eurypylus is smitten, and I now

Bring home this warrior with an arrow-wound.
Yet doth Achilles, valiant as he is,
Care nothing for the Greeks. Will he then wait
Till our swift galleys, moored upon the shore, 810
After a vain defence shall feed the flames
Lit by the enemy's hand, and we be slain,
And perish, heaps on heaps? My strength is now
Not that which dwelt in these once active limbs.
Would I were strong and vigorous as of yore, 815
When strife arose between our men and those
Of Elis for our oxen driven away,
And, driving off their beeves in turn, I slew
The Elean chief, the brave Itymoneus,
Son of Hypirochus! For, as he sought 820
To save his herd, a javelin from my arm
Smote him the first among his band. He fell;
His rustic followers fled on every side;
And mighty was the spoil we took: of beeves
We drave off fifty herds, as many flocks 825
Of sheep, of swine as many, and of goats
An equal number, and of yellow steeds
Thrice fifty;—these were mares, and by their sides
Ran many a colt. We drave them all within
Neleian Pylos in the night. Well pleased 830
Was Neleus, that so large a booty fell
To me, who entered on the war so young.
When morning brake, the heralds' cry was heard
Summoning all the citizens to meet
To whom from fruitful Elis debts were due; 835
And then the princes of the Pyleans came,
And made division of the spoil. For much
The Epeians owed us: we were yet but few
In Pylos, and had suffered grievously.
The mighty Hercules in former years 840
Had made us feel his wrath, and of our men
Had slain the bravest: of the twelve who drew
Their birth from Neleus, I alone am left;
The others fell. The Epeians brazen-mailed
Saw this, delighted, and insulted us 845

And did us wrong. When now the spoil was shared
The old man for himself reserved a herd
Of oxen, and a numerous flock of sheep,—
Three hundred, with their shepherds,—for to him
Large debts were due in Elis. He had sent 850
Four horses once, of peerless speed, with cars,
To win a tripod, the appointed prize.
Augeias, king of men, detained them there,
And sent the grieving charioteer away.
My father, angered at the monarch's words 855
And acts, took large amends, and gave the rest
To share among the people, that no one
Might leave the ground, defrauded of his right.
All this was justly done, and we performed
Due sacrifices to the gods, throughout 860
The city;—when the third day came, and brought
The Epeians all at once, in all their strength,—
Both men on foot and prancing steeds. With these
Came the Molions twain, well armed, though young
And yet untrained to war. There is a town 865
Named Thryoëssa, on a lofty hill
Far off beside Alpheius, on the edge
Of sandy Pylos. They beleaguered this,
And sought to overthrow it. As they crossed
The plain, Minerva came, a messenger, 870
By night from Mount Olympus, bidding us
Put on our armor. Not unwillingly
The Pyleans mustered, but in eager haste
For battle. Yet did Neleus not consent
That I should arm myself,—he hid my steeds; 875
For still he deemed me inexpert in war.
Yet even then, although I fought on foot,
I won great honor even among the knights;
For so had Pallas favored me. A stream
Named Minyëius pours into the sea 880
Near to Arena, where the Pylean knights
Waited the coming of the holy morn,
While those who fought on foot came thronging in.
Thence, with our host complete, and all in arms,

We marched, and reached at noon the sacred stream 885
Alpheius, where to Jove Omnipotent
We offered chosen victims, and a bull
To the river-god, another to the god
Of ocean, and a heifer yet unbroke
To blue-eyed Pallas. Then we banqueted, 890
In bands, throughout the army, and lay down
In armor by the river-side to sleep.
Meantime the brave Epeians stood around
The city, resolute to lay it waste.
But first was to be done a mighty work 895
Of war; for as the glorious sun appeared
Above the earth we dashed against the foe,
Praying to Jove and Pallas. When the fight
Between the Eleans and the Pylean host
Was just begun, I slew a youthful chief,— 900
Mulius,—and bore away his firm-paced steeds.
The fair-haired Agamedè, eldest-born
Of King Augeias' daughters, was his spouse;
And well to her each healing herb was known
That springs from the great earth. As he drew near, 905
I smote him with my brazen lance: he fell
To earth: I sprang into his car, and stood
Among the foremost warriors; while, around,
The brave Epeians, as they saw him fall,—
The leader of their knights, their mightiest 910
In battle,—turned and, panic-stricken, fled,
Each his own way. I followed on their flight
Like a black tempest; fifty cars I took,
And from each car I dashed two warriors down,
Pierced by my spear. And now I should have slain 915
The young Molions also, Actor's sons,
Had not their father, he who shakes the earth,
Enshrouded them in mist, and hidden them
From all pursuit. Then with victorious might
Did Jove endue our arms, while we pursued 920
The foe across a region strewn with shields,—
Slaying, and gathering spoil,—until our steeds
Came to Buprasium, rich in fields of wheat,

And to the Olenian rock, and to the hill
Alesium in Colonè. Pallas there   925
Stayed our pursuit, and bade our host return.
There slew I the last man, and left him there.
And then the Achaians, guiding their swift steeds
Homeward to Pylos from Buprasium, gave
Great thanks to Jupiter among the gods,   930
And Nestor among men. Such was I then
Among the heroes; but Achilles keeps
His valor for himself alone,—and yet
Bitterly must he grieve when he beholds
Our people perish. O my friend! how well   935
Menœtius charged thee when he sent thee forth,
From Phthia, to Atrides! We were both—
The nobly-born Ulysses and myself—
Within the palace, and we clearly heard
What he commanded thee. For we had come   940
To Peleus' stately dwelling, on our way
Gathering a host in fertile Greece, and saw
The great Menœtius there, and there we found
Achilles with thee. There the aged knight
Peleus was burning, in the palace-court,   945
A steer's fat thighs to Jove the Thunderer,
And lifted up a golden cup and poured
Dark wine upon the blazing sacrifice.
And both of you were busy with the flesh
When we were at the threshold. As he saw   950
Our coming, in surprise Achilles sprang
Toward us, and took our hands and led us in,
Bade us be seated, and before us placed
The generous banquet due to stranger-guests.
Then, having feasted, I began discourse,   955
Exhorting you to join us. Both of you
At once consented, and your fathers gave
Their admonitions. Aged Peleus charged
His son Achilles to excel the rest
In valor, while Menœtius, in his turn,   960
The son of Actor, gave thee this command:—
   "'My son, Achilles is the nobler born,

But thou art elder. He surpasses thee
By far in warlike might, but thou must prompt
His mind with prudent counsels; thou must warn 965
And guide him; he will hearken to thy words
Meant for his good.' The old man charged thee thus.
Thou hast forgotten it. Yet speak thou now
To Peleus' warlike son; and haply he
May heed thy counsels. Thou perchance may'st bend 970
His will—who knows?—by thy persuasive words;
For wholesome are the warnings of a friend.
Yet, if he shrink from some predicted doom,
Or if his goddess-mother have revealed
Aught of Jove's counsels to him, then, at least 975
Let him send thee to war, and let his troop
Of Myrmidons go with thee, so that thou
May'st carry succor to the Greeks. Yet more,—
Let him permit thee in the field to wear
His glorious armor, that the Trojan host, 980
Beholding thee so like to him, may shun
The combat, and the warlike sons of Greece,
Hard-pressed, may breathe again, and find at length
A respite from the conflict. Ye, who still
Are fresh and vigorous, shall assault and drive 985
Townward the weary foe from camp and fleet."
   He spake. The spirit of the youth took fire,
And instantly he hastened toward the ships
Of Peleus' son. But when he came where lay
The galleys of Ulysses the divine, 990
Where was the assembly-place and judgment-seat,
And where the altars of the immortals stood,
Evæmon's noble son, Eurypylus,
Met him as from the battle-field he came
Halting, and with an arrow in his thigh. 995
The sweat ran down his shoulders and his brow,
And the black blood was oozing from his wound,
Yet was his spirit untamed. The gallant youth,
Son of Menœtius, saw with grief, and said:—
   "Unhappy chiefs and princes of the Greeks! 1000
Are ye then doomed to feast with your fair limbs

The famished dogs of Ilium, far away
From friends and country? Tell me, child of Jove,
Gallant Eurypylus, will yet the Greeks
Withstand the mighty Hector, or give way   1005
And perish, overtaken by his spear?"
   And thus the wise Eurypylus replied:—
"Nursling of Jove, Patroclus! for the Greeks
There is no help, and all at their black ships
Must perish; for within them even now   1010
All those who were our bravest warriors lie,
Wounded in close encounter, or from far,
By Trojan hands, whose strength with every hour
Becomes more terrible. Give now thine aid
And take me to my ship, and cut away   1015
The arrow from my thigh, and from the part
Cleanse with warm water the dark blood, and shed
Soothing and healing balms upon the wound,
As taught thee by Achilles, who had learned
The art from Chiron, righteous in his day   1020
Beyond all other Centaurs. Now the leech
Machaon lies, I think, among the tents,
Wounded, and needs the aid of others' skill,
And Podalirius out upon the plain
Helps stem the onset of the Trojan host."   1025
   Then spake the valiant Menœtiades:—
"O brave Eurypylus! what yet will be
The end of this, and what are we to do?
Even now I bear a message on my way
From reverend Nestor, guardian of the Greeks,   1030
To the great warrior, Peleus' son; and yet
I must not leave thee in thine hour of need."
   He spake; and, lifting in his arms the prince,
He bore him to his tent. A servant spread,
Upon his entering, hides to form a couch;   1035
And there Patroclus laid him down and cut
The rankling arrow from his thigh, and shed
Warm water on the wound to cleanse away
The purple blood, and last applied a root
Of bitter flavor to assuage the smart,   1040

Bruising it first within his palms: the pangs
Ceased; the wound dried; the blood no longer flowed.

BOOK XII

THUS in the camp Menœtius' valiant son
Tended Eurypylus, and dressed his wounds;
While yet in mingled throngs the warriors fought,—
Trojans and Greeks. Nor longer was the trench
A barrier for the Greeks, nor the broad wall   5
Which they had built above it to defend
Their fleet; for all around it they had drawn
The trench, yet not with chosen hecatombs
Paid to the gods, that so it might protect
The galleys and the heaps of spoil they held.   10
Without the favor of the gods it rose,
And therefore was not long to stand entire.
As long as Hector lived, and Peleus' son
Was angered, and King Priam's city yet
Was not o'erthrown, so long the massive wall   15
Built by the Greeks stood firm. But when at length
The bravest of the Trojans had been slain,
And many of the Greeks were dead,—though still
Others survived,—and when in the tenth year
The city of Priam fell, and in their ships   20
The Greeks went back to their beloved land,
Then did Apollo and the god of sea
Consult together to destroy the wall
By turning on it the resistless might
Of rivers, all that from the Idæan heights   25
Flow to the ocean,—Rhesus, Granicus,

Heptaporus, Caresus, Rhodius,
Æsepus, and Scamander's hallowed stream,
And Simoïs, in whose bed lay many shields
And helms and bodies of slain demigods.   30
Phœbus Apollo turned the mouths of these
All toward one spot; nine days against the wall
He bade their currents rush, while Jupiter
Poured constant rain, that floods might overwhelm
The rampart; and the god who shakes the earth,   35
Wielding his trident, led the rivers on.
He flung among the billows the huge beams
And stones which, with hard toil, the Greeks had laid
For the foundations. Thus he levelled all
Beside the hurrying Hellespont, destroyed   40
The bulwarks utterly, and overspread
The long broad shore with sand; and then he brought
Again the rivers to the ancient beds
In which their gently flowing waters ran.
   This yet was to be done in time to come   45
By Neptune and Apollo. Meanwhile raged
Battle and tumult round that strong-built wall.
The towers in all their timbers rang with blows;
And, driven as by the scourge of Jove, the Greeks,
Hemmed closely in beside their roomy ships,   50
Trembled at Hector, the great scatterer
Of squadrons, fighting, as he did before,
With all a whirlwind's might. As when a boar
Or lion mid the hounds and huntsmen stands,
Fearfully strong, and fierce of eye, and they   55
In square array assault him, and their hands
Fling many a javelin;—yet his noble heart
Fears not, nor does he fly, although at last
His courage cause his death; and oft he turns,
And tries their ranks; and where he makes a rush   60
The ranks give way;—so Hector moved and turned
Among the crowd, and bade his followers cross
The trench. The swift-paced horses ventured not
The leap, but stood upon the edge and neighed
Aloud, for the wide space affrighted them;   65

And hard it was to spring across, or pass
From side to side, for on each side the brink
Was steep, and bristled with sharp stakes, close set
And strong, which there the warrior sons of Greece
Had planted, a defence against the foe. 70
No steed that whirled the rapid car along
Could enter, but the soldiery on foot
Eagerly sought to pass, and in these words
Polydamas to daring Hector spake:—
   "Hector, and ye who lead the troops of Troy 75
And our auxiliars! rashly do we seek
To urge our rapid steeds across the trench
So hard to pass, beset with pointed stakes,—
And the Greek wall so near. The troops of horse
Cannot descend nor combat there: the space 80
Is narrow: they would all be slain. If Jove,
The Thunderer of the skies, design to crush
The Greeks and succor Troy, I should rejoice
Were the design at once fulfilled, and all
The sons of Greece ingloriously cut off, 85
Far from their Argos. But if they should turn
Upon us, and repulse us from their fleet,
And we become entangled in the trench,
I deem no messenger would e'er go back
To Troy from fighting with the rallied Greeks. 90
Heed, then, my words, and let the charioteers
Stay with the coursers at the trench, while we,
Armed, and on foot, and all in close array,
Follow our Hector. For the Greeks in vain
Will strive to stem our onset if, in truth, 95
The hour of their destruction be at hand."
   So spake Polydamas; and Hector, pleased
To hear the prudent counsel, leaped to earth
With all his arms, and left his car. The rest
Rode with their steeds no more, but, hastily 100
Dismounting, as they saw their noble chief,
Each bade his charioteer hold back his steeds,
Reined at the trench, in ranks. And then, apart,
They mustered in five columns, following close

Their leaders. First, the largest, bravest band,   105
Those who, with resolute daring, longed to break
The rampart and to storm the fleet, were led
By Hector and the good Polydamas,
Joined with Cebriones,—for Hector left
His chariot to the care of one who held   110
An humbler station than Cebriones.
Paris, Alcathoüs, and Agenor led
A second squadron. Helenus, a son
Of Priam, and Deïphobus, a youth
Of godlike form, his brother, took command   115
Of yet a third,—with whom in rank was joined
The hero Asius, son of Hyrtacus,
Whose bright-haired coursers, of majestic size,
Had borne him from Arisba and the banks
Of Selleïs. Æneas led the fourth,—   120
The brave son of Anchises; and with him
Were joined Archilochus and Acamas,
Sons of Antenor, skilled in arts of war.
The band of Troy's illustrious allies
Followed Sarpedon, who from all the rest   125
Had chosen, to partake in the command,
Glaucus and brave Asteropæus. These
He deemed the bravest under him; yet he
Stood foremost of them all in warlike might.

   Then all, with their stout bucklers of bull's-hide   130
Adjusted to each other, bravely marched
Against the Greeks, who, as they deemed, must fly
Before them, and must fall by their black ships.
Then all the other Trojans, and the allies
From foreign shores, obeyed the counsel given   135
By good Polydamas; but Asius, son
Of Hyrtacus, and prince of men, chose not
To leave his chariot and his charioteer,
But drave with them against the roomy ships.
Vain youth!—he was not destined to return,   140
Borne by his steeds and chariot, from the fleet,
And from the fate he braved, to wind-swept Troy,
His evil fate o'ertook him from the spear

Of great Idomeneus, Deucalion's son;
For toward the galleys moored upon the left   145
He hastened by the way in which the Greeks,
With steeds and cars, retreated from the plain.
Thither he drave his coursers; there he found
The gates not closed, nor the long bar across,
But warriors held them open to receive   150
In safety their companions as they fled
From battle to the fleet. Exultingly
He turned his coursers thither, and his men
Followed him, shouting; for they thought the Greeks
Could not abide their onset, but must yield,   155
And perish by their ships. Deluded men!—
They met two mighty warriors at the gate,—
The brave descendants of the Lapithæ,
That warlike tribe: Pirithoüs' gallant son
Was one, named Polypœtes; with him stood   160
Leonteus, strong as Mars the slayer of men.
By the tall gates they stood, as giant oaks
Stand on the mountains and abide the wind
And the tempestuous rains of all the year,
Firm-planted on their strong and spreading roots. 165
So they, confiding in their strength of arm,
Waited for mighty Asius hasting on,
And fled not. Onward came the hostile troop,
With their tough shields uplifted, and with shouts:
All rushing toward the massive wall they came,   170
Following King Asius, and Iamenus,
Orestes, Thoön, Acamas the son
Of Asius, and Œnomaus. Meanwhile
Leonteus and his comrade had retired
Within, encouraging the well-armed Greeks   175
To combat for the fleet; but when they saw
The rout and panic of their flying host,
They darted forth and fought before the gates,—
Fought like wild boars that in the mountains meet
A clamorous troop of men and dogs, and dart   180
Sideway at their assailants, break the trees
Close to the root, and fiercely gnash their tusks,

Until some javelin strikes them, and they die.
So on the breasts of the two warriors rang
The shining brass, oft smitten; for they fought 185
Fearlessly, trusting in the aid of those
Who held the wall, and their own valiant arms.
And they who stood on the strong towers hurled down
Stones, to defend the Achaians and their tents
And their swift ships. As snow-flakes fall to earth 190
When strong winds, driving on the shadowy cloud,
Shower them upon the nourishing glebe, so thick
Were showered the weapons from the hands of Greeks
And Trojans; and the helms and bossy shields,
Beaten by stones, resounded. Asius then— 195
The son of Hyrtacus—in anger groaned,
And smote his thighs impatiently, and said:—
   "O Father Jove! thou then art wholly false.
I did not look to see the men of Greece
Stand thus before our might and our strong arms; 200
Yet they, like pliant-bodied wasps or bees,
That build their cells beside the rocky way,
And quit not their abode, but, waiting there
The hunter, combat for their young—so these,
Although but two, withdraw not from the gates, 205
Nor will, till they be slain or seized alive."
   He spake; but moved not thus the will of Jove,
Who planned to give the glory of the day
To Hector. Meanwhile, at the other gates
Fought other warriors,—but 'twere hard for me, 210
Were I a god, to tell of all their deeds;
For round the wall on every side there raged,
Fierce as consuming fire, a storm of stones.
The Greeks, in bitter anguish, yet constrained,
Fought for their fleet; and sorrowful were all 215
The gods who in the battle favored Greece.
   Now the two Lapithæ began the fight.
Pirithoüs' son, brave Polypœtes, cast
His spear at Damasus; it broke its way
Through the helm's brazen cheek,—nor that alone: 220
Right through the temple went the brazen blade,

And crushed the brain within. He left him slain,
And next struck Pylon down, and Ormenus.
Leonteus, of the stock of Mars, assailed
Hippomachus, who from Antimachus 225
Derived his birth; he pierced him at the belt,
And, drawing forth his trenchant sword, hewed down,
In combat hand-to-hand, Antiphates;
He dashed him backward to the ground, and next
Smote Menon and Iamenus; and last 230
He slew Orestes: at his feet they lay,
A pile of dead, upon their mother Earth.
   Then, as the twain were stripping from the dead
Their glittering arms, the largest, bravest band
Of those who eagerly desired to break 235
The rampart and to burn the ships with fire,
Following Polydamas and Hector, stood
Consulting at the trench. An augury,
Just as they were in act to cross, appeared
Upon the left: an eagle high in air, 240
Between the armies, in his talons bore
A monstrous serpent, bleeding, yet alive
And palpitating,—nor disabled yet
For combat; for it turned, and on the breast
Wounded the eagle, near the neck. The bird 245
In pain let fall his prize amid the host,
And flew away, with screams, upon the wind.
The Trojans shuddered at the spotted snake
Lying among them, and Polydamas
Said thus to fearless Hector, standing near:— 250
   "Hector, thou almost ever chidest me
In council, even when I judge aright.
I know it ill becomes the citizen
To speak against the way that pleases thee,
In war or council,—he should rather seek 255
To strengthen thy authority; yet now
I will declare what seems to me the best:
Let us not combat with the Greeks, to take
Their fleet; for this, I think, will be the end,—
If now the omen we have seen be meant 260

For us of Troy who seek to cross the trench;—
This eagle, flying high upon the left,
Between the hosts, that in his talons bore
A monstrous serpent, bleeding, yet alive,
Hath dropped it mid our host before he came   265
To his dear nest, nor brought it to his brood;—
So we, although by force we break the gates
And rampart, and although the Greeks fall back,
Shall not as happily retrace our way;
For many a Trojan shall we leave behind,   270
Slain by the weapons of the Greeks, who stand
And fight to save their fleet. Thus will the seer,
Skilled in the lore of prodigies, explain
The portent, and the people will obey."
   Sternly the crested Hector looked, and spake:—   275
"Polydamas, the thing that thou hast said
Pleases me not, and easily couldst thou
Frame better counsels. If thy words convey
Thy earnest thought, the gods assuredly
Have made thee lose thy senses. Thou dost ask   280
That I no longer reverence the decree
Of Jove, the Thunderer of the sky, who gave
His promise, and confirmed it. Thou dost ask
That I be governed by the flight of birds,
Which I regard not, whether to the right   285
And toward the morning and the sun they fly,
Or toward the left and evening. We should heed
The will of mighty Jupiter, who bears
Rule over gods and men. One augury
There is, the surest and the best,—to fight   290
For our own land. Why dreadest thou the war
And conflict? Though we all should fall beside
The galleys of the Greeks, there is no fear
That thou wilt perish, for thou hast no heart
To stand against the foe;—no warrior thou!   295
Yet, if thou dare to stand aloof, or seek
By words to turn another from the fight,
The spear I wield shall take thy life at once."
   He spake, and went before; and all his band

Followed with fearful clamor. Jupiter, 300
The God of thunders, sending a strong wind
From the Idæan summits, drave the dust
Full on the galleys, and made faint the hearts
Of the Greek warriors, and gave new renown
To Hector and the men of Troy. For these, 305
Trusting in portents sent from Jupiter,
And their own valor, labored to break through
The massive rampart of the Greeks: they tore
The galleries from the towers, and levelled down
The breastworks, heaved with levers from their place 310
The jutting buttresses which Argive hands
Had firmly planted to support the towers,
And brought them to the ground; and thus they hoped
To force a passage to the Grecian camp.
Not yet did they of Greece give way: they fenced 315
The rampart with their ox-hide shields, and smote
The enemy from behind them as he came
Under the wall. The chieftains Ajax flew
From tower to tower, and cheered the Achaians on,
And roused their valor,—some with gentle words, 320
And some with harsh rebuke,—whome'er they saw
Skulk from the toils and dangers of the fight.
  "O friends!" they said, "ye great in war, and ye
Of less renown, and ye of little note!—
For all are not alike in war,—the time 325
Demands the aid of all, as well ye know:
And now let no man turn him toward the fleet
Before the threats of Hector, but press on,
And each exhort his fellow: so may Jove,
Who flings the lightning from Olympus, grant 330
That, driving back their onset, we may chase
The enemy to the very walls of Troy."
  Thus in the van they shouted, and awoke
New courage in the Greeks. As when the flakes
Of snow fall thick upon a winter-day, 335
When Jove the Sovereign pours them down on men,
Like arrows, from above;—he bids the wind
Breathe not; continually he pours them down,

And covers every mountain-top and peak,
And flowery mead, and field of fertile tilth, 340
And sheds them on the havens and the shores
Of the gray deep; but there the waters bound
The covering of snows,—all else is white
Beneath that fast-descending shower of Jove;—
So thick the shower of stones from either side 345
Flew toward the other,—from the Greeks against
The Trojans, and from them against the Greeks;
And fearful was the din along the wall.
   Yet would illustrious Hector and the men
Of Troy have failed to force the gates and burst 350
The bar within, had not all-seeing Jove
Impelled his son Sarpedon to attack
The Greeks as falls a lion on a herd
Of hornèd beeves. The warrior held his shield,
A brazen orb, before him,—beautiful, 355
And fenced with metal; for the armorer laid
Broad plates without, while under these he sewed
Bull's-hides the toughest, edged with golden wires
Upon the rim. With this the warrior came,
Wielding two spears. As when a lion, bred 360
Among the mountains, fasting long from flesh,
Comes into the fenced pastures, without fear,
To prey upon the flock; and though he meet
The shepherds keeping watch with dogs and spears,
Yet will he not be driven thence until 365
He makes a spring into the fold and bears
A sheep away, or in the act is slain,
Struck by a javelin from some ready hand;—
Sarpedon, godlike warrior, thus was moved
By his great heart to storm the wall and break 370
Through the strong barrier; and to Glaucus, son
Of Lycia's king Hippolochus, he said:—
   "Why, Glaucus, are we honored, on the shores
Of Lycia, with the highest seat at feasts,
And with full cups? Why look men up to us 375
As to the gods? And why do we possess
Broad, beautiful enclosures, full of vines

And wheat, beside the Xanthus? Then it well
Becomes us, foremost in the Lycian ranks
To stand against the foe, where'er the fight 380
Is hottest; so our well-armed Lycian men
Shall say, and truly: 'Not ingloriously
Our kings bear rule in Lycia, where they feast
On fallings of the flock, and drink choice wine;
For they excel in valor, and they fight 385
Among our foremost.' O my friend, if we,
Leaving this war, could flee from age and death,
I should not here be fighting in the van,
Nor would I send thee to the glorious war;
But now, since many are the modes of death 390
Impending o'er us, which no man can hope
To shun, let us press on and give renown
To other men, or win it for ourselves!"

   He spake; and Glaucus not unwillingly
Heard and obeyed. Right on the warriors pressed, 395
Leading the Lycian host. Menestheus, son
Of Peteus, saw, and trembled; for they came
With evil menace toward his tower. He looked
Along the Grecian lines in hope to see
Some chieftain there whose ready help might save 400
His comrades from their danger. He beheld
The rulers Ajax, never tired of war,
Standing with Teucer, who just then had left
His tent; and yet they could not hear his shout,
So fearful was the din that rose to heaven 405
From all the shields, and crested helms, and gates,
Smitten with missiles,—for at all the gates
The Lycians thundered, struggling hard to break
A passage through them. Then Menestheus called
A herald near, and bade Thoötes bear 410
A message to the leaders Ajax, thus:—

   "Go, nobly-born Thoötes, and in haste
Call Ajax,—call them both, for that were best,—
Since terrible will be the slaughter here,
So fiercely are the Lycians pressing on, 415
Impetuous ever in assault. If there

The fight be also urgent, then at least
Let the brave Telamonian Ajax come,
And Teucer, the great archer, follow him."
    He spake. The herald listened and obeyed,   420
And flew along the summit of the wall
Built by the Greeks. He reached, and stood beside,
The chieftains Ajax, and addressed them thus:—
    "Ajaces, leaders of the warlike Greeks,
The honored son of noble Peteus asks   425
That ye will come, though for a little space,
To aid him and to share his warlike toils;
For terrible will be the slaughter there,
So fiercely are the Lycians pressing on,
Impetuous ever in assault. If here   430
The fight be also urgent, then at least
Let the brave Telamonian Ajax come,
And Teucer, the great archer, follow him."
    He ended. Ajax, son of Telamon,
Hearkened, and to his fellow-warrior said:—   435
    "Here, where the gallant Lycomedes stands,
Ajax! remain, and, cheering on the Greeks,
Lead them to combat valiantly. I go
To stem the battle there, and when our friends
Are succored I will instantly return."   440
    So speaking, Ajax, son of Telamon,
Departed thence, and with him Teucer, sprung
From the same father. With them also went
Pandion, carrying Teucer's crooked bow.
They came to brave Menestheus at his tower,   445
And went within the wall and met their friends,
Hard-pressed,—for gallantly the Lycian chiefs
And captains, like a gloomy tempest, rushed
Up the tall breastworks; while the Greeks withstood
Their onset, and a mighty clamor rose.   450
    Then Telamonian Ajax smote to death
Epicles, great of soul, Sarpedon's friend:
Against that chief he cast a huge, rough stone,
That lay high up beside a pinnacle
Within the wall. No man with both his hands,—   455

Such men as now are,—though in prime of youth,
Could lift its weight; and yet he wielded it
Aloft, and flung it. Through the four-coned helm
It crashed, and brake the skull within. Down plunged
The Lycian, like a diver, from his place   460
On the high tower, and life forsook his limbs.
Then Teucer also wounded with a shaft
Glaucus, the brave son of Hippolochus,
As he leaped forth to scale the lofty wall,—
Wounded him where the naked arm was seen,   465
And made him leave the combat. Back he sprang,
Hiding amid the crowd, that so the Greeks
Might not behold the wounded limb, and scoff.
With grief Sarpedon saw his friend withdraw,
Yet paused not from the conflict, but took aim   470
At Thestor's son, Alcmaon, with his spear;
Pierced him; and drew the weapon out. The Greek,
Following the spear, fell headlong; and his arms,
Studded with brass, clashed round him as he fell.
Then did Sarpedon seize, with powerful hands,   475
The battlement; he wrenched it, and it came
To earth, and laid the rampart's summit bare,
To make a passage for the assailing host.
Ajax and Teucer saw, and both took aim
Together at Sarpedon: Teucer's shaft   480
Struck in the midst the buckler's glittering belt,
Just at the bosom; but Jove warded off
The death-stroke from his son, lest he should fall
Beside the galleys. Ajax, springing, struck
The buckler with his spear, and pierced its folds,   485
And checked the eager warrior, who gave way
A little, yet retreated not, but turned,
Encouraging the godlike Lycians thus:—
 "Where, Lycians, is your fiery valor now?
Were I the bravest, it were hard, alone,   490
For me to force a passage to the fleet,
Though I have cleared the way. Come on with me!
Light is the task when many share the toil."
 He spake; and they who reverenced his words

Of exhortation drew more closely round 495
Their counsellor and sovereign, while the Greeks
Above them made their phalanxes more strong
Within the wall,—for urgent was the need;
Since neither could the gallant Lycians break
The barrier of the Greeks, and cut their way 500
Through to the fleet, nor could the warlike Greeks
Drive back the Lycians when they once had reached
The rampart. As two men upon a field,
With measuring-rods in hand, disputing stand
Over the common boundary, in small space, 505
Each one contending for the right he claims,
So, kept asunder by the breastwork, fought
The warriors over it, and fiercely struck
The orbèd bull's-hide shields held up before
The breast, and the light targets. Many a one 510
Was smitten when he turned and showed the back
Unarmed, and many wounded through the shield.
The towers and battlements were steeped in blood
Of heroes,—Greeks and Trojans. Yet were not
The Greeks thus put to flight; but, as the scales 515
Are held by some just woman, who maintains,
By spinning wool, her household,—carefully
She poises both the wool and weights, to make
The balance even, that she may provide
A pittance for her babes,—thus equally 520
Were matched the warring hosts, till Jupiter
Conferred the eminent glory of the day
On Hector, son of Priam. He it was
Who first leaped down into the space within
The Grecian wall, and, with far-reaching voice, 525
Thus shouted, calling to the men of Troy:—
    "Rush on, ye knights of Troy! rush boldly on,
And break your passage through the Grecian wall,
And hurl consuming flames against their fleet!"
    So spake he, cheering on his men. They heard, 530
And rushed in mighty throngs against the wall,
And climbed the battlements, to charge the foe
With spears. Then Hector stooped, and seized a stone

Which lay before the gate, broad at the base
And sharp above, which two, the strongest men,—　　535
As men are now,—could hardly heave from earth
Into a wain. With ease he lifted it,
Alone, and brandished it: such strength the son
Of Saturn gave him, that it seemed but light.
As when a shepherd carries home with ease　　540
A wether's fleece,—he bears it in one hand,
And little is he cumbered with its weight,—
So Hector bore the lifted stone, to break
The beams that strengthened the tall folding-gates.
Two bars within, laid crosswise, held them firm,—　　545
Both fastened with one bolt. He came and stood
Before them; with wide-parted feet he stood,
And put forth all his strength, that so his arm
Might drive the missile home; and in the midst
He smote the folding-gates. The blow tore off　　550
The hinges; heavily the great stone fell
Within; the portals crashed; nor did the bars
Withstand the blow: the shattered beams gave way
Before it; and illustrious Hector sprang
Into the camp. His look was stern as night;　　555
And terribly the brazen armor gleamed
That swathed him. With two spears in hand he came,
And none except the gods—when once his foot
Was on the ground—could stand before his might.
His eyes shot fire, and, turning to his men,　　560
He bade them mount the wall; and they obeyed:
Some o'er the wall, some through the sculptured gate,
Poured in. The Achaians to their roomy ships
Fled, and a fearful uproar filled the air.

BOOK XIII

WHEN Jove had brought the Trojans and their chief,
Hector, beside the ships, he left them there
To toil and struggle and endure, while he
Turned his resplendent eyes upon the land
Of Thracian horsemen, and the Mysians, skilled   5
To combat hand to hand, and the famed tribe
Of long-lived Hippomulgi, reared on milk,
And the most just of men. On Troy no more
He turned those glorious eyes, for now he deemed
That none of all the gods would seek to aid   10
Either the Greeks or Trojans in the strife.
  The monarch Neptune kept no idle watch;
For he in Thracian Samos, dark with woods,
Aloft upon the highest summit sat,
O'erlooking thence the tumult of the war;   15
For thence could he behold the Idæan mount,
And Priam's city, and the Grecian fleet.
There, coming from the ocean-deeps, he sat,
And pitied the Greek warriors put to rout
Before the Trojans, and was wroth with Jove.   20
Soon he descended from those rugged steeps,
And trod the earth with rapid strides; the hills
And forests quaked beneath the immortal feet
Of Neptune as he walked. Three strides he took,
And at the fourth reached Ægæ, where he stopped,   25
And where his sumptuous palace-halls were built,

Deep down in ocean, golden, glittering, proof
Against decay of time. These when he reached,
He yoked his swift and brazen-footed steeds,
With manes of flowing gold, to draw his car,
And put on golden mail, and took his scourge,
Wrought of fine gold, and climbed the chariot-seat,
And rode upon the waves. The whales came forth
From their deep haunts, and frolicked round his way:
They knew their king. The waves rejoicing smoothed
A path, and rapidly the coursers flew;
Nor was the brazen axle wet below.
And thus they brought him to the Grecian fleet.
   Deep in the sea there is a spacious cave,
Between the rugged Imbrus and the isle
Of Tenedos. There Neptune, he who shakes
The shores, held back his steeds, took off their yoke,
Gave them ambrosial food, and, binding next
Their feet with golden fetters which no power
Might break or loosen, so that they might wait
Their lord's return, he sought the Grecian host.
   Still did the Trojans, rushing on in crowds,
Like flames or like a tempest, follow close
Hector, the son of Priam; still their rage
Abated not; with stormy cries they came;
They hoped to seize the fleet and slay the Greeks
Beside it. But the power who swathes the earth
And shakes it, Neptune, coming from the deep,
Revived the valor of the Greeks. He took
The shape of Calchas and his powerful voice,
And thus to either Ajax, who yet stemmed
The battle with a resolute heart, he spake:—
   "O chieftains! yours it is to save the host,
Recalling your old valor, with no thought
Of fatal flight. Elsewhere I feel no dread
Of what the daring sons of Troy may do
Who climb the wall in throngs; the well-greaved Greeks
Will meet them bravely. But where Hector leads,
Fierce as a flame, his squadrons, he who boasts
To be a son of sovereign Jove, I fear

Lest we should sorely suffer. May the gods
Strengthen your hearts to stand against the foe,
And flinch not, and exhort the rest to stand,
And drive him back, audacious as he is,
From the swift ships, though Jove should urge him on." 70
    Thus earth-surrounding Neptune said, and touched
Each hero with his sceptre, filled their hearts
With valor, gave new lightness to their limbs
And feet and hands, and then, as when a hawk
Shoots swiftly from some lofty precipice 75
And chases o'er the plain another bird,
So swiftly Neptune, shaker of the shores,
Darted from them away. Oïleus' son
Perceived the immortal presence first, and thus
At once to Telamonian Ajax spake:— 80
    "Some god, O Ajax, from the Olympian hill,
Wearing the augur's form, hath bid us fight
Beside the ships; nor can it be the seer
Calchas, for well I marked his feet and legs
As he departed; easily by these 85
The gods are known. I feel a spirit roused
In my own bosom eager to engage
In the fierce strife; my very feet below,
And hands above, take part in the desire."
    And thus the son of Telamon replied:— 90
"So also these strong hands that grasp the spear
Burn eagerly to wield it, and my heart
Is full of courage. I am hurried on
By both my feet, and vehemently long
To try alone the combat with this chief 95
Of boundless valor, Hector, Priam's son."
    Thus they conferred, rejoicing as they felt
That ardor for the battle which the god
Had breathed into their hearts. Meantime he roused
The Achaians at the rear, who in their ships 100
Sought respite, and whose limbs were faint with toil,
And their hearts sad to see the Trojan host
With tumult pouring o'er the lofty wall.
As they beheld, the tears came gushing forth

From underneath their lids; they little hoped 105
For rescue from destruction; but when came
The power that shakes the shores, he woke anew
The spirit of their valiant phalanxes.
Teucer he first addressed, and Leïtus,
The hero Peneleus and Thoas next, 110
Deïpyrus, Meriones expert
In battle, and Antilochus his peer,
And thus exhorted them with wingèd words:—
   "Shame on you, Argive youths! I put my trust
In your tried valor to defend our fleet; 115
But if ye fear to face the perilous fight,
The day has risen which shall behold us fall
Vanquished before the Trojans. O ye gods!
These eyes have seen a marvel, a strange sight
And terrible, which I had never thought 120
Could be,—the Trojans close upon our ships,
They who, erewhile, were like the timid deer
That wander in the wood an easy prey
To jackals, pards, and wolves,—weak things, unapt
For combat, fleeing, but without an aim. 125
Such were the Trojans, who till now ne'er dared
Withstand the might and prowess of the Greeks
Even for an hour. But now, afar from Troy
They give us battle at the hollow ships,
All through our general's fault, and through the sloth 130
Of the Greek warriors, who, displeased with him,
Fight not for their swift galleys, but are slain
Beside them. Yet although our sovereign chief,
Atrides Agamemnon, may have done
Foul wrong, dishonoring the swift-footed son 135
Of Peleus, still ye cannot without blame
Decline the combat. Let us then repair
The mischief done; the hearts of valiant men
Are soon appeased. And not without the loss
Of honor can your fiery courage sleep, 140
Since ye are known the bravest of the host.
I would not chide the weak, unwarlike man
For shrinking from the combat; but for you,—

I look on you with anger in my heart.
Weaklings! ye soon will bring upon yourselves 145
Some sorer evil if ye loiter thus.
Let each of you bethink him of the shame
And infamy impending. Terrible
The struggle is before us. Hector storms
The ships, loud-shouting Hector; he has burst 150
The gate and broken the protecting bar."
  So Neptune spake, encouraging the Greeks.
While firmly stood the serried phalanxes
Round either Ajax, nor could Mars himself,
Nor Pallas, musterer of armèd hosts, 155
Reprove their order. There the flower of Greece
Waited the Trojans and their noble chief,
Spear beside spear, and shield by shield, so close
That buckler pressed on buckler, helm on helm,
And man on man. The plumes of horse-hair touched 160
Each other as they nodded on the crests
Of the bright helms, so close the warriors stood.
The lances quivered in the fearless hands
Of warriors eager to advance and strike
The enemy. But the men of Troy began 165
The assault; the fiery Hector was the first
To rush against the Greeks. As when a stone
Rolls from a cliff before a wintry flood
That sweeps it down the steep, when mighty rains
Have worn away the props that held it fast; 170
It rolls and bounds on high; the woods around
Crash, as it tears its unresisted way
Along the slope until it reach the plain,
And there, however urged, moves on no more;—
So Hector, menacing to cut his way 175
Through tents and galleys to the very sea,
Slaying as he went forward, when he now
Met the firm phalanxes and pressed them close,
Stopped suddenly; the sons of Greece withstood
His onset and repulsed it, striking him 180
With swords and two-edged spears, and made the chief
Give way before the shock. He lifted up

His voice and shouted to the Trojans thus:—
    "Trojans and Lycians and Dardanians skilled
In fighting hand to hand, stand firm. Not long   185
Will the Greeks bide my onset, though drawn up
Square as a tower in close array. My spear,
I trust, will scatter them, if true it be
That Juno's husband, Sovereign of the gods,
And Lord of thunders, prompts my arm to-day."   190
    He spake, and kindled in the breasts of all
Fresh courage. In the band Deïphobus
Marched proudly, Priam's son, with his round shield
Before him, walking with a quick, light step
Behind its shelter. Then Meriones   195
Aimed at the chief his glittering spear; the point
Missed not; it struck the orb of bullock's hide,
Yet did not pierce it, for the weapon broke
Just at the neck. Deïphobus held forth
His shield far from him, dreading to receive   200
A spear-thrust from the brave Meriones.
Vexed thus to lose the victory, and the spear
Snapped by the blow, Meriones fell back
Into the column of his friends, and passed
Hastily toward the camp and ships, to bring   205
A powerful spear that stood within his tent,
While others fought, and fearful was the din.
    Then Teucer first, the son of Telamon,
Smote gallant Imbrius, son of Mentor, lord
Of many steeds. He, ere the Greeks had come   210
To Troy, dwelt at Pedæum and espoused
Medesicasta, Priam's spurious child.
But when the well-oared galleys of the Greeks
Mustered at Troy, he also came, and there
Was eminent among her chiefs, and dwelt   215
With Priam, and was honored as his son.
The son of Telamon beneath the ear
Pierced him with his long javelin, and drew forth
The weapon. Headlong to the earth he fell.
As on a mountain height, descried from far,   220
Hewn by a brazen axe, an ash is felled

And lays its tender sprays upon the ground,
Thus Imbrius fell, and round him in his fall
Clashed his bright armor. Teucer sprang in haste
To spoil the dead, but Hector hurled at him 225
His shining spear; the wary Teucer stepped
Aside, and just escaped the brazen blade.
It struck Amphimachus, Cteatus' son,
And Actor's grandson; as he came to join
The battle, he was smitten in the breast, 230
And fell, his armor clashing round his limbs.
Then Hector flew in haste to tear away
From the large-souled Amphimachus the helm
That cased his temples. Ajax saw, and hurled
His glittering spear at Hector as he came: 235
It made no wound; for Hector stood equipped
All o'er in formidable brass. The spear
Struck on the bossy shield with such a shock
As forced him to recoil, and leave unspoiled
The bodies, which the Achaians dragged away. 240
For Stichius and Menestheus, chief among
The Athenians, bore the dead Amphimachus
To the Greek camp, while the two men of might,
The Chieftains Ajax, lifted Imbrius up;
And as two lions, bearing off among 245
The close-grown shrubs a goat, which they have snatched
From sharp-toothed dogs, uplift it in their jaws
Above the ground, so the two warriors raised
The corpse of Imbrius, and stripped off the mail,
While, angered that Amphilochus was slain, 250
Oïleus' son struck from the tender neck
The head, and sent it far among the crowd,
Whirled like a ball, to fall at Hector's feet.
   Meantime was Neptune moved with grief to see
His grandson perish in that desperate fray, 255
And passed among the Achaian tents and ships
Encouraging the men, and planning woes
For Ilium. There he met Idomeneus,
Expert to wield the spear, as he returned
From caring for a comrade who had left 260

The battle, wounded in the knee, and whom
His friends had carried in. Idomeneus
Had called the surgeons to his aid, and now
Was hastening to the field, intent to bear
His part in battle. Him the monarch god 265
Of ocean thus addressed, but first he took
The voice of Thoas, King Andræmon's son,
Whose father ruled the Ætolians through the bounds
Of Pleuron, and in lofty Calydon,
And like a god was honored in the land. 270
  "O counsellor of Crete, Idomeneus!
Where are the threats which late the sons of Greece
Uttered against the Trojans?" Promptly came
The Cretan leader's answer: "No man here,
O Thoas, seems blameworthy, for we all 275
Are skilled in war, nor does unmanly fear
Hold any back; nor from the difficult strife
Does sloth detain one warrior. So it is
Doubtless that it seems good to Saturn's son,
The All-disposer, that the Greeks, afar 280
From Argos, should ingloriously fall
And perish. Thoas, thou wert ever brave,
And didst exhort the laggards. Cease not now
To combat, cease not to exhort the rest."
  And Neptune, he who shakes the earth, rejoined:— 285
"Idomeneus, whoever keeps aloof
From battle, willingly, to-day, may he
Never return from Troy, but be the prey
Of dogs. Take thou thy arms and come with me,
For we must quit ourselves like men, and strive 290
To aid our cause, although we be but two.
Great is the strength of feeble arms combined,
And we can combat even with the brave."
  So speaking, Neptune turned to share the toils
Of war. Idomeneus, who now had reached 295
His princely tent, put on his glorious mail,
And seized two spears, and flew upon his way,
Like lightning grasped by Saturn's son and flung
Quivering above Olympus' gleaming peak,

A sign to mortals, dazzled by the blaze,   300
So glittered, as he ran, his brazen mail.
His fellow-warrior, good Meriones,
Met him beside the tent, for he had come
To fetch a brazen javelin thence, and thus
The stout Idomeneus addressed his friend:—   305
    "O son of Molus, swift Meriones,
Dearest of all my comrades! Why hast thou
Thus left the battle-field? Hast thou a wound,—
A weapon's point that galls thee? Dost thou bring
A message to me? Think not that I sit   310
Within my tent an idler; I must fight."
    Discreetly did Meriones reply:—
"Idomeneus, whose sovereign counsels rule
The well-armed Cretans, I am come to seek
A spear if one be left within thy tents.   315
I broke the one I bore, in hurling it
Against the shield of fierce Deïphobus."
    The Cretan chief, Idomeneus, rejoined:—
"If spears thou seek, there stand within my tent
Twenty and one against the shining walls.   320
I took them from slain Trojans. 'Tis my wont
Never to fight at distance from the foe,
And therefore have I spears, and bossy shields,
And helms, and body-mail of polished brass."
    Then spake in turn discreet Meriones:—   325
"Within my tent are also many spoils
Won from the Trojans, and in my black ship;
But they are far away. I do not think
That I forget what valor is. I fight
Among the foremost in the glorious strife   330
Where'er the battle calls me. Other men
Among the well-armed Greeks may not have seen
What I perform, but thou must know me well."
    Idomeneus, the Cretan leader, spake:—
I know thy courage well. What need hast thou   335
To speak as thou hast done? If all of us,
The bravest of the Greeks, were set apart
To form an ambush;—for an ambush tries

And shows men's valor; there the craven, there
The brave, is known; the coward's color comes 340
And goes; his spirit is not calm within
His bosom, so that he can rest awhile
And tremble not; he shifts his place; he sits
On both his feet; his heart beats audibly
Within his breast; his teeth at thought of death 345
Chatter; the brave man's color changes not,
Nor when with other warriors he sits down
In ambush is he troubled, but he longs
To rise and mingle in the desperate fray;—
For thee, in such an ambush, none could blame 350
Thy courage or thy skill. If there the foe
Should wound thee from afar, or smite thee near,
The weapon would not strike thy neck behind,
Or pierce thy back, but enter at thy breast
Or stomach, as thou wert advancing fast 355
Among the foremost. But enough of this.
Come! stand we here no longer, idiot-like,
Lest some one chide us sharply. Hasten thou,
And bring a sturdy javelin from the tent."

He spake. Meriones, like Mars in port 360
And swiftness, hastened to the tent and brought
A brazen spear, and joined Idomeneus,
Eager for battle. As the god of war,
The man-destroyer, comes into the field,
With Terror, his strong-limbed and dauntless son, 365
Following and striking fear into the heart
Of the most resolute warrior, when from Thrace
They issue armed against the Ephyri,
Or else against the Phlegyans large of soul,
And hearken not to both the hosts, but give 370
To one the victory; so Meriones
Advanced to battle with Idomeneus,
Leaders of heroes both, and both equipped
In glittering helms. And first Meriones
Spake and addressed his fellow-warrior thus:— 375

"Son of Deucalion, at which point wilt thou
Enter the throng? Upon the army's right,

Its centre, or its left? The long-haired Greeks
Seem most to need our aid upon the left."
   Then spoke Idomeneus, in turn, the prince   380
Of Cretans: "At the centre of the fleet
Are others who will guard it. Posted there
Are either Ajax and the most expert
Of Grecian archers, Teucer, not less skilled
In standing fight, and amply will they task   385
The arm of Hector, Priam's son, though bent
On desperate conflict, and though passing fierce.
With all his fierceness, he will find it hard
To quell their prowess, never yet o'ercome,
And fire the ships, unless Saturnian Jove   390
Himself should cast on them the flaming torch.
Nor yet will Telamonian Ajax yield
To any man of mortal birth, or reared
Upon the grains of Ceres, or whom brass
Or ponderous stones can wound. He would not own   395
The warlike son of Peleus mightier
Than he in standing fight, although in speed
He vies not with him. Lead us then to join
The army's left, that we may learn at once
Whether our fate in battle shall confer   400
Glory on other men, or theirs on us."
   So spake the chief. Meriones, the peer
Of Mars in swiftness, hastened till he joined
The army where his comrade bade. The foe
Beheld Idomeneus, who like a flame   405
Swept on with his companion all in arms
Gloriously wrought; they raised from rank to rank
The battle-cry, and met him as he came,
And hand to hand, before the galleys' sterns
Was waged the combat. As when storms arise,   410
Blown up by piping winds, when dust lies loose
Along the roads, a spreading cloud of dust
Fills the wide air, so came the battle on
Between the bands that struggled eagerly
To slay each other. All along the line   415
The murderous conflict bristled with long spears

That tore the flesh; the brazen splendor, shot
From gleaming helmets and from burnished mail
And shining bucklers, all in narrow space,
Dazzled the eyes. Brave-hearted would he be,   420
The man who, gazing on it, could have seen
The furious strife rejoicing or unmoved.
   Meantime the potent sons of Saturn each
Favored a different side, and planned new toils
For all the warriors. Jupiter had willed   425
That Hector and the Trojans should prevail,
Yet had he not decreed the Achaian host
To perish before Troy; he only sought
To honor Thetis and her large-souled son.
But Neptune, mingling with the Greeks, aroused   430
Their martial spirit. From the hoary deep
He came unmarked, for deeply was he grieved
To see the Greeks give way before the host
Of Troy, and he was wroth with Jupiter.
Both gods were of one race, and owed their birth   435
To the same parents; but the elder-born
Was Jupiter, and wiser. For that cause
Not openly did Neptune aid the Greeks,
But, as by stealth, disguised in human form,
Moved through their army and encouraged them   440
To combat. Thus it was the potent twain
Each drew, with equal hand, the net of strife
And fearful havoc, which no power could break
Or loosen, stretched o'er both the warring hosts,
And laying many a warrior low in death.   445
And now, although his brows were strewn with gray,
Idomeneus, encouraging the Greeks,
Rushed on the Trojans, and revived the fight.
He slew Orthryoneus, who just before,
Drawn by the rumor of the war, had left   450
Cabesus, and now made a lover's suit
For Priam's fairest daughter. Without dower
He sought to wed Cassandra, promising
A vast exploit,—to drive the Greeks from Troy,
In spite of all their valor. The old king   455

Consented that the maiden should be his;
And now he fought, and trusted to fulfil
His promise. But Idomeneus took aim,
And cast his glittering javelin at the youth.
It struck him marching proudly on, nor stopped 460
The weapon at the brazen mail, but pierced
The stomach. With a clash the warrior fell,
And thus the victor boasted over him:—
    "Orthryoneus, I deem thee worthy of praise
Beyond all other men, if thou perform 465
What thou hast undertaken,—to defend
Dardanian Priam, who has promised thee
His daughter. We would make a compact too,
And will perform it,—to bestow on thee
A spouse, the fairest daughter of the house 470
Of Atreus' son, and we will send for her
To Argos, if thou join us, and lay waste
The well-built Ilium. Now, then, follow me,
And at the ships which brought us we will treat
Of marriage, and will make no niggard terms." 475
    So spake Idomeneus, and dragged the slain
Through the sharp conflict by the foot. He met
Asius, who walked before his car, and came
To avenge his friend. The attending charioteer
Behind him reined the steeds, that they should breathe 480
Over the shoulders of their lord, who sought
To smite Idomeneus. The Greek was first
To strike; he plunged the spear into his throat
Below the chin, and drave the weapon through.
The Trojan fell to earth as falls an oak, 485
Poplar, or stately pine, which woodmen fell
With their sharp axes on the mountain-side,
To form a galley's beam. So there he lay
Stretched out before his coursers and his car,
And gnashed his teeth, and clenched the bloody dust. 490
The charioteer, amazed, and losing power
Of action, dared not turn the horses back
To bear him from the foe. Antilochus
The warlike cast his spear, and in the midst

Transfixed him. Little did the brazen mail 495
Avail to stay the blade, which cleft its way
Into the stomach. With a sudden gasp
He toppled from the sumptuous chariot-seat,
And large-souled Nestor's son, Antilochus,
Drave with the chariot to the well-armed Greeks. 500
Deïphobus, who sorrowed for the fate
Of Asius, drawing near Idomeneus,
Hurled at him his bright spear. The Greek beheld,
As face to face they stood, and scaped the stroke,
Covered by his round shield, two-handled, strong 505
With bullocks' hides and glittering brass. With this
He hid himself, close couched within, and turned
The brazen point aside. The buckler rang
Shrilly; the weapon glanced away, yet flew
Not vainly from the Trojan's powerful hand: 510
It struck Hypsenor, son of Hippasus,
The shepherd of the people, on the side
Where lies the liver, just below the breast.
His knees gave way; he fell; Deïphobus
Thus shouted o'er the dead his empty boast:— 515
   "Not unavenged lies Asius, and no doubt,
In journeying to the massy gates and wall
Of Hades, will rejoice that I have sent
A soul to be companion of his way."
   He spake; and at his boast the Greeks were moved 520
With anger,—most of all Antilochus
The warlike; yet he left not to the foe
His slain companion, but made haste to hold
His shield above him. His beloved friends,
Mecisteus, son of Echius, and the prince 525
Alastor, lifted up, with many a groan,
The corpse, and bore it to the roomy ships.
   Meantime the valor of Idomeneus
Remitted not; he vehemently longed
To cover many a Trojan with the night 530
Of death, or fall himself with clashing arms,
In warring to defend the ships of Greece.
The brave Alcathoüs, the beloved son

Of Æsyetus, whom Anchises made
His son-in-law,—for he had given to him 535
Hippodameia, eldest-born of all
His daughters, whom her parents, while she dwelt
With them, loved dearly, fair and wise beyond
All other maidens of her age, and skilled
In household arts; so that the noblest prince 540
Of the broad Trojan kingdom made her his;—
Him, by the weapon of Idomeneus,
Did Neptune bring to death. The sparkling eyes
Grew dim, and stiffened were the shapely limbs,
For neither could he flee nor turn aside; 545
But as he stood before him, column-like,
Or like a towering tree, Idomeneus
Transfixed him in the bosom with his spear.
The brazen coat of mail gave way, which oft
Had saved him, breaking with a sharp, shrill sound 550
Before the severing blade. He fell to earth
With noise; the spear stood planted in his heart,
And as he panted quivered through its length,
Yet soon its murderous force was spent and still.
And then the victor boasted thus aloud:— 555
    "Deïphobus, does this appear to thee
A fair return, when three are slain for one,
Or hast thou boasted idly? Yet do thou,
Vain as thou art, stand forth and face me here,
And I will teach thee of what race I am,— 560
An offshoot of the stock of Jove, whose son
Was Minos, guardian of our Crete, and he
Was father of the good Deucalion.
Deucalion's son am I, and I am king
O'er many men in the broad isle of Crete. 565
My galleys brought me thence to be the dread
Of thee, thy father, and the men of Troy."
    He spake. Deïphobus, irresolute,
Stood doubting whether to retreat and bring
Some other of the heroic sons of Troy 570
To aid him, or to try the fight alone.
As thus he mused, it seemed most wise to seek

Æneas. Him he found withdrawn among
The rear of the army, for he was displeased
With noble Priam, who had paid his worth 575
With light esteem. Deïphobus approached,
And thus with wingèd words accosted him:—
   "Æneas, counsellor of Troy, if thou
Hadst ever a regard to him who was
Thy sister's husband, it becomes thee now 580
To avenge him. Follow me, and help avenge
Alcathoüs, guardian of thy tender years,
Slain by the spear of famed Idomeneus."
   He spake; and at his words Æneas felt
His courage rise. Impatient for the fight, 585
He went to meet Idomeneus; yet fear
Fell not upon the Greek as if he were
A puny boy: he stood and kept his ground.
As, when a mountain boar, unterrified,
Waits in the wilderness the hunter-crew, 590
That come with mighty din, his bristly back
Rises, his eyes shoot fire, he whets his tusks,
And fiercely keeps both dogs and men at bay,—
So did Idomeneus, expert to wield
The spear, await Æneas hastening on 595
With fury. Not a backward step he made,
But called upon his warrior-friends aloud,
Looking at Aphareus, Ascalaphus,
Deïpyrus, Meriones, and last
Antilochus, all skilled in arts of war, 600
And thus exhorted them with wingèd words:—
   "Haste hither, O my friends, and bring me aid.
I stand alone, in dread of the approach
Of swift Æneas, who comes fiercely on,
Powerful to slay, and in his prime of youth, 605
The highest vigor of the human frame.
Yet, were our years the same, that chief or I
Would quickly triumph at the other's cost."
   He spake, and all with one accord drew near
And stood by him, with shields obliquely held 610
Upon their shoulders. On the other side

Æneas cheered his comrades on. He fixed
His look on Paris, and Deïphobus,
And nobly-born Agenor, who, like him,
Were leaders of the Trojans. After these   615
The soldiers followed, as the thronging flock
Follow the ram that leads them to the fount
From pasture, and the shepherd's heart is pleased.
So was Æneas glad at heart to see
The multitude of warriors following him.   620
  Then mingled they in battle hand to hand
Around Alcathoüs, with their ponderous spears,
And fearfully upon their bosoms rang
The brass, as through the struggling crowd they aimed
Their weapons at each other. Two brave men,   625
Æneas and Idomeneus, the peers
Of Mars, conspicuous o'er their fellows, strove
With cruel brass to rend each other's limbs.
And first Æneas cast his spear to smite
Idomeneus, who saw it as it came,   630
And shunned it. Plunging in the earth beyond,
It stood and quivered; it had left in vain
The Trojan's powerful hand. Idomeneus
Next smote Œnomaüs: the spear brake through
His hollow corslet at the waist; it pierced   635
And drank the entrails: down amid the dust
He fell, and grasped the earth with dying hand.
Idomeneus plucked forth the massy spear,
But, pressed by hostile weapons, ventured not
To strip the sumptuous armor from the dead;   640
Since now no more the sinews of his feet
Were firm to bear him rushing to retake
His spear, or start aside from hostile spears.
Wherefore in standing fight he warded off
The evil hour, nor trusted to his feet   645
To bear him fleetly from the field. He moved
Slowly away, and now Deïphobus,
Who long had hated him and bitterly,
Aimed at him his bright spear; it missed its mark,
And struck Ascalaphus, the son of Mars.   650

The weapon cleft the shoulder of the Greek,
Who fell amid the dust, and clenched the earth.
  Not yet the clamorous Mars, of passionate mood,
Had heard that in the fray his son was slain;
But on the summit of the Olympian mount   655
He sat, o'ercanopied by golden clouds,
Restrained from combat by the will of Jove,
With other gods, forbidden, like himself,
To aid the combatants. Meantime around
Ascalaphus the combat hand to hand   660
Still raged. Deïphobus had torn away
The slain man's shining helm, when suddenly
Meriones sprang forward, spear in hand,
And smote him on the arm; the wounded limb
Let fall the helm, resounding as it fell,   665
And with a vulture's leap Meriones
Rushed toward him, plucking out from the torn flesh
The spear, and falling back among the crowd.
Polites, brother of the wounded, threw
Both arms around his waist, and bore him off   670
From the loud din of conflict, till he reached
His swift-paced steeds, that waited in the rear
Of battle, with their chariot nobly wrought
And charioteer. These took him back to Troy,
Heavily groaning and in pain, the blood   675
Yet gushing from the newly wounded limb.
   Still fought the other warriors, and the noise
Of a perpetual tumult filled the air.
Æneas, rushing upon Aphareus,
Caletor's son, who turned to face him, thrust   680
A sharp spear through his throat. With drooping head,
And carrying shield and helmet to the ground,
He fell, and rendered up his soul in death.
Antilochus, as Thoön turned away,
Attacked and smote him, cutting off the vein   685
That passes through the body to the neck.
This he divided sheer; the warrior fell
Backward, and lay in dust, with hands outstretched
To his beloved friends. Antilochus

Flew to the slain, and from his shoulders stripped 690
The armor, casting cautious glances round;
While toward him pressed the Trojans on all sides,
Striking the fair broad buckler with their darts,
Yet could not even score with pointed brass
The tender skin of Nestor's son; for still 695
Neptune, the shaker of the sea-coast, kept
Watch o'er him while the weapons round him showered.
Yet he withdrew not from his foes, but moved
Among the crowd, nor idle was his spear,
But wielded right and left, and still he watched 700
With resolute mind the time to strike the foe
At distance, or assault him near at hand.
   The son of Asius, Adamas, beheld
The hero meditating thus, and struck,
In close attack, the middle of his shield 705
With a sharp brazen spear. The dark-haired god
Who rules the deep denied to Adamas
The life he sought, and weakened the hard stroke.
Part of the Trojan's weapon, like a stake
Hardened by fire, stood fixed within the shield, 710
Part lay on earth, and he who cast it slunk
Among his comrades to avoid his fate.
Meriones, pursuing with his spear,
Smote him between the navel and the groin,
Where deadliest are the wounds in battle given 715
To man's unhappy race. He planted there
The cruel blade, and Adamas, who fell,
Writhed panting round it, as a bullock bound
By cowherds on the mountain with strong cords
Pants as they lead him off against his will. 720
So wounded, Adamas drew heavy breath,
And yet not long. The brave Meriones,
Approaching, plucked the weapon forth, and night
Came o'er the eyes of Adamas. At hand
Stood Helenus, and struck Deïpyrus 725
Upon the temple with his ponderous sword,
Of Thracian make, and cut the three-coned helm
Away, and dashed it to the ground; it rolled

Between a Grecian warrior's feet, who stooped
And took it up, while o'er its owner's eyes 730
The darkness gathered. Grieved at this, the son
Of Atreus, Menelaus great in war,
Rushed forward, threatening royal Helenus.
He brandished his sharp spear; the Trojan drew
His bow; advancing, one to hurl a lance, 735
And one to send an arrow. Priam's son
Let fly a shaft at Menelaus' breast.
The bitter missile from the hollow mail
Glanced off. As when from the broad winnowing-fan
On some wide threshing-floor the swarthy beans, 740
Or vetches, bound before the whistling wind
And winnower's force, so, bounding from the mail
Of gallant Menelaus, flew afar
The bitter shaft. Then Menelaus, great
In battle, smote the hand of Helenus 745
That held the polished bow; the brazen spear
Passed through the hand, and reached the bow, and there
Stood fixed, while Helenus, avoiding death,
Drew back among his comrades, with his hand
Held low, and trailing still the ashen stem. 750
Magnanimous Agenor from the wound
Drew forth the blade, and wrapped the hand in wool,
Carefully twisted, taken from a sling
Carried by an attendant of the chief.
   To meet the glorious Menelaus sprang 755
Pisander, led by his unhappy fate
To perish, Menelaus! by thy hand
In that fierce conflict. When the two were near,
Advancing toward each other, Atreus' son
Took aim amiss; his spear flew far aside. 760
Pisander smote the buckler on the arm
Of mighty Menelaus, yet drave not
The weapon through. The broad shield stopped its force,
And broke it at the neck; yet hoped he still
For victory, and exulted. Then the son 765
Of Atreus drew his silver-studded sword
And sprang upon his foe, who from beneath

His buckler took a brazen battle-axe,
With a long stem of polished olive-wood.
Both struck at once. Pisander hewed away,   770
Below the crest, the plumèd helmet-cone
Of Atreus' son, who smote, above the nose,
Pisander's forehead, crashing through the bones.
Both bleeding eyes dropped to the ground amid
The dust; he fell; he writhed; the conqueror,   775
Advancing, set his heel upon his breast,
And stripped the armor off, and, boasting, said:—
   "Thus shall ye leave unharmed the fleet that brought
The knights of Greece, ye treaty-breaking sons
Of Ilium, never satisfied with war!   780
Yet lack ye not still other guilt and shame,—
Wrong done to me, ye dogs! Ye have not feared
The wrath of Hospitable Jove, who flings
The thunder, and will yet destroy your town,
With all its towers,—ye who, without a cause,   785
Bore off my youthful bride, and heaps of wealth,
When she had given you welcome as our guests.
And now ye seek to burn with fire the fleet
With which we cross the ocean, and to slay
The Grecian heroes. Ye shall yet be forced,   790
Eager for battle as ye are, to pause.
O Father Jupiter, who hast the praise
Of highest wisdom among gods and men!
All this is of thy ordering. How hast thou
Favored this arrogant crew of Troy, in love   795
With violence, who never have enough
Of war and all its many miseries!
All other things soon satisfy desire,—
Sleep, love, and song, and graceful dance, which most
Delight in more than warlike toils,—yet they   800
Of Troy are never satisfied with war."
   So spake the illustrious man, and, having stripped
The bloody armor from the dead, he gave
The spoil to his companions, and rejoined
The warriors in the van. Harpalion then,   805
A son of King Pylæmenes, with whom

He left his home to join the war at Troy,
Assaulted him. He never saw again
His native land. Close to Atrides' shield,
He struck it in the centre with his lance, 810
Yet could not drive the weapon through the brass,
And backward shrank, in fear of death, among
His comrades, looking round him lest some foe
Should wound him with the spear. Meriones
Let fly a brazen arrow after him, 815
Which, entering his right flank below the bone,
Passed through and cleft the bladder. Down he sank
Where the shaft struck him, breathing out his life
In the arms of his companions. Like a worm
He lay extended on the earth; his blood 820
Gushed forth, a purple stream, and steeped the soil.
The large-souled Paphlagonians came around,
And placed him in a chariot, sorrowing,
And bore him to the gates of sacred Troy.
The father followed weeping, but no hand 825
Was raised to avenge the slaughter of his son.
   Yet deeply moved was Paris at his death,
For he had been Harpalion's guest among
The Paphlagonians. Grieving for the slain,
He sent a brazen arrow from his bow. 830
Now there was one Euchenor, rich and brave,
The son of Polyïdus, hoary seer;
His dwelling was in Corinth, and he came,
Forewarned and conscious of his fate, to Troy;
For often Polyïdus, good old man, 835
Warned him that he within his palace halls
Should perish by a grievous malady,
Or else be slain by Trojan hands beside
The Grecian fleet. So, to escape at once
The censure of the Achaians and disease, 840
He came, lest he in after times might rue
His choice. And now between the jaw and ear
Did Paris smite him; from the warrior's limbs
Life fled, and darkness gathered o'er his eyes.
   And then they fought; like a devouring fire 845

That battle was; but Hector, dear to Jove,
Had not yet learned that on the left the Greeks
Made havoc of his men; for in that hour
The Greeks had almost made the victory theirs,
So greatly had the god who shakes the shores   850
Kindled their courage, and with his own arm
Brought timely aid. Still Hector, pressing on
Where first he leaped within the gates and wall,
Broke the close phalanxes of shielded Greeks.
There, ranged beside the hoary deep, the ships   855
Of Ajax and Protesilaüs lay.
The wall that guarded them was low, and there
Warriors and steeds in fiercest conflict met;
There the Bœotians, there in their long robes
The Iäonians, there the Locrians, there   860
The men of Phthia, and the Epeians famed
For valor, held back Hector, struggling on
To reach the ships, yet found they had no power
To drive the noble warrior from the ground,
For he was like a flame. The chosen men   865
Of Athens formed the van. Menestheus, son
Of Peteus, was their leader, after whom
Phidas and Stichius followed, and with them
The gallant Bias. Meges, Phyleus' son,
With Dracius and Amphion, marshalled there   870
The Epeians; while the Phthian band were led
By Medon and Podarces, warlike chief.
And Medon was the great Oïleus' son,
And brother of the lesser Ajax, born
Without the tie of wedlock, and he dwelt   875
Far from his native land, in Phylacè;
For by his violent hand the brother died
Of Eryopis, whom Oïleus made
His lawful spouse. Podarces was the son
Of Iphiclus, and dwelt in Phylacè.   880
These, at the head of Phthia's valiant youth,
And cased in massive armor, fought beside
Bœotia's warriors for the Grecian fleet.
  But Ajax swift of foot, Oïleus' son,

From him of Telamon departed not 885
Even for an instant. As when two black steers
Of equal vigor o'er a fallow draw
The strongly jointed plough, till near their horns
Streams the warm sweat; the polished yoke alone
Holds them asunder, as they move along 890
The furrow, and the share divides the soil
That lies between them;—so the heroic twain
Kept near each other. Many men and brave
Followed to Troy the son of Telamon
As his companions, and, when weariness 895
Came o'er his sweaty limbs, relieved their chief
Of his broad buckler. But the Locrian host
Attended not Oïleus' great-souled son,
Nor could they ever venture to engage
In combat hand to hand. No brazen helms 900
Were theirs, with horse-hair plumes, no orbèd shields,
Nor ashen spears. They came with him to Troy,
Trusting in their good bows, and in their slings
Of twisted wool, from which they showered afar
Stones that dispersed the phalanxes of Troy. 905
The chieftains Ajax, warring in the van,
Clad in their shining armor, fought to check
The Trojans and their leader, brazen-mailed,
While in the rear the Locrians lurked unseen,
And sent their shafts, so that the men of Troy, 910
All order lost, were fain to cease from fight.
   Then had the Trojans from the ships and tents
Turned back, and fled, with fearful loss of life,
To lofty Ilium, if Polydamas
Had not accosted valiant Hector thus:— 915
   "Hector, thou hearkenest not to warning words.
Deem'st thou, because a god has given thee strength
Beyond all other men for feats of war,
That therefore thou art wiser than they all
In council? Think not for thyself to claim 920
All gifts at once. On one the god bestows
Prowess in war, upon another grace
In dance, upon another skill to touch

The harp and sing. In yet another, Jove
The Thunderer, implants the prudent mind, 925
By which the many profit, and by which
Communities are saved; and well doth he
Who hath it know its worth. Now let me speak
What seems to me the wisest. Round thee flames
The encircling war; the valiant sons of Troy, 930
Since they have crossed the ramparts, stand aloof,
Armed as they are, or fight against large odds
Scattered among the galleys. Yield thou now
The ground, and, summoning the chiefs, decide
What plan to follow,—whether we shall storm 935
The well-oared galleys, should the God vouchsafe
The victory to us,—or else depart
In safety from the fleet. I greatly fear
The Achaians may repay to us the debt
Of yesterday. There yet is at the fleet 940
One who, I think, no longer will refrain
Wholly from battle." Thus Polydamas
Spake, and the sage advice pleased Hector well,
Who, leaping from his chariot to the ground,
With all his weapons, said these wingèd words:— 945
    "Remain with all the bravest warriors here,
Polydamas, while I depart to give
The due commands, and instantly return."
    He spake, and with a shout he rushed away,
Seen from afar, like a snow-mountain's peak, 950
And flew among the Trojans and allies,
Who crowded round the brave Polydamas,
The son of Panthoüs, at Hector's call.
Among the foremost combatants he sought
Deïphobus, and mighty Helenus, 955
The king; he looked for Adamas, the son
Of Asius, and for Asius of the house
Of Hyrtacus. Some not unharmed he found,
Yet not o'ercome; while others lay in death
Beneath the galley-sterns, where Grecian hands 960
Had slain them; others on the wall, struck down
By missiles, or in combat hand to hand.

There on the left of that disastrous fray
He met the noble Alexander, spouse
Of fair-haired Helen, as he cheered his men, 965
And rallied them to battle. Hector thus
Addressed his brother with reproachful words:—
   "Accursed Paris! noble but in form,
Effeminate seducer! where are now
Deïphobus, and mighty Helenus? 970
And Adamas, the son of Asius, where?
And Asius, son of Hyrtacus? and where
Orthryoneus? Now towering Ilium sinks
From her high summit, and thy fate is sure."
And then the godlike Paris answered thus:— 975
   "Since it hath pleased thee, Hector, thus to cast
Reproach on me, though innocent, I may
Another day neglect the toils of war,
Although in truth my mother brought me forth
Not quite unapt for combat. Since the hour 980
When thou didst lead the battle to the ships
With thy companions, we have held our ground,
Here on this spot, contending with the Greeks.
Three chiefs for whom thou askest have been slain.
Deïphobus and mighty Helenus, 985
Both wounded in the hand by massive spears,
Have left the field; the son of Saturn saved
Their lives. Now lead us wheresoe'er thou wilt,
And we will follow thee with resolute hearts,
Nor deem that thou wilt find in us a lack 990
Of valor while our strength of arm remains.
The boldest cannot fight beyond his strength."
   With such persuasive words the warrior calmed
His brother's anger, and they went where raged
The hottest conflict round Cebriones, 995
Phalces, Orthæus, and the excellent
Polydamas, with Palmys at his side,
And Polyphœtes, godlike in his form,
And where Ascanius and Morys fought,
Sons of Hippotion. They the day before 1000
Came marching from Ascania's fertile fields,

Moved by the will of Jove to share the war.
All these swept on, as when a hurricane,
A thunder-gust, from Father Jupiter
Buffets the plain, and mingles with the deep, 1005
In mighty uproar, and the billows rise
All over the resounding brine, and swell,
Whitening with foam, and chase each other on.
So moved the Trojans on, man after man,
In close array, all armed in glittering brass, 1010
Following their generals. Hector, Priam's son,
And peer of Mars in battle, led the van,
His round shield held before him, tough with hides
And overlaid with brass. Upon his brow
The gleaming helmet nodded as he moved. 1015
On every side he tried the phalanxes,
If haply they might yield to his assault,
Made from beneath that buckler; but the Greeks
In spirit or in order wavered not.
And Ajax, striding forth, defied him thus:— 1020
    "Draw nearer, friend! Think'st thou to frighten thus
The Greeks? We are not quite so inexpert
In war, although so cruelly chastised
By Jupiter. Thou thinkest in thy heart
That thou shalt make our ships thy spoil; but we 1025
Have also our strong arms to drive thee back,
And far more soon the populous town of Troy,
Captured and sacked, shall fall by Grecian hands.
And now I warn thee that the hour is near
When, fleeing, thou shalt pray to Father Jove 1030
And all the immortals, that thy long-maned steeds,
Bearing thee townward mid a cloud of dust
Along the plain, may be more swift than hawks."
    As thus he spake, an eagle, to the right,
High in the middle heaven, flew over him, 1035
And, gladdened by the omen, all the Greeks
Shouted; but then illustrious Hector spake:—
    "Babbler and boaster, what wild words are these?
O Ajax I would that I were but as sure
To be the child of ægis-bearing Jove, 1040

Brought forth by Juno the august, and held
In honor everywhere like that which crowns
Apollo and Minerva, as I know
That to the Greeks this very day will bring
Destruction, and that thou shalt also lie 1045
Slain with the others, if thou dare abide
The stroke of my long spear, which yet shall tear
Thy dainty flesh, and thou, with thy full limbs,
Shalt be the feast of Trojan dogs and birds,
Unburied by the galleys of the Greeks." 1050
  So Hector spake, and led his warriors on.
They followed with a mighty shout; the rear
Sent up as loud a cry. On the other side
Shouted the Greeks, nor intermitted now
Their wonted valor, but stood firm to breast 1055
The onset of the chosen men of Troy.
The mingled clamor of both hosts went up
To heaven, and to the shining seat of Jove.

BOOK XIV

THE mighty uproar was not unperceived
By Nestor's ear, who sitting at the wine,
Addressed the son of Æsculapius thus:—
"Noble Machaon, what will happen now?
Bethink thee: for the clamor grows more loud   5
From our young warriors at the ships. Stay here
And drink the purple wine, while for thy limbs
The fair-haired Hecamede warms the bath
And washes the dark blood away, and I
Will climb the watch-tower, and will know the worst."   10
   He spake, and took a buckler, fairly wrought,
Glittering with brass, and left within the tent
By Thrasymedes, his own knightly son,
Who to the war had borne his father's shield;
He grasped a ponderous spear, with brazen blade,   15
And stood without the tent, and saw a sight
Of shame,—the routed Greeks, and close behind
The haughty Trojans putting them to flight,
And the Greek wall o'erthrown. As when the face
Of the great deep grows dark with weltering waves, 20
That silently forbode the swift descent
Of the shrill blast, the yet uncertain seas
Roll not to either side, till from the seat
Of Jupiter comes down the violent wind,—
So paused the aged chief, uncertain yet   25
Of purpose,—whether he should join the throng

Of Greeks, with their swift coursers, or repair
To sovereign Agamemnon, Atreus' son.
This to his thought seemed wiser, and he went
To seek Atrides. Meantime both the hosts 30
Urged on the work of slaughter; still they fought,
And still the solid brass upon their limbs
Rang, smitten with the swords and two-edged spears.
    Then, coming from the fleet, the wounded kings,
Nurslings of Jove, met Nestor; toward him came 35
Tydides, and Ulysses, and the son
Of Atreus, Agamemnon. On the beach
Of the gray deep their ships were ranged afar
From that fierce conflict. There the Greeks had drawn,
To the plain's edge, the first that touched the land, 40
And built a rampart at their sterns. Though long
The shore-line, it sufficed not to contain
The galleys, and the host had scanty room;
Wherefore they drew the galleys up in rows,
Row behind row, and filled the shore's wide mouth 45
Between the promontories. There the kings
Walked, leaning on their lances, to behold
The tumult and the fight, and inly grieved.
The sight of aged Nestor startled them,
And thus the royal Agamemnon spake:— 50
    "Neleian Nestor, glory of the Greeks,
Why hast thou left the murderous fray, and why
Come hither? Much I fear the fiery chief,
Hector, will make the menace good which once
He uttered, speaking to the men of Troy,— 55
Not to return to Ilium from the fleet
Till he had burned our ships with fire, and slain
Us also; thus he spake, and now fulfils
His menace. O ye gods! the other Greeks,
And not Achilles only, cherish hate 60
Against me in their hearts, and now refuse
To combat even where our galleys lie."
    And Nestor, the Gerenian knight, replied:—
"Thus is the threat accomplished, nor can Jove
The Thunderer reverse the event. The wall 65

In which we trusted as impregnable,
Our fleet's defence and ours, is overthrown;
But obstinately still the Greeks maintain
The combat at the ships, nor couldst thou now
Distinguish with thy sharpest sight where most   70
The ranks are routed, so confusèdly
They fall, and the wild uproar reaches heaven.
Meantime consult we what may yet be done,
If counsel aught avail; yet can I not
Advise to mingle in the strife again.   75
It is not meet that wounded men should fight."
   And then the royal Agamemnon said:—
"Since at our ships, beneath their very sterns,
The combat rages; since the wall we built
Avails not, nor the trench, at which the Greeks   80
Labored and suffered, hoping it might be
A sure defence for us and for our fleet,
Certain it is that to Almighty Jove
It hath seemed good that here the Greeks, afar
From Argos, should be shamefully cut off;   85
For well was I aware when he designed
To aid the Greeks, and well can I perceive
That he is honoring now the men of Troy
Like to the blessed gods, and fettering
Our valor and our hands. Hear my advice,   90
And follow it. Let us draw down the ships
Nearest the sea, and launch them on the deep,
And moor them, anchored, till the lonely night
Shall come, when, if the Trojans pause from war,
Haply we may draw down the other barks;   95
For he who flees from danger, even by night,
Deserves no blame; and better is his fate
Who flees from harm than his whom harm o'ertakes."
   Then wise Ulysses, with stern look, replied:—
"What words, Atrides, have escaped thy lips?   100
Unhappy man, thou shouldst have held command
O'er some effeminate army, and not ours,—
Ours to whom Jupiter, from youth to age,
Hath granted to accomplish difficult wars,

Until we pass away. And wouldst thou then 105
Depart from Troy, the city of broad streets,
For which we have endured so much and long?
Nay, be thou silent, lest the other Greeks
Hear words that never should be said by one
Who knows to speak with wisdom, and who bears 110
The sceptre, and who rules so many Greeks
As thou dost. I contemn with my whole soul
The counsel thou hast given, commanding us,
While yet the battle rages, to draw down
Our good ships to the sea, that so the foe 115
May see his wish more easily fulfilled,
Even in the hour of triumph, and our fate
Be certain ruin; for the Greeks no more
Will combat when they draw their galleys down,
But, looking backward to the shore, will leave 120
The battle there; and thus, O king of men!
Will mischief flow from what thou counsellest."
  And Agamemnon, king of men, rejoined:—
"Thou touchest me, Ulysses, to the heart
With thy harsh censure; yet I did not give 125
Command to drag our good ships to the sea,
Against the will of the Greeks. And would there were
Some other, young or old, to counsel them
More prudently, for that would please me well."
  Then spake the great in battle, Diomed:— 130
"The man is here, nor have ye far to look
If ye will be persuaded, and refrain
To blame me angrily, because my years
Are fewest midst you all. I too can boast
Of noble birth; my father, Tydeus, lies 135
Buried beneath a mound of earth at Thebes.
To Portheus three illustrious sons were born,
Who dwelt in Pleuron, and in Calydon
The lofty,—Agrius, Melas, and the knight,
My father's father, Œneus, eminent 140
Among the rest for valor; he remained
At home, but, wandering thence, my father went
To Argos, for the will of Jove was such,—

Jove and the other gods. He wedded there
A daughter of Adrastus, and he dwelt   145
Within a mansion filled with wealth; broad fields
Fertile in corn were his, and many rows
Of trees and vines around him; large his flocks,
And great his fame as one expert to wield,
Beyond all other Greeks, the spear in war.   150
This should ye know, for this is true; nor yet
Contemn my counsel given with careful thought
And for your good, nor deem it comes from one
Unwarlike and low-born. Now let us join
The battle, wounded as we are, for much   155
It needs our presence, keeping carefully
Beyond the reach of weapons, to avoid
Wound upon wound, and, cheering on the rest,
Send back into the combat those who stand
Apart, indulgent to their weariness."   160
   He spake: they hearkened, and with hasty steps
Went on, King Agamemnon at their head.
   Nor was the glorious power that shakes the earth
Unmindful of his charge. He went among
The warriors in the semblance of a man   165
Stricken in years, and, seizing the right hand
Of Agamemnon, spake these wingèd words:—
   "O son of Atreus, the revengeful heart
Of Peleus' son must leap within his breast
For joy, to see the slaughter and the rout   170
Of the Achaians, since with him there dwells
No touch of pity. May he perish too,
Like us, and may some god o'erwhelm his name
With infamy. With thee the blessed gods
Are not so far incensed, and thou shalt see   175
The Trojan chiefs and princes of their host
Raising the dust-clouds on the spacious plain
In fleeing from our ships and tents to Troy."
   He spake, and, shouting, strode across the field.
As loud a cry as from nine thousand men,   180
Or from ten thousand hurrying to engage
In battle, such the cry that ocean's king

Uttered from his deep lungs. It woke anew
Invincible resolve in every heart
Among the Greeks to combat to the end.   185
   Now, Juno of the golden throne beheld
As, standing on the Olympian height, she cast
Downward her eyes to where her brother moved,
Bearing his part with glory in the fray;
And inly she rejoiced. She also saw   190
Jove on the peak of Ida, down whose side
Glide many brooks, and greatly was displeased.
Then the majestic goddess with large eyes
Mused how to occupy the mind of him
Who bears the ægis. This at length seemed best: 195
To deck herself in fair array, and haste
To Ida, that the God might haply yield
To amorous desire, and in that hour
Her hand might pour into his lids, and o'er
His watchful mind, a soft and pleasant sleep.   200
She went to her own chamber, which her son
Vulcan had framed, with massive portals made
Fast to the lintels by a secret bolt,
Which none but she could draw. She entered in
And closed the shining doors; and first she took 205
Ambrosial water, washing every stain
From her fair limbs, and smoothed them with rich oil,
Ambrosial, soft, and fragrant, which, when touched
Within Jove's brazen halls, perfumed the air
Of earth and heaven. When thus her shapely form   210
Had been anointed, and her hands had combed
Her tresses, she arranged the lustrous curls,
Ambrosial, beautiful, that clustering hung
Round her immortal brow. And next she threw
Around her an ambrosial robe, the work   215
Of Pallas, all its web embroidered o'er
With forms of rare device. She fastened it
Over the breast with clasps of gold, and then
She passed about her waist a zone which bore
Fringes an hundred-fold, and in her ears   220
She hung her three-gemmed ear-rings, from whose gleam

She won an added grace. Around her head
The glorious goddess drew a flowing veil,
Just from the loom, and shining like the sun;
And, last, beneath her bright white feet she bound   225
The shapely sandals. Gloriously arrayed
In all her ornaments, she left her bower,
And calling Venus to herself, apart
From all the other gods, addressed her thus:—
    "Wilt thou, dear child, comply with what I ask?   230
Or, angered that I aid the Greeks, while thou
Dost favor Troy, wilt thou deny my suit?"
    And thus Jove's daughter, Venus, made reply:—
"O Juno, whom I reverence, speak thy thought,
Daughter of mighty Saturn! for my heart   235
Commands me to obey thy wish in all
That I can do, and all that can be done."
    And thus imperial Juno, planning guile,
Rejoined: "Give me the charm and the desire
With which thou overcomest gods and men.   240
I go to the far end of this green earth,
To visit Ocean, father of the gods,
And Mother Tethys, who, receiving me
From Rhea, cherished me, and brought me up
In their abodes, when Jove the Thunderer   245
Cast Saturn down to lie beneath the earth
And barren sea. I go to visit them,
And end their hateful quarrel. For too long
Have they been strangers to the marriage-bed.
But if my words persuade them, and bring back   250
Their hearts to their old love, my name will be
Honored by them, and dear throughout all time."
    And laughter-loving Venus answered thus:—
"What thou desirest should not be denied,
And shall not, for thou sleepest in the arms   255
Of Jupiter, the mightiest of the gods."
    She spake, and from her bosom drew the zone,
Embroidered, many colored, and instinct
With every winning charm—with love, desire,
Dalliance, and gentle speech—that stealthily   260

O'ercomes the purpose of the wisest mind,
And, placing it in Juno's hands, she said:—
    "This many-colored zone, and all that dwells
Within it, take, and in thy bosom hide,
And thou, I deem, wilt not return and leave   265
Thy purpose unfulfilled." As thus she spake,
The large-eyed stately Juno smiled and took,
And, smiling, in her bosom placed the zone,
While Venus, daughter of the Thunderer,
Went to the palace. Juno took her way   270
From high Olympus o'er Pieria's realm
And rich Emathia, o'er equestrian Thrace,
With snowy peaks exceeding high; her feet
Touched not the ground. From Athos suddenly
She stooped upon the tossing deep, and came   275
To Lemnos, seat of Thoas the divine,
And there she met Death's brother, Sleep, and took
His hand in hers, and thus accosted him:—
    "O Sleep, whose sway is over all the gods
And all mankind, if ever thou didst heed   280
My supplication, hearken to me now,
And I shall be forever grateful. Close
The glorious eyes of Jove beneath his lids
Midst our embracings, and for thy reward
Thou shalt possess a sumptuous throne of gold   285
Imperishable. Vulcan, my lame son,
Shall forge it for thee, and adorn its sides,
And place below a footstool, upon which
Thy shining feet shall rest in banqueting."
    Then gentle Sleep made answer, speaking thus:—   290
"Great Saturn's daughter, Juno the august,
On any other of the deathless gods
Could I bring slumber,—even on the tides
Of the swift Ocean, parent of them all;
Yet may I not approach Saturnian Jove   295
If he command me not. Already once
He made me quail with fright before his threats,
When his magnanimous son, Alcides, sailed
From Troy, which he had ravaged. Then I lulled

The senses of the Ægis-bearer, Jove, 300
Wrapping myself around him, while thy mind
Was planning mischiefs for his son, and thou
Didst wake the blasts of all the bitter winds
To sweep the ocean, and to bear away
The hero on its billows from his friends 305
To populous Cos. When Jupiter awoke
His anger rose; he seized and flung the gods
Hither and thither; me he chiefly sought,
And would have cast me to destruction, down
From the great heavens into the deep, if Night, 310
Whose power o'ercomes the might of gods and men,
Had not preserved me, fleeing to her shade.
So Jove refrained, indignant as he was,
For much he feared to offend the swift-paced Night.
And now thou bid'st me tempt my fate again." 315
  Imperial, large-eyed Juno thus rejoined:—
"Why rise such thoughts, O Sleep, within thy heart?
Deem'st thou that Jove the Thunderer favors Troy
As much as he was angered for the sake
Of Hercules, his son? Do what I ask, 320
And thou shalt have from me a wedded spouse.
One of the younger Graces shall be thine,—
Pasithea, whom thou hast desired so long."
  She spake, and Sleep, delighted, answered thus:—
"Swear now to me, O goddess, by the Styx, 325
The inviolable river. Lay one hand
Upon the food-producing earth, and place
The other on the glimmering sea, that all
The gods below, round Saturn, may attest
Thy promise,—that thou wilt bestow on me 330
One of the younger Graces for my bride,—
Pasithea, whom I have desired so long."
  He spake, and white-armed Juno willingly
Complied; she took the oath, and called on all
The gods who dwell in Tartarus below, 335
And bear the name of Titans. When the oath
Was taken, and the accustomed rites performed,
From Lemnos and from Imbrus forth they went,

Shrouded in mist; and swiftly moving on
Toward Ida, seamed with rivulets and nurse   340
Of savage beasts, they came to Lectos first,
And there they left the sea. Their way was now
Over the land, and underneath their feet
The forest summits shook. Sleep halted there
Ere yet the eye of Jupiter descried   345
His coming, and upon a lofty fir,
The tallest growing on the Idæan mount,
High in the air among the clouds of heaven,
Springing from earth, he took his perch within
The screen of branches, like the shrill-voiced bird,   350
Called Chalcis by the immortals, and by men
Cymindis, haunting the high mountain-side.

   And Juno hastened on to Gargarus,
The peak of lofty Ida. Jupiter
The Cloud-compeller, saw her, and at once   355
Love took possession of his mighty heart,
As when they first were wedded, and withdrew
From their dear parents' sight. The God drew near
And stood before her, and addressed her thus:—

   "Why art thou hastening from Olympus thus,   360
And whither; yet without thy steeds and car?"

   And Juno answered with dissembled guile:—
"To the far ends of the green earth I go,
To visit Ocean, father of the gods,
And Mother Tethys, in whose palace halls   365
They nourished me, and brought me up. I go
To end their hateful quarrels, for too long
Have they been strangers to the marriage-bed,
Incensed against each other. Now my steeds,
Waiting to bear me over land and sea,   370
Stand at the foot of Ida seamed with rills,
And now I come to thee, lest thou perchance
Be wroth if I unknown to thee repair
To where old Ocean dwells amid his deeps."

   The Cloud-compeller, Jupiter, rejoined:—   375
"Hereafter, Juno, there will be a time
For such a journey; meantime let us give

This hour to rest and dalliance. Never yet
Did love of goddess or of mortal maid
Possess and overcome my heart as now; 380
Not even when I loved Ixion's dame,
Who bore Pirithoüs, prudent as a god
Among the counsellors; nor when I loved
Acrisius' daughter with the dainty feet,
Danaë who brought forth Perseus, eminent 385
Above the other warrior-chiefs; nor when
I carried off from Phœnix the renowned
His daughter, who bore Minos afterward,
And Rhadamanthus. Never so I loved
Semele, nor Alcmena who in Thebes 390
Brought forth to me the great-souled Hercules,
My valiant son, while Bacchus, the delight
Of men, was born of Semele; nor yet
So loved I Ceres, fair-haired queen, nor yet
Latona, gloriously beautiful, 395
Nor even thee, as now I love, and yield
My spirit to the sweetness of desire."
    Imperial Juno artfully replied:—
"Importunate Saturnius, what is this
That thou hast said? If on this summit height 400
Of Ida we recline, where all around
Is open to the sight, how will it be
Should any of the ever-living gods
Behold us sleeping, and to all the rest
Declare it? I could never, rising thence, 405
Enter again thy palace, save with shame.
Yet if thou truly speakest thy desire,
Thou hast a marriage-chamber of thine own,
Which Vulcan, thy beloved son, for thee
Framed, fitting to its posts the solid doors; 410
And thither let us go to take our rest
Within it, since thou hast declared thy will."
    Then spake again the Cloud-compeller Jove:—
"O Juno! fear thou not that any god
Or man will look upon us. I shall throw 415
A golden cloud around us, which the Sun

Himself cannot look through, although his eye
Is piercing, far beyond all other eyes."
   The son of Saturn spake, and took his wife
Into his arms, while underneath the pair   420
The sacred Earth threw up her freshest herbs,—
The dewy lotus, and the crocus-flower,
And thick and soft the hyacinth. All these
Upbore them from the ground. Upon this couch
They lay, while o'er them a bright golden cloud   425
Gathered, and shed its drops of glistening dew.
   So slumbered on the heights of Gargarus
The All-Father, overcome by sleep and love,
And held his consort in his arms. Meanwhile
The gentle Sleep made haste to seek the fleet   430
Of Greece. He bore a message to the god
Neptune, who shakes the shores, and, drawing near,
He thus accosted him with wingèd words:—
   "Now, Neptune, give the Greeks thy earnest aid,
And though it be but for a little space,   435
While Jupiter yet slumbers, let them win
The glory of the day; for I have wrapt
His senses in a gentle lethargy,
To which he is betrayed by Juno's wiles."
   He spake, and took his way, departing thence   440
Among the tribes of men. These words inflamed
The god's desire to aid the Greeks; he sprang
Far on among the foremost, and exclaimed:—
   "O Greeks! do ye again submit to yield
The victory to Hector, Priam's son,   445
That he may seize our fleet and bear away
The glory of the day? This is his hope,
And this his boast, since now Achilles lies
Inactive at his ships, in sullen wrath.
Yet little should we need him, if the rest   450
Stood bravely by each other. Hear me now,
And do what I advise. Let all of us,
The best and bravest, bearing shields, and capped
With glittering helms, and wielding in our hands
The longest spears, advance, and I will lead   455

The charge; nor do I think that Hector, son
Of Priam, daring as he seems, will yet
Abide our onset. Whoso has the heart
To make a stand with me, and yet who bears
A narrow shield, let it be given to one   460
Less warlike, and a broader shield be found."
   He spake; they hearkened and obeyed. The kings
Tydides, and Ulysses, and the son
Of Atreus, Agamemnon, though their wounds
Still galled them, marshalled and reviewed the ranks,   465
And changed their arms; they made the braver wear
The better armor, and the worse they gave
To the less warlike. Now, when o'er their breasts
The burnished mail was girded, they began
Their march; the great earth-shaker, Neptune, led   470
The onset, grasping in his sinewy hand
A sword of fearful length and flashing blade,
Like lightning. No man dared encounter it
In combat; every arm was stayed by fear.
   Right opposite, illustrious Hector ranged   475
His Trojans. Dark-haired Neptune and the son
Of Priam now engaged in desperate strife,
One on the side of Troy, and one for Greece.
The sea swelled upward toward the Grecian tents
And fleet, while both the armies flung themselves   480
Against each other with a loud uproar.
Not with such noise the ocean-billows lash
The mainland, when the violent north wind
Tumbles them shoreward; not with such a noise
Roar the fierce flames within the mountain glen,   485
When leaping upward to consume the trees;
And not so loudly howls the hurricane
Among the lofty branches of the oaks
When in its greatest fury, as now rose
The din of battle from the hosts that rushed   490
Against each other with terrific cries.
   At Ajax glorious Hector cast his spear,
As face to face they stood. It missed him not,
But struck him where two belts upon his breast

O'erlapped each other,—that which held the shield 495
And that which bore the silver-studded sword.
These saved the tender muscles. Hector, vexed
That thus his weapon should have flown in vain,
Retreated toward his comrades, shunning death.
As he drew back, the Telamonian hurled 500
A stone,—for stones in multitude, that propped
The galleys, lay around, and rolled among
The feet of those who struggled. One of these
He lifted, smiting Hector on the breast,
Above the buckler's orb and near the neck. 505
He sent it spinning like a top; it fell
And whirled along the ground. As when beneath
The stroke of Father Jupiter an oak
Falls broken at the root, and from it fumes
A stifling smell of sulphur, and the heart 510
Of him who stands and sees it sinks with dread,—
For fearful is the bolt of mighty Jove,—
So dropped the valiant Hector to the earth
Amid the dust; his hand let fall the spear;
His shield and helm fell with him, and his mail 515
Of shining brass clashed round him. Then the Greeks
Rushed toward him, yelling fiercely, for they hoped
To drag him thence; and many a lance they cast;
But none by javelin or by thrust could wound
The shepherd of the people, for there came 520
Around him all the bravest of his host,—
Polydamas, Æneas, and the great
Agenor, and Sarpedon, he who led
The Lycian bands, and Glaucus the renowned;
These flung themselves into the strife, while none 525
Of all the rest refrained, but firmly held
Their broad round shields before him. Then his friends
Lifted him in their arms, and bore him off,
Out of the conflict, to his fiery steeds
That waited for him in the battle's rear, 530
With charioteer and sumptuous car; and these
Bore him to Ilium, sorely suffering.
    But when they now had reached the crossing-place

Of Xanthus, full of eddies, pleasant stream,
The progeny of ever-living Jove, 535
They lifted out the hero from the car,
And laid him on the ground, and on him poured
Water, at which his breath and sight returned.
He sat upon his knees, and from his throat
Gave forth the purple blood, and then he fell 540
Back to the ground, and darkness veiled his eyes,
For still his senses felt the stunning blow.
    The Greeks saw Hector leave the field, and pressed
The foe more hotly, and bethought themselves
Of their old valor. Then the swift of foot, 545
Oïlean Ajax, darted to the van,
And with his fir-tree spear smote Satnius, son
Of Enops, whom a Naiad eminent
For beauty among all the nymphs brought forth
To Enops, when on Satnio's banks he kept 550
His flocks. Oïleus' son, expert to wield
The spear, drew near, and pierced him in the flank.
Prostrate he fell, and suddenly the Greeks
And Trojans gathered round in desperate fray.
Polydamas, the mighty spearman, son 555
Of Panthoüs, coming to avenge him, smote
On the right shoulder Prothoënor, son
Of Areïlochus. The pitiless spear
Passed through, and falling in the dust he grasped
The earth with dying hands. Polydamas 560
Shouted aloud, exulting over him:—
    "Not vainly, as I think, hath flown the spear
From the strong hand of the magnanimous son
Of Panthoüs. Some Achaian hath received
The weapon in his side, to lean upon 565
In going down to Pluto's dim abode."
    He spake; the Achaians chafed to hear his boast,
And most the warlike son of Telamon;
For the slain Greek fell near him. Instantly,
Just as the Trojan moved away, he hurled 570
His shining lance. Polydamas, to escape
The death-stroke, sprang aside. Archilochus,

Antenor's son, received the blow: the gods
Had doomed him to be slain. It pierced the spine
Where the head joins the neck, and severed there   575
The tendons on each side. His head and mouth
And nostrils struck the ground before his knees.
   And thus to excellent Polydamas
Did Ajax shout in turn: "Bethink thee now,
And tell me truly, was not this a man   580
Worthy to die for Prothoënor's sake?
No man of mean repute or meanly born
He seems, but either brother to the knight
Antenor, or his son; for certainly
His looks declare him of Antenor's race."   585
   He spake; but well he knew the slain. Meanwhile
The Trojans heard and grieved. Then Acamas,
Stalking around his fallen brother, slew
Promachus, the Bœotian, with his spear,
While dragging off the dead man by the feet.   590
   Then o'er the fallen warrior, Acamas
Boasted aloud: "O measureless in threats!
Bowmen of Argos! not to us alone
Shall woe and mourning come; ye also yet
Will perish. See your Promachus o'erthrown,   595
And by my spear, that so my brother's death
May not be unrequited. Every man
Should wish a brother left to avenge his fall."
   He ended, and the Greeks were vexed to hear
His boast; the brave Peneleus most of all   600
Was angered, and he rushed on Acamas,
Who waited not the onset of the king,
And in his stead was Ilioneus slain,
The son of Phorbas, who was rich in flocks,
Whom Mercury, of all the sons of Troy,   605
Loved most, and gave him ample wealth; his wife
Brought Ilioneus forth, and only him;
And him Peneleus smote beneath the brow,
In the eye's socket, forcing out the ball;
The spear passed through, and reappeared behind.   610
Down sat the wounded man with arms outstretched,

While, drawing his sharp sword, Peneleus smote
The middle of his neck, and lopped away
The helmed head, which fell upon the ground,
The spear still in the eye. He lifted it   615
As one would lift a poppy up, and thus
He shouted, boasting, to the Trojan host:—
    "Go now, ye Trojans, and inform from me
The father and the mother of the slain
That they may mourn within their palace walls   620
Illustrious Ilioneus. After this
Shall the sad wife of Promachus, the son
Of Alegenor, never hasten forth
To meet her husband with glad looks, when we
The Greeks return from Ilium with our fleet."   625
    He spake; the Trojans all grew pale with fear,
And gazed around for an escape from death.
    Say, Muses, ye who on the Olympian height
Inhabit, who was first among the Greeks
To gather bloody spoil, when now the power   630
That shakes the shores had turned the tide of war.
    First, Ajax, son of Telamon, struck down
Hyrtius, the leader of the Mysian band,
And son of Gyrtias, while Antilochus
Spoiled Mermerus and Phalces. Morys next,   635
Slain by the weapon of Meriones,
Fell with Hippotion. Teucer overthrew
Prothoüs and Periphœtes. Atreus' son
Smote Hyperenor, prince among his tribe,
Upon the flank; the trenchant weapon drank   640
The entrails, and the soul, driven forth, escaped
Through the deep wound, and darkness veiled his eyes.
But Ajax swift of foot, Oïleus' son,
O'erthrew the most, for none could equal him
In swift pursuit when Jove ordained a flight.   645

BOOK XV

NOW when the Trojans in their flight had crossed
Rampart and trench, and many had been slain
By the pursuing Greeks, they made a halt
Beside their chariots, in despair and pale
With terror. Meanwhile Jupiter awoke, 5
On Ida's height, from slumber by the side
Of Juno, goddess of the golden throne.
At once he rose and saw the Trojan host
Routed, and, following close upon their flight,
The Argive warriors putting them to rout, 10
Aided by Neptune, sovereign of the sea,
And Hector lying on the field among
His fellow-warriors, breathing painfully,
Vomiting blood, and senseless, for the arm
That smote was not the feeblest of the Greeks. 15
The Father of immortals and of men
Beheld and pitied him, and terribly
Frowned upon Juno, and bespake her thus:—
   "O evil-minded Juno, full of guile!
Thy arts have made the noble Hector leave 20
The combat, and have forced his troops to flee.
I know not whether 'twere not well that thou
Shouldst taste the fruit of thy pernicious wiles,
Chastised by me with stripes. Dost thou forget
When thou didst swing suspended, and I tied 25
Two anvils to thy feet, and bound a chain

Of gold that none could break around thy wrists?
Then didst thou hang in air amid the clouds,
And all the gods of high Olympus saw
With pity. They stood near, but none of them
Were able to release thee. Whoso came
Within my reach I seized, and hurled him o'er
Heaven's threshold, and he fell upon the earth
Scarce breathing. Yet the passion of my wrath,
Caused by the wrongs of godlike Hercules,
Was not to be so calmed; for craftily
Hadst thou called up the violent northern blast,
To chase him far across the barren deep,
And drive him from his course to populous Cos.
I rescued him at length, and brought him back
To Argos famed for steeds, though after long
And many hardships. I remind thee now
Of this, that thou mayst see of what avail
Hereafter thy dissembled love and all
Thy cunning strategies will be to thee."
   He spake, and Juno, large-eyed and august,
Shuddered, and answered Jove with wingèd words:—
   "Be witness, Earth, and the great Heavens above,
And waters of the Styx that glide beneath,—
That dreadful oath which most the blessed gods
Revere,—be witness, too, that sacred head
Of thine, and our own nuptial couch, by which
I would not rashly swear at any time,
That not by my persuasion Neptune went—
The shaker of the shores—to harass Troy
And Hector, and to aid the cause of Greece.
He went self-counselled; he had seen the Greeks
Pressed grievously beside their fleet, and took
Compassion on them. Yet would I advise
That he obey thy word, and take his place
Where thou, the Cloud-compeller, bid'st him go."
   She ended, and the Father of the gods
And mortals smiled, and said, in wingèd words:—
   "Large-eyed, imperial Juno, wouldst thou sit
In council with the immortals, and assist

My purposes, then Neptune, though at heart
He were averse, would yet conform his will
To mine and thine. If thou dost truly speak,
And from thy heart, go now to where the gods
Assemble, summon Iris, and with her   70
The archer-god Apollo. Give in charge
To Iris that she hasten to the host
Of the mailed Greeks, and bid king Neptune leave
The battle for his palace. Let the god
Phœbus, preparing Hector for the fight,   75
Breathe strength into his frame, that so he lose
The sense of pain which bows his spirit now,
And he shall force the Greeks again to flee
In craven fear. Then shall their flying host
Fall back upon the galleys of the son   80
Of Peleus, who shall send into the fight
His friend Patroclus. Him the mighty spear
Of Hector shall o'erthrow before the walls
Of Ilium, after many a Trojan youth
Shall by his hand have fallen, and with them   85
My noble son, Sarpedon. Roused to rage,
Then shall the great Achilles take the life
Of Hector. Be it from this time my care
That all the assaults of Trojans in the fleet
Be beaten back, till by Minerva's aid   90
The Greeks possess the lofty town of Troy.
Still am I angry, nor will I allow
One of the ever-living gods to aid
The Greeks, until the prayer of Peleus' son
Shall fully be accomplished, as my word   95
And nod were given, when Thetis clasped my knees,
Entreating me to honor, signally,
Her son, Achilles, spoiler of walled towns."
  He spake; the white-armed goddess willingly
Obeyed him, and from Ida's summit flew   100
To high Olympus. As the thought of man
Flies rapidly, when, having travelled far,
He thinks, "Here would I be, I would be there,"
And flits from place to place, so swiftly flew

Imperial Juno to the Olympian mount, 105
And there she found the ever-living gods
Assembled in the halls of Jupiter.
These, as they saw her, starting from their seats,
Reached forth their cups to greet her. All the rest
She overlooked, and took the beaker held 110
By blooming Themis, who in haste had run
To meet her, and in wingèd accents said:—
  "Why comest thou, O Juno! with the look
Of one o'ercome with fear. Hath Saturn's son,
Thy lord, disquieted thy soul with threats?" 115
  The white-armed goddess Juno answered her:—
"Ask me not, heavenly Themis,—thou dost know
The cruel, arrogant temper that is his,—
But sit presiding at the common feast,
In this fair palace of the gods, and thou 120
And all in heaven shall hear what evils Jove
Has threatened. All, I think, will not rejoice
To hear the tidings, be they gods or men,
Though some contentedly are feasting now."
  Thus having said, imperial Juno took 125
Her place, and all the gods within the halls
Of Jupiter were grieved. The goddess smiled,
But only with the lips; her forehead wore
Above the jetty brows no sign of joy,
While thus she spake in anger to the rest:— 130
  "Vainly, and in our madness, do we strive
With Father Jove. We come and seek by craft
Or force to move his stubborn will; he sits
Apart, unyielding, unregarding, proud
Of the vast strength and power in which he stands 135
Above all other of the deathless gods.
Bear therefore patiently whatever ill
He sends to each. Already, as I learn,
Hath Mars his share of sorrow. In the war
Ascalaphus hath perished, whom he loved 140
Dearly, beyond all other men, and whom
The fiery god acknowledged as his son."
  As thus she spake, Mars smote his sinewy thighs

With his dropped hands, and sorrowfully said:—
"Be not offended with me, ye who make   145
Your dwelling on Olympus, if I go
Down to the Achaian fleet, and there avenge
The slaughter of my son, though I be doomed
To fall before the thunderbolt of Jove,
And lie in blood and dust among the dead."   150
    He spake, and summoned Fear and Flight to yoke
His steeds, and put his glorious armor on.
Then greater and more terrible had been
The avenging wrath of Jupiter inflamed
Against the gods, if Pallas in her fear   155
For all the heavenly dwellers had not left
Her throne, and, rushing through the portals, snatched
The helmet from his head, and from his arm
The shield, and from his brawny hand the spear,
And laid the brazen weapon by, and thus   160
Rebuked the fiery temper of the god:—
    Thou madman, thou art frantic, thou art lost!
Hast thou not ears to hear, nor any shame
Nor reason left? Hast thou not heard the words
Of white-armed Juno, who so lately left   165
Olympian Jupiter? Wouldst thou return
In pain and sorrow to the Olympian heights,
Driven back ingloriously, and made the cause
Of many miseries to all the gods?—
For Jove would leave the Trojans and their foes, 170
The gallant Greeks, and turn on us, and bring
Ruin upon Olympus. He would seize
Guilty and guiltless in his rage alike.
Wherefore I counsel thee to lay aside
Resentment for the slaughter of thy son,   175
Since braver men and stronger have been slain,
And will be slain hereafter. Vain it were
To seek from death to save the race of man."
    She said, and, leading back the fiery Mars,
Seated him on his throne, while Juno called   180
Apollo forth, with Iris, messenger
Of heaven, and thus in wingèd accents spake:—

"Jove calls you both to Ida. When ye reach
Its heights, and look upon his countenance,
Receive his sovereign mandate and obey." 185
  So spake imperial Juno, and withdrew
And took her seat again, while they in haste
Flew toward the mount of Ida, seamed with rills
And nurse of savage beasts. Upon the top
Of Gargarus they found the Thunderer, 190
The son of Saturn, sitting. In a cloud
Of fragrant haze he sat concealed; the twain
Entered and stood before the God of Storms,
Who saw them not displeased, so speedily
Had they obeyed his consort. First he turned 195
To Iris, and in wingèd accents said:—
  "Haste thee, swift Iris, and report my words
To royal Neptune, and report them right.
Bid him, withdrawing from the battle-field,
Repair to the assembly of the gods, 200
Or the great ocean. If he disobey,
Contemning my command, then bid him think
Maturely, whether, mighty though he be,
He can withstand when I put forth my power
Against him. Greater is my strength than his, 205
And elder-born am I. Yet in his pride
Of heart he dares to call himself my peer,
Though all the others look on me with awe."
  Thus spake the god, and Iris, whose swift feet
Are like the wind, obeyed, and downward plunged 210
From Ida's height to sacred Troy. As when
Snow-flakes or icy hail are dropped to earth
From clouds before the north wind when it sweeps
The sky, so darted Iris to the ground,
And stood by mighty Neptune's side, and said:— 215
  "O dark-haired shaker of the shores, I bring
A message from the Ægis-bearer, Jove,
That thou, withdrawing from the battle-field,
Repair to the assembly of the gods,
Or the great ocean. If thou disobey, 220
Contemning his command, then hear his threat:

He will come hither and put forth his power
Against thee, and he warns thee not to tempt
The strife; for greater is his power than thine,
And he is elder-born, though in thy pride
Of heart thou dost declare thyself the peer
Of him whom all the rest regard with awe."

   Illustrious Neptune answered with disdain:—
"In truth an arrogant speech; he seeks by force
To bar me from my purpose, who can claim
Rights equal to his own, though great his power.
We are three brothers,—Rhea brought us forth,—
The sons of Saturn,—Jupiter, and I,
And Pluto, regent of the realm below.
Three parts were made of all existing things,
And each of us received his heritage.
The lots were shaken; and to me it fell
To dwell forever in the hoary deep,
And Pluto took the gloomy realm of night,
And, lastly, Jupiter the ample heaven
And air and clouds. Yet doth the earth remain,
With high Olympus, common to us all.
Therefore I yield me not to do his will,
Great as he is; and let him be content
With his third part. He cannot frighten me
With gestures of his arm. Let him insult
With menaces the daughters and the sons
Of his own loves, and give them law, since they
Perforce must hear, and patiently submit."

   Then the fleet-footed Iris spake again:—
"O dark-haired Neptune, shall I bear from thee
This harsh, defiant answer back to Jove,
Or shall it yet be changed? The prudent mind
Yields to the occasion, and thou knowest well
The Furies wait upon the elder-born."

   Then spake in turn the god who shakes the shores:—
"O goddess Iris, thou hast wisely said.
An excellent thing it is when messengers
Know how to counsel well. But in my heart
And soul a wrathful sense of injury

Arises when he chides with insolent words
Me, who was equal with him in my lot,
And born to equal destinies. Yet now,
Although offended, I give way; but this
I tell thee, and 'tis from my heart,—if he, 265
In spite of me and Pallas, spoiler-queen,
And Juno, Mercury, and Vulcan, spare
The towers of Troy,—if he refuse to bring
Ruin on her, and glory on the Greeks,
Then let him know that hatred without end 270
Or intermission is between us two."
   As thus he spake, the shaker of the shores
Quitted the Grecian army, took his way
Seaward, and plunged into the deep. The host
Perceived their loss. Then Cloud-compelling Jove 275
Turned to Apollo and addressed him thus:—
   "Now go at once to Hector, mailed in brass,
Belovèd Phœbus, for the god who shakes
The earth, departing to the ocean-deeps,
Avoids our wrath; else had the other gods, 280
Even they who far beneath the earth surround
Old Saturn, heard our quarrel. Well it is
For both of us that he, although enraged,
Braved not my arm, for otherwise the strife
Had not been ended without sweat. Now take 285
The fringèd ægis in thy hands, and shake
Its orb before the warrior Greeks, to fill
Their hearts with fear. I give, O archer-god,
Illustrious Hector to thy charge. Revive
The might that dwelt within him, till the Greeks 290
Reach, in their flight, the fleet and Hellespont;
Then shall it be my care, by word and deed,
To give them rest and respite from their toils."
   He spake: Apollo hearkened and obeyed
His father, darting down from Ida's height 295
Like the fleet falcon, chaser of the dove,
And swiftest of the race of birds. He found
Hector, the warlike Priam's noble son,
No longer on his bed. He sat upright;

The life was coming back; he knew again
His friends; the heavy breathing ceased; the sweat
Was stanched; the will of ægis-bearing Jove
Revived the warrior's strength. The archer-god,
Phœbus, approached, and, standing by him, said:—
    "Why, Hector, son of Priam, dost thou sit
Languishing thus, apart from all the host?
Has aught of evil overtaken thee?"
    And then the crested Hector feebly said:—
"Who may'st thou be, O kindest of the gods,
That thus dost question me? Hast thou not heard
That the great warrior Ajax, with a stone,
Smote me upon the breast, and made me leave
The battle-field, where I o'ertook and slew
His comrades by the galleys of the Greeks?
I thought to be this day among the dead
In Pluto's mansion; even now it seemed
That I was breathing my dear life away."
    Then spake again Apollo, archer-god:—
"Take courage, for the son of Saturn sends
From Ida's summit one who will attend
And aid thee,—Phœbus of the golden sword,
Long practised to defend thy Troy and thee.
Rise now, encouraging thy numerous host
Of charioteers to press with their swift steeds
Straight toward the roomy galleys of the Greeks.
I go before to smooth for them the way,
And turn the Achaian bands, and make them flee."
    He spake, and into the great ruler's breast
Breathed strength and courage. As a stabled horse,
Fed at his crib with barley, breaks the thong
That fastened him, and, issuing, scours the plain
Where he was wont in some smooth-flowing stream
To bathe his sides,—he holds his head aloft
Proudly, and o'er his shoulders streams the mane,—
Consciously beautiful, he darts away
On nimble knees, that bear him to the fields
He knows so well, and pastures of the mares;—
So after he had hearkened to the god

Moved the swift feet of Hector, and he flew
To cheer his horsemen on. As peasant men   340
Rush with their dogs in chase of hornèd stag
Or mountain goat, whose refuge is among
Thickets and lofty rocks, nor can they take
Their prey, for at their clamor there appears
A manèd lion in the way, and turns   345
The chasers back, although in hot pursuit,—
Thus did the Greeks embattled close pursue
The men of Ilium, striking with their swords
And two-edged spears; but when at length they saw
Hector among the ranks of armèd men,   350
Their hearts were troubled, and their courage sank.
   Thoas, Andræmon's son, the bravest far
Among the Ætolians, skilled to cast the spear
And combat hand to hand, addressed the Greeks.
In council few excelled him, when the youths   355
Assembled for debate. With prudent speech
Thoas bespake his fellow-warriors thus:—
"Gods! what a marvel do mine eyes behold;
Hector has risen from death! We fully thought,
Each one of us, that, smitten by the hand   360
Of Telamonian Ajax, he had died.
Some god hath rescued and restored to strength
This Hector who hath slain, and yet will slay,
I fear, so many Greeks. He comes not thus
Leading the charge without the aid of Jove,   365
The God of Thunders. Now let all of us
Follow this counsel: bid the multitude
Retreat upon the ships, and let the rest,
Who boast ourselves the bravest of the host,
Stand firm and breast his onset, and so break   370
Its fury with our lifted spears. I think,
With all his rage, he will be slow to fling
Himself into a band of armèd Greeks."
   He spake; they hearkened and at once complied;
The Ajaxes, the Prince Idomeneus,   375
Teucer, Meriones, and Meges, peer
Of Mars, assembled all the chiefs, and ranked

Their files to encounter Hector and his band
Of Trojans, while the multitude fell back
To the Greek galleys. Then, in close array, 380
The Trojan host moved forward. Hector led
The van in rapid march. Before him walked
Phœbus, the terrible ægis in his hands
Dazzlingly bright within its shaggy fringe,
By Vulcan forged, the great artificer, 385
And given to Jupiter, with which to rout
Armies of men. With this in hand he led
The assailants on. The Achaians kept their ground
In serried ranks, and a sharp yell arose
From Greeks and Trojans. Arrows from the string 390
Flew through the air, and spears from valiant hands.
Some pierced the breasts of warrior-youths, but more
Fell half-way ere they reached their aim, and plunged
Into the ground, still hungering for their prey.
As long as Phœbus held the ægis still, 395
The weapons reached and wounded equally
Both armies, and in both the people fell;
But ever when the god looked face to face
On the Greek knights, and shook the orb, and gave
A mighty shout, he made their hearts to sink 400
Within their bosoms, and their courage fled.
As when two beasts of prey at dead of night
Suddenly, while their keeper is away,
Scatter a herd of beeves or flock of sheep,
So the disheartened Greeks were put to rout, 405
For Phœbus sent among them fear, and gave
Victory to Hector and the men of Troy.
  Then, as the lines were broken, man slew man.
First Stichius fell by Hector's hand, and next
Arcesilaus; one was chief among 410
The mailed Bœotians, one the trusty friend
Of brave Menestheus. Medon fell before
Æneas, and with him Iasus died.
Medon was great Oïleus' base-born son,
And Ajax was his brother, and he dwelt 415
In Phylacè, an exile, for his hand

Had slain the brother of his father's wife,
The step-dame Eriopis, late espoused.
Iasus was appointed to command
The warriors sent from Athens, and he claimed   420
His birth from Sphelus, son of Bucolus.
Mecistes fell before Polydamas.
Polites struck down Echius in the van,
And Clonius died by great Agenor's hand;
And Paris, when Deïochus had turned   425
To flee, among the foremost combatants,
Smote him upon the shoulder from behind,
And drave the brazen weapon through his heart.
   Then, while the Trojans stripped the dead, the Greeks
Fled every way, and, falling as they ran   430
Into the trench and on the stakes, were driven,
Back o'er the rampart. Hector lifted up
His mighty voice, and bade the Trojans leave
The bloody spoil and hasten to the ships.
"And whomsoever I shall find apart   435
In any place, at distance from the ships,
There will I slay him. None of all his kin,
Women or men, shall build his funeral pile,
But dogs shall tear his limbs in sight of Troy."
   He spake; and on the shoulders of his steeds   440
He laid the lash, and urged them toward the foe,
And cheered the Trojans on. They joined their shouts
To his, and charged with all their steeds and cars;
And fearful was the din. Apollo marched
Before them, treading down with mighty feet   445
The banks of the deep ditch, and casting them
Back to the middle, till a causey rose,
Broad, and of length like that to which a spear
Reaches when thrown by one who tries his strength.
O'er this the Trojans poured into the camp   450
By squadrons, with Apollo still in front,
Holding the marvellous ægis. He with ease
O'erthrew the rampart. As a boy at play
Among the sea-shore sands in childish sport
Scatters with feet and hands the little mounds   455

He reared, thus didst thou cause the mighty work,
O archer Phœbus, which the Greeks had reared
With so much toil, to crumble. Thou didst fill
Their hearts with eager thoughts of flight, till, hemmed
Between the assailants and their ships, they stopped 460
And bade each other stand, and raised their hands
To all the gods, and offered vows aloud.
Gerenian Nestor, guardian of the Greeks,
With arms extended toward the starry skies,
Prayed earnestly: "O Father Jove, if e'er 465
In fruitful Argos there were burned to thee
The thighs of fattened oxen or of sheep,
By one who asked a safe return to Greece,
And thou didst promise it, remember him,
God of Olympus, and avert from us 470
The day of evil. Suffer not the Greeks
To perish, slaughtered by the sons of Troy."
   So spake he supplicating. Jupiter
The All-disposer thundered as he heard
The old man's prayer. The Trojans by that voice 475
Of ægis-bearing Jove were moved to press
The Greeks more resolutely, and were filled
With fiercer valor. As a mighty wave
On the great ocean, driven before a gale
Such as rolls up the hugest billow, sweeps 480
O'er the ship's side, so swept the Trojan host
With dreadful tumult o'er the wall. They drave
Their steeds into the camp, and there they fought
Beside the galley-sterns, and hand to hand,
With two-edged spears,—they from their cars, the Greeks 485
From their black ships on high with long-stemmed poles
Which lay upon the decks, prepared for fight
At sea, and strongly joined to blades of brass.
   Patroclus, while the Greeks and Trojans fought
Around the wall, at distance from the fleet 490
Sat with the brave Eurypylus in his tent,
Amusing him with pleasant talk, and dressed
His wound with balms that calmed the bitter pain.
But when he saw the Trojans bursting in

Over the wall, and heard the din, and saw 495
The Achaians put to rout, he gave a cry
Of sudden grief, and with his open hands
Smote both his thighs, and sorrowfully said:—
　"Eurypylus, I cannot stay with thee,
Much as thou needest me, for desperate grows 500
The struggle. Now let thine attendant take
The charge of thee. I hasten to persuade
Achilles to the field. Who knows but I,
With Jove's good help, may change his purpose yet?
For potent are the counsels of a friend." 505
　The hero spake, and instantly his feet
Bore him away. Meanwhile the Achaian host
Firmly withstood the onset of their foes.
And yet, though greater was their multitude,
They could not drive the Trojans from the fleet, 510
Nor could the Trojans break, with all their power,
The serried lines, and reach the tents and ships.
As when a plumb-line, in the skilful hands
Of shipwright well instructed in his art
By Pallas, squares the beam that builds a bark, 515
So even was the fortune of the fray.
　While some beside one galley waged the war,
And others round another, Hector came
To encounter Ajax the renowned, and both
Fought for one ship. The Trojan could not drive 520
The Greek away, and burn his ship with fire,
Nor the Greek drive the Trojan, for a god
Had brought him thither. Then did Ajax smite
Caletor, son of Clytius, with his spear
Upon the breast, as he was bringing fire 525
To burn the ship; he dropped the torch, and fell,
With clashing armor. Hector, as he saw
His kinsman lying slain amid the dust
By the black galley, raised his voice, and thus
Called to the Lycians and the men of Troy:— 530
　"Hear, men of Troy and Lycia, and ye sons
Of Dardanus, who combat hand to hand,
Stand firm, and never yield this narrow ground.

Rescue the son of Clytius, who has fallen
Before the ships, nor let the Achaians make   535
His arms their spoil." The hero spake, and aimed
His shining spear at Ajax, whom it missed,
But smote Lycophron, Mastor's son, who served
Ajax, and dwelt with him, for he had left
His native land, Cythera, having slain   540
One of the gallant Cytherean race.
Him Hector smote upon the head beneath
The ear with his keen weapon, as he stood
Near Ajax; from the galley's stern he fell
Headlong upon the ground, with lifeless limbs.   545
Then to his brother Teucer Ajax spake:—
    "Dear Teucer, see, our faithful friend is gone,
The son of Mastor, from Cythera's isle,
Whom we had learned to honor equally
With our own parents in our palaces.   550
He falls before the great-souled Hector's hand.
Where, then, are now thy shafts that carry death,
And where the bow that Phœbus gave to thee?"
    He spake, and Teucer, hearkening, came in haste,
With his bent bow, and quiver full of shafts,   555
And, standing near him, sent his arrows forth
Among the Trojan warriors. There he smote
Clitus, Pisenor's eminent son, the friend
Of the renowned Polydamas, who claimed
His birth from Panthoüs. Clitus held the reins,   560
Guiding the coursers of Polydamas
Where most the crowded Grecian phalanxes
Wavered and broke, that so he might support
Hector and his companions. Soon he met,
Brave as he was, disaster which no hand   565
Had power to avert: the bitter arrow struck
His neck behind, and from the chariot-seat
He fell to earth; the startled steeds sprang back;
The empty chariot rattled. This the king
Polydamas perceived, and came to meet   570
His steeds, and gave them to Astinous,
The son of Protiäon, charging him

To keep them ever near, and in his sight,
While he, returning, mingled with the throng
That struggled in the van. Then Teucer aimed 575
Another shaft at Hector mailed in brass,
Which, had it reached him fighting gallantly,
Had made him leave the battle, for his life
Had ended there. The act was not unseen
By All-disposing Jupiter, whose power 580
Protected Hector, and denied the Greek
The glory hoped for; for he snapped in twain
The firmly twisted cord as Teucer drew
That perfect bow; the brazen arrow flew
Aside; the warrior's hands let fall the bow, 585
And, shuddering, he bespake his brother thus:—
  "Now woe is me! some deity, no doubt,
Brings all our plans to nought. 'Tis he whose touch
Strikes from my hand the bow, and snaps in twain
The cord just twisted, which I bound myself 590
This morning to the bow, that it might bear
The frequent arrow bounding toward the foe."
  He spake, and thus replied the man of might,
The Telamonian Ajax: "Lay aside
Thy bow, my brother, and thy store of shafts, 595
Since, in displeasure with the Greeks, a god
Has made them useless. Haste to arm thy hand
With a long spear, and on thy shoulders lay
A buckler, and with these attack the foe,
And bid thy fellows stand. Let Trojans see 600
That, even though the day thus far be theirs,
They cannot lay their hands on our good ships
Without a mighty struggle. Let us all
Be mindful of our fame for gallant deeds."
  He spake, and Teucer went to place the bow 605
Within the tents, and on his shoulders hung
A fourfold shield, and placed on his grand brows
A stately helmet with a horse-hair crest
That nodded fearfully. He took in hand
A ponderous spear with brazen blade, and sprang 610
Forward with hasty steps, and stood beside

His brother Ajax. Hector, when he saw
That Teucer's shafts had failed him, called aloud
Upon the men of Lycia and of Troy:—
   "Ye men of Troy and Lycia, and ye sons 615
Of Dardanus who combat hand to hand,
Acquit yourselves like men, my friends, and prove
Your fiery valor by these roomy ships;
For I have seen with mine own eyes the shafts
Of their chief warrior rendered impotent 620
By Jupiter. His hand is plainly seen
Among the sons of men; to some he gives
Glory above the rest; from some he takes
The glory, and withdraws from their defence.
He withers now the courage of the Greeks, 625
And succors us. Press closely round the fleet,
And combat. Whosoe'er among you all,
Wounded or beaten down, shall meet his death,
So let him die; 'tis no inglorious fate
To perish fighting in his country's cause; 630
And he shall leave his wife and children safe,
His home and household store inviolate,
If now the Greeks depart to their own land."
   With words like these he filled their hearts anew
With strength and courage. On the other side 635
Ajax exhorted thus his warrior friends:—
   "Shame on you, Greeks! We perish here, unless
We rescue with strong arms our host and fleet.
Think ye that, should the crested Hector seize
Our galleys, ye may reach your homes on foot? 640
Hear ye not Hector's voice, who, fiercely bent
To burn our ships with fire, is cheering on
His warriors? To no dance he summons them,
But to the battle. Nought is left for us,
And other counsel there is none, save this: 645
Close with the foe; let every hand put forth
Its strength; far better 'twere to die at once,
Or make at once our safety sure, than thus
To waste away, in lingering fight, beside
Our ships, destroyed by weaker arms than ours." 650

So spake the chief, and all who heard received
Courage and strength. Then Hector put to death
Schedius, the son of Perimedes, prince
Of the Phocæans. Ajax also slew
Laodamas, Antenor's honored son, 655
A chief of infantry. Polydamas
Struck down Cyllenian Otus, who had come,
The comrade of Phylides, at the head
Of the high-souled Epeians. Meges saw,
And rushed upon Polydamas, who sprang 660
Aside unharmed, for Phœbus suffered not
The son of Panthoüs thus to be o'erthrown,
Fighting among the foremost. But the spear
Of Meges wounded Crœsmus in the breast;
He fell with clanging arms. The slayer stripped 665
The corpse; but Dolops, son of Lampus, skilled
To wield the spear, leaped on him in the act.
Lampus, the father, best of men, was son
Of king Laomedon, and eminent
For warlike prowess. Dolops struck the shield 670
Of Meges in the midst; the corselet stayed
The blade with its close-jointed plates, and saved
The warrior's life. That corselet Phyleus brought
From Ephyrè, beside the Selleïs,
Given by his host, Euphetes, king of men, 675
For his defence in battle, and it now
Preserved his son from death. Then Meges smote
With his sharp spear the helm that Dolops wore,
And from its summit struck the horse-hair crest,
New-tinged with purple, and the cone entire 680
Fell midst the dust. While Meges, standing firm,
Fought thus, and hoped the victory, to his aid
Came warlike Menelaus, unobserved,
And, standing near, smote Dolops from behind,
Beneath the shoulder, and drave through the spear 685
Till it appeared beyond. The Trojan fell
Upon his face, and both the Greeks rushed on
To wrench the brazen armor from his limbs,
When Hector saw his fall and called aloud

Upon the kindred of the slain. He first 690
Rebuked the valiant Melanippus, son
Of Hicetaon, who but lately fed
His slow-paced beeves at Percotè, while yet
The enemy was far from Troy; but when
The Achaians landed from their well-oared barks, 695
He came to Troy, and took an eminent place
Among the Trojans. Near to Priam's halls
He had his dwelling, honored equally
With Priam's sons. Him Hector thus rebuked:—
    "Why, Melanippus; are we loitering thus? 700
Grievest thou not to see thy kinsman slain?
And see'st thou not how eagerly the Greeks
Are spoiling Dolops of his arms? Come on
With me. No time is this for distant fight,
But either we must rout the Greeks, or they 705
Will level to the ground the lofty towers
Of Ilium, and will slay its citizens."
    He spake, and led the way; his godlike friend
Followed him, while the son of Telamon,
Ajax, exhorted thus the sons of Greece:— 710
    "Be men, my friends, and let a noble dread
Of shame possess your hearts, and jealously
Look to each other's honor in the heat
Of battle; for to men who flee there comes
No glory, and that way no safety lies." 715
    He spake, and all were eager to drive back
The assaulting foe; they heeded well his words,
And drew around their barks a fence of mail,
While Jove urged on the Trojans. Then it was
That Menelaus, brave in battle, spake 720
To rouse the courage of Antilochus:—
    "Antilochus, there is no other Greek
Younger than thou, or fleeter; none so strong
For combat. Would that, springing on the foe,
Thou mightest strike some Trojan warrior down." 725
    So speaking, he drew back; but he had roused
The courage of his friend, who, springing forth
From midst the foremost combatants, took aim,

First looking keenly round, with his bright spear,
From which the Trojans shrank as they beheld 730
The hero cast it. Not in vain he threw
The weapon, for it struck upon the breast
Brave Melanippus, Hicetaon's son;
Beneath the pap it smote him as he came.
He fell with ringing arms; Antilochus 735
Sprang toward him like a hound that springs to seize
A wounded fawn, which, leaping from its lair,
Is stretched disabled by the hunter's dart.
So sprang the stout Antilochus on thee,
O Melanippus!—sprang to spoil thy limbs 740
Of armor; but the noble Hector saw,
And, hastening through the thick of battle, came
Against him. Mighty as he was in war,
Yet ventured not Antilochus to wait
His coming; but as flees a savage beast, 745
Conscious of guilty deed, when, having slain
Herdsman or hound, that kept the pastured kine,
He steals away before a crowd of men,
So fled the son of Nestor. On his rear
The Trojans under Hector poured a storm 750
Of weapons, and the din was terrible.
Yet when he reached the serried ranks of Greece
He turned and stood. Meanwhile the Trojan host,
Like ravening lions, fiercely rushed against
The galleys, that the will of Jupiter 755
Might be fulfilled; for now he nerved their limbs
With vigor ever new, while he denied
Stout hearts and victory to the Greeks, and cheered
Their foes with hope. His purpose was to give
The victory to Hector, Priam's son, 760
Till he should cast upon the beakèd ships
The fierce, devouring fire, and bring to pass
The end for which the cruel Thetis prayed.
   Therefore did Jove the All-disposer wait
Till from a burning galley he should see 765
The flames arise. Then must the Trojan host,—
Such was his will,—retreating from the fleet,

Yield to the Greeks the glory of the day.
For this he moved the already eager heart
Of Hector, son of Priam, to attack
The roomy ships. The hero was aroused
To fury fierce as Mars when brandishing
His spear, or as a desolating flame
That rages on a mountain-side among
The thickets of a close-grown wood. His lips
Were white with foam; his eyes from underneath
His frowning brows streamed fire; and as he fought,
Upon the hero's temples fearfully
The helmet nodded. Jupiter himself
Sent aid from his high seat, and heaped on him
Honor and fame beyond the other chiefs,—
And they were many,—for his term of life
Was to be short. Minerva even now
Was planning to bring on its closing day,
Made fatal by the might of Peleus' son.
And now he strove to break the Grecian ranks,
Assaulting where he saw the thickest crowd
And the best weapons; yet in vain he strove
With all his valor. Through the serried lines
He could not break; the Greeks in solid squares
Resisted, like a rock that huge and high
By the gray deep abides the buffetings
Of the shrill winds and swollen waves that beat
Against it. Firmly thus the Greeks withstood
The Trojan host, and fled not. In a blaze
Of armor, Hector, rushing toward their ranks,
Fell on them like a mighty billow raised
By the strong cloud-born winds, that flings itself
On a swift ship, and whelms it in its spray,
While fearfully among the cordage howls
The blast; the sailors tremble and are faint
With fear, as men who deem their death-hour nigh.
So the Greek warriors were dismayed at heart.
    As when a hungry lion suddenly
Springs on a herd of kine that crop the grass
By hundreds in the broad moist meadow-grounds,

Beneath the eye of one who never learned
To guard his hornèd charge from beasts of prey,
But ever walks before them or behind,
While the grim spoiler bounds into the midst 810
And makes a prey of one, and all the rest
Are scattered in affright, so all the Greeks
Were scattered by the will of heaven before
Hector and Father Jove. Yet only one,
Young Periphœtes of Mycenæ, fell, 815
The son of Copreus. Once his father went
An envoy from Eurystheus to the court
Of mighty Hercules. The son excelled
The father in all gifts of form and mind,
In speed, in war, in council eminent 820
Among the noblest of his land. His death
Brought Hector new renown; for as he turned,
Stepping by chance upon his buckler's rim,
That reached the ground,—the buckler which had been
His fence against the enemy's darts,—he fell 825
Backward, his helmet clashing fearfully
Around his temples. Hector saw, and came
In haste, and pierced his bosom with his spear,
Among his fellow-warriors, who with grief
Beheld, yet dared not aid him, such their awe 830
Of noble Hector. Now the Greeks retired
Among that row of galleys which were first
Drawn up the beach; the foe poured after them,
In hot pursuit; again the Greeks fell back,
Constrained, and left that foremost row behind, 835
And stood beside their tents in close array,
And not dispersed throughout the camp, for shame
And fear restrained them, and unceasingly
With shouts they bade each other bravely stand.
Chiefly Gerenian Nestor, wise to guide 840
The counsels of the Greeks, adjured them all,
And in their parents' name, to keep their ground.

   "O friends, be men; so act that none may feel
Ashamed to meet the eyes of other men.
Think each one of his children and his wife, 845

His home, his parents, living yet or dead.
For them, the absent ones, I supplicate,
And bid you rally here, and scorn to fly."
   He spake, and his brave words to every heart
Carried new strength and courage. Pallas then   850
Lifted the heaven-sent cloud that veiled the fight,
And all things in the clear full light were seen
On either side, both where the galleys lay
And where the warriors struggled. They beheld
Hector the great in war, and all his host,   855
Both those who formed the rear and wielded not
Their arms, and those who combated in front
Beside the ships. And now it pleased no more
The soul of valiant Ajax to remain
In the thick squadrons with the other Greeks,   860
But, striding on the galley-decks, he bore
A sea-pike two and twenty cubits long,
Huge, and beset with iron nails. As when
One who is skilled to vault on running steeds
Chooses four horses from a numerous herd,   865
And on the highway to a populous town
Drives them, while men and women in a crowd
Behold his feats with wonder, as he leaps
Boldly, without a fall, from steed to steed,
And back again, and all the while they run,   870
So on the lofty decks of those good ships
From ship to ship flew Ajax, lifting up
His mighty voice,—a shout that reached to heaven,—
And bade the Greeks defend their fleet and tents
Nor loitered Hector in those armèd throngs   875
Of Troy, but as a tawny eagle swoops
Upon a flock of birds that seek their food
Along a river's border,—geese or cranes,
Or long-necked swans,—so Hector in hot haste
Sprang toward a galley with an azure prow,   880
While mightily the power of Jove impelled
The hero onward, and inflamed his train
With courage. Fiercely then around the ships
The struggle was renewed. Thou wouldst have said

No toils of war could tire those resolute arms, 885
So stubbornly they fought. In every mind
The thought was this: the Greeks were in despair
Of rescue, and believed their hour had come
To perish; every Trojan hoped to give
The fleet to flames, and slay the sons of Greece. 890
With thoughts like these the hostile warriors closed.
   Then Hector laid his hand upon the stern
Of a stanch galley, beautiful and swift,
In which Protesilaüs came to Troy,—
It never bore him back. Around its keel 895
The Trojans and the Greeks fought hand to hand,
And slew each other. For no more they sent
The arrow or the javelin from afar,
Waiting to see the wound it gave, but each
With equal fury pressed upon his foe 900
With halberd and with trenchant battle-axe,
Huge sword and two-edged spear. Upon the ground
Had fallen many a fair black-hilted sword
With solid handles, some from slain men's hands,
Some from lopped arms of warriors; the dark earth 905
Ran red with blood. But Hector, having laid
His hand upon the galley's stern, held fast
To the carved point, and called upon his men:—
   "Bring fire, and press in throngs upon the foe;
For now doth Jove vouchsafe to us a day 910
Worth all the past,—a day on which we make
The ships our prey. Against the will of Heaven
They landed on our coast, and brought on us
Disasters many, through the coward fears
Of our own elders, who denied my wish 915
To combat at the galleys, and held back
The people. But if then the Thunderer
Darkened our minds, his spirit moves us now
In what we do, and we obey his will."
   He spake; and they with fiercer valor fell 920
Upon the Greeks. Even Ajax could no more
Withstand the charge, but, fearing to be slain,
Amid a storm of darts withdrew a space,

To where the seven-foot bench of rowers lay,
And left the galley's stern. There, as he stood, 925
He watched the assailants keenly, and beat back
With thrusts of his long spear whoever brought
The firebrand. With terrific shouts he called
Upon the Greeks to combat manfully:—
  "O friends, Achaian heroes, ministers 930
Of Mars, be men, be mindful of your fame
For valor. Do ye dream that in your rear
Are succors waiting us, or firmer walls
That may protect us yet? Nay, no fenced town
Have we for refuge, flanked with towers from which 935
Fresh troops may take our place. Between the sea
And country of the well-armed Trojans lie
Our tents; our native land is far away;
And now our only hope of safety left
Is in our weapons: there is no retreat." 940
  He spake, and mightily with his sharp spear
Thrust at whoever of the men of Troy
At Hector's bidding came with fire to burn
The galleys. On the blade of that long spear
The hero took them as they came, and slew 945
In close encounter twelve before the fleet.

BOOK XVI

SUCH was the struggle for that gallant bark.
Meanwhile Patroclus stood beside his friend,
The shepherd of the people, Peleus' son,
And shed hot tears, as when a fountain sheds
Dark waters streaming down a precipice. 5
The great Achilles, swift of foot, beheld
And pitied him, and spake these wingèd words:—
    "Why weepest thou, Patroclus, like a girl,—
A little girl that by her mother's side
Runs, importuning to be taken up, 10
And plucks her by the robe, and stops her way,
And looks at her, and cries, until at last
She rests within her arms? Thou art like her,
Patroclus, with thy tears. Dost thou then bring
Sad tidings to the Myrmidons or me? 15
Or hast thou news from Phthia? It is said
That still Menœtius, son of Actor, lives,
And Peleus also, son of Æacus,
Among the Myrmidons. Full bitterly
Should we lament to hear that either died, 20
Or mournest thou because the Achaians fall
Through their own folly by the roomy ships?
Speak, and hide nothing, for I too would know."
    And thou, O knight Patroclus, with a sigh
Deep-drawn, didst answer thus: "Be not displeased, 25
Achilles, son of Peleus, bravest far

Of all the Achaian army! for the Greeks
Endure a bitter lot. The chiefs who late
Were deemed their mightiest are within the ships,
Wounded or stricken down. There Diomed,
The gallant son of Tydeus, lies, and there
Ulysses, the great spearman, wounded both;
And Agamemnon; and Eurypylus,
Driven from the field, an arrow in his thigh.
Round them the healers, skilled in remedies,
Attend and dress their painful wounds, while thou,
Achilles, sittest here implacable.
O, never be such fierce resentments mine
As thou dost cherish, who art only brave
For mischief! Whom wilt thou hereafter aid,
If now thou rescue not the perishing Greeks?
O merciless! it cannot surely be
That Peleus was thy father, or the queen
Thetis thy mother; the green sea instead
And rugged precipices brought thee forth,
For savage is thy heart. But if thou heed
The warning of some god, if thou hast heard
Aught which thy goddess-mother has received
From Jove, send me at least into the war,
And let me lead thy Myrmidons, that thus
The Greeks may have some gleam of hope. And give
The armor from thy shoulders. I will wear
Thy mail, and then the Trojans, at the sight,
May think I am Achilles, and may pause
From fighting, and the warlike sons of Greece,
Tired as they are, may breathe once more, and gain
A respite from the conflict. Our fresh troops
May easily drive back upon their town
The weary Trojans from our tents and fleet."

   So spake he, sighing; rash and blind, he asked
Death for himself and evil destiny.
Achilles the swift-footed also drew
A heavy sigh, and thus in turn he spake:—

   "What, O divine Patroclus, hast thou said?
I fear no omen yet revealed to me;

Nor has my goddess-mother told me aught
From Jove; but ever in my heart and soul
Rankles the painful sense of injury done
By one who, having greater power, deprives
An equal of his right, and takes away 70
The prize he won. This is my wrong, and this
The cause of all my bitterness of heart.
Her whom the sons of Greece bestowed on me
As my reward, a trophy of my spear,
After the sack of a fenced city,—her 75
Did Agamemnon, son of Atreus, take
Out of my hands, as if I were a wretch,
A worthless outcast. But let that affront
Be with the things that were. It is not well
To bear a grudge forever. I have said 80
My anger should not cease to burn until
The clamor of the battle and the assault
Should reach the fleet. But go thou and put on
My well-known armor; lead into the field
My Myrmidons, men that rejoice in war, 85
Since like a lowering cloud the men of Troy
Surround the fleet, and the Achaians stand
In narrow space close pressed beside the sea,
And all the city of Ilium flings itself
Against them, confident of victory, 90
Now that the glitter of my helm no more
Flashes upon their eyes. Yet very soon
Their flying host would fill the trenches here
With corpses, had but Agamemnon dealt
Gently with me; and now their squadrons close 95
Around our army. Now no more the spear
Is wielded by Tydides Diomed
In rescue of the Greeks; no more the shout
Of Agamemnon's hated throat is heard;
But the man-queller Hector, lifting up 100
His voice, exhorts the Trojans, who, in throngs,
Raising the war-cry, fill the plain, and drive
The Greeks before them. Gallantly lead on
The charge, Patroclus; rescue our good ships;

Let not the enemy give them to the flames,
And cut us off from our desired return.
Follow my counsel; bear my words in mind;
So shalt thou win for me among the Greeks
Great honor and renown, and they shall bring
The beautiful maiden back with princely gifts.
When thou hast driven the assailants from the fleet,
Return thou hither. If the Thunderer,
Husband of Juno, suffer thee to gain
That victory, seek no further to prolong
The combat with the warlike sons of Troy,
Apart from me, lest I be brought to shame,
Nor, glorying in the battle and pursuit,
Slaying the Trojans as thou goest, lead
Thy men to Troy, lest from the Olympian mount
One of the ever-living gods descend
Against thee: Phœbus loves the Trojans well.
But come as soon as thou shalt see the ships
In safety; leave the foes upon the plain
Contending with each other. Would to Jove
The All-Father, and to Pallas, and the god
Who bears the bow, Apollo, that of all
The Trojans, many as they are, and all
The Greeks, not one might be reprieved from death,
While thou and I alone were left alive
To overthrow the sacred walls of Troy."
   So talked they with each other. Ajax, whelmed
Beneath a storm of darts, meantime but ill
Endured the struggle, for the will of Jove
And the fierce foe prevailed. His shining helm
Rang fearfully, as on his temples fell,
Stroke following after stroke, the weapons hurled
Against its polished studs. The buckler borne
Firmly on his left arm, and shifted oft
From side to side, had wearied it, and yet
The Trojans, pressing round him, could not drive,
With all their darts, the hero from his place.
Heavily heaved his panting chest; his limbs
Streamed with warm sweat; there was no breathing-time;

On danger danger followed, toil on toil.
   Now, Muses, dwellers of Olympus, tell   145
How first the galleys of the Greeks were fired.
   Hector drew near, and smote with his huge sword
The ashen spear of Ajax just below
The socket of the blade, and cut the stem
In two. The son of Telamon in vain   150
Brandished the severed weapon, while afar
The brazen blade flew off, and ringing fell
To earth. Then Ajax in his mighty mind
Acknowledged that the gods were in the war,
And shuddered, knowing that the Thunderer   155
Was thwarting all his warlike purposes,
And willed the victory to Troy. The chief
Withdrew beyond the reach of spears, while fast
The eager enemy hurled the blazing brands
At the swift ship, and wrapped the stern in flames   160
Unquenchable. Achilles saw, and smote
His thigh, and spake: "Patroclus, noble friend
And knight, make haste: already I behold
The flames that rage with fury at the fleet.
Now, lest the enemy seize our ships and we   165
Be barred of our return, put quickly on
Thy armor; be my task to call the troops."
   He spake: Patroclus then in glittering brass
Arrayed himself; and first around his thighs
He put the beautiful greaves, and fastened them   170
With silver clasps; around his chest he bound
The breastplate of the swift Æacides,
With star-like points, and richly chased; he hung
The sword with silver studs and blade of brass
Upon his shoulders, and with it the shield   175
Solid and vast; upon his gallant head
He placed the glorious helm with horsehair plume,
That grandly waved on high. Two massive spears
He took, that fitted well his grasp, but left
The spear which great Achilles only bore,   180
Heavy and huge and strong, and which no arm
Among the Greeks save his could poise; his strength

Alone sufficed to wield it. 'Twas an ash
Which Chiron felled in Pelion's top, and gave
To Peleus, that it yet might be the death 185
Of heroes. Then he called, to yoke with speed
The steeds, Automedon, whom he esteemed
Next to Achilles, that great scatterer
Of armies; for he found him ever firm
In battle, breasting faithfully its shock. 190
Automedon led forth to take the yoke
Xanthus and Balius, coursers that in speed
Were like the wind. Podargè brought them forth
To Zephyrus, while she, the Harpy, grazed
By ocean's streams. Upon the outer side 195
He joined to them the noble Pedasus,
Brought by Achilles from the captured town
Where ruled Eëtion. Though of mortal stock,
Well might he match with those immortal steeds.
    Meanwhile Achilles armed the Myrmidons, 200
Passing from tent to tent. Like ravening wolves,
Terribly strong, that, having slain among
The hills an antlered stag of mighty size,
Tear and devour it, while their jaws are stained
With its red blood, then gather in a herd 205
About some darkly flowing stream, and lap
The sullen water with their slender tongues,
And drop the clots of blood from their grim mouths,
And, although gorged, are fierce and fearless still,—
So came the leaders of the Myrmidons, 210
In rushing crowds, about the valiant friend
Of swift Æacides. Among them stood
Achilles, great in war, encouraging
The charioteers and warriors armed with shields.
    Achilles, dear to Jupiter, had led 215
Fifty swift barks to Ilium, and in each
Were fifty men, companions at the oar.
O'er these he gave command to five; himself,
Supreme in power, was ruler over all.
One band, the nobly armed Menestheus led, 220
Son of Spercheius. To that river-god,

Beautiful Polydora brought him forth,
Daughter of Peleus; she, a mortal maid,
Met an immortal's love. Yet Borus, son
Of Periëres, owned the boy and took 225
The mother for his bride, with princely dower.
Eudorus led the second band, a youth
Of warlike mould, whom Polymela bore,
Daughter of Phylas, graceful in the dance.
In secrecy she brought him forth, for once 230
The mighty Argus-queller saw the maid
Among the choir of those who danced and sang
At Dian's festival, the huntress-queen,
Who bears the golden shafts; he saw and loved
And, climbing to her chamber, met by stealth 235
The damsel, and she bore a gallant son,
Eudorus, swift of foot and brave in war.
When Ilithyia, midwife goddess, gave
The boy to see the pleasant light of day,
The stout Echecleus, son of Actor, brought 240
The mother to his house, with liberal dower.
The aged Phylas reared the child she left
Tenderly as a son, and loved him well.
Pisander, warlike son of Mæmalus,
Commanded the third squadron; none like him 245
Among the Myrmidons could wield the spear
Except Pelides. Phœnix, aged knight,
Led the fourth squadron. With the fifth and last
There came Alcimedon, Laerceus' son,
As leader. When their ranks were duly formed, 250
Achilles spake to them in earnest words:—
    "Now, Myrmidons, forget no single word
Of all the threats ye uttered against Troy
Since first my wrath began. Ye blame me much,
And say: 'Hard-hearted son of Peleus, sure 255
Thy mother must have suckled thee on gall;
For sternly thou dost keep us in the ships,
Unwilling as we are. We might, at least,
Crossing the sea, return in our good ships,
If thus thine anger is to last.' These words 260

Ye utter oft when our assemblies meet,
And now the great occasion is at hand
Which ye have longed for; now let him whose heart
Is fearless meet the Trojans valiantly."
    He spake, and roused their courage and their might; 265
And as they heard their king they brought their ranks
To closer order. As an architect
Builds up, with closely fitting stones, the wall
Of some tall mansion, proof against the blast,
So close were now the helms and bossy shields. 270
Shield leaned on shield, and helm on helm, and man
On man, and on the glittering helmet-cones
The horse-hair plumes with every motion touched
Each other, so compact the squadrons stood.
Two heroes, nobly armed, were at their head, 275
Patroclus and Automedon, and both
Had but one thought,—to combat in the van.
    Entering his tent, Achilles raised the lid
Of a fair coffer, beautifully wrought,
Which silver-footed Thetis placed on board 280
His bark, and filled with tunics, cloaks well lined,
And fleecy carpets. There he also kept
A goblet richly chased, from which no lip
Of man, save his, might drink the dark red wine,
Nor wine be poured to any god save Jove, 285
The mighty Father. This he took in hand
And purified with sulphur first, and then
Rinsed with clear water. Next, with washen hands,
He drew the dark red wine, and stood without,
In the open space, and, pouring out the wine, 290
Prayed with his eyes turned heavenward, not unheard
By Jupiter, who wields the thunderbolt.
    "Dodonian Jove, Pelasgian, sovereign King,
Whose dwelling is afar, and who dost rule
Dodona winter-bound, where dwell thy priests, 295
The Selli, with unwashen feet, who sleep
Upon the ground! Thou once hast heard my prayer,
And thou hast honored me, and terribly
Avenged me on the Greeks. Accomplish yet

This one request of mine. I shall remain   300
Among the rows of ships, but in my stead
I send my comrade, who will lead to war
My vast array of Myrmidons. With him,
O God of Thunders, send the victory.
Make his heart bold; let even Hector learn   305
Whether my follower, though alone, can wage
Successful war, or conquer only then
When I go forth with him into the field
Of slaughter. When he shall have beaten back
The assailants from the fleet, let him return   310
Unharmed to my good galleys and to me,
With all his arms and all his valiant men."

  So spake he, offering prayer, and Jupiter,
The Great Disposer, hearkened. Half the prayer
The All-Father granted him, and half denied: 315
To drive the storm of battle from the fleet
He granted, but denied his friend's return
In safety. When the warrior thus had prayed,
And poured the wine to Father Jove, he went
Into his tent again, and there replaced   320
The goblet in the coffer. Coming forth,
He stood before the entrance to behold
The terrible encounter of the hosts.

    The newly armed, led by their gallant chief,
Patroclus, marched in warlike order forth,   325
And in high hope, to fall upon the foe.
As wasps, that by the wayside build their cells,
Angered from time to time by thoughtless boys,—
Whence mischief comes to many,—if by chance
Some passing traveller should unwittingly   330
Disturb them, all at once are on the wing,
And all attack him, to defend their young;
So fearless and so fierce the Myrmidons
Poured from their fleet, and mighty was the din.
Patroclus with loud voice exhorted them:—   335

  "O Myrmidons, companions of the son
Of Peleus, bear in mind, my friends, your fame
For valor, and be men, that we who serve

Achilles, we who combat hand to hand,
May honor him by our exploits, and teach 340
Wide-ruling Agamemnon how he erred
Slighting the bravest warrior of the Greeks."
  These words awoke the courage and the might
Of all who heard them, and in close array
They fell upon the Trojans. Fearfully 345
The fleet around them echoed to the sound
Of Argives shouting. When the Trojans saw,
In glittering arms, Menœtius' gallant son
And his attendant, every heart grew faint
With fear; the close ranks wavered; for they thought 350
That the swift son of Peleus at the fleet
Had laid aside his wrath, and was again
The friend of Agamemnon. Eagerly
They looked around for an escape from death.
  Then first Patroclus cast his shining spear 355
Into the crowd before him, where they fought
Most fiercely round the stern of the good ship
Of brave Protesilaüs. There it smote
Pyræchmes, who had led from Amydon,
On the broad Axius, his Pæonian knights. 360
Through his right shoulder went the blade; he fell,
Heavily groaning, to the earth. His band
Of warriors from Pæonia, panic-struck,
Fled from Patroclus as they saw their chief
Cut off, their bravest in the battle-field. 365
So from the ship he drave the foe, and quenched
The blazing fire. There lay the half-burnt bark,
While with a mighty uproar fled the host
Of Troy, and from between the beakèd ships
Poured after them with tumult infinite 370
The Greeks. As when from some high mountain-top
The God of Lightnings, Jupiter, sweeps off
The overshadowing cloud, at once appear
The watch-towers and the headland heights and lawns
All in full light, and all the unmeasured depth 375
Of ether opens, so the Greeks, when thus
Their fleet was rescued from the hostile flame,

Breathed for a space; and yet they might not cease
From battle, for not everywhere alike
Were chased the Trojans from the dark-hulled ships 380
Before the Greeks, but struggled still to keep
The mastery, and yielded but to force.
   Then in that scattered conflict of the chiefs
Each Argive slew a warrior. With his spear
The brave son of Menœtius made a thrust 385
At Areïlochus, and pierced his thigh,
Just as he turned away, and through the part
Forced the keen weapon, splintering as it went
The bone, and brought the Trojan to the ground;
And warlike Menelaus pierced the breast 390
Of Thoas where the buckler left it bare,
And took his life. The son of Phyleus saw
Amphiclus rushing on, and with his spear
Met him and pierced his leg below the knee,
Where brawniest is the limb. The blade cut through 395
The sinews, and his eyes were closed in night.
There fought the sons of Nestor. One of these,
Antilochus, transfixed with his good spear
Atymnius through the flank, and brought him down
At his own feet. With sorrow Maris saw 400
His brother fall, and toward Antilochus
Flew to defend the corpse; but ere he strook,
The godlike Thrasymedes, with a blow
That missed not, smote his shoulder, tearing off
With the spear's blade upon the upper arm 405
The muscles from the bone. With ringing arms
He fell, and darkness gathered o'er his eyes.
Thus were two brothers by two brothers slain,
And sent to Erebus; two valiant friends
Were they of King Sarpedon, and the sons 410
Of Amisodarus, who reared and fed
Chimera, the destroyer of mankind.
   Oïlean Ajax, springing forward, seized
On Cleobulus, for the struggling crowd
Hindered his flight. He took the Trojan's life, 415
Smiting the neck with his huge-handled sword;

The blade grew warm with blood, and cruel fate
Brought darkness o'er the dying warrior's eyes.
Peneleus fought with Lycon; each had cast
His spear and missed his aim, and now with swords 420
The twain encountered. Lycon dealt a stroke
Upon the crested helmet of his foe,
And the blade failed him, breaking at the hilt.
Meantime Peneleus smote beneath the ear
The neck of Lycon: deep the weapon went; 425
The severed head, held only by the skin,
Dropped to one side, and life forsook the limbs.
Meriones, o'ertaking Acamas,
In rapid flight, discharged a mighty blow
On his left shoulder as he climbed his car; 430
He fell, and darkness gathered o'er his eyes.
Then plunged Idomeneus the cruel spear
Into the mouth of Erymas. The blade
Passed on beneath the brain, and pierced the neck,
And there divided the white bones. It dashed 435
The teeth out; both the eyes were filled with blood,
Which gushed from mouth and nostrils as he breathed;
And the black cloud of death came over him.
Thus every Grecian leader slew his man.
   As ravening wolves that spring on lambs and kids, 440
And seize them, wandering wide among the hills
Beyond the keeper's care, and bear them off,
And rend with cruel fangs their helpless prey,
So fiercely did the Achaians fling themselves
Upon the men of Troy, who only thought 445
Of flight from that tumultuous strife, and quite
Forgot their wonted valor. All the while
The greater Ajax sought to hurl his spear
At Hector, clad in brazen mail, who yet,
Expert in battle, kept his ample chest 450
Hid by his bull's-hide shield, and, though he heard
The hiss of darts and clash of spears, and saw
The fortune of the field deserting him,
Lingered to rescue his beloved friends.
   As from the summit of Olympus spreads 455

A cloud into the sky that late was clear,
When Jove brings on the tempest, with such speed
In clamorous flight the Trojans left the fleet,
Yet passed they not the trench in seemly plight.
The rapid steeds of Hector bore him safe   460
Across with all his arms, while, left between
The high banks of the trench, the Trojan host
Struggled despairingly. The fiery steeds,
Harnessed to many a chariot, left it there
With broken pole. Patroclus followed close,   465
With mighty voice encouraging the Greeks,
And meditating vengeance on the foe,
That noisily ran on, and right and left
Were scattered, filling all the ways. The dust
Rose thick and high, and spread, and reached the clouds,   470
As with swift feet the Trojan coursers held
Their way to Ilium from the tents and ships.
Patroclus where he saw the wildest rout
Drave thither, shouting threats. Full many a chief
Fell under his own axle from his car,   475
And chariots with a crash were overthrown.
The swift, immortal horses which the gods
Bestowed on Peleus leaped the trench at once,
Eager to reach the plain. As eagerly
Patroclus longed to overtake and smite   480
Hector, whose steeds were hurrying him away.
   As when, in autumn time, the dark-brown earth
Is whelmed with water from the stormy clouds,
When Jupiter pours down his heaviest rains,
Offended at men's crimes who override   485
The laws by violence, and drive justice forth
From the tribunals, heedless of the gods
And their displeasure,—all the running streams
Are swelled to floods,—the furious torrents tear
The mountain slopes, and, plunging from the heights   490
With mighty roar, lay waste the works of men,
And fling themselves into the dark-blue sea,—
Thus with loud tumult fled the Trojan horse.
   Patroclus, having cut the nearest bands

Of Troy in pieces, made his warriors turn 495
Back to the fleet, and, eager as they were,
Stopped the pursuit that led them toward the town.
Then, in the area bounded by the sea,
River, and lofty wall, he chased and smote
And took full vengeance. With his glittering spear 500
He wounded Pronoüs where the buckler left
The breast exposed; the Trojan with a clash
Fell to the earth, and life forsook his limbs.
Advancing in his might, Patroclus smote
Thestor, the son of Enops, as he sat 505
Cowering upon his sumptuous seat, o'ercome
With fear, and dropped the reins. Through his right cheek
Among the teeth Patroclus thrust his spear,
And o'er the chariot's border drew him forth
With the spear's stem. As when an angler sits 510
Upon a jutting rock, and from the sea
Draws a huge fish with line and gleaming hook,
So did Patroclus, with his shining spear,
Draw forth the panting Trojan from his car,
And shook him clear: he fell to earth and died. 515
   As Eryalus then came swiftly on,
Patroclus flung a stone, and on the brow
Smote him; the Trojan's head, beneath the blow,
Parted in two within the helm; he fell
Headlong to earth, a prey to ghastly death. 520
Then slew he Erymas, Amphoterus,
Epaltes, Pyris, Ipheus, Echius,
Tlepolemus, Damastor's son, and next
Euippus; nor was Polymelus spared,
The son of Argias,—smitten all, and thrown, 525
Slain upon slain, along their mother earth.
   And now Sarpedon, as he saw his friends,
The unbelted Lycians, falling by the hand
Of Menœtiades, exhorted thus
The gallant Lycians: "Shame upon you all, 530
My Lycians! whither do you flee? Be bold!
For I myself will meet this man, and learn
Who walks the field in triumph thus, and makes

Such havoc in our squadrons; for his hand
Has laid full many a gallant warrior low." 535
   He spake, and from his car with all his arms
Sprang to the ground, while on the other side
Patroclus, as he saw him come, leaped down
And left his chariot. As on some tall rock
Two vultures, with curved talons and hooked beaks, 540
Fight screaming, so these two with furious cries
Advanced against each other. When the son
Of crafty Saturn saw them meet, his heart
Was touched with pity, and he thus bespake
His spouse and sister Juno: "Woe is me! 545
Sarpedon, most beloved of men, is doomed
To die, o'ercome by Menœtiades.
And now I halt between two purposes,—
Whether to bear him from this fatal fight,
Alive and safe, to Lycia's fertile fields, 550
Or let him perish by his enemy's hand."
   Imperial, large-eyed Juno answered thus:—
"What words, dread son of Saturn, hast thou said!
Wouldst thou deliver from the common lot
Of death a mortal doomed long since by fate? 555
Do as thou wilt, but be thou sure of this,—
The other gods will not approve. And bear
In mind these words of mine. If thou shouldst send
Sarpedon home to Lycia safe, reflect
Some other god may claim the right, like thee, 560
To rescue his beloved son from death
In battle; for we know that in the war
Round Priam's noble city are many sons
Of gods, who will with vehement anger see
Thy interposing hand. Yet if he be 565
So dear to thee, and thou dost pity him,
Let him in mortal combat be o'ercome
By Menœtiades, and when the breath
Of life has left his frame, give thou command
To Death and gentle Sleep to bear him hence 570
To the broad realm of Lycia. There his friends
And brethren shall perform the funeral rites;

There shall they build him up a tomb, and rear
A column,—honors that become the dead."
    He ceased, nor did the All-Father disregard   575
Her words. He caused a bloody dew to fall
Upon the earth in sorrow for the son
Whom well he loved, and whom Patroclus soon
Should slay upon the fertile plain of Troy,
Far from the pleasant land that saw his birth.   580
    The warriors now drew near. Patroclus slew
The noble Thrasymelus, who had been
Sarpedon's valiant comrade in the war.
Below the belt he smote him, and he fell
Lifeless. Sarpedon threw his shining lance;   585
It missed, but struck the courser Pedasus
In the right shoulder. With a groan he fell
In dust, and, moaning, breathed his life away.
Then the two living horses sprang apart,
And the yoke creaked, and the entangled reins   590
Were useless, fastened to the fallen horse.
Automedon, the mighty spearman, saw
The remedy, and from his brawny thigh
He drew his sword, and cut the outside horse
Loose from his fellows. They again were brought   595
Together, and obeyed the reins once more;
And the two chiefs renewed the mortal fight.
    And now, again, Sarpedon's shining spear
Was vainly flung; the point, in passing o'er
Patroclus's left shoulder, gave no wound.   600
In turn, Patroclus, hurling not in vain
His weapon, smote him where the midriff's web
Holds the tough heart. He fell as falls an oak
Or poplar or tall pine, which workmen hew
Among the mountains with their sharpened steel   605
To frame a ship. So he before his steeds
And chariot fell upon the bloody dust,
And grasped it with his hands, and gnashed his teeth.
As when a lion coming on a herd
Seizes, amid the crowd of stamping beeves,   610
A tawny and high-mettled bull, that dies

Bellowing in fury in the lion's jaws,—
Like him, indignant to be overcome,
The leader of the bucklered Lycian host,
Laid prostrate by Patroclus, called by name   615
His dear companion, and addressed him thus:—
   "Beloved Glaucus, mighty among men!
Now prove thyself a hero, now be bold.
Now, if thou have a warrior's spirit, think
Of naught but battle. Go from rank to rank,   620
Exhorting all the Lycian chiefs to fight
Around Sarpedon. Combat thou for me
With thy good spear, for I shall be to thee
A shame and a reproach through all thy days,
If here the Greeks, beside whose ships I fall,   625
Bear off my armor. Stand thou firm, and stir
Thy people up to combat valiantly."
   While he was speaking, death crept o'er his sight
And stopped his breath. Patroclus set his heel
Against his bosom, and plucked out the spear;   630
The midriff followed it, and thus he drew
The life and weapon forth at once. Meantime
The Myrmidons held fast the snorting steeds,
That, loosened from the Lycian's car, were bent
On flight. The grief of Glaucus as he heard   635
His comrade's voice was bitter, and his heart
Ached at the thought that he could bring no aid.
He seized his arm and pressed it in his grasp,
For there the wound which Teucer's arrow left,
When Glaucus stormed the wall and Teucer's shafts   640
Defended it, still pained him grievously,
And thus he prayed to Phœbus, archer-god:—
   "Give ear, O king! wherever thou abide
In the opulent realm of Lycia, or in Troy;
For everywhere thou hearest those who cry   645
To thee in sorrow, and great sorrow now
Is on me. Grievous is the wound I bear;
Sharp are the pains that pierce my hand; the blood
Cannot be stanched; my very arm becomes
A burden; I can wield the spear no more   650

With a firm grasp, nor combat with the foe.
A mighty chief—Sarpedon, son of Jove—
Has perished, and the father came not nigh
To aid his son. Yet come thou to my aid,
O monarch-god! and heal this painful wound, 655
And give me strength to rally to the fight
The Lycian warriors, and myself contend
Valiantly for the rescue of the dead."

So prayed he: Phœbus hearkened, and at once
Assuaged the pain, and stanched the purple blood 660
In the deep wound, and filled his frame with strength.
The warrior felt the change, rejoiced to know
That with such friendly speed the mighty god
Granted his prayer. And first he went among
The Lycian chiefs, exhorting them to wage 665
Fierce battle for Sarpedon. Then he sought,
Walking with rapid strides, the Trojan chiefs,
Agenor, nobly born, Polydamas,
The son of Panthoüs, Æneas next,
And Hector mailed in brass. By him he stood, 670
And thus accosted him with wingèd words:—

"O Hector, thou art careless of the fate
Of thine allies, who for thy sake, afar
From those they love, and from their native land,
Pour out their lives; thou bringest them no aid. 675
Sarpedon lies in death, the chief who led
The bucklered Lycians, who with justice swayed
The realm of Lycia, and defended it
With valor. Him hath brazen Mars beneath
The weapon of Patroclus smitten down. 680
Come then, my friends, repulse we gallantly
These Myrmidons; else will they bear away
His armor and insult his corpse, to avenge
The havoc we have made among the Greeks
Who perished by our weapons at the fleet." 685

He spake, and grief immitigable seized
The Trojans; for the slain, though stranger-born,
Had been a pillar of the realm of Troy,
And many were the troops that followed him,

And he was bravest of them all in war. 690
   Then rushed the Trojans fiercely on the Greeks,
With Hector, sorrowing for Sarpedon's fall,
Leading them on, while the bold-hearted chief
Patroclus Menœtiades, aroused
The courage of the Greeks. He thus addressed 695
The warriors Ajax, eager like himself
For combat: "Be it now your welcome task,
O warriors Ajax, to drive back the foe;
He who first sprang across the Grecian wall,
Sarpedon, lies a corpse, and we must now 700
Dishonor the dead chief, and strip from him
His armor, and strike down with our good spears
Whoever of his comrades shall resist."
   He spake, and all were resolute to beat
The enemy back; and when, on either side, 705
Trojans and Lycians, Myrmidons and Greeks,
Had put their phalanxes in firm array,
They closed, with dreadful shouts and horrid clash
Of arms, in fight around the dead, while Jove
Drew o'er that deadly fray an awful veil 710
Of darkness, that the struggle for the corpse
Of his dear son might rage more furiously.
The Trojans first drave back the dark-eyed Greeks,
For one was in the onset smitten down,
Not the least valiant of the Myrmidons,— 715
The son of brave Agacles, nobly born
Epeigeus, who aforetime, when he ruled
The populous Budeium, having slain
A noble kinsman, fled a suppliant
To Peleus and the silver-footed queen, 720
Thetis, his consort, and by them was sent,
With terrible Achilles, to the coast
Of courser-breeding Ilium and the siege
Of Troy. As now he stooped to seize the dead,
Illustrious Hector smote him with a stone 725
Upon the forehead, cleaving it in two
In the strong helmet; headlong on the corse
He fell, and cruel death crept over him.

With grief Patroclus saw his comrade slain,
And broke his way among the foremost ranks.   730
As a swift hawk that chases through the air
Starlings and daws, so didst thou dart among
Trojans and Lycians, for thy wrath was roused,
O knight Patroclus! by thy comrade's death.
And now his hand struck Sthenelaüs down,   735
The dear son of Ithæmenes; he flung
A stone that crushed the sinews of the neck.
Back drew illustrious Hector, and with him
The warriors who were fighting in the van.
As far as one can send a javelin,   740
When men contend in martial games, or meet
Their deadly enemies in war, so far
Withdrew the Trojans, and the Greeks pursued.
The leader of the bucklered Lycian host,
Glaucus, was first to turn against his foes.   745
He slew the brave Bathycles, the dear son
Of Chalcon, who in Hellas had his home,
And was the richest of the Myrmidons.
The Lycian, turning on him suddenly
As he drew near pursuing, sent his spear   750
Right through his breast, and with a clash he fell.
Great was the sorrow of the Greeks to see
That valiant warrior fall; the men of Troy
Exulted, and pressed round him in a crowd.
Nor lacking was the valor of the Greeks,   755
Who met them manfully. Meriones
Struck down a Trojan chief, Laogonus,
Onetor's valiant son. His father stood
Priest at the altar of Idæan Jove,
And like a god was honored by the realm.   760
Below the jaw and ear Meriones
Smote him, and instantly the life forsook
His limbs, and fearful darkness shrouded him.
Straight at Meriones Æneas aimed
His brazen spear to smite him, as he came,   765
Beneath his buckler; but the Greek beheld
The weapon in the air, and, stooping low,

Escaped it; over him it passed, and stood
Fixed in the earth behind him, where its stem
Trembled, for now the rapid steel had spent 770
Its force. As thus it quivered in the ground,
Æneas, who perceived that it had left
His powerful hand in vain, was vexed, and said:
"Had I but struck thee, dancer as thou art,
Meriones, my spear had suddenly 775
Ended thy dancing." Then Meriones,
The skilful spearman, answered: "Thou art brave,
But thou wilt find it hard to overcome
The might of all who gather to repulse
Thy onset. Thou art mortal, and if I, 780
Aiming at thee with my good spear, should pierce
Thy bosom, valiant as thou art and proud
Of thy strong arm, thy death would bring me praise,
And send thy soul where gloomy Pluto dwells."

   He spake; the brave Patroclus heard, and thus 785
Rebuked him: "Why wilt thou, Meriones,
With all thy valor, stand to make a speech.
The foe, my friend, will not be forced to leave
The corpse by insults; some of them must die.
In deeds the issue of a battle lies; 790
Words are for counsel. Now is not the time
To utter swelling phrases, but to fight."

   He ended, and went on; the godlike man
Followed his steps. As when from mountain dells
Rises, and far is heard, a crashing sound 795
Where woodmen fell the trees, such was the noise
From those who fought on that wide plain,—the din
Of brass, of leather, and of tough bull's-hide
Smitten with swords and two-edged spears. No eye,
Although of keenest sight, would then have known 800
Noble Sarpedon, covered as he lay,
From head to foot, with weapons, blood, and dust;
And still the warriors thronged around the dead.
As when in spring-time at the cattle-stalls
Flies gather, humming, when the milk is drawn, 805
Round the full pails, so swarmed around the corpse

The combatants; nor once did Jove withdraw
His bright eyes from the stubborn fray, but still
Gazed, planning how Patroclus should be slain.
Uncertain whether, in the desperate strife   810
Over the great Sarpedon, to permit
Illustrious Hector with his spear to lay
The hero dead, and make his arms a spoil,
Or spare him yet a while, to make the war
More bloody. As he pondered, this seemed best: 815
That the brave comrade of Achilles first
Should put to flight the Trojans and their chief,
Hector the brazen-mailed, pursuing them
Toward Troy with slaughter. To this end he sent
Into the heart of Hector panic fear,   820
Who climbed his car and fled, and bade the rest
Flee also, for he saw how Jove had weighed
The fortunes of the day. Now none remained,
Not even the gallant Lycians, when they saw
Their monarch lying wounded to the heart   825
Among a heap of slain; for Saturn's son
In that day's strife had caused a multitude
To fall in death. Now when the Greeks had stripped
Sarpedon of the glittering brazen mail,
The brave son of Menœtius bade his friends   830
Convey it to the hollow ships. Meanwhile
The Cloud-compeller spake to Phœbus thus:—
    "Go now, beloved Phœbus, and withdraw
Sarpedon from the weapons of the foe;
Cleanse him from the dark blood, and bear him thence,   835
And lave him in the river-stream, and shed
Ambrosia o'er him. Clothe him then in robes
Of heaven, consigning him to Sleep and Death,
Twin brothers, and swift bearers of the dead,
And they shall lay him down in Lycia's fields,   840
That broad and opulent realm. There shall his friends
And kinsmen give him burial, and shall rear
His tomb and column,—honors due the dead."
    He spake: Apollo instantly obeyed
His father, leaving Ida's mountain height,   845

And sought the field of battle, and bore off
Noble Sarpedon from the enemy's spears,
And laved him in the river-stream, and shed
Ambrosia o'er him. Then in robes of heaven
He clothed him, giving him to Sleep and Death, 850
Twin brothers and swift bearers of the dead,
And they, with speed conveying it, laid down
The corpse in Lycia's broad and opulent realm.
    Meantime Patroclus, urging on his steeds
And charioteer, pursued, to his own hurt, 855
Trojans and Lycians. Madman! had he then
Obeyed the counsel which Pelides gave,
The bitter doom of death had not been his.
But stronger than the purposes of men
Are those of Jove, who puts to flight the brave, 860
And takes from them the victory, though he
Impelled them to the battle; and he now
Urged on Patroclus to prolong the fight.
    Who first, when thus the gods decreed thy death,
Fell by thy hand, Patroclus, and who last? 865
Adrastus first, Autonoüs next, and then
Echeclus; then died Perimus, the son
Of Meges; then with Melanippus fell
Epistor; next was Elasus o'ercome,
And Mulius, and Pylartes. These he slew, 870
While all the rest betook themselves to flight.
    Then had the Greeks possessed themselves of Troy,
With all its lofty portals, by the hand
And valor of Patroclus, for his rage
Was terrible beyond the rage of all 875
Who bore the spear, had not Apollo stood
On a strong tower to menace him with ill,
And aid the Trojans. Thrice Patroclus climbed
A shoulder of the lofty wall, and thrice
Apollo, striking his immortal hands 880
Against the glittering buckler, thrust him down;
And when, for the fourth time, the godlike man
Essayed to mount the wall, the archer-god,
Phœbus, encountered him with fearful threats:

"Noble Patroclus, hold thy hand, nor deem   885
The city of the warlike Trojans doomed
To fall beneath thy spear, nor by the arm
Of Peleus' son, though mightier far than thou."
    He spake; Patroclus, fearful of the wrath
Of the archer-god, withdrew, and stood afar,   890
While Hector, at the Scæan gates, restrained
His coursers, doubtful whether to renew
The fight by mingling with the crowd again,
Or gather all his host within the walls
By a loud summons. As he pondered thus,   895
Apollo stood beside him in the form
Of Asius, a young warrior and a brave,
Uncle of Hector, the great horse-tamer,
And brother of Queen Hecuba, and son
Of Dymas, who in Phrygia dwelt beside   900
The streams of the Sangarius. Putting on
His shape and aspect, thus Apollo said:—
    "Why, Hector, dost thou pause from battle thus?
Nay, it becomes thee not. Were I in might
Greater than thou, as I am less, full soon   905
Wouldst thou repent this shrinking from the war.
Come boldly on, and urge thy firm-paced steeds
Against Patroclus; slay him on the field,
And Phœbus will requite thee with renown."
    He spake, and mingled in the hard-fought fray,   910
While noble Hector bade his charioteer,
The brave Cebriones, ply well the lash,
And join the battle. Phœbus went before,
Entering the crowd, and spread dismay among
The Greeks, and gave the glory of the hour   915
To Hector and the Trojans. Little heed
Paid Hector to the rest, nor raised his arm
To slay them, but urged on his firm-paced steeds
To meet Patroclus, who, beholding him,
Leaped from his car. In his left hand he held   920
A spear, and with the other lifting up
A white, rough stone, the largest he could grasp,
Flung it with all its force. It flew not wide,

Nor flew in vain, but smote Cebriones,
The warlike chief who guided Hector's steeds, 925
A spurious son of Priam the renowned.
The sharp stone smote his forehead as he held
The reins, and crushed both eyebrows in; the bone
Resisted not the blow; the warrior's eyes
Fell in the dust before his very feet. 930
Down from the sumptuous seat he plunged, as dives
A swimmer, and the life forsook his limbs.
And this, Patroclus, was thy cruel jest:—
   "Truly a nimble man is this who dives
With such expertness. Were this, now, the sea, 935
Where fish are bred, and he were searching it
For oysters, he might get an ample store
For many men, in leaping from a ship,
Though in a storm, so skilfully he dives
Even from the chariot to the plain. No doubt 940
There must be divers in the town of Troy."
   He spake, and sprang upon Cebriones.
With all a lion's fury, which attacks
The stables and is wounded in the breast,
And perishes through his own daring; thus, 945
Patroclus, didst thou fall upon the slain,
While Hector, hastening also, left his steeds,
And both contended for Cebriones.
As lions for the carcass of a deer
Fight on a mountain summit, hungry both, 950
And both unyielding, thus two mighty men
Of war, Patroclus Menœtiades
And glorious Hector, eager each to smite
His adversary with the cruel spear,
Fought for Cebriones. The slain man's head 955
Was seized by Hector's powerful hand, whose grasp
Relaxed not, while Patroclus held the foot;
And, thronging to the spot, the other Greeks
And Trojans mingled in the desperate strife.
   As when the east wind and the south contend 960
In the open mountain grounds, and furiously
Assail the deep old woods of beech and ash

And barky cornel, flinging their long boughs
Against each other with a mighty roar,
And crash of those that break, so did the Greeks 965
And Trojans meet with mutual blows, and slay
Each other; nor had either host a thought
Of shameful flight. Full many a trenchant spear
Went to its mark beside Cebriones,
And many a wingèd arrow that had left 970
The bowstring; many a massive stone was hurled
Against the ringing bucklers, as they fought
Around the dead, while he, the mighty, lay
Stretched on the ground amid the eddying dust,
Forgetful of his art of horsemanship. 975
   While yet the sun was climbing to his place
In middle heaven, the men of either host
Were smitten by the weapons, and in both
The people fell; but when he stooped to the west
The Greeks prevailed, and from that storm of darts 980
And tumult of the Trojans they drew forth
Cebriones, and stripped him of his arms.
   Still rushed Patroclus onward, bent to wreak
His fury on the Trojans. Fierce as Mars,
He charged their squadrons thrice with fearful shouts, 985
And thrice he laid nine warriors in the dust.
But as with godlike energy he made
The fourth assault, then clearly was it seen,
Patroclus, that thy life was near its end,
For Phœbus terribly in that fierce strife 990
Encountered thee. Patroclus saw him not
Advancing in the tumult, for he moved
Unseen in darkness. Coming close behind,
He smote, with open palm, the hero's back
Between the ample shoulders, and his eyes 995
Reeled with the blow, while Phœbus from his head
Struck the tall helm, that, clanking, rolled away
Under the horses' feet; its crest was soiled
With blood and dust, though never till that hour
Had dust defiled its horse-hair plume; for once 1000
That helmet guarded an illustrious head,

The glorious brows of Peleus' son, and now
Jove destined it for Hector, to be worn
In battle; and his death was also near.
The spear Patroclus wielded, edged with brass, 1005
Long, tough, and huge, was broken in his hands;
And his broad buckler, dropping with its band,
Lay on the ground, while Phœbus, son of Jove,
Undid the fastenings of his mail. With mind
Bewildered, and with powerless limbs, he stood 1010
As thunderstruck. Then a Dardanian named
Euphorbus, son of Panthoüs, who excelled
His comrades in the wielding of the spear,
The race, and horsemanship, approaching, smote
Patroclus in the back with his keen spear, 1015
Between the shoulder-blades. Already he
Had dashed down twenty warriors from their cars,
Guiding his own, a learner in the art
Of war. The first was he who threw a lance
At thee, Patroclus, yet o'ercame thee not; 1020
For, plucking from thy back its ashen stem,
He fled, and mingled with the crowd, nor dared
Await thy coming, though thou wert unarmed,
While, weakened by that wound and by the blow
Given by the god, Patroclus turned and sought 1025
Shelter from danger in the Grecian ranks;
But Hector, when he saw the gallant Greek
Thus wounded and retreating, left his place
Among the squadrons, and, advancing, pierced
Patroclus with his spear, below the belt, 1030
Driving the weapon deep. The hero fell
With clashing mail, and all the Greeks beheld
His fall with grief. As when a lion bears
A stubborn boar to earth, what time the twain
Fight on the mountains for a slender spring, 1035
Both thirsty and both fierce, the lion's strength
Lays prone his panting foe, so Priam's son
Slew, fighting hand to hand, the valiant Greek,
Son of Menœtius, who himself had slain
So many. Hector gloried over him 1040

With wingèd words: "Patroclus, thou didst think
To lay our city waste, and carry off
Our women captive in thy ships to Greece.
Madman! in their defence the fiery steeds
Of Hector sweep the battle-field, and I,   1045
Mightiest of all the Trojans, with the spear
Will guard them from the doom of slavery.
Now vultures shall devour thee, wretched youth!
Achilles, mighty though he be, has brought
No help to thee, though doubtless when he sent   1050
Thee forth to battle, and remained within,
He charged thee thus: 'Patroclus, flower of knights,
Return not to the fleet until thy hand
Hath torn the bloody armor from the corpse
Of the man-queller Hector.' So he spake,   1055
And filled with idle hopes thy foolish heart."
   Then thou, Patroclus, with a faltering voice,
Didst answer thus: "Now, Hector, while thou mayst,
Utter thy boast in swelling words, since Jove
And Phœbus gave the victory to thee,   1060
Easily have they vanquished me; 'twas they
Who stripped the armor from my limbs, for else,
If twenty such as thou had met me, all
Had perished by my spear. A cruel fate
O'ertakes me, aided by Latona's son,   1065
The god, and by Euphorbus among men.
Thou who shalt take my spoil art but the third;
Yet hear my words, and keep them in thy thought.
Not long shalt thou remain alive; thy death
By violence is at hand, and thou must fall,   1070
Slain by the hand of great Æacides."
   While he was speaking, death stole over him
And veiled his senses, while the soul forsook
His limbs and flew to Hades, sorrowing
For its sad lot, to part from life in youth   1075
And prime of strength. Illustrious Hector thus
Answered the dying man: "Why threaten me,
Patroclus, with an early death? Who knows
That he, thy friend, whom fair-haired Thetis bore

Achilles, may not sooner lose his life, 1080
Slain by my spear?" He spake, and set his heel
Upon the slain, and from the wound drew forth
His brazen spear and pushed the corpse aside,
And with the weapon hurried on to smite
Godlike Automedon, the charioteer 1085
Of swift Æacides; but him the steeds
Fleet-footed and immortal, which the gods
Bestowed on Peleus, swiftly bore away.

BOOK XVII

THE warlike Menelaus, Atreus' son,
Beheld Patroclus fall by Trojan hands,
And came in glittering armor to the van
To guard the body of the slain. As walks
A heifer moaning round her new-born young,   5
So fair-haired Menelaus stalked around
The body of Patroclus, holding forth
His spear and great round shield, intent to slay
Whoever came against him. But the son
Of Panthoüs, mighty spearman, not the less   10
Intent to spoil the illustrious dead, drew near,
And spake to warlike Menelaus thus:—
  "Atrides Menelaus, reared by Jove,
And leader of thy host, give way and leave
The dead, and quit to me his bloody spoil;   15
For none of our brave Trojans and allies
Smote him in deadly combat with the spear,
Before me. Leave me therefore to receive
The glory due me from the sons of Troy,
Else will I smite thee too, and thou wilt lose   20
Thy precious life!" Indignant at the word,
The fair-haired Menelaus answered him;—
  "O Father Jove! unseemly boasts are these!
For not the panther's nor the lion's might,
Nor that of the fierce forest-boar whose rage   25
Is heightened into fury, is as great

As that which these distinguished spearmen, sons
Of Panthoüs, utter with their lips. And yet
The horseman Hyperenor did not long
Enjoy his youth when he with insolent words 30
Assailed me, and withstood me,—when he said
That I was the most craven wretch who bore
Arms in the Grecian host. He never turned,
I think, his footsteps homeward to delight
His reverend parents and beloved wife; 35
And I, like his, will take thy life, if thou
Oppose me. Heed my counsel, and withdraw
Among the crowd, and so avoid my stroke
Before thou come to harm. He is a fool
Who only sees the mischiefs that are past." 40
 He said: Euphorbus, heeding not his words
Of warning, spake again: "Now is my time,
Jove-nurtured Menelaus, to avenge
My brother, slain by thee, and over whom
Thou utteredst such swelling words, whose wife 45
In her new bridal chamber thou hast made
A widow, and upon her parents brought
Mourning and endless sorrow. It may make
The sorrow less, should I into the hands
Of Panthoüs and the noble Phrontis give 50
Thy head and armor. Let us now delay
The strife no longer: it will show with whom
The valor dwells, and who is moved by fear."
 He spake, and smote his enemy's round shield,
But pierced it not; the stubborn metal turned 55
The weapon's point. Then Menelaus, son
Of Atreus, with a prayer to Jupiter,
Struck, as Euphorbus made a backward step,
His throat, and drave the weapon with strong hand
Through the soft neck. He fell with clashing arms. 60
His locks, which were like those the Graces wear,
And ringlets, bound with gold and silver bands,
Were drenched with blood. As when some husbandman
Rears in a lonely and well-watered spot
An olive-tree with widely spreading boughs, 65

Beautiful with fresh shoots, and putting forth
White blossoms, gently waved by every wind,
A sudden blast descends with mighty sweep
And tears it from its bed, and lays it prone
Upon the earth,—so lay Euphorbus, skilled 70
To wield the spear and son of Panthoüs, slain
And spoiled by Menelaus, Atreus' son.
As when a lion of the mountain wilds,
Fearless and strong, bears from the browsing herd
The fairest of the kine, and breaks her neck 75
With his strong teeth, and, tearing her, devours
The bloody entrails, while a clamorous throng
Of dogs and herdsmen, with incessant cries,
Gather around him, yet approach him not,
Withheld by fear, so of the warriors round 80
The gallant Menelaus none could find
The courage to encounter him; and then
Atrides easily had borne away
The sumptuous armor worn by Panthoüs' son,
If envious Apollo had not moved 85
Hector to meet him. Putting on the form
Of Mentes, chief of the Ciconian band,
He said to him aloud, with wingèd words:—
  "Hector, thou art pursuing what thy feet
Will never overtake, the steeds which draw 90
The chariot of Achilles. Hard it were
For mortal man to tame them or to guide,
Save for Achilles, goddess-born. Meanwhile
Hath warlike Menelaus, Atreus' son,
Guarding the slain Patroclus, overthrown 95
Euphorbus, bravest of the Trojan host,
A son of Panthoüs; he will fight no more."
  Thus spake the god, and disappeared among
The warring squadrons. Bitter was the grief
That seized the heart of Hector as he looked 100
Along the ranks and saw the Greek bear off
The sumptuous arms, and saw the Trojan lie
Weltering in blood. At once he made his way
To the front rank, all armed in glittering brass,

And with loud shouts. As terrible he came 105
As Vulcan's inextinguishable fires.
The son of Atreus heard that mighty shout,
And thus to his great soul lamenting said:—
    "If I abandon these rich spoils and leave
Patroclus, who has perished in my cause, 110
I fear the Greeks will look upon the act
With indignation. If, through dread of shame,
I fight alone with Hector and his men,
I fear to be o'erwhelmed by multitudes,
For crested Hector leads the whole array 115
Of Trojans hither. Yet why question thus?
For when a warrior ventures to assault
One whom a god protects, a bitter doom
Is his. Then none of all the Greeks should blame
If I give way to Hector, whom a god 120
Hath sent against me. Yet could I but hear
The voice of mighty Ajax, we would both
Return, and even against a god renew
The combat, that we haply might restore
Patroclus to Achilles, Peleus' son. 125
Such in this choice of evils were the least."
    As thus he mused, the men of Troy came on,
With Hector at their head. The Greek gave way
And left the slain. As when a lion, driven
With pikes and clamor from the herdsman's stalls 130
By men and dogs, unwillingly retreats,
His valiant heart still raging in his breast,
So did the fair-haired Menelaus leave
Patroclus. When he reached the Grecian ranks,
He turned and stood and looked about to find 135
The mighty Ajax, son of Telamon,
And him he soon beheld on the left edge
Of battle, rallying there and heartening
His men; for Phœbus from above had sent
A panic fear among them. To him then 140
The son of Atreus went in haste and said:—
    "Ajax, my friend, come hither where we fight
Around Patroclus. Let us strive at least

To bring Achilles back the hero's corpse,
Though stripped; for crested Hector hath his arms." 145
    He spake; the courage of the warlike son
Of Telamon was kindled by his words.
To the front rank he hastened, and with him
Went fair-haired Menelaus. Hector there
Had spoiled Patroclus of his glorious arms, 150
And now was dragging him apart to hew
The head away with his keen sword, and give
The body to the dogs of Troy. Just then
Came Ajax, bearing, like a tower, his shield,
And Hector mingled with the Trojan ranks, 155
And leaped into his car; but first he gave
His friends the glittering spoil to bear away
To Troy,—a glory to the conqueror;
While Ajax, over Menœtiades
Holding his ample shield, stood firm as stands 160
A lion o'er his whelps, when, as he comes
Leading them through the wood, the hunters rush
Upon him, and his look is terrible
As his knit eyebrows cover his fierce eyes.
So Ajax moved around the hero's corpse, 165
While warlike Menelaus by his side,
The son of Atreus, stood in bitter grief.
    Then, with a look of anger, Glaucus spake—
Son of Hippolochus, and chief among
The Lycians—thus to Hector: "Though thy form, 170
Hector, be noble, yet in prowess thou
Art wanting, and thy fame in feats of war
Is not deserved, since thou dost fly the foe.
Think whether thou alone, with others born
In Troy, canst save the city and the state. 175
For henceforth will no Lycian fight for Troy
Against the Greeks; this conflict without end
Has never earned them thanks. Inglorious chief!
How wilt thou be the shield of humbler men,
If thou canst leave Sarpedon, who has been 180
Thy comrade and thy guest, to be the prey
And spoil of the Greek warriors? While he lived,

Great was the aid he brought thy cause and thee,
And now thou dost not seek to drive away
The dogs from his neglected corpse. For this, 185
If any of the Lycians heed my words,
They will go home, and imminent will be
The ruin of thy city. If that firm
And resolute valor lived in Trojan hearts
Which they should cherish who in the defence 190
Of their own country bear the toils and face
The dangers of the field, we might this hour
Drag off the slain Patroclus into Troy.
And should we bear him from the thick of fight
To the great city of Priam, soon the Greeks 195
Would let us ransom the rich armor worn
By our Sarpedon, and bring back his corpse;
For he lies slain who was the bosom friend
Of the most valiant chieftain at the fleet
Of Greece, and leader of her bravest men. 200
But thou, when great-souled Ajax fixed his eye
Upon thee, didst not venture to remain
And fight with him; he is more brave than thou."
   The crested Hector frowned and thus replied:—
"Why, Glaucus, should a warrior such as thou 205
Utter such violent words? My friend, I deemed
That thou wert wise above all other men
Of fertile Lycia, but I now must blame
Thy judgment when thou say'st I shrink to meet
The mighty Ajax. I do neither dread 210
The battle's fury nor the rush of steeds;
But all-prevailing are the purposes
Of ægis-bearing Jove, who makes the brave
To flee, and takes from him the victory,
And then again impels him to the fight. 215
Come then, my friend, stand by me; see if I
Skulk this time from the conflict, as thou say'st,
Or tame the courage of whatever Greek,
The bravest, who defends Patroclus slain."
   He spake, and, shouting, cheered the Trojans on: 220
"Trojans and Lycians and Dardanians, trained

To combat hand to hand, let it be seen,
My friends, that ye are men, and still retain
Your ancient valor; while I buckle on
The glorious armor of the illustrious son   225
Of Peleus, taken from Patroclus slain."
   So spake the crested Hector, and withdrew
From the fierce conflict, and with rapid steps
O'ertook his comrades as they bore away
Townward the glorious arms of Peleus' son.   230
There from that deadly strife apart he stood,
And changed his coat of mail. He gave his own
To his companions, to be carried thence
To sacred Ilium, and he buckled on
The immortal armor of Achilles, son   235
Of Peleus, which the gods of heaven bestowed
Upon his father, who in his old age
Consigned them to Achilles; but the son
Was never in that armor to grow old.
   And when the Cloud-compeller Jove beheld   240
Hector apart, accoutred in the arms
Of Peleus' godlike son, he shook his head,
And to himself he said: "Unhappy man!
Death even now is near to thee, and yet
Is not in all thy thoughts. Thou puttest on   245
The heavenly armor of the terrible chief,
Before whom others tremble; thou hast slain
His friend, the brave and gentle, and hast stripped,
To do him shame, the armor from his limbs.
Yet will I for the moment give to thee   250
Fresh triumphs, since Andromache shall ne'er
Receive, when thou returnest from the field,
The armor of Pelides from thy hands."
   The son of Saturn spake, and gave the nod
With his dark brows. Well did that coat of mail   255
Suit Hector's form. Meantime the god of war
In all his fierceness entered Hector's breast:
Fresh vigor filled and nerved his frame; he went
Along the ranks of his renowned allies
With shouts; that glittering armor made him seem   260

The large-souled son of Peleus. To them all
He spake in turn, encouraging their hearts,—
To Mesthles, Glaucus, and Thersilochus,
Medon, Deisenor, and Hippothoüs,
Asteropæus, Phorcys, Chromius, 265
And Ennomus the Augur; these the chief
Exhorted to the fight with wingèd words:—
   "Hear me, ye mighty throng of our allies,
Dwellers of nations round us! Not to make
Our army vast in numbers did I send 270
To summon you, each from his native town,
But that your willing valor might defend
The wives and children of the sons of Troy
From the assailing Greeks. I therefore give
Most freely of our substance in large gifts 275
And banquets, that ye all may be content;
And now let some of you move boldly on
To do or die, which is the chance of war.
To him who from the field will drag and bring
The slain Patroclus to the Trojan knights, 280
Compelling Ajax to give way,—to him
I yield up half the spoil; the other half
I keep, and let his glory equal mine."
   He spake, and all that mighty multitude
With lifted lances threw themselves against 285
The Grecian ranks. They hoped to bear away
The dead from Ajax, son of Telamon.
Ah, idle hope! that hero o'er the dead
Took many a Trojan's life. Then Ajax thus
To Menelaus, great in battle, spake:— 290
   "O friend, O Menelaus, reared by Jove,
No longer now I hope our safe return
From battle. Not the greatest of my fears
Is for Patroclus, whom the dogs of Troy
And birds of prey full quickly will devour, 295
But for my life and thine. That cloud of war,
Hector, o'ershadows all, and over us
Impends the doom of death. Yet let us call
Our mighty men, if they perchance may hear."

He spake, and Menelaus, great in war, 300
Obeyed his wish and shouted to the Greeks:—
  "O friends, the princes and the chiefs of Greece,
Who at the public feasts with Atreus' sons—
King Agamemnon and his brother chief—
Drink wine,—who each command a host, and hold 305
Your honors and your state from Jove,—my eyes
Cannot discern you in the thick of fight;
But some of you, who cannot bear to leave
Patroclus to the dogs of Troy, draw near!"
  He spake; Oïlean Ajax, swift of foot, 310
Heard and came forward, hastening through the fight;
And after him Idomeneus, who brought
Meriones, his armor-bearer, fierce
As the man-slayer Mars. But who could tell
The names of all the other Greeks that sprang 315
To mingle in the strife? The Trojans made
The first assault, and Hector led them on.
  As at the mouth of some great river, swoln
By rains from Jove, the mighty ocean-wave
Meets it with roaring, and the cliffs around 320
Rebellow, while the surges toss without,
With such a clamor came the Trojans on,
While round Patroclus closed, with one accord,
The Greeks, protected by their brazen shields,
And o'er their shining helmets Saturn's son 325
Poured darkness. For when Menœtiades
Yet lived, attendant upon Peleus' son,
Jove looked on him with no unkind regard,
And now he would not that his corse should feed
The enemy's dogs, and therefore moved his friends 330
To rescue him. At first the Trojans drave
The dark-eyed Greeks before them; back they fell
And left the dead; yet, fiercely as they came,
The Trojans slew no man, but dragged away
The dead. A moment, and no more, the Greeks 335
Fell back; for Ajax quickly rallied them,—
Ajax, who, next to Peleus' valiant son,
Excelled them all in form and feats of war;

He through the foremost warriors brake, as strong
As a wild boar that on the mountain's side   340
Breaks through the shrubs, and scatters with a bound
A band of youths and dogs. The illustrious son
Of honored Telamon thus put to rout
The Trojan phalanxes environing
Patroclus, in the hope to bear him thence   345
Townward with glory. There Hippothoüs, son
Of Lethus the Pelasgian, having bound
A thong about the sinewy ankle, toiled
To drag away the slain man by the foot
From that fierce strife,—a grateful spectacle   350
To Hector and the Trojans. Yet on him
A vengeance which no friendly arm could ward
Fell suddenly. The son of Telamon
Rushed through the crowd, and in close combat smote
His helmet's brazen cheek. That plumèd helm   355
Was cleft by the huge spear and vigorous hand,
And where the weapon struck Hippothoüs,
Mingled with blood the brain gushed forth; the life
Forsook his limbs; he dropped from nerveless hands
The foot of brave Patroclus, and beside   360
The corpse fell headlong,—far from the rich fields
Of his Larissa, never to repay
With gentle cares in their old age the love
Of his dear parents; for his life was short,
Slain by the spear of Ajax, large of soul.   365
   Then Hector aimed again his shining spear
At Ajax, who perceived it as it came,
And just avoided it. The weapon struck
Schedius, the valiant son of Iphitus,
And bravest of the Phocians, whose abode   370
Was Panopeus the famous, where he ruled
O'er many men. Beneath the collar-bone
It pierced him, and passed through; the brazen point
Came out upon the shoulder; to the ground
He fell, his armor clashing with his fall.   375
Then Ajax smote the valiant Phorcys, son
Of Phœnops, in the navel. Through the mail

The brazen weapon broke, and roughly tore
The entrails. In the dust he fell, and clenched
The earth with dying hands. The foremost ranks,   380
Led by illustrious Hector, at the sight
Yielded the ground; the Greeks with fearful shouts
Dragged off the bodies of Hippothoüs
And Phorcys, and despoiled them of their arms.
    Then would the Trojans have been put to flight   385
Before the warlike Greeks, and, craven-like,
Gone up to Troy, and great had been the fame
Gained by the might and courage of the Greeks,
Beyond what Jupiter designed to give,
Had not Apollo brought Æneas forth   390
By putting on the form of Periphas,
The herald and the son of Epytus,
Who in that office as a prudent friend
And counsellor had served, till he grew old,
The father of Æneas. In his shape   395
Thus spake Apollo, son of Jupiter:—
    "Æneas, ye might even hold the towers
Of lofty Ilium safe against a god,
Were ye to act as some whom I have seen,—
Valiant, and confident in their own might   400
And multitude of dauntless followers.
And now Jove favors us and offers us
The victory o'er the Greeks, and yet ye flee
In abject terror, and refuse to fight."
    He spake; Æneas, looking at him, knew   405
The archer-god, and with a mighty voice
Called out to Hector: "Hector! thou and all
Who lead the troops of Troy, and our allies,
Great shame it were if we were put to rout
Before the warlike Greeks, and beaten back   410
To Troy like cowards. Standing by my side,
One of the gods already hath declared
That Jupiter, All-wise, is our ally
In battle. Let us therefore boldly fall
Upon the Greeks, nor suffer them to bear   415
Patroclus unmolested to their fleet."

He spake, and, springing to the foremost ranks,
Stood firm; the Trojans also turned and faced
The Achaians. Then Æneas with his spear
Struck down Leocritus, the gallant friend   420
Of Lycomedes and Arisbas' son.
The warlike Lycomedes saw his fall
With grief, and came and cast his shining spear
At Apisaon, son of Hippasus,
A shepherd of the people. Underneath   425
The midriff, through the liver went the spear,
And he fell lifeless. He had come to Troy
From rich Pæonia, and was great in war,
Next to Asteropæus. As he saw
His comrade fall, Asteropæus, moved   430
By grief, advanced to combat with the Greeks,
But could not; for the group that stood around
Patroclus showed a fence of shields, and held
Their spears before them. Ajax moved among
The warriors, charging them that none should leave 435
The corpse, and none should step beyond the rest
To strike the foe, but stay to guard the dead,
And combat hand to hand. Such was the charge
Of mighty Ajax. All the earth around
Was steeped with blood, and many a corpse was heaped 440
On corpse of Trojans and their brave allies,
And of the Greeks, for even on their side
The strife was not unbloody, though of Greeks
There perished fewer; each was on the watch
To ward the battle's dangers from the rest.   445
    Then did they fight like fire. You could not say
The sun was safe, nor yet the moon, so thick
A darkness gathered over the brave men
Around the corpse of Menœtiades.
The other Trojans and the well-armed Greeks   450
Fought freely under the clear sky; the sun
Shed o'er them his full brightness; not a cloud
Shadowed the earth, or rested on the hills.
From time to time they paused, and warily
They shunned each other's cruel darts, and kept 455

Far from each other, while in the mid-war
Struggled the combatants in darkness, galled
By the remorseless weapons of their foes.
Yet Thrasymedes and Antilochus,
Two famous Grecian warriors, had not learned 460
That excellent Patroclus was no more,
But thought that, still alive, he led the war
Against the Trojans, fighting in the van.
They watched the flight and slaughter of the Greeks,
And fought apart, for Nestor so enjoined, 465
Who sent them to the battle from the fleet.
   But they who held the middle space around
The friend of swift Æacides, maintained
A desperate strife all day; the knees, the thighs,
The feet, the hands, the eyes of those who fought 470
Were faint with weariness and foul with sweat.
As when an ample ox-hide, steeped in fat,
Is given to workmen to be stretched, they stand
Around it in a circle, pulling it,
Till forth the moisture issues, and the oil 475
Enters the skin, and by that constant strain
From many hands the hide is duly stretched,
So in small space the warriors drew the dead
Hither and thither; they of Ilium strove
To drag it to the city, they of Greece 480
To bear it to the fleet. The tumult then
Was terrible, and neither Mars himself,
The musterer of hosts, nor Pallas, roused
To her intensest wrath, had they been near
The struggle, would have seen it with disdain. 485
Such deadly strife of steeds and men was held
O'er slain Patroclus by the will of Jove.
   The great Achilles knew not yet the fate
Of his Patroclus, for the warriors fought
Far from the fleet, beside the wall of Troy. 490
He never thought of him as one whose death
Was near, but trusted that, when once he reached
The Trojan wall, he would return alive;
Nor ever deemed he that without his aid,

Or even with it, would Patroclus sack 495
The city. This was what he oft had heard
From Thetis, who disclosed to him apart
The counsel of Almighty Jupiter.
Yet had his mother never once revealed
The present evil,—that the one whom most 500
He loved of all his friends should perish thus.
   Still round the dead they fought with their keen spears,
And slew each other. Then of the mailed Greeks
Some one would say: "O friends, it were disgrace
Should we fall back upon our roomy ships. 505
First let the dark earth swallow us; for this
Were better than to let the Trojan knights
Drag off the dead in triumph to their town."
   And some among the large-souled sons of Troy
Would say: "O friends, though all of us should fall 510
Beside this corpse, let no one turn and flee."
Thus they, encouraging each other, spake,
And thus the fight went on. The iron din
Rose through the waste air to the brazen heaven.
   Meantime aloof from battle stood the steeds 515
Of Peleus' son, and sorrowed when they knew
That he who guided them lay stretched in dust
By Hector's slaughtering hand. Automedon,
The brave son of Diores, often tried
The lash, and gentle words as oft, and oft 520
Shouted forth threats; yet neither would they move
Toward the broad Hellespont, where lay the fleet,
Nor toward the Greeks in combat, but remained
Motionless as a funeral column, reared
To mark a man's or woman's tomb. So stood 525
The coursers yoked to that magnificent car,
With drooping heads, and tears that from their lids
Flowed hot, for sorrow at the loss of him
Who was their charioteer, and their fair manes,
Sweeping the yoke below, were foul with dust. 530
The son of Saturn saw their grief, and shook
His head in pity, saying to himself:—
   "Why did the gods bestow you, luckless pair,

On Peleus,—on a king of mortal birth,—
You who shall never feel old age or death? 535
Was it that ye might share with human-kind
Their sorrows? for the race of mortal men
Of all that breathe and move upon the earth
Is the most wretched. Yet of this be sure,—
That ye shall never in that sumptuous car 540
Bear Hector. Is it not enough that he
Should wear that armor, uttering idle boasts?
And now will I infuse into your limbs
Spirit and strength, that ye may safely bear
Automedon across the battle-field 545
To where the roomy galleys lie. I yet
Must give more glory to the men of Troy,
And they must slay until they come again
To the good ships of Greece,—until the sun
Goes down and sacred darkness covers all." 550
  So spake the god, and breathed into the steeds
New life and vigor. From their manes they shook
The dust, and flew with that swift car among
The Greeks and Trojans. With the Trojan throng,
Automedon, though mourning his slain friend, 555
Maintained the fight; he rushed upon their ranks,
A vulture pouncing on a flock of geese.
Swiftly he passed from out the Trojan throng;
Swiftly again he charged their phalanxes
In fierce pursuit. Yet slew he none of those 560
Whom he pursued; he could not guide at once
The steeds and cast the spear, when seated thus
Alone within that sacred car. At last
A friend, the valorous Alcimedon,
Laerces' son, of Æmon's line, beheld 565
His plight, and, standing near his chariot, said:—
  "What god, Automedon, hath prompted thee
To these mad acts, and stolen thy better sense,
Fighting alone among the foremost ranks
Of Trojan warriors, thy companion slain, 570
And Hector in the field, who boastfully
Stalks in the armor of Æacides?"

And thus Automedon, Diores' son,
Made answer: "Who is there among the Greeks
Able like thee, Alcimedon, to rein 575
And curb the spirit of immortal steeds?
None were there save Patroclus while he lived,
Wise as a god in council. Death and fate
Now hold him. To thy hand I give the lash
And shining reins, while I descend and fight." 580
   He spake, and into his swift chariot sprang
Alcimedon, and took the lash and reins.
Automedon leaped down. As Hector saw,
He thus bespake Æneas at his side:—
   "Æneas, leader of the men of Troy, 585
Equipped in brazen armor, I have seen
Those coursers of the swift Æacides
Driven through the battle by unwarlike hands,
And 'tis my hope, if thou wilt give thine aid,
To seize them. They who guide them will not dare 590
To stand and face us when we make the charge."
   He spake; Anchises' valiant son complied,
And, sheltered by their shields of tough ox-hide,
Well dried and firm, and strong with plates of brass,
The twain went forward. With them at their side 595
Went Chromius and Aretus, nobly formed,
In hope to lead away the high-necked steeds,
Their guardians slain. Vain dreamers! they were doomed
Not without bloody penance to return
From that encounter with Automedon, 600
Who prayed to Father Jove, and whose faint heart
Was strengthened and made bold. And thus the chief
Said to his faithful friend Alcimedon:—
   "Keep not the steeds thou guidest far from me,
Alcimedon, but let them ever breathe 605
Upon my shoulders. Hector, Priam's son,
I think, will not give over this assault
Before he either slays us, and ascends
The car to which these steeds with flowing manes
Are yoked, and puts to flight the phalanxes 610
Of Argive warriors, or himself is slain."

He spake, and called to both the Ajaxes
And Menelaus: "Ye who lead the Greeks,"
He said, and named the chieftains, "give in charge
The dead to your best warriors, to surround   615
And guard the corpse, and drive away the foe;
But hasten to avert the evil day
From us who are alive. For even now
Hector comes rushing through the deadly fight,
And brings Æneas; these are the most brave   620
Of all the Trojan army. On the knees
Of the great gods the issue rests. I too
Will cast the spear, and leave the rest to Jove."
   He spake, and lifting his huge spear he smote
The round shield of Aretus. There the blade   625
Stopped not, but, entering, pierced him through the belt.
As, when a vigorous youth with a keen axe
Strikes a wild bull behind the horns, and there
Severs the sinews, forward leaps the beast
And falls,—Aretus, springing forward thus,   630
Fell headlong. In the Trojan's entrails still
Quivered the spear, and life forsook his limbs.
   Then Hector aimed, to smite Automedon,
His shining spear. The Greek beheld and stooped,
And shunned the brazen weapon. Down it came,   635
And plunged into the earth, and stood, its stem
Still shaken with the blow, and spent its force.
Now would the twain have turned, and hand to hand
Fought with their swords, when suddenly came up
The warriors Ajax, hastening, at the call   640
Of their companion, through the crowd, and stayed
The combat. Hector and Æneas then,
And Chromius, of the godlike form, withdrew
Through caution, leaving on the battle-field
Aretus lying mangled. The fierce chief   645
Automedon despoiled the dead, and spake
Boastfully: "Somewhat lighter on my heart
Lies now my grief for Menœtiades,
Though I have slain a man of meaner note."
   As thus he spake, he threw the bloody spoils   650

Into his chariot, mounting to the seat,
His feet and hands all crimson with the blood,
As when a lion has devoured an ox.
Then round Patroclus raged the strife again,
Murderous and sad to see; for Pallas there 655
Inflamed the strife, sent down from heaven by Jove,
To rouse the courage of the Greeks, since such
Was now his will. As when the god displays
To men a purple rainbow in the skies,
A sign of war or of a bitter storm, 660
Which drives the laborer from his task, and makes
The cattle droop, so, in a purple cloud
Concealed, she went among the Greeks, and filled
Their hearts with valor. Taking first the form
Of Phœnix, and his clear, unwearied voice, 665
She spake in stirring words to Atreus' son,
The gallant Menelaus, standing near:
"Shame and dishonor will it be to thee,
O Menelaus, if, beneath the walls
Of Troy, the hungry dogs should tear the corpse 670
Of him who was in life the faithful friend
Of great Achilles. Fight thou therefore on
Bravely, and bid the other Greeks be brave."

   And Menelaus, great in war, rejoined:
"O Phœnix, aged father, who wert born 675
In days long past, would but Minerva give
The needed strength, and ward from me the stroke
Of weapons, then would I stand by and guard
Patroclus, for his death hath filled my heart
With grief. But Hector's rage is like the rage 680
Of fire; he ceases not to slay; for Jove
Gives to his spear the glory of the day."

   He spake, and well was blue-eyed Pallas pleased
That first to her of all the deities
He prayed; and therefore did she nerve his chest 685
And knees with strength, and put into his heart
The daring of the fly, that, often driven
From man, returns and bites, and finds how sweet
Is human blood. Such resolute zeal she woke

In his stern soul, as quickly he approached 690
Patroclus, and sent forth his shining spear.
Among the Trojans was Eëtion's son,
Podes, the rich and brave, whom Hector held
In highest honor, choosing him to be
Companion of his feasts. Him in the waist 695
The fair-haired Menelaus, as he fled,
Smote, driving home the weapon. With a clash
He fell to earth, and Menelaus drew
The slain away among the Grecian ranks.
Then came Apollo, putting on the form 700
Of Phænops, son of Asius, whose abode
Was in Abydos, and whom Hector most
Esteemed of all his guests. The archer-god
Drew near to Hector, and bespake him thus:—
  "Hector, what other Greek will fear thee now, 705
Since thou dost shrink from Menelaus, deemed
Effeminate in war? Behold, he drags
Away a warrior from thy host; his hand
Hath slain thy faithful friend, Eëtion's son,
Brave Podes, fighting in the foremost ranks." 710
  He spake: a cloud of sorrow overspread
The soul of Hector. Armed in glittering brass,
He went among the warriors in the van.
Then did the son of Saturn lift on high
His fringèd ægis, gleaming; with a cloud 715
He covered Ida, sent his lightnings down,
And thundered terribly, and made the mount
Shake to its base, and gave the victory
To Troy, and put to rout the Grecian host.
  Peneleus of Bœotia led the fight. 720
A spear that lighted on the shoulder-tip,
As he came forward, wounded him. The blade,
Hurled by Polydamas in close assault,
Entered and grazed the bone. Then Hector pierced
The wrist of Leïtus, Alectryon's son, 725
And made him leave the combat. As he fled
He looked around in fear, nor hoped again
To wield the spear against the men of Troy.

As Hector followed Leïtus, he met
The long spear of Idomeneus, which struck 730
His corselet near the pap; the weapon broke
Sheer at the socket, and the Trojans raised
A shout, while Hector at Idomeneus
Let fly his spear. It missed the chief, but smote
Cœranus, who from pleasant Lyctus came, 735
The friend and follower of Meriones.
For on that day Idomeneus had come
From his good ships on foot, and great had been
The triumph of the Trojans at his fall,
If Cœranus had not with his swift steeds 740
Passed near and bid him mount. 'Twas thus he came
To save Idomeneus from death, and yield
To the man-queller Hector his own life;
The javelin entered underneath the ear,
By the jaw-bone, where, forcing out the teeth, 745
It cleft the tongue in twain. He fell to earth,
And dropped the reins. Meriones stooped down
And took them from the dust in his own hands,
And thus bespake Idomeneus: "Ply well
The lash, until thy coursers reach the fleet, 750
For thou mayst clearly see that victory
To-day is not upon the Grecian side."

   He spake: Idomeneus, fear-smitten, lashed
The long-maned steeds that hurried toward the fleet.
Nor now did Menelaus nor his friend, 755
The valiant Ajax, fail to see that Jove
Had changed the vantage to the side of Troy.
And thus the son of Telamon began:—

   "Alas! the feeblest mind can now perceive
That Father Jove is with the sons of Troy, 760
And gives to them the glory of the day.
Their weapons smite, whoever sends them forth,
Coward or brave, for Jove directs them all;
Ours fell to earth in vain. But let us now
Consult how best to bear the corpse away, 765
And how, returning, we may meet our friends
With joy; for they are grieved as they behold

Our plight, and fear that we may not withstand
The fiery onset and invincible arm
Of the man-queller Hector. Would there were   770
Some comrade who would bear to Peleus' son
The tidings of the day! for he, I think,
Has not yet heard that his dear friend is slain.
None such can I behold of all the Greeks,
For they are shrouded all—their steeds and they—   775
In darkness. Father Jove, deliver us
From darkness; clear the heavens and give our eyes
Again to see. Destroy us if thou wilt,
But O destroy us in the light of day!"
   He spake: the All-Father saw him shedding tears, 780
And pitied him, and bade the shadows flee,
And swept away the cloud. The sun looked forth,
And all the battle lay in light. Then thus
To warlike Menelaus Ajax said:—
   "O Menelaus, foster-child of Jove,   785
Look round and see if yet Antilochus,
The large-souled son of Nestor, is alive,
And bid him bear the tidings in all haste
To the great son of Peleus, that the one
Of all his friends whom most he loved is slain."   790
   He spake, and Menelaus, great in war,
Complied, and hastened forth, as from a fold
A lion stalks away, that long has kept
In fear the hounds and herdsmen, who all night
Have watched to drive him from their well-fed beeves, 795
While, eager for his prey, he rushes oft
Against them, but in vain, for many a spear
Is hurled at him, and many a blazing brand,
Which, fierce for ravin as he is, he dreads,
Till sullenly at early morn he goes.   800
So from Patroclus went unwillingly
The valiant Menelaus, for he feared
Lest, panic-struck, the Greeks should leave his corpse
The enemy's prey. Thus earnestly he prayed
The warriors Ajax and Meriones:—   805
   "Ye warriors Ajax, leaders of the Greeks!

And thou, Meriones! let each of you
Bear well in mind how kindly was the mood
Of poor Patroclus; gentle in his life
Was he to all, and now is with the dead." 810
    The fair-haired Menelaus, speaking thus,
Withdrew. He looked around him as he went,
As looks an eagle, bird of sharpest sight—
So men declare—of all the fowls of air,
From which, though high in heaven, the nimble hare 815
Beneath the thicket is not hid; he stoops,
And takes the creature's life. Thy piercing eyes,
O Menelaus, thus on every side
Were turned, in eager scrutiny, to find
Among the multitude of Greeks the son 820
Of Nestor living. Him he soon descried
Upon the battle's left, where manfully
He cheered his fellows on. The fair-haired son
Of Atreus came and stood by him, and said:—
    "Stay, foster-child of Jove, Antilochus! 825
And listen to the sorrowful news I bring
Of what should ne'er have been. Thou must have well
Perceived, I think, that some divinity
Doth heap disaster on our host, and give
The victory to the Trojans. He is dead,— 830
Patroclus,—the most valiant of the Greeks,
And great their sorrow is. Now hasten thou
To the Greek galleys; let Achilles know
The tidings; he may haply bring the corpse,
Stripped as it is, unmangled to the fleet, 835
For crested Hector has the arms he wore."
    He spake, and at his words Antilochus
Was horror-struck; in grief too great for speech,
Tears filled his eyes, and his clear voice was choked.
Yet heeded he the mandate. Laying off 840
His arms, he gave them to his blameless friend,
Laodocus, who with his firm-paced steeds
Came toward him. Thus prepared he ran; his feet
Carried him swiftly from the battle-field
To bear the evil news to Peleus' son. 845

    Yet Menelaus, foster-child of Jove,
Thy spirit did not prompt thee to remain
And aid thy hard-pressed comrades at the spot
Whence thou didst send Antilochus, and where
The Pyleans longed to keep him. Yet he sent 850
The noble Thrasymedes to their aid,
While he returned to where Patroclus lay,
And stood beside the warriors there, and said:—
    "I sent to swift Achilles at the fleet
A messenger, yet think he will not come. 855
Though royal Hector's deed hath roused his rage,
Unarmed he cannot meet the sons of Troy.
Consult we then how we may best convey
The body to the ships, and how ourselves
Escape the doom of death by Trojan hands." 860
    The mighty Ajax, son of Telamon,
Replied: "O Menelaus far-renowned,
Well hast thou spoken. Lift thou now the corse,
Thou and Meriones, and place yourselves
Beneath it, and convey it from the field. 865
We, following you, will combat with the sons
Of Troy and noble Hector,—we who, named
Alike and one in spirit, oft have borne
The fury of the battle side by side."
    He ended, and the warriors in their arms 870
Raised with main strength the body from the ground.
The Trojans, as they saw it borne away,
Shouted behind them, rushing on like hounds
That spring upon a wounded forest-boar
Before the hunter-youths now pressing close 875
Upon his flank, to tear him, then again,
Whene'er he turns upon them in his strength,
Retreating in dismay, and put to flight
Hither and thither. Thus, in hot pursuit
And close array, the Trojans following strook 880
With swords and two-edged spears; but when the twain
Turned and stood firm to meet them, every cheek
Grew pale, and not a single Trojan dared
Draw near the Greeks to combat for the corse.

   Thus rapidly they bore away the dead 885
Toward their good galleys from the battle-field.
Onward with them the furious battle swept,
As spreads a fire that, kindled suddenly,
Seizes a city, and the dwellings sink
In the consuming blaze, and a strong wind 890
Roars through the flame. Such fearful din of steeds
And warriors followed the retreating Greeks.
As from a mountain summit strong-backed mules
Drag over the rough ways a ponderous beam
Or mast, till weary with the mighty strain 895
And streaming sweat, so they with resolute toil
Bore off the dead. Behind them as they went
Their two defenders kept the foe aloof.
As when a river-dike o'ergrown with trees
Crosses a plain, and holds the violent course 900
Of the swoln stream in check, and, driving back
The waters, spreads them o'er the level fields,
Nor can their fury force a passage through,—
So did the warriors Ajax hold in check
The Trojans; yet they followed close, and two 905
More closely than the rest,—Æneas, son
Of old Anchises, and the illustrious chief,
Hector. As when a company of daws
Or starlings, startled at a hawk's approach,
The murderous enemy of the smaller birds, 910
Take wing with piercing cries, so, driven before
The might of Hector and Æneas, fled
The Greeks with clamorous cries, and thought no more
Of combat. In the trench and near it lay
Many fair weapons, which the fugitive Greeks 915
Had dropped in haste, and still the war went on.

BOOK XVIII

AS thus they fought with all the rage of fire,
Antilochus, the nimble-footed, came
With tidings to Achilles. Him he found
Before his lofty galleys, deep in thought
Of what he knew had happened. With a sigh
The hero to his mighty spirit said:—
  "Ah me! why should the Grecians thus be driven
In utter disarray across the plain?
I tremble lest the gods should bring to pass
What most I dread. My mother told me once
That the most valiant of the Myrmidons,
While yet I live, cut off by Trojan hands,
Shall see the sun no more. It must be so:
The brave son of Menœtius has been slain.
Unhappy! 'Twas my bidding that, when once
The enemy with his firebrands was repulsed,
He should not think to combat gallantly
With Hector, but should hasten to the fleet."
  As thus he mused, illustrious Nestor's son
Drew near Achilles, and with eyes that shed
Warm tears he gave his sorrowful message thus:—
  "Son of the warlike Peleus, woe is me!
For bitter are the tidings thou must hear
Of what should not have been, Patroclus lies
A naked corpse, and over it the hosts
Are fighting; crested Hector hath his arms."

 He spake, and a black cloud of sorrow came
Over the chieftain. Grasping in both hands
The ashes of the hearth, he showered them o'er
His head, and soiled with them his noble face.   30
They clung in dark lumps to his comely vest.
Prone in the dust of earth, at his full length,
And tearing his disordered hair, he lay.
Then wailed aloud the maidens whom in war
He and Patroclus captured. Forth they came,   35
And, thronging round him, smote their breasts and swooned.
Antilochus mourned also, and shed tears,
Holding Achilles by the hand, for much
His generous nature dreaded that the chief
Might aim at his own throat the sword he wore.   40
 Loud were the hero's cries, and in the deep
His gracious mother, where she sat beside
Her aged father, heard them. She too raised
A wail of sorrow. All the goddesses,
Daughters of Nereus, dwelling in the depths   45
Of ocean, gathered to her side. There came
Glaucè, Thaleia, and Cymodocè,
Nesæa, Speio, Halia with large eyes,
And Thoa, and Cymothöè; nor stayed
Actæa, Limnoreia, Melita,   50
Amphithöè, Iæra, Agavè,
Doto, and Proto, and Dynamenè.
There came Dexamenè, Amphinomè,
Pherusa, Callianira, Panopè,
Doris, and Galateia, the renowned.   55
With these Nemertes and Apseudes came,
And Callianassa. Clymenè was there,
Janeira and Janassa, and with them
Mæra, and Amatheia with bright hair,
And Orithya, and whoever else,   60
Children of Nereus, bide within the deep.
The concourse filled the glimmering cave; they beat
Their bosoms, while the sorrowing Thetis spake:—
 "Hear, sister Nereids, that ye all may know
The sharpness of my sorrows. Woe is me,   65

Unhappy! Woe is me! in evil hour,
The mother of a hero,—me who gave
Birth to so noble and so brave a son,
The first among the warriors, saw him grow
Like a green sapling, reared him like a plant   70
Within a fruitful field, and sent him forth
With his beaked ships to Ilium and the war
Against the Trojans. Never shall I see
That son returning to his home, the halls
Of Peleus. While he lives and sees the light   75
Of day his lot is sorrow, nor can I
Help him in aught, though at his side; and yet
I go to look on my beloved son,
And learn from him what grief, while he remains
Aloof from war, o'ertakes him in his tent."   80
   She spake, and left the cavern. All the nymphs
Went with her weeping. Round their way the waves
Of ocean parted. When they reached the fields
Of fertile Troas, up the shore they went
In ordered files to where, a numerous fleet,   85
Drawn from the water, round Achilles lay
The swift ships of the Myrmidons. To him
His goddess mother came, and with a cry
Of grief embraced the head of her dear son,
And, mourning o'er him, spake these wingèd words:—   90
   "Why weepest thou, my son? What sorrow now
O'ercomes thy spirit? Speak, and hide it not.
All thou didst pray for once, with lifted hands,
Has been fulfilled by Jove; the sons of Greece,
Driven to their galleys, and with thy good help   95
Withdrawn from them, are routed and disgraced."
   The swift Achilles, sighing deeply, made
This answer: "O my mother! true it is
Olympian Jove hath done all this for me;
But how can that delight me, since my friend,   100
My well-beloved Patroclus, is no more?
He whom, of all my fellows in the war,
I prized the most, and loved as my own self,
Is lost to me, and Hector, by whose hand

He was cut off, has spoiled him of his arms,— 105
His dreaded arms, a wonder to the sight
And glorious, which the gods of heaven bestowed
On Peleus, sumptuous bridal gifts, when thou
Wert led by them to share a mortal's bed.
Yet would that thou hadst evermore remained 110
Among the immortal dwellers of the deep,
And Peleus had espoused a mortal maid,
Since now thy heart must ache with infinite grief
For thy slain son, whom thou shalt never more
Welcome returning to his home. No wish 115
Have I to live or to concern myself
In men's affairs, save this: that Hector first,
Pierced by my spear, shall yield his life, and pay
The debt of vengeance for Patroclus slain."
    And Thetis, weeping, answered: "O my son! 120
Soon must thou die; thou sayest true; that fate
Hangs over thee as soon as Hector dies."
    Again the swift Achilles, sighing, spake:
"Then quickly let me die, since fate denied
That I should aid my friend against the foes 125
That slew him. Far from his own land he fell,
And longed for me to rescue him. And now,
Since I am never more to see the land
I love, and since I went not to defend
Patroclus, nor the other Greeks, my friends, 130
Of whom so many have fallen by the hand
Of noble Hector, but beside the fleet
Am sitting here, a useless weight on earth,
Mighty in battle as I am beyond
The other Grecian warriors, though excelled 135
By other men in council,—would that Strife
Might perish among gods and men, with Wrath,
Which makes even wise men cruel, and, though sweet
At first as dropping honey, growing, fills
The heart with its foul smoke. Such was my rage, 140
Aroused by Agamemnon, king of men.
Yet now, though great my wrong, let things like these
Rest with the past, and, as the time requires,

Let us subdue the spirit in our breasts.
I go in quest of Hector, by whose hand   145
My friend was slain. My death will I accept
Whene'er to Jove and to the other gods
It shall seem good to send it. Hercules,
Though mighty and beloved of Jupiter,
The son of Saturn, could not shun his death,   150
For fate and Juno's cruel wrath prevailed
Against him. I shall lie in death like him,
If a like fate be measured out for me.
Yet now shall I have glory; I shall do
What many a Trojan and Dardanian dame,   155
Deep-bosomed, wiping with both hands the tears
From their fair cheeks, shall bitterly lament;
And well shall they perceive that, till this hour,
I paused from war. Thou lov'st me; but seek not
To keep me from the field, for that were vain."   160
  The silver-footed Thetis thus rejoined:
"Truly, my son, thy purpose is not ill,
To rescue thy endangered friends from death.
But with the Trojans are thy beautiful arms,
Brazen and dazzling bright; their crested chief,   165
Hector, exults to wear them: no long space,
I think, will he exult; his death is near.
Yet go not to the battle-field until
Thine eyes shall look upon me yet again.
I come to-morrow with the sun, and bring   170
Bright arms, the work of Vulcan's royal hand."
  So having said, and turning from her son,
She thus bespake her sisters of the sea:
"Return to the broad bosom of the deep,
To its gray Ancient and my father's halls,   175
And tell him all. I hasten to ascend
The summits of Olympus, there to ask
Of Vulcan, the renowned artificer,
Armor of glorious beauty for my son."
  She spake: at once they plunged into the deep,   180
While Thetis, silver-footed goddess, sought
Olympus, whence it was her hope to bring

New armor for her son. As thus her feet
Bore her toward heaven, the Achaians, fleeing fast,
With infinite clamor, driven before the arm 185
Of the man-queller Hector, reached the ships
And Hellespont. Nor could the well-armed Greeks
Bear off Patroclus from the shower of darts;
For rushing on them came both foot and horse,
And Hector, son of Priam, like a flame 190
In fury. Thrice illustrious Hector seized
The body by the heels to drag it off,
And called his Trojans with a mighty shout.
Thrice did the chieftains Ajax, terrible
In resolute valor, drive him from the dead. 195
Yet kept he to his purpose, confident
In his own might, now charging through the crowd,
Now standing firm and shouting to his men,
And never losing ground. As when, at night,
Herdsmen that watch their cattle strive in vain 200
To drive a lion, fierce and famine-pinched,
From some slain beast, so the two Ajaxes,
With all their valor, vainly strove to keep
Hector, the son of Priam, from the corpse.
And now would he have dragged it thence, and won 205
Infinite glory, had not Iris come—
The goddess whose swift feet are like the wind—
To Peleus' son, a messenger from heaven,
In haste, unknown to Jupiter and all
The other gods,—for Juno sent her down,— 210
To bid the hero arm. She came and stood
Beside him, speaking thus with wingèd words:—
   "Pelides, rise, most terrible of men,
In rescue of Patroclus, over whom
They struggle fiercely at the fleet; for there 215
They slay each other,—these who fight to keep
The dead, and those, the men of Troy, who charge
To drag him off to Ilium's airy heights;
And chief, illustrious Hector longs to seize
The corpse, and from the delicate neck to hew 220
The head, and fix it on a stake. Arise,

Loiter no longer;—rise, ashamed to leave
Patroclus to be torn by Trojan dogs.
For thine will be the infamy, if yet
The corpse be brought dishonored to thy tent." 225
    The swift Achilles listened and inquired;
"Which of the gods, O Iris, speaks by thee?"
And Iris, whose swift feet are like the wind,
Answered: "The glorious spouse of Jupiter,
Juno, hath sent me. Even Saturn's son, 230
On his high throne, knows not that I am sent,
Nor any other of the gods who dwell
Upon Olympus overspread with snow."
    "But how," the swift Achilles asked again,
"Shall I go forth to war? They have my arms, 235
And my beloved mother strictly bade
That I should put no armor on until
I saw her face again. She promised me
A suit of glorious mail from Vulcan's hand.
Nor know I any warrior here whose arms 240
Might serve me, save, perhaps, it were the shield
Of Telamonian Ajax, who, I hope,
Is in the van, and dealing death among
The foe, in vengeance for Patroclus slain."
    Then the swift-footed Iris spake again: 245
"They have thy glorious armor; that we know.
But go thou to the trench, and show thyself
To them of Troy, that, haply smit with fear,
They may desist from battle, and the host
Of Grecian warriors, overtoiled, may breathe 250
In a brief respite from the stress of war."
    So the fleet Iris spake, and passed away,
And then arose Achilles, dear to Jove,
While o'er his ample shoulders Pallas held
Her fringèd ægis. The great goddess caused 255
A golden cloud to gather round his head
And kindled in the cloud a dazzling flame.
And as when smoke, ascending to the sky,
Hangs o'er some city in a distant isle,
Which enemies beleaguer, swarming forth 260

From their own city, and in hateful strife
Contend all day, but when the sun goes down
Forthwith blaze many bale-fires, sending up
A brightness which the neighboring realms may see,
That haply they may send their ships and drive 265
The war away,—so from the hero's head
That flame streamed upward to the sky. He came
Without the wall and stood beside the trench,
Nor mingled with the Greeks, for he revered
His mother's words. He stood and called aloud, 270
And Pallas, from the host, returned his shout,—
A shout that carried infinite dismay
Into the Trojan squadrons. As the sound
Of trumpet rises clear when deadly foes
Lay siege to a walled city, such was heard 275
The clear shout uttered by Æacides.
The hearts of all who heard that brazen voice
Were troubled, and their steeds with flowing manes
Turned backward with the chariots,—such the dread
Of coming slaughter. When the charioteers 280
Beheld the terrible flame that played unquenched
Upon the brow of the magnanimous son
Of Peleus, lighted by the blue-eyed maid
Minerva, they were struck with panic fear.
Thrice o'er the trench Achilles shouted; thrice 285
The men of Troy and their renowned allies
Fell into wild disorder. Then there died,
Entangled midst their chariots, and transfixed
By their own spears, twelve of their bravest chiefs.
The Greeks bore off Patroclus from the field 290
With eager haste, and placed him on a bier,
And there the friends that loved him gathered round
Lamenting. With them swift Achilles came,
The hot tears on his cheeks, as he beheld
His faithful comrade lying on his bier, 295
Mangled with many wounds, whom he had sent
With steeds and car to battle, never more
To welcome him alive on his return.
   Now Juno, large-eyed and august, bade set

The never-wearied sun; unwillingly 300
He sank into the ocean streams. Then paused
The noble Greeks from that ferocious strife,
Deadly in equal measure to both hosts.
The Trojans also paused, and from their cars
Unharnessed the fleet steeds, and ere they took 305
Their evening meal assembled to consult.
Standing they held the council; no man cared
To sit, for all were trembling from the hour
When, long a stranger to the bloody field,
Achilles showed himself again. And now 310
The son of Panthoüs, wise Polydamas,
Began to speak. Beyond the rest he saw
Things past and things to come, and he had been
Hector's companion, born in the same night,
Mighty in speech as Hector with the spear. 315
With prudent admonitions thus he spake:—
 "Consider well, my friends. My counsel is
That we return, nor wait the holy morn
Here, by the fleet and in the open plain,
Far from our city ramparts. While this man 320
Was wroth with Agamemnon, we maintained
A strife of far less peril with the Greeks,
And I was ever ready to encamp
By night beside the galleys, which we hoped
To make our prize; but now I fear the might 325
Of swift Pelides. He will not remain
Content upon the space between the fleet
And town, where Greeks and Trojans wage a war
Of changeful fortune, but will strive to take
The city, and to carry off our wives. 330
March we then homeward. Let my words prevail,—
It must be so. The gentle Night now keeps
The nimble-footed hero from the war.
But if to-morrow, issuing forth in arms,
He find us here, there are among us those 335
Who will have cause to know him. Gladly then
Will he find refuge who escapes his arm
In sacred Troy, and many a Trojan corpse

Will feed the dogs and vultures. May mine ear
Hear of it never. But if ye will heed340
My words, though sorrowful, ye shall be safe
Assembled in the city squares at night.
The lofty towers and gates, with massive beams
Polished and strongly fitted each to each,
Will keep the town. To-morrow we shall take,345
At dawn, our station on the towers, arrayed
In armor, and his difficult task will be,
Far from his ships, to fight us from below;
And after he has tired his high-necked steeds
With coursing round the ramparts to and fro,350
Back to his galleys he must go; nor yet
With all his valor can he force his way
Into the town to lay its dwellings waste,—
The dogs will feed upon his carcass first."

    And crested Hector answered with a frown:355
"The counsel thou hast given, Polydamas,
Pleases me not,—that we return to be
Pent up in Troy. Are ye not weary yet
Of lying long imprisoned within walls
And towers? The time has been that in all lands,360
Wherever human speech is heard, the fame
Of Priam's city, for its treasured gold
And brass, was in all mouths. Those treasures now
Have passed away; our dwellings have them not.
Much that we had was sold on Phrygia's coast,365
And in Mæonia's pleasant land, for Jove
The mighty was displeased with us. But now,
When politic Saturn's son hath granted me
To win great glory at the fleet, and hold
The Greeks imprisoned by the sea, refrain,370
Idler, from laying counsels such as these
Before the people. Not a Trojan here
Will follow them, nor would I suffer it.
Now hearken all, and act as I advise:
First banquet, rank by rank, throughout the host,375
And set your guards, and each of you keep watch;
And then, if any Trojan stands in fear

For his possessions, let him bring them all
Into the common stock, to be consumed;
Better that we enjoy them than the Greeks.　　380
To-morrow with the dawn and all in arms,
We will do battle at the roomy ships
Valiantly. If in truth the noble son
Of Peleus choose to rise and to defend
The ships, so much the worse for him, since I　　385
Shall not for him desert the field, but stand
Firmly against him, whether he obtain
The victory or I. The chance of war
Is equal, and the slayer oft is slain."
　　So Hector spake: the Trojans shouted forth　　390
Applause, the madmen! Pallas took away
Their reason; all approved the fatal plan
Of Hector; no one ventured to commend
The sober counsel of Polydamas.
And then they banqueted throughout the host;　　395
But all night long the Achaians mourned with tears
Patroclus, while Pelides in the midst,
Leading the ceaseless lamentation, placed
His slaughter-dealing hands upon the breast
Of his companion with continual sighs.　　400
As a maned lion, from whose haunt within
The thick, dark wood a hunter has borne off
The whelps, returning finds them gone, and grieves,
And roams the valleys, tracking as he goes
The robber, bent to find him, for his rage　　405
Is fierce,—with such fierce sorrow Peleus' son
Spake, deeply sighing, to his Myrmidons:—
　　"O, idle were the words which once I spake,
When in our palace-halls I bade the chief
Menœtius bear a cheerful heart. I said　　410
That I would bring to Opus yet again,
Laden with spoil from Ilium overthrown,
His valiant son. But Jove doth not fulfil
The plans of men. That both of us should stain
Earth with our blood in Troy was the decree　　415
Of fate, and never will the aged knight

Peleus receive me in his palace-halls,
Returning from the war, nor Thetis, she
Who gave me birth; the earth will hold me here.
And now, since after thee I take my place 420
In earth, Patroclus, I will not perform
Thy funeral rites before I bring to thee
The arms and head of the magnanimous chief
Hector, who slew thee. By thy funeral pile
I will strike off in vengeance for thy death 425
The heads of twelve illustrious Trojan youths.
Thou meanwhile, lying at the beakèd ships,
Shalt be lamented night and day, with tears,
By many a Trojan and Dardanian maid,
Deep-bosomed, won by our victorious spears 430
After hard wars and opulent cities sacked."
 Thus having said, the great Achilles bade
Place a huge tripod on the fire in haste,
To cleanse Patroclus from the clotted blood.
They brought and set upon the glowing hearth 435
A tripod for the bath, and in it poured
Water, and piled the wood beneath. The flame
Crept up the vessel's rounded sides and warmed
The water. When within the murmuring brass
It boiled, they washed the dead, and with rich oil 440
Anointed him, and filled the open wounds
With ointment nine years old; and laying him
Upon a couch, they spread from head to foot
Fine linen over him, and covered all
With a white mantle. Through the hours of night 445
The Myrmidons, lamenting their dead chief,
Wept round the swift Achilles. Then did Jove
Thus to his wife and sister Juno speak:—
 "Large-eyed, imperial Juno, thou hast now
Accomplished thy desire, for thou hast roused 450
The swift Achilles. There is not a doubt
The long-haired Argives owe their birth to thee."
 And large-eyed Juno answered: "What strange words,
Austere Saturnius, hast thou said? A man,
A mortal far less skilled in shaping means 455

To compass ends, might do what I have done
Against his fellow-man. Then should not I—
Who boast to be the chief of goddesses
By birthright, and because I bear the name
Of wife to thee who rulest o'er the gods— 460
Plan evil to the Trojans, whom I hate?"
   So talked they. Silver-footed Thetis came
Meanwhile to Vulcan's halls, eternal, gemmed
With stars, a wonder to the immortals, wrought
Of brass by the lame god. She found him there 465
Sweating and toiling, and with busy hand
Plying the bellows. He was fashioning
Tripods, a score, to stand beside the wall
Of his fair palace. All of these he placed
On wheels of gold, that, of their own accord, 470
They might roll in among the assembled gods,
And then roll back, a marvel to behold.
So far they all were finished; but not yet
Were added the neat handles, and for these
The god was forging rivets busily. 475
While thus he labored, with a mind intent
Upon his skilful task, on silver feet
Came Thetis. Charis, of the snowy veil,
The beautiful, whom the great god of fire,
Vulcan, had made his wife, beheld, and came 480
Forward to meet her, seized her hand, and said:—
   "O Thetis of the flowing robe, beloved
And honored, what has brought thee to our home?
Thou dost not often visit us. Come in,
That I may pay the honors due a guest." 485
   So the bright goddess spake, and led the way,
And seated Thetis on a sumptuous throne,
With silver studs divinely wrought, and placed
A footstool, and called out to Vulcan thus:
"Come, Vulcan; Thetis here hath need of thee." 490
   And the great artist, Vulcan, thus replied:
"Then of a truth a goddess is within
Whom I must ever honor and revere;
Who from the danger of my terrible fall

Saved me, what time my shameless mother sought 495
To cast me from her sight, for I was lame.
Then great had been my misery, had not
Eurynomè and Thetis in their laps
Received me as I fell,—Eurynomè,
Daughter of billowy Ocean. There I dwelt 500
Nine years, and many ornaments I wrought
Of brass,—clasps, buckles, bracelets, necklaces,—
Within a vaulted cave, round which the tides
Of the vast ocean murmured and flung up
Their foam; nor any of the gods or men 505
Knew of my hiding-place, save only they
Who saved me, Thetis and Eurynomè.
And now, as she is with us, I must make,
To fair-haired Thetis some thank-offering
For having rescued me. Haste, spread the board 510
Amply with generous fare, while I shall lay
Aside my bellows and my implements."
   He spake, and from his anvil-block arose,
A mighty bulk; his weak legs under him,
Halting, moved painfully. He laid apart 515
His bellows from the fire, and gathered up
The scattered implements with which he wrought,
And locked them in a silver chest, and wiped
With a moist sponge his face and both his hands,
Stout neck and hairy chest. He then put on 520
His tunic, took his massive regal wand
Into his hand, and, tottering, sallied forth.
Two golden statues, like in form and look
To living maidens, aided with firm gait
The monarch's steps. And mind was in their breasts, 525
And they had speech and strength, and from the gods
Had learned becoming arts. Beside their lord
They walked and tended him. As he drew near,
Halting, to Thetis on the shining throne,
He took the goddess by the hand and said:— 530
   "What cause, O Thetis of the flowing robe,
Honored and dear, has brought thee to our home?
Not often com'st thou hither. Freely say

Whatever lies upon thy mind. My heart
Commands me to obey, if it be aught   535
That can be done and may be done by me."
   And Thetis answered, with a gush of tears:
"O Vulcan! of the goddesses who dwell
Upon Olympus, is there one who bears
Such bitter sorrows as Saturnian Jove   540
Inflicts on me, distressed above them all?
Me, of the ocean deities, he forced
To take a mortal husband,—Peleus, son
Of Æacus,—and to his bed I came
Unwillingly. Within his palace halls,   545
Worn with a late old age, my husband lies.
Now I have other woes; for when a son
Was granted me, and I had brought him forth
And reared him, flourishing like a young plant,
A sapling in a fertile field, and great   550
Among the heroes,—thus maturely trained,
I sent him with his beakèd ships to Troy,
To combat with her sons; but never more
Will it be mine to welcome him returned
Home to the halls of Peleus. While to me   555
He lives, and sees the sunshine, he endures
Affliction, nor can I, though at his side,
Aid him in aught. The maiden whom the Greeks
Decreed him as his prize, the king of men,
Atrides, took away, and grief for her   560
Consumes his heart. The Trojans keep the Greeks
Beleaguered by their ships, nor suffer them
To pass beyond their gates. The elder chiefs
Implored him to relent, and offered him
Large presents; he refused to avert the doom   565
That threatened them himself, but sent instead
Patroclus to the war with his own arms,
And with him sent much people. All the day
They fought before the Scæan gates; and then
Had Ilium fallen, but that Apollo slew   570
The brave son of Menœtius, who had caused
Vast slaughter,—slew him fighting in the van

Of war, and gave the glory of his death
To Hector. Therefore I approach thy knees,
And ask for him, my son, so soon to die, 575
Buckler and helm, and beautiful greaves, shut close
With clasps, and all the other arms complete,
Which in the war my son's companion lost.
For now Achilles lies upon the ground
Bitterly grieving in his inmost soul." 580
    And Vulcan, the great artist, answered her:
"Be comforted, and take no further thought
Of this; for would I could as certainly
Shield him from death's dread summons when his hour
Is come at last, as I shall have for him 585
Beautiful armor ready to put on,
And such as every man, of multitudes
Who look on it hereafter, shall admire."
    So speaking he withdrew, and went where lay
The bellows, turned them toward the fire, and bade 590
The work begin. From twenty bellows came
Their breath into the furnaces,—a blast
Varied in strength as need might be; for now
They blew with violence for a hasty task,
And then with gentler breath, as Vulcan pleased 595
And as the work required. Upon the fire
He laid impenetrable brass, and tin,
And precious gold and silver; on its block
Placed the huge anvil, took the ponderous sledge,
And held the pincers in the other hand. 600
    And first he forged the huge and massive shield,
Divinely wrought in every part,—its edge
Clasped with a triple border, white and bright.
A silver belt hung from it, and its folds
Were five; a crowd of figures on its disk 605
Were fashioned by the artist's passing skill,
For here he placed the earth and heaven, and here
The great deep and the never-resting sun
And the full moon, and here he set the stars
That shine in the round heaven,—the Pleiades, 610
The Hyades, Orion in his strength,

And the Bear near him, called by some the Wain,
That, wheeling, keeps Orion still in sight,
Yet bathes not in the waters of the sea.
  There placed he two fair cities full of men. 615
In one were marriages and feasts; they led
The brides with flaming torches from their bowers,
Along the streets, with many a nuptial song.
There the young dancers whirled, and flutes and lyres
Gave forth their sounds, and women at the doors 620
Stood and admired. Meanwhile a multitude
Was in the forum, where a strife went on,—
Two men contending for a fine, the price
Of one who had been slain. Before the crowd
One claimed that he had paid the fine, and one 625
Denied that aught had been received, and both
Called for the sentence which should end the strife.
The people clamored for both sides, for both
Had eager friends; the heralds held the crowd
In check; the elders, upon polished stones, 630
Sat in a sacred circle. Each one took,
In turn, a herald's sceptre in his hand,
And, rising, gave his sentence. In the midst
Two talents lay in gold, to be the meed
Of him whose juster judgment should prevail. 635
  Around the other city sat two hosts
In shining armor, bent to lay it waste,
Unless the dwellers would divide their wealth,—
All that their pleasant homes contained,—and yield
The assailants half. As yet the citizens 640
Had not complied, but secretly had planned
An ambush. Their beloved wives meanwhile,
And their young children, stood and watched the walls,
With aged men among them, while the youths
Marched on, with Mars and Pallas at their head, 645
Both wrought in gold, with golden garments on,
Stately and large in form, and over all
Conspicuous, in bright armor, as became
The gods; the rest were of an humbler size.
And when they reached the spot where they should lie 650

394   ILIAD

In ambush, by a river's side, a place
For watering herds, they sat them down, all armed
In shining brass. Apart from all the rest
They placed two sentries, on the watch to spy
The approach of sheep and hornèd kine. Soon came   655
The herds in sight; two shepherds walked with them,
Who, all unweeting of the evil nigh,
Solaced their task with music from their reeds.
The warriors saw and rushed on them, and took
And drave away large prey of beeves, and flocks   660
Of fair white sheep, whose keepers they had slain.
When the besiegers in their council heard
The sound of tumult at the watering-place,
They sprang upon their nimble-footed steeds,
And overtook the pillagers. Both bands   665
Arrayed their ranks and fought beside the stream,
And smote each other. There did Discord rage,
And Tumult, and the great Destroyer, Fate.
One wounded warrior she had seized alive,
And one unwounded yet, and through the field   670
Dragged by the foot another, dead. Her robe
Was reddened o'er the shoulders with the blood
From human veins. Like living men they ranged
The battle-field, and dragged by turns the slain.
    There too he sculptured a broad fallow field   675
Of soft rich mould, thrice ploughed, and over which
Walked many a ploughman, guiding to and fro
His steers, and when on their return they reached
The border of the field the master came
To meet them, placing in the hands of each   680
A goblet of rich wine. Then turned they back
Along the furrows, diligent to reach
Their distant end. All dark behind the plough
The ridges lay, a marvel to the sight,
Like real furrows, though engraved in gold.   685
    There, too, the artist placed a field which lay
Deep in ripe wheat. With sickles in their hands
The laborers reaped it. Here the handfuls fell
Upon the ground; there binders tied them fast

With bands, and made them sheaves. Three binders went 690
Close to the reapers, and behind them boys,
Bringing the gathered handfuls in their arms,
Ministered to the binders. Staff in hand,
The master stood among them by the side
Of the ranged sheaves and silently rejoiced. 695
Meanwhile the servants underneath an oak
Prepared a feast apart; they sacrificed
A fatling ox and dressed it, while the maids
Were kneading for the reapers the white meal.
   A vineyard also on the shield he graved, 700
Beautiful, all of gold, and heavily
Laden with grapes. Black were the clusters all;
The vines were stayed on rows of silver stakes.
He drew a blue trench round it, and a hedge
Of tin. One only path there was by which 705
The vintagers could go to gather grapes.
Young maids and striplings of a tender age
Bore the sweet fruit in baskets. Midst them all,
A youth from his shrill harp drew pleasant sounds,
And sang with soft voice to the murmuring strings. 710
They danced around him, beating with quick feet
The ground, and sang and shouted joyously.
   And there the artist wrought a herd of beeves,
High-horned, and sculptured all in gold and tin.
They issued lowing from their stalls to seek 715
Their pasture, by a murmuring stream, that ran
Rapidly through its reeds. Four herdsmen, graved
In gold, were with the beeves, and nine fleet dogs
Followed. Two lions, seizing on a bull
Among the foremost cattle, dragged him off 720
Fearfully bellowing; hounds and herdsmen rushed
To rescue him. The lions tore their prey,
And lapped the entrails and the crimson blood.
Vainly the shepherds pressed around and urged
Their dogs, that shrank from fastening with their teeth 725
Upon the lions, but stood near and bayed.
   There also did illustrious Vulcan grave
A fair, broad pasture, in a pleasant glade,

Full of white sheep, and stalls, and cottages,
And many a shepherd's fold with sheltering roof.   730
   And there illustrious Vulcan also wrought
A dance,—a maze like that which Dædalus,
In the broad realm of Gnossus once contrived
For fair-haired Ariadne. Blooming youths
And lovely virgins, tripping to light airs,   735
Held fast each other's wrists. The maidens wore
Fine linen robes; the youths had tunics on
Lustrous as oil, and woven daintily.
The maids wore wreaths of flowers; the young men swords
Of gold in silver belts. They bounded now   740
In a swift circle,—as a potter whirls
With both his hands a wheel to try its speed,
Sitting before it,—then again they crossed
Each other, darting to their former place.
A multitude around that joyous dance   745
Gathered, and were amused, while from the crowd
Two tumblers raised their song, and flung themselves
About among the band that trod the dance.
   Last on the border of that glorious shield
He graved in all its strength the ocean-stream.   750
   And when that huge and massive shield was done,
He forged a corselet brighter than the blaze
Of fire; he forged a solid helm to fit
The heroes temples, shapely and enchased
With rare designs, and with a crest of gold.   755
And last he forged him greaves of ductile tin.
   When the great artist Vulcan saw his task
Complete, he lifted all that armor up
And laid it at the feet of her who bore
Achilles. Like a falcon in her flight,   760
Down plunging from Olympus capped with snow,
She bore the shining armor Vulcan gave.

BOOK XIX

IN saffron-colored mantle from the tides
Of Ocean rose the Morning to bring light
To gods and men, when Thetis reached the fleet,
Bringing the gift of Vulcan. There she found
Her son, who, bending o'er Patroclus, wept   5
Aloud, and all around a troop of friends
Lamented bitterly. Beside him stood
The glorious goddess, took his hand, and said:—
   "Leave we the dead, my son, since it hath pleased
The gods that he should fall; and now receive   10
This sumptuous armor, forged by Vulcan's hand,
Beautiful, such as no man ever wore."
   The goddess spake, and laid the armor down
Before Achilles; as they touched the earth,
The well-wrought pieces clanked, and terror seized 15
The Myrmidons. No one among them all
Dared fix his gaze upon them; all shrank back.
Achilles only, as he saw them, felt
His spirit roused within him. In his eyes
A terrible brightness flashed, as if of fire.   20
He lifted up the god's magnificent gift
Rejoicing, and, when long his eyes had dwelt
Delighted on the marvellous workmanship,
Thus to his mother said, in wingèd words:—
   "A god indeed, my mother, must have given   25
These arms, the work of heavenly hands: no man

Could forge them. Now I arm myself for war.
But for the valiant Menœtiades
I greatly fear that flies will gather round
The wounds inflicted by the spear, and worms
Be bred within them, to pollute the corpse
Now that the life is gone, and taint the whole."
   And silver-footed Thetis answered thus:
"Son, have no care for that. The task be mine
To drive away the importunate swarm that feed
On heroes slain in battle. Though it lie
The whole year long, the body shall remain
Even more than uncorrupted. Call thou now
To council all the Achaian chiefs; renounce
Thy feud with Agamemnon, king of men,
And arm for war, and put on all thy might."
   She spake, and called a fiery courage up
Within the hero's breast. The goddess then
Infused ambrosia and the ruddy juice
Of nectar through the nostrils of the dead
Into the frame, to keep it from decay.
   Along the beach the great Achilles went,
Calling with mighty shouts the Grecian chiefs.
Then even they who till that day remained
Beside the fleet,—the pilots and the men
Who held the helm, the stewards of the ships,
And the purveyors,—all made haste to swell
The assembly, for they knew that he who long
Had borne no part in the disastrous war
Had now come forth. Two ministers of Mars,
The brave Tydides and the nobly born
Ulysses, both supported by their spears,
Came halting, for their wounds were painful yet;
They came and sat among the foremost chiefs.
And last came Agamemnon, king of men,
Wounded, for he had felt in thick of fight
The edge of the sharp spear which Coön bore,
Antenor's son. Now when the Greeks were all
Assembled, swift Achilles rose and said:—
   "Atrides, of a truth it would have been

Better for both of us had we done this
At first, though sorely angered, when we strove
For a girl's sake so fiercely. Would that she
Had perished in my ships, by Dian's shaft,
The day on which I laid Lyrnessus waste!   70
So many Greeks would then have not been forced,
Slain by the enemy's hand, to bite the dust
Of the great earth, while I was brooding o'er
My wrath. All that was for the good of Troy
And Hector; but the Greeks, I think, will long   75
Remember our contention. Let us leave
These things among the things that were, and, though
They make us grieve, let us subdue our minds
To what the time requires. Here then my wrath
Shall end; it is not meet that it should burn   80
Forever. Hasten thou and rouse to war
The long-haired Greeks, that I may yet again
Go forth among the men of Troy, and learn
If they design to encamp another night
Before the fleet. There is among them all   85
No man, I ween, who will not joyfully
Sit down when he escapes my deadly spear."

  He ended, and the Achaians all rejoiced
To hear the brave Pelides thus renounce
His anger. Agamemnon, king of men,   90
Then rose. He came not forth into the midst,
But stood beside his seat, and thus he spake:—

  "O friends, Achaian heroes, ministers
Of Mars! Whoever rises up to speak
'Tis well to hear him through, and not break in   95
Upon his speech, else is the most expert
Confounded. Who amid a clamorous throng
Can listen or can speak? The orator
Of clearest voice must utter it in vain.
Now I address Pelides; for the rest,   100
Hearken ye all, and ponder what I say.
The Greeks speak often of this feud, and cast
The blame on me. Yet was I not the cause,
But Jupiter and Fate, and she who walks

In darkness, dread Erynnis. It was they 105
Who filled my mind with fury in the hour
When from Achilles I bore off his prize.
What could I do? A deity prevails
In all things, Atè, mighty to destroy,
Daughter of Jove, and held in awe by all. 110
Delicate are her feet; she never comes
Near to the ground, but glides above the heads
Of men, to do them harm, and in her net
Entangles one at least of two who strive.
Jove, deemed the mightiest among men and gods, 115
Once felt her power of mischief. Him his spouse,
Juno, entrapped by cunning, when within
The massive walls of Thebes Alcmena lay
In childbed, and the mighty Hercules
Was near his birth. For Jupiter had said 120
Boastfully to the immortals: 'Hear, ye gods
And goddesses, what I am moved to speak:
This day shall Ilithyia, who presides
At births, bring into light a prince whose rule
The neighboring tribes shall own; he shall be one 125
Who bears the blood of my illustrious race.'
  "Imperial Juno thus, with words of guile,
Made answer: 'What thou sayest will prove false,
Nor wilt thou keep thy word. Now swear to me,
Olympius, with the irrevocable oath, 130
That whosoever of thy race shall fall
This day between a woman's feet shall bear
The rule o'er all the neighboring tribes.' She spake,
And Jove, perceiving not her craft, complied,
And took the mighty oath, but afterward 135
Found himself wronged. For Juno, darting forth,
Shot from the Olympian summit, and at once
Alighted at Achaian Argos. There
She found the noble wife of Sthenelus,
The son of Perseus, pregnant with a son, 140
In the seventh month. She caused him to be born,
The number of his months yet incomplete,
And kept Alcmena's hour of childbirth back,

And stayed her pangs. The goddess then made haste
To bear the tidings to Saturnian Jove.   145
  "'O Father Jupiter, by whom are hurled
The ruddy lightnings, I have news for thee.
A man-child of a generous stock is born,—
Eurystheus, whom the Argives shall obey,—
Born at this hour to Sthenelus, the son   150
Of Perseus, who is thine. And well it is
That such a prince should rule the Argive race.'
  "She ended: Jupiter was deeply grieved,
And, seizing Atè by her shining locks,
In his great wrath, he swore a mighty oath,—   155
That Atè, whose delight it is to bring
Mischief to all, should never tread again
Olympus and the starry floor of heaven.
Thus having sworn, he swung her, with raised arm,
On high, and hurled her from the starry heaven   160
Downward, where soon she reached the haunts of men;
Yet oft in after time because of her
He sighed, beholding his beloved son
Doomed by Eurystheus to unworthy tasks.
So I, while crested Hector in his might   165
Made havoc at our fleet among the Greeks
Even by their prows, remembered well my fault.
And now since I have borne the penalty,
And Jupiter it was who took away
My reason, I would gladly make amends   170
With liberal gifts. But rise and join the war;
Inflame the courage of the rest; the gifts
Will I supply,—all that were promised thee
When nobly-born Ulysses yesterday
Went to thy tents. Or, if it please thee, wait,   175
Though armed for battle, and my train shall bring
The treasures from my ship, that thou mayst see
My presents are peace-offerings indeed."
  The swift of foot, Achilles, answered thus:
"Most glorious son of Atreus, king of men!   180
Whether, O Agamemnon, thou wilt give
Gifts, as is meet, or keep them, rests with thee.

Now let us think of war; it is not well
To waste the hour in talking, and put off
The mighty work that we have yet to do.   185
Let every Greek among you, as he sees
Achilles fighting in the foremost ranks,
And slaughtering the Trojan phalanxes,
Take heart and boldly combat with his man."
   And then Ulysses, wise in council, spake,   190
Answering Achilles: "Nay, thou shouldst not thus,
Brave as thou art, lead on the sons of Greece,
Yet fasting, to the conflict with the men
Of Troy beside their city. No brief space
The struggle will endure when once the foes   195
Rush on each other, and a god inspires
Both hosts with fury. Bid the Achaians take
In their swift galleys food and wine; in these
Are force and vigor. No man can endure
To combat all the day till set of sun,   200
Save with the aid of food, however great
The promptings of his valor; for his limbs
Grow heavy, thirst and hunger weaken him,
And his knees fail him as he walks. Not so
The warrior well supplied with food and wine: 205
He fights the foe all day; a resolute heart
Is in his bosom; nor does weariness
O'ertake him till all others leave the field.
Now let the people be dismissed awhile,
And a repast be ordered. Let the king,   210
Atrides, bring into the assembly here
His gifts, that all the Greeks may look on them,
And thou rejoice to see them. Let him rise
Among the Greeks, and take a solemn oath
That he has ne'er approached the maiden's bed   215
To claim a husband's right. Thus let thy heart
Be satisfied. Yet let the monarch spread
A sumptuous banquet in his tent for thee,
That thy redress may be complete. And thou,
Atrides, wilt hereafter be more just   220
To others. It dishonors not a king

To make amends to one whom he has wronged."
   And then King Agamemnon spake in turn:
"Son of Laertes, gladly have I heard
What thou hast said, and well hast thou discoursed 225
Of all things in their order. I will take
The oath of which thou speakest,—so my heart
Commands me. In the presence of a god
I take it, and commit no perjury.
Now let Achilles, though he longs for war, 230
Delay awhile; and all assembled here,
Remain ye on the ground till from my ship
The gifts are brought. This charge and this command
I give to thee, Ulysses. Take with thee
A band of youths, the noblest of the host, 235
And bring the presents promised yesterday
To Peleus' son, and hither let them lead
The women. Meantime let Talthybius haste
To bring from our broad camp a boar, which I
Will offer up to Jove and to the Sun." 240
   The swift of foot, Achilles, thus replied:
"Most glorious son of Atreus, king of men,
These things are for the time when there shall come
A pause from battle, and this warlike heat
Within my breast shall cool. They whom the spear 245
Of Hector, son of Priam, has o'ercome
Lie mangled on the earth, since Jupiter
Awarded him the glory of the day:—
And ye propose a banquet. I would call
The sons of Greece to rush into the war 250
Unfed and fasting, and when this disgrace
Shall be avenged, I would, at sunset, spread
A liberal feast. Be sure that I, till then,
Taste neither food nor drink, while my slain friend
Lies gashed with weapons in my tent, amidst 255
His sorrowing comrades. Little I regard
The things of which thou speakest, for my thoughts
Are all of bloodshed and of dying groans."
   Ulysses, the sagacious, thus rejoined:
"Achilles, son of Peleus, bravest far 260

Of all the Achaians, mightier with the spear
By no small odds than I, yet do I stand
In prudence much above thee; I have lived
More years, and more have learned. Let then thy mind
Accept what I shall say. Men soon become 265
Weary of warfare, even when the sword
Lays its most ample harvest on the earth.
But fewer sheaves are reaped when Jupiter,
The arbiter of battles, turns the scale.
It is not well that we of Greece should mourn 270
The dead with fasting, since from day to day
Our warriors fall in numbers. Where were then
Respite from daily fasts? Lay we our slain
In earth and mourn a day. We who outlive
The cruel combat should refresh ourselves 275
With food and wine, that we may steadily
Maintain in arms the conflict with the foe.
And then let no man idly wait to hear
A further call to war,—for it will come
Freighted with evil to the man who skulks 280
Among the ships,—but let us all go forth
To wage fierce battle with the knights of Troy."
   He spake, and summoned to his side the sons
Of glorious Nestor, and Meriones,
And Meges, son of Phyleus, and with them 285
Thoas, and Lycomedes, Creon's son,
And Melanippus. Straight they took their way
To Agamemnon's tent, and there their task
Was done as quickly as the word was given.
They brought seven tripods forth, the promised gifts, 290
And twenty burnished caldrons, and twelve steeds,
And led away seven graceful women trained
In household arts,—the maid with rosy cheeks,
Briseis, was the eighth. Ulysses came,
Leading the way, and bearing, duly weighed, 295
Ten talents, all of gold. The Achaian youths
Followed, and placed the presents in the midst
Of that assembly. Agamemnon rose;
And then Talthybius, who was like a god

In power of voice, came near and took his place   300
Beside the monarch, holding in his hands
A boar. The son of Atreus drew a knife,
Which hung by the great scabbard of his sword,
And, cutting off the forelock of the boar,
Prayed with uplifted hands to Jupiter: 305
Meantime the Greeks in silence kept their seats,
And, as became them, listened to the king,
Who looked into the sky above, and said:—
  "Now first bear witness, Jove, of all the gods
Greatest and best, and also Earth and Sun,   310
And Furies dwelling under Earth, who take
Vengeance on men forsworn, that never I
Have laid, for purpose of unchaste desire,
Or other cause, my hand upon the maid
Briseis. She hath dwelt inviolate   315
Within my tents. If yet in aught I say
Lurk perjury, then may the blessed gods
Heap on my head the many miseries
With which they punish those who falsely swear!"
  He spake, and drew the unrelenting blade   320
Across the animal's throat. Talthybius took
And swung the carcass round, and cast it forth
Into the gray sea's depths, to be the food
Of fishes. Then again Achilles rose
Among the warlike sons of Greece, and said:—   325
  "Great sorrows thou dost send, O Father Jove!
Upon mankind; for never would the son
Of Atreus have provoked the wrath that burned
Within my bosom, never would have thought
To bear away the maiden from my tent   330
In spite of me, had it not been the will
Of Jupiter that many a Greek should die.
But banquet now, and then prepare for war."
  So spake Achilles, and at once dissolved
The assembly, each repairing to his ship   335
Save the large-hearted Myrmidons, who still
Were busy with the gifts, and carried them
Toward their great general's galley. These they laid

Carefully in the tents, and seated there
The women, while the attentive followers drave 340
The coursers to the stables. When the maid
Briseis, beautiful as Venus, saw
Patroclus lying gashed with wounds, she sprang
And threw herself upon the dead, and tore
Her bosom, her fair cheeks and delicate neck; 345
And thus the graceful maiden, weeping, said:—
　"Patroclus, dear to my unhappy heart!
I left thee in full life, when from this tent
They led me; I return and find thee dead,
chieftain of the people! Thus it is 350
That sorrow upon sorrow is my lot.
Him to whose arms my father, in my youth,
And gracious mother gave me as a bride,
I saw before our city pierced and slain,
And the three brothers whom my mother bore 355
Slain also,—brothers whom I dearly loved.
Yet thou, when swift Achilles struck to earth
My hapless husband, and laid waste the town
Of godlike Mynes, wouldst not suffer me
To weep despairingly; for thou didst give 360
Thy word to make me yet the wedded wife
Of great Achilles, bear me in the fleet
To Phthia, and prepare the wedding feast
Among the Myrmidons. O ever kind!
I mourn thy death, and cannot be consoled." 365
　Weeping she spake; the women wept with her,
Seemingly for the dead, but each, in truth,
For her own griefs. Meanwhile the elders came
Around Achilles, praying him to join
The banquet, but the chief, with sighs, refused. 370
　"Dear comrades, if ye love me, do not thus
Press me to sit and feast. A mighty woe
Weighs down my spirit; it is my resolve
To wait and bear until the setting sun."
　So saying, he dismissed the other kings. 375
The sons of Atreus, and the high-born chief
Ulysses, Nestor, and Idomeneus,

And Phœnix, aged knight, alone remained,
And anxiously they sought to comfort him
In his great grief; but comfort would he none 380
Ere entering the red jaws of war. He drew
Deep sighs, and, thinking on Patroclus, spake:—
   "The time has been when thou too, hapless one,
Dearest of all my comrades, wouldst have spread
With diligent speed before me in my tent 385
A genial banquet, while the Greeks prepared
For desperate battle with the knights of Troy.
Thou liest now a mangled corse, and I,
Through grief for thee, refrain from food and drink,
Though they are near. No worse calamity 390
Could light on me, not even should I hear
News of my father's death, who haply now
Tenderly mourns with tears his absent son
In Phthia, while upon a foreign coast
I wage for hated Helen's sake the war 395
Against the Trojans; or were I to hear
Tidings that my beloved son had died,
The noble Neoptolemus, who now,
If living, is in Scyros, growing up
To manhood. Once the hope was in my heart 400
That I alone should perish here at Troy,
Far from the Argive pastures full of steeds,
And thou return to Phthia and bring home
My son from Scyros in thy ship, and show
The youth my wealth, my servants, and my halls, 405
High-roofed and spacious. For my mind misgives
That Peleus either lives not, or endures
A painful age, and hardly lives, yet waits
To hear the sorrowful news that I am slain."
   So spake he weeping, and the elders sighed 410
To see his tears, as each recalled to mind
Those whom he left at home, while Saturn's son
Beheld their grief with pity, and bespake
His daughter Pallas thus with wingèd words:—
   "My child, wilt thou desert that valiant man? 415
And shall Achilles be no more thy care?

Lo, by his ships, before their lofty prows,
He sits, lamenting his beloved friend.
The rest are at the banquet; he remains
Apart from them, and fasting. Hasten thou;   420
With nectar and ambrosial sweets refresh
His frame, that hunger overtake him not."
  As thus he spake he sent the goddess forth
Eager to do her errand. Plunging down,
In form a shrill-voiced harpy with broad wings,   425
She cleft the air. The Greeks throughout the camp
Were putting on their armor. She infused
Into the hero's frame ambrosial sweets
And nectar, that his limbs might not grow faint
With hunger. Then the goddess sought again   430
The stable mansion of Almighty Jove,
While all the Greeks came pouring from the fleet.
  As when the flakes of snow fall thick from heaven,
Driven by the north wind sweeping on the clouds
Before it, so from out the galleys came   435
Helms crowding upon helms that glittered fair,
Strong hauberks, bossy shields, and ashen spears.
The gleam of armor brightened heaven and earth,
And mighty was the sound of trampling feet.
Amidst them all the great Achilles stood,   440
Putting his armor on; he gnashed his teeth;
His eyes shot fire; a grief too sharp to bear
Was in his heart, as, filled with rage against
The men of Troy, he cased his limbs in mail,
The gift of Vulcan, from whose diligent hand   445
It came. And first about his legs he clasped
The beautiful greaves, with silver fastenings,
Fitted the corselet to his bosom next,
And from his shoulders hung the brazen sword
With silver studs, and then he took the shield,   450
Massive and broad, whose brightness streamed as far
As the moon's rays. And as at sea the light
Of beacon, blazing in some lonely spot
By night, upon a mountain summit, shines
To mariners whom the tempest's force has driven   455

Far from their friends across the fishy deep,
So from that glorious buckler of the son
Of Peleus, nobly wrought, a radiance streamed
Into the sky. And then he raised and placed
Upon his head the impenetrable helm   460
With horse-hair plume. It glittered like a star,
And all the shining tufts of golden thread,
With which the maker's hand had thickly set
Its cone, were shaken. Next the high-born chief
Tried his new arms, to know if they were well   465
Adjusted to his shape, and left his limbs
Free play. They seemed like wings, and lifted up
The shepherd of the people. Then he drew
From its ancestral sheath his father's spear,
Heavy and huge and tough. No man of all   470
The Grecian host could wield that weapon save
Achilles only. 'Twas a Pelian ash,
Which Chiron for his father had cut down
On Pelion's highest peak, to be the death
Of heroes. Meantime, busy with the steeds,   475
Automedon and Alcimus put on
Their trappings and their yoke, and round their necks
Bound the fair collars, thrust into their mouths
The bit, and backward drew the reins to meet
The well-wrought chariot. Then Automedon   480
Took in his hand the showy lash, and leaped
Into the seat. Behind him, all equipped
For war, Achilles mounted, in a blaze
Of arms that dazzled like the sun, and thus
Called to his father's steeds with terrible voice:—   485
   "Xanthus and Balius, whom Podargè bore,—
A noble stock,—I charge you to bring back
Into the Grecian camp, the battle done,
Him whom ye now are bearing to the field,
Nor leave him, as ye left Patroclus, dead."   490
   Swift-footed Xanthus from beneath the yoke
Answered him with bowed head and drooping mane
That, flowing through the yoke-ring swept the ground,—
For Juno gave him then the power of speech:—

"For this one day, at least, we bear thee safe, 495
O fiery chief, Achilles! but the hour
Of death draws nigh to thee, nor will the blame
Be ours; a mighty god and cruel fate
Ordain it. Not through our neglect or sloth
Did they of Troy strip off thy glorious arms 500
From slain Patroclus. That invincible god,
The son of golden-haired Latona, smote
The hero in the foremost ranks, and gave
Glory to Hector. Even though our speed
Were that of Zephyr, fleetest of the winds, 505
Yet certain is thy doom to be o'ercome
In battle by a god and by a man."
    Thus far he spake, and then the Furies checked
His further speech. Achilles, swift of foot,
Replied in anger: "Xanthus, why foretell 510
My death? It is not needed; well I know
My fate,—that here I perish, far away
From Peleus and my mother. I shall fight
Till I have made the Trojans sick of war."
    He spake, and, shouting to his firm-paced steeds, 515
Drave them, among the foremost, toward the war.

BOOK XX

THUS, O Pelides, did the sons of Greece,
Impatient for the battle, arm themselves,
By their beaked ships, around thee. Opposite,
Upon a height that rose amidst the plain,
The Trojans waited. Meantime Jupiter   5
Sent Themis from the Olympian summit, ploughed
With dells, to summon all the immortal ones
To council. Forth she went from place to place,
Bidding them to the palace halls of Jove.
Then none of all the Rivers failed to join   10
The assembly, save Oceanus, and none
Of all the Nymphs were absent whose abode
Is in the pleasant groves and river-founts
And grassy meadows. When they reached the halls
Of Cloud-compelling Jove they sat them down   15
On shining thrones, divided each from each
By polished columns, wrought for Father Jove
By Vulcan's skill. Thus all to Jove's abode
Were gathered. Neptune had not disobeyed
The call. He left the sea, and took his seat   20
Among them, and inquired the will of Jove.
    "Why, wielder of the lightning, dost thou call
The gods again to council? Do thy plans
Concern the Greeks and Trojans? For the war
Between their hosts will be rekindled soon."   25
    And thus the Cloud-compeller Jove replied:

"Thou who dost shake the shores, thou knowest well
The purpose of my mind, and for whose sake
I call this council. Though so soon to die,
They are my care. Yet will I keep my place,
Seated upon the Olympian mount, and look
Calmly upon the conflict. All of you
Depart, and aid the Trojans or the Greeks,
As it may list you. For should Peleus' son
Alone do battle with the men of Troy,
Their squadrons could not stand before the assault
Of the swift-footed warrior for an hour.
Beforetime, at the sight of him they fled,
O'ercome with Fear, and now, when he is roused
To rage by his companion's death, I fear
Lest, though it be against the will of fate,
He level with the ground the walls of Troy."

 Saturnius spake, and moved the hosts to join
In desperate conflict. All the gods went forth
To mingle with the war on different sides.
Juno and Pallas hastened to the fleet
With Neptune, he who makes the earth to shake,
And Hermes, god of useful arts, and shrewd
In forecast. Vulcan also went with them,
Strong and stern-eyed, yet lame, his feeble legs
Moving with labor. To the Trojan side
Went crested Mars, Apollo with his locks
Unshorn, Diana mighty with the bow,
Latona, Xanthus, and the Queen of smiles,
Venus; for while the gods remained apart
From men, the Achaian host was high in hope
Because Achilles, who so long had left
The war, now reappeared upon the field,
And terror shook the limbs of every son
Of Troy when he beheld the swift of foot,
Pelides, terrible as Mars—that curse
Of human-kind—in glittering arms again.
But when the dwellers of Olympus joined
The crowd of mortals, Discord, who makes mad
The nations, rose and raged; Minerva raised

Her war-cry from the trench without the wall,
And then she shouted from the sounding shore;
While, like a cloudy whirlwind, opposite,
Moved Mars, and fiercely yelled, encouraging
The men of Troy, as on the city heights 70
He stood, or paced with rapid steps the hill
Beside the Simoïs, called the Beautiful.
  Thus, kindling hate between the hosts, the gods
Engaged, and hideous was the strife that rose
Among them. From above, with terrible crash, 75
Thundered the father of the blessed gods
And mortal men, while Neptune from below
Shook the great earth and lofty mountain peaks.
Then watery Ida's heights and very roots,
The city of Troy, and the Greek galleys, quaked. 80
Then Pluto, ruler of the nether world,
Leaped from his throne in terror, lest the god
Who makes the earth to tremble, cleaving it
Above him, should lay bare to gods and men
His horrible abodes, the dismal haunts 85
Which even the gods abhor. Such tumult filled
The field of battle when the immortals joined
The conflict. Then against King Neptune stood
Phœbus Apollo, with his wingèd shafts,
And Pallas, goddess of the azure eyes, 90
Confronted Mars. Encountering Juno came
The sister of Apollo, archer-queen
And huntress, Dian of the golden bow.
The helpful Hermes, god of useful arts,
Opposed Latona, and the mighty stream 95
Called Xanthus by the immortals, but by men
Scamander, with his eddies strong and deep,
Stood face to face with Vulcan in the field.
  So warred the gods with gods. Meantime the son
Of Peleus, ranging through the thick of fight, 100
Sought only Hector, Priam's son, whose blood
He meant to pour to greedy Mars, the god
Of carnage. But Apollo, who impels
Warriors to battle, stirred Æneas up

To meet Pelides. First he filled his heart 105
With resolute valor, and then took the voice
Of Priam's son, Lycaon. In his shape
Thus spake Apollo, son of Jupiter:—
  "Æneas, prince of Troy, where now are all
The boasts which thou hast made before the chiefs 110
Of Troy at banquets, that thou yet wouldst meet
Pelides in the combat hand to hand?"
  Æneas made reply: "Priamides,
Why dost thou bid me, when thou knowest me
Unwilling, meet in combat Peleus' son, 115
The mighty among men? It will not be
For the first time if I confront him now.
He chased me once from Ida with his spear,—
Me and my fellows, when he took our herds
And laid Lyrnessus waste and Pedasus. 120
But Jove, who gave me strength and nimble feet,
Preserved me; I had else been slain by him
And by Minerva, for the goddess went
Before him, giving him the victory
And moving him to slay the Leleges 125
And Trojans with the brazen spear he bore.
'Tis not for mortal man to fight the son
Of Peleus, at whose side there ever stands
One of the immortal gods, averting harm.
And then his weapon flies right on, nor stops 130
Until it bites the flesh. Yet were the god
To weigh the victory in an equal scale,
Achilles would not vanquish me with ease,
Though he might boast his frame were all of brass."
  Then spake the king Apollo, son of Jove: 135
"Pray, warrior, to the eternal gods. They say
That Venus gave thee birth, who has her own
From Jove. His mother is of lower rank
Than thine. Thine is a child of Jove, but his
A daughter of the Ancient of the Deep. 140
Strike at him with that conquering spear of thine,
Nor let him scare thee with stern words and threats."
  He said, and breathed into the prince's breast

Fresh valor, as, arrayed in glittering arms,
He pressed to where the foremost warriors fought; 145
Yet not unseen by Juno's eye went forth
The son of old Anchises. She convened
The gods in council, and addressed them thus:—
   "Neptune and Pallas, what shall now be done?
Consider ye. Æneas, all arrayed 150
In glittering arms, is pressing on to meet
Pelides. Phœbus sends him. Let us join
To turn him back, or let some one of us
Stand near Achilles, fill his limbs with strength,
Nor let his heart grow faint, but let him see 155
That we, the mightiest of the immortals, look
On him with favor, and that those who strive
Amid the war and bloodshed to protect
The sons of Troy are empty boasters all.
For this we came from heaven to interpose 160
In battle, that Achilles may endure
No harm from Trojan hands, although, no doubt,
Hereafter he must suffer all that Fate
Spun for him when his mother brought him forth.
But if he hear not, from some heavenly voice, 165
Of this assurance, fear may fall on him
When, haply, in the battle he shall meet
Some god; for when revealed to human sight
The presence of the gods is terrible."
   And then did Neptune, he who shakes the earth, 170
Make answer: "Juno, it becomes thee ill
To be so greatly vexed, I cannot wish
A contest with the other gods, though we
In power excel them. Rather let us sit
Apart, where we can look upon the war, 175
And leave it to mankind. And yet, if Mars
Or Phœbus should begin the fight, or seek
To thwart Achilles or restrain his arm,
There will be cause for us to join the strife
In earnest, and I deem that they full soon, 180
The contest ended, will return to join
The assembled gods upon the Olympian mount,

Forced to withdraw by our all-potent hands."
   So spake the dark-haired god, and led the way
To the high mound of godlike Hercules, 185
Raised from the earth by Trojans, with the aid
Of Pallas, that the hero there might find
A refuge when the monster of the deep
Should chase him from the sea-beach to the plain.
With other gods beside him Neptune there 190
Sat down and drew a shadow, which no sight
Could pierce, around their shoulders. Other gods,
Upon the hill called Beautiful, were grouped
Round thee, Apollo, archer-god, and Mars,
Spoiler of cities. On both sides they sat, 195
Devising plans, unwilling to begin
The fierce encounter, though Almighty Jove
From where he sat in heaven commanded it.
   The warriors thronged into the field, which shone
With brazen armor and caparisons 200
Of steeds; earth trembled with the sounding tramp
Of marching squadrons. From the opposing ranks
Two chieftains, each the bravest of his host,
Impatient to engage,—Anchises' son,
Æneas, and the great Achilles,—came. 205
And first Æneas, with defiant mien
And nodding casque, stood forth. He held his shield
Before him, which he wielded right and left,
And shook his brazen spear. On the other side,
Pelides hurried toward him, terrible 210
As is a lion, which the assembled hinds
Of a whole village chase and seek to slay,
While on he stalks, contemning their assault;
But if the arrow of some strong-armed youth
Have smitten him, he stands, and gathers all 215
His strength to spring, with open jaws and teeth
Half hid in foam, and uttering fearful growls
From his deep chest; he lashes with his tail
His sides and sinewy thighs to rouse himself
To combat, and then, grimly frowning, leaps 220
To slay, or by the foremost youths be slain,

So sprang Achilles, moved by his bold heart
To meet the brave Æneas. As the twain
Drew near each other, the swift-footed chief,
The great Achilles, was the first to speak:— 225
   "Why, O Æneas, hast thou come so far
Through this vast crowd to seek me? Does thy heart
Bid thee confront me in the hope to gain
The place which Priam holds, and to bear rule
Over the knights of Troy? Yet shouldst thou take 230
My life, think not that Priam in thy hand
Will place such large reward. He has his sons,
Nor is he fickle, but of stable mind.
Or will the Trojans, if thou slayest me,
Bestow on thee broad acres, of a soil 235
Fruitful exceedingly, and suited well
To vines or to the plough, which thou mayst till?
That also, as I hope, thou wilt obtain
With difficulty; for, unless I err,
I forced thee once to flee before my spear. 240
Dost thou remember, when thou wert alone
Among thy beeves, I drave thee, running fast,
Down Ida's steeps? Then didst thou never turn
To face me, but didst seek a hiding-place
Within Lyrnessus, which I also took 245
And wasted, with the aid of Father Jove
And Pallas. From the town I led away
The women, never to be free again.
Jove and the other gods protected thee
That day. Yet will they not protect thee now, 250
As thou dost vainly hope. Withstand me not,
I counsel thee, but hide thyself among
The crowd before thou suffer harm, for he
Who sees past evils only is a fool."
   And then Æneas answered: "Do not think, 255
Pelides, with such words to frighten me,
As if I were a beardless boy. I too
Might use reproach and taunt; but well we know
Each other's birth and lineage, through report
Of men, although by sight I know not thine, 260

Nor know'st thou mine. They say that thou art sprung
From Peleus the renowned, and from the nymph
Of ocean, fair-haired Thetis, while I boast
My birth from brave Anchises, and can claim
Venus as mother. Two of these to-day 265
Must weep the death of a beloved son,
For we are not to part, I think, nor end
The combat after a few childish words;
Yet let me speak, that thou mayst better know
Our lineage, known already far and wide. 270
Jove was the father, Cloud-compelling Jove,
Of Dardanus, by whom Dardania first
Was peopled, ere our sacred Troy was built
On the great plain,—a populous town; for men
Dwelt still upon the roots of Ida fresh 275
With many springs. To Dardanus was born
King Erichthonius, richest in his day
Of mortal men, and in his meadows grazed
Three thousand mares, exulting in their brood
Of tender foals. Of some of this vast herd 280
Boreas became enamored as they fed.
He came to them in likeness of a steed
That wore an azure mane, and they brought forth
Twelve foals, which all were females, of such speed
That when they frolicked on the teeming earth 285
They flew along the topmost ears of wheat
And broke them not, and when they sported o'er
The mighty bosom of the deep they ran
Along the hoary summits of its waves.
To Erichthonius Tros was born, who ruled 290
The Trojans, and from Tros there sprang three sons
Of high renown,—Ilus, Assaracus,
And godlike Ganymede, most beautiful
Of men; the gods beheld and caught him up
To heaven, so beautiful was he, to pour 295
The wine to Jove, and ever dwell with them.
And Ilus had a son, Laomedon,
Of mighty fame, to whom five sons were born,
Tithonus, Priam, Lampus, Clytius,

And Hicetaon, trained to war by Mars.   300
Assaracus begat my ancestor,
Capys, to whom Anchises owes his birth.
Anchises is my father; Priam's son
Is noble Hector. Such I claim to be
My lineage and my blood; but Jove at will   305
Gives in large measure, or diminishes,
Men's warlike prowess; and the power of Jove
Is over all. But let us talk no more
Of things like these, as if we were but boys,
While here in the mid-field we stand between   310
The warring armies. Both of us might cast
Reproaches at each other, many and foul,
Such as no galley of a hundred oars
Could bear and float. Men's tongues are voluble,
And endless are the modes of speech, and far   315
Extends from side to side the field of words.
Such as thou utterest it will be thy lot
To hear from others. But what profits it
For us to rail and wrangle, in high brawl,
Like women angered to the quick, that rush   320
Into the middle of the street and scold
With furious words, some true and others false,
As rage may prompt them? Me thou shalt not move
With words from my firm purpose ere thou raise
Thy arm against me. Let us hasten first   325
To prove the temper of our brazen spears."
   He spake, and hurled his brazen spear to smite
The dreadful shield, a terror in men's eyes;
That mighty buckler rang with the strong blow.
Achilles, as it came, held forth his shield   330
With nervous arm far from him, for he feared
That the long javelin of his valiant foe
Might pierce it. Idle fear; he had not thought
That the bright armor given him by the gods
Not easily would yield to force of man.   335
Nor could the rapid spear that left the hand
Of brave Æneas pierce the shield; the gold,
The gift of Vulcan, stopped it. Through two folds

It went, but three remained; for Vulcan's skill
Fenced with five folds the disk,—the outer two 340
Of brass, the inner two of tin; between
Was one of gold, and there the brazen spear
Was stayed. And then in turn Achilles threw
His ponderous spear, and struck the orbèd shield
Borne by Æneas near the upper edge, 345
Where thinnest was the brass and thinnest lay
The bullock's hide. The Pelian ash broke through;
The buckler crashed; Æneas, stooping low,
Held it above him, terrified; the spear,
Tearing both plate and hide of that huge shield, 350
Passed over him, and, eager to go on,
Plunged in the earth and stood. He, when he saw
The massive lance which he had just escaped
Fixed in the earth so near him, stood awhile
As struck with fear, and with despairing looks. 355
Achilles drew his trenchant sword and rushed
With fury on Æneas, uttering
A fearful shout. Æneas lifted up
A stone, a mighty weight, which no two men,
As men are now, could raise, yet easily 360
He wielded it. Æneas then, to save
His threatened life, had smitten with the stone
His adversary's buckler or his helm,
And with his sword Pelides had laid dead
The Trojan, had not he who shakes the earth, 365
Neptune, beheld him in that perilous hour,
And instantly addressed the immortal gods:—
   "My heart, ye gods, is heavy for the sake
Of the great-souled Æneas, who will sink
To Hades overcome by Peleus' son. 370
Rash man! he listened to the archer-god
Apollo, who has now no power to save
The chief from death. But, guiltless as he is,
Why should he suffer evil for the wrong
Of others? He has always sought to please 375
With welcome offerings the gods who dwell
In the broad heaven. Let us withdraw him, then,

From this great peril, lest, if he should fall
Before Achilles, haply Saturn's son
May be displeased. And 'tis the will of fate   380
That he escape; that so the Dardan race,
Beloved by Jove above all others sprung
From him and mortal women, may not yet
Perish from earth and leave no progeny.
For Saturn's son already holds the house   385
Of Priam in disfavor, and will make
Æneas ruler o'er the men of Troy,
And his sons' sons shall rule them after him."
    Imperial Juno with large eyes replied:
"Determine, Neptune, for thyself, and save   390
Æneas, or, all blameless as he is,
Abandon him to perish by the hand
Of Peleus' son, Achilles. We have sworn—
Minerva and myself—that never we
Would aid in aught the Trojans to escape   395
Their day of ruin, though the town of Troy
Sink to the dust in the destroying flames,—
Flames kindled by the warlike sons of Greece."
    And then did Neptune, shaker of the shores,
Go forth into the battle and amidst   400
The clash of spears, and come where stood the chiefs,
Æneas and his mighty foe, the son
Of Peleus. Instantly he caused to rise
A darkness round the eyes of Peleus' son,
And from the buckler of Æneas drew   405
The spear with ashen stem and brazen blade,
And laid it at Achilles' feet, and next
He lifted high Æneas from the ground
And bore him thence. O'er many a warrior's head,
And many a harnessed steed, Æneas flew,   410
Hurled by the god, until he reached the rear
Of that fierce battle, where the Caucons stood
Arrayed for war. The shaker of the shores
Drew near, and said to him in wingèd words:—
    "What god, Æneas, moved thee to defy   415
Madly the son of Peleus, who in might

Excels thee, and is dearer to the gods?
Whenever he encounters thee in arms
Give way, lest thou, against the will of fate,
Pass down to Hades. When he shall have met   420
His fate and perished, thou mayst boldly dare
To face the foremost of the enemy;
No other of the Greeks shall take thy life."
   He spake, and having thus admonished him
He left Æneas there, and suddenly   425
Swept off the darkness that so thickly rose
Around Achilles, who, with sight now clear,
Looked forth, and, sighing, said to his great soul:—
   "How strange is this! My eyes have seen to-day
A mighty marvel. Here the spear I flung   430
Is lying on the earth, and him at whom
I cast it, in the hope to take his life,
I see no longer. Well beloved, no doubt,
Is this Æneas by the immortal gods.
Yet that, I thought, was but an empty boast   435
Of his. Well, let him go; I cannot think
That he who gladly fled from death will find
The courage to encounter me again.
And now will I exhort the Greeks to fight
This battle bravely, while I go to prove   440
The prowess of the other chiefs of Troy."
   He spake, and, cheering on the soldiery,
He sprang into the ranks: "Ye noble Greeks,
Avoid no more the Trojans; press right on.
Let each man single out his man, and fight   445
With eager heart. 'Tis hard for me to chase,
With all my warlike might, so many men,
And fight with all. Not even Mars, the god,
Although immortal, nor Minerva's self,
Could combat with so vast a multitude   450
Unwearied; yet whatever I can do,
With hands and feet and strength, I give my word
Not to decline, or be remiss in aught.
I go to range the Trojan files, where none,
I think, will gladly stand to meet my spear."   455

Such stirring words he uttered, while aloud
Illustrious Hector called, encouraging
The men of Troy, and promising to meet
Achilles: "Valiant Trojans, do not quail
Before Pelides. In the strife of words　　　　　　　　　460
I too might bear my part against the gods;
But harder were the combat with the spear,
For greater is their might than ours. The son
Of Peleus cannot make his threatenings good.
A part will he perform and part will leave　　　　　465
Undone. I go to wait him; I would go
Although his hands were like consuming flame,—
His hands like flame, his strength the strength of steel."
　　He spake: the Trojans at his stirring words
Lifted their lances, and the adverse hosts　　　　　470
Joined battle with a fearful din. Then came
Apollo and admonished Hector thus:—
　　"Hector, encounter not Achilles here
Before the armies, but amidst the throng
And tumult of the battle, lest perchance　　　　　　475
He strike thee with the javelin or the sword."
　　He spake: the Trojan chief, dismayed to hear
The warning of the god, withdrew among
The crowded ranks. Meantime Achilles sprang
Upon the Trojans with a terrible cry,　　　　　　　480
And slew a leader of the host, the brave
Iphition, whom a Naiad, at the foot
Of snowy Tmolus, in the opulent vale
Of Hyda, bore to the great conqueror
Of towns, Otrynteus. As he came in haste,　　　　　485
The noble son of Peleus with his spear
Smote him upon the forehead in the midst,
And cleft the head in two. He fell; his arms
Clashed, and Achilles boasted o'er him thus:—
　　"Son of Otrynteus, terrible in arms,　　　　　　490
Thou art brought low; thou meetest here thy death,
Though thou wert born by the Gygæan lake
Where lie, by fishy Hyllus and the stream
Of eddying Hermus, thy paternal fields."

Thus boastfully he spake, while darkness came　　495
Over Iphition's eyes, and underneath
The chariots of the Greeks who foremost fought
His corse was mangled. Next Achilles smote
Antenor's son, Demoleon, gallantly
Breasting the onset of the Greeks. He pierced　　500
His temple through the helmet's brazen cheek;
The brass stayed not the blow; the eager spear
Brake through the bone, and crushed the brain within,
And the brave youth lay dead. Achilles next
Struck down Hippodamas; he pierced his back　　505
As, leaping from his car, the Phrygian fled
Before him. With a moan he breathed away
His life, as moans a bull when dragged around
The altar of the Heliconian king
By youths on whom the god that shakes the earth　　510
Looks down well pleased. With such a moaning sound
The fiery spirit left the Phrygian's frame.
　　Then sprang Achilles with his spear to slay
The godlike Polydorus, Priam's son,
Whose father bade him not to join the war,　　515
For he was younger than the other sons,
And dearest of them all. In speed of foot
He had no peer. Yet, with a boyish pride
To show his swiftness, in the foremost ranks
He ranged the field, until he lost his life.　　520
Him with a javelin the swift-footed son
Of Peleus smote as he was hurrying by.
The weapon pierced the middle of his back,
Where, by its golden rings, the belt was clasped
Above the double corselet; the keen blade　　525
Came forth in front; the Trojan with a cry
Fell forward on his knees, and, bending, clasped
His bowels in his hands. When Hector saw
His brother thus upon the earth, there came
A darkness o'er his eyes, nor could he bear　　530
Longer to stand aloof, but, brandishing
His spear, came forward like a rushing flame
To meet the son of Peleus, who beheld

And bounded toward him, saying boastfully:
"So, he is near whose hand hath given my heart   535
Its deepest wound, who slew my dearest friend.
No more are we to shun each other now,
Timidly stealing through the paths of war."
   And then he said to Hector with a frown:
"Draw nearer, that thou mayst the sooner die."   540
   The crested Hector, undismayed, replied:
"Pelides, do not hope with empty words
To frighten me, as if I were a boy.
Insults and taunts I could with ease return.
I know that thou art brave; I know that I   545
In might am not thy equal; but the event
Rests in the laps of the great gods, and they
May, though I lack thy prowess, give thy life
Into my hands when I shall cast my spear.
The weapon that I bear is keen like thine."   550
   Thus having spoken, brandishing his spear,
He sent it forth; but with a gentle breath
Minerva turned it from the glorious Greek,
And laid it at the noble Hector's feet.
Then did Achilles, resolute to slay   555
His enemy, rush against him with a shout
Of fury; but Apollo, with such power
As gods put forth, withdrew him thence, and spread
A darkness round him. Thrice the swift of foot,
Achilles, rushed against him with his spear,   560
And thrice he smote the cloud. But when once more,
In godlike might, he made the assault, he spake
These wingèd words of menace and reproach:—
   "Hound as thou art, thou hast once more escaped
Thy death; for it was near. Again the hand   565
Of Phœbus rescues thee; to him thy vows
Are made ere thou dost trust thyself amidst
The clash of javelins. I shall meet thee yet
And end thee utterly, if any god
Favor me also. I will now pursue   570
And strike the other Trojan warriors down."
   He spake, and in the middle of the neck

Smote Dryops with his spear. The Phrygian fell
Before him at his feet. He left him there,
And wounding with his spear Philetor's son, 575
Demuchus, tall and valiant, in the knee,
Stayed him until he slew him with his sword.
Then from their chariot to the ground he cast
Laogonus and Dardanus, the sons
Of Bias, piercing with a javelin one, 580
And cutting down the other with his sword.

   And Tros, Alastor's son, who came to him
And clasped his knees, in hope that he would spare
A captive,—spare his life, nor slay a youth
Of his own age,—vain hope! he little knew 585
That not by prayers Achilles could be moved,
Nor was he pitiful, nor mild of mood,
But hard of heart,—while Tros embraced his knees
And passionately sued, Pelides thrust
His sword into his side; the liver came 590
Forth at the wound; the dark blood gushing filled
The Phrygian's bosom; o'er his eyes there crept
A darkness, and his life was at an end.

   Approaching Mulius next, Achilles smote
The warrior at the ear; the brazen point 595
Passed through the other ear; and then he slew
Agenor's son, Echeclus, letting fall
His heavy-hilted sword upon his head
Just in the midst; the blade grew warm with blood,
And gloomy death and unrelenting fate 600
Darkened the victim's eyes. Achilles next
Wounded Deucalion, thrusting through his arm
The brazen javelin, where the sinews met
That strung the elbow. While with powerless arm
The wounded Trojan stood awaiting death, 605
Achilles drave his falchion through his neck.
Far flew the head and helm, the marrow flowed
From out the spine, and stretched upon the ground
Deucalion lay. Pelides still went on,
O'ertaking Rigmus, the renownèd son 610
Of Peireus, from the fruitful fields of Thrace,

And smote him in the stomach with his lance.
There hung the weapon fixed; the wounded man
Fell from the car. At Areïthoüs
The charioteer, who turned his steeds to flee,   615
Achilles sent his murderous lance, and pierced
His back, and dashed him from the car, and left
His horses wild with fright. As when, among
The deep dells of an arid mountain-side,
A great fire burns its way, and the thick wood   620
Before it is consumed, and shifting winds
Hither and thither sweep the flames, so ranged
Achilles in his fury through the field
From side to side, and everywhere o'ertook
His victims, and the earth ran dark with blood.   625
  As when a yeoman underneath the yoke
Brings his broad-fronted oxen to tread out
White barley on the level threshing-floor,
The sheaves are quickly trodden small beneath
The heavy footsteps of the bellowing beasts,   630
So did the firm-paced coursers, which the son
Of Peleus guided, trample with their feet
Bucklers and corpses, while beneath the car
Blood steeped the axle, and the chariot-seat
Dripped on its rim with blood, that from below   635
Was splashed upon them by the horses' hoofs
And by the chariot-wheels. Such havoc made
Pelides in his ardor for renown,
Till his invincible hands were foul with blood.

BOOK XXI

NOW when they reached the pleasant banks through
which
The eddying Xanthus runs, the river sprung
From deathless Jove, Achilles drave his foes
Asunder. Part he chased across the plain
Townward, along the way by which the Greeks   5
In terror fled the day before, pursued
By glorious Hector. Panic-struck they ran
Along that way, while, to restrain their flight,
Before them Juno hung a veil of cloud
And darkness. Meanwhile half the flying crowd   10
Leaped down to that deep stream and rolled among
Its silver eddies. With a mighty noise
They plunged; the torrent dashed; the banks around
Remurmured shrilly to the cries of those
Who floated struggling in the current's whirl,   15
As when before the fierce, devouring flames
A swarm of locusts, springing into air,
Fly toward a river, while the fire behind
Crackles with sudden fierceness, and in fright
They fall into the waves, the roaring stream   20
Of the deep-eddied Xanthus thus was filled
Before Achilles with a mingled crowd
Of steeds and men. The Jove-descended man
Left leaning on the tamarisks his spear
Upon the river's border, and leaped in,   25

Armed only with his sword, intent to deal
Death on the fugitives; on every side
He smote, and from the smitten by the sword
Rose lamentable cries; the waves around
Grew crimson with their blood. As when before   30
A dolphin of huge bulk the fishes flee
In fear, and crowd the creeks that lie around
The sheltered haven,—for their foe devours
All that he overtakes,—the Trojans thus
Hid from his sight among the hollow rocks   35
Beside the rushing river. When his hand
Was weary with the work of death, he took
Twelve youths alive, whose blood was yet to pay
The penalty for Menœtiades,
His slaughtered friend. He led them from the stream, 40
Passive with fear like fawns, and tied their hands
Behind them with the well-twined cords that bound
Their tunics. Then he gave them to his friends,
Who led the captives to the roomy ships.

   Again Achilles rushed upon the foe   45
Intent on slaughter. One he met who climbed
The river's bank, Dardanian Priam's son,
Lycaon, whom in former days he made
His captive, by surprise, when in the night
He found him lopping with an axe the boughs   50
Of a wild fig-tree, that the trunk might form
The circle of a wheel. Achilles came,
An unexpected foe, and bore him off
To sea, and sold him in the populous isle
Of Lemnos. He was bought by Jason's son,   55
The Imbrian prince, Eëtion, who had been
His host, and now redeemed him with large gifts,
And sent him to Arisba's noble town.
Yet thence he stole, and reached his father's house
Again, and there made merry with his friends   60
Eleven days, but on the twelfth a god
Delivered him again into the hands
Of Peleus' son, who now would send his soul
Repining down to Hades. When the chief,

The swift of foot, beheld him stand unarmed, 65
With neither helm nor shield nor spear,—for these
He had thrown down,—faint with the sweaty toil
Of clambering up the bank, and every limb
Unstrung with weariness, then wrathfully
Thus said Achilles to his mighty soul:— 70
   "O strange! my eyes behold a miracle.
Sure, the brave sons of Troy whom I have slain
Will rise up from the nether darkness yet,
Since this man, whom I once reprieved from death
And sold in Lemnos the divine, comes back. 75
Nor could the ocean's gray abyss of brine,
Beyond which many long in vain to pass,
Detain him in that isle. But he shall taste
The sharpness of my spear, that I may prove
Whether he after that will reappear, 80
And whether the kind earth, which holds so well
The valiant dead, can keep him in her womb."
   So pondered he and stood. The Trojan drew
Close to him, with intent to clasp his knees,
Fear-struck, yet hoping to avoid the doom 85
Of bitter death. The great Achilles raised
His ponderous spear to strike. Lycaon stooped,
And, darting underneath the weapon, seized
The hero's knees; behind him in the ground
The spear stood fixed, though eager yet for blood; 90
One arm was round his adversary's knees,
The other held—and would not let it go—
The spear, while thus with wingèd words he prayed:—
   "I clasp thy knees, Achilles; look on me
Kindly and pity me, O foster-child 95
Of Jove. I am thy suppliant, and may claim
Thy mercy, I partook with thee the fruits
Of Ceres, when amid my fruitful fields
Thou madest me a captive, carrying me
From friends and kindred to the sacred isle 100
Of Lemnos. Thou didst sell me there,—my price
A hundred beeves,—and thou shalt now receive,
For ransom, thrice as many. It is yet

But the twelfth morning since I came to Troy
After much hardship, and a pitiless fate   105
Betrays me to thy hands. I must believe
That Father Jove in wrath delivers me
To thee again. Laothoë brought me forth
To a brief life; that mother was the child
Of aged Altes,—Altes ruling o'er   110
The warlike Leleges, by whom are tilled
The heights of Pedasus, where Satnio flows,—
And Priam wedded her with other maids.
She bore two children to be slain by thee;
One was the godlike Polydore, whom thou   115
Didst smite with thy keen spear, in the front rank
Of those who fought on foot. His evil fate
Must overtake me now, for, since a god
Has brought me near thee, there is no escape.
Yet let me tell thee this, and weigh it well,   120
And let it save my life. I came not forth
From the same womb with Hector, by whose hand
Thy brave and gentle friend, Patroclus, died."
   The illustrious son of Priam ended here
His prayer, and heard a merciless reply:—   125
   "Fool! never talk of ransom,—not a word.
Before the evil day on which my friend
Was slain, it pleased me oftentimes to spare
The Trojans. Many a one I took alive
And sold; but now no man of all their race,   130
Whom any god may bring within my reach,
Shall leave the field alive, and least of all
The sons of Priam. Die thou, then; and why
Shouldst thou, my friend, lament? Patroclus died,
And greatly he excelled thee. Seest thou not   135
How eminent in stature and in form
Am I, whom to a prince renowned for worth
A goddess mother bore; yet will there come
To me a violent death at morn, at eve,
Or at the midday hour, whenever he   140
Whose weapon is to take my life shall cast
The spear or send an arrow from the string."

He spake: the Trojan's heart and knees grew faint;
His hand let go the spear; he sat and cowered
With outstretched arms. Achilles drew his sword, 145
And smote his neck just at the collar-bone;
The two-edged blade was buried deep. He fell
Prone on the earth; the black blood spouted forth
And steeped the soil. Achilles by the foot
Flung him to float among the river-waves, 150
And uttered, boastfully, these wingèd words:—
"Lie there among the fishes, who shall feed
Upon thy blood unscared. No mother there
Shall weep thee lying on thy bier; thy corpse
Scamander shall bear down to the broad sea, 155
Where, as he sees thee darkening its face,
Some fish shall hasten, darting through the waves,
To feed upon Lycaon's fair white limbs.
So perish ye, till sacred Troy be ours,
You fleeing, while I follow close and slay. 160
This river cannot aid you,—this fair stream
With silver eddies, to whose deity
Ye offer many beeves in sacrifice,
And fling into its gulfs your firm-paced steeds;
But thus ye all shall perish, till I take 165
Full vengeance for Patroclus of the Greeks,
Whom, while I stood aloof from war, ye slew."
 He spake: and, deeply moved with inward wrath,
The River pondered how to render vain
The prowess of Achilles, and avert 170
Destruction from the Trojans. Now the son
Of Peleus rushed, his ponderous spear in hand,
To slay Asteropæus, who was sprung
From Pelegon, and Pelegon was born
To the broad river Axius, of a maid, 175
The eldest-born of Acessamenus,
Named Peribœa; for the river-god
Was joined with her in love. Achilles sprang
To meet the youth, as, rising from the stream,
Armed with two spears, he stood, his heart made strong 180
And resolute by Xanthus, who had seen

Indignantly so many Trojans die,—
Youths whom Achilles slaughtered in his stream,
And had no pity on them. When the twain
Were near each other, standing face to face,   185
The swift Achilles was the first to speak:—
"Who and whence art thou that dost venture thus
To meet me? They who seek to measure strength
With me are sons of most unhappy men."
   And thus the illustrious son of Pelegon   190
Made answer: "Brave Pelides, why inquire
My lineage? I am from a distant coast,—
Pæonia's fertile fields; I lead to war
Pæonia's warriors with long spears, and this
Is now the eleventh morning since I came   195
To join the war at Troy. I claim descent
From Axius, the broad Axius, who pours forth
The fairest river on the earth. His son
Was Pelegon, expert to wield the spear,
And I was born to Pelegon. And now,   200
Illustrious son of Peleus, let us fight."
   He spake: Achilles raised the Pelian ash
To smite; Asteropæus aimed at him
Both lances, for he used both hands alike.
One struck the Grecian's shield, yet passed not through,   205
Stopped by the god-given gold; the other gashed
Lightly the elbow of his dexter arm;
The black blood spouted forth, the spear passed on
Beyond him, and, still eager for its prey,
Stood fixed in earth. Achilles then, intent   210
To slay Asteropæus, hurled at him
His trusty spear. The weapon missed its mark,
And, striking the high bank, was buried there
Up to the middle of its ashen staff.
Achilles drew the keen sword from his thigh,   215
And flew with fury toward his foe, who toiled
In vain with sinewy arm to pluck that spear
From out the bank; and thrice he shook the beam
Fiercely, and thrice desisted, lacking strength,
And last he sought, by bending it, to break   220

The ashen weapon of Æacides.
But ere it snapped Achilles took his life,
Smiting him at the navel with the sword.
Forth gushed the entrails to the ground, and o'er
His dying eyes the darkness came; and then 225
Achilles, leaping on his breast, tore off
The armor, and exultingly exclaimed:—
  "Lie there! a perilous task it was for thee
To combat with a son of Jove, though born
Thyself to a great River. I can boast 230
Descent from sovereign Jove. I owe my birth
To Peleus, ruler of the Myrmidons.
His father was Æacus, who was born
To Jupiter, a god more potent far
Than all the rivers flowing to the sea. 235
And mightier is the race of Jupiter
Than that of any stream. Here close at hand
Is a great river, if such aid can aught
Avail thee; but to strive with Jupiter
Is not permitted. Acheloüs, king 240
Of rivers, cannot vie with him, nor yet
The great and mighty deep from which proceed
All streams and seas and founts and watery depths.
He trembles at the bolt of mighty Jove
And his hoarse thunder crashing in the sky." 245
  As thus he spake he plucked from out the bank
His brazen spear, and left the lifeless chief
Stretched in the sand, where the dark water steeped
His limbs, and eels and fishes came and gnawed
The warrior's reins. Achilles hastened on, 250
Pursuing the Pæonian knights, who now,
When they beheld their bravest overthrown
In desperate battle by the mighty arm
And falchion of Pelides, took to flight
Along the eddying river. There he slew 255
Mydon, Thersilochus, Astypylus,
Mnesus, and Thrasius, and struck down in death
Ænius and Ophelestes. Many more
Of the Pæonians the swift-footed Greek

Had slain, had not the eddying River, roused   260
To anger, put a human semblance on,
And uttered from its whirling deeps a voice:—
  "O son of Peleus! thou who dost excel
All other men in might and dreadful deeds,—
For the gods aid thee ever,—if the son   265
Of Saturn gives thee to destroy the race
Of Trojans, drive them from me to the plain,
And there perform thy terrible exploits.
For now my pleasant waters, in their flow,
Are choked with heaps of dead, and I no more   270
Can pour them into the great deep, so thick
The corpses clog my bed, while thou dost slay
And sparest not. Now then, withhold thy hand,
Prince of the people! I am horror-struck."
  Achilles the swift-footed made reply: 275
"Be it as thou commandest, foster-child
Of Jove, Scamander! Yet I shall not cease
To slay these treaty-breakers till at length
I shut them up within their town, and force
Hector to meet me, that we may decide   280
Which shall o'ercome the other,—he or I."
  He spake, and rushed upon the men of Troy,
Terrible as a god, while from his bed
The eddying River called to Phœbus thus:—
  "Why this, thou bearer of the silver bow,   285
Thou son of Jove? Thou heedest not the will
Of Saturn's son, who strictly bade that thou
Shouldst aid the Trojans till the latest gleam
Of sunset, and till night is on the fields."
  And then Achilles, mighty with the spear,   290
From the steep bank leaped into the mid-stream,
While, foul with ooze, the angry River raised
His waves, and pushed along the heaps of dead
Slain by Achilles. These, with mighty roar
As of a bellowing ox, Scamander cast   295
Aground; the living with his whirling gulfs
He hid, and saved them in his friendly streams.
In tumult terribly the surges rose

Around Achilles, beating on his shield,
And made his feet to stagger, till he grasped 300
A tall, fair-growing elm upon the bank.
Down came the tree, and in its loosened roots
Brought the earth with it; the fair stream was checked
By the thick branches, and the prostrate trunk
Bridged it from side to side. Achilles sprang 305
From the deep pool, and fled with rapid feet
Across the plain in terror. Nor did then
The mighty river-god refrain, but rose
Against him with a darker crest, to drive
The noble son of Peleus from the field, 310
And so deliver Troy. Pelides sprang
A spear's cast backward,—sprang with all the speed
Of the black eagle's wing, the hunter-bird,
Fleetest and strongest of the fowls of air.
Like him he darted; clashing round his breast, 315
The brazen mail rang fearfully. Askance
He fled; the water with a mighty roar
Followed him close. As, when a husbandman
Leads forth, from some dark spring of earth, a rill
Among his planted garden-beds, and clears 320
Its channel, spade in hand, the pebbles there
Move with the current, which runs murmuring down
The sloping surface and outstrips its guide,—
So rushed the waves where'er Achilles ran,
Swift as he was; for mightier are the gods 325
Than men. As often as the noble son
Of Peleus made a stand in hope to know
Whether the deathless gods of the great heaven
Conspired to make him flee, so often came
A mighty billow of the Jove-born stream 330
And drenched his shoulders. Then again he sprang
Away; the rapid torrent made his knees
To tremble, while it swept, where'er he trod,
The earth from underneath his feet. He looked
To the broad heaven above him, and complained:— 335
   "Will not some god, O Father Jove, put forth
His power to save me in my hour of need

From this fierce river? Any fate but this
I am resigned to suffer. None of all
The immortal ones is more in fault than she 340
To whom I owe my birth; her treacherous words
Deluded me to think that I should fall
Beneath the walls of Troy by the swift shafts
Of Phœbus. Would that Hector, the most brave
Of warriors reared upon the Trojan soil, 345
Had slain me; he had slain a brave man then,
And a brave man had stripped me of my arms.
But now it is my fate to perish, caught
In this great river, like a swineherd's boy,
Who in the time of rains attempts to pass 350
A torrent, and is overwhelmed and drowned."

 He spake, and Neptune and Minerva came
Quickly and stood beside him. In the form
Of men they came, and took his hand, and cheered
His spirit with their words. And thus the god 355
Neptune, who makes the earth to tremble, said:—

 "Fear not, Pelides, neither let thy heart
Be troubled, since thou hast among the gods,
By Jove's consent, auxiliars such as I
And Pallas. It is not thy doom to be 360
Thus vanquished by a river. Soon its rage
Will cease, as thou shalt see. Meantime we give
This counsel; heed it well: let not thy hand
Refrain from slaughter till the Trojan host
Are all shut up—all that escape thy arm— 365
Within the lofty walls of Troy. Then take
The life of Hector, and return on board
Thy galleys; we will make that glory thine."

 Thus having spoken, they withdrew and joined
The immortals, while Achilles hastened on, 370
Encouraged by the mandate of the gods,
Across the plain. The plain was overflowed
With water; sumptuous arms were floating round,
And bodies of slain youths. Achilles leaped,
And stemmed with powerful limbs the stream, and still 375
Went forward; for Minerva mightily

Had strengthened him. Nor did Scamander fail
To put forth all his power, enraged the more
Against the son of Peleus; higher still
His torrent swelled and tossed with all its waves, 380
And thus he called to Simoïs with a shout:—
   "O brother, join with me to hold in check
This man, who threatens soon to overthrow
King Priam's noble city; for no more
The Trojan host resist him. Come at once 385
And aid me; fill thy channel from its springs,
And summon all thy brooks, and lift on high
A mighty wave, and roll along thy bed,
Mingled in one great torrent, trees and stones,
That we may tame this savage man, who now 390
In triumph walks the field, and bears himself
As if he were a god. His strength, I deem,
Will not avail him, nor his noble form,
Nor those resplendent arms, which yet shall lie
Scattered along the bottom of my gulfs, 395
And foul with ooze. Himself too I shall wrap
In sand, and pile the rubbish of my bed
In heaps around him. Never shall the Greeks
Know where to gather up his bones, o'erspread
By me with river-slime, for there shall be 400
His burial-place; no other tomb the Greeks
Will need when they perform his funeral rites."
   He spake, and wrathfully he rose against
Achilles,—rose with turbid waves, and noise,
And foam, and blood and bodies of the dead. 405
One purple billow of the Jove-born stream
Swelled high and whelmed Achilles. Juno saw,
And trembled lest the hero should be whirled
Downward by the great river, and in haste
She called to Vulcan, her beloved son:— 410
   "Vulcan, my son, arise! We deemed that thou
And eddying Xanthus were of equal might
In battle. Come with instant aid, and bring
Thy vast array of flames, while from the deep
I call a tempest of the winds,—the West 415

And the swift South,—and they shall sweep along
A fiery torrent to consume the foe,
Warriors and weapons. Thou meantime lay waste
The groves along the Xanthus; hurl at him
Thy fires, nor let him with soft words or threats   420
Avert thy fury. Pause not from the work
Of ruin till I shout and give the sign,
And then shalt thou restrain thy restless fires."
   She spake, and Vulcan at her word sent forth
His fierce, devouring flames. Upon the plain   425
They first were kindled, and consumed the dead
That strewed it, where Achilles struck them down.
The ground was dried; the glimmering flood was stayed.
As when the autumnal north-wind, breathing o'er
A newly watered garden, quickly dries   430
The clammy mould, and makes the tiller glad,
So did the spacious plain grow dry on which
The dead were turned to ashes. Then the god
Seized on the river with his glittering fires.
The elms, the willows, and the tamarisks   435
Fell, scorched to cinders, and the lotus-herbs,
Rushes, and reeds that richly fringed the banks
Of that fair-flowing current were consumed.
The eels and fishes, that were wont to glide
Hither and thither through the pleasant depths   440
And eddies, languished in the fiery breath
Of Vulcan, mighty artisan. The strength
Of the great River withered, and he spake:—
   "O Vulcan, there is none of all the gods
Who may contend with thee. I combat not   445
With fires like thine. Cease then. With my consent
The noble son of Peleus may drive out
The Trojans from their city. What have I
To do with war,—the attack or the defence?"
   Thus in that fiery glow he spake, while seethed   450
His pleasant streams. As over a strong fire
A caldron filled with fat of pampered swine
Glows bubbling on all sides, while underneath
Burns the dry fuel, thus were his fair streams

Scorched by the heat, and simmered, while the blast 455
Sent forth by Vulcan, the great artisan,
Tormented him, and he besought the aid
Of Juno with these supplicating words:—
   "Why should thy son, O Juno, wreak on me
His fury, more than on the other gods? 460
My fault is less than theirs who give their aid
To Troy; and I will cease, if thou command.
Bid him desist, and here I pledge my oath
Not to attempt to save the Trojan race
From ruin, though their city sink in flames 465
Before the torches of the warlike Greeks."
   This when the white-armed goddess Juno heard,
She said to Vulcan, her beloved son:—
   "Dear son, refrain; it is not well that thus
A god should suffer for the sake of men." 470
   She spake, and Vulcan quenched his dreadful fires,
And back the pleasant waters to their bed
Went gliding. Xanthus had been made to yield,
And the two combatants no longer strove
Since Juno, though offended, bade them cease. 475
   Yet was the conflict terrible among
The other gods, as zeal for different sides
Impelled them. With a loud uproar they met
Each other in the field; the spacious earth
Rebellowed to the noise, and the great heaven 480
Returned it. To the ear of Jove it rose,
Who, sitting on Olympus, laughed within
His secret heart as he beheld the gods
Contending, for not long they stood apart.
Shield-breaking Mars began the assault; he rushed 485
Toward Pallas, brandishing his brazen spear,
And thus accosted her with insolent words:—
   "Thou shameless one, thou whose effrontery
Is boundless, why wilt thou provoke the gods
To strife? Thy temper is most arrogant. 490
Rememberest thou the time when thou didst prompt
Tydides Diomed to strike at me?
It was thy hand that held his shining spear,

And aimed it well, and gave the wound; but now
Will I take vengeance on thee for that wrong." 495
　He spake, and smote Minerva's fringèd shield,
The dreadful ægis, which not even Jove
Could pierce with thunderbolts. The murderous Mars
Smote it with his huge spear. She only stepped
Backward a space, and with her powerful hand 500
Lifted a stone that lay upon the plain,
Black, huge, and jagged, which the men of old
Had placed there for a landmark. This she hurled
At Mars, and struck him on the neck; he fell
With nerveless limbs, and covered, as he lay, 505
Seven acres of the field: his armor clashed
Around him in his fall; his locks all soiled
Lay in the trodden dust. The goddess stood
O'er him, and boasted thus with wingèd words:—
　"Fool that thou art, hast thou not learned how much 510
The might I boast excels thine own, that thus
Thou measurest strength with me? Now dost thou feel
Thy mother's curse fulfilled, who meditates
Thy chastisement, since thou hast left the Greeks
And joined the treaty-breaking sons of Troy." 515
　She spake, and turned away her glorious eyes.
Jove's daughter, Venus, took the hand of Mars,
And led him groaning thence, while hardly yet
His strength came back. The white-armed Juno saw,
And spake to Pallas thus, with wingèd words:— 520
　"See, daughter of the Ægis-bearer, Jove,
Unconquerable maid! that shameless one,
Through all the tumult, from the thick of fight,
Leads hence the murderous Mars; but follow her."
　She spake, and Pallas gladly hastened forth, 525
And, overtaking Venus, dealt at her
A mighty buffet on the breast; her heart
Fainted, her knees gave way; and, as she lay
Prostrate with Mars upon the fruitful earth,
Exulting Pallas spake these wingèd words:— 530
　"Would that all those who aid the cause of Troy
And combat with the mailèd Greeks were thus!

Would that they were as hardy and as brave
As Venus here, who ventured to the help
Of Mars, and met the force of my right arm!   535
Then had the stately Ilium been o'erthrown
Long since, and we had rested from the war."
   She spake: the white-armed Juno gently smiled,
And then King Neptune to Apollo said:—
   "Why, Phœbus, stand we thus aloof? it ill   540
Becomes us, while the other gods engage
In conflict. 'Twere a shame should we return
Up to Olympus and the brazen halls
Of Jove with no blow struck. Begin, for thou
Art younger born, and I, who both in years   545
And knowledge am before thee, must not make
The assault. O silly god, and slow of thought!
Hast thou indeed forgotten all the wrongs
We suffered once in Troy, and only we
Of all the gods, when, sent to earth by Jove,   550
We served a twelvemonth for a certain hire
The proud Laomedon, by whom our tasks
Were set? I built a city and a wall
Of broad extent, and beautiful, and strong
To stand assault; and, Phœbus, thou didst feed   555
His stamping oxen, with curved horns, among
The lawns of woody Ida seamed with glens.
But when the welcome hours had brought the day
Of our reward, the ruffian king refused
The promised wages, and dismissed us both   560
With menaces; to bind thee hand and foot
He threatened, and to sell thee as a slave
In distant isles, and to cut off the ears
Of both of us. So we returned to heaven,
Incensed at him who thus withheld the hire   565
He promised. Dost thou favor Troy for this?
Wilt thou not rather act with us until
These treaty-breakers, with their children all
And their chaste matrons, perish utterly?"
   Then thus the archer-king, Apollo, spake: 570
"Thou wouldst not deem me wise, should I contend

With thee, O Neptune, for the sake of men,
Who flourish like the forest-leaves awhile,
And feed upon the fruits of earth, and then
Decay and perish. Let us quit the field,   575
And leave the combat to the warring hosts."
   He spake, and turned, afraid to meet in arms
His uncle; but the sylvan Dian heard,—
His sister, mistress of the beasts that range
The wilds,—and harshly thus upbraided him:—   580
   "O mighty Archer, dost thou flee and yield
The victory to Neptune, who bears off
A glory cheaply earned? Why dost thou bear
That idle bow, thou coxcomb? I shall hope
No more to hear thee in our father's halls,   585
And in the presence of the immortals, boast
That thou wilt fight with Neptune hand to hand."
   The archer-god, Apollo, answered not;
But thus the imperial wife of Jupiter,
Indignantly and with reproachful words,   590
Rebuked the quivered goddess of the chase:—
   "How is it that thou darest, shameless one,
Resist me? Thou wilt find it hard, though trained
In archery, to match thy strength with mine,
Though Jove has made thee among womankind   595
A lioness, and though he gives thee power
To slay whomever of thy sex thou wilt;
Yet wilt thou find it easier to strike down
The mountain beasts of prey, and forest deer,
Than combat with thy betters. If thou choose   600
To try the event of battle, then put forth
Thy strength against me, and thou shalt be taught
How greatly I excel in might of arm."
   Thus Juno spake, and grasped in her left hand
Both Dian's wrists, and, plucking with her right   605
The quiver from her shoulders, beat with it
Her ears, and smiled as under her quick blows
The sufferer writhed. To earth the arrows fell,
And Dian weeping fled. As when a dove,
Not fated to be overtaken yet,   610

Flees from a hawk to find her hiding-place,
The hollow rock, so Dian fled in tears,
And left her arrows. To Latona, then,
Heaven's messenger, the Argus-queller, spake:—
   "Far be it from me to contend with thee,   615
Latona; perilous it were to meet
A consort of the Cloud-compeller, Jove,
In combat. Go and freely make thy boast
Among the gods that thou hast vanquished me."
   He spake: Latona gathered from the ground   620
The bow and shafts which in that whirl of dust
Had fallen here and there, and, bearing them,
Followed her daughter, who meantime had reached
Olympus and the brazen halls of Jove.
And there, a daughter at her father's knees,   625
She sat her down, while, as she wept, her robe
Of heavenly texture trembled. Graciously
Jove smiled, and drew her toward him and inquired:
"What dweller of the sky has dared do this,
Dear child, as though some flagrant guilt were thine?"   630
   And thus replied the mistress of the chase
Crowned with the crescent: "Father, 'twas thy queen,
The white-armed Juno; she who causes strife
And wrath among the gods has done me wrong."
   So talked they, while to sacred Ilium came   635
Phœbus Apollo; 'twas his charge to watch
The well-built city's ramparts, lest the Greeks
That day should lay it waste against the will
Of fate. The other gods went back to heaven,
Some angry, some exulting. They sat down   640
Beside the All-Father, him who darkens heaven
With gathered clouds. Meantime Achilles chased
And slew the Trojans and their firm-paced steeds.
As, when the smoke rolls heavenward from a town
Given by the angry gods a prey to fire,   645
Toil is the lot of all, and bitter woe
The fate of many, such the woe and toil
Caused by Achilles to the sons of Troy.
   The aged Priam from a lofty tower

Beheld the large-limbed son of Peleus range 650
The field, and all the Trojans helplessly
Fleeing in tumult. With a cry of grief
He came from that high station to the ground,
And gave commandment to the sturdy men
Who stood to watch the gates along the wall:— 655
   "Hold the gates open while the flying host
Enter the city; for Achilles comes,
Routing them, near at hand, and we may see
Terrible havoc. But when all our troops
Are once within the walls, and breathe again, 660
Shut the close-fitting portals; for I dread
Lest that fierce warrior rush into our streets."
   He spake: they drew the bolts and opened wide
The gates, and gave a refuge to the host.
Then leaped Apollo forth to meet their flight 665
And rescue them. All faint with burning thirst,
And grimed with dust, they hurried o'er the plain,
And toward the city and its lofty walls,
While eagerly Achilles on their track
Pressed with his spear; his heart was full of rage, 670
And all on fire his spirit with desire
For glory. Then the Greeks had overthrown
The towery Troy, if Phœbus had not moved
Agenor, a young hero, nobly born,
Blameless, and brave, Antenor's son, to meet 675
Achilles. Phœbus breathed into his heart
Courage, as, standing by the youth, he leaned
Against a beechen tree, and, wrapped from sight
In darkness, watched to rescue him from death.
Agenor stood as he beheld approach 680
The mighty spoiler, and, perplexed in mind,
Sighed heavily, and said to his great soul:—
   "Ah me! if with the routed troops I flee
From fierce Achilles, he will overtake
And slay me; I shall die as cowards die. 685
But if I leave the host to be pursued
By Peleus' son, and by another way
Flee from the wall across the plain, until

I reach the lawns of Ida, and am hid
Among its thickets, then I may at eve 690
Bathe in the river and return refreshed
To Troy. But why give way to thoughts like these?
For he may yet observe me as I haste
From Ilium o'er the plain, and his swift feet
May follow; there will then be no escape 695
From death and fate, since he in might of arm
Excels all other men. If now I here
Confront him before Troy, I cannot think
That he is weapon-proof; one life alone
Dwells in him, though Saturnian Jupiter 700
Bestows on him the glory of the day."

   He spake, and firmly waited for the son
Of Peleus; eagerly his fearless heart
Longed for the combat. As a panther leaves
The covert of the wood and comes to meet 705
A huntsman, nor is scared nor put to flight
By noise of baying hounds, not even though
A spear's thrust or a javelin flung from far
Have wounded him, yet, wounded, he fights on,
Until he grapples with his enemy 710
Or perishes,—thus did the noble son
Of the renowned Antenor press to try
His prowess with Achilles, and disdained
To flee before him. Holding his round shield
Before his face, and with his lifted spear 715
Aimed at the Greek, he shouted thus aloud:—

   "Renowned Achilles! thou dost fondly hope
That thou today wilt overthrow the town
Of the magnanimous Trojans. Many toils,
Thou fool! must be endured ere that can be; 720
For we are many and are brave who dwell
Within it, and shall well defend the town
For our beloved parents and our wives
And little ones. Here shalt thou meet thy doom,
Brave as thou art, and terrible in war." 725

   As thus he spake, his powerful hand dismissed
The keen-edged spear, nor missed his aim; it struck

The son of Peleus just below the knee.
The tin of which the greave was newly forged
Rang shrilly, and sent back the brazen point;   730
It could not pierce the armor which a god
Had given. And then the son of Peleus aimed
His weapon at Agenor. Phœbus came
And snatched away his triumph, bearing off
The godlike youth, Agenor, in a veil   735
Of darkness from the perils of the war.
Then he decoyed Achilles from the host
Of Troy; the archer of the skies put on
Agenor's perfect semblance, and appeared
Before the Greek, and fled; his hasty flight   740
Was followed close. Achilles chased the god
Ever before him, yet still near, across
The fruitful fields, to the deep-eddied stream
Of Xanthus; for Apollo artfully
Made it to seem that he should soon o'ertake   745
His flying foe, and thus beguiled him on.
Meantime the routed Trojans gladly thronged
Into the city, filled the streets, and closed
The portals. None now dared without the walls
To wait for others, or remain to know   750
Who had escaped with life, and who were slain
In battle; eagerly they flung themselves
Into the city,—every one whose feet
And knees had borne him from the field alive.

BOOK XXII

THUS were they driven within the city walls
Like frighted fawns, and there dispersing cooled
Their sweaty limbs, and quenched their eager thirst,
And rested on the battlements. The Greeks,
Bearing their shields upon their shoulders, came   5
Close to the ramparts. Hector's adverse fate
Detained him still without the walls of Troy,
And near the Scæan gates. Meantime the god
Apollo to the son of Peleus said:—
   "O son of Peleus! why pursue me thus   10
With thy swift feet,—a mortal man in chase
Of an immortal? That I am a god
Thou seest not yet, but turnest all thy rage
On me, and, having put the host of Troy
To rout, dost think of them no more. They find   15
A refuge in their town, while far astray
Thou wanderest hither. Thou hast not the power
To slay me; I am not of mortal birth."
   The swift Achilles angrily replied:
"O archer-god, thou most unjust of all   20
The immortals! thou hast wronged me, luring me
Aside; since many a warrior I had forced
To bite the dust before they reached the gates
Of Ilium but for thee, who from my grasp
Hast snatched the glory and hast rescued them.   25
Thou didst not fear my vengeance; yet if power

Were given me, I would punish thee for this."
   He spake, and with heroic purpose turned
Toward Ilium. As a steed that wins the race
Flies at his utmost speed across the plain,   30
And whirls along the chariot, with such speed
The son of Peleus moved his rapid feet.
   The aged monarch Priam was the first
To see him as he scoured the plain, and shone
Like to the star which in the autumn time   35
Rises and glows among the lights of heaven
With eminent lustre at the dead of night,—
Orion's Hound they call it,—bright indeed,
And yet of baleful omen, for it brings
Distressing heat to miserable men.   40
So shone the brass upon the warrior's breast
As on he flew. The aged Priam groaned,
And smote his head with lifted hands, and called
Aloud, imploring his beloved son,
Who eagerly before the city gate   45
Waited his foe Achilles. Priam thus,
With outstretched hands, besought him piteously:—
   "O wait not, Hector, my beloved son,
To combat with Pelides, thus alone
And far from succor, lest thou meet thy death,   50
Slain by his hand, for he is mightier far
Than thou art. Would that he, the cruel one,
Were but as much the favorite of the gods
As he is mine! then should the birds of prey
And dogs devour his carcass, and the grief   55
That weighs upon my spirit would depart.
I have been robbed by him of many sons,
Brave youths, whom he has slain or sold as slaves
In distant isles; and now I see no more
Among our host on whom the gates are closed   60
My Polydorus and Lycaon, whom
The peerless dame Laothoë bore to me.
If yet they are within the Grecian camp,
I will redeem their lives with brass and gold;
For I have store, which Altes, the renowned   65

And aged, gave his daughter. If they live
No longer, but have passed to the abode
Of Hades, bitter will our sorrow be,—
Mine and their mother's,—but the popular grief
Will sooner be consoled if thou fall not, 70
Slain by Achilles. Come within the walls,
My son, that thou mayst still be the defence
Of Ilium's sons and daughters, nor increase
The glory of Pelides with the loss
Of thine own life. Have pity upon me, 75
Who only live to suffer,—whom the son
Of Saturn, on the threshold of my age,
Hath destined to endure a thousand griefs,
And then to be destroyed,—to see my sons
Slain by the sword, my daughters dragged away 80
Into captivity, their chambers made
A spoil, our infants dashed against the ground
By cruel hands, the consorts of my sons
Borne off by the ferocious Greeks; and last,
Perchance the very dogs which I have fed 85
Here in my palaces and at my board,
The guardians of my doors, when, by the spear
Or sword, some enemy shall take my life,
And at my threshold leave me stretched a corpse,
Will rend me, and, with savage greediness, 90
Will lap my blood, and in the porch lie down.
When one in prime of youth lies slain in war,
Gashed with the spear, his wounds become him well,
And honor him in all men's eyes; but when
An aged man is slain, and his white head 95
And his white beard and limbs are foully torn
By ravening dogs, there is no sadder sight."
   So the old monarch spake, and with his hands
Tore his gray hair, but moved not Hector thus.
Then came, with lamentations and in tears, 100
The warrior's mother forward. One hand laid
Her bosom bare; she pressed the other hand
Beneath it, sobbed, and spake these wingèd words:—
   "Revere this bosom, Hector, and on me

Have pity. If when thou wert but a babe   105
I ever on this bosom stilled thy cries,
Think of it now, beloved child; avoid
That dreadful chief; withdraw within the walls,
Nor madly think to encounter him alone,
Son of my love and of my womb! If he   110
Should slay thee, I shall not lament thy death
Above thy bier,—I, nor thy noble wife,—
But far from us the greedy dogs will throng
To mangle thee beside the Grecian fleet."
    Thus, weeping bitterly, the aged pair   115
Entreated their dear son, yet moved him not.
He stood and waited for his mighty foe
Achilles, as a serpent at his den,
Fed on the poisons of the wild, awaits
The traveller, and, fierce with hate of man,   120
And glaring fearfully, lies coiled within.
So waited Hector with a resolute heart,
And kept his ground, and, leaning his bright shield
Against a tower that jutted from the walls,
Conferred with his great soul impatiently:—   125
    "Ah me! if I should pass within the walls,
Then will Polydamas be first to cast
Reproach upon me; for he counselled me
To lead the Trojans back into the town
That fatal night which saw Achilles rise   130
To join the war again. I yielded not
To his advice; far better if I had.
Now, since my fatal stubbornness has brought
This ruin on my people, I most dread
The censure of the men and long-robed dames   135
Of Ilium. Men less brave than I will say,
'Foolhardy Hector in his pride has thrown
His people's lives away.' So will they speak,
And better were it for me to return,
Achilles slain, or, slain myself by him,   140
To perish for my country gloriously.
But should I lay aside this bossy shield
And this stout helm, and lean against the wall

This spear, and go to meet the gallant son
Of Peleus, with a promise to restore   145
Helen and all the treasure brought with her
To Troy by Paris, in his roomy ships,—
All that the war was waged for,—that the sons
Of Atreus may convey it hence, besides
Wealth drawn from all the hoards within the town,   150
And to be shared among the Greeks; for I
Would bind the Trojans by a solemn oath
To keep back nothing, but divide the whole—
Whate'er of riches this fair town contains—
Into two parts— But why should I waste thought   155
On plans like these? I must not act the part
Of suppliant to a man who may not show
Regard or mercy, but may hew me down
Defenceless, with my armor laid aside
As if I were a woman. Not with him   160
May I hold parley from a tree or rock,
As youths and maidens with each other hold
Light converse. Better 'twere to rush at once
To combat, and the sooner learn to whom
Olympian Jove decrees the victory."   165
    Such were his thoughts. Achilles now drew near.
Like crested Mars, the warrior-god, he came.
On his right shoulder quivered fearfully
The Pelian ash, and from his burnished mail
There streamed a light as of a blazing fire,   170
Or of the rising sun. When Hector saw,
He trembled, nor could venture to remain,
But left the gates and fled away in fear.
Pelides, trusting to his rapid feet,
Pursued him. As, among the mountain wilds,   175
A falcon, fleetest of the birds of air,
Darts toward a timid dove that wheels away
To shun him by a sidelong flight, while he
Springs after her again and yet again,
And screaming follows, certain of his prey,—   180
Thus onward flew Achilles, while as fast
Fled Hector in dismay, with hurrying feet,

Beside the wall. They passed the Mount of View,
And the wind-beaten fig-tree, and they ran
Along the public way by which the wall   185
Was skirted, till they came where from the ground
The two fair springs of eddying Xanthus rise,—
One pouring a warm stream from which ascends
And spreads a vapor like a smoke from fire;
The other, even in summer, sending forth   190
A current cold as hail, or snow, or ice.
And there were broad stone basins, fairly wrought,
At which, in time of peace, before the Greeks
Had landed on the plain, the Trojan dames
And their fair daughters washed their sumptuous robes.   195
Past these they swept; one fled, and one pursued,—
A brave man fled, a braver followed close,
And swiftly both. Not for a common prize,
A victim from the herd, a bullock's hide,
Such as reward the fleet of foot, they ran,—   200
The race was for the knightly Hector's life.
As firm-paced coursers, that are wont to win,
Fly toward the goal, when some magnificent prize,
A tripod or a damsel, is proposed
In honor of some hero's obsequies,   205
So these flew thrice on rapid feet around
The city of Priam. All the gods of heaven
Looked on, and thus the Almighty Father spake:—
   "Alas! I see a hero dear to me
Pursued around the wall. My heart is grieved   210
For Hector, who has brought so many thighs
Of bullocks to my altar on the side
Of Ida ploughed with glens, or on the heights
Of Ilium. The renowned Achilles now
Is chasing him with rapid feet around   215
The city of Priam. Now bethink yourselves,
And answer. Shall we rescue him from death?
Or shall we doom him, valiant as he is,
To perish by the hand of Peleus' son?"
   Minerva, blue-eyed goddess, answered thus: 220
"O Father, who dost hurl the thunderbolt,

And hide the sky in clouds, what hast thou said?
Wouldst thou reprieve from death a mortal man,
Whose doom is fixed? Then do it; but know this,
That all the other gods will not approve." 225
    Then spake again the Cloud-compeller Jove:
"Tritonia, my dear child, be calm. I spake
Of no design. I would be kind to thee.
Do as thou wilt, and be there no delay."
    He spake; and Pallas from the Olympian peaks, 230
Encouraged by his words in what her thought
Had planned already, downward shot to earth.
Still, with quick steps, the fleet Achilles pressed
On Hector's flight. As when a hound has roused
A fawn from its retreat among the hills, 235
And chases it through glen and forest ground,
And to close thickets, where it skulks in fear
Until he overtake it. Hector thus
Sought vainly to elude the fleet pursuit
Of Peleus' son. As often as he thought, 240
By springing toward the gates of Troy, to gain
Aid from the weapons of his friends who stood
On the tall towers, so often was the Greek
Before him, forcing him to turn away
From Ilium toward the plain. Achilles thus 245
Kept nearest to the city. As in dreams
The fleet pursuer cannot overtake,
Nor the pursued escape, so was it now;
One followed but in vain, the other fled
As fruitlessly. But how could Hector thus 250
Have put aside the imminent doom of death,
Had not Apollo met him once again,
For the last time, and given him strength and speed?
    The great Achilles nodded to his host
A sign that no man should presume to strike 255
At Hector with his weapon, lest perchance
Another, wounding him, should bear away
The glory, and Pelides only wear
The second honors. When the twain had come
For the fourth time beside Scamander's springs, 260

The All-Father raised the golden balance high,
And, placing in the scales two lots which bring
Death's long dark sleep,—one lot for Peleus' son,
And one for knightly Hector,—by the midst
He poised the balance. Hector's fate sank down   265
To Hades, and Apollo left the field.
   The blue-eyed goddess Pallas then approached
The son of Peleus with these wingèd words:—
   "Renowned Achilles, dear to Jupiter!
Now may we, as I hope, at last return   270
To the Achaian army and the fleet
With glory. Hector slain, the terrible
In war. Escape he cannot, even though
The archer-god Apollo fling himself
With passionate entreaty at the feet   275
Of Jove the Ægis-bearer. Stay thou here
And breathe a moment, while I go to him
And lure him hither to encounter thee."
   She spake, and he obeyed, and gladly stood
Propped on the ashen stem of his keen spear;   280
While, passing on, Minerva overtook
The noble Hector. In the outward form,
And with the strong voice of Deïphobus,
She stood by him and spake these wingèd words:—
   "Hard pressed I find thee, brother, by the swift 285
Achilles, who, with feet that never rest,
Pursues thee round the walls of Priam's town.
But let us make a stand and beat him back."
   And then the crested Hector spake in turn:
"Deïphobus, thou ever hast been dear   290
To me beyond my other brethren, sons
Of Hecuba and Priam. Now still more
I honor thee, since thou hast seen my plight,
And for my sake hast ventured forth without
The gates, while all the rest remain within."   295
   And then the blue-eyed Pallas spake again:
"Brother! 'tis true, my father, and the queen,
My mother, and my comrades, clasped my knees
In turn, and earnestly entreated me

That I would not go forth, such fear had fallen 300
On all of them; but I was grieved for thee.
Now let us combat valiantly, nor spare
The weapons that we bear, and we shall learn
Whether Achilles, having slain us both,
Will carry to the fleet our bloody spoil, 305
Or die himself, the victim of thy spear."
   The treacherous goddess spake, and led the way;
And when the advancing chiefs stood face to face,
The crested hero, Hector, thus began:—
   "No longer I avoid thee as of late, 310
O son of Peleus! Thrice around the walls
Of Priam's mighty city have I fled,
Nor dared to wait thy coming. Now my heart
Bids me encounter thee; my time is come
To slay or to be slain. Now let us call 315
The gods to witness, who attest and guard
The covenants of men. Should Jove bestow
On me the victory, and I take thy life,
Thou shalt meet no dishonor at my hands;
But, stripping off the armor, I will send 320
The Greeks thy body. Do the like by me."
   The swift Achilles answered with a frown:
"Accursed Hector, never talk to me
Of covenants. Men and lions plight no faith,
Nor wolves agree with lambs, but each must plan 325
Evil against the other. So between
Thyself and me no compact can exist,
Or understood intent. First, one of us
Must fall and yield his life-blood to the god
Of battles. Summon all thy valor now. 330
A skilful spearman thou hast need to be,
And a bold warrior. There is no escape,
For now doth Pallas doom thee to be slain
By my good spear. Thou shalt repay to me
The evil thou hast done my countrymen,— 335
My friends whom thou hast slaughtered in thy rage."
   He spake, and, brandishing his massive spear,
Hurled it at Hector, who beheld its aim

From where he stood. He stooped, and over him
The brazen weapon passed, and plunged to earth.   340
Unseen by royal Hector, Pallas went
And plucked it from the ground, and brought it back
And gave it to the hands of Peleus' son,
While Hector said to his illustrious foe:—
  "Godlike Achilles, thou hast missed thy mark;   345
Nor hast thou learned my doom from Jupiter,
As thou pretendest. Thou art glib of tongue,
And cunningly thou orderest thy speech,
In hope that I who hear thee may forget
My might and valor. Think not I shall flee,   350
That thou mayst pierce my back; for thou shalt send
Thy spear, if God permit thee, through my breast
As I rush on thee. Now avoid in turn
My brazen weapon. Would that it might pass
Clean through thee, all its length! The tasks of war   355
For us of Troy were lighter for thy death,
Thou pest and deadly foe of all our race!"
  He spake, and, brandishing his massive spear,
Hurled it, nor missed, but in the centre smote
The buckler of Pelides. Far away   360
It bounded from the brass, and he was vexed
To see that the swift weapon from his hand
Had flown in vain. He stood perplexed and sad;
No second spear had he. He called aloud
On the white-bucklered chief, Deïphobus,   365
To bring another; but that chief was far,
And Hector saw that it was so, and said:—
  "Ah me! the gods have summoned me to die.
I thought my warrior-friend, Deïphobus,
Was by my side; but he is still in Troy,   370
And Pallas has deceived me. Now my death
Cannot be far,—is near; there is no hope
Of my escape, for so it pleases Jove
And Jove's great archer-son, who have till now
Delivered me. My hour at last is come;   375
Yet not ingloriously or passively
I die, but first will do some valiant deed,

Of which mankind shall hear in after time."
   He spake, and drew the keen-edged sword that hung,
Massive and finely tempered, at his side,   380
And sprang—as when an eagle high in heaven,
Through the thick cloud, darts downward to the plain
To clutch some tender lamb or timid hare,
So Hector, brandishing that keen-edged sword,
Sprang forward, while Achilles opposite   385
Leaped toward him, all on fire with savage hate,
And holding his bright buckler, nobly wrought,
Before him. On his shining helmet waved
The fourfold crest; there tossed the golden tufts
With which the hand of Vulcan lavishly   390
Had decked it. As in the still hours of night
Hesper goes forth among the host of stars,
The fairest light of heaven, so brightly shone,
Brandished in the right hand of Peleus' son,
The spear's keen blade, as, confident to slay   395
The noble Hector, o'er his glorious form
His quick eye ran, exploring where to plant
The surest wound. The glittering mail of brass
Won from the slain Patroclus guarded well
Each part, save only where the collar-bones   400
Divide the shoulder from the neck, and there
Appeared the throat, the spot where life is most
In peril. Through that part the noble son
Of Peleus drave his spear; it went quite through
The tender neck, and yet the brazen blade   405
Cleft not the windpipe, and the power to speak
Remained. The Trojan fell amid the dust,
And thus Achilles boasted o'er his fall:—
   "Hector, when from the slain Patroclus thou
Didst strip his armor, little didst thou think   410
Of danger. Thou hadst then no fear of me,
Who was not near thee to avenge his death.
Fool! there was left within the roomy ships
A mightier one than he, who should come forth,
The avenger of his blood, to take thy life.   415
Foul dogs and birds of prey shall tear thy flesh;

The Greeks shall honor him with funeral rites."
    And then the crested Hector faintly said:
"I pray thee by thy life, and by thy knees,
And by thy parents, suffer not the dogs   420
To tear me at the galleys of the Greeks.
Accept abundant store of brass and gold,
Which gladly will my father and the queen,
My mother, give in ransom. Send to them
My body, that the warriors and the dames   425
Of Troy may light for me the funeral pile."
    The swift Achilles answered with a frown:
"Nay, by my knees entreat me not, thou cur,
Nor by my parents. I could even wish
My fury prompted me to cut thy flesh   430
In fragments, and devour it, such the wrong
That I have had from thee. There will be none
To drive away the dogs about thy head,
Not though thy Trojan friends should bring to me
Tenfold and twenty-fold the offered gifts,   435
And promise others,—not though Priam, sprung
From Dardanus, should send thy weight in gold.
Thy mother shall not lay thee on thy bier,
To sorrow over thee whom she brought forth;
But dogs and birds of prey shall mangle thee."   440
    And then the crested Hector, dying, said:
"I know thee, and too clearly I foresaw
I should not move thee, for thou hast a heart
Of iron. Yet reflect that for my sake
The anger of the gods may fall on thee,   445
When Paris and Apollo strike thee down,
Strong as thou art, before the Scæan gates."
    Thus Hector spake, and straightway o'er him closed
The night of death; the soul forsook his limbs,
And flew to Hades, grieving for its fate,—   450
So soon divorced from youth and youthful might.
Then said the great Achilles to the dead:—
    "Die thou; and I, whenever it shall please
Jove and the other gods will meet my fate."
    He spake, and, plucking forth his brazen lance,   455

He laid it by, and from the body stripped
The bloody mail. The thronging Greeks beheld
With wonder Hector's tall and stately form,
And no one came who did not add a wound;
And, looking to each other, thus they said:—   460
  "How much more tamely Hector now endures
Our touch than when he set the fleet on fire!"
  Such were the words of those who smote the dead;
But now, when swift Achilles from the corpse
Had stripped the armor, he stood forth among   465
The Achaian host, and spake these wingèd words:—
  "Leaders and princes of the Grecian host!
Since we, my friends, by favor of the gods,
Have overcome the chief who wrought more harm
To us than all the rest, let us assault   470
The town, and learn what they of Troy intend,—
Whether their troops will leave the citadel
Since he is slain, or hold it with strong hand,
Though Hector is no more. But why give thought
To plans like these while yet Patroclus lies   475
A corse unwept, unburied, at the fleet?
I never will forget him while I live
And while these limbs have motion. Though below
In Hades they forget the dead, yet I
Will there remember my beloved friend.   480
Now then, ye youths of Greece, move on and chant
A pæan, while, returning to the fleet,
We bring great glory with us; we have slain
The noble Hector, whom, throughout their town,
The Trojans ever worshipped like a god."   485
  He spake, and, planning in his mind to treat
The noble Hector shamefully, he bored
The sinews of his feet between the heel
And ankle; drawing through them leathern thongs
He bound them to the car, but left the head   490
To trail in dust. And then he climbed the car,
Took in the shining mail, and lashed to speed
The coursers. Not unwillingly they flew.
Around the dead, as he was dragged along,

The dust arose; his dark locks swept the ground. 495
That head, of late so noble in men's eyes,
Lay deep amid the dust, for Jove that day
Suffered the foes of Hector to insult
His corse in his own land. His mother saw,
And tore her hair, and flung her lustrous veil 500
Away, and uttered piercing shrieks. No less
His father, who so loved him, piteously
Bewailed him; and in all the streets of Troy
The people wept aloud, with such lament
As if the towery Ilium were in flames 505
Even to its loftiest roofs. They scarce could keep
The aged king within, who, wild with grief,
Struggled to rush through the Dardanian gates,
And, rolling in the dust, entreated all
Who stood around him, calling them by name:— 510
    "Refrain, my friends, though kind be your intent.
Let me go forth alone, and at the fleet
Of Greece will I entreat this man of blood
And violence. He may perchance be moved
With reverence for my age, and pity me 515
In my gray hairs; for such a one as I
Is Peleus, his own father, by whose care
This Greek was reared to be a scourge to Troy,
And, more than all, a cause of grief to me,
So many sons of mine in life's fresh prime 520
Have fallen by his hand. I mourn for them,
But not with such keen anguish as I mourn
For Hector. Sorrow for his death will bring
My soul to Hades. Would that he had died
Here in my arms! this solace had been ours,— 525
His most unhappy mother and myself
Had stooped to shed these tears upon his bier."
    He spake, and wept, and all the citizens
Wept with him. Hecuba among the dames
Took up the lamentation, and began:— 530
    "Why do I live, my son, when thou art dead,
And I so wretched?—thou who wert my boast
Ever, by night and day, where'er I went,

And whom the Trojan men and matrons called
Their bulwark, honoring thee as if thou wert   535
A god. They glory in thy might no more,
Since Fate and Death have overtaken thee."
    Weeping she spake. Meantime Andromache
Had heard no tidings of her husband yet.
No messenger had even come to say   540
That he was still without the gates. She sat
In a recess of those magnificent halls,
And wove a twofold web of brilliant hues,
On which were scattered flowers of rare device;
And she had given her bright-haired maidens charge   545
To place an ample caldron on the fire,
That Hector, coming from the battle-field,
Might find the warm bath ready. Thoughtless one!
She knew not that the blue-eyed archer-queen,
Far from the bath prepared for him, had slain   550
Her husband by the hand of Peleus' son.
She heard the shrieks, the wail upon the tower,
Trembled in every limb, and quickly dropped
The shuttle, saying to her bright-haired maids:—
    "Come with me, two of you, that I may learn   555
What now has happened. 'Tis my mother's voice
That I have heard. My heart leaps to my mouth;
My limbs fail under me. Some deadly harm
Hangs over Priam's sons; far be the hour
When I shall hear of it. And yet I fear   560
Lest that Achilles, having got between
The daring Hector and the city gates,
May drive him to the plain alone, and quell
The desperate valor that was ever his;
For never would he keep the ranks, but ranged   565
Beyond them, and gave way to no man's might."
    She spake, and from the royal mansion rushed
Distractedly, and with a beating heart.
Her maids went with her. When she reached the tower
And throng of men, and, standing on the wall,   570
Looked forth, she saw her husband dragged away
Before the city. Toward the Grecian fleet

The swift steeds drew him. Sudden darkness came
Over her eyes, and in a breathless swoon
She sank away and fell. The ornaments   575
Dropped from her brow,—the wreath, the woven band,
The net, the veil which golden Venus gave
That day when crested Hector wedded her,
Dowered with large gifts, and led her from her home,
Eëtion's palace. Round her in a throng   580
Her sisters of the house of Priam pressed,
And gently raised her in that deathlike swoon.
But when she breathed again, and to its seat
The conscious mind returned, as in their arms
She lay, with sobs and broken speech she said:—   585
　"Hector,—O wretched me!—we both were born
To sorrow; thou at Troy, in Priam's house,
And I at Thebè in Eëtion's halls,
By woody Placos. From a little child
He reared me there,—unhappy he, and I   590
Unhappy! O that I had ne'er been born!
Thou goest down to Hades and the depths
Of earth, and leavest me in thine abode,
Widowed, and never to be comforted.
Thy son, a speechless babe, to whom we two   595
Gave being,—hapless parents!—cannot have
Thy loving guardianship now thou art dead,
Nor be a joy to thee. Though he survive
The cruel warfare which the sons of Greece
Are waging, hard and evil yet will be   600
His lot hereafter; others will remove
His landmarks and will make his fields their own.
The day in which a boy is fatherless
Makes him companionless; with downcast eyes
He wanders, and his cheeks are stained with tears. 605
Unfed he goes where sit his father's friends,
And plucks one by the cloak, and by the robe
Another. One who pities him shall give
A scanty draught, which only wets his lips,
But not his palate; while another boy,   610
Whose parents both are living, thrusts him thence

With blows and vulgar clamor: 'Get thee gone!
Thy father is not with us at the feast.'
Then to his widowed mother shall return
Astyanax in tears, who not long since 615
Was fed, while sitting in his father's lap,
On marrow and the delicate fat of lambs.
And ever when his childish sports had tired
The boy, and sleep came stealing over him,
He slumbered, softly cushioned, on a couch 620
And in his nurse's arms, his heart at ease
And satiate with delights. But now thy son
Astyanax,—whom so the Trojans name
Because thy valor guarded gate and tower,—
Thy care withdrawn, shall suffer many things. 625
While far from those who gave thee birth, beside
The roomy ships of Greece, the restless worms
Shall make thy flesh their banquet when the dogs
Have gorged themselves. Thy garments yet remain
Within the palace, delicately wrought 630
And graceful, woven by the women's hands;
And these, since thou shalt put them on no more,
Nor wear them in thy death, I burn with fire
Before the Trojan men and dames; and all
Shall see how gloriously thou wert arrayed." 635
    Weeping she spake, and with her wept her maids.

BOOK XXIII

SO mourned they in the city; but the Greeks,
When they had reached the fleet and Hellespont,
Dispersed, repairing each one to his ship,
Save that Achilles suffered not his band
Of Myrmidons to part in disarray.　　　　　　　　　5
And thus the chief enjoined his warrior friends:—
　"Myrmidons, gallant knights, my cherished friends!
Let us not yet unyoke our firm-paced steeds,
But bring them with the chariots, and bewail
Patroclus with the honors due the dead,　　　　　10
And, when we have indulged in grief, release
Our steeds and take our evening banquet here."
　He spake, and led by him the host broke forth
In lamentation. Thrice around the dead,
Weeping, they drave their steeds with stately manes,　15
While Thetis in their hearts awoke the sense
Of hopeless loss; their tears bedewed the sands,
And dropped upon their arms, so brave was he
For whom they sorrowed. Peleus' son began
The mourning; on the breast of his dead friend　　20
He placed his homicidal hands, and said:—
　"Hail thou, Patroclus, even amid the shades!
For now shall I perform what once I vowed:
That, dragging Hector hither, I will give
His corse to dogs, and they shall rend his flesh;　　25
And at thy funeral pile there shall be slain

Twelve noble Trojan youths, to avenge thy death."
   So spake he, meditating outrages
To noble Hector's corse, which he had flung
Beside the bier of Menœtiades,
Amid the dust. The Myrmidons unbraced
Their shining brazen armor, and unyoked
Their neighing steeds, and sat in thick array
Beside the ship of swift Æacides,
While he set forth a sumptuous funeral feast.
Many a white ox, that day, beneath the axe
Fell to the earth, and many bleating goats
And sheep were slain, and many fattened swine,
White-toothed, were stretched to roast before the flame
Of Vulcan, and around the corse the earth
Floated with blood. Meantime the Grecian chiefs
To noble Agamemnon's royal tent
Led the swift son of Peleus, though he went
Unwillingly, such anger for the death
Of his companion burned within his heart.
As soon as they had reached his tent, the king
Bade the clear-throated heralds o'er the fire
Place a huge tripod, that Pelides there
Might wash away the bloody stains he bore.
Yet would he not, and with an oath replied:—
   "No! by the greatest and the best of gods,
By Jupiter, I may not plunge my head
Into the bath before I lay my friend
Patroclus on the fire, and heap his mound,
And till my hair is shorn; for never more
In life will be so great a sorrow mine.
But now attend we to this mournful feast.
And with the morn, O king of men, command
That wood be brought, and all things duly done
Which may beseem a warrior who goes down
Into the lower darkness. Let the flames
Seize fiercely and consume him from our sight,
And leave the people to the tasks of war."
   He spake; they hearkened and obeyed, and all
Prepared with diligent hands the meal, and each

Sat down and took his portion of the feast.
And when their thirst and hunger were allayed,
Most to their tents betook them and to rest.
But Peleus' son, lamenting bitterly,
Lay down among his Myrmidons, beside					70
The murmuring ocean, in the open space,
Where plashed the billows on the beach. And there,
When slumber, bringing respite from his cares,
Came softly and enfolded him,—for much
His shapely limbs were wearied with the chase					75
Of Hector round the windy Ilium's walls,—
The soul of his poor friend Patroclus came,
Like him in all things,—stature, beautiful eyes,
And voice, and garments which he wore in life.
Beside his head the vision stood and spake:—					80
  "Achilles, sleepest thou, forgetting me?
Never of me unmindful in my life,
Thou dost neglect me dead. O, bury me
Quickly, and give me entrance through the gates
Of Hades; for the souls, the forms of those					85
Who live no more, repulse me, suffering not
That I should join their company beyond
The river, and I now must wander round
The spacious portals of the House of Death.
Give me thy hand, I pray; for never more					90
Shall I return to earth when once the fire
Shall have consumed me. Never shall we take
Counsel together, living, as we sit
Apart from our companions; the hard fate
Appointed me at birth hath drawn me down.					95
Thou too, O godlike man, wilt fall beneath
The ramparts of the noble sons of Troy.
Yet this I ask, and if thou wilt obey,
This I command thee,—not to let my bones
Be laid apart from thine. As we were reared					100
Under thy roof together, from the time
When first Menœtius brought thee, yet a boy,
From Opus, where I caused a sorrowful death;—
For by my hand, when wrangling at the dice,

Another boy, son of Amphidamas, 105
Was slain without design,—and Peleus made
His halls my home, and reared me tenderly,
And made me thy companion;—so at last
May one receptacle, the golden vase
Given by thy gracious mother, hold our bones." 110
  The swift Achilles answered: "O most loved
And honored, wherefore art thou come, and why
Dost thou command me thus? I shall fulfil
Obediently thy wish; yet draw thou near,
And let us give at least a brief embrace, 115
And so indulge our grief." He said, and stretched
His longing arms to clasp the shade. In vain;
Away like smoke it went, with gibbering cry,
Down to the earth. Achilles sprang upright,
Astonished, clapped his hands, and sadly said:— 120
  "Surely there dwell within the realm below
Both soul and form, though bodiless. All night
Hath stood the spirit of my hapless friend
Patroclus near me, sad and sorrowful,
And asking many duties at my hands, 125
A marvellous semblance of the living man."
  He spake, and moved the hearts of all to grief
And lamentation. Rosy-fingered Morn
Dawned on them as around the hapless dead
They stood and wept. Then Agamemnon sent 130
In haste from all the tents the mules and men
To gather wood, and summoned to the task
Meriones, himself a gallant chief,
Attendant on the brave Idomeneus.
These went with woodmen's axes and with ropes 135
Well twisted, and before them went the mules.
O'er steep, o'er glen, by straight, by winding ways,
They journeyed till they reached the woodland wilds
Of Ida fresh with springs, and quickly felled
With the keen steel the towering oaks that came 140
Crashing to earth. Then, splitting the great trunks,
They bound them on the mules, that beat the earth
With hasty footsteps through the tangled wood,

Impatient for the plain. Each woodcutter
Shouldered a tree, for so Meriones, 145
Companion of the brave Idomeneus,
Commanded, and at last they laid them down
In order on the shore, where Peleus' son
Planned that a mighty sepulchre should rise
Both for his friend Patroclus and himself. 150
    So brought they to the spot vast heaps of wood,
And sat them down, a numerous crowd. But then
Achilles bade his valiant Myrmidons
Put on their brazen mail and yoke their steeds.
At once they rose, and put their harness on, 155
And they who fought from chariots climbed their seats
With those who reined the steeds. These led the van,
And after them a cloud of men on foot
By thousands followed. In the midst was borne
Patroclus by his comrades. Cutting off 160
Their hair, they strewed it, covering the dead.
Behind the corpse, Achilles in his hands
Sustained the head, and wept, for on that day
He gave to Hades his most cherished friend.
    Now when they reached the spot which Peleus' son 165
Had chosen, they laid down the dead, and piled
The wood around him, while the swift of foot,
The great Achilles, bent on other thoughts,
Standing apart, cut off his amber hair,
Which for the river Sperchius he had long 170
Nourished to ample growth, and, sighing, turned
His eyes upon the dark-blue sea, and said:—
    "Sperchius, in vain my father made a vow
That I, returning to my native shore,
Should bring my hair, an offering to thee, 175
And slay a consecrated hecatomb,
And burn a sacrifice of fifty rams,
Beside the springs where in a sacred field
Thy fragrant altar stands. Such was the vow
Made by the aged man, yet hast thou not 180
Fulfilled his wish. And now, since I no more
Shall see my native land, the land I love,

Let the slain hero bear these locks away."
   He spake, and in his dear companion's hands
He placed the hair, and all around were moved   185
To deeper grief; the setting sun had left
The host lamenting, had not Peleus' son
Addressed Atrides, standing at his side:—
   "Atrides, thou whose word the Greeks obey
Most readily, all mourning has an end.   190
Dismiss the people from the pyre to take
Their evening meal, while we with whom it rests
To pay these mournful duties to the dead
Will close the rites; but let the chiefs remain."
   This when the monarch Agamemnon heard,   195
Instantly he dismissed to their good ships
The people. They who had the dead in charge
Remained, and heaped the wood, and built a pyre
A hundred feet each way from side to side.
With sorrowful hearts they raised and laid the corse   200
Upon the summit. Then they flayed and dressed
Before it many fallings of the flock,
And oxen with curved feet and crooked horns.
From these magnanimous Achilles took
The fat, and covered with it carefully   205
The dead from head to foot. Beside the bier,
And leaning toward it, jars of honey and oil
He placed, and flung, with many a deep-drawn sigh,
Twelve high-necked steeds upon the pile. Nine hounds
There were, which from the table of the prince   210
Were daily fed; of these Achilles struck
The heads from two, and laid them on the wood,
And after these, and last, twelve gallant sons
Of the brave Trojans, butchered by the sword;
For he was bent on evil. To the pile   215
He put the iron violence of fire,
And, wailing, called by name the friend he loved:—
   "Rejoice, Patroclus, even in the land
Of souls. Lo! I perform the vow I made;
Twelve gallant sons of the brave men of Troy   220
The fire consumes with thee. For Hector's corse,

The flames shall not devour it, but the dogs."
  Such was his threat; but Hector was not made
The prey of dogs, for Venus, born to Jove,
Drave off by night and day the ravenous tribe,   225
And with a rosy and ambrosial oil
Anointed him, that he might not be torn
When dragged along the earth. Above the spot,
And all around it, where the body lay,
Phœbus Apollo drew a veil of clouds   230
Reaching from heaven, that on his limbs the flesh
And sinews might not stiffen in the sun.
  The flame seized not upon the funeral pile
Of the dead chief. Pelides, swift of foot,
Bethought him of another rite. He stood   235
Apart, and offered vows to the two winds,
Boreas and Zephyr. Promising to bring
Fair offerings to their shrines, and pouring out
Libations from a golden cup, he prayed
That they would haste and wrap the pile in flames,   240
And burn the dead to ashes. At his prayer
Fleet Iris on a message to the Winds
Took instant wing. They sat within the halls
Of murmuring Zephyr, at a solemn feast.
There Iris lighted on the threshold-stone.   245
As soon as they beheld her, each arose
And bade her sit beside him. She refused
To seat her at the banquet, and replied:—
  "Not now; for I again must take my way
Over the ocean currents to the land   250
Where dwell the Æthiopians, who adore
The gods with hecatombs, to take my share
Of sacrifice. Achilles supplicates,
With promise of munificent offerings,
Boreas and sounding Zephyrus to come   255
And blow the funeral structure into flames
On which, bewailed by all the Grecian host,
Patroclus lies, and waits to be consumed."
  So spake she, and departed. Suddenly
Arose the Winds with tumult, driving on   260

The clouds before them. Soon they reached the deep;
Beneath the violence of their sounding breath
The billows heaved. They swept the fertile fields
Of Troas, and descended on the pyre,
And mightily it blazed with fearful roar.   265
All night they howled and tossed the flames. All night
Stood swift Achilles, holding in his hand
A double beaker; from a golden jar
He dipped the wine, and poured it forth, and steeped
The earth around, and called upon the soul   270
Of his unhappy friend. As one laments
A newly married son upon whose corse
The flames are feeding, and whose death has made
His parents wretched, so did Peleus' son,
Burning the body of his comrade, mourn,   275
As round the pyre he moved with frequent sighs.

  Now when the star that ushers in the day
Appeared, and after it the morning, clad
In saffron robes, had overspread the sea,
The pyre sank wasted, and the flames arose   280
No longer, and the winds, departing, flew
Homeward across the Thracian sea, which tossed
And roared with swollen billows as they went.
And now Pelides from the pyre apart
Weary lay down, and gentle slumber soon   285
Came stealing over him. Meantime the Greeks
Gathered round Agamemnon, and the stir
And bustle of their coming woke the chief,
Who sat upright and thus addressed his friends:—
    "Atrides, and all ye who lead the hosts   290
Of Greece! our task is, first to quench the pyre
With dark red wine where'er the flames have spread,
And next to gather, with discerning care,
The bones of Menœtiades. And these
May well be known; for in the middle space   295
He lay, and round about him, and apart
Upon the border, were the rest consumed,—
The bodies of the captives and the steeds.
Be his enclosed within a golden vase,

And wrapped around with caul, a double fold, 300
Till I too pass into the realm of Death.
And be a tomb not over-spacious reared,
But of becoming size, which afterward
Ye whom we leave behind in our good ships,
When we are gone, will build more broad and high." 305
  So spake the swift Pelides, and the chiefs
Complied; and first they quenched with dark red wine
The pyre, where'er the flames had spread, and where
Lay the deep ashes; then, with many tears,
Gathered the white bones of their gentle friend, 310
And laid them in a golden vase, wrapped round
With caul, a double fold. Within the tents
They placed them softly, wrapped in delicate lawn,
Then drew a circle for the sepulchre,
And, laying its foundations to enclose 315
The pyre, they heaped the earth, and, having reared
A mound, withdrew. Achilles yet detained
The multitude, and made them all sit down,
A vast assembly. From the ships he brought
The prizes,—caldrons, tripods, steeds, and mules, 320
Oxen in sturdy pairs, and graceful maids,
And shining steel. Then for the swiftest steeds
A princely prize he offered first,—a maid
Of peerless form, and skilled in household arts,
And a two-handled tripod of a size 325
For two-and-twenty measures. He gave out
The second prize,—a mare unbroken yet,
Of six years old, and pregnant with a mule.
For the third winner in the race he staked
A caldron that had never felt the fire, 330
Holding four measures, beautiful, and yet
Untarnished. For the fourth, he offered gold,
Two talents. For the fifth, and last, remained
A double vessel never touched by fire.
He rose and stood, and thus addressed the Greeks:— 335
  "Atrides, and ye other well-armed Greeks,
These prizes lie within the chariot-course,
And wait the charioteers. Were but these games

In honor of another, then would I
Contend, and win and carry to my tent   340
The first among these prizes. For my steeds,
Ye know, surpass the rest in speed, since they
Are of immortal birth, by Neptune given
To Peleus, and by him in turn bestowed
On me his son. But I and they will keep   345
Aloof; they miss their skilful charioteer,
Who washed in limpid water from the fount
Their manes, and moistened them with softening oil.
And now they mourn their friend, and sadly stand
With drooping heads and manes that touch the ground.   350
Let such of you as trust in their swift steeds
And their strong cars prepare to join the games."
   Pelides spake: the abler charioteers
Arose, and, first of all, the king of men,
Eumelus, eminent in horsemanship,   355
The dear son of Admetus. Then arose
The valiant son of Tydeus, Diomed,
And led beneath the yoke the Trojan steeds
Won from Æneas when Apollo saved
That chief from death. The son of Atreus next,   360
The noble Menelaus, yellow-haired,
Brought two swift coursers underneath the yoke,
King Agamemnon's Æthè, and with her
His own Podargus. Echepolus once,
Anchises' son, sent Æthè as a gift   365
To Agamemnon, that he might be free
From following with the army to the heights
Of Ilium, and enjoy the ease he loved;
For Jove had given him wealth, and he abode
On Sicyon's plains. Now, eager for the race,   370
She took the yoke. Antilochus, the fourth,
The gallant son of the magnanimous king,
Neleian Nestor, harnessed next his steeds
With stately manes. Swift coursers that were foaled
At Pylus drew his chariot. To his side   375
His father came and stood, and spake and gave
Wise counsels, though the youth himself was wise:—

"Antilochus, I cannot doubt that Jove
And Neptune both have loved thee, teaching thee,
Young as thou art, all feats of horsemanship. 380
Small is the need to instruct thee. Thou dost know
Well how to turn the goal, and yet thy steeds
Are slow, and ill for thee may be the event.
Their steeds are swift, yet have they never learned
To govern them with greater skill than thou. 385
Now then, dear son, bethink thee heedfully
Of all precautions, lest thou miss the prize.
By skill the woodman, rather than by strength,
Brings down the oak; by skill the pilot guides
His wind-tossed galley over the dark sea; 390
And thus by skill the charioteer o'ercomes
His rival. He who trusts too much his steeds
And chariot lets them veer from side to side
Along the course, nor keeps a steady rein
Straight on, while one expert in horsemanship, 395
Though drawn by slower horses, carefully
Observes the goal, and closely passes it,
Nor fails to know how soon to turn his course,
Drawing the leathern reins, and steadily
Keeps on, and watches him who goes before. 400
Now must I show the goal which, easily
Discerned, will not escape thine eye. It stands
An ell above the ground, a sapless post,
Of oak or larch,—a wood of slow decay
By rain, and at its foot on either side 405
Lies a white stone; there narrow is the way,
But level is the race-course all around.
The monument it is of one long dead,
Or haply it has been in former days
A goal, as the swift-footed Peleus' son 410
Has now appointed it. Approach it near,
Driving thy chariot close upon its foot,
Then in thy seat lean gently to the left
And cheer the right-hand horse, and ply the lash,
And give him a loose rein, yet firmly keep 415
The left-hand courser close beside the goal,—

So close that the wheel's nave may seem to touch
The summit of the post; yet strike thou not
The stone beside it, lest thou lame thy steeds
And break the chariot, to thy own disgrace   420
And laughter of the others. My dear son,
Be on thy guard; for if thou pass the goal
Before the rest, no man in the pursuit
Can overtake or pass thee, though he drave
The noble courser of Adrastus, named   425
Arion the swift-footed, which a god
Bade spring to life, or those of matchless speed
Reared here in Ilium by Laomedon."
   Neleian Nestor spake, and, having thus
Given all the needful cautions, took his seat   430
In his own place. Meriones, the fifth,
Harnessed his steeds with stately manes, and all
Mounted their chariots. Lots were cast; the son
Of Peleus shook the helmet, and the lot
Of Nestor's son, Antilochus, leaped forth;   435
And next the lot of King Eumelus came;
And Menelaus, mighty with the spear,
Had the third lot; Meriones was next;
And to the bravest of them all, the son
Of Tydeus, fell the final lot and place.   440
They stood in order, while Achilles showed
The goal far off upon the level plain,
And near it, as the umpire of the race,
He placed the godlike Phœnix, who had been
His father's armor-bearer, to observe   445
With judging eye, and bring a true report.
   All raised at once the lash above their steeds,
And smote them with the reins, and cheered them on
With vehement cries. Across the plain they swept,
Far from the fleet; beneath them rose the dust,   450
A cloud, a tempest, and their tossing manes
Were lifted by the wind. And now the cars
Touched earth, and now were flung into the air.
Erect the drivers stood, with beating hearts,
Eager for victory, each encouraging   455

His steeds, that flew beneath the shroud of dust.
  But when they turned their course, and swiftly ran
Back to the hoary deep to close the course,
Well did the skill of every chief appear.
They put their horses to the utmost speed, 460
And then did the quick-footed steeds that drew
Eumelus bear him on beyond the rest.
But with his Trojan coursers Diomed
Came next, so near it seemed that they would mount
The car before them, and upon the back 465
And ample shoulders of Eumelus smote
Their steaming breath; for as they ran their heads
Leaned over him. And then would Diomed
Have passed him by, or would at least have made
The victory doubtful, had not Phœbus struck, 470
In his displeasure, from the hero's hand
The shining scourge. It fell, and to his eyes
Started indignant tears; for now he saw
The others gaining on him, while the speed
Of his own steeds, which feared the lash no more, 475
Was slackened. Yet Apollo's strategem
Was not unseen by Pallas, who o'ertook
The shepherd of the people, and restored
The scourge he dropped, and put into his steeds
New spirit. In her anger she approached 480
Eumelus, snapped his yoke, and caused his mares
To start asunder from the track; the pole
Was dashed into the ground, and from the seat
The chief was flung beside the wheel, his mouth,
Elbows, and nostrils torn, his forehead bruised. 485
Grief filled his eyes with tears and choked his voice,
While Diomed drave by his firm-paced steeds,
Outstripping all the rest; for Pallas nerved
Their limbs with vigor, and bestowed on him
Abundant glory. After him the son 490
Of Atreus, fair-haired Menelaus, came,
While Nestor's son cheered on his father's steeds:—
  "On, on! press onward with your utmost speed!
Not that I bid you strive against the steeds

Of warlike Diomed, for Pallas gives 495
Swiftness to them and glory to the man
Who holds the reins; but let us overtake
The horses of Atrides, nor submit
To be thus distanced, lest the victory
Of the mare Æthè cover you with shame. 500
Fleet as ye are, why linger? This at least
I tell you, and my words will be fulfilled:
Look not for kindly care at Nestor's hands,
That shepherd of the people, but for death
With the sharp steel, if through your fault we take 505
A meaner prize. Then onward and away,
With all your strength, for this is my design,—
To pass by Menelaus where the way
Is narrow, and he cannot thwart my plan."

   He spake, and they who feared their master's threat 510
Mended their speed awhile. The warlike son
Of Nestor saw just then the narrow pass
Within the hollow way, a furrow ploughed
By winter floods, which there had torn the course
And deepened it. Atrides, to avoid 515
The clash of wheels, drave thither; thither too
Antilochus—who turned his firm-paced steeds
A little from the track in which they ran—
Followed him close. Atrides saw with fear,
And shouted to Antilochus aloud:— 520

   "Antilochus, thou drivest rashly; rein
Thy horses in. The way is narrow here,
But soon will broaden, and thou then canst pass.
Beware lest with thy chariot-wheels thou dash
Against my own, and harm befall us both." 525

   He spake; but all the more Antilochus
Urged on his coursers with the lash, as if
He had not heard. As far as flies a quoit
Thrown from the shoulder of a vigorous youth
Who tries his strength, so far they ran abreast. 530
The horses of Atrides then fell back;
He slacked the reins; for much he feared the steeds
Would dash against each other in the way,

And overturn the sumptuous cars, and fling
The charioteers contending for the prize   535
Upon the dusty track. With angry words
The fair-haired Menelaus chided thus:—
  "Antilochus, there is no man so prone
As thou to mischief, and we greatly err,
We Greeks, who call thee wise. Go now, and yet   540
Thou shalt not take the prize without an oath."
  Again he spake, encouraging his steeds:
"Check not your speed, nor sorrowfully stand:
Their feet and knees will fail with weariness
Before your own; they are no longer young."   545
  He spake; the coursers, honoring his voice,
Ran with fresh speed, and soon were near to those
Of Nestor's son. Meantime the assembled Greeks
Sat looking where the horses scoured the plain
And filled the air with dust. Idomeneus,   550
The lord of Crete, descried the coursers first,
For on a height he sat above the crowd.
He heard the chief encouraging his steeds,
And knew him, and he marked before the rest
A courser, chestnut-colored save a spot   555
Upon the middle of the forehead, white,
And round as the full moon. And then he stood
Upright, and from his place harangued the Greeks:—
  "O friends, the chiefs and leaders of the Greeks,
Am I the sole one that descries the steeds,   560
Or do ye also? Those who lead the race,
I think, are not the same, and with them comes
A different charioteer. The mares, which late
Were foremost, may have somewhere come to harm.
I saw them first to turn the goal, and now   565
I can no more discern them, though my sight
Sweeps the whole Trojan plain from side to side.
Either the charioteer has dropped the reins,
And could not duly round the goal, or else
Met with disaster at the turn, o'erthrown,   570
His chariot broken, and the affrighted mares
Darting, unmastered, madly from the way.

But rise: look forth yourselves. I cannot well
Discern, but think the charioteer is one
Who, born of an Ætolian stock, commands   575
Among the Argives,—valiant Diomed,
A son of Tydeus, tamer of wild steeds."
   And Ajax, swift of foot, Oïleus' son,
Answered with bitter words: "Idomeneus,
Why this perpetual prating? Far away   580
The mares with rapid hoofs are traversing
The plain, and thou art not the youngest here
Among the Argives, nor hast such sharp eyes
Beneath thy brows, yet must thou chatter still.
Among thy betters here it ill becomes   585
A man like thee to be so free of tongue.
The coursers of Eumelus, which at first
Outran the rest, are yet before them all,
And he is drawing near and holds the reins."
   The Cretan leader angrily rejoined: 590
"Ajax, thou railer, first in brawls, yet known
As in all else below the other Greeks,
A man of brutal mood, come, let us stake
A tripod or a caldron, and appoint
As umpire Agamemnon, to decide   595
Which horses are the foremost in the race,
That when thou losest thou mayst be convinced."
   He spake: Oïlean Ajax, swift of foot,
Started in anger from his seat, to cast
Reproaches back, and long and fierce had been   600
The quarrel if Achilles had not risen,
And said: "No longer let this strife go on,
Idomeneus and Ajax! Ill such words
Become you; ye would blame in other men
What now ye do. Sit then among the rest,   605
And watch the race; for soon the charioteers
Contending for the victory will be here,
And each of you—for well ye know the steeds
Of the Greek chieftains—for himself will see
Whose hold the second place, and whose are first."   610
   He spake: Tydides rapidly drew near,

Lashing the shoulders of his steeds, and they
Seemed in the air as, to complete the course,
They flew along, and flung the dust they trod
Back on the charioteer. All bright with tin   615
And gold, the car rolled after them; its tires
Made but a slender trace in the light dust,
So rapidly they ran. And now he stopped
Within the circle, while his steeds were steeped
In sweat, that fell in drops from neck and breast.   620
Then from his shining seat he leaped, and laid
His scourge against the yoke. Brave Sthenelus
Came forward, and at once received the prize
For Diomed, and bade his comrades lead
The maid away, and in their arms bear off   625
The tripod, while himself unyoked the steeds.
    Next the Neleian chief, Antilochus,
Came with his coursers. More by fraud than speed
He distanced Menelaus, yet that chief
Drave his fleet horses near him. Just so far   630
As runs the wheel behind a steed that draws
His master swiftly o'er the plain, his tail
Touching the tire with its long hairs, and small
The space between them as the spacious plain
Is traversed, Menelaus just so far   635
Was distanced by renowned Antilochus.
For though at first he fell as far behind
As a quoit's cast, yet was he gaining ground
Rapidly, now that Agamemnon's mare,
Æthè the stately-maned, increased her speed,   640
And Menelaus, had the race for both
Been longer, would have passed his rival by,
Nor left the victory doubtful. After him,
A spear's throw distant, came Meriones,
The gallant comrade of Idomeneus,   645
Whose full-maned steeds were slower than the rest,
And he unskilled in contests such as these.
And last of all Eumelus came. He drew
His showy chariot after him, and drave
His steeds before him. Great Achilles saw   650

With pity, and from where he stood among
The Greeks addressed him thus with wingèd words:—
  "The ablest horseman brings his steeds the last,
But let us, as is just, confer on him
The second prize; Tydides takes the first."   655
  He spake, and all approved his words; and now
The mare, to please the Greeks, had been bestowed
Upon Eumelus, if Antilochus,
Son of magnanimous Nestor, had not risen
To plead for justice with Achilles thus:—   660
  "Achilles, I shall deem it grave offence
If thou fulfil thy word; for thou wilt take
My prize, because thou seest that this man's car
And his fleet steeds have suffered injury,
Though he be skilful. Yet he should have prayed   665
To the good gods; then had he not been seen
Bringing his steeds the last. But if thou feel
Compassion for him, and if so thou please,
Large store of brass and gold is in thy tent,
And thine are cattle, and handmaidens thine,   670
And firm-paced steeds; hereafter give of these
A nobler largess, or bestow it now,
And hear the Greeks applaud thee. But this prize
I yield not; let the warrior who may claim
To take it try with me his strength of arm."   675
  He ceased: the noble son of Peleus smiled,
And, pleased to see Antilochus succeed,—
For he was a beloved friend,—he spake
These wingèd words: "Since, then, Antilochus,
Thou wilt that I bestow some recompense   680
Upon Eumelus from my store, I give
The brazen corselet which my arm in war
Took from Asteropæus, edged around
With shining tin,—a gift of no mean price."
  He ceased, and sent his friend Automedon   685
To bring it from the tent. He went and brought
The corselet, and Eumelus joyfully
Received it from Achilles. Then arose,
Among them Menelaus, ill at ease,

And angry with Antilochus. He took
The sceptre from a herald's hand, who hushed
The crowd to silence, and the hero spake:—
  "Antilochus, who wert till now discreet,
What hast thou done? Thou hast disgraced my skill
And wronged my steeds by thrusting in thine own,
Which were less fleet, before them. Now, ye chiefs
And leaders of the Achaians, judge between
This man and me, and judge impartially,
Lest that some warrior of the Greeks should say
That Menelaus, having overcome
Antilochus by falsehood, led away
The mare a prize; for his were slower steeds,
But he the mightier man in feats of arms.
Nay, I myself will judge; and none of all
The Greeks will censure me, for what I do
Will be but just. Antilochus, step forth,
Illustrious as thou art, and in due form,
Standing before thy horses and thy car,
And taking in thy hand the pliant scourge
Which thou just now hast wielded, touch thy steeds,
And swear by Neptune, whose embrace surrounds
The earth, that thou hast wittingly employed
No stratagem to break my chariot's speed."
  And thus discreet Antilochus replied:
"Have patience with me: I am younger far
Than thou. King Menelaus; thou art both
My elder and my better. Thou dost know
The faults to which the young are ever prone;
The will is quick to act, the judgment weak.
Bear with me then. The mare which I received
I cheerfully make over to thy hands.
And if thou wilt yet more of what I have,
I give it willingly and instantly,
Rather, O loved of Jove, than lose a place
In thy good-will, and sin against the gods."
  The son of large-souled Nestor, speaking thus,
Led forth the mare, and gave her to the hand
Of Menelaus, o'er whose spirit came

A gladness. As upon a field of wheat
Bristling with ears gathers the freshening dew,   730
So was his spirit gladdened in his breast,
And he bespake the youth with wingèd words:—
  "Antilochus, now shall my anger cease,
For hitherto thou hast not shown thyself
Foolish or fickle, though the heat of youth   735
Just now hath led thee wrong. In time to come,
Beware to practise stealthy arts on men
Of higher rank than thou. No other Greek
Would easily have made his peace with me.
But thou hast suffered much, and much hast done,—   740
Thou, and thy worthy father, and his son,
Thy brother,—for my sake, I therefore yield
To thy petition; yet I give to thee
The mare, though mine she be, that these who stand
Around us may perceive that I am not   745
Of unforgiving or unyielding mood."
  He spake, and to Noëmon gave the mare,—
Noëmon, comrade of Antilochus,—
To lead her thence, while for himself he took
The shining caldron. Then Meriones,   750
Fourth in the race, received the prize of gold,—
Two talents. But the fifth prize and the last,
The double goblet, still was left unclaimed;
And this Achilles carried through the crowd
Of Greeks, and placed in Nestor's hands, and said:—   755
  "Receive thou this, O ancient man, to keep
In memory of the funeral honors paid
Patroclus, whom thou never more shalt see
Among the Greeks. I give this prize, which thou
Hast not contended for, since thou wilt wield   760
No more the cestus, nor wilt wrestle more,
Nor hurl the javelin at the mark, nor join
The foot-race; age lies heavy on thy limbs."
  He spake, and gave the prize, which Nestor took,
Well pleased, and thus with wingèd words replied:—   765
  "Son, thou hast spoken rightly, for these limbs
Are strong no longer; neither feet nor hands

Move on each side with vigor as of yore.
Would I were but as young, with strength as great,
As when the Epeians in Buprasium laid 770
King Amarynceus in the sepulchre,
And funeral games were offered by his sons!
Then of the Epeians there was none like me,
Nor of the Pylian youths, nor yet among
The brave Ætolians. In the boxing match 775
I took the prize from Clytomedes, son
Of Enops, and in wrestling overcame
Ancæus the Pleuronian, who rose up
Against me. In the foot-race I outstripped,
Fleet as he was, Iphiclus, and beyond 780
Phyleus and Polydore I threw the spear.
Only the sons of Actor won the race
Against me with their chariot, and they won
Through force of numbers. Much they envied me,
And feared lest I should bear away the prize; 785
For largest in that contest of the steeds
Was the reward, and they were two,—one held,
Steadily held, the reins, the other swung
The lash. Such was I once. Now feats like these
Belong to other, younger men, and I, 790
Though eminent among the heroes once,
Must do as sad old age admonishes.
Go thou, and honor thy friend's funeral
With games. Thy gift I willingly accept,
Rejoicing that thy thoughts revert to one 795
Who loves thee, and that thou forgettest not
To pay the honor due to me among
The Greeks. The gods will give thee thy reward."
   He ceased. The son of Peleus, having heard
This praise from Nestor, left him, and passed through 800
The mighty concourse of the Greeks. He laid
Before them prizes for the difficult strife
Between the boxers. To the middle space
He led a mule, and bound him, six years old
And strong for toil, unbroken and most hard 805
To break, while to the vanquished he assigned

A goblet. Rising, he addressed the host:—
   "Ye sons of Atreus and ye well-armed Greeks,
We call for two of the most skilled to strive
For these, by striking with the lifted fist;   810
And he to whom Apollo shall decree
The victory, acknowledged by you all,
Shall have this sturdy mule to lead away.
The vanquished takes this goblet as his meed."
   He spake. A warrior strong and huge of limb,   815
Skilled in the cestus, named Epeius, son
Of Panopeus, rose at the word, and laid
His hand upon the sturdy mule, and said:—
   "Let him appear whose lot will be to take
The goblet. No man of the Grecian host   820
Will get the mule by overcoming me
In combat with the cestus,—so I deem.
In that I claim to be the best man here.
And should it not suffice that in the war
Others surpass me? All cannot excel   825
In everything alike. I promise this,
And shall fulfil my word,—that I will crush
His body, and will break his bones. His friends
Should all remain upon the ground to bear
Their comrade off when beaten by my hand."   830
   He spake, and all were silent. Only rose
Euryalus, whose father was the king
Mecisteus of Talaïon's line, the same
Who went to Thebes and overcame, of old,
In all the funeral games of Œdipus,   835
The sons of Cadmus. To Euryalus
Came Diomed, the spearman, bidding him
Expect the victory which he greatly wished
His friend might gain. Around his waist he drew
A girdle, adding straps that from the hide   840
Of a wild bull were cut with dextrous care.
And, fully now arrayed, the twain stepped forth
Into the middle space, and both began
The combat. Lifting their strong arms, they brought
Their heavy hands together. Fearfully   845

Was heard the crash of jaws; from every limb
The sweat was streaming. As Euryalus
Looked round, his noble adversary sprang
And smote him on the cheek,—too rude a blow
To be withstood; his shapely limbs gave way   850
Beneath him. As upon the weedy shore,
When the fresh north-wind stirs the water's face,
A fish leaps forth to light, and then again
The dark wave covers it, so sprang and fell
The chief. Magnanimous Epeius gave   855
His hands and raised him up; his friends came round
And led him thence with dragging feet, and head
That drooped from side to side, while from his mouth
Came clotted blood. They placed him in the midst,
Unconscious still, and sent and took the cup.   860
   Then, third in order, for the wrestling-match
The son of Peleus brought and showed the Greeks
Yet other prizes. To the conqueror
A tripod for the hearth, of ample size,
He offered; twice six oxen, as the Greeks   865
Esteemed it, were its price. And next he placed
In view a damsel for the vanquished, trained
In household arts; four beeves were deemed her price.
   Then rose Achilles, and addressed the Greeks:
"Ye who would try your fortune in this strife,   870
Arise." He spake, and mighty Ajax rose,
The son of Telamon, and after him
The wise Ulysses, trained to stratagems.
They, girding up their loins, came forth and stood
In the mid space, and there with vigorous arms   875
They clasped each other, locked like rafters framed
By some wise builder for the lofty roof
Of a great mansion proof against the winds.
Then their backs creaked beneath the powerful strain
Of their strong hands; the sweat ran down their limbs; 880
Large whelks upon their sides and shoulders rose,
Crimson with blood. Still eagerly they strove
For victory and the tripod. Yet in vain
Ulysses labored to supplant his foe,

And throw him to the ground, and equally 885
Did Ajax strive in vain, for with sheer strength
Ulysses foiled his efforts. When they saw
That the Greeks wearied of the spectacle,
The mighty Telamonian Ajax said:—
   "Son of Laertes, nobly born and trained 890
To wise expedients, lift me up, or I
Will lift up thee; and leave the rest to Jove."
   He spake, and raised Ulysses from the ground,
Who dealt, with ready stratagem, a blow
Upon the ham of Ajax, and the limb 895
Gave way; the hero fell upon his back,
And on his breast Ulysses, while the host
Stood wondering and amazed. Ulysses strove,
In turn, to lift his rival, but prevailed
Only to move him from his place; he caught 900
The knee of Ajax in his own, and both
Came to the ground together, soiled with dust.
They rose to wrestle still, but from his seat
Achilles started, and forbade them thus:—
   "Contend no longer, nor exhaust your strength 905
With struggling; there is victory for both,
And equal prizes. Now depart, and leave
The field of contest to the other Greeks."
   He spake: they listened and obeyed, and wiped
The dust away, and put their garments on. 910
And then the son of Peleus placed in sight
Prizes of swiftness,—a wrought silver cup
That held six measures, and in beauty far
Excelled all others known; the cunning hands
Of the Sidonian artisans had given 915
Its graceful shape, and over the dark sea
Men of Phœnicia brought it, with their wares,
To the Greek harbors; they bestowed it there
On Thoas. Afterward Euneüs, son
Of Jason, gave it to the hero-chief, 920
Patroclus, to redeem a captive friend,
Lycaon, Priam's son. Achilles now
Brought it before the assembly as a prize,

For which, in honor of the friend he loved,
The swiftest runners of the host should strive.   925
Next, for the second in the race, he showed
A noble fatling ox; and for the last,
Gold, half a talent. Then he stood and said
To the Achaians: "Those who would contend
For these rewards, rise up." And then arose   930
Oïlean Ajax, fleet of foot; and next
Ulysses the sagacious; last upstood
Antilochus, the son of Nestor, known
As swiftest of the youths. In due array
They stood; Achilles showed the goal. At once   935
Forward they sprang. Oïlean Ajax soon
Gained on the rest, but close behind him ran
The great Ulysses. As a shapely maid
Flinging the shuttle draws with careful hand
The thread that fills the warp, and so brings near   940
The shuttle to her bosom, just so near
To Ajax ran Ulysses, in the prints
Made by his rival's feet, before the dust
Fell back upon them. As he ran, his breath
Smote on the head of Ajax. All the Greeks   945
Shouted applause to him, encouraging
His ardor for the victory; but when now
They neared the goal, Ulysses silently
Prayed thus to Pallas: "Goddess, hear my prayer,
And help these feet to win." The goddess heard,   950
And lightened all his limbs, his feet, his hands;
And just as they were rushing on the prize,
Ajax, in running, slipped and fell—the work
Of Pallas—where in heaps the refuse lay
From entrails of the bellowing oxen slain   955
In honor of Patroclus by the hand
Of swift Achilles. Mouth and nostrils both
Were choked with filth. The much-enduring man
Ulysses, coming first, received the cup,
While Ajax took the ox, and as he stood   960
Holding the animal's horn and spitting forth
The dirt, he said to those around: "'Tis plain

The goddess caused my feet to slide; she aids
Ulysses like a mother." So he said,
And the Greeks laughed. And then Antilochus 965
Received the third reward, and with a smile
Said to the Greeks: "I tell you all, my friends,
What you must know already, that the gods
Honor the aged ever. Ajax stands
Somewhat in years above me, but this chief 970
Who takes the prize is of a former age
And earlier race of men; they call him old,
But hard it were for any Greek to vie
With him in swiftness, save Achilles here."
  Such praise he gave Pelides, fleet of foot, 975
Who answered: "Thy good word, Antilochus,
Shall not be vainly spoken. I will add
Yet half a talent to thy gold." He said,
And gave the gold; Antilochus, well pleased,
Received it. Then Pelides brought a spear 980
Of ponderous length into the middle space,
And laid it down, and placed a buckler near
And helmet, which had been Sarpedon's arms,
And which Patroclus won of him in war.
Then stood Achilles and addressed the Greeks:— 985
  "I call on two, the bravest of the host,
To arm themselves and take their spears in hand,
And in a contest for these weapons put
Each other to the proof. Whoever first
Shall wound his adversary, piercing through 990
The armor to the delicate skin beneath,
And draw the crimson blood, to him I give
This beautiful sword of Thrace, with silver studs,
Won from Asteropæus. And let both
Bear off these arms, a common gift, and both 995
Shall sit and banquet nobly in my tent."
  He spake, and Telamonian Ajax rose,
The large of limb; Tydides Diomed,
The strong, rose also. When they had put on
Their arms apart from all the host, they came, 1000
All eager for the combat, to the lists,

And fearful was their aspect. All the Greeks
Looked on with dread and wonder, and when now
Stood face to face the warriors, thrice they rushed
Against each other; thrice they dealt their blows. 1005
Then Ajax thrust through Diomed's round shield
His weapon, but it wounded not; the mail
Beyond it stopped the stroke. Tydides aimed
Over his adversary's mighty shield
A blow to reach his neck. The Greeks, alarmed 1010
For Ajax, shouted that the strife should cease,
And both divide the prize. Achilles heard,
But gave to Diomed the ponderous sword,
Its sheath, and the fair belt from which it hung.
    Again Pelides placed before the host 1015
A mass of iron, shapeless from the forge,
Which once the strong Eëtion used to hurl;
But swift Achilles, when he took his life,
Brought it with other booty in his ships
To Troas. Rising, he addressed the Greeks:— 1020
    "Stand forth, whoever will contend for this,
And if broad fields and rich be his, this mass
Will last him many years. The man who tends
His flocks, or guides his plough, need not be sent
To town for iron; he will have it here." 1025
    He spake, and warlike Polypœtes rose.
Uprose the strong Leonteus, who in form
Was like a god. The son of Telamon
Rose also, and Epeius nobly born;
Each took his place. Epeius seized the mass, 1030
And sent it whirling. All the Achaians laughed.
The loved of Mars, Leonteus, flung it next,
And after him the son of Telamon,
The large-limbed Ajax, from his vigorous arm
Sent it beyond the mark of both. But when 1035
The sturdy warrior Polypœtes took
The mass in hand, as far as o'er his beeves
A herdsman sends his whirling staff, so far
This cast outdid the rest. A shout arose;
The friends of sturdy Polypœtes took 1040

The prize, and bore it to the hollow ships.
    Achilles for the archers brought forth steel,
Tempered for arrow-heads,—ten axes, each
With double edge, and single axes ten,—
And from a galley's azure prow took off 1045
A mast, and reared it on the sands afar,
And, tying to its summit by the foot
A timorous dove, he bade them aim at her:
"Whoever strikes the bird shall bear away
The double axes to his tent; while he 1050
Who hits the cord, but not the bird, shall take
The single axes, as the humbler prize."
    He ceased, and then arose the stalwart king,
Teucer; then also rose Meriones,
The valiant comrade of Idomeneus. 1055
The lots were shaken in a brazen helm,
And Teucer's lot was first. He straightway sent
A shaft with all his strength, but made no vow
Of a choice hecatomb of firstling lambs
To Phœbus, monarch-god. He missed the bird, 1060
Such was the will of Phœbus, but he struck,
Close to her foot, the cord that made her fast.
The keen shaft severed it; the dove flew up
Into the heavens; the fillet dropped to earth
Amid the loud applauses of the Greeks. 1065
And then Meriones made haste to take
The bow from Teucer's hand. Long time he held
The arrow aimed, the while he made a vow
To Phœbus, the great archer, promising
A chosen hecatomb of firstling lambs; 1070
Then, looking toward the dove, as high in air
She wheeled beneath the clouds, he pierced her breast
Beneath the wing; the shaft went through and fell,
Fixed in the ground, beside Meriones,
While the bird settled on the galley's mast 1075
With drooping head and open wings. The breath
Forsook her soon, and down from that high perch
She fell to earth. The people all looked on,
Admiring and amazed. Meriones

Took up the double axes as his prize, 1080
While Teucer bore the others to the fleet.
    And then Pelides brought into the midst
A ponderous spear, and laid a caldron down
Which never felt the fire, inwrought with flowers,
Its price an ox. And then the spearmen rose. 1085
Atrides Agamemnon, mighty king,
First rose, and after him Meriones,
The brave companion of Idomeneus;
And thus to both the swift Achilles said:—
    "O son of Atreus, for we know how far 1090
Thou dost excel all others, and dost cast
The spear with passing strength and skill, bear thou
This prize, as victor, to the roomy ships,
And if it please thee, let us, as I wish,
Give to our brave Meriones the spear." 1095
    He spake, and Agamemnon, king of men,
Complied, and gave Meriones in hand
The brazen spear, while to Talthybius,
The herald, he consigned the greater prize.

BOOK XXIV

THE assembly was dissolved, the people all
  Dispersed to their swift galleys, and prepared
With food and gentle slumber to refresh
Their wearied frames. But still Achilles wept,
Remembering his dear comrade. Sleep, whose sway   5
Is over all, came not; he turned and tossed,
Still yearning for his strong and valiant friend
Patroclus. All that they had ever done
Together, all the hardships they had borne,
The battles fought with heroes, the wild seas   10
O'erpassed, came thronging on his memory.
He shed warm tears, as now upon his sides,
Now on his back, now on his face he lay.
Then, starting from his couch, he wandered forth
In sorrow by the margin of the deep.   15
Nor did the morn that rose o'er sea and shore
Dawn unperceived by him; for then he yoked
His fleet steeds to the chariot, and made fast
The corse of Hector, that it might be dragged
After the wheels. Three times around the tomb   20
Of Menœtiades he dragged the slain,
Then turned and sought his tent, again to rest,
And left him there stretched out amid the dust
With the face downward. Yet Apollo, moved
With pity for the hero, kept him free   25
From soil or stain, though dead, and o'er him held

The golden ægis, lest, when roughly dragged
Along the ground, the body might be torn.
  So in his anger did Achilles treat
Unworthily the noble Hector's corse. 30
The blessed gods themselves with pity looked
Upon the slain, and bade the vigilant one,
The Argus-queller, bear him thence by stealth.
This counsel pleased the immortals all, except
Juno and Neptune and the blue-eyed maid, 35
And these persisted in their wrath. To them
Ilium, the hallowed city, and its king,
Priam, and all his people, from the first
Were hateful; 'twas for Alexander's fault,
Affronting the two goddesses what time 40
They sought his cottage, and preferring her
Who ministered to his calamitous love.
But now, when the twelfth morning from that day
Arose, Apollo spake among the gods:—
  "Cruel are ye, O gods, and prone to wrong. 45
For was not Hector wont before your shrines
To burn the thighs of chosen bulls and goats?
And now that he is dead ye venture not
To rescue him, and let his wife and son
And mother and King Priam look again 50
Upon his face. Soon would they light the pile,
And burn the dead, and pay the funeral rite.
Ye seek to favor, O ye gods, that pest,
Achilles, in whose breast there dwells no love
Of justice, nor a temper to be moved 55
By prayers, but who delights in savage deeds.
And as a lion, conscious of vast strength
And scornful of resistance, falls upon
The shepherd's flock, and slays for his repast,
Thus with Achilles neither mercy dwells 60
Nor shame, which often profits, often harms
Mankind. For when another man has met
A greater grief than he,—has lost, perchance,
A brother or a son,—he dries at length
His tears, and ceases to lament; for fate 65

Bestows the power to suffer patiently.
But this Achilles, after he has spoiled
The godlike Hector of his life in war,
Hath bound him to his chariot, and hath dragged
The corse around his dear companion's tomb. 70
Unseemly is the deed, and small will be
The good it brings him. Brave although he be,
We may be angry with him when he thus
Insults a portion of insensible earth."
   The white-armed Juno was incensed, and spake: 75
"So mightst thou say, God of the silver bow,
Were equal honor to Achilles due
And Hector. Hector is a mortal man,
And suckled at a woman's breast. Not so
Achilles; he was born of one of us, 80
A goddess whom I nurtured and brought up
And gave to Peleus. Ye were present all,
Ye gods, when they were wedded. Thou wert there
To share the marriage banquet, harp in hand,
Thou plotter with the vile, thou faithless one!" 85
   Then answered cloud-compelling Jove, and said:
"Let not thy anger rise against the gods,
O Juno, for the honor of the chiefs
Shall not be equal. Yet of all the race
Of mortals dwelling in the city of Troy 90
Was Hector dearest to the gods; to me
He ever was; and never did he fail
To offer welcome gifts. My altar ne'er
Lacked fitting feast, libation, and the fume
Of incense,—hallowed rites which are our due. 95
Yet seek we not to steal away the corse
Of valiant Hector; that we could not do
Without his slayer's knowledge, who by night
And day is ever near to him and keeps
Watch o'er him like a mother. Let some god 100
Call hither Thetis. I will counsel her
Prudently, that Achilles may receive
Ransom from Priam, and restore his son."
   He ceased, and with the swiftness of the storm

Rose Iris up, to be his messenger.   105
Half-way 'twixt Samos and the rugged coast
Of Imbrus down she plunged to the dark sea,
Entering the deep with noise. Far down she sank
As sinks the ball of lead, that, sliding o'er
A wild bull's horn, bears into ocean's depths   110
Death to the greedy fishes. There she found
Thetis within her roomy cave, among
The goddesses of ocean, seated round
In full assembly. Thetis in the midst
Bewailed the fate of her own blameless son,   115
About to perish on the fertile soil
Of Troy, and far from Greece. The swift of wing,
Iris, approached her and addressed her thus:—
   "Arise, O Thetis. Father Jupiter,
Whose counsel stands forever, sends for thee."   120
   And silver-footed Thetis answered him:
"Why should that potent deity require
My presence, who have many griefs, and shrink
From mingling with immortals? Yet I go,
Perforce, for never doth he speak in vain."   125
So spake the goddess-queen, and, speaking, took
Her mantle,—darker web was never worn,—
And onward went. Wind-footed Iris led
The way; the waters of the sea withdrew
On either side. They climbed the steepy shore,   130
And took their way to heaven. They found the son
Of Saturn, him of the far-sounding voice,
With all the blessed, ever-living gods
Assembled round him. Close to Father Jove
She took her seat, for Pallas yielded it,   135
And Juno put a beautiful cup of gold
Into her hand, and spake consoling words.
She drank and gave it back, and thus began
The father of immortals and of men:—
   "Thou comest to Olympus, though in grief,   140
O goddess Thetis, and I know the cause
That makes thee sad and will not from thy thoughts;
Yet let me now declare why I have called

Thee hither. For nine days the immortal gods
Have been at strife concerning Hector's corse   145
And Peleus' son, the spoiler. They have asked
The vigilant Argus-queller to remove
The dead by stealth. But I must yet bestow
Fresh honor on Achilles, and thus keep
Thy love and reverence. Now descend at once   150
Into the camp and carry to thy son
My message: say that it offends the gods,
And me the most, that in his spite he keeps
The corse of Hector at the beakèd ships,
Refusing to restore it. He perchance   155
Will listen, and, revering me, give back
The slain. And I will send a messenger,
Iris, to large-souled Priam, bidding him
Hasten in person to the Grecian fleet,
To ransom his beloved son, and bring   160
Achilles gifts that shall appease his rage."
  He spake: the goddess of the silver feet,
Thetis, obeyed, and with precipitate flight
Descended from the mountain-peaks. She came
To her son's tent, and found him uttering moans   165
Continually, while his beloved friends
Were busy round him; they prepared a feast,
And had just slain within the tent a ewe
Of ample size and fleece. She took her seat
Beside her son, and smoothed his brow, and said:—   170
  "How long, my son, wilt thou lament and grieve
And pine at heart, abstaining from the feast
And from thy couch? Yet well it is to seek
A woman's love. Thy life will not be spared
Long time to me, for death and cruel fate   175
Stand near thee. Listen to me; I am come
A messenger from Jove, who bids me say
The immortals are offended, and himself
The most, that thou shouldst in thy spite detain
The corse of Hector at the beakèd ships,   180
Refusing its release. Comply thou then,
And take the ransom and restore the dead."

And thus Achilles, swift of foot, replied:
"Let him who brings the ransom come and take
The body, if it be the will of Jove." 185
   Thus did the mother and the son confer
Among the galleys, and between them passed
Full many a wingèd word, while Saturn's son
Bade Iris go with speed to sacred Troy:—
   "Fleet Iris, haste thee. Leave the Olympian seats, 190
And send magnanimous Priam to the fleet,
To ransom his dear son, and bear him back
To Ilium. Let him carry gifts to calm
The anger of Achilles. He should go
Alone, no Trojan with him, save a man 195
In years, a herald, who may guide the mules
And strong-wheeled chariot, harnessed to bear back
Him whom the great Achilles has o'erthrown;
And let him fear not death nor other harm,
For we will send a guide to lead him safe, 200
The Argus-queller, till he stand beside
Achilles; and when once he comes within
The warrior's tent, Achilles will not raise
His hand to slay, but will restrain the rest.
Nor mad, nor rash, nor criminal is he, 205
And will humanely spare a suppliant man."
   He spake, and Iris, the swift messenger,
Whose feet are like the wind, went forth with speed,
And came to Priam's palace, where she found
Sorrow and wailing. Round the father sat 210
His sons within the hall, and steeped with tears
Their garments. In the midst the aged man
Sat with a cloak wrapped round him, and much dust
Strewn on his head and neck, which, when he rolled
Upon the earth, he gathered with his hands. 215
His daughters and the consorts of his sons
Filled with their cries the mansion, sorrowing
For those, the many and brave, who now lay slain
By Grecian hands. The ambassadress of Jove
Stood beside Priam, and in soft, low tones, 220
While his limbs shook with fear, addressed him thus:—

"Be comforted, and have no fear; for I
Am come, Dardanian Priam, not to bring
Mischief, but blessing. I am sent to thee
A messenger from Jove, who, though afar,   225
Pities thee and will aid thee. He who rules
Olympus bids thee ransom thy slain son,
The noble Hector, carrying gifts to calm
The anger of Achilles. Thou shouldst go
Alone, no Trojan with thee, save a man   230
In years, a herald, who shall guide the mules
And strong-wheeled chariot, harnessed to bring back
Him whom the great Achilles has o'erthrown.
And have no fear of death or other harm;
A guide shall go with thee to lead thee safe,   235
The Argus-queller, till thou stand beside
Achilles, and when once thou art within
The warrior's tent, Achilles will not raise
His hand to slay, but will restrain the rest.
He is not mad, nor rash, nor prone to crime,   240
And will humanely spare a suppliant man."
   Thus the swift-footed Iris spake, and then
Departed. Priam bade his sons prepare
The strong-wheeled chariot, drawn by mules, and bind
A coffer on it. He descended next   245
Into a fragrant chamber, cedar-lined,
High-roofed, and stored with many things of price,
And calling Hecuba, his wife, he said:—
   "Dear wife, a message from Olympian Jove
Commands that I betake me to the fleet,   250
And thence redeem my slaughtered son with gifts
That may appease Achilles. Tell me now
How this may seem to thee? for I am moved
By a strong impulse to approach the ships,
And venture into the great Grecian camp."   255
   He spake: his consort wept, and answered thus:
"Ah me! the prudence which was once so praised
By strangers and by those who own thy sway,
Where is it now? Why wouldst thou go alone
To the Greek fleet, to meet the eye of him   260

Who slew so many of thy gallant sons?
An iron heart is thine. If that false man,
Remorseless as he is, should see thee there
And seize thee, neither pity nor respect
Hast thou to hope from him. Let us lament   265
Our Hector in these halls. A cruel fate
Spun, when I brought him forth, his thread of life,—
That far from us his corse should feed the hounds
Near that fierce man, whose liver I could tear
From out his bosom. Then the indignities   270
Done to my son would be repaid, for he
Was slain, not shunning combat, coward-like,
But fighting to defend the men of Troy
And the deep-bosomed Trojan dames. He fell
Without a thought of flight or of retreat."   275
  And thus the aged, godlike king rejoined:
"Keep me not back from going, nor be thou
A bird of evil omen in these halls,
For thou shalt not persuade me. This I say:
If any of the dwellers of the earth,   280
Soothsayer, seer, or priest, had said to me
What I have heard, I well might deem the words
A lie, and heed them not. But since I heard
Myself the mandate from a deity,
And saw her face to face, I certainly   285
Will go, nor shall the message be in vain.
And should it be my fate to perish there
Beside the galleys of the mail-clad Greeks,
So be it; for Achilles will forthwith
Put me to death embracing my poor son,   290
And satisfying my desire to weep."
  He spake, and, raising the fair coffer-lids,
Took out twelve robes of state most beautiful,
Twelve single cloaks, as many tapestried mats,
And tunics next and mantles twelve of each,   295
And ten whole talents of pure gold, which first
He weighed. Two burnished tripods from his store
He added, and four goblets and a cup
Of eminent beauty, which the men of Thrace

Gave him when, as an envoy to their coast, 300
He came from Troy,—a sumptuous gift, and yet
The aged king reserved not even this
To deck his palace, such was his desire
To ransom his dear son. And then he drave
Away the Trojans hovering round his porch, 305
Rebuking them with sharp and bitter words:—
    "Hence with you, worthless wretches! have ye not
Sorrow enough at home, that ye are come
To vex me thus? Or doth it seem to you
Of little moment, that Saturnian Jove 310
Hath sent such grief upon me in the loss
Of my most valiant son? Ye yet will know
How great that loss has been; for it will be
A lighter task for the beleaguering Greeks
To work our ruin, now that he is dead. 315
But I shall sink to Hades ere mine eyes
Behold the city sacked and made a spoil."
    He spake, and with his staff he chased away
The loiterers; forth before the aged man
They went. With like harsh words he chid his sons. 320
Helenus, Paris, noble Agathon,
Pammon, Antiphonus, Deïphobus,
Polites, great in war. Hippothoüs,
And gallant Dios, nine in all he called,
And thus bespake them with reproachful words:— 325
    "Make haste, ye idle fellows, my disgrace!
Would ye had all been slain beside the fleet
Instead of Hector! Woe is me! the most
Unhappy of mankind am I, who had
The bravest sons in all the town of Troy, 330
And none of them, I think, are left to me.
Mestor, divine in presence, Troïlus,
The gallant knight, and Hector, he who looked
A god among his countrymen,—no son
Of man he seemed, but of immortal birth,— 335
Those Mars has slain, but these who are my shame
Remain,—these liars, dancers, excellent
In choirs, whose trade is public robbery

Of lambs and kids. Why haste ye not to get
My chariot ready, and bestow these things   340
Within it, that my journey may begin?"
  He spake, and they, in fear of his rebuke,
Lifted from out its place the strong-wheeled car,
Framed to be drawn by mules, and beautiful,
And newly built, and on it they made fast   345
The coffer. From its pin they next took down
The boxwood mule-yoke, fitted well with rings,
And carved with a smooth boss. With this they brought
A yoke-band nine ells long, which carefully
Adjusting to the polished pole's far end,   350
They cast the ring upon the bolt, and thrice
Wound the long band on each side of the bolt
Around the yoke, and made it fast, and turned
The loose ends under. Then they carried forth
The treasures that should ransom Hector's corse;   355
And having piled them in the polished car,
They yoked the hardy, strong-hoofed mules which once
The Mysians gave to Priam, princely gifts.
To bear the yoke of Priam they led forth
The horses which the aged man himself   360
Fed at the polished manger. These the king
Yoked, aided by the herald, while in mind,
Within the palace court, they both revolved
Their prudent counsels. Hecuba, the queen,
Came to them in deep sorrow. In her hand   365
She bore a golden cup of delicate wine,
That they might make libations and depart.
She stood before the steeds, and thus she spake:—
  "Take this, and pour to Father Jove, and pray
That thou mayst safely leave the enemy's camp   370
For home, since 'tis thy will, though I dissuade,
To go among the ships. Implore thou then
The god of Ida and the gatherer
Of the black tempest, Saturn's son, who looks
Down on all Troy, to send his messenger,   375
His swift and favorite bird, of matchless strength,
On thy right hand, that, with thine eye on him,

Thou mayst with courage journey to the ships
Of the Greek horsemen. But if Jupiter
All-seeing should withhold his messenger, 380
I cannot bid thee, eager as thou art,
Adventure near the galleys of the Greeks."
   And thus the godlike Priam made reply:
"Dear wife, indeed, I will not disobey
Thy counsel; meet it is to raise our hands 385
To Jove, and ask him to be merciful."
   He spake, and bade the attendant handmaid pour
Pure water on his hands, for near him stood
A maid who came and held a basin forth
And ewer. When his hands were washed, he took 390
The goblet from the queen, and then, in prayer,
Stood in the middle of the court, and poured
The wine, and, looking heavenward, spake aloud:—
   "O Father Jove, most glorious and most great,
Who rulest all from Ida, let me find 395
Favor and pity with Achilles. Send
A messenger, thy own swift, favorite bird,
Of matchless strength, on my right hand, that I,
Beholding him, may confidently pass
To where the fleet of the Greek horsemen lies!" 400
   Thus in his prayer he spake, and Jupiter,
The All-disposer, hearkened, and sent forth
An eagle, bird of surest augury,
Named the Black Chaser, and by others called
Percnos, with wings as broad as is the door 405
Skilfully fashioned for the lofty hall
Of some rich man, and fastened with a bolt.
Such ample wings he spread on either side
As townward on the right they saw him fly.
They saw and they rejoiced; their hearts grew light 410
Within their bosoms. Then the aged king
Hastened to mount the polished car, and drave
Through vestibule and echoing porch. The mules,
Harnessed to draw the four-wheeled car, went first,
Driven by the sage Idæus; after them, 415
The horses, urged by Priam with the lash

Rapidly through the city. All his friends
Followed lamenting, as for one who went
To meet his death. And now when they had reached
The plain descending from the town, the sons 420
And sons-in-law of Priam all returned
To Ilium, and the twain proceeded on,
Yet not unmarked by all-beholding Jove,
Who, moved with pity for the aged man,
Turned to his well-beloved son and said:— 425
    "Hermes, who more than any other god
Delightest to consort with human-kind,
And willingly dost listen to their prayers,
Haste, guide King Priam to the Grecian fleet,
Yet so that none may see him, and no Greek 430
Know of his coming, till he stand before
Pelides." Thus he spake: the messenger
Who slew the Argus hearkened and obeyed;
And hastily beneath his feet he bound
The fair, ambrosial, golden sandals worn 435
To bear him over ocean like the wind,
And o'er the boundless land. His wand he took
Wherewith he seals in sleep the eyes of men,
And opens them at will. With this in hand,
The mighty Argus-queller flew, and soon 440
Was at the Troad and the Hellespont.
Like to some royal stripling seemed the god,
In youth's first prime, when youth has most of grace.
And there the Trojans twain, when they had passed
The tomb of Ilus, halted with their mules 445
And horses, that the beasts might drink the stream;
For twilight now was creeping o'er the earth.
The herald looked, and saw that Mercury
Was near, and thus, addressing Priam, said:—
    "Be on thy guard, O son of Dardanus, 450
For here is cause for wariness. I see
A warrior, and I think he seeks our lives.
Now let us urge our steeds and fly, or else
Descend and clasp his knees, and sue for grace."
    He spake, and greatly was the aged king 455

Bewildered by his words; with hair erect
He stood, and motionless, while Mercury
Drew near, and took the old man's hand, and asked:—
  "Whither, O father, guidest thou thy mules
And steeds in the dim night, while others sleep? 460
Fearest thou nothing from the warlike Greeks,
Thy foes, who hate thee, and are near at hand?
Should one of them behold thee bearing off
These treasures in the swiftly darkening night,
What wouldst thou do? Thou art not young, and he 465
Who comes with thee is old; ye could not make
Defence against the foe. Fear nought from me,
And I will save thee, since thou art so like
To my own father, from all other harm."
  Priam, the godlike ancient, answered thus: 470
"Thou sayest true, dear son; but sure some god
Holds over me his kind, protecting hand,
Who sends a guide like thee to join me here,
So noble art thou both in form and air,
And gracious are thy thoughts, and blessed they 475
Who gave thee birth." With that the messenger,
The Argus-queller, spake again, and said:
"Most wisely hast thou spoken, aged man.
But tell, and truly, why thou bearest hence
This store of treasures among stranger men? 480
Is it that they may be preserved for thee?
Or are ye all deserting in alarm
Your hallowed Troy? for such a man of might
Was thy brave son who died, that I may say
The Greeks in battle had no braver man." 485
  And Priam, godlike ancient, spake in turn:
"Who then art thou, and of what parents born,
Excellent youth, who dost in such kind words
Speak of the death of my unhappy son?"
  The herald, Argus-queller, answered him: 490
"I see that thou wouldst prove me, aged man,
By questions touching Hector, whom I oft
Have seen with mine own eyes in glorious fight,
Putting the Greeks to rout and slaying them

By their swift ships with that sharp spear of his. 495
We stood and marvelled, for Achilles, wroth
With Agamemnon, would not suffer us
To join the combat. I attend on him;
The same good galley brought us to this shore,
And I am one among his Myrmidons. 500
Polyctor is my father, who is rich,
And now as old as thou. Six are his sons
Beside me, I the seventh. In casting lots
With them, it fell to me that I should come
To Ilium with Achilles. I am here 505
In coming from the fleet, for with the dawn
The dark-eyed Greeks are planning to renew
The war around the city. They have grown
Impatient of long idleness; their chiefs
Seek vainly to restrain their warlike rage." 510
   Then spake the godlike ancient, Priam, thus:
"If thou indeed dost serve Pelides, tell,
And truly tell me, whether yet my son
Is at the fleet, or has Achilles cast,
Torn limb from limb, his body to the hounds?" 515
   The herald, Argus-queller, thus replied:
"O aged monarch, neither have the hounds
Devoured thy son, nor yet the birds of prey;
But near the galleys of Achilles still
He lies neglected and among the tents. 520
Twelve mornings have beheld him lying there,
Nor hath corruption touched him, nor the worms
That make the slain their feast begun to feed.
'Tis true that, when the holy morning dawns
Achilles drags him fiercely round the tomb 525
Of his dear friend; yet that disfigures not
The dead. Shouldst thou approach him, thou wouldst see
With marvelling eyes how fresh and dewy still
The body lies, the blood all cleansed away,
Unsoiled in every part, and all the wounds 530
Closed up wherever made; for many a spear
Was thrust into his sides. Thus tenderly
The blessed gods regard thy son, though dead,

For dearly was he loved by them in life."
   He spake; the aged man was comforted,   535
And said: "'Tis meet, O son, that we should pay
Oblations to the immortals; for my son
While yet alive neglected not within
His palace the due worship of the gods
Who dwell upon Olympus; therefore they   540
Are mindful of him, even after death.
Take this magnificent goblet; be my guard,
And guide me, by the favor of the gods,
Until I reach Pelides in his tent."
   Again the herald, Argus-queller, spake: 545
"Thou seekest yet to try me, aged man,
Who younger am than thou. Yet think thou not
That I, without the knowledge of my chief,
Will take thy gifts; for in my heart I fear
Achilles, nor would wrong him in the least,   550
Lest evil come upon me. Yet I go
Willingly with thee, as thy faithful guide.
Were it as far as Argos the renowned,
In a swift galley, or on foot by land,
Yet none would dare to harm thee while with me."   555
   So Hermes spake, and leaped into the car,
And took into his hands the lash and reins,
And breathed into the horses and the mules
Fresh vigor. Coming to the wall and trench
About the ships, they found the guard engaged   560
With their night-meal. The herald Argicide
Poured sleep upon them all, and quickly flung
The gates apart, and pushed aside the bars,
And led in Priam, with the costly gifts
Heaped on the car. They went until they reached   565
The lofty tent in which Achilles sat,
Reared by the Myrmidons to lodge their king,
With timbers of hewn fir, and over-roofed
With thatch, for which the meadows had been mown,
And fenced for safety round with rows of stakes.   570
One fir-tree bar made fast its gate, which three
Strong Greeks were wont to raise aloft, and three

Were needed to take down the massive beam.
Achilles wielded the vast weight alone;
Beneficent Hermes opened it before 575
The aged man, and brought the treasures in,
Designed for swift Achilles. Then he left
The car and stood upon the ground, and said:—
 "O aged monarch, I am Mercury,
An ever-living god; my father, Jove, 580
Bade me attend thy journey. I shall now
Return, nor must Achilles look on me;
It is not meet that an immortal god
Should openly befriend a mortal man.
Enter, approach Pelides, clasp his knees; 585
Entreat him by his father, and his son,
And fair-haired mother; so shall he be moved."
 Thus having spoken, Hermes took his way
Back to the Olympian summit. Priam then
Sprang from the chariot to the ground. He left 590
Idæus there to guard the steeds and mules,
And, hastening to the tent where, dear to Jove,
Achilles lodged, he found the chief within,
While his companions sat apart, save two,—
Automedon the brave, and Alcimus, 595
Who claimed descent from Mars. These stood near by,
And ministered to Peleus' son, who then
Was closing a repast, and had just left
The food and wine, and still the table stood.
Unmarked the royal Priam entered in, 600
And, coming to Achilles, clasped his knees,
And kissed those fearful slaughter-dealing hands,
By which so many of his sons had died.
And as, when some blood-guilty man, whose hand
In his own land has slain a fellow-man, 605
Flees to another country, and the abode
Of some great chieftain, all men look on him
Astonished,—so, when godlike Priam first
Was seen, Achilles was amazed, and all
Looked on each other, wondering at the sight. 610
And thus King Priam supplicating spake:—

"Think of thy father, an old man like me,
Godlike Achilles! On the dreary verge
Of closing life he stands, and even now
Haply is fiercely pressed by those who dwell
Around him, and has none to shield his age
From war and its disasters. Yet his heart
Rejoices when he hears thou yet dost live,
And every day he hopes that his dear son
Will come again from Troy. My lot is hard,
For I was father of the bravest sons
In all wide Troy, and none are left me now.
Fifty were with me when the men of Greece
Arrived upon our coast; nineteen of these
Owned the same mother, and the rest were born
Within my palaces. Remorseless Mars
Already had laid lifeless most of these,
And Hector, whom I cherished most, whose arm
Defended both our city and ourselves,
Him didst thou lately slay while combating
For his dear country. For his sake I come
To the Greek fleet, and to redeem his corse
I bring uncounted ransom. O, revere
The gods, Achilles, and be merciful,
Calling to mind thy father! happier he
Than I; for I have borne what no man else
That dwells on earth could bear,—have laid my lips
Upon the hand of him who slew my son."
  He spake: Achilles sorrowfully thought
Of his own father. By the hand he took
The suppliant, and with gentle force removed
The old man from him. Both in memory
Of those they loved were weeping. The old king,
With many tears, and rolling in the dust
Before Achilles, mourned his gallant son.
Achilles sorrowed for his father's sake,
And then bewailed Patroclus, and the sound
Of lamentation filled the tent. At last
Achilles, when he felt his heart relieved
By tears, and that strong grief had spent its force,

Sprang from his seat; then lifting by the hand
The aged man, and pitying his white head
And his white chin, he spake these wingèd words:—
  "Great have thy sufferings been, unhappy king!
How couldst thou venture to approach alone   655
The Grecian fleet, and show thyself to him
Who slew so many of thy valiant sons?
An iron heart is thine. But seat thyself,
And let us, though afflicted grievously,
Allow our woes to sleep awhile, for grief   660
Indulged can bring no good. The gods ordain
The lot of man to suffer, while themselves
Are free from care. Beside Jove's threshold stand
Two casks of gifts for man. One cask contains
The evil, one the good, and he to whom   665
The Thunderer gives them mingled sometimes falls
Into misfortune, and is sometimes crowned
With blessings. But the man to whom he gives
The evil only stands a mark exposed
To wrong, and, chased by grim calamity,   670
Wanders the teeming earth, alike unloved
By gods and men. So did the gods bestow
Munificent gifts on Peleus from his birth,
For eminent was he among mankind
For wealth and plenty; o'er the Myrmidons   675
He ruled, and, though a mortal, he was given
A goddess for a wife. Yet did the gods
Add evil to the good, for not to him
Was born a family of kingly sons
Within his house, successors to his reign.   680
One short-lived son is his, nor am I there
To cherish him in his old age; but here
Do I remain, far from my native land,
In Troy, and causing grief to thee and thine.
Of thee too, aged king, they speak, as one   685
Whose wealth was large in former days, when all
That Lesbos, seat of Macar, owns was thine,
And all in Phrygia and the shores that bound
The Hellespont; men said thou didst excel

All others in thy riches and thy sons.   690
But since the gods have brought this strife on thee
War and perpetual slaughter of brave men
Are round thy city. Yet be firm of heart,
Nor grieve forever. Sorrow for thy son
Will profit nought; it cannot bring the dead   695
To life again, and while thou dost afflict
Thyself for him fresh woes may fall on thee."
   And thus the godlike Priam, aged king,
Made answer: "Bid me not be seated here,
Nursling of Jove, while Hector lies among   700
Thy tents unburied. Let me ransom him
At once, that I may look on him once more
With my own eyes. Receive the many gifts
We bring thee, and mayst thou possess them long,
And reach thy native shore, since by thy grace   705
I live and yet behold the light of day."
   Achilles heard, and, frowning, thus rejoined:
"Anger me not, old man; 'twas in my thought
To let thee ransom Hector. To my tent
The mother came who bore me, sent from Jove,   710
The daughter of the Ancient of the Sea,
And I perceive, nor can it be concealed,
O Priam, that some god hath guided thee
To our swift galleys; for no mortal man,
Though in his prime of youthful strength, would dare   715
To come into the camp; he could not pass
The guard, nor move the beams that bar our gates.
So then remind me of my griefs no more,
Lest, suppliant as thou art, I leave thee not
Unharmed, and thus transgress the laws of Jove."   720
   He spake: the aged man in fear obeyed.
And then Pelides like a lion leaped
Forth from the door, yet not alone he went;
For of his comrades two—Automedon,
The hero, and his comrade Alcimus,   725
He whom Achilles held in most esteem
After the slain Patroclus—followed him.
The mules and horses they unyoked, and led

The aged monarch's clear-voiced herald in,
And bade him sit. Then from the polished car 730
They took the costly ransom of the corse
Of Hector, save two cloaks, which back they laid
With a fair tunic, that their chief might give
The body shrouded to be borne to Troy.
And then he called the maidens, bidding them 735
Wash and anoint the dead, yet far apart
From Priam, lest, with looking on his son,
The grief within his heart might rise uncurbed
To anger, and Achilles in his rage
Might stay him and transgress the laws of Jove. 740
And when the handmaids finished, having washed
The body and anointed it with oil,
And wrapped a sumptuous cloak and tunic round
The limbs, Achilles lifted it himself
And placed it on a bier. His comrades gave 745
Their aid, and raised it to the polished car.
When all was done, Achilles groaned, and called
By name the friend he dearly loved, and said:—
    "O my Patroclus, be not wroth with me
Shouldst thou in Hades hear that I restore 750
Hector to his dear father, since I take
A ransom not unworthy; but of this
I yield to thee the portion justly thine."
    So spake the godlike warrior, and withdrew
Into his tent, and took the princely seat 755
From which he had arisen, opposite
To that of Priam, whom he thus bespake:—
    "Behold thy son is ransomed, aged man,
As thou hast asked, and lies upon his bier.
Thou shalt behold him with the early dawn, 760
And bear him hence. Now let us break our fast,
For even Niobe, the golden-haired,
Refrained not from her food, though children twelve
Perished within her palace,—six young sons
And six fair daughters. Phœbus slew the sons 765
With arrows from his silver bow, incensed
At Niobe, while Dian, archer-queen,

Struck down the daughters; for the mother dared
To make herself the peer of rosy-cheeked
Latona, who, she boastfully proclaimed, 770
Had borne two children only, while herself
Had brought forth many. Yet, though only two,
The children of Latona took the lives
Of all her own. Nine days the corses lay
In blood, and there was none to bury them, 775
For Jove had changed the dwellers of the place
To stone; but on the tenth the gods of heaven
Gave burial to the dead. Yet Niobe,
Though spent with weeping long, did not refrain
From food. And now forever mid the rocks 780
And desert hills of Sipylus, where lie,
Fame says, the couches of the goddess-nymphs,
Who lead the dance where Acheloüs flows,
Although she be transformed to stone, she broods
Over the woes inflicted by the gods. 785
But now, O noble Ancient, let us sit
At our repast, and thou mayst afterward
Mourn thy beloved son, while bearing him
Homeward, to be bewailed with many tears."
   Achilles, the swift-footed, spake, and left 790
His seat, and, slaying a white sheep, he bade
His comrades flay and dress it. Then they carved
The flesh in portions which they fixed on spits,
And roasted carefully, and drew them back.
And then Automedon distributed 795
The bread in shapely canisters around
The table, while Achilles served the flesh,
And all put forth their hands and shared the feast.
But when their thirst and hunger were appeased,
Dardanian Priam fixed a wondering look 800
Upon Achilles, who in nobleness
Of form was like the gods. Achilles fixed
A look of equal wonder on his guest,
Dardanian Priam, for he much admired
His gracious aspect and his pleasant speech. 805
And when at length they both withdrew their gaze,

Priam, the godlike Ancient, spake, and said:—
  "Nursling of Jove, dismiss me speedily
To rest, that we may lie, and be refreshed
With gentle slumbers. Never have these eyes 810
Been closed beneath their lids, since by thy hand
My Hector lost his life; and evermore
I mourn and cherish all my griefs, and writhe
Upon the ground within my palace courts;
But I have taken food at last, and drunk 815
Draughts of red wine, untasted till this hour."
  Achilles bade the attending men and maids
Place couches in the porch, and over them
Draw sumptuous purple mats on which to lay
Embroidered tapestries, and on each of these 820
Spread a broad, fleecy mantle, covering all.
Forth went the train with torches in their hands,
And quickly spread two couches. Then the swift
Achilles pleasantly to Priam said:—
  "Sleep, excellent old man, without the tent, 825
Lest some one of our counsellors arrive,
Such as oft come within my tent to sit
And talk of warlike matters. Seeing thee
In the dark hours of night, he might relate
The tale to Agamemnon, king of men, 830
And hinder thus the ransom of thy son.
But say, and truly say, how many days
Requirest thou to pay the funeral rites
To noble Hector, so that I may rest
As many, and restrain the troops from war." 835
  Then answered godlike Priam, aged king:
"Since, then, thou wilt, Achilles, that we pay
The rites of burial to my noble son,
I own the favor. Well thou knowest how
We Trojans are constrained to keep within 840
The city walls, for it is far to bring
Wood from the mountains, and we fear to dare
The journey. Nine days would we mourn the dead
Within our dwellings, and upon the tenth
Would bury him, and make a solemn feast, 845

And the next day would rear his monument,
And on the twelfth, if needful, fight again."
   And swift Achilles, godlike chief, rejoined:
"Be it, O reverend Priam, as thou wilt,
And for that space will I delay the war."   850
   He spake, and that the aged king might feel
No fear, he grasped his right hand at the wrist;
And then King Priam and the herald went
To sleep within the porch, but wary still.
Achilles slumbered in his stately tent,   855
The rosy-cheeked Briseis at his side,
And all the other gods and men who fought
In chariots gave themselves to slumber, save
Beneficent Hermes; sleep came not to him,
For still he meditated how to bring   860
King Priam back from the Achaian fleet
Unnoticed by the watchers at the gate.
So at the monarch's head he stood, and spake:—
   "O aged king, thou givest little heed
To danger, sleeping thus amid thy foes,   865
Because Achilles spares thee. Thou hast paid
Large ransom for thy well-beloved son,
And yet the sons whom thou hast left in Troy
Would pay three times that ransom for thy life,
Should Agamemnon, son of Atreus, learn—   870
Or any of the Greeks—that thou art here."
   He spake: the aged king in fear awaked
The herald. Hermes yoked the steeds and mules,
And drave them quickly through the camp unmarked
By any there. But when they reached the ford   875
Where Xanthus, progeny of Jupiter,
Rolls the smooth eddies of his stream, the god
Departed for the Olympian height, and Morn
In saffron robes o'erspread the Earth with light.
Townward they urged the steeds, and as they went   880
Sorrowed and wailed: the mules conveyed the dead,
And they were seen by none of all the men
And graceful dames of Troy save one alone.
Cassandra, beautiful as Venus, stood

On Pergamus, and from its height discerned 885
Her father, standing on the chariot-seat,
And knew the herald, him whose voice so oft
Summoned the citizens, and knew the dead
Stretched on a litter drawn by mules. She raised
Her voice, and called to all the city thus:— 890
   "O Trojan men and women, hasten forth
To look on Hector, if ye e'er rejoiced
To see him coming from the field alive,
The pride of Troy, and all who dwell in her."
   She spake, and suddenly was neither man 895
Nor woman left within the city bounds.
Deep grief was on them all; they went to meet,
Near to the gates, the monarch bringing home
The dead. And first the wife whom Hector loved
Rushed with his reverend mother to the car 900
As it rolled on, and, plucking out their hair,
Touched with their hands the forehead of the dead,
While round it pressed the multitude, and wept,
And would have wept before the gates all day,
Even to the set of sun, in bitter grief 905
For Hector's loss, had not the aged man
Addressed the people from his chariot-seat:
"Give place to me, and let the mules pass on,
And ye may weep your fill when once the dead
Is laid within the palace." As he spake, 910
The throng gave way and let the chariot pass;
And having brought it to the royal halls,
On a fair couch they laid the corse, and placed
Singers beside it, leaders of the dirge,
Who sang a sorrowful, lamenting strain, 915
And all the women answered it with sobs.
White-armed Andromache in both her hands
Took warlike Hector's head, and over it
Began the lamentation midst them all:—
   "Thou hast died young, my husband, leaving me 920
In this thy home a widow, and one son,
An infant yet. To an unhappy pair
He owes his birth, and never will, I fear,

Bloom into youth; for ere that day will Troy
Be overthrown, since thou, its chief defence, 925
Art dead, the guardian of its walls and all
Its noble matrons and its speechless babes,
Yet to be carried captive far away,
And I among them, in the hollow barks;
And thou, my son, wilt either go with me, 930
Where thou shalt toil at menial tasks for some
Pitiless master; or perhaps some Greek
Will seize thy little arm, and in his rage
Will hurl thee from a tower and dash thee dead,
Remembering how thy father, Hector, slew 935
His brother, son, or father; for the hand
Of Hector forced full many a Greek to bite
The dust of earth. Not slow to smite was he
In the fierce conflict; therefore all who dwell
Within the city sorrow for his fall. 940
Thou bringest an unutterable grief,
O Hector, on thy parents, and on me
The sharpest sorrows. Thou didst not stretch forth
Thy hands to me, in dying, from thy couch,
Nor speak a word to comfort me, which I 945
Might ever think of night and day with tears."

   So spake the weeping wife: the women all
Mingled their wail with hers, and Hecuba
Took up the passionate lamentation next:—

   "O Hector, thou who wert most fondly loved 950
Of all my sons! While yet thou wert alive,
Dear wert thou to the gods, who even now,
When death has overtaken thee, bestow
Such care upon thee. All my other sons
Whom swift Achilles took in war he sold 955
At Samos, Imbrus, by the barren sea,
And Lemnos harborless. But as for thee,
When he had taken with his cruel spear
Thy life, he dragged thee round and round the tomb
Of his young friend, Patroclus, whom thy hand 960
Had slain, yet raised he not by this the dead;
And now thou liest in the palace here,

Fresh and besprinkled as with early dew,
Like one just slain with silent arrows aimed
By Phœbus, bearer of the silver bow."   965
    Weeping she spake, and woke in all who heard
Grief without measure. Helen, last of all,
Took up the lamentation, and began:—
    "O Hector, who wert dearest to my heart
Of all my husband's brothers,—for the wife   970
Am I of godlike Paris, him whose fleet
Brought me to Troy,—would I had sooner died!
And now the twentieth year is past since first
I came a stranger from my native shore,
Yet have I never heard from thee a word   975
Of anger or reproach. And when the sons
Of Priam, and his daughters, and the wives
Of Priam's sons, in all their fair array,
Taunted me grievously, or Hecuba
Herself,—for Priam ever was to me   980
A gracious father,—thou didst take my part
With kindly admonitions, and restrain
Their tongues with soft address and gentle words.
Therefore my heart is grieved, and I bewail
Thee and myself at once,—unhappy me!   985
For now I have no friend in all wide Troy,—
None to be kind to me: they hate me all."
    Weeping she spake: the mighty throng again
Answered with wailing. Priam then addressed
The people: "Now bring wood, ye men of Troy,   990
Into the city. Let there be no fear
Of ambush from the Greeks, for when of late
I left Achilles at the dark-hulled barks,
He gave his promise to molest no more
The men of Troy till the twelfth morn shall rise." 995
    He spake, and speedily they yoked the mules
And oxen to the wains, and came in throngs
Before the city walk. Nine days they toiled
To bring the trunks of trees, and when the tenth
Arose to light the abodes of men, they brought   1000
The corse of valiant Hector from the town

With many tears, and laid it on the wood
High up, and flung the fire to light the pile.
   Now when the early rosy-fingered Dawn
Looked forth, the people gathered round the pile   1005
Of glorious Hector. When they all had come
Together, first they quenched the funeral fires,
Wherever they had spread, with dark-red wine,
And then his brothers and companions searched
For the white bones. In sorrow and in tears,   1010
That streaming stained their cheeks, they gathered them,
And placed them in a golden urn. O'er this
They drew a covering of soft purple robes,
And laid it in a hollow grave, and piled
Fragments of rock above it, many and huge.   1015
In haste they reared the tomb, with sentries set
On every side, lest all too soon the Greeks
Should come in armor to renew the war.
When now the tomb was built, the multitude
Returned, and in the halls where Priam dwelt,   1020
Nursling of Jove, were feasted royally.
Such was the mighty Hector's burial rite.

GENEALOGIES

522　ILIAD

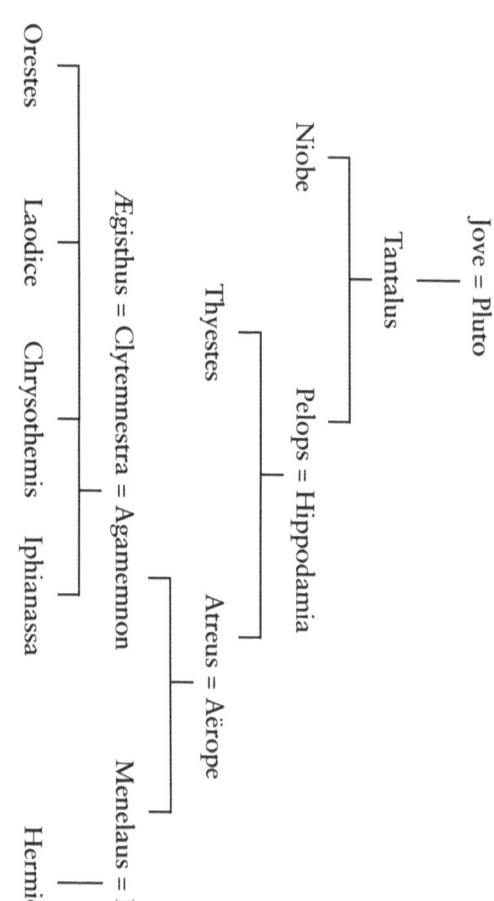

GENEALOGIES 523

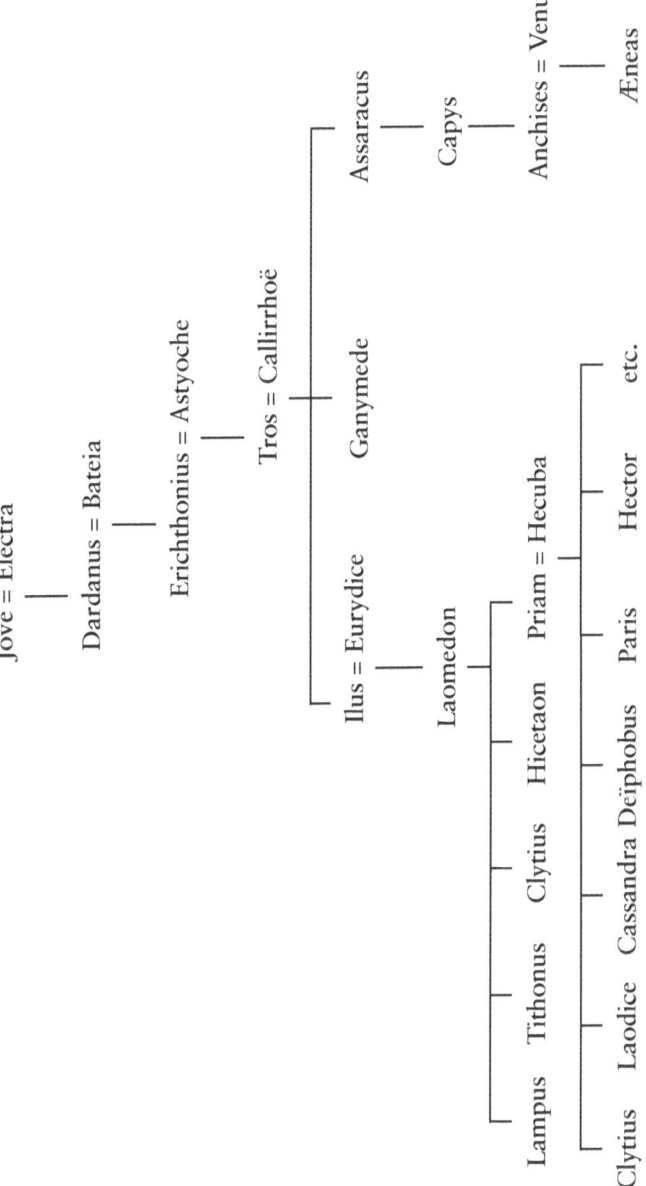

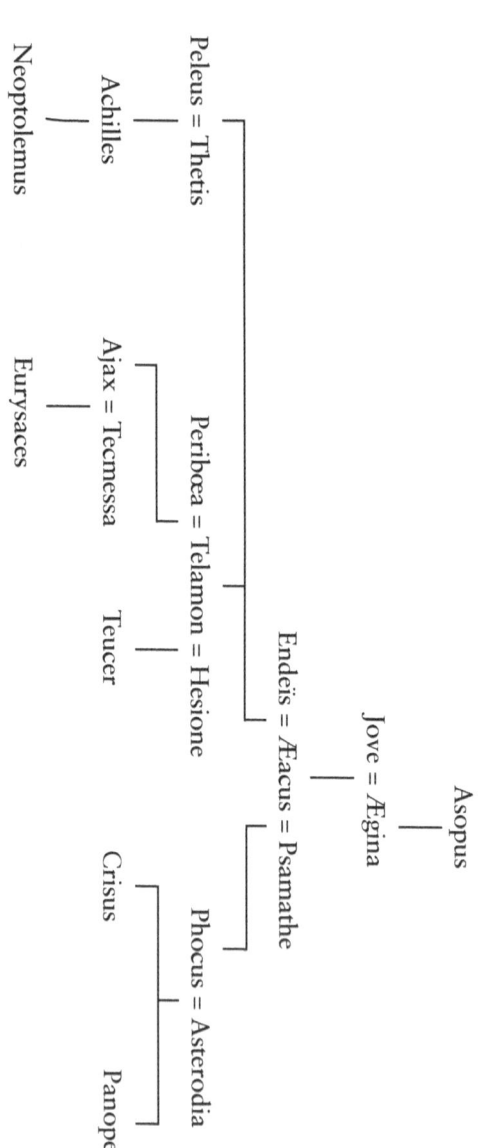

BIBLIOGRAPHY

EDITIONS

F. A. Paley, ed. **The Iliad of Homer,** 2nd ed. Vols. I-II. (London: Whitaker & Co., 1884).

D. B. Monro and T. W. Allen, eds. **Homeri Opera,** 3rd ed. Vols. I-II. (Oxford: Clarendon Press, 1920)

Walter Leaf. **The Iliad; ed., with apparatus criticus, prolegomena, notes, and appendices,** 2nd ed. Vols. I-II. (London: Macmillan & Co., 1902)

COMMENTARIES

Anton Bierl, Joachim Latacz eds. **Homer's Iliad: The Basel Commentary.** Vols. I-XI. (Berlin: De Gruyter, 2000-2016)

G.S. Kirk et al. **The Iliad: A Commentary.** Vols. I-VI. (Cambridge: Cambridge University Press, 1985-1993)

CRITICISM AND INTERPRETATION

Adam Nicolson. **Why Homer Matters: A History.** (London: Macmillan, 2015)

Richard Claverhouse Jebb. **Homer: An Introduction to the Iliad and the**

Odyssey. (Boston: Ginn and Company 1894)

Walter Leaf. **A Companion to the Iliad, for English Readers.** (London: Macmillan & Co., 1892)

Ian Morris and Barry B. Powell. **A New Companion to Homer.** (Leiden: Brill, 1997)

Cedric H. Whitman. **Homer and the Heroic Tradition.** (New York: W. W. Norton & Co., 1958)

Matthew Arnold. **On Translating Homer.** (London: Longman, Green, Longman, and Roberts, 1861)

Albert B. Lord. **The Singer of Tales,** 3rd ed. (Cambridge: Harvard University Press, 2019)

T. B. L. Webster. **From Mycenae to Homer: A Study in Early Greek Literature and Art.** (London: Methuen & Co. Ltd., 1958)

S. E. Bassett. **The Poetry of Homer.** (Berkeley, University of California Press, 1938)

M. P. Nilsson. **Homer and Mycenae.** (London: Methuen & Co Ltd., 1933)

John A. Scott. **The Unity of Homer.** (Berkeley: University of California Press, 1921)

Leonard Muellner. **The Anger of Achilles: Mēnis in Greek Epic.** (Ithaca: Cornell University Press, 1996)

Irene J. F. de Jong, ed. **Homer, Critical Assessments. Vols. I–IV.** (London and New York: Routledge, 1999)

M. M. Willcock. **A Companion to The Iliad.** (Chicago: University of Chicago Press, 2013)

Douglas L. Cairns. **Oxford Readings in Homer's Iliad.** (Oxford: Oxford University Press, 2001)

G. S. Kirk. **The Songs of Homer.** (Cambridge: Cambridge University Press, 2005)

BACKGROUND

Jacob Burckhardt, tr. Palmer Hilty. **History of Greek Culture.** (New York: Frederick Ungar, 1963)

Gregory Nagy. **Greek Mythology and Poetics.** (Ithaca: Cornell University

Press, 1992)

W. K. C. Guthrie. **The Greeks and Their Gods.** (London: Methuen & Co. Ltd., 1950)

André Bonnard. **Greek Civilization: From the Iliad to the Parthenon.** (London: Macmillan, 1962)

H. V. Routh. **God, Man, & Epic Poetry: A Study in Comparative Literature. Vol. I: Classical.** (Cambridge: Cambridge University Press, 1927)

E. R. Dodds. **The Greeks And The Irrational.** (Berkeley: University of California Press, 1951)

A. M. Snodgrass. **The Dark Age of Greece: An Archaeological Survey of the Eleventh to the Eighth Centuries BC.** (Edinburgh: Edinburgh University Press, 1971)

Erwin Rohde, tr. W. B. Hillis. **Psyche: The Cult of Souls and the Belief in Immortality among the Greeks.** (London: Routledge & Kegan Paul, 1925)

Bernard Williams. **Shame and Necessity.** (Berkeley: University of California Press, 1993)

Eric H. Cline, ed. **The Oxford Handbook of the Bronze Age Aegean.** (Oxford: Oxford University Press, 2012)

Eric H. Cline, ed. **The Oxford Handbook of Ancient Anatolia.** (Oxford: Oxford University Press, 2011)

ARTICLES AND EXTRACTS

Ricardo Duchesne. "**The Masculine Preconditions of Individualism, the Indo-Europeans, and the Modern Hegelian Concept of Collective Freedom,**" Council of European Canadians. May 1, 2018. https://www.eurocanadian.ca/2018/05/masculine-preconditions-of-individualism-indo-europeans-hegelian-concept-collective-freedom.html

Eric Voegelin. "**Homer and Mycenae**" in Order and History. Vol. II: The World of the Polis. Ch.3. (Columbia and London: University of Missouri Press, 2000).

Douglas Frame. "**Achilles and Patroclus as Indo-European Twins: Homer's Take,**" Center for Hellenic Studies, Harvard. 2013. http://nrs.harvard.edu/urn-3:hlnc.essay:Frame.Achilles_and_Patroclus_as_Indo-European_Twins.2013

Erwin F. Cook. "**The Mythological Background of Homer: The Eter-**

nal Return of Killing Dragons," Trinity University. 2015. https://www.semanticscholar.org/paper/The-Mythological-Background-of-Homer%3A-The-Eternal-Cook/

Dominique Venner. "**Homer: The European Bible,**" Counter Currents Publishing. September 7, 2010. https://www.counter-currents.com/2010/09/homer-the-european-bible-part-1/

Barbara Graziosi and Johannes Haubold. "**Homeric Masculinity: Énorén and Ágenorín,**" The Journal of Hellenic Studies, 2003. https://www.jstor.org/stable/3246260?seq=1#page_scan_tab_contents

PRE-MODERN CRITICISM

J. Lundon. "**Homeric Commentaries on Papyrus: A Survey**" in Ancient Scholarship and Grammar: Archetypes, Concepts and Contexts. Trends in Classics: Supplementary Volume 8. (Berlin and New York: De Gruyter, 2011).

F. Montanari, L. Pagani, eds. **From Scholars to Scholia: Chapters in the History of Ancient Greek Scholarship.** Trends in Classics, Supplementary Volume 9. (Berlin and New York: De Gruyter, 2011).

H. Erbse, ed. **Scholia Graeca in Homeri Iliadem (Scholia vetera).** Vols. I-VII. (Berlin: De Gruyter, 1969)

J. A. García Landa. **Homer in the Renaissance: The Troy Stories.** (Providence: Brown University, 1988).

Philip Ford. "**Homer In The French Renaissance,**" Renaissance Quarterly. Spring 2006.

Filippomaria Pontani. "**From Budé to Zenodotus: Homeric Readings in the European Renaissance,**" International Journal of the Classical Tradition. December 2007.

Marc Bizer. **Homer and the Politics of Authority in Renaissance France.** (Oxford: Oxford University Press, 2011)

GLOSSARY OF NAMES

Abantes — Euboœan tribe originating in Thrace, led by Elephenor, son of Chalcodon (2.664).

Abarbareïa — Naiad who bore Æsepus and Pedasus to Bucolion (6.27).

Abas — Trojan son of the seer Eurydamas, brother of Polyeidus, slain by Diomed (5.180).

Ablerus — Trojan slain by Antilochus (6.41).

Abydos — City in Mysia, situated at Nagara Point on the Hellespont, ally to Troy (2.1043).

Acamas — [1] Trojan son of Antenor and Theano, brother of Archelochus, cousin of Æneas, slain by Meriones or possibly Philoctetes (2.1032). [2] Thracian son of Eussorus, co-commander of the Thracians along with Piroüs, slain by Telamonian Ajax or Idomeneus (6.10).

Acessamenus — King of Pieria, father of Periboea, grandfather of Pelagon and Telamonian Ajax, great-grandfather of Asteropæus (21.176).

Achaia — Northernmost region of the Peloponnese, but used in Iliad as a collective name for the Greeks (2.650).

Achaians — Inhabitants of Achaia, Greeks collectively (1.23).

Acheloüs — [1] The largest river in Greece, dividing Acarnania from Ætolia, and chief of all river gods (21.240). [2] River in Lydia, near Mount Sipylos (24.783).

Achilles — King of the Myrmidons, son of Peleus and Thetis, grandson of Æacus, slayer of Hector (1.2).

Acrisius — King of Argos and of Ocalea, father of Danaë, grandfather of

ILIAD

Perseus (14.384).

Actæa — A Nereid (18.50).

Actor — [1] King of the Minyans of Orchomenus, son of Azeus, father of Astyoche, grandfather of Ascalaphus and Ialmenus (2.627). [2] Son of Deioneus of Phocis and Diomedè, father of Menœtius, grandfather of Patroclus (11.961). [3] King of Elis, son of Phorbas and Hyrmine, cuckolded husband of Molion, nominal father of Eurytus and Cteatus, the Molions (2.769). [4] Myrmidon, father of Echecles (16.240).

Adamas — Trojan son of Asius, nephew of Hecuba, slain by Meriones (13.703).

Admetus — King of Thessaly, son of Pheres, husband of Alcestis, father of Eumelus, took part in the Calydonian Hunt and the expedition of the Argonauts (2.890).

Adrasteia — City in Mysia, traditionally sited between Priapus and Parium (2.1038).

Adrastus — [1] King of Sicyon during the war of the Seven Against Thebes, father of Ægialeia, father-in-law of Diomed (2.703). [2] Co-commander of Trojan ally force, son of Merops, brother of Amphius, slain by Diomed (2.1041). [3] Trojan captured by Menelaus, slain by Agamemnon (6.48). [4] Trojan slain by Patroclus (16.866).

Æacus — King of Ægina, son of Jove, grandson of Asopus, father of Peleus and Telamon, grandfather of Achilles and Telamonian Ajax (16.18).

Ægæ — City in Eubœa on the Eubœan Gulf, sacred to Neptune (8.255).

Ægeon — Epithet used by mortals for Briareus (1.506).

Ægeus — King of Athens after whom the Ægean Sea is named, son of Pandion II, father of Theseus (1.336).

Ægialeia — Daughter of Adrastus, adulterous wife of Diomed (5.511).

Ægialus — City in Paphlagonia west of the river Halys and east of Carambis, ally to Troy (2.1075).

Ægilips — City on the island of Lefkada near Ithaca, in the realm of Ulysses (2.784).

Ægina — Island in the Saronic Gulf off the southern Argolid peninsula, in the realm of Argos (2.690).

Ægium — One of the 12 Achaian cities, sited on the coast west of the river Selinus, in the realm of Agamemnon (2.690).

Æmon — Father of Laerces (17.565).

GLOSSARY OF NAMES 531

Æneas — King of the Dardanians, son of Anchises and Venus, second cousin to Hector and Paris, destined to become king of the Trojans and, in Vergil's Æneid, to become the ancestor of the Romans (2.1026).

Ænius — Pæonian slain by Achilles (21.258).

Ænus — City on the south-eastern coast of Thrace (4.659).

Æpeia — City in Messinia east of Pylos (9.183).

Æpy — City in Messinia near Pylos, in the realm of Nestor (2.732).

Æsculapius — Achaian father of Machaon and Podalirius, renowned healer, deified in Roman times (2.913).

Æsepus — [1] River originating near Skepsis and emptying into the Hellespont near Zelea (2.1035). [2] Trojan son of Bucolion and Abarbareïa, twin brother of Pedasus, slain by Euryalus (6.26).

Æsyeta — [1] Trojan hero (2.902). [2] Trojan father of Alcathoüs (13.534).

Æsyma — City in Thrace (8.384).

Æsymnus — Achaian slain by Hector (11.360).

Æthè — Mare of Agamemnon (23.363).

Æthicæ — Seat of the Æthices, a Thessalian tribe near Mount Pindus (2.930).

Æthon — Horse of Hector (8.234).

Æthra — Daughter of Pittheus, mother of Theseus, abducted by Castor and Pollux, later handmaid of Helen (3.181).

Ætolians — Tribe dwelling in Ætolia, a region on the north coast of the Gulf of Corinth (9.652).

Agacles — Trojan father of the Achaian Epeigeus, by whom he was slain (16.716).

Agamedè — Daughter of Augeias, wife of Mulius, skilled in healing herbs (11.902).

Agamemnon — King of Mycenæ, son of Atreus and Aërope, brother of Menelaus, husband of Clytemnestra, father of Orestes, Iphigenia, and Electra, general of the Achaian armies (1.32).

Agapenor — King of Arcadia, grandson of Lycurgus, son of Ancæus, later founder of Paphos (2.755).

Agasthenes — Son of Augeias, father of Polyxenus, later king of Elis (2.772).

Agastrophus — Trojan son of Pæon, slain by Diomed (11.408).

Agathon — Trojan son of King Priam (24.321).

Agavè — A Nereid (18.51).

Agelaus — [1] Trojan son of Phradmon, slain by Diomed (8.325). [2] Achaian slain by Hector (11.360).

Agenor — Trojan son of Antenor and Theano, father of Echeclus (4.588).

Aglaia — Nymph, mother of Nireus by King Charopus (2.837).

Agrius — Son of King Portheus of Calydon, brother of Œneus whom his sons overthrew; Diomed reinstated Œneus, his grandfather, and later slew all Agrius' sons but Thersites (14.137).

Ajax — [1] Achaian son of Telamon and Periboea, grandson of Æacus and Acessamenus, brother of Teucer, renowned for his towering shield, commander of the Salamian contingent, known as Telamonian or Greater Ajax (1.181). [2] Achaian son of Oïleus by Eriopis, commander of the Locrian contingent, raped Cassandra in the temple of Minerva at Troy, known as Oïlean or Lesser Ajax (2.497).

Alastor — [1] Achaian commander from Pylos (4.375). [2] Lycian comrade of Sarpedon, slain by Ulysses (5.849). [3] Achaian comrade of Ajax and Teucer (8.418). [4] Trojan father of Tros (20.582).

Alcander — Lycian slain by Ulysses (5.850).

Alcathoüs — Trojan son of Æsyeta, husband of Hippodameia, brother-in-law of Æneas, slain by Idomeneus (12.112).

Alcestis — Daughter of Pelias, wife of Admetus, mother of Eumelus, an exemplar of the devoted wife, rescued from the underworld by Hercules as depicted in her eponymous play by Euripides (2.889).

Alcimedon — Myrmidon son of Laerceus, commander of the Myrmidons under Patroclus (16.249).

Alcimus — Achaian groom to Achilles, possibly the same Alcimus as was slain by Deïphobus (19.476).

Alcmaon — Achaian son of Thestor, slain by Sarpedon (12.471).

Alcmena — Theban wife of King Amphitryon, mother of Iphicles, Laonome, and Hercules (14.390).

Alectryon — Bœotian son of Itonus, father of Leïtus (17.725).

Alegenor — Bœotian son of Itonus, brother to Alectryon, father of Clonius and Promachus, uncle of Leïtus (14.623).

GLOSSARY OF NAMES 533

Aleian Fields — Plain in Cilicia in which Bellerophon wandered (6.262).

Alisium — City in Elis, on the road leading to Olympia (2.764, called "Alesium" at 11.925).

Alexander — See Paris.

Aloëus — Son of Neptune and Canace, husband of Iphimedeia, father of the giants Otus and Ephialtes (5.477).

Alope — City near Argos, in the realm of Achilles (2.849).

Alpheus — River in the western Peloponnese and its associated deity, father of Orsilochus, grandfather of Diocles (2.731).

Altes — King of the Leleges, father of Laothoë (21.108).

Althæa — Daughter of Thestius and Eurythemis, sister of Leda and Hypermnestra, wife of Œneus, mother of Meleager (9.683).

Alos — City in Thessaly, in the realm of Achilles (2.849).

Alyba — City of the Halezonians in Asia Minor, possibly Chalybe according to Strabo (2.1079).

Amarynceus — Achaian commander of the Eleans, son of Onesimachus, Acetor, or Pyttius, father of Diores (2.771).

Amazons — A warlike race of women located on the banks of the river Thermodon and Themiscyra, said to have invaded Thrace, Asia Minor, the islands of the Ægean, mainland Greece, and various other locations in the Near East (3.239).

Amisodarus — King of Caria or Lycia, father of Atymnius and Maris (16.411).

Ampheius — Trojan ally, son of Selagus, slain by Telamonian Ajax (5.702).

Amphiclus — Trojan slain by Meges (16.393).

Amphidamas — [1] Cytheran (10.313). [2] Trojan from Opus, his son slain by Patroclus over a game of dice (23.105).

Amphigeneia — City in Messinia, in the realm of Nestor (2.733).

Amphimachus — [1] Achaian son of Cteatus, grandson of Neptune, chief of the Epeans, slain by Hector (2.767). [2] Co-commander of the Carians along with his brother Nastes, son of Nomion (2.1097).

Amphinomè — A Nereid (18.53).

Amphion — Achaian chief of the Epeans (13.870).

Amphithöe — A Nereid (18.51).

Amphitryon — Cuckolded husband of Alcmena, nominal father of Hercules (5.487).

Amphius — Co-commander of a Trojan ally force, son of Merops, brother of Adrastus, slain by Diomed (2.1041).

Amphoterus — Trojan slain by Patroclus (16.521).

Amyclæ — City in Lacedæmon, said to have been the abode of Tyndarus and of Castor and Pollux (2.719).

Amydon — Capital of Pæonia on the river Axius (2.1067).

Amyntor — King of Eleon or Ormenium, son of Ormenus, father of Phœnix (9.557).

Ancæus — [1] Father of Arcadian commander Agapenor, son of King Lycurgus of Arcadia, took part in the Calydonian Hunt and the expedition of the Argonauts (2.756). [2] Pleuronian, defeated by Nestor in a wrestling match (23.778).

Anchialus — Achaian slain by Hector (5.766).

Anchises — [1] Trojan son of King Capys of Dardania and Themis, second cousin of King Priam, father of Æneas by Venus, father-in-law of Alcathoüs (2.1027). [2] Achaian from Sicyon, father of Echepolus (23.365).

Andræmon — King of Ætolia, husband of Gorge, father of Thoas, succeeded his father-in-law Œneus upon Diomed reinstating him, his tomb at Amphissa still stood in the time of Pausanias (2.7390).

Andromache — Daughter of King Eëtion of Thebes, sister of Podes, wife of Hector, mother of Astyanax (6.480).

Anemoreia — City in Phocis near Delphi (2.638).

Anteia — Wife of King Prœtus of Corinth, spurned seductress of Bellerophon (6.205).

Antenor — Trojan counselor to King Priam, son of Æsyetus and Cleomestra, husband of Theano on whom he fathered many children (2.1031).

Anthedon — City in Bœotia (2.620).

Antheia — City in Messinia (9.182).

Anthemion — Father of Simoïsius (4.598).

Antilochus — Achaian son of Nestor and Anaxibia or Eurydice, brother of Thasymedes, comrade of Achilles (4.576).

Antimachus — Trojan father of Pisander, Hippolochus, and Hippomachus, rejects Menelaus' and Ulysses' petition to return Helen (11.148).

GLOSSARY OF NAMES 535

Antiphates — Trojan slain by Leonteus (12.228).

Antiphonus — Son of Priam, slain by Neoptolemus during the siege of Troy (24.322).

Antiphus — [1] Achaian son of King Thessalus, grandson of Hercules, co-commander of the contingent from Carpathos, Casos, Cos, and other islands along with his brother Phidippus (2.845). [2] Mæonian son of Talæmenes, co-commander of the Mæonians along with his brother Mesthles (2.1088). [3] Trojan son of Priam, taken prisoner by Achilles, later slain by Agamemnon (4.618).

Antrona — City in Thessaly, in the realm of Protesilaüs (2.868).

Apæsus — City in ancient Mysia at the entrance of the Propontis, between Lampsacus and Parium (2.1039).

Aphareus — Achaian chief, son of Caletor, slain by Æneas (9.99).

Aphrodite — See Venus.

Apisaon — [1] Trojan son of Phausias, slain by Eurypylus (11.702). [2] Pæonian son of Hippasus, slain by Lycomedes (17.424).

Apollo — God of the sun, archery, music and poetry, prophecy, and disease, son of Jove and Latona, twin brother of Diana, favours the Trojans; the Oracle at Delphi was consecrated to him (1.18).

Apseudes — A Nereid (18.56).

Aræthyrea — City near Corinth, in the realm of Agamemnon (2.702).

Arcadia — Region in the central and eastern Peloponnese, named after Arcas (2.757).

Arcesilaus — Bœotian commander, son of Lycus and Theobule, brother of Prothoënor, comrade of Menestheus, slain by Hector (2.601).

Archelochus — Trojan son of Antenor, brother of Acamas, slain by Telamonian Ajax (2.1031).

Archeptolemus — Trojan son of Iphitus, charioteer to Hector, slain by Teucer (8.157).

Areïlochus — [1] Achaian father of Prothoënor (14.558). [2] Trojan slain by Patroclus (16.386).

Areïthoüs — [1] King of Arnè, father of Menestheus, husband of Philomedusa, called "Mace-bearer", fighting only with a club, slain by Lycurgus (7.12). [2] Trojan charioteer to Rigmus, slain by Achilles (20.614).

Arenè — City in Pylos, in the realm of Nestor (2.730).

Ares — See Mars.

Aretaon — Trojan slain by Teucer (6.39).

Aretus — Trojan chief, slain by Automedon (17.596).

Argias — Trojan father of Polymelus (16.525).

Argissa — City in Thessaly on the river Peneus, in the realm of Polypœtes (2.921).

Argives — An epithet for the Greeks; see also Achaians (1.101).

Argos — [1] The Argolid as a whole, the area under the dominion of Agamemnon (2.148). [2] A general term for mainland Greece (2.353). [2] City in Thessaly, in the realm of Diomed (2.685). [4] Pelasgian Argos, home of the Myrmidons (2.848).

Argos-queller — See Hermes.

Ariadne — Daughter of King Minos of Crete, sister of Phædra, helped Theseus slay the Minotaur (18.734).

Arimi — The burial place in Cilicia of the monsrous serpent Typhœus (2.983).

Arion — Immortal racehorse mounted by Adrastus (23.426).

Arisbas — Achaian father of Leocritus (17.421).

Arisba — City in Mysia (2.1050).

Arnè — City in Bœotia (2.619).

Arsinoüs — King of Tenedos, father of Hecamedè (11.759).

Artemis — See Diana.

Asæus — Achaian slain by Hector (11.357).

Ascalaphus — Achaian son of Mars and Astyoche, co-commander of the Minyan contingent from Orchomenus along with his brother Ialmenus, slain by Deïphobus (2.625).

Ascania — City in Nicæa (2.1087).

Ascanius — Phrygian son of Hippotion, co-commander of the Phrygians along with his brother Phorcys (2.1085).

Asine — City on the coast of Argolis (2.687).

Asius — [1] Commander of Trojan ally force from Percote, Practium, Sestus, Abydus, and Arisba, son of Hyrtacus, slain by Idomeneus (2.1050). [2] Trojan father of Adamas and Phænops, son of Dymas, brother of Hecuba, uncle of Hector (16.897).

GLOSSARY OF NAMES 537

Asopus — River in Bœotia and its associated deity (4.486).

Aspledon — City in Bœotia near Orchomenus (2.623).

Assaracus — King of Dardania and of Troy, son of Tros, brother of Ilus and Ganymede, father of Capys, grandfather of Anchises, great-grandfather of Æneas (20.292).

Asterium — City in Thessaly, possibly near Arnè, in the realm of Eurypylus (2.917).

Asteropæus — Pæonian son of Pelegon, grandson of the river Axius, co-commander of the Pæonians along with Pyræchmes, slain by Achilles (12.127).

Astinous — Trojan son of Protiäon, charioteer to and comrade of Polydamas (15.571).

Astyalus — Trojan slain by Polypœtes (6.37).

Astyanax — Infant son of Hector and Andromache, tradition has him thrown from the walls of Troy, but some later traditions have him survive and found later nations, e.g. the Franks; "Astyanax" is a nickname meaning "Overlord of the City"; see also Scamandrius (6.520).

Astynous — Trojan slain by Diomed (5.174).

Astyoche — [1] Daughter of Actor, mother of Ascalaphus and Ialmenus by Mars (2.628). [2] Daughter of King Phylas of Ephyrè, mother of Tlepolemus by Hercules (2.817).

Astypylus — Pæonian slain by Achilles (21.256).

Athena — See Minerva, Pallas, and Tritonia.

Athens — Chief city of Attica, founded by Erechtheus (2.667).

Athos — Mount Athos in Macedonia (14.274).

Atreus — King of Mycenæ, son of Pelops, father of Agamemnon and Menelaus (1.14).

Atrides — "Sons of Atreus," patronymic for Agamemnon and Menelaus (1.7).

Atymnias — Trojan father of Mydon, brother of Maris (5.730).

Atymnius — Trojan son of Amisodarus, brother of Maris, slain by Antilochus (16.399).

Augeia — [1] City in Locris (2.653). [2] City in Lacedæmon (2.718).

Augeias — King of Elis, son of Phorbas and Hyrmine, known for the Augeian stables in connection with the fifth labour of Hercules (2.773).

Aulis — Coastal city in Bœotia opposite Eubœa, the muster point for the entire Achaian fleet before sailing for Troy, and the site at which Agamemnon sacrificed Iphigenia (2.374).

Autolycus — Son of Hermes, husband of Mestra, father of Anticlea, grandfather of Ulysses, renowned for his cunning and the power of shapeshifting (10.309).

Automedon — Achaian son of Diores, charioteer to Achilles and Patroclus (9.257).

Autonoüs — [1] Achaian slain by Hector (11.358). [2] Trojan slain by Patroclus (16.866).

Autophonos — Theban father of Lycophontes (4.501).

Axius — River in Pæonia and its associated deity, father of Pelegon by Peribœa (2.1067).

Axylus — Wealthy Trojan ally from Arisba, son of Teuthras, slain by Diomed (6.15).

Azis — King of the Minyans of Orchomenus, son of Clymenus, father of Actor, grandfather of Astyoche, great-grandfather of Ascalaphus and Ialmenus (2.627).

Bacchus — God of wine, fertility, madness, and theatre, son of Jove and Semele (6.168).

Balius — An immortal horse sired by Zephyrus on Podargè (16.192).

Bathycles — Achaian son of Chalcon, slain by Glaucus (16.746).

Batiea — Prominent promontory near Troy (2.1090).

Bear, The — Constellation of Ursa Major, the Great Bear, also called the Big Dipper (18.612).

Beautiful, The — Epithet for Callicolone, a hill beside the river Simoïs (20.72).

Bellerophon — Corinthian son of Glaucus and Eurynome, grandson of Sisyphus, father of Laodameia and Hippolochus, grandfather of Sarpedon and Glaucus, slayer of the Chimæra (6.199).

Bellona — Goddess of war, destruction, conquest, and bloodlust (5.408).

Bessa — City in Locris (2.651).

Bias — [1] Pylian commander under Nestor (4.377). [2] Athenian commander under Menestheus (13.869). [3] Trojan son of King Priam, father of Laogonus and Dardanus (20.580).

GLOSSARY OF NAMES 539

Bienor — Trojan chief slain by Agamemnon (11.110).

Boagrius — River in Locris rising in Mount Cnemis, and flowing into the sea between Scarpheia and Thronium (2.623).

Bœbe — City in Thessaly in the realm of Eumelus, home to Lake Bœbeis (2.886).

Bœotians — Tribe dwelling in Bœotia, formerly Cadmeis, a region north of the eastern part of the Gulf of Corinth (2.602)

Boreas — God of winter and the North Wind (20.281).

Borus — [1] Mæonian father of Phæstus (5.50). [2] Achaian son of Periëres, husband of Polydora, nominal father of Menesthius (16.224).

Briareus — Hundred-handed giant, instrumental in Jove's deposing of the Titans; see also Ægeon (1.505).

Briseis — Daughter of Briseus, widow of Mynes of Lyrnessus, prize of Achilles (1.241).

Bryseiæ — City in Lacedæmon (2.718).

Bucolion — Bastard Trojan son of Laomedon and Calybe, father of Æsepus and Pedasus (6.29).

Bucolus — Achaian father of Sphelus, grandfather of Iasus (15.421).

Budeium — City in Thessaly under the dominion of the Myrmidons (16.718).

Buprasium — City in Elis, north of the city of Elis (2.761).

Cabesus — City of site unknown, likely on on the border between Macedonia and Thrace (13.451).

Cadmeans — The descendants of Cadmus, founding father of Thebes (5.1008).

Cæneus — King of the Lapiths, originally a woman until raped by Neptune and granted a wish, father of Coronus, slain fighting against the Centaurs (1.308).

Calchas — Achaian seer and priest of Apollo, son of Thestor (1.89).

Calysius — Trojan charioteer to Axylus, slain by Diomed (6.23).

Caletor — [1] Achaian father of Aphareus (13.680). [2] Trojan son of Clytius, slain by Telamonian Ajax (15.524).

Callianassa — A Nereid (18.57).

Callianira — A Nereid (18.54).

Calliarus — City in eastern Locris (2.652).

Calydnian Isles — Islands in the Sporades (2.844).

Calydon — City in Ætolia on the river Evenus, plagued by the Calydonian Boar and host to the Calydonian Hunt patronized by Œneus (2.794).

Camirus — City on the northwest coast of Rhodes (2.815).

Capaneus — Achaian son of Hipponoüs, father of Sthenelaüs (2.693).

Capys — King of the Dardanians, son of Assaracus and Hieromneme, father of Anchises, grandfather of Æneas (20.302).

Cardamyle — City in Messinia, offered by Agamemnon to Achilles (9.180).

Caresus — River in the Troad, flowing down from Ida into the river Æsepus (12.27).

Carians — Trojan allies from a region in southwestern Asian Minor from Mycalè south to Lycia and east to Phrygia (2.1092).

Cassandra — Daughter of Priam, gifted with prophecy but cursed never to be believed, raped by Oïlean Ajax in the temple of Minerva (13.453).

Castianira — Wife of Priam, mother of Trojan Gorgythion (8.383).

Castor — Brother of Helen, twin brother of Pollux, renowned for horsemanship; together the twins are known as the Dioscuri (3.296).

Casus — Island in the southeastern Ægean southwest of Crapathus and northeast of Crete (2.844).

Caucons — Trojan allies, dwelling in Asia Minor and eventually displaced by the Bithynians (10.506).

Caÿster — River in Asia Minor, upon which Ephesus was once situated (2.566).

Ceas — Father of Trœzenus (2.1065).

Cebriones — Bastard Trojan son of Priam, brother of and charioteer to Hector, slain by Patroclus (8.401).

Celadon — River in Arcadia, possible tributary of the river Alpheus (7.177).

Centaurs — Half-man, half-horse creatures, sons of Ixion and Juno, living in the mountains of Thessaly (1.339).

Cephallenians — Tribe dwelling in Cephallenia, called "Samos" in earlier times, an island off the western coast of Greece in the realm of Ulysses; see also Samos (2.781).

GLOSSARY OF NAMES 541

Cephissus — River rising in Phocis and flowing through Bœotia (2.639).

Cephissus, Lake — Lake Copais in Bœotia, west of Thebes (5.889).

Ceres — Goddess of harvest and agriculture, sister of Jove and mother of Proserpine (13.394).

Cerinthus — City on the northeastern coast of Eubœa (2.660).

Chalcis — [1] City of the Abantes in Eubœa (2.658). [2] City of the Abantes in Ætolia (2.793).

Chalcodon — King of the Abantes, son of Abas, father of Elephenor, along with Telamon he assisted Hercules in his campaign against Elis (2.663).

Chalcon — Myrmidon father of Bathycles (16.747).

Charis — One of the Graces, personification of Grace and Beauty, wife of Vulcan, possibly identical with Venus (18.478).

Charops — Trojan son of Hippasus, brother of Socus, slain by Ulysses (11.516).

Charopus — King of Syme, father of Nireus (2.837).

Chersidamas — Lycian slain by Ulysses (11.511).

Chimæra — Monstrous creature with the body of a lion, the head of a goat on its back, and a tail ending in a snake's head, offspring of Typhœus and Echidna, sibling of Cerberus and the Lernæan Hydra, slain by Bellerophon (6.231).

Chiron — Son of Saturn and Philyra, wisest of the Centaurs, teacher of Æsculapius and Achilles, dwelling on Mount Pelion (4.283).

Chromis — Mysian son of Arsinoüs, co-commander of the Mysian contingent along with his brother Ennomus, slain by Achilles (2.1080).

Chromius — [1] Pylian chief, brother of Nestor (4.376). [2] Trojan son of Priam, slain by Diomed (5.193). [3] Lycian slain by Ulysses (5.849). [4] Trojan slain by Teucer (8.348). [5] Trojan chief (17.265).

Chrysa — Home to Chryses, possibly a town in the Troad, possibly the island off Lemnos where Philoctetes was bitten by a snake (1.49).

Chryseis — Daughter of Chryses, prize of Agamemnon (1.188).

Chryses — Trojan priest of Apollo, father of Chryseis (1.15).

Chrysothemis — Daughter of Agamemnon (9.173).

Cicones — Thracian tribe living in Ismarus, Trojan allies (2.1063).

Cilicia — Region surrounding Thebè in southeastern Asian minor north of Cyprus (6.514).

Cilla — Town in Æolis, said to be near the plain of Thebè (1.50).

Cinyras — King of Cyprus, son of Apollo, priest of the Paphian Venus, gave a breastplate to Agamemnon (11.25).

Cisseus — King of Thrace, father of Theano, grandfather of Iphidamas (6.390).

Cleobulus — Trojan slain by Oïlean Ajax (16.414).

Cleonæ — City near Corinth, in the realm of Agamemnon (2.701).

Cleopatra - Daughter of Idas and Marpessa, wife of Meleager; also known as "Alcyone" (9.684).

Clitus — Trojan son of Pisenor, charioteer to Polydamas, slain by Teucer (15.558).

Clonius — Achaian chief of the Bœotians, slain by Agenor (2.601).

Clymene — Relative of Menelaus, handmaid to Helen with whom she was abducted (3.182).

Clytemnestra — Daughter of King Tyndareus and Leda, wife of Agamemnon, sister of Helen and the Dioscuri, mother of Orestes, Electra, and Iphigenia, slew Agamemnon on his return from Troy (1.148).

Clytis — Achaian father of Dolops (11.353).

Clytius — Trojan elder, son of Laomedon, brother of Priam, father of Caletor and Procleia (3.185).

Clytomedes — Elian son of Enops, defeated by Nestor in a boxing match (23.776).

Cœranus — [1] Lycian son of Iphitus, slain by Ulysses (5.849). [2] Achaian charioteer to Meriones, slain by Hector (17.735).

Coön — Trojan son of Antenor, brother of Iphidamas, slain by Agamemnon (11.294).

Copæ — City in Bœotia (2.611).

Copreus — Achaian son of Pelops, father of Periphetes, herald of Eurystheus, slew Iphitus and fled from Elis to Mycenæ (15.816).

Corinth — City on the Isthmus of Corinth, in the realm of Agamemnon (2.700).

Coronæa — City in Bœotia, near Mount Helicon (2.613).

Coronus — Achaian son of Cæneus, father of Leonteus, took part in the expedition of the Argonauts (2.932).

GLOSSARY OF NAMES 543

Cos — Island in the southeastern Ægean, part of the Dodecanese (2.843).

Cranaë — Island off the coast of Gythium in Lacedæmon, where Helen and Paris spent their first night (3.546).

Crapathus — Island in the southeastern Ægean near Casus, between Rhodes and Crete (2.842).

Creon — Achaian father of Lycomedes (9.100).

Cretans — Tribe dwelling in Crete, the large island in the southern Ægean and the seat of Minoan culture, the realm of Idomeneus (2.801).

Crethon — Achaian son of Diocles, slain by Æneas (5.680).

Crissa — City in Phocis near Delphi (2.636).

Crocyleia — City in Ithaca (2.727).

Crœsmus — Trojan slain by Meges (15.664).

Cromna — City in Paphlagonia in the region of Sesamus (2.1075).

Cronus — See Saturn.

Cteatus — Nominal son of Actor, father of the Trojan Amphimachus, twin brother of Eurytus; the two together are known as the Molions (2.768).

Curetes — Ætolians dweling in Pleuron, quarreled with the Calydonians concerning the Calydonian Hunt (9.651).

Cyllene — Mountain in northern Arcadia, birthplace of Hermes (2.746).

Cymodocè — A Nereid (18.47).

Cymothöè — A Nereid (18.48).

Cynus — City in Locris, principal sea-port of the Locrians (2.641).

Cyparissus — [1] City in Phocis (2.635). [2] City in Messinia near Pylos, in the realm of Nestor (2.732).

Cyprus — Island in the eastern Mediterranean, sacred to Venus (11.26).

Cythera — Island off the southern coast of the Peloponnese near Cape Malea, sacred to Venus (10.313).

Cytorus — City in Paphlagonia on the southern coast of the Black Sea near Mount Cytorus (2.1073).

Cythus — City in Thessaly (2.936).

Dædalus — Craftsman in the service of King Minos of Crete, father of Icarus, built the famous labyrinth, his name means "cunningly wrought" (18.732).

Dætor — Trojan slain by Teucer (8.347).

Damastor — Trojan father of Tlepolemus (16.496).

Damasus — Trojan slain by Polypœtes (12.219).

Danaë — Daughter of Acrisius, mother of Perseus by Jove (14.385).

Dardanian Gates — One of the gates of Troy (22.508).

Dardanians — Descendants of Dardanus, inhabitants of a precursor kingdom to Troy, ruled by Æneas (2.1027).

Dardanus — [1] Son of Jove and Electra, brother of Jason, father of Erichthonius, ancestor of Priam and the Trojans and through them the Romans (3.379). [2] Trojan son of Bias, slain by Achilles (20.579).

Dares — Trojan priest of Vulcan, father of Phegeus and Idæus, traditionally said to have been the author of an account of the destruction of Troy (5.11).

Daulis — City in Phocis near Apollo's shrine in Pytho, site where Philomela was raped and transformed into a nightingale (2.637

Dawn — Goddess of the morning, daughter of Hyperion and Theia, sister of Helios and Selene, mother of the winds, wife of Tithonus (1.602).

Death — God, son of Night and Erebos, twin brother of Sleep (14.277).

Deïcoön — Trojan son of Pergasis, comrade of Æneas, slain by Agamemnon (5.670).

Deïochus — Achaian slain by Paris (15.425).

Deïopites — Trojan son of Priam, slain by Ulysses (11.497).

Deïphobus — Trojan, greatest of Priam's sons after Hector and Paris, married Helen after Paris' death (12.114).

Deipylus — Achaian comrade of Sthenelus (5.399).

Deïpyrus — Achaian chief slain by Helenus (9.98).

Demeter — See Ceres.

Democoön — Bastard Trojan son of Priam, slain by Ulysses (4.631).

Demoleon — Trojan son of Antenor and Theano, slain by Achilles (20.499).

Demuchus — Trojan son of Philetor, slain by Achilles (20.576).

Deucalion — [1] King of Crete, son of Minos, brother of Ariadne, father of Idomeneus, took part in the Calydonian Hunt and the expedition of the Argonauts (12.144). [2] Trojan slain by Achilles (20.602).

GLOSSARY OF NAMES 545

Dexius — Achaian father of Iphinous (7.20).

Diana — Goddess of the hunt, childbirth, and of women's matters more generally, daughter of Jove and Latona, sister of Apollo (5.63).

Dexamenè — A Nereid (18.53).

Diocles — King of Pheræ, son of Ortilochus, father of Crethon and Orsilochus (5.679).

Diomedè — Daughter of Phorbas of Lesbos, mistress of Achilles (9.812).

Diomed — King of Argos, son of Tydeus, second only to Achilles in fighting prowess (2.692).

Dium — City of the Abantes in Eubœa (2.660).

Dione — Titaness, beloved by Jove and possibly his ancient consort, mother of Venus (5.456).

Dionysus — See Bacchus.

Diores — [1] Achaian co-commander of the Epeans along with Amphimacus and Thalpius, son of Amarynceus, slain by Piroüs (2.770). [2] Achaian father of Automedon (17.519).

Deisenor — Trojan ally (17.264).

Dios — Trojan son of Priam (24.324).

Dodona — Site of an ancient oracle of Jove in Epirus; possibly a city in Thessaly near Mount Olympus, as suggested by the likely extent of Guneus' dominion (2.939).

Dolon — Trojan spy, son of Eumedes, slain on a night mission by Diomed and Ulysses (10.366).

Dolopians — Tribe in Phthia ruled by Phœnix (9.596).

Dolopion — Trojan priest of Scamander, father of Hypsenor (5.94).

Dolops — [1] Achaian son of Clytius, slain by Hector (11.351). [2] Trojan son of Lampus, slain by Menelaus (15.666).

Doris — A Nereid (18.55).

Dorium — City in Messinia, the realm of Nestor (2.734).

Doryclus — Bastard Trojan son of Priam, slain by Telamonian Ajax (11.596).

Doto — A Nereid (18.52).

Dracius — Achaian chief of the Epeans (13.870).

Dresus — Trojan slain by Euryalus (6.24).

Dryas — Father of Lycurgus (6.166).

Dryops — Trojan slain by Achilles (20.573).

Dulichium — Island near Ithaca in the Ionian sea off western Greece, in the realm of Meges (2.774).

Dymas — Phyrigian father of Hecuba and Asius, father-in-law to Priam (16.900).

Earystus — City of Eubœa inhabited by the Abantes; also known as "Carystus" (2.661).

Dynamenè — A Nereid (18.52).

Earth — Primal Mother Earth goddess, mother of Uranus and the Titans (2.571).

Echecleus — Achaian nominal father of Eudorus, son of Actor, husband of Polymela (16.240).

Echeclus — [1] Trojan slain by Patroclus (16.867). [2] Trojan son of Agenor, slain by Achilles (20.597).

Echemon — Trojan son of Priam, slain by Diomed (5.193).

Echepolus — [1] Trojan son of Thalysias, slain by Antilochus (4.577). [2] Achaian son of Anchises of Sicyon (23.364).

Echinades — Islands east of Ithaca, in the realm of Meges (2.774).

Echius — [1] Achaian father of Mecisteus (8.418). [2] Achaian slain by Polites (15.423). [3] Lycian slain by Patroclus (16.522).

Eribœa — Wife of Aloëus, stepmother of Otus and Ephialtes (5.483).

Eëtion — [1] King of Cilician Thebè, father of Andromache, slain in a raid by Achilles (1.458). [2] Trojan father of Podes (17.692). [3] Prince of Imbros, ransomed Lycaon (21.56).

Eïonæ — City in the Argolid (2.688).

Eïoneus — [1] Achaian slain by Hector (7.15). [2] Thracian father of Rhesus (10.515).

Elasus — Trojan slain by Patroclus (16.869).

Elatus — Trojan ally from Pedasus, slain by Agamemnon (6.43).

Eleon — City in Bœotia (2.609).

Elphenor — Achaian commander of the Abantes, slain by Agenor; also known as "Elephenor" (2.662).

Elis — Region of the Epeans in the western Peloponnese (2.762).

GLOSSARY OF NAMES 547

Emathia — Ancient Macedonia, bordering on Orestis and Pieria (14.272).

Eneti — Tribe dwelling in Paphlagonia, Trojan allies (2.1070).

Enienes — Thessalian tribe dwelling on the banks of the river Spercheios (2.937).

Eniopeus — Trojan son of Thebæus, charioteer to Hector, slain by Diomed (8.150).

Enispe — City in Arcadia (2.751).

Ennomus — [1] Mysian seer, son of Arsinoüs, co-commander of the Mysians along with Chromis, slain by Achilles (2.1080). [2] Trojan slain by Ulysses (11.510).

Enope — City in Messinia east of Pylos (9.181).

Enops — [1] Trojan father of Satnius (14.550). [2] Trojan father of Thestor (16.505). [3] Father of Clytomedes (23.777).

Enyëus — King of Scyros (9.827).

Enyo — See Bellona.

Epaltes — Lycian slain by Patroclus (16.495).

Epeans — The royal house of Elis (4.681).

Epeius — Achaian son of Panopeus, grandson of Phocus, builder of the Trojan horse (23.816).

Ephialtes — Son of Neptune by Iphimedia, nominal son of Aloëus, from whom he and his brother Otus received their patronymic Aloadæ, imprisoned Mars (5.478).

Ephyrè — City in Elis on the river Selleïs, ancient capital of Augeias (2.819).

Ephyri — A tribe dwelling in Thessaly (13.368).

Epicles — Lycian slain by Telamonian Ajax (12.452).

Epidaurus — City on the northeastern Argolid, in the realm of Diomed (2.689).

Epeigeus — Myrmidon son of Agacles, slain by Hector (16.717).

Epistor — Trojan slain by Patroclus (16.869).

Epistrophus — [1] Phocian son of Iphitus and Hippolyte, co-commander of the Phocians along with his brother Schedius (2.632). [2] Lyrnessian son of Evenus, slain by Achilles (2.861). [3] Co-commander of the Halezonians along with Hodius (2.1077).

Epytus — King of Arcadia and originally of Phæsana on the river Alpheius, son of Elatus, his tomb near Mount Cyllene still stood in the time of Pausanias (2.741).

Erechtheus — Founder of Athens, son of Pandion, father of Orithyia and Procris (2.670).

Eretria — City of the Abantes in Eubœa (2.658).

Ereuthalion — Arcadian slain by Nestor (4.408).

Erichthonius — King of Dardania and Batea, son of Dardanus, brother of Ilus and Zacynthus, husband of Astyoche, father of Tros, progenitor of the royal house of Priam (20.277).

Erinnys — See Furies.

Eriopis — Wife of Oïleus, stepmother of Medon, who slew her brother (15.418).

Eryalus — Trojan slain by Patroclus (16.516).

Erymas — [1] Trojan slain by Idomeneus (16.433). [2] Trojan slain by Patroclus (16.521).

Erythini — City in Paphlagonia near Sesamus (2.1076).

Erythræ — City in Bœotia south of the Asopus at the foot of Mount Cithæron (2.589).

Eteocles — Son of Œdipus, king of Thebes, defender thereof against his brother Polynices, by whom he was slain (4.490).

Eteonus — City in Bœotia, traditional site of Œdipus' burial (2.605).

Eubœa — Large island off the coast of eastern Greece, home to Eretria and Ægæ. Also called Euripos and Negropont (2.656).

Euchenor — Corinthian son of Polyïdus, slain by Paris (13.831).

Eudorus — Myrmidon chief, son of Hermes and Polymela (16.227).

Euippus — Lycian slain by Patroclus (16.524).

Eumedes — Trojan herald, father of Dolon (10.372).

Eumelus — King of Pheræ, son of Admetus and Alcestis, husband of Iphthime, Thessalian chief (2.815).

Euneus — King of Lemnos, son of Jason and Hypsipyle, ransomed Lycaon from Patroclus (7.581).

Euphemus — Thracian son of Trœzenus, chief of the Cicones (2.1063).

Euphetes — King of Ephyrè (15.675).

GLOSSARY OF NAMES 549

Euphorbus — Trojan son of Panthoüs and Phrontis, wounded Patroclus, slain by Menelaus (16.1012).

Euryalus — Achaian son of Mecisteus (2.694).

Eurybates — [1] Achaian herald of Agamemnon (1.402). [2] Ithacan herald of Ulysses (2.224).

Eurydamas — Trojan interpreter of dreams, father of Abas and Polyeidus (5.181).

Eurymedon — [1] Achaian son of Ptolemy Piraides, charioteer to Agamemnon (4.294). [2] Achaian charioteer to Nestor (8.141).

Eurynomè — Oceanid, mother to the Graces by Jove (18.499).

Eurypylus — [1] King of Cos (2.843). [2] King of Thessaly, son of Evæmon, commander of the Thessalians from Ormenion (2.918).

Eurystheus — King of Argos, son of Sthenelus, grandson of Perseus, set Hercules the Twelve Labours (8.455).

Eurytus — [1] King of Œchalia (2.735). [2] Nominal son of Actor, father of the Achaian Thalpius, twin brother of Cteatus; the two together are known as the Molions (2.769).

Eussorus — Thracian father of Acamas (6.11).

Eutresis — City in Bœotia (2.612).

Evæmon — Father of Eurypylus of Ormenion (2.919).

Evenus — [1] Lyrnessian son of Selepius, father of Mynes and Epistrophus (2.862). [2] Father of Marpessa (9.686).

Exadius — Lapith, fought at the marriage feast of Pcirithous (1.334).

Fates — Weaving goddesses who apportion destinies to mortals at birth (2.1046).

Furies — Chthonic deities of vengeance, originally a personification of curses pronounced on the guilty; also euphemistically known as Eumenides ("beneficent ones") (9.565).

Galateia — A Nereid (18.55).

Ganymede — Son of Tros, most beautiful of mortals, immortalized as cupbearer to Jove (5.322).

Gargarus — Summit of Mount Ida, beloved of Jove (8.57).

Glaphyræ — City in Thessaly, in the realm of Eumelus (2.886).

Glaucus — [1] Lycian son of Hippolochus, co-commander of the Lycians along with Sarpedon, ancestral guest of Diomed (2.1106). [2] Son of

Sisyphus and Merope, grandson of Æolus, father of Bellerophon, great-grandfather of Glaucus, angered the gods by feeding his horses human flesh to imbue them with spirit (6.198).

Glissa — City in Bœotia, burial place of Argive chiefs who fell in battle (2.615).

Gnossus — Principal city in Crete, site of the Minoan culture, home to Minos, Ariadne, and the labyrinth of Dædalus; also known as "Cnosus" (2.733).

Gonoessa — Achaian city near Cornith, in the realm of Agamemnon (2.705).

Gorgon — Monstrous female creature with hair made of living snakes, whose visage could turn its beholder to stone (5.927).

Gorgythion — Trojan son of Priam and Castianira, charioteer to Hector, slain by Teucer (8.381).

Gortyna — City in Crete, perhaps a term for the surrounding region (2.802).

Graces — Goddesses of beauty, daughters of Jove and Eurynome, part of the retinue of Venus (5.414).

Graia — City in Bœotia, traditionally held to be of great antiquity, said by Aristotle to have preceded the deluge (2.606).

Granicus — River in the Troad, flowing down from Ida into the Hellespont (12.26).

Guneus — Achaian commander of the Enienes and Peribœans, Pseudo-Apollodorus has him journeying to Libya after the war and settling near the river Cinyps (2.935).

Gygæa — Naiad of Lake Gyges in Magonia, mother of Mesthles and Antiphus by Talæmenes (2.1090).

Gyrtias — Mysian father of Hyrtius (14.634).

Gyrtonè — City in Thessaly, in the realm of Polypœtes (2.840).

Hades — God of the dead, king of the underworld, son of Saturn and Rhea, brother of Jove, Ceres, and Neptune; also a title for the underworld in general, the destination of the dead, of particularly fallen warriors (1.4).

Hæmon — [1] Pylian chief under Nestor, son of Creon of Thebes, father of Maion (4.376).

Halezonians — Trojan allies, a tribe of unknown origin, led by Hodius

GLOSSARY OF NAMES 551

and Epistrophus (2.1078, called "Halizonians" at 5.45).

Haliartus — City in Bœotia (2.614).

Halius — Lycian slain by Ulysses (5.850).

Hamopaon — Trojan son of Polyæmon, slain by Teucer (8.349).

Harmonius — Trojan blacksmith (5.71).

Harpalion — Paphlagonian son of King Pylæmenes, slain by Meriones (13.805).

Hebe — Goddess of youth, daughter of Jove and Juno, cupbearer for the gods on Olympus (4.3).

Hecamedè — Daughter of Arsinoüs, captive servant woman of Nestor (11.757).

Hector — Trojan son of Priam and Hecuba, chief Trojan hero and general of the allied armies (1.309).

Hecuba — Daughter of Dymas, wife of Priam, mother of Hector (6.577).

Helen — Daughter of Jove and Leda, sister of Clytemnestra and the Dioscuri, wife of Menelaus, abducted by Paris from Lacedæmon, instigating the Trojan War (2.197).

Helemes — Achaian son of Œnops, slain by Hector (5.886).

Helenus — Trojan son of Priam, skilled in augury (6.93).

Helicaon — Trojan son of Antenor, husband of Laodice (3.156).

Helicè — City or region on the Gulf of Corinth in the realm of Agamemnon, home to a sanctuary of Neptune, seat of the First Achaian League (2.707).

Hellenes — Tribe dwelling in Hellas, a region in southeastern Thessaly, in the realm of Peleus and Achilles (2.851).

Hellespont — Narrow strait linking the Black Sea with the Ægean Sea; also known as the "Dardanelles" (2.1062).

Helonè — City in Thessaly near Mount Olympus, in the realm of Polypœtes (2.841).

Helos — [1] City in Lacedæmon east of the mouth of the Eurotas (2.719). [2] City in Messinia in the realm of Nestor (2.734).

Hephæstus — See Vulcan.

Heptaporus — River in the Troad (12.27).

Hercules — Deified hero, son of Jove and Alcmena, father of Tlepolemus, performed the Twelve Labours, rescued Prometheus, sacked Troy on account of Laomedon breaking his word (2.811).

Herma — City in Bœotia (2.607).

Hermes — God of trade, wealth, luck, thieves, and travel, son of Jove, herald messenger of the gods; also known as "Argos-queller", alluding to his slaying a primordial giant (2.131).

Hermione — City in the southern Argolid, in the realm of Diomed (2.686).

Hermus — River in Mæonia, flowed past Tmolus and Sardis (20.494).

Hicetaon — Trojan elder, son of Laomedon, father of Melanippus and Thymœtes (3.185).

Hippasus — [1] Trojan father of Charops and Socus (11.516). [2] Achaian father of Hypsenor (13.511). [3] Trojan father of Apisaon (17.424).

Hippomulgi — Nomadic tribe of the north, likely Scythians, called by Hesiod "mare-milkers" (13.7).

Hippocoön — Trojan ally, cousin of Rhesus (10.612).

Hippodamas — Trojan son of Priam, slain by Achilles (20.505).

Hippodameia — [1] Daughter of Atrax, wife of Pirithoüs, mother of Polypœtes, (2.926). [2] Eldest daughter of Anchises, wife of Alcathoüs (13.536).

Hippodamus — Trojan slain by Ulysses (11.403).

Hippolochus — [1] Trojan son of Bellerophon, father of Glaucus (6.152). [2] Trojan son of Antimachus, slain by Agamemnon (11.146).

Hippomachus — Trojan son of Antimachus, slain by Leonteus (12.225).

Hipponoüs — Achaian slain by Hector (11.361).

Hippothoüs - [1] Larissan son of Lethus, grandson of Teutamus, co-commander of the Pelasgians along with his brother Pylæus, slain by Telamonian Ajax (2.1054). [2] Trojan son of Priam (24.323).

Hippotion — Trojan father of Ascanius and Morys, slain by Meriones (13.1000).

Hira — City in Messinia, east of Pylos (9.181).

Histiæa — City of the Abantes, in Eubœa (2.627).

Hodius [1] Co-commander of the Halezonians along with Epistrophus, slain by Agamemnon (2.1077). [2] Achaian herald (9.206).

Hours — Goddesses of the seasons, wardens at the gates of Mount

Olympus (5.941).

Hyades — Constellation forming the face of the bull Taurus, named after the nymph half sisters of the Pleiades (18.611).

Hyampolis — City in Phocis (2.637).

Hyda — Region of Mæonia in the Hermus valley (20.484).

Hyla — City in Bœotia on the shores of Lake Hylica (2.609).

Hyllus — Tributary of the river Hermus in Mæonia, later known as the river Phrygius (20.493).

Hyperenor — Trojan son of Panthoüs, brother of Euphorbus, slain by Menelaus (14.639).

Hyperesia — Corinthian city, in the realm of Agamemnon (2.704).

Hyperian Fount — Spring in Thessaly, in the realm of Euryplus (2.916).

Hypirochus — [1] Trojan slain by Ulysses (11.403). [2] Chief of Elis, father of Itymoneus (11.820).

Hypenor — Trojan slain by Diomed (5.174).

Hypothebæ — Settlement to the north of Thebes built after its destruction in the War of the Seven (2.616).

Hypsenor — [1] Trojan son of the priest Dolopion, slain by Eurypylus (5.93). [2] Achaian son of Hippasus, slain by Deïphobus (13.511).

Hypsipyle — Daughter of Thoas, wife of Jason, mother of Euneus (7.582).

Hyria — City in Bœotia (2.603).

Hyrmine — City of the Epeans in Elis, named after Hyrmine, daughter of Epeius (2.762).

Hyrtacus — Trojan husband of Arisba, father of Asius and Nisus (2.1051).

Hyrtius — Mysian son of Gyrtius, Mysian chief, slain by Telamonian Ajax (14.633).

Ialmenus — Achaian son of Mars and Astyoche, co-commander of the Minyan contingent from Orchomenus along with his brother Ascalaphus (2.626).

Iæra — A Nereid (18.51).

Ialassa — City in the north of Rhodes (2.816).

Iamenus — Trojan slain by Leonteus (12.171).

Iapetus — Titan brother of Saturn, father of Prometheus (8.598).

Iardan — River in the western Peloponnese, in Odyssey a river of the same name in Crete is mentioned (7.178).

Iasus — Athenian chief, son of Sphelus, grandson of Bucolus, slain by Æneas (15.413).

Icarian Sea — Sea south of Chios, between the Cyclades and Asia Minor (2.179).

Ida — Mountain and range southeast of Troy, also the name of a sacred mount in Crete (2.1029).

Idæus — [1] Trojan herald of Priam (3.308). [2] Trojan son of Dares, brother of Phegeus (5.13).

Idas — Son of Aphareus and Arene, husband of Marpessa, and father of Cleopatra (9.687).

Idomeneus — Cretan son of Deucalion, grandson of Minos and Pasiphæ, commander of the contingent from Crete (1.189).

Ilesius — City in Bœotia (2.607).

Ilioneus — Trojan son of Phorbas, slain by Peneleus (14.603).

Ilium — The citadel of Troy, so named after Ilus, great-grandson of Dardanus; alternative name for Troy itself (2.197).

Ilus — Son of Tros and Calirrhoë, grandson of Erichthonius, father of Laomedon, grandfather of Priam, founder of Troy (10.490).

Ilythian Maids — The Eileithyiæ, goddesses of childbirth and midwifery, possibly related to the cult of Eleusis (11.318).

Imbrasus — Thracian father of Piroüs (4.658).

Imbrius — Trojan ally from Pedæum, son of Mentor, husband of Medesicasta, son-in-law of Priam, slain by Teucer (13.209).

Imbrus — Island at the entrance to Saros Bay in the Ægean, northwest of Troy (13.40).

Iolchos — City in Thessaly, in the realm of Eumelus (2.887).

Ipheus — Lycian slain by Patroclus (16.522).

Iphianassa — Daughter of Agamemnon (9.174).

Iphiclus — Achaian son of Phylacus, father of Protesilaüs and Podarces, defeated by Nestor in a foot-race (2.879).

Iphidamas — Trojan son of Antenor and Theano, reared in Thrace, slain by Agamemnon (11.260).

GLOSSARY OF NAMES 555

Iphinous — Achaian son of Dexius, slain by Glaucus (7.20).

Iphis — Mistress of Patroclus, captured at the taking of Scyros (9.825).

Iphition — Trojan general, son of Otrynteus and a Naiad, slain by Achilles (20.482).

Iphitus — [1] Achaian son of Naubolus, father of Schedius, Epistrophus, and Eurynome, took part in the expedition of the Argonauts (2.633). [2] Trojan father of Archeptolemus (8.158).

Iris — Goddess of the rainbow, minister of the gods, messenger of Jove (2.985).

Isandrus — Son of Bellerophon, slain by Mars (6.256).

Isus — Bastard Trojan son of Priam, ransomed by Achilles, slain by Agamemnon (11.120).

Ithaca — Island in the Ionian Sea off western Greece, seat of Ulysses (2.224).

Ithæmenes — Trojan father of Sthenelaüs (16.736).

Ithome — City in Thessaly, in the realm of Podalirius and Machaon (2.909).

Itona — City in Thessaly, in the realm of Protesilaüs (2.867).

Itymoneus — Epean chief of Elis, son of Hypirochus, slain by Nestor (11.819).

Ixion — Nominal father of Pirithoüs (14.381).

Janassa — A Nereid (18.58).

Janeira — A Nereid (18.58).

Jason — Son of Æson, commander of the Argonauts, father of Euneus by Hypsipyle, quested after the Golden Fleece (7.583).

Jove — King of the gods, son of Saturn and Rhea, brother and husband of Juno, father of the Olympians, shares dominion of the world with Neptune, who rules the sea, and Hades, who rules the underworld (1.6, called "Jupiter" at 1.305).

Juno — Goddess of women, marriage, and childbirth, daughter of Saturn and Rhea, wife and sister of Jove, favours the Achaians (1.72).

Läas — City in Lacedæmon (2.721).

Lacedæmon — City and kingdom of Menelaus (2.716).

Laerces — Myrmidon son of Æmon, father of Alcimedon (17.565).

Laertes — Son of Arceisius, father of Ulysses (2.201).

Lampus — [1] Trojan elder, son of Laomedon, father of Dolops (3.185). [2] Horse of Hector (8.233).

Laodamas — Trojan son of Antenor, slain by Telamonian Ajax (15.655).

Laodameia — Daughter of Bellerophon, sister of Hippolochus and Isander, mother of Sarpedon by Jove, slain by Diana (6.257).

Laodice — [1] Trojan daughter of Priam, wife of Helicaon (3.155). [2] Daughter of Agamemnon (9.174).

Laodocus — [1] Trojan son of Antenor (4.108). [2] Achaian charioteer to Antilochus (17.842).

Laogonus [1] Trojan son of Onetor, slain by Meriones (16.757). [2] Trojan son of Bias, slain by Achilles (20.579).

Laomedon — King of Troy, son of Ilus, father of Priam, Tithonus, Lampus, Clytius, Hicetaon, Bucolion, and Astyoche, possibly of Tithonus and Ganymede (3.311).

Laothoë — Trojan daughter of Altes, wife of Priam, mother of Polydorus and Lycaon (21.108).

Lapithæ — Tribe dwelling in Thessaly in the valley of the Peneus and on Mount Pelion, commanded by Polypœtes and Leonteus (12.158).

Larissa — City of the Pelasgians in Asia Minor (2.1056).

Lectos — Cape and promontory in the Troad between Tenedos and Lesbos (14.341).

Leïtus — Achaian son of Alectryon by Cleobule, co-commander of the Bœotians along with Peneleus, took part in the expedition of the Argonauts (2.600).

Leleges — Trojan allies, tribe dwelling in northwestern Asia Minor, conquered by the Carians (20.125, called "Lelegans" at 10.506).

Lemnos — Island in the northeastern Ægean Sea, sacred to Vulcan (1.714).

Leocritus — Achaian son of Arisbas, comrade to Lycomedes, slain by Æneas (17.420).

Leonteus — Achaian son of Coronus, co-commander of the Lapiths from Argissa along with Polypœtes (2.931).

Lesbos — Island in the northeastern Ægean Sea south of Troy, home to Sappho (9.823).

Lethus — Larissan son of Teutamus, father of Hippothoüs and Pylæus (2.1059).

Latona — Goddess of feminine demure and motherhood, daughter of the Titan Cœus, mother of Apollo and Diana by Jove (1.10).

Leucus — Achaian comrade of Ulysses, slain by Antiphus (4.623).

Lycimnius — Bastard son of Electryon, uncle of Hercules, slain by his great-nephew Tlepolemus, some sources say unintentionally (2.826).

Lilæa — City in Phocis (2.640).

Limnoreia — A Nereid (18.50).

Lindus — City in Rhodes (2.814).

Locrians — Tribe dwelling in Locris in northeastern Greece, the kingdom of Oïlean Ajax (2.645).

Lycaon — [1] Trojan father of Pandarus (2.1036). [2] Trojan son of Priam and Laothoë, slain by Achilles (3.412).

Lycastus — City in Crete (2.804).

Lycians — Trojan allies, a tribe dwelling in Lycia in southern Asia Minor, in the realm of Sarpedon and Glaucus (2.1107).

Lycomedes — Theban son of Creon, brother of Megareus, Hæmon, Megara (9.100).

Lycon — Trojan slain by Peneleus (16.419).

Lycophontes — [1] Theban son of Autophonus, slain by Tydeus (4.500). [2] Trojan slain by Teucer (8.348).

Lycophron — Cytheran son of Mastor, comrade of Telamonian Ajax, slain by Hector (15.538).

Lyctus — City in Crete, birthplace of Jove (2.803).

Lycurgus — [1] Thracian king of the Edones, son of Dryas, persecuted the cult of Bacchus, blinded therefor by Jove (6.165). [2] King of Arcadia, son of Aleus and Neæra, slayer of Areïthoüs (7.186).

Lyrnessus — Cilician city in Dardania, home of Briseis (2.858).

Lysander — Trojan slain by Telamonian Ajax (11.598).

Macar — Son of Helios and Rhodos, king and founder of Lesbos (24.688).

Machaon — Thessalian son of Æsculapius, healer and co-commander of the Thessalian contingent from Tricca and Œchalia along with his brother Podalirius (2.914).

Mæander — River in Caria, near Miletus (2.1095).

Mæmalus — Myrmidon father of Pisander (16.244).

Mæonians — Trojan allies, tribe dwelling in Mæonia, a region in Lydia (2.1089).

Mæra — A Nereid (18.59).

Magnesians — Tribe dwelling in Magnesia, a region on the southeastern coast of Thessaly, led by Prothoüs (2.946).

Mantinea — City in Arcadia (2.753).

Maris — Lycian son of Amisodarus, brother of Atymnius, slain by Thrasymedes (16.400).

Marpessa — Daughter of Evenus and Alcippe, husband of Idas, mother of Cleopatra (9.686).

Mars — God of war, son of Jove and Juno, consort of Venus, favours the Trojans (2.140).

Mases — City in the southern Argolid, in the realm of Diomed (2.691).

Mastor — Cytheran father of Lycophron (15.538).

Mecisteus — [1] Achaian son of Talaus and Lysimache, brother of Adrastus, father of Euryalus (2.695). [2] Achaian son of Echius, comrade of Telamonian Ajax and Teucer, slain by Polydamas (8.525, called "Menestheus" at 8.417).

Medeon — City in Bœotia (2.611).

Medesicasta — Trojan illegitimate daughter of Priam, wife of Imbrius (13.212).

Medon — [1] Achaian bastard son of Oïleus, leader of the Thessalians from Methonè in absence of Philoctetes, slain by Æneas (2.906). [2] Chief of the Phthians (13.871).

Megas — Achaian son of Phyleus, grandson of Augeias, commander of the men from Dulichium and the Echinades (2.776).

Meges — Trojan father of Perimus (16.867).

Melanippus — [1] Trojan slain by Teucer (8.350). [2] Trojan son of Hicetaon, slain by Antilochus (15.691). [3] Trojan slain by Patroclus (16.868). [4] Achaian chief (19.287).

Melanthius — Trojan slain by Eurypylus (6.46).

Melas — Son of Portheus, brother of Œneus (14.139).

Meleager — Son of Œneus and Althæa, Ætolian prince, took part in the

GLOSSARY OF NAMES   559

Calydonian Hunt and the expedition of the Argonauts (2.797).

Melibœa — City in Thessaly, in the realm of Philoctetes (2.893).

Melita — A Nereid (18.50).

Menelaus — King of Lacedæmon, son of Atreus, brother of Agamemnon, husband of Helen (1.207).

Menesthes — Achaian slain by Hector (5.699).

Menestheus — [1] Athenian son of Peteus, commander of the Athenian contingent (2.677). [2] Myrmodon chief, son of the river Spercheius, nominal son of Borus (16.220).

Menesthius — Achaian son of Areïthoüs, slain by Paris (7.11).

Menœtius — Opœian son of Actor, father of Patroclus, comrade of Hercules (9.248).

Menon — Trojan slain by Leonteus (12.230).

Mentes — Ciconian commander (17.87).

Mentor — Trojan father of Imbrius, horse breeder (13.209).

Meriones — Cretan son of Molus, comrade of and second in command to Idomeneus (2.746).

Mermerus — Trojan slain by Antilochus (14.635).

Merops — Percosian prophet, father of Cleite, Arisbe, Adrestus, and Amphius (2.1043).

Messa — City in Lacedæmon (2.717).

Messeis — Spring, perhaps in Thessaly (6.585).

Mesthles — Mæonian son of Talæmenes, co-commander of the Mæonians along with Antiphus (2.1088).

Mestor — Trojan son of Priam (24.332).

Methonè — City in Thessaly, in the realm of Philoctetes (2.817).

Midea — City in Bœotia (2.619).

Miletus — [1] City in Crete (2.803). [2] City in Caria, a seaport in southern Asia Minor near Samos (2.1094).

Minerva — Goddess of wisdom, craft, and warfare, daughter of Jove, favours the Achaians and especially Ulysses (4.388).

Minos — King of Crete, son of Jove and Europa, father of Deucalion (13.562).

Minyas — Tribe dwelling in Orchomenus, commanded by Ascalaphus and Ialmenus, associated with the Pelasgians but probably post-dating them; also known as the "Minyans" (2.624).

Minyëius — River in the western Peloponnese flowing into the sea near Arenè (11.880).

Mnesus — Pæonian slain by Achilles (21.257).

Molion — Trojan charioteer to Thymbræus, slain by Ulysses (11.385).

Molions — Twin brothers Cteatus and Eurytus, nominal sons of Actor but sired by Neptune, nephews of Augeias (11.864).

Molus — Achaian son of Deucalion, father of Meriones (10.315).

Morys — Phrygian son of Hippotion, slain by Meriones (13.999).

Mulius — [1] Epean chief, son-in-law of Augeias, slain by Nestor (11.901). [2] Trojan slain by Patroclus (16.870). [3] Trojan slain by Achilles (20.594).

Muses — Nine inspirational goddesses of literature, science, and the arts, daughters of Jove and Mnemosyne (1.764).

Mycalè — Mountain in Caria, north of the mouth of the river Mæander, divided from Samos by the Mycale Strait (2.1096).

Mycalesian Plain — Plain in Bœotia in the region of Tanagra, near Thebes (2.606).

Mycenæ — City in the Argolid north of Argos and Tiryns, royal capital of Agamemnon, seat of Mycenæan culture (2.699).

Mydon — [1] Paphlagonian son of Atymnius, charioteer to Pylæmenes, slain by Antilochus (5.730). [2] Pæonian slain by Achilles (21.256).

Mygdon — Son of Acmon, commander of the Phrygians against the Amazons (3.235).

Mynes — King of Lyrnessus, son of Evenus, husband of Briseis, slain by Achilles (2.861).

Myrinna — Queen of the Amazons, believed to have founded the city of Myrina in Lemnos (2.1020).

Myrmidons — Tribe dwelling in Phthia in southern Thessaly, ruled by Peleus, commanded by Achilles (1.235).

Myrsinus — City in Elis, later known as "Myrtuntium" (2.763).

Mysians — [1] Trojan allies, tribe dwelling to the east of the Troad (2.1081). [2] Tribe dwelling in Thrace (13.5).

GLOSSARY OF NAMES 561

Naiads — Feminine spirits or nymphs presiding over bodies of fresh water (14.548).

Nastes — Carian son of Nomion, co-commander of the Carians along with his brother Amphimachus, slain by Achilles (2.1092).

Naubolus — King of Phocis, son of Ornytus, father of Iphitus (2.633).

Neleus — King of Pylos, son of Neptune and Tyro, father of Nestor (2.26).

Nemertes — A Nereid (18.56).

Neoptolemus — Son of Achilles, slayer of Priam and Astyanax (19.398).

Neptune — God of the sea and earthquakes, son of Saturn and Rhea, brother of Jove, Ceres, and Hades (1.501).

Nereids — Water nymphs, daughters of Nereus, presiding over primarily the Ægean Sea, as opposed to Naiads who preside over fresh water, and Oceanides who preside over the great ocean (18.64).

Nereus — Primordial water god, the Old Man of the Sea, father of Thetis and the Nereids (18.45).

Neritus — Mountain on Ithaca (2.783).

Nesæa — A Nereid (18.48).

Nestor — King of Pylos, son of Neleus, father of Antilochus and Thrasymedes, took part in the Calydonian Hunt and the expedition of the Argonauts, an elder statesman and emblematic of wisdom and experience (1.290).

Night — Primordial goddess of the night, mother of Sleep, Death, and Darkness (14.310).

Niobe — Phrygian daughter of Tantalus, sister of Pelops, wife of King Amphion, her insult to Latona prompted Diana and Apollo to slay all her children (24.762).

Nireus — Achaian son of Charopus and Aglaia, commander of the contingent from Syma (2.836).

Nyssa — [1] City in Bœotia (2.620). [2] Mountain on Eubœa, birthplace of Bacchus (6.169).

Nisyrus — Island in the southeastern Ægean, part of the Dodecanese (2.842).

Noëmon — [1] Lycian slain by Ulysses (5.851). [2] Achaian comrade of Antilochus (23.747).

Nomion — Carian father of Amphimachus and Nastes (2.1099).

Ocalea — City in Bœotia near Mantinea (2.591).

Ocean — Colossal river encircling the world, and its associated deity (1.532).

Ochesius — Ætolian father of Periphas (5.1056).

Odysseus — See Ulysses.

Œchalia — City in Thessaly, seat of Eurytus, in the realm of Machaon and Podalirius (2.735).

Œdipus — King of Thebes, son of Laius and Jocasta, subject of Sophocles' Œdipus Rex (23.835).

Œneus — King of Pleuron and Calydon, son of Portheus, father of Tydeus and Meleager, grandfather of Diomed (2.795).

Œnomaus — [1] Achaian slain by Hector (5.885). [2] Trojan slain by Idomeneus (12.173).

Œnops — Achaian father of Helenus (5.886).

Œtylus — City in Lacedæmon on the eastern shore of the Messinian Gulf (2.721).

Oïleus — [1] King of Locris, son of Hodœdocus and Laonome, father of Oïlean Ajax and Medon (2.644). [2] Trojan charioteer to Bienor, slain by Agamemnon (11.111).

Olenian Precipice — Mountain near the river Peiros on the border of Elis (2.763).

Olenus — City in Ætolia between the rivers Acheloüs and Evenus (2.792).

Olizon — City in Thessaly, in the realm of Philoctetes (2.892).

Oloösson — City in Thessaly, in the realm of Polypœtes (2.923).

Olympus — Mountain in northern Thessaly, seat of the Olympian gods (1.24).

Onchestus — City in Bœotia in the region of Haliartus, home to a sanctuary of Neptune (2.617).

Onetor - Trojan father of Laogonus, priest of Idæan Jove (16.758).

Ophelestes — [1] Trojan slain by Teucer (8.347). [2] Pæonian slain by Achilles (21.258).

Opheltius — [1] Trojan slain by Euryalus (6.25). [2] Achaian slain by Hector (11.359).

GLOSSARY OF NAMES 563

Opites — Achaian slain by Hector (11.359).

Opus — City in Locris, home of Menœtius and Patroclus (2.651).

Orchomenus — [1] City of the Minyans bordering on Bœotia (2.624). [2] City in Arcadia (2.749).

Orithya — A Nereid (18.60).

Oresbius — Bœotian slain by Hector (5.887).

Orestes — [1] Achaian slain by Hector (5.884). [2] Trojan son of Agamemnon, slew Clytemnestra to avenge his father, subject of Æschylus' Oresteia (9.171). [3] Trojan slain by Leonteus (12.172).

Orion — Constellation named after the great huntsman, fell in love with Meriope, slain by a scorpion; the constellation is pursued by Scorpio (18.611).

Orion's Hound — Sirius, the Dog-star (22.38).

Ormenium — City in Thessaly, the realm of Eurypylus (2.915).

Ormenus — [1] Trojan slain by Teucer (8.347). [2] King of Ormenium, son of Cercaphus, grandson of Æolus, father of Amyntor (9.557). [3] Trojan slain by Polypœtes (12.223).

Orneia — City in the northern Argolid near Corinth, in the realm of Agamemnon (2.702).

Orsilochus — [1] Achaian son of Diocles, slain by Æneas (5.680). [2] Achaian son of Alpheus, father of Diocles (5.685). [3] Trojan slain by Teucer (8.346).

Orthæus — Trojan chief (13.996).

Orthè — City in Thessaly, in the realm of Polypœtes (2.922).

Orus — Achaian slain by Hector (11.360).

Orthryoneus — Trojan suitor of Cassandra, slain by Idomeneus (13.449).

Otreus — King of Phrygia (3.235).

Otrynteus — Trojan father of Iphition (20.485).

Otus — [1] Nominal son of Aloëus, from whom he and his brother Ephialtes received their patronymic Aloadæ, imprisoned Mars (5.478). [2] Cyllenian commander of the Epeans, slain by Polydamas (15.657).

Pæon — [2] Trojan father of Agastrophus (11.409). God of medicine, later an epithet of Apollo (5.1125).

Pæonians — Tribe dwelling in Pæonia, in the region of Thrace, later part of Macedonia (2.1066).

Pæsus — City in the Troad (5.772).

Pallas — Epithet of Minerva (1.251).

Palmys — Trojan chief (13.997).

Pammon — Trojan son of Priam (24.322).

Pandarus — Lycian son of Lycaon, commander of the Zeleian contingent, slain by Diomed; portrayed quite differently in later literature, as a conniving figure who facilitates the affair between Troilus and Cressida (2.1036).

Pandion — Achaian comrade of Teucer (12.444).

Pandocus — Trojan slain by Telamonian Ajax (11.597).

Panope — City in Phocis (2.636, called "Panopeus" at 17.371).

Panopè — A Nereid (18.54).

Panopeus — Achaian father of Epeus (23.817).

Panthoüs — Trojan elder and priest of Apollo, husband of Phrontis, father of Polydamas, Euphorbus, and Hyperenor (3.184).

Paphlagonians — Tribe dwelling in Paphlagonia, a region between Bithynia and Pontus on the north coast of Asia Minor (2.1072).

Paris — Trojan son of Priam, his abduction of Helen sparked the Trojan war; also known as "Alexander" (3.19).

Parrhasia — City or region in southern Arcadia (2.754).

Parthenius — River marking the western boundary of Paphlagonia (2.1074).

Pasithea — One of the Graces, promised to Sleep by Juno (14.323).

Patroclus — Achaian son of Menœtius, beloved comrade of Achilles, slain by Hector (1.385).

Pedæum — City in the Troad (13.211).

Pedæus — Bastard Trojan son of Antenor, slain by Meges (5.82).

Pedasus — [1] Trojan son of Bucolion and Abarbareïa, twin brother of Æsepus, slain by Euryalus (6.26). [2] City in the Troad on the river Satnio (6.43). [3] City in Messinia near Pylos (9.183). [4] Horse captured from Eëtion by Achilles when he took Thebè (16.196).

Pelagon — [1] Pylian captain (4.375). [2] Lycian comrade of Sarpedon (5.869).

Pelasgians — Tribe dwelling in Asia Minor, the name of the pre-Greek

GLOSSARY OF NAMES 565

race inhabiting northern Greece to Thrace (2.848).

Pelegon — Trojan son of Axius and Peribœa, father of Asteropæus (21.174).

Peleus — King of the Myrmidons, son of Æacus, father of Achilles (1.1).

Pelion — Mountain range in Thessaly, home of the Centaurs; often refers to the ash tree from which the spear of Achilles was fashioned (2.929).

Pelias — King of Iolchos, son of Neptune and Tyro, brother of Neleus, father of Alcestis (2.891).

Pelides — "Son of Peleus", patronymic of Achilles (1.190).

Pellenè — Achaian city near Corinth, in the realm of Agamemnon (2.705).

Pelops — King of Argos, son of Tantalus, father of Atreus, grandfather of Agamemnon and Menelaus, from whom the Peloponnesus takes its name (2.132).

Peneleus — Son of Hippalcimus and Asterope, co-commander of the Bœotians along with Leïtus, took part in the expedition of the Argonauts (2.600).

Peneus — River in Thessaly flowing down from the Pindaros mountains (2.941).

Peribœans — Race from Dodona, commanded by Guneus (2.938).

Percote — City in the Troad northeast of Troy (2.1048).

Pergamus — The citadel of Troy (4.643).

Pergasis — Trojan father of Deïcoön (5.670).

Peribœa — Daughter of Acessamenus, mother of Pelegon by the river Axius (21.177).

Periëres — King of Messene, father of Borus (16.225).

Perimedes — Phocian father of Schedius (15.653).

Perimus — Trojan son of Megas, slain by Patroclus (16.867).

Periphas — [1] Achaian son of Ochesius, Ætolian slain by Mars (5.1055). [2] Trojan son of Epytus, herald of Anchises (17.375).

Periphœtes — [1] Trojan slain by Teucer (14.638). [2] Mycenæan son of Copreus, slain by Hector (15.815).

Persephone — See Proserpine.

Perseus — Son of Jove and Danaë, grandfather of Eurystheus, father of Sthenelus, founder of Mycenæ and the Perseid dynasty (14.385).

Peteona — City in Bœotia (2.610).

Peteus — Achaian son of Orneus, father of Menestheus, founded the town of Stiris (2.677).

Phæa — City in Elis in the Pisatis, near Iardan (7.178).

Phænops — [1] Trojan father of Xanthus and Thoön (5.185). [2] Trojan son of Asius (17.701).

Phæstus — City in southern Crete (2.804). [2] Mæonian son of Bolus, slain by Idomeneus (5.49).

Phalces — Trojan chief, slain by Antilochus (13.996).

Phare — City in Lacedæmon (2.717).

Phausias — Trojan father of Apisaon (11.703).

Phegeus — Trojan son of Dares, brother of Idæus, slain by Diomed (5.13).

Pheneus — City in northeastern Arcadia (2.748).

Pheræ — [1] City in Thessaly, seat of Admetus and Eumelus (2.885). [2] City in the southwestern Peloponnese between Pylos and Sparta (5.681).

Phereclus — Trojan son of Tecton, grandson of Harmon, artificer who built the fleet of ships used by Paris to abduct Helen, slain by Meriones (5.70).

Pherusa — A Nereid (18.54).

Phidas — Athenian chief under Menestheus (13.868).

Phidippus — Achaian son of King Thessalus, grandson of Hercules, co-commander of the contingent from Carpathos, Casos, Cos, and other islands along with his brother Antiphus (2.845).

Philetor - Trojan father of Demuchus (20.575).

Philoctetes — Son of Pœas, took up the bow and arrows that would vanquish Troy, original leader of the Thessalians from Methonè but bitten by a snake on Lemnos and abandoned there, subsequently rescued by Ulysses and brought to Troy (2.894).

Phlegyans — Tribe in dwelling Thessaly, identified with the Gyrtonians (13.369).

Phocians — Tribe dwelling in Phocis, region north of the Gulf of Corinth and west of Bœotia (17.370, called "Phocean" at 2.615).

Phœbus — Epithet of Apollo (1.56).

Phœnicians — Race living on the coast of Lebanon and Syria (23.917).

GLOSSARY OF NAMES 567

Phœnix — [1] Son of Amyntor, guardian and comrade of Achilles, took part in the Calydonian Hunt (9.203). [2] Grandfather of Minos and Rhadamanthus, father of Europa (14.387).

Phœnops — Trojan father of Phorcys (17.360).

Phorbas — [1] Father of Diomedè (9.822). [2] Trojan father of Ilioneus (14.604).

Phorcys — Phrygian son of Phænops, co-commander of the Phrygians of Ascania, slain by Telamonian Ajax (2.1085).

Phradmon — Trojan father of Agelaus (8.325).

Phrontis — Wife of Panthoüs (17.50).

Phrygians — Tribe dwelling in Phrygia, a region in the west of Asia Minor (2.1086).

Phthians — Tribe dwelling in Phthia, a region in Thessaly near the Eubœan Gulf, the kingdom of Peleus, birthplace of Achilles (13.871).

Phthirians — Tribe dwelling in Caria, probably near Mount Latmus in southern Asia Minor (2.1095).

Phylacè — City in Thessaly, in the realm of Protesilaüs (2.865).

Phylacus — [1] Son of Deion and Diomedè, father of Iphiclus, grandfather of Podarces, founder of the city of Phylacè (2.880). [2] Trojan slain by Leïtus (6.45).

Phylas — Father of Polymela, surrogate father to Eudorus, his daughter's son by Hermes (16.229).

Phyleus — Achaian son of Augeias, father of Megas, defeated by Nestor in a spear-throwing contest (2.777).

Philomedusa — Achaian wife of Areïthoüs, mother of Menesthius (7.14).

Pidytes — Percosian slain by Ulysses (6.38).

Pieria — [1] Region in Thessaly, probably Hypereia at Pheræ (2.959). [2] Region containing Mount Olympus (14.271).

Piraides — Patronymic of Ptolemy (4.294).

Peireus — Thracian son of Imbrasus, father of Rigmus, commander of the Thracian contingent allied with Troy (20.611).

Pirithoüs — Thessalian king of the Lapiths, son of Jove, father of Polypœtes (1.333).

Piroüs — Thracian son of Imbrasus, co-commander of the Thracians along with Acamas, slain by Thoas (4.658, called "Peiroüs" at 2.1060).

Pisander — [1] Trojan son of Antimachus, slain by Agamemnon (11.146). [2] Trojan slain by Menelaus (13.756). [3] Myrmidon chief, son of Mæmalus (16.244).

Pisenor — Trojan chief, father of Clitus (15.558).

Pitheus — King of Trœzene, son of Pelops and Dia, father of Æthra, grandfather of Theseus (3.182).

Pityeia — City in Mysia (2.1040).

Placos — Mountain in Mysian Cilicia above Thebè (6.514).

Platæa — City in Bœotia (2.615).

Pleiades — Constellation, seven sisters named after their Oceanid mother Pleione (18.610).

Pleuron — City in Ætolia (2.792).

Pluto — See Hades.

Podalirius — Thessalian son of Æsculapius, healer and co-commander of the Thessalian contingent from Tricca and Œchalia along with his brother Machaon (2.913).

Podarces — Thessalian son of Iphiclus, brother of Protesilaüs, after whose death he assumed command of the Thessalian contingent from Phylacè (2.870).

Podes — Trojan son of Eëtion, slain by Menelaus (17.693).

Polites — Trojan son of Priam, father of Priam the younger, slain by Neoptolemus (2.991).

Pollux — Brother of Helen, twin brother of Castor, renowned for horsemanship; together the twins are known as the Dioscuri (3.297).

Polyæmon — Trojan father of Hamopaon (8.349).

Polybus — Trojan son of Antenor, slain by Neoptolemus (11.71).

Polyctor — Myrmidon, the son of whom Hermes impersonates (24.501).

Polydamas — Trojan son of Panthoüs, brother of Euphorbus, Trojan chief (11.67).

Polydeuces — See Pollux.

Polydora — Daughter of Peleus, sister of Achilles, mother of Menesthius by the river Spercheus (16.222).

Polydorus — Trojan son of Priam, slain by Achilles (20.514).

Polydore — Elian defeated by Nestor in a spear-throwing contest

(23.710).

Polyeidus — Trojan son of Eurydamas, slain by Diomed (5.165).

Polyïdus — Corinthian seer, father of Euchenor (13.832).

Polymela — Achaian daughter of Phylas, wife of Echecles, mother of Eudorus by Hermes (16.228).

Polymelus — Lycian son of Argias, slain by Patroclus (16.525).

Polynices — Son of Œdipus and Jocasta, brother of Eteocles and Antigone, led the expedition of the Seven against Thebes (4.477).

Polypheme — Arcadian son of Elatus, took part in the expedition of the Argonauts (1.335).

Polyphœtes — Trojan chief (13.998).

Polypœtes — Thessalian son of Pirithoüs, co-commander of the Lapiths from Argissa (2.924).

Polyxenus — Epean son of Agasthenes, grandson of Augeias, co-commander of the Epeans (2.771).

Portheus — Ætolian son of Agenor, father of Agrius, Melas, and Œneus, grandfather of Tydeus (14.137).

Poseidon — See Neptune.

Practium — City in Mysia on the Hellespont (2.1048).

Pramnian wine — Strong red wine with medicinal properties (11.776).

Priam — King of Troy, son of Laomedon, husband of Hecuba, father of Hector, Helenus, Paris, Polydorus, Deïphobus, Cassandra and Polyxena (1.25).

Prœtus — King of Argos, son of Abas, twin-brother of Acrisius, persecuted Bellerophon (6.201).

Promachus — Bœotian son of Alegenor, slain by Acamas (14.589).

Pronoüs — [1] Thessalian son of Tenthredon, commander of the Thessalian contingent from Magnesia (2.945). [2] Trojan slain by Patroclus (16.474).

Proserpine — Goddess of the underworld, daughter of Jove and Ceres, wife of Hades (9.568).

Protesilaüs — Thessalian son of Iphiclus, brother of Podarces, original commander of the men of Phylacè (2.870).

Prothoënor — Bœotian son of Areïlochus, commander of the Bœotians, slain by Polydamas (2.600).

Prothoüs — Trojan slain by Teucer (14.638).

Protiäon — Trojan father of Astynous (15.572).

Proto — A Nereid (18.52).

Prytanis — Lycian slain by Ulysses (5.850).

Pteleum — [1] City in Messinia, in the realm of Nestor (2.733). [2] City in Thessaly, in the realm of Protesilaüs (2.868).

Ptolemy — Achaian son of Piræus, father of Eurymedon (4.294).

Pylæmenes — [1] King of the Paphlagonians, father of Harpalion, slain by Menelaus (2.1069). [2] Mæonian father of Mesthles and Antiphus (2.1091).

Pylæus — Larissan son of Lethus, grandson of Teutamus, co-commander of the Pelasgians from Larissa along with his brother Hippothoüs (2.1057).

Pylartes — [1] Trojan slain by Telamonian Ajax (11.599). [2] Trojan slain by Patroclus (16.870).

Pylene — City in Ætolia (2.792).

Pylon — Trojan slain by Polypœtes (12.223).

Pylos — City in Elis, the royal seat of Nestor (1.320).

Pyræchmes — Co-commander of the Pæonians along with Asteropæus, slain by Patroclus (2.1061).

Pyrasus — [1] City in Thessaly, in the realm of Protesilaüs (2.865). [2] Trojan slain by Telamonian Ajax (11.599).

Pyris — Trojan slain by Patroclus (16.522).

Pytho — Site in Phocis on the slope of Mount Parnassus, home to a sanctuary sacred to Apollo, later called Delphi (9.504).

Rhadamanthus — Son of Jove and Europa, brother of Minos (14.389).

Rhea — Titaness, wife of Saturn, mother of Jove, Neptune, Hades, Juno, Ceres, and Hestia (14.244).

Rhene — Achaian mother of Medon by Oïleus (2.830).

Rhesus — [1] King of Thrace, son of Eïoneus, slain by Diomed (10.515). [2] River in the Troad, flowing down from Ida (12.26).

Rhodians — Tribe dwelling in Rhodes, an island in the eastern Ægean, settled by Tlepolemus after slaying Licymnius, the maternal uncle of Hercules (2.813).

GLOSSARY OF NAMES   571

Rhodius — River in the Troad, flowing down from Ida (12.27).

Rhytium — City in Crete, home to the Gortynians (2.804).

Rigmus — Thracian son of Peireus, slain by Achilles (20.610).

Ripa — City in Arcadia (2.750).

Rumor — Messenger goddess of Jove, personification of rumour or report (2.119)

Salamis — Island west of Athens in the Saronic Gulf, birthplace of Telamonian Ajax (2.683).

Samos — [1] Island off the west coast of Greece near Ithaca, in the realm of Ulysses (2.786). [2] Island in the northern Ægean near Thrace, home of the Sanctuary of the Great Gods, later called Samothrace (13.13).

Sangarius — River in Phrygia and Bithynia (3.237).

Sarpedon — Lycian son of Jove and Laodamia, brother of Clarus and Themon, co-commander of the Lycian contingent along with Glaucus, slain by Patroclus (2.1106).

Satnio — River in the Troad (6.44).

Satnius — Trojan son of Enops, slain by Oïlean Ajax (14.547).

Scæan Gates — The main gates of Troy (3.183).

Saturn — God of time, son of Uranus, father of Jove, Hades, Neptune, Juno, and Ceres (1.498).

Scamander — Chief river of the Trojan plain and its associated deity, son of Oceanus and Tethys, brother of the river Simoïs, called Xanthus by the gods (2.570).

Scamandrius — [1] Trojan son of Strophius, slain by Menelaus (5.58). [2] Birth name of Astyanax, son of Hector and Andromache (6.520).

Scandeia — Port city on the island of Cythera (10.314).

Scarpha — City in Locris (2.652).

Schedius — [1] Phocian son of Iphitus and Hippolyte, co-commander of the Phocians along with his brother Epistrophus, slain by Hector (2.632). [2] Phocian chief, son of Perimedes, slain by Hector (15.653).

Schœnus — City in Bœotia (2.604).

Scolus — City in Bœotia (2.604).

Scyros — Island in the central Ægean off the coast of Eubœa, ruled by Pyrrhus (9.827).

Selagus — Trojan father of Amphius (5.703).

Selapius — Lyrnessian father of Evenus (2.863).

Selleïs — [1] River in Elis (2.820). [2] River in the Troad near Arisba (2.1053).

Selli — Priests of Jove, intepreters of the oracle at Dodona (16.296).

Semele — Theban Daughter of Cadmus and Harmonia, mother of Dionysus by Jove, the full glory of whom consumed her (14.390).

Sesamus — City in Paphlagonia (2.1073).

Sestus — City on the Thracian shore of the Hellespont (2.1049).

Sicyon — City near Cornith, ruled by Adrastus, in the realm of Agamemnon (2.662).

Sidonians — Race in Sidon, city in Phœnicia (23.915).

Simoïs — River in Troy and its associated god, brother of Scamander, which it joins in the plain of Troy (4.600).

Simoïsius — Trojan son of Anthemion, named after the river Simoïs, slain by Telamonian Ajax (4.597).

Sintians — Thracian tribe dwelling in Lemnos (1.752).

Sipylus — Mountain in Lydia (24.781).

Sisyphus — Corinthian son of Æolus, grandfather of Bellerophon, punished for his cunning, doomed to roll an immense boulder up a hill in Hades eternally (6.180).

Sleep — God, son of Night and Erebos, twin brother of Death (14.277).

Smintheus — Epithet of Apollo, derived by some from the Greek word for mouse, thus suggesting a connection with plague, and by others from the town of Sminthe in the Troad (1.51).

Socus — Trojan son of Hippasus, brother of Charops, slain by Ulysses (11.517).

Solymi — Tribe dwelling in Milyas in Asia Minor (6.238).

Sparta — Chief city of Lacedæmon, seat of Menelaus (2.674).

Spercheius — River in Phthia and its associated god, father of Menesthius by Polydora (16.221).

Sphelus — Achaian son of Bucolus, father of Iasus (15.421).

Stentor — Achaian herald, renowned for his powerful voice (5.986).

Sthenelaüs — Trojan son of Ithæmenes, slain by Patroclus (16.736).

GLOSSARY OF NAMES 573

Sthenelus — [1] Argolid son of Capaneus, father of Cylarabes, co-commander along with Diomed and Euryalus of the Argolid contingent (2.692). [2] Argolid son of Perseus, father of Eurystheus (19.139).

Stichius — Athenian chief, slain by Hector (13.241).

Stratia — City in Arcadia (2.750).

Strophius — Trojan father of Scamandrius (5.59).

Stymphalus — City in northeastern Arcadia (2.753).

Styra — City of the Abantes in Eubœa (2.661).

Styx — River forming the boundary between earth and the underworld, upon which the gods swear oaths (8.462).

Syma — Island in the Dodecanese northwest of Rhodes (2.836).

Talaus — King of Argos, son of Bias and Pero, father of Mecisteus, took part in the expedition of the Argonauts (2.696).

Talthybius — Achaian herald of Agamemnon (1.402).

Tarna — City in Mæonia (5.51).

Tarpha — City in Locris on the river Boagrius (2.653).

Tartarus — The deepest abyss in the underworld, place of torment and suffering, prison for the Titans (8.15).

Tegea — City in Arcadia (2.752).

Telamon — Son of Æacus, brother of Peleus, father of Telamonian Ajax and Teucer, took part in the Calydonian Hunt and the expedition of the Argonauts (2.647).

Telemachus — Son of Ulysses and Penelope (2.321).

Tenedos — Island in the northeastern Ægean, near Troy (1.50).

Tenthredon — Father of Prothoüs (2.945).

Tereia — Mountain in Mysia, northeast of Troy (2.1040).

Tethys — Titaness, daughter of Uranus and Gaia, wife and sister of Ocean (14.243).

Teucer — Bastard Achaian son of Telamon, half-brother of Telamonian Ajax, renowned for skill in archery (6.39).

Teutamus — Father of Lethus (2.1059).

Teuthras — [1] Magnesian slain by Hector (5.883). [2] Trojan father of Axylus (6.16).

Thalpius — Achaian commander of the Epeans, son of Eurytus (2.768).

Thalysius — Trojan father of Echepolus (4.578).

Thamyris — Thracian son of Philammon and Argiope, bard whose hubris led to punishment by the Muses (2.687).

Thaumacia — City in Thessaly near Mount Pelion, in the realm of Philoctetes (2.893).

Theano — Thracian daughter of Cisseus, wife of Antenor, priestess of Minerva at Troy (6.389, called "Threno" at 5.77).

Thebæus — Trojan father of Eniopeus (8.150).

Thebè — City in Mysia, ruled by Eëtion, home of Andromache, sacked by Achilles (1.458).

Thebes — [1] City in Bœotia, founded by Cadmus, attacked by Polynices in the War of the Seven (2.860). [2] City in Egypt, famed for wealth and its hundred gates (9.474).

Themis — Titaness, goddess of order, law, and custom (15.111).

Thersilochus — Pæonian son of Antenor, slain by Achilles (17.263).

Thersites — Calydonian son of Agrius, vulgar dissenter who questions the kings (2.264).

Theseus — King of Athens, son of Ægeus and Æthra (1.309).

Thespeia — City in Bœotia (2.605).

Thessalus — Achaian son of Hercules, father of Phidippus and Antiphus (2.851).

Thestor — [1] Achaian father of Calchas (1.89). [2] Achaian father of Alcmaon (12.471). [3] Trojan son of Enops, slain by Patroclus (16.505).

Thetis — Nereid, wife of Peleus, mother of Achilles (1.518).

Thisbè — City in Bœotia (2.611).

Thoa — A Nereid (18.49).

Thoas — [1] Ætolian son of Andræmon, commander of the Ætolian contingent (2.791). [2] King of Lemnos, son of Dionysus and Ariadne, father of Hypsipyle and Sicinus (14.276). [3] Trojan slain by Menelaus (16.391).

Thoön — [1] Trojan son of Phænops, slain by Diomed (5.185). [2] Trojan slain by Ulysses (11.510). [3] Trojan slain by Antilochus (13.684).

Thoötes — Achaian herald (12.410).

Thracians — Tribes dwelling in Thrace, region north of Thessaly and the Hellespont (2.1061)

Thrasius — Pæonian slain by Achilles (21.257).

Thrasymedes — Pylian son of Nestor, co-commander of the Pylian contingent along with Antilochus (9.95).

Thrasymelus — Trojan charioteer to Sarpedon, slain by Patroclus (16.582).

Thronium — City in Locris on the river Boagrius (2.654).

Thrya — City in Elis by the river Alpheius, in the realm of Nestor (2.730, called "Thryoëssa" at 11.866).

Thyestes — Son of Pelops, brother of Atreus, with whom he engaged in blood feud (2.135).

Thymbra — City on the river Scamander near Troy (10.508).

Thymbræus — Trojan slain by Diomed (11.383).

Thymœtes — Trojan elder and soothsayer, son of Laomedon (3.184).

Tiryns — City in the Argolid near Argos, in the realm of Diomed (2.686).

Titanus — Mountain range and city Thessaly, in the realm of Eurypylus (2.918).

Titans — The second generation of gods, children of Uranus and Gaia, imprisoned by Jove in Tartarus (14.336).

Titaresius — River in Thessaly, major tributary of the river Peneus (2.940).

Tithonus — Trojan son of Laomedon, brother of Priam, husband of the Dawn (11.2).

Tlepolemus — [1] Rhodian son of Hercules, commander of the Rhodian contingent, slain by Sarpedon (2.810). [2] Lycian son of Damastor, slain by Patroclus (16.523).

Tmolus — Mountain in Mæonia (2.1090).

Trachys — City near the river Spercheus, in the realm of Peleus and Achilles (2.849).

Trechus — Ætolian slain by Hector (5.884).

Tricca — Thessalian city in the realm of Machaon (2.909).

Tritonia — Epithet of Minerva, likely meaning "third born", or "thrice born" (4.652).

Trœzene — City and region in the Argolid on the Saronic Gulf, in the realm of Diomed (2.688).

Trœzenus — Trojan son of Ceas, father of Euphemus (2.1065).

Troïlus — Trojan son of Priam (24.332).

Trojans — Race of Greek speaking peoples in the Troad, ruled by Priam (1.214).

Tros — [1] Son of Erichthonius and Astyoche, father of Ilus, Assaracus, and Ganymede, great-grandfather of Priam, namesake of Troy (5.321). [2] Trojan son of Alastor, slain by Achilles (20.582).

Troy — City of the Trojans, also known as Ilus or Ilium (1.169).

Tychius — Currier and artificer, made the bronze-plated battle-shield of Telamonian Ajax (7.286).

Tydeus — King of Argos and Calydon, Son of Œneus, father of Diomed, one of the Seven Against Thebes (2.498).

Tydides — "Son of Tydeus," patronymic of Diomed (4.464).

Typhœus — Monstrous creature, son of Gaia and Tartarus, antagonist in a cataclysmic battle with Jove, also known as Typhon (2.982).

Ucalegon — Trojan elder whose home was set ablaze during the sack of Troy (3.186).

Ulysses — King of Ithaca, son of Laertes, husband of Penelope, father of Telemachus, hero of the Odyssey, renowned for verbal skill (1.181).

Venus — Goddess of love, daughter of Jove and Dione, lover of Anchises, mother of Æneas, favours the Trojans (2.1027).

Vulcan — God of fire, master craftsman, son of Juno, cuckolded husband of Venus, cast from Olympus by Jove and thereby crippled (1.722).

Waggon, Wain, The — See Bear, The.

Xanthus — [1] River in Lycia (2.1084). [2] Chief river of the Trojan plain and its associated deity, son of Oceanus and Tethys, brother of the river Simoïs, called Scamander by mortals (6.5). [3] Trojan son of Phænops, slain by Diomed (5.185).

Zacynthus — Island near Ithaca, in the realm of Ulysses (2.785).

Zeleia — Lycian city in the northwestern Troad (2.1034).

Zephyrus — The West Wind, father of Xanthus and Balius by Podargè (16.194).

Zeus — See Jove.

www.ingramcontent.com/pod-product-compliance
Lightning Source LLC
Chambersburg PA
CBHW032020290426
44110CB00012B/613